HANDBOOK ON PARTICIPATORY ACTION RESEARCH AND COMMUNITY DEVELOPMENT

To everyone who works to create a more just, healthy, and sustainable world for all.

Handbook on Participatory Action Research and Community Development

Edited by

Randy Stoecker

Professor and Director of the Applied Population Laboratory, Department of Community and Environmental Sociology, University of Wisconsin-Madison, USA

Adrienne Falcón

Professor and Director of the Masters of Advocacy and Political Leadership, Chair of the Public and Nonprofit Leadership Department, Metropolitan State University, USA

Edward Elgar
PUBLISHING

Cheltenham, UK • Northampton, MA, USA

Published by
Edward Elgar Publishing Limited
The Lypiatts
15 Lansdown Road
Cheltenham
Glos GL50 2JA
UK

Edward Elgar Publishing, Inc.
William Pratt House
9 Dewey Court
Northampton
Massachusetts 01060
USA

Paperback edition 2023

A catalogue record for this book
is available from the British Library

Library of Congress Control Number: 2022931721

This book is available electronically in the **Elgar**online
Sociology, Social Policy and Education subject collection
http://dx.doi.org/10.4337/9781839100970

ISBN 978 1 83910 096 3 (cased)
ISBN 978 1 83910 097 0 (eBook)
ISBN 978 1 0353 2744 7 (paperback)

Printed and bound by CPI Group (UK) Ltd, Croydon, CR0 4YY

Contents

PART III BUILDING ORGANIZATIONS AND NEIGHBORHOODS

PART IV GROWING YOUTH POWER

PART V RESPONDING TO CRISIS

Figures

Contributors

Nova Ahmed is Associate Professor at North South University in Dhaka, Bangladesh. She is particularly interested in distributed sensing systems with unreliable sensors. Her passion for social justice has driven her to work on social problems in Bangladesh, resulting in an interest in feminist human-centered computing, and in ensuring social justice using science and enlightenment in her country. Other areas of interest include women's electronic privacy and safety issues in traditional, patriarchal environments.

Giovanna Alvarez works as the director of a non-profit organization that serves thousands of vulnerable international immigrants with a focus on the Hispanic/Latino community. Giovanna is glad to participate in the Communities Acting for Kids' Empowerment (CAKE) initiative to be the voice of communities that are traditionally underrepresented. She strives for social justice for the most vulnerable in society.

Misita Anwar is Lecturer in the Faculty of Information Technology at Monash University. She has been conducting research in development informatics for the last ten years in Indonesia and Bangladesh. Currently, Anwar is working with the joint Monash–Oxfam PROTIC project in Bangladesh and a health information project in Indonesia. Anwar also explores human-centered design working with people with disabilities and digital literacy in a development context and community engagement in data governance.

Monica Arenas-Losacker is a social worker and community outreach specialist for a community agency that supports adults who care for young children. She has been working in Carthage and Roselawn since 2004. She is motivated to be a part of CAKE because her experience in these neighborhoods makes her confident that we can make change by working together for a common goal. In CAKE, she is a liaison for the Hispanic and immigrant communities.

Ana Elisa Astudillo graduated with an undergraduate degree in sociology from the University of Cuenca, Ecuador, a master's in anthropology from the Autonomous University of Barcelona, and is currently working on her PhD in anthropology from KU Leuven as part of the Interculturalism, Migration, and Minorities Center. She works as a social researcher at the University of Cuenca on Right to the City projects and with the World Heritage City Research Group of the Faculty of Architecture and Urbanism.

Todd Barr has a background in education and community development. Todd has held senior management positions in non-profit organizations for close to 20 years and has been an independent coach and consultant since 2014 – a practice that supports individuals and teams to define and achieve their goals. Recently Todd launched Condition Shift, an initiative supporting networks, coalitions, and collaboratives to shift the conditions that hold complex problems in place. For good.

Katelyn Baumann is Coordinator of Academic Service Learning within the Link Center at the University of Wisconsin-Superior (UW-S). She received her degree in international peace studies and mass communication from UW-S. She started her professional career at UW-S in 2012. Following this, Katelyn obtained her Nonprofit Administration Certificate in 2014 and completed Leadership Superior-Douglas County in 2015. She is a dedicated community engagement practitioner with nine years of experience building mutually beneficial partnerships with the community and UW-S through academic service learning.

Dana Beasley-Brown has been a community advocate for working families across Kentucky for the last 17 years. She is a founder of the Homeless and Housing Coalition of South Central Kentucky and served as editor-in-chief for the *Barren River Area Renters' Handbook*. Dana currently serves families as the coordinator of the Youth Services Center at Bowling Green Junior High School and is currently serving her second term as a city commissioner in Bowling Green, KY.

Isabel Bernier is a community organizer, University Integrated Health and Social Service Centre, Capitale Nationale, Québec.

Lakisha A. Best works in early childcare training, operates a consulting firm for preschools, and recently opened her own Family Childcare Center. For eight years, she worked in a preschool that served the communities of Roselawn and Carthage. Lakisha is motivated by her passion to change impoverished children's view of the world by empowering parents. She wants to be the advocate she never had in her childhood. Lakisha's motto is "Give children a childhood they do not have to recover from."

Nicole Bouchard is a community organizer, University Integrated Health and Social Service Centre, Capitale Nationale, Québec.

Nicole Breazeale is Associate Professor of Community and Leadership Development at the University of Kentucky. Formerly a sociology professor at Western Kentucky University-Glasgow, Nicole is committed to engaged learning experiences that build community capacity, democratize knowledge, and reduce social inequality.

Megan Brown is Assistant Professor of Advocacy and Political Leadership at Metropolitan State University in St. Paul, Minnesota. She was the first director of the Liberal Arts Action Lab, serving from 2017 to 2020.

Daniel Bryan is an educator, activist, artist, and scholar specializing in the use of participatory theater as a means of education, conflict transformation, and knowledge creation. Originally from the United States, he has lived for over 20 years in Quito, Ecuador where he has directed community-based and university-based study abroad programs. He is Co-Founder and Executive Director at Fundación Pachaysana and a regular lecturer and scholar/artist in residence at colleges and universities in the United States.

Brian D. Christens studies organizations' efforts to change systems and benefit their communities. He conducts research into the mechanisms linking civic participation to individual and community well-being, and into how different organizational approaches to civic action can lead to different outcomes. He is especially interested in young people's involvement and leadership in efforts to change systems, and the ways that these experiences relate to other aspects of human development.

Shanah Cole is a parent of two children who attended the YMCA, Valley Early Learning Center in Roselawn over a five-year period. Shanah is passionate to take part in the CAKE initiative to give a parent's perspective. She strives for comprehensiveness and is an advocate for children with disabilities.

Kimberly S. Compton is a faculty member at Virginia Commonwealth University's School of Social Work. Her research, teaching, and practice aims to center the margins. Compton's radical hope is that participatory action research will flip the script on what we think we know, how we think we know it, and what actions we will take accordingly.

Cristian Cuevas is a 2018 Stetson University graduate who worked as the AmeriCorps VISTA at the Stetson Center for Community Engagement from 2018 to 2019. He worked closely with members of the Spring Hill Gardeners Association and the Artisan Alley Farmers Market to slowly transition power back into the community's hands with these projects. He now works as a health coach and is planning to pursue a master's degree in dietetics studies and nutrition.

Crystal Davis works as a community educator and mentor to students and families in Roselawn. As a mother, she has learned that if you show genuine love and care to a child, he/she will respond by demonstrating how well he/she can behave, perform academically in school, and more. CAKE enables her to be surrounded by great people who serve the same purpose and helps broaden her view regarding children's health and education as she pursues her doctorate in leadership studies.

Marie-Hélène Deshaies is a professor at the School of Social Work and Criminology of Laval University, Québec. With a doctorate in sociology, she has diverse experience in collective intervention with community non-profit organizations. Her research interests focus on community organizing, collective action and social movements, the fight against poverty and inequality, and participatory and collaborative research processes.

Alan Dicken serves as the senior pastor at Carthage Christian Church. Part of his calling is service to the community and the needs of the neighborhood. He doesn't live in Carthage, but is involved with youth, parents, and community organizations that strive to improve the lives of those in that community.

Shilretha Dixon is Director of the Joyce M. Cusack Resource Center, located in the Spring Hill community of DeLand, FL. Through the center, she provides health, nutrition, education, employment, social, and income-based assistance to the residents of the community where she lives. In addition to the center, Shilretha is involved in numerous non-profit and civic organizations including the Spring Hill Neighborhood Association and Spring Hill Community Redevelopment Agency.

Jack Dougherty is Professor of Educational Studies at Trinity College in Hartford, CT. He served as Trinity's first faculty director of the Liberal Arts Action Lab and also the first director of the Center for Hartford Engagement and Research.

Maxwell Droznin began serving as an AmeriCorps VISTA at its Center for Community Engagement after graduating from Stetson University (2016). He obtained a master's in public health from Rollins College (2018) and continued his work at Stetson as a community engagement Fellow and adjunct professor of Public Health. Maxwell is currently completing his degree at the University of Central Florida College of Medicine and hopes to pursue a career at the intersection of healthcare and poverty reduction.

Sophie Dupéré is Associate Professor in the Faculty of Nursing at Laval University, Québec, specializing in community health and health promotion. She has worked with ATD Fourth World and the Collectif pour un Québec sans pauvreté. She has thus acquired experience with the methods of cross-fertilization of knowledge and practices. In addition, she is a founding member of midi-RAP, a community of practice in Quebec City on participatory action research that has been organizing seminars since 2011.

Adrienne Falcón is a professor in and director of the Masters of Advocacy and Political Leadership and chair of the Public and Nonprofit Leadership Department at Metropolitan State University. She trained as a community organizer in Chicago and studied higher education civic engagement in Ecuador on a Fulbright scholarship. She has been doing community-engaged work, within and outside of academia, for over 30 years, always inspired by people's potential to transform their worlds.

Viviane Frings-Hessami is a DECRA Fellow in the Digital Equity and Digital Transformation Group, Faculty of Information Technology at Monash University. Between 2016 and 2020, she was a lecturer in the Faculty of Information Technology, Monash University, teaching in the archives and information science programs. Her current research, supported by an Australian Research Council DECRA Fellowship, 2021–2023, aims to design a framework for culturally sensitive and gender-sensitive information dissemination and information preservation for disadvantaged rural communities in Bangladesh.

Marie-Jade Gagnon is a community organizer, University Integrated Health and Social Service Centre, Capitale Nationale, Québec.

Lucie Gélineau is Professor of Social Work at the Université du Québec in Rimouski, Canada, trained in social anthropology. Most of her work is on social exclusion issues. For nearly 30 years she has co-developed expertise on participatory research and collective analysis methods, initiating seminars, training, and communities of practice. As a founding researcher with the Participatory Research Collective on Poverty in Rural Areas, she accompanies stakeholders doing independent research projects seen as an intervention opportunity.

Melody Gibson is Education Director at the Civic Design Center where she leads the Design Your Neighborhood youth education program. After studying architecture in college and then teaching high school math, Melody discovered a passion for engaging youth in shaping the spaces they inhabit. Through her leadership, Design Your Neighborhood has grown to impact over 3,000 young people annually in Metro Nashville in both the classroom and extra-curricular settings.

Lyne Gilbert is a community organizer, University Integrated Health and Social Service Centre, Capitale Nationale, Québec.

Nancy E. Gordon is Chair of the Graduate Department of Counseling, Leadership, and Expressive Arts at Salve Regina University, Program Director of the Holistic Leadership Program, and Associate Professor. She received her doctorate from Harvard University. Her professional and research interests lie in the intersection between leadership, whole system change, and personal mastery.

Alexa Hatcher is an Economic Justice Organizer at Kentuckians for the Commonwealth. She works on policy change in support of fair budgets and taxes, also ensuring the continuation of critical welfare programs at the state level. While obtaining a degree in sociology from Western Kentucky University (with a minor in citizenship and social justice), she began her career in organizing for food justice and access to healthcare. Alexa was a founding member of Breaking Ground: A Sustainable Jail Garden and Food Justice project.

Tiffany S. Haynes is a researcher and organizer with Advocates for Richmond Youth.

Dadit G. Hidayat is a policy and engagement specialist at Kids Forward, a research policy and advocacy non-profit organization based in Madison, WI. Dadit has been practicing participatory action research for over a decade, facilitating community–university partnerships through research, course instruction, and service. Throughout his professional career, he has been uniquely situated as both an academic and community partner experiencing the dynamic of the partnerships in both roles.

Ming Hu is Assistant Professor in Social Work and Social Policy at Nanjing University in China. His research interests include non-profit management, philanthropy, and community development. His recent articles on these themes have been published in *Administration and Society* and *Voluntas: International Journal of Voluntary and Nonprofit Organizations*.

Farrah Jacquez works as a professor and engages in research with CAKE. Her Latina identity and her personal experiences as a first-generation college student and a mother motivate her participation in the work, but she does not live in Carthage or Roselawn and does not have the lived experience of raising children in these neighborhoods.

Asal M. Johnson joined Stetson University in 2014. She has a PhD in urban and regional planning from Florida State University, a master's degree in urban planning from the University of Tehran and a master's in public health-epidemiology from Georgia Southern University. With her unique background that connects neighborhood planning to public health, she has involved herself in undergraduate public health education at Stetson and community-building efforts within the Spring Hill community of DeLand, FL.

Samantha Johnson is a 2016 graduate of WKU-Glasgow and former correctional officer/ rehabilitation facilitator. She is a lifelong resident of Barren County with strong community ties and has continually worked to fight for social justice.

Tetiana Kidruk is the director of a charitable organization in Rivne City, Ukraine. She has been involved with community development for more than five years, and implemented eight Rivne-based youth initiatives in cooperation with the Peace Corps in Ukraine, IREX, and IRI. She was a language and cross-cultural facilitator at Peace Corps Ukraine, and is a Fulbright Foreign Language Teacher's Assistant Program alumna at the University of Kansas (2019–2020).

Celeste Koppe is a Community Planner for West Central Initiative in rural Minnesota. Previously, she worked as an independent researcher, writer, and teacher in Tunis, Tunisia.

She holds an M.A. in Political Science from Central European University and a B.A. in History from Carleton College.

Jae Lange (they/them) is a creator, researcher, and organizer with Advocates for Richmond Youth.

Laura Jessee Livingston is a community-based researcher and evaluator collaborating with farmers and food systems educators. She is a PhD candidate in the Nelson Institute for Environmental Studies at the University of Wisconsin-Madison where she received a Master's of Science in Agroecology. Before graduate school, Laura served in the Peace Corps in Ghana and worked on farms in Massachusetts, Ohio, and Costa Rica. She returned to school to research supporting farmers in addressing systemic issues in the food system.

Kelsey Maglio served as an AmeriCorps VISTA in Stetson's Center for Community Engagement after graduating from Stetson University's Bonner Program in 2019, overseeing the university's partnerships with education-related institutions and conducting research to expand the university's community-based research program. Having received her BA in philosophy from Stetson, Kelsey is now pursuing her PhD in philosophy at Baylor University, where she hopes to continue integrating her academic and community engagement interests through public philosophy initiatives.

Manuel Martínez Casanova is Professor Emeritus at Central University "Marta Abreu" of Las Villas, Cuba. His PhD in philosophy is from Taras Chevchenko University, Kyiv. He served at the Academy of the History of Cuba, as Executive Secretary of the National Project of Science-Technology and Innovation "Cuban and Latin American Cultural Identity," and from 2008 to 2018 as President of the National Commission on the "Sociocultural Management for Development" degree. He has taught in Colombian, Venezuelan, Ecuadorian, Spanish, and Ukrainian Universities.

Ihsan Mejdi is a PhD student at the University of Exeter. His research focuses on the social and political transformations in Tunisia since the 2011 revolution. He holds a master's degree in sociology and social anthropology from the Central European University and a bachelor's degree in political science from Hacettepe University. Mejdi also published on party politics in Tunisia with a focus on the tension between the secular and Islamist parties from 2011 to 2019.

Jenice Meyer is a passionately committed higher education professional with 15 years of progressive leadership experience. At the University of Wisconsin-Superior she serves as Senior Officer for Community Engagement and Strategic Partnerships. Her areas of expertise include campus–community partnerships, relationship building, community development, community engagement curriculum development, and leading institutional change. She facilitates workshops and presents to local, state, and national audiences. Her work has been recognized most recently with the distinguished University of Wisconsin System Regents Academic Staff Award for Excellence.

Kathryn Y. Morgan's research explores community-based efforts to increase leadership, empowerment, and active citizenship among youth. She studies youth civic empowerment across community and organizational settings, particularly focusing on place-based experiential education and youth-driven primary prevention efforts that address disparities in the built environment. She also supports capacity building among youth activists as they engage in youth participatory action research and claim their right to participate in community decision making.

Jamie-Lee Morris is Educational Programming Coordinator at Elementz, a Hip Hop youth organization. As the community partner on the project, she uses her understanding of organizing to bring the community into the process of engagement. She aims to help the community interact with stakeholders regarding the educational issues that affect their families and neighborhoods as a whole.

Laura L. O'Toole is Professor of Sociology and Senior Faculty Fellow for Community Engagement at Salve Regina University. She is a co-editor of *Gender Violence: Interdisciplinary Perspectives*, 3rd edition (2020) with Jessica R. Schiffman and Rosemary Sullivan. O'Toole is active in numerous community development initiatives, most notably those focused on youth leadership development and food access, equity, and sovereignty on Aquidneck Island, RI.

Rae Caballero Obejero is a seasoned social worker who has been in the field for over seven years addressing homelessness, youth and adult behavioral health, LGBTQ+ advocacy, the destigmatization of mental health, and ending systemic poverty. Rae is passionate about decolonizing the world around him and raising his dog, Cebu.

Gillian Oliver is Associate Professor of Information Management, Digital Equity and Digital Transformation Group, in the Faculty of Information Technology, Monash University. Previously, she led teaching and research into archives and records in New Zealand. Her research interests focus on data cultures, including the information cultures of workplaces and issues relating to the continuity of digital information, particularly in development contexts. She is the author of four books and is co-editor-in-chief of the journal *Archival Science*.

Jeff Partridge is Professor of English at Capital Community College in Hartford and Director of the Hartford Heritage Project, a place-based education initiative. Jeff serves as the college's faculty director at the Liberal Arts Action Lab.

Oleh Petrus has a master's in psychology and in the past seven years he has collaborated with local government and non-governmental organizations, Peace Corps Ukraine, and the United Nations Procurement Division to develop, implement, and promote the principles of civil society and an actively engaged citizenry. Apart from his work in the community, he also worked closely with Ukrainian and international youth through the Erasmus+ program. Oleh is dedicated to strengthening communities and advocating for underrepresented groups.

Julie Richard is a doctoral student in community health (Université Laval) and Professor in Social Work at the University of Quebec at Rimouski campus in Lévis, Québec. Anchored in the practice of community organizing, she has been involved for more than 20 years in supporting the inclusion and sociopolitical participation of youth, particularly those considered marginalized, in Canada and elsewhere in the world. She sees her research practice as a tool for activism and a lever to support collective intervention.

Ana Cecilia Salazar worked with indigenous women and liberation theology for 18 years. She served as a Cuenca City Council member (2000–2004), founded Cuenca City to Live Collective, defends water rights, and teaches sociology at the University of Cuenca. She did postgraduate studies in Leuven and has a master's in participatory social research from Madrid. She has directed the Sociology Department, the university-wide Community Engagement Program, and the Social Development Organizational Support program at the University of Cuenca.

Anindita Sarker received her PhD from the Faculty of Information Technology at Monash University (2021). Her research area is information and communication technologies, gender, and development. She works as a research assistant with the Digital Equity and Digital Transformation Group at Monash and with the joint Monash–Oxfam PROTIC project in Bangladesh. She also teaches there. Previously she worked in international development for many years in Bangladesh with major non-governmental organizations. She has a bachelor's and master's in anthropology from Jahangirnagar University.

Molly Schwebach is Lecturer and Research Program Coordinator with dual appointments at the University of Wisconsin-Madison's Nelson Institute for Environmental Studies and School of Nursing. She works to institutionalize high-quality civic engagement through research, graduate and undergraduate academic programs and curriculum, and in coordinating community events, in partnership with staff colleagues. In 2010, she developed and administered the Zieve Fellowship Program that supported the development of the service learning courses described in her chapter.

Alessandra Seiter is the Community Engagement Librarian at Harvard Kennedy School Library and Knowledge Services. Informed by her academic background in the geography of social movements and direct experience in movement organizing, she is primarily interested in how libraries can be leveraged to support the visionary knowledge production of counter-hegemonic social formations.

Alexander Shelton serves as a community organizer that uses yoga and creative place making to create spaces that prioritize the mindfulness and illness of people of color. As a parent and eco-activist, community matters, access matters, children matter. CAKE allows Alexander to continue the efforts of the Preschool Promise in a more localized way.

Mark Skinner is Dean of Humanities and Social Sciences at Trent University, where he is also Professor in the Trent School of the Environment. A leading rural aging scholar, Mark was the founding director of the Trent Centre for Aging and Society and recently completed his appointment as Canada Research Chair in Rural Aging, Health and Social Care.

José Wellington Sousa is an emerging community development scholar and practitioner placed in Canada. He is Assistant Professor of Management at Crandall University, New Brunswick and a PhD candidate in Adult Education and Community Engagement at the University of Regina, Saskatchewan. His current research interests include asset-based and community-led development, participatory research facilitation, and the social formation of community-based facilitators and organic intellectuals.

Danielle Stevens has a bachelor's in anthropology from the University of Utah and a master's in political science and applied community and economic development from Illinois State University. She is a dedicated service learner and served as an AmeriCorps VISTA with a statewide non-profit in Boise, ID and as a United States Peace Corps volunteer in Ukraine from 2017 to 2019. She believes strongly in collaborative, grassroots efforts that challenge the status quo and encourage systemic change.

Larry Stillman is Senior Research Fellow, Digital Equity and Digital Transformation Group, Faculty of Information Technology, Monash University. He has been a practitioner and researcher in community and development informatics since 1994, in Australia, South Africa, and the Bangladeshi PROTIC project. He has been involved with the Community Informatics Research Network conferences at Monash Prato, Italy since 2003. He is a member of the research group Cuneiform Texts in Australia and New Zealand.

Randy Stoecker is Professor of Community and Environmental Sociology at the University of Wisconsin-Madison, and has been "practicing" (meaning, trying to get it right) the integration of participatory action research and community development for more than three decades. He hopes to escape academia as soon as he can find a producer for his rock opera, *Apocalypse Optimism*, so he can retire rich and famous.

Michael Topmiller is a researcher who helps lead CAKE as part of his job. He is motivated to do this work through his experiences seeing inequities and wanting that all kids have the same opportunities to succeed as his own children. Michael does not live in Carthage or Roselawn.

Chelsea Viteri is an activist, educator, youth worker, and artist. Born and raised in Quito, Ecuador, she completed her undergraduate and graduate studies at Clark University in theater arts and community development and planning. She has worked with diverse communities in both Ecuador and the United States, utilizing theater, music, poetry, and Hip Hop as a means for collective empowerment and creative conflict transformation. She is the resident director of Pachaysana's "Rehearsing Change" study abroad program.

M. Alex Wagaman is Associate Professor in the School of Social Work at Virginia Commonwealth University and a co-researcher with Advocates for Richmond Youth, a participatory action research team that conducts research and engages in advocacy to end youth and young adult homelessness.

Jessica L. Walsh is Executive Director of the Women's Resource Center in Newport, RI, the backbone organization of the Newport Health Equity Zone collaborative.

Elaine G. Williams is a researcher and organizer with Advocates for Richmond Youth.

Cynthia Wooten is a mother and grandmother with a purpose. She has worked in early childhood for over 40 years. As a director of an early childhood center, she sees the world as a window of opportunity for all, especially our children. She strives to be a voice for the voiceless, a hand to lift up when down. CAKE represents everything about who she is and has given her a renewed sense of hope that community matters.

1. Introduction: reflecting upon the development of participatory action research and community development efforts

Randy Stoecker and Adrienne Falcón

This collection is a first-of-its-kind attempt to carefully consider the possibilities and challenges of strategically integrating participatory action research (PAR) and community development (CD).[1] It's not that people haven't been connecting the two in practice for a very long time. But they by and large have not documented how to connect them and where the overlap can enrich the practices of each and point to the transformative nature of both.

To begin, we first need to define how we are using the two terms. We use *participatory action research* as a generic term for all research that is guided by and generates knowledge for use by civil society organizations for local community projects or groups of individuals who have come together to improve their communities. We are well aware that there are many different labels for this practice (Chandler and Torbert, 2003) including, most commonly, community-based participatory research, community-based research, action research, participatory research, and popular education. We choose PAR because it explicitly names the three important components of the practice – participation, action, and research. *Participation* refers to the principle that a civil society group or organization has power to guide and use a research process and an action process. It does not refer to token "advising" and it especially does not refer to people "participating" in any researcher-defined study. *Action* refers to the principle that the group is involved in some kind of community development process that the research is designed to support in a tangible and meaningful way. And *research* refers to any process of knowledge development that a group engages in that directly supports the action. This can be formal research, such as natural science research studying air or water quality, or social science research studying people, organizations, communities, or societies. It can also be information collection to support groups telling their own stories in prose or visual art.

We use *community development* as an inclusive term for projects led by community members that focus on the physical, cultural, environmental, and social development of rural and urban place-based communities. This term has been used for widely varying practices that include everything from massive-scale developments wholly controlled by governments, corporations, and international funders to tiny little grass-roots social change efforts. By using the term "community," we are excluding projects that are imposed upon place-based communities by outsiders. Even given that more restrictive definition, however, we will see that there is much to discuss in both the theory and practice of CD. Much like taking apart the key ideas behind each of the terms in *participatory action research*, analyzing the terms *community* and *development* separately provides a fuller understanding of their implications. The term "community" is used unreflectively for so many different collections of people that it has become meaningless. For our purposes, *community* refers to a face-to-face collective of people who interact through multiple intersecting roles to support each other and who sustain those interactions over time (Stoecker, 2016). The most obvious manifestations of this form of community are the rural village or the urban neighborhood, but there are many others. In such communities, people interact with each other as parents, workers, worshippers, consumers, volunteers, and many other roles. This distinguishes the community from single-interest associations. The face-to-face characteristic distinguishes the community from online networks whose members may provide significant support to each other but, because of their geographic dispersal, cannot engage collectively in place-based development. The temporal characteristic "over time" distinguishes the community from the temporary gathering.

Likewise, we limit the term *development* to the process of the community engaged in guiding its own improvement, as community members define such improvement. We acknowledge that the term development can have a problematic understanding based in a linear form with expected outcomes that highlight valuing global north capitalist ideals. We challenge that Euro-centric notion of development and instead offer to reclaim the word for processes of growth led by and for communities of individuals and their organizations. Our understanding of development does not exclude the involvement of outsiders or government, but it does mean that community members lead the process. And improvement can refer to physical, social, or cultural changes. Thus, community organizing that reconnects community members and allows them to have more societal power as a group is included in this definition.

Why bring these two models/practices together? We see great synergy between them. As societies across the globe become more complex, community development must deal with many consequent complexities – funding, negotiations with various levels of government and with funders, relations with non-governmental organizations, knowledge of new techniques and strategies, and understanding of many other contextual factors that affect the success of any community development effort. All of these things require forms of research, involving information, knowledge, and skills. This can involve anything from trying to recognize that there is even a problem, to understanding current conditions, informing community development priorities, choosing the best community development option for a given condition, or evaluating the success of the chosen option (Stoecker, 2013). Indeed, sometimes the community development project can itself be a research project, such as a community history project (Twells, 2008).

We now have a large literature on the many forms of PAR, though the practice has only recently generated its own journal, *Action Research*, and the publications have taken an increasingly higher education standpoint. Additionally, the more recent literature has pushed aside some of the early global south literature and focused on the research process, not how it is connected to producing actual community outcomes. The emphasis has been on the relationships between researchers and community members, and the process of carrying out research projects (Beran and Lubin, 2012; Sandy and Holland, 2006). We are lacking good models of how to choose what research to do, and how to design research so it is directly tied to effective community change strategy. In sum, PAR lacks a community development framework.

Likewise, there is an enormous literature on community development extending well back in history, with its own journals like *The Community Development Journal* or *Community Development*. That literature has run the gamut from the process of bringing people together to do actual development projects to deepening theoretical analysis of social and political contexts. But it has not, except in passing, attended deeply to the role of knowledge development in those projects. That may be because there is often little formal research done as part of the project itself, though community development practitioners may draw upon past research to inform their projects (Stoecker, 2013). So when we look, for example, at collections purporting to discuss the intersection, such as Mayo et al. (2013) we see a concentration of papers on evaluating projects, or reflecting on their group process, rather than discussions of how research was used strategically in the conduct of the community development itself.

These two practices of PAR and CD seem wholly complementary of each other, and each seems quite lacking without the other. To fully understand both their complementarity and their individual insufficiency, we must look closely at each, recognizing the key role that power plays in both. Each seeks to offer new forms of power and knowledge to the participants, and thus challenge the existing social structural power system. Consequently, both the form and the content of these two approaches face significant obstacles to operating in ways that could be truly transformative.

We also recognize that both practices too often take a "global north" standpoint rather than fully include the insights and experiences of those doing engaged research and community development in the wide variety of cultures around the globe. Therefore, this handbook is intentionally international, including chapters from Latin America, Africa, and Asia, as well as North America and Europe. We also solicited chapters from people at a range of places in their career trajectories, and even in different careers (especially activists and academics), so that we could incorporate people who are in the thick of doing and discovering their practice as well as individuals with decades of experience to bridge not only cultural and national boundaries, but also generational differences and the practice–theory divide.

Along with seeking to include a multiplicity of voices, we have engaged ourselves as editors with the authors in a participatory process to edit and learn from each other. Each of the chapters was reviewed not only by the editors but also by other authors to enable a community of researchers/activists to learn from each other and produce a shared endeavor. The core of our commitment is to work in a way that engages with others in a respectful way so as to learn, grow, and be transformed through processes of engaging with PAR and CD in a global way.

We developed this project in this way because of our commitment as academics and practitioners. Each of us comes from a background of combining PAR and CD. We offer both of our stories here as a way to make visible our standpoints as editors.

ADRIENNE'S STORY

My first job out of college in 1990 was doing a version of PAR. I worked for the Urban Coalition of the Twin Cities doing research with communities of color in ways that would empower them to do their own research projects in the future. The first project involved doing research with community members about the hopes, dreams, and life experiences of undocumented and newly legalized immigrants in order to inform policy decisions at the state capitol. While we incorporated community members as researchers with us, and the report was used to protect food access for immigrants during the time of welfare reform, the project was not sustained nor did it lead to long-term community change. Nevertheless, a few of the leaders from that time are still active in their causes today. At the time, I knew that my work was inspired by Paulo Freire and others, but I did not have all the language that has since developed and which, to be truthful, must also be unpacked to understand how these terms are used to describe practices by individuals seeking to bring about community change.

In 1998, when I was doing participant observation research in graduate school, I was employed as a community organizer on the North Side of Chicago. Working with a group of teenagers, we created a group, YPMC, Young People Making a Change, so that they could have an organizational context for doing the work that was important to them on issues of police brutality. They knew that they and their friends were being affected negatively by their interactions with police. They shared stories among themselves about the "bad cops." I was new at organizing, but already in my fourth year of graduate school. I knew that if we wanted to convince others, we needed to move beyond individual stories or rumors.

During the summer after their sophomore year, six members of YPMC and I worked together on an organizing research and strategy project to try to raise awareness of the conflicts occurring between police and young people. We gathered data on youth and police interactions so that we could share findings, publicize issues, and provide evidence for making changes in the police system. Together with two youth interns, Billy and Yolanda, we designed a survey and spread it through their high school and diverse immigrant neighborhood to learn about their peers' experiences.

After we had gathered over 200 surveys, they entered the data and did some simple analysis of experiences. What we found was that, although there were some examples of clear-cut abuse – one of the members of the club experienced a police officer pulling down his pants "so I can see how big he is" said one cop to another – the majority of the abuse was not as extreme. It was in the daily small mistreatments that the breakdown was taking place. As one young person explained it, "when you are on the hood of a cop car in the summer, it gets hot." We also learned that some police officers were covering their badge numbers so that you could not report them.

We used our data to help us try to make a case to the Chicago Police Chief to try to force them to give business cards to police officers so we could track down who the "bad apples" were and to change how the Office of Professional Standards (OPS) – the reporting group within the police force for police brutality complaints – operated. We organized a community-wide meeting with the chief and OPS representatives. At this meeting, attended by over 300 people from all walks of life, young people and others who were recognized as community leaders shared the stories and experiences from their lives and the data in order to raise awareness of the conflicts on the streets. We asked the police department to provide business cards to officers so that we could find out who would and would not give out their cards and use that to identify who was mistreating young people. While in the end we did not win on our "asks" to the Police Chief, we did change awareness in the neighborhood. The young people who participated went on to organize more activities in their high school and community, engaging in community development in their neighborhood as they sought to make it safer for all.

In many ways, this project was a more successful version of PAR. The project from the start was owned by young people who were being affected by the police brutality. They created the survey, gathered the data, analyzed it, and shared it at a large community meeting. Through this collaboration, they built a group of friends that is still connected. They went on to work on other projects, challenging standardized tests in the Chicago Public Schools, and the youth police work has continued in the community. Therefore, this project stands as a much finer example of CD and PAR and yet still could be critiqued for not bringing about systemic change.

In 2020, I returned to this work, doing a survey in rural Minnesota where I now live with and through a local League of Women Voters committee with a group of young people and older adults, working intergenerationally in order to understand current interactions between young people and police. Recognizing the impact that this work has had on me and the participants over the years, including the Latino community leaders researching immigrants and the young people in Chicago who are still connected, raises questions about how this kind of approach impacts people's lives over the long haul.

Through this work one encounters challenges, and figures out when and how to persist. As a community organizer, I have learned the importance of building shared knowledge through PAR, strategizing to bring about community change; and through it all sharing ideas with a community of peers. That is what Randy and I have done in pulling together this book with our fellow authors, to try and learn from each other about how to keep improving not only the practices of PAR and CD, but also to address the ongoing social structural inequalities.

RANDY'S STORY

I first became aware of a PAR-style practice in graduate school in 1985, but in a very different way from Adrienne. I was just completing a class assignment when a community activist called me out. I was taking a qualitative research methods class, and the assignment was to do an in-depth interview with someone. At the time I was living in the Cedar-Riverside neighborhood in Minneapolis, and all around me there was sawing and hammering as old run-down houses were getting rehabbed. Wondering what was happening, I found out there was a neighborhood organization involved, and I set out to interview someone there. When I got to the organization's office, however, the person I asked to interview told me about how he was regularly bothered by students who wanted to do similar interviews, but none of those students so much as gave him a copy of anything they wrote from those interviews. He made me promise that I would be the exception, after which he politely answered my neophyte graduate student questions. When I came back a week or so later, obsessed with a still somewhat amorphous guilt about what I represented, I felt compelled to ask him if there was anything else I could do. Tim Mungavan pointed to a door in the corner of his office, beyond which was a short hallway. He explained that was the fire exit, but between his door and the outside door was a pile of stuff in the way and the fire marshal was leaning on him. With a twinkle in his eye, he asked if I could clean it all up. Feeling both guilt-ridden and intimidated I could only meekly nod yes. What I found between those doors were neighborhood newspapers and documents of all sorts that told the story of a neighborhood destined to be wiped off the map by a government-funded developer, but which organized and then created one of the strongest alternative housing development programs in the country. By the time I finished cleaning up that hallway, I realized I had found my dissertation, and began a relationship with the neighborhood that continues to this day, more than three decades later.

If Tim Mungavan and the residents of Cedar-Riverside turned me from traditional extractive and exploitive academic research, it was Dave Beckwith and the residents of Toledo, Ohio who taught me how to be truly useful. When I started my career at the University of Toledo as a young assistant professor, Dave asked me to lunch, where he presented to me a whole page of research projects. I negotiated my way down to one – a resources and needs assessment of Toledo's struggling neighborhood-based development organizations. The goal was to understand what they were and were not accomplishing in terms of neighborhood development, and what they needed to do better. We had a small team of folks from the neighborhood groups guiding the research, but I was charged with the actual labor.

I went from neighborhood to neighborhood interviewing the directors of these tiny community-based development organizations and looking through their records. And because Dave, who was known as a highly skilled community organizer with an unchallenged reputation in Toledo, led the effort, I got all the information I wanted. But the story was horribly depressing. I had arrived in Toledo after having written about an amazingly successful neighborhood, and now was tasked with writing what looked like failure. Still, I dutifully put together my report, which Dave promptly sent off to the printer, after declaring "I know exactly what we'll do!" A few weeks later, I and my report were the keynote at an all-day city-wide neighborhood development meeting. After I recited the depressing findings, Dave sent all the government officials and funders into one room and all the neighborhood groups to another room to talk about what they wanted from the other group and what they were willing to do for it. Miraculously (so I thought, but Dave had prepped a few people in each room in advance, like a good organizer), both groups agreed that funding had to be dramatically increased, and that the neighborhood groups had to significantly ramp up their skills and capacity. Out of this formed the Working Group on Neighborhoods (WGN), which then commissioned my next research project – a study of foundation philanthropy in Toledo. In some ways it was another depressing project, showing just how little funding went to community development. But Dave once again reached into his community organizer toolbox and a couple of years later that report helped WGN leverage $2 million to support capacity building and other support for the neighborhood groups. A few years after that you could drive down the streets of those neighborhoods and see new and rehabbed housing.

So I learned my PAR practice directly from a community development context. And it gave me a model that I have continued to learn more about and feel like I am becoming more successful at. More recently I have been figuring out how to do this by involving students. I have been able to go beyond using communities to train students and instead have been able to learn how students can dramatically expand my own research capacity. As a consequence, I have seen community groups put our research to work for environmental improvements, a new community center, and reduced local discrimination against Hip Hop artists.

But I have not seen a lot of work like mine being done through higher education institutions and I've consequently always felt like a Martian in academic meetings about all this "scholarship of engagement" stuff. So my goal for this volume is to have a discussion I can't find elsewhere – how to integrate PAR and CD to achieve the kinds of outcomes I have witnessed.

BACKGROUND ON PARTICIPATORY ACTION RESEARCH

One way to think about the history of PAR is to recognize that it has origins in both the global south and global north and that the two origin stories are very different in ways that reflect their understandings of power and resistance and the role of information in maintaining the current system versus challenging it.

History

The documented practice of PAR began later in the global south than in the north, but is worth beginning with because its influence in the north seems to have been greater. It may also be that additional documents on its origins in the global south are harder to encounter and as such merit future additional excavation. In the east, Rajesh Tandon in India and Muhammad Anisur Rahmin in Bangladesh have been leaders in the literature and the conversations about the practice. In the west, the practice has been made most visible by Paulo Freire and Augusto Boal in Brazil and Orlando Fals Borda in Colombia.

All of these practitioners emphasized a kind of knowledge mobilization that sometimes used formal research procedures but also commonly drew on people's experiential knowledge to inform organizing and action against various oppressive social conditions being imposed on the people. Action drove the desire for information and research that could lead to social change.

Paulo Freire (1970) in particular became famous for the practice of popular education and conscientization – a process of facilitating people to engage in a participatory education process that starts from their own experience. The phrase *pedagogy of the oppressed* that titled one of his books (Freire, 1970) was adapted by Augusto Boal (1979) to what he called *theatre of the oppressed*. Rajesh Tandon's (Brown and Tandon, 1983) work, which he labeled *participatory research*, involved more formal research processes, but focused on grass-roots people developing knowledge to fight oppression. Fals-Borda (1991) used the phrase *participatory action research*. Similarly to Tandon, he emphasized more formal research, and set up principles for the co-construction of knowledge with grass-roots people. Rahman may have been the strongest advocate for people leading not just their own research processes (1991) but also their own community development (1993).

In the global south from the beginning, then, the vision for PAR was liberatory and even revolutionary. The purpose was to change structural conditions of oppression, and the practice lived the goals. If the people were to be liberated, they could not be led by the privileged. All of these practitioners believed that the people themselves must lead. And while they believed that the people must lead in an educated and informed way, they were wise in realizing that such education could not be imposed on them but that even the education process must be led by the people.

In the global north there was a distinct lack of revolutionary goals in the official version of the history of PAR. Kurt Lewin (1946, 1948) is perhaps the most notable and cited historical influence. His practice of *action research* focused on engaging people across structural divides – workers and managers, and people from structurally unequal racial groups. In Lewin's process the researcher was a central figure, often leading both the research process and the action process with the goal of improving production, very much in line with maintaining structural hierarchies. In working across structural divides, Lewin can be seen as operating in a conflict resolution mode without a willingness to directly confront structural power differentials.

Lewin's approach, as well as the action research label, has been picked up most prominently in the field of education (Kemmis, 1960; Sherman et al., 2004). And in sociology, William Foote Whyte's (1990) work, which he labeled *participatory action research*, expressed very much a Lewinian process.

Of course, not all work in the global north has been researcher-led and oriented to conflict resolution. Indeed if one extracts an alternative history, there is a long-standing tradition of other community-engaged research projects primarily led by women and people of color. Going back to the early twentieth century, one of the more participatory-oriented research projects was Hull House maps and papers (Residents of Hull House, 2007). This project, led primarily by residents of the famous settlement house in Chicago at the close of the nineteenth century, remains a role model for community-based ethnography.

Another overlooked tradition, especially in academia, is the work of Myles Horton, through the Highlander Folk School in Appalachia. He drew on some of the practices of Hull House but also the Danish folk schools. Horton's work, consequently, looked much more like Paulo Freire than Kurt Lewin. Highlander's process was very much popular education – bringing together people experiencing a common issue to tell their own stories about the issue and devise their own strategies for dealing with it (Horton and Freire, 1990). The organization was central to the founding and growth of the racially integrated Congress of Industrial Organizations and to the Civil Rights Movement.

When John Gaventa took over the directorship of Highlander, he added an explicit participatory research approach, most famously with the Appalachian Land Ownership study (Appalachian Land Ownership Task Force, 1983) that exposed the oppressive influence of mining in the region. Gaventa, a sociologist, also brought a theoretical perspective to the work that emphasized the importance of structural power relationships in the research itself and in the role of the research in social change efforts (Gaventa and Cornwall, 2001). Indeed, his work on knowledge and power informs this text in many ways, recognizing that knowledge is a form of power and that even the definition of what is considered knowledge, data, and information is in and of itself an act of power.

Contemporary Practice

The global south and global north veins of practice have remained in PAR. David Brown and Rajesh Tandon (1983) were the first to contrast the approaches, referring to them by their original labels, *action research* and *participatory research*. They were followed by Stoecker (2003a), who added more theoretical framing to their differences. In basic terms, the Lewinian model is comfortable having the researcher lead the research process, and follows a functionalist theory of change. In functionalism, the important standard for the good society is that all its members are socially sorted into appropriate roles and that the system remains stable. Conflict is seen as a symptom of an unhealthy society and groups challenging the system are seen as expressing deviance. Within these theoretical frameworks, Lewinian-style action research is designed more to maintain system stability through minor, gradual adjustments that may involve only token demobilizing participation by oppressed groups (Arnstein, 1969).

The global south model in contrast puts much greater emphasis on the empowerment and liberation of oppressed people, following a conflict theory of change. In conflict theory, superficial stability is not an indicator of a healthy society when there are inequalities in access to the resources and amenities of that society. Open conflict, in such societies, is a positive development as it indicates the potential for progressive change (Morrow, 1978; Eitzen et al., 2012; Downes and Rock, 2011). Participatory research is designed to support the organization and mobilization of oppressed groups pressing for dramatic changes in the social system.

The youth participatory action research (YPAR) efforts from the 1990s to today stand in sharp contrast to much of the more mainstream work in the United States (U.S.). In these efforts, young people are invited to study their communities and processes which affect them in order to bring about change. These efforts are often linked to community organizing and honoring the wisdom of diverse young people. This is in part why we have one section of the book dedicated to models adopting this approach.[2]

But in general, we can't tell today what model a practitioner is following by the label they use. Indeed, even going decades back we see "participatory action research" being used by both the more conflict-oriented Fals Borda and the functionalist-oriented Whyte. Stringer's (2014) "action research" looks more like Tandon's "participatory research." The labels are simply not helpful for more than perhaps orienting the discipline of the practitioner. The term "action research" still tends to be used more in education, "community-based participatory research" in public health, and "community-based research" in the liberal arts. But within each label the variations in actual practice are so wide that there is more variation within than between.

The challenge facing PAR, beyond the diversity of practice, is figuring out how to enhance the action component. Practitioners have focused much more on the "P" and the "R" than the "A." Public health has made some strides in connecting the action component (Minkler and Wallerstein, 2008) but hasn't built robust theoretical how-to models.

And thus the gap between PAR and CD remains unfilled.

BACKGROUND ON COMMUNITY DEVELOPMENT

CD, on the global stage, has been a comprehensive practice that includes both social and physical forms of development. Since its inception it has been a contested term. The practice of CD, of course, dates back to the beginning of collective action by people to improve their existence. But the professionalization of the practice has been more recent.

History

In both the global north and south people have long-standing traditions that could be understood as CD. From barn raisings in the U.S. to *mingas* in the Andes mountains where indigenous people would come together to accomplish community projects, people have always worked together to improve communities. While barn raisings are rare now in the U.S., the practice of *mingas* continues in Peru, Ecuador, and Bolivia. In Quito, for example, people came together in low-income neighborhoods in the 1980s to build childcare centers for the community in response to family needs.

Two starting points for professional community development in the global north would be the settlement movement in the United Kingdom and Cooperative Extension in the U.S. In 1884 Toynbee Hall (Till, 2013) was the first in a wave of settlement houses that would sweep Britain and the U.S. Established in buildings located in marginalized neighborhoods, settlement houses brought together college-educated professors, students, and recent graduates to provide services and build on the existing cultures of their host communities. Settlement house staff often lived on the premises, thus often building strong relationships with residents (Matthews and Kimmis, 2001; Davis, 1984). Looking back on the settlement house movement in the U.S. we can also see its colonizing tendencies, as those institutions often acted out the pressures on them to assimilate immigrants (Mieras, 2008).

At about the same time, a practice known in England as "university extension" focused on bringing university research to farmers. This practice was formalized in the U.S. through a variety of legislative acts establishing the land grant university system (McDowell, 2001) and then Cooperative Extension in 1914 that expanded university engagement with communities from agriculture to home economics and community development more generally (Rasmussen, 1989; Somersan, 1997). And while the land grant system attempted to integrate the knowledge mission of higher education with community development, it must be noted that the "land grants" that funded such universities came from the sale of land stolen from indigenous people (Lee and Ahtone, 2020), fundamentally contradicting its purpose.

British and U.S. governments and professional practitioners then spread the practice globally where it became further entangled with colonization. The principles of empowering local communities to develop themselves became confused with imposing Western development models on them. As the global north practices of community development spread across the global south they began clashing with community development practices already emerging in the global south. Among the most important alternatives to the colonizing development models in the early twentieth century was the Swaraj movement promoted by Gandhi (1909) which focused on developing communities of local self-reliance, against imposed statist authority and especially colonial authority. In practice that meant organizing and developing the skills and knowledge of local community residents to do the work required for self-development.

The post-World War II era saw the waning of statist colonization, as many colonized nations regained at least their political independence. But neocolonial forms of development persisted, as global north standards of development persisted among nations whose global corporations benefited from continued resource extraction and whose development funding schemes imposed western standards of consumption on newly legally independent nations (Willis, 2011). But because this historical moment saw a new need for community development as newly independent nations, and other war-ravaged nations, worked to rebuild their societies, neocolonialism exposed contradictions and created space for challenges. Significantly, by 1955 the United Nations chose to define community development as "a process designed to create conditions of economic and social progress of the whole community, with its active participation and the fullest possible reliance on the community's initiative" (United Nations, 1955: 6).

But the shift in rhetoric to such participatory development is not free of contradiction. Mallence Bart-Williams from Sierra-Leone notes "It's quite evident that the aid is in fact not coming from the West to Africa, but from Africa to the Western world. The Western world depends on Africa in every possible way, since alternative resources are scarce out here … While one hand gives under the flashing lights of cameras, the other takes, in the shadows" (Pangambam, 2018).

Contemporary Models

How can we understand contemporary community development? There are so many varied practices in so many parts of the world. One starting point is to follow Boothroyd and Davis' (1993) distinction between three forms of what they call "community economic development." They use the acronym with a carefully structured creativity, asking what the practice looks like when it emphasizes the economic (cEd), the development (ceD), or the community (Ced). In their analysis, *cEd* looks most like the capital-intensive colonizing development projects that allow little community input and prop up existing power relations. Its focus is on economic growth, without regard to externalities. Moving to *ceD*, the emphasis can still be economic, but the process is more rooted in the locale, focusing on local resources and processes for a more customized intervention that takes into account the quality of development. It is in *Ced* that alternatives blossom, as the focus is on community-led processes that build the bonds of community itself and can work much further outside of the box.

Another way to distinguish the practices is through a two-dimensional model that focuses on the degree of social change on one axis and the degree of constituency control on the other (Beckwith, 1997). Community organizing has high constituency control and a high social change focus. Forms of community-led physical community development have high constituency control but low social change focus. Advocacy has a high social change focus but low constituency control. Advocacy, as defined in this model, does focus on systems change, but the advocate is usually a professional who is again separate from the constituency. Finally, traditional social services have low constituency control and a low social change focus. In the U.S., social services are typically developed by professionals who are separated from the constituencies they serve, and such service professionals focus on filling the gaps in the existing system rather than changing it.

Community organizing and physical community development stand in contrast from advocacy and social services in that they both attempt to be driven by their constituencies in terms of what issues they take on and what strategies they use. The theoretical and practical distinction is that physical community development works within the system and its existing rules to create jobs, housing, and other community amenities, while community organizing emphasizes changing the system rules, often so that community members can engage in forms of community development that leads to better jobs, housing, and other community amenities (Callahan et al., 1999).

Global North Community Development

The CD box, then, in the U.S., is quite specialized. It has even led to a specific form of organization called a community development corporation (CDC). CDCs were formed partly as a response to a massive wave of community organizing in the 1970s, and could even be portrayed as attempts by elites to dilute community organizing into more acceptable forms of community work that didn't challenge the existing system (Siriani and Friedland, 2001). As the model became popular especially in the U.S. urban "rustbelt" stretching from the Midwest to the northeast, more and more neighborhood-based constituencies started forming their own CDCs, partly taking control back from outsiders (Yin, 1998). And while CDCs tried their hand at a wide variety of community development activities, most of them found that what they were best at was housing development (von Hoffman, 2013). But over time economies of scale caught up with them, and into the 1990s and beyond there was a wave of CDC downsizings, failures, and mergers that diluted grass-roots control over neighborhood development (Rohe et al., 2003).

This model is pretty unique to the U.S. So yet another way to think about the variations in practice is to consider one of the forms that U.S. exceptionalism takes – the splitting of community organizing and CD into separate practices and even separate organizations. In much of the world, organizing and development are combined (Kenny, 2002), and sometimes the term social development is applied to it (Binswanger-Mkhize et al., 2010). But in the U.S. the practices are usually split. Community organizing developed a culture of confrontation and opposition in the U.S., while community development grew to mostly refer to physical development, especially in the arena of housing (von Hoffman, 2013). This is, of course, partly due to the other form of U.S. exceptionalism – the anti-government culture and glorified unfettered capitalism that characterizes the country (Lipset, 1996). The few attempts to recombine organizing and development have been sporadic and short-lived (Greenberg, 2005; Stoecker, 2003b).

In the rest of the global north, and including the settler colonies of Canada, Australia, and New Zealand imposed by Britain in the seventeenth–nineteenth centuries, government is not as suspect, the government-sponsored safety net is stronger, and community organizing is less confrontational and oppositional (see for example, Community Organisers, 2020). In addition, stronger welfare states provide for more citizen needs (van Kersbergen and Vis, 2013) reducing the need for a strong non-profit sector for things like housing development. But devolution and austerity have in recent decades created a need for more U.S.-style community organizing in places with previously strong welfare states (Harries et al., 2020; Hande and Kelly, 2015; Bailey et al., 2017). In recent years, this has resulted in CD around immigrant, refugee, and Roma communities increasing in prominence (Ryder et al., 2014; Kirwan and Jacob, 2016).

Global South Community Development

In the global south, however, CD continues to operate in the tension between large outside forces and community-based efforts. The largest and least accountable outside forces, of course, exist in the form of the International Monetary Fund and the World Bank. There are also massively large non-governmental development organizations like Oxfam that operate in communities across the global south with grass-roots groups. National development efforts are also often designed in country capitals in order to promote the incursion of capitalism into rural and indigenous communities in order to make them "civilized" or "correct." How much community control exists in such efforts can vary tremendously, though there is increasing support for stronger forms of community control. Even the World Bank promotes their research findings that show greater success with greater community control (Binswanger-Mkhize et al., 2010). It is important to note that in general the World Bank is viewed with skepticism if not explicit criticism by many in the global south, especially those who would embrace a more transformation approach to PAR and CD.

These efforts can contrast with the most home-grown efforts at CD, many of which are informed by indigenous culture. As Sillitoe (2006) describes, development that starts from indigenous knowledge allows for local definitions of both problems and strategies to prevail over outsider-imposed definitions. There are more formal local community development programs such as the barefoot doctors movement in China (Rosenthal and Greiner, 1982). In Aotearoa/New Zealand, the practice of Kaupapa Maori is deeply informed by Maori culture (Mane, 2009). In this book Asturias and Salazar demonstrate this in their chapter about Cuenca, Ecuador.

One of the important characteristics of much international development is the inclusion of human rights as an integral part of CD. Indeed, much international CD focuses on power and even systems change (Kenny et al., 2018; Gaventa and Cornwall, 2001). In the global south, as a consequence, those who focus on process, rather than just physical development have a more prominent role in CD. Even some of the historical figures associated with forms of participatory action research – Paulo Freire, Augusto Boal, and others – are included in the field of CD (Ledworth, 2016; Sloman, 2012).

THE NEOLIBERAL TURN IN COMMUNITY DEVELOPMENT

One of the most important trends in CD led by the global north has been the increasing influence of neoliberalism on the field. Neoliberalism manifests itself in the elimination of both government regulation over economic actors and government services for those harmed by such economic actors. Philosophically, neoliberalism replaces values about collective action and the community good with values about individualistic achievement and responsibility, and human values with economic values. At the government level, this means dismantling the welfare state (Hartman, 2005; Hasenfeld and Garrow, 2012) and imposing austerity measures (Conway, 2014), restricting various forms of protest and collective action, including union organizing (Blum, 2019; Peters, 2011), and dramatically scaling back environmental and health protections (Castree, 2010). In CD, neoliberalism replaces collective forms of development such as cooperative housing, worker and consumer cooperatives, and community agriculture with new practices emphasizing collective impact, community capitals, asset-based CD (ABCD), resilience, social entrepreneurship, and capacity building. Here we expand on Stoecker and Witkovsky's (2020) discussion of these neoliberal influences over CD.

Collective impact may seem to be the CD approach least influenced by neoliberalism, as it usually involves both government and non-profit agencies in coordinating efforts around ameliorating social problems (Kania and Kramer, 2011). Indeed, the critiques of collective impact often come from those who see the model as privileging professionals in devising and implementing solutions, and excluding constituency groups from the process (Christens and Inzeo, 2015). Looking at the neoliberal influences on collective impact, however, Christens and Inzeo (2015) also see the practice as avoiding any analysis of root problems or challenging existing power structures, and adopting a form of neoliberal managerialism that can legitimize cuts in government services.

The community capitals approach (Flora et al., 2016) adds cultural, human, political, economic, financial, and environmental capitals to the social capital model and turns them into exchangeable commodities. But most important and problematic is social capital, which begins by thinking about social networks as literally a form of "capital" that can be invested for either individual gain (Fukuyama, 1999) or, in our case, community improvement. In particular this model advocates that, to achieve such goals, communities should switch from emphasizing "bonding capital" – close relationships of trust within a community – to "bridging" or "linking" social capital that can connect the community to external actors with access to resources (Putnam, 2000). Thus it takes human relationships and transforms them from what Marx would call "use values" – things that are valued in and of themselves – to "exchange values" – things whose value is determined by exchange in a market setting. In addition, it requires communities to frame themselves in such a way as to appear attractive to such outsiders, limiting their development options (DeFilippis, 2001; Van den Berk-Clark and Pyles, 2012; Stoecker, 2004). The other community capitals then become similarly transformed.

The association of ABCD with neoliberalism is controversial (Roy, 2017). The approach initially develops as Kretzmann and McKnight (1993) critique the social welfare approach to poverty alleviation, arguing that the social welfare approach sees marginalized people as needy and deficient and thus needing help from professionals. Kretzmann and McKnight then argue that we should see people in poverty, and their communities, as having assets or "gifts" instead. But such an analysis can show a neoliberal bias in two ways. First, charging that social welfare approaches portray people in poverty as somehow deficient is not only inaccurate but distracts us from the structural argument that the fault lies not in the individuals but in a system that puts up barriers to success. Second, ABCD's solution is for those individuals to deploy their assets to do their own development, again distracting us from structural analysis that could illuminate the systemic barriers to doing so and replacing it with a neoliberal ideology of individualization and privatization (MacLeod and Emejulu, 2014). Thus, people's failure to develop their communities without outside assistance could lead to a form of neoliberal victim blaming (Stoecker, 2004).

Resilience is a close relative of ABCD, even replacing sustainability as a standard among some CD practitioners (Axel-Lute, 2019). The focus of resilience has individualistic underpinnings, promoting strategies for how individuals can be resilient, but then expanding the idea to communities. The concept of resilience itself emphasizes individual responsibility for coping with the uncertainties and disruptions that are endemic to a deregulated capitalist economy devoid of significant safety nets, along with climate chaos and the increasing global challenges that seem to surround us (Joseph, 2013; Tierney, 2015). Thus, like ABCD, it places responsibility on the individual, or individual communities to fend for themselves, avoiding any analysis of the social structural roots of the threats all around.

Social entrepreneurship is the most clearly neoliberal form of CD. It takes the idea of the self-made person to the extreme, showing that it is not only possible to take responsibility for one's own fate, but then help others at the same time. The concept is deeply hegemonic, emphasizing the social good of the social entrepreneur, and distracting us away from how the social entrepreneur also could exploit wage workers (Lazzarato, 2009). It is to these individual social entrepreneurs that we now turn for housing development, job development, token environmental protection, and social services (Hamschmid and Pirson, 2011). This model is promoted across the globe (Mayer and Rankin, 2002) and another indicator of the hegemony involved is the lengths to which authoritarian governments in developing countries will go to create support structures for a select chosen subset of the supposedly hyper-individualistic social entrepreneurs (Kreitmeyr, 2019).

Finally, capacity building then becomes the focus for technical assistance to CD organizations. And given the increasing dominance of neoliberal-influenced models such as collective impact, community capitals, ABCD, resilience, and social entrepreneurship, capacity building becomes training in neoliberalism. Additionally, within neoliberalism, CDCs and other such organizations must operate like businesses, putting the economic bottom line before the human and environmental bottom line. As CD organizations "professionalize," the technical financial aspects of development take precedence, CDCs become more easily controlled by funders (Thibault, 2007) and embedded in the non-profit industrial complex (INCITE!, 2007), and they become more removed from their constituencies (Stoecker, 1997).

Within the neoliberal context, we are consequently seeing important shifts in on-the-ground practice of CD. Instead of CDCs producing housing, community development financial institutions are now supporting social entrepreneurs who are acting as developers (Doshna,

2015). Farmers' markets, branded as the apex of direct-to-consumer community agriculture, are also physical manifestations of the pure neoliberal market unfettered by collective controls, excluding those who cannot pay the often higher prices of such a neoliberal market setting (Joassart-Marcelli and Bosco, 2014).

MOVING TOWARD PROGRESSIVE COMMUNITY DEVELOPMENT PRACTICE

These trends show a CD practice unreflectively driven more by neoliberal ideology than knowledge about the structural conditions affecting marginalized communities. Neoliberal CD models are glorifying the isolated individual, or the isolated individual community, over the reality that we are all connected and need to organize collectively if we are to develop strong, sustainable communities that build into strong, sustainable societies.

Good CD practice needs to be guided by deep knowledge – of social structures and power relations, of forms of collective action, of policy options, and of criteria for social, environmental, and other forms of sustainability.

As CD becomes more technical, driven by exclusionary technical knowledge and led by professionals, it risks becoming even more of a colonizing practice propping up capitalism rather than empowering people. And in a more complicated world, the kinds of development that CD can accomplish require even more access to information and knowledge. In order to roll back the neoliberalization of CD and return the practice to the people's control, we need to expand and integrate the practice of PAR because the people will only be able to control their own development when they have access to the means of knowledge production that can build their power and inform community development practice. This collection attempts to inform that goal.

ABOUT THIS COLLECTION

We are very proud of all the contributions to this book. Our authors gathered together with us to talk about their work in a virtual meeting, gave each other feedback on their drafts in a peer-review process, wrote and revised their chapters multiple times, and worked tirelessly to help us through all the details in the final stretches of submitting the manuscript. We express our deepest appreciation to the authors for their work in the world and on this collection.

Though a plurality of chapters in this collection come from the global north, reflecting inequalities in the global political economic and higher education system, we also have chapters from work being done on five continents. These chapters represent the commitment of our authors to writing through a global pandemic, sometimes as their own projects were impacted by that pandemic. Some of them explore the challenges of integrating PAR and CD while navigating the baggage of colonization. Others explore how jettisoning the baggage of colonization allows for new innovations in PAR/CD. The chapters range incredibly widely across varying PAR methods and varying CD approaches. Our grouping of the chapters is thus probably arbitrary. But they help us at least to feel some coherence in the volume. You will see that the early chapters mostly review institutionalized PAR/CD in the global north, and then gradually transition to the global south, with the final chapters presenting what we think are the most provocative perspectives on PAR/CD practice. But no chapter is only about the topic it's listed under. So if you are interested in urban development, for example, you will find chapters across the parts. Nevertheless, here is the organization we have chosen.

Part I, Structures and processes for integrating participatory action research and community development, looks at some of the infrastructure we can create in order to bring the two practices together. Megan Brown, Jack Dougherty, and Jeff Partridge explore the Liberal Arts Action Lab – a unique partnership between a liberal arts college and a community college in the northeastern U.S. that has committed to community-driven processes and supported community groups to achieve real community development outcomes. Randy Stoecker, Todd Barr, and Mark Skinner then discuss an almost singularly unique model of integrating PAR and CD managed by three community-based non-profit organizations in Ontario, Canada that connect university research resources with community groups to advance their community development goals. Jenice Meyer and Katelyn Baumann look at how university, local government, education, and non-profit actors came together to facilitate a community-based visioning project in a small northern U.S. city. Manuel Martínez Casanova and Adrienne Falcón develop a theory based on work at the University of Santa Clara, Cuba that focuses on social development of communities as "protagonists" in society.

Part II, Organizing communities, focuses on PAR/CD projects that emphasize building people's power and capacity. Dadit Hidayat and Molly Schwebach compare one project organizing a white community around environmental sustainability with another organizing Black men returning from prison around urban agriculture in the northern U.S., showing how PAR supported these two very different projects in perhaps surprisingly similar ways. Lucie Gélineau et al. explore PAR/CD projects facilitated by community organizers who themselves were supported through a community of practice to do PAR in Québec, Canada. Finally, Nicole Breazeale et al. look at how story telling as a form of PAR, in a rural community college where the students were members of the communities with whom they were collaborating, supports community organizing and social change in the southern U.S.

Part III, Building organizations and neighborhoods, discusses the integration of PAR and CD in relation to community and organization capacity building. Maxwell Droznin and colleagues tell a fascinating story of a university–community PAR/CD relationship in the southern U.S. that gradually transformed from being university-led to being community-led. Laura O'Toole, Nancy Gordon, and Jessica Walsh exhibit how PAR can be used for organizational development in a neighborhood-based community organization in the northeastern U.S. Farrah Jacquez et al. describe how a neighborhood-based organization came together in the northern U.S. to guide early childhood education efforts, and its use of participatory evaluation as part of its organizational development. Larry Stillman et al. then explore the challenges involved in bringing together universities, non-governmental organizations, and local community groups to facilitate a Bangladesh community informatics project to support women-led commerce using mobile phones and project-based PAR.

Part IV, Growing youth power, includes perspectives on the practice of YPAR. M. Alex Wagaman et al. discuss the integration of YPAR and CD around a youth homelessness community education and advocacy effort led by young people experiencing homelessness in the U.S. Danielle Stevens, Tetiana Kidruk, and Oleh Petrus analyze a Ukraine YPAR project to enhance youth volunteerism that ended up turning into a youth leadership development project. Kathryn Morgan, Brian Christens, and Melody Gibson explore an ambitious project in the southern U.S. combining urban design and YPAR with middle schoolers.

Part V, Responding to crisis, came together partly because of the COVID-19 pandemic, but is more about how PAR/CD projects respond to mass disruption. Ming Hu's chapter focuses on how a coalition of community groups came together to support a community struck by the Szechuan earthquake of 2008 in China, employing an innovative PAR/CD strategy. Laura Livingston compares two PAR/CD projects, one university-led and the other community-led, that carried on through the COVID-19 epidemic in the northern U.S., with counter-intuitive findings. And Alessandra Seiter shows us how mutual aid groups that sprang up to support communities disrupted by COVID-19 innovated PAR/CD strategies.

Part VI, Expanding our thinking, includes the most provocative chapters in this collection that involve the deepest questioning of PAR/CD practice and show us community-led PAR/CD that we may otherwise not even include in the practice. Ana Elisa Astudillo and Ana Cecilia Salazar tell the story of a community collective in Cuenca, Ecuador that uses PAR in support of its Right to the City efforts. Ihsan Mejdi and Celeste Koppe tell us about a community in Tunisia that, in the wake of the revolution, reclaimed agricultural land from colonization and used it to expand human rights and community development, using community historical knowledge as its PAR support. José Wellington Sousa uses global south PAR philosophy and reflexive experience in the Amazon to rethink PAR/CD practice by focusing on relationship building as not just a path toward development but as a form of development in itself. Daniel Bryan and Chelsea Viteri then round out the collection by promoting a decolonizing PAR/CD built on stories as both knowledge and relationship, reflecting on experience in Ecuador.

Through these chapters we invite you to reconsider the relationship between CD and PAR and become involved in reflection and practice on the possibilities that emerge when these approaches are intentionally combined.

NOTES

1. Thanks to Larry Stillman for comments on an earlier draft of this chapter.
2. For more on critical YPAR see http://yparhub.berkeley.edu/, which provides a perspective on the field as well as tools for those seeking to launch their own YPAR projects. See also the book edited by Julio Cammarota and Michelle Fine (2008), key leaders in the field of YPAR.

REFERENCES

Appalachian Land Ownership Task Force. 1983. *Who Owns Appalachia? Landownership and Its Impact*. Lexington, KY: University Press of Kentucky.

Arnstein, Sherry. 1969. A Ladder of Citizen Participation. *Journal of the American Institute of Planners*, 35(4), 216–224.

Axel-Lute, Miriam. 2019. Editor's Note: From Sustainability to Resilience. Shelterforce, May 13. https://shelterforce.org/2019/05/13/from-sustainability-to-resilience/

Bailey, David J., Mònica Clua-Losada, Nikolai Huke, and Olatz Ribera-Almandoz. 2017. *Beyond Defeat and Austerity: Disrupting (the Critical Political Economy of) Neoliberal Europe*. New York: Routledge.

Beckwith, Dave. 1997. Community Organizing: People Power from the Grassroots. COMM-ORG Papers. https://comm-org.wisc.edu/papers97/beckwith.htm

Beran, J. and A. Lubin. 2012. Shifting Service-Learning from Transactional to Relational. *Journal of Jewish Communal Service*, 87(1/2), 88–92.

Binswanger-Mkhize, Hans P., Swaminathan S. Anklesaria Aiyar, Jacomina P. de Regt et al. 2010. Historical Roots and Evolution of Community Driven Development. In Hans P. Binswanger-Mkhize, Jacomina P. de Regt, and Stephen Spector (Eds). *Local and Community Driven Development*. Washington, DC: World Bank, pp. 27–72. http://documents.worldbank.org/curated/en/128661468343731149/pdf/533000PUB0comm1B1Official0Use0Only1.pdf

Blum, Richard. 2019. Labor Picketing, the Right to Protest, and the Neoliberal First Amendment. *New York University Review of Law and Social Change*, 42(4), 595–648.

Boal, Augusto. 1979. *Theatre of the Oppressed*. New York: Theater Communications Group.

Boothroyd, Peter and H. Craig Davis. 1993. Community Economic Development: Three Approaches. *Journal of Planning Education and Research*, 12(3), 230–240.

Brown, L. David and Rajesh Tandon. 1983. Ideology and Political Economy in Inquiry: Action Research and Participatory Research. *Journal of Applied Behavioral Science*, 19(3), 277–294.

Callahan, Steve, Neil Mayer, Kris Palmer, and Larry Ferlazzo. 1999. Rowing the Boat with Two Oars. COMM-ORG Papers. https://comm-org.wisc.edu/papers99/callahan.htm

Cammarota, Julio and Michelle Fine, Eds. 2008. *Revolutionizing Education: Youth Participatory Action Research in Motion*. New York: Routledge.

Castree, Noel. 2010. Neoliberalism and the Biophysical Environment: A Synthesis and Evaluation of the Research. *Environment and Society*, 1(1), 5–45.

Chandler, Dawn, and Bill Torbert. 2003. Transforming Inquiry and Action: Interweaving 27 Flavors of Action Research. *Action Research*, 1, 33–52.

Christens, Brian D., and Pamela Tran Inzeo. 2015. Widening the View: Situating Collective Impact among Frameworks for Community-Led Change. *Community Development*, 46(4), 420–435.

Community Organisers. 2020. About Us. www.corganisers.org.uk/about-us/

Conway, Dennis. 2014. Neoliberalism: Globalization's Neoconservative Enforcer of Austerity. In Vandana Desai and Rob Potter (Eds). *The Companion to Development Studies*, 3rd Edition. New York: Routledge, pp. 106–111.

Davis, Allen. F. 1984. *Spearheads for Reform: The Social Settlements and the Progressive Movement, 1890 to 1914*, Revised Edition. New Brunswick, NJ: Rutgers University Press.

DeFilippis, James. 2001. The Myth of Social Capital in Community Development. *Housing Policy Debate*, 12, 781–806.

Doshna, Jeffrey Peter. 2015. *Community Development in the Age of Neoliberalism: The Case of the Pennsylvania Fresh Food Financing Initiative*. PhD, Rutgers, State University of New Jersey. https://rucore.libraries.rutgers.edu/rutgers-lib/47357

Downes, David and Paul Rock. 2011. *Understanding Deviance: A Guide to the Sociology of Crime and Rule-Breaking*, 6th Edition. Oxford: Oxford University Press.

Eitzen, D. Stanley, Maxine Baca Zinn, and Kelly Eitzen Smith. 2012. *In Conflict and Order: Understanding Society*, 13th Edition. New York: Pearson.

Fals-Borda, Orlando. 1991. Some Basic Ingredients. In Orlando Fals-Borda and Muhammad Anisur Rahman (Eds). *Action and Knowledge: Breaking the Monopoly with Participatory Action Research*. New York: Apex Press, pp. 3–12.

Flora, Cornelia Butler, Jan L. Flora, and Stephen P. Gasteyer. 2016. *Rural Communities: Legacy and Change*. Boulder, CO: Westview Press.

Freire, Paulo. 1970. *Pedagogy of the Oppressed*. New York: Herder and Herder.

Fukuyama, Francis. 1999. Social Capital and Civil Society. Paper prepared for delivery at the IMF Conference on Second Generation Reforms, Washington, DC, October 1. www.imf.org/external/pubs/ft/seminar/1999/reforms/fukuyama.htm

Gandhi, Mohandas K. 1909. *Hind Swaraj or Indian Home Rule*. Ahmedabad: Jitendra T. Desai Navajivan Publishing House. www.mkgandhi.org/ebks/hind_swaraj.pdf

Gaventa, John and Andrea Cornwall. 2001. Power and Knowledge. In Peter Reason and Hilary Bradbury (Eds). *Handbook of Action Research: Participative Inquiry and Practice*. London: Sage, pp. 70–80.

Greenberg, David. 2005. Ricanne Hadrian Initiative for Community Organizing Documentation and Evaluation Report. Massachusetts Association for Community Development Corporations.

Hamschmid, Jost and Michael Pirson (Eds). 2011. *Case Studies in Social Entrepreneurship and Sustainability: The Oikos Collection*, Vol. 2. London: Routledge.

Hande, Mary Jean and Christine Kelly. 2015. Organizing Survival and Resistance in Austere Times: Shifting Disability Activism and Care Politics in Ontario, Canada. *Disability and Society*, 30(7), 961–975.

Harries, Bethan, Bridget Byrne, Lindsey Garratt, and Andy Smith. 2020. "Divide and Conquer": Anti-Racist and Community Organizing under Austerity. *Ethnic and Racial Studies*, 43(16), 20–38.

Hartman, Yvonne. 2005. In Bed with the Enemy: Some Ideas on the Connections between Neoliberalism and the Welfare State. *Current Sociology*, 53(1), 57–73.

Hasenfeld, Yeheskel and Eve E. Garrow. 2012. Nonprofit Human-Service Organizations, Social Rights, and Advocacy in a Neoliberal Welfare State. *Social Service Review*, 86(2), 295–322.

Horton, Myles and Paulo Freire. 1990. *We Make the Road by Walking: Conversations on Education and Social Change*. Philadelphia, PA: Temple University Press.

INCITE! Women of Color Against Violence. 2007. *The Revolution Will Not Be Funded: Beyond the Non-Profit Industrial Complex*. Cambridge, MA: South End Press.

Joassart-Marcelli, Pascale and Fernando. J. Bosco. 2014. Alternative Food Projects, Localization and Neoliberal Urban Development: Farmers' Markets in Southern California. *Metropoles* 15. https://journals.openedition.org/metropoles/4970

Joseph, Jonathan. 2013. Resilience as Embedded Neoliberalism: A Governmentality Approach. *Resilience*, 1(1), 38–52.

Kania, John and Mark Kramer. 2011. Collective Impact. *Stanford Social Innovation Review*. https://ssir.org/articles/entry/collective_impact

Kemmis, Stephen. 1960. Action Research in Retrospect and Prospect. Paper presented to the Annual Meeting of the Australian Association for Research in Education, Sydney, November 6–9.

Kenny, Sue. 2002. Tensions and Dilemmas in Community Development: New Discourses, New Trojans? *Community Development Journal*, 37(4), 284–299.

Kenny, Sue, Brian McGrath, and Rhonda Phillips. 2018. *The Routledge Handbook of Community Development: Perspectives from around the Globe*. New York: Routledge.

Kirwan, Gloria and Deirdre Jacob. 2016. Addressing Barriers to Healthcare Access for Roma: A Community Development Approach. *Administration*, 64(2), 157–177.

Kreitmeyr, Nadine. 2019. Neoliberal Co-optation and Authoritarian Renewal: Social Entrepreneurship Networks in Jordan and Morocco. *Globalizations*, 16(3), 289–303.

Kretzmann, John P. and John L. McKnight. 1993. *Building Communities from the Inside Out: A Path toward Finding and Mobilizing a Community's Assets*. Chicago, IL: ACTA Publications.

Lazzarato, Maurizio. 2009. Neoliberalism in Action: Inequality, Insecurity and the Reconstitution of the Social. *Theory, Culture and Society*, 26, 109–133.

Ledworth, Margaret. 2016. *Community Development in Action: Putting Freire into Practice*. Bristol: Policy Press.

Lee, Robert and Tristan Ahtone. 2020. Land Grab Universities. *High Country News*, March 30. www.hcn.org/issues/52.4/indigenous-affairs-education-land-grab-universities

Lewin, Kurt. 1946. Action Research and Minority Problems. *Journal of Social Issues*, 2, 34–46.

Lewin, Kurt. 1948. *Resolving Social Conflicts: Selected Papers on Group Dynamics*, Ed. G. W. Lewin. New York: Harper and Row.

Lipset, Seymour Martin. 1996. *American Exceptionalism: A Double-Edged Sword*. New York: W. W. Norton & Co.

MacLeod, Mary Anne, and Akwugo Emejulu. 2014. Neoliberalism with a Community Face? A Critical Analysis of Asset-Based Community Development in Scotland. *Journal of Community Practice*, 22(4), 430–450.

Mane, Jo. 2009. Kaupapa Maori: A Community Approach. *MAI Review*, 9. www.review.mai.ac.nz/mrindex/MR/article/download/243/243-1710-1-PB.pdf

Matthews, John and James Kimmis. 2001. Development of the English Settlement Movement. In Ruth Gilchrist and Tony Jeffs (Eds). *Settlements, Social Change and Community Action: Good Neighbours*. London: Jessica Kingsley, pp. 54–68.

Mayer, Margit and Katharine N. Rankin. 2002. Social Capital and (Community) Development: A North/South Perspective. *Antipode*, 34, 804–808.

Mayo, Marjorie, Zoraida Mendiwelso-Bendek, and Carol Packham. 2013. *Community Research for Community Development*. New York: Palgrave Macmillan.

McDowell, George R. 2001. *Land-Grant Universities and Extension into the 21st Century: Renegotiating or Abandoning a Social Contract*. Ames, IA: Iowa State University Press.

Mieras, Emily. 2008. College Students, Social Responsibility, and Settlement House Work. Paper presented at the annual meeting of the American Studies Association, Albuquerque, NM.

Minkler, Meredith and Nina Wallerstein. 2008. *Community-Based Participatory Research for Health: Process and Outcomes*. San Francisco, CA: Jossey-Bass.

Morrow, Paula C. 1978. Functionalism, Conflict Theory and the Synthesis Syndrome in Sociology. *International Review of Modern Sociology*, 8, 209–225.

Pangambam, S. 2018. Mallence Bart-Williams: Change Your Channel at TEDxBerlinSalon (Transcript). *The Singju Post*. https://singjupost.com/mallence-bart-williams-change-your-channel-at -tedxberlinsalon-transcript/?singlepage=1

Peters, John. 2011. Neoliberal Convergence in North America and Western Europe: Fiscal Austerity, Privatization, and Public Sector Reform. *Review of International Political Economy*, 19(2), 208–235.

Putnam, Robert D. 2000. *Bowling Alone: The Collapse and Revival of American Community*. New York: Simon and Schuster.

Rahman, Muhammad Anisur. 1991. The Theoretical Standpoint of PAR. In Orlando Fals-Borda and Muhammad Anisur Rahman (Eds). *Action and Knowledge: Breaking the Monopoly with Participatory Action Research*. New York: The Apex Press, pp. 13–23.

Rahman, Muhammad Anisur. 1993. *People's Self-Development: Perspectives on Participatory Action Research: A Journey through Experience*. London: Zed Books.

Rasmussen, Wayne D. 1989. *Taking the University to the People: Seventy-Five Years of Cooperative Extension*. Ames, IA: Iowa State University Press.

Residents of Hull House. 2007. *Hull House Maps and Papers*. Champaign, IL: University of Illinois Press.

Rohe, William M., Rachel G. Bratt, and Protip Biswas. 2003. *Evolving Challenges for Community Development Corporations: The Causes and Impacts of Failures, Downsizings and Mergers*. Chapel Hill, NC: University of North Carolina. https://curs.unc.edu/wp-content/uploads/sites/400/2013/04/cdcreport.pdf

Rosenthal, Marlynn M. and Jay R. Greiner. 1982. The Barefoot Doctors of China: From Political Creation to Professionalization. *Human Organization*, 41(4), 330–341.

Roy, Michael J. 2017. The Assets-Based Approach: Furthering a Neoliberal Agenda or Rediscovering the Old Public Health? A Critical Examination of Practitioner Discourses. *Critical Public Health*, 27, 455–464.

Ryder, Andrew Richard, Iulius Rostas, and Marius Taba. 2014. "Nothing about us without us": The Role of Inclusive Community Development in School Desegregation for Roma communities. *Race Ethnicity and Education*, 17(4), 518–539.

Sandy, Marie and Barbara A. Holland. 2006. Different Worlds and Common Ground: Community Partner Perspectives on Campus-Community Partnerships. *Michigan Journal of Community Service Learning*, 13(1), 30–43.

Sherman, Lawrence W., Richard Schmuck, and Patrica Schmuck. 2004. Kurt Lewin's Contribution to the Theory and Practice of Education in the United States: The Importance of Cooperative Learning. Paper presented to the International Conference on Kurt Lewin: Contribution to Contemporary Psychology. Casimirus The Great University of Bydgoszcz, September 10–12.

Sillitoe, Paul. 2006. Introduction: Indigenous Knowledge in Development. *Anthropology in Action*, 13(3), 1–12.

Siriani, Carmen and Lewis Friedland. 2001. Community Organizing and Development. In Carmen Siriani and Lewis Friedland (Eds). *Civic Innovation in America: Community Empowerment, Public Policy, and the Movement for Civic Renewal*. Berkeley, CA: University of California Press, pp. 35–84.

Sloman, Annie. 2012. Using Participatory Theatre in International Community Development. *Community Development Journal*, 47(1), 42–57.

Somersan, Ayse. 1997. *Distinguished Service*. Friendship WI: New Past Press.

Stoecker, Randy. 1997. The Community Development Corporation Model of Urban Redevelopment: A Critique and an Alternative. *Journal of Urban Affairs*, 19, 1–23.

Stoecker, Randy. 2003a. Community-Based Research: From Theory to Practice and Back Again. *Michigan Journal of Community Service Learning*, 9, 35–46.

Stoecker, Randy. 2003b. Understanding the Development-Organizing Dialectic. *Journal of Urban Affairs*, 25, 493–512.

Stoecker, Randy. 2004. The Mystery of the Missing Social Capital and the Ghost of Social Structure: Why Community Development Can't Win. In Rob Silverman (Ed.). *Community-Based Organizations in Contemporary Urban Society: The Intersection of Social Capital and Local Context*. Detroit, MI: Wayne State University Press.

Stoecker, Randy. 2013. *Research Methods for Community Change: A Project-Based Approach*, 2nd Edition. Thousand Oaks, CA: Sage.

Stoecker, Randy. 2016. *Liberating Service Learning, and the Rest of Higher Education Civic Engagement*. Philadelphia, PA: Temple University Press.

Stoecker, Randy and Benny Witkovsky. 2020. From Inclusionary to Exclusionary Populism in the Transformation of U.S. Community Development. In Sue Kenny, Peter Westoby, and Jim Ife (Eds). *Populism, Democracy and Community Development*. Bristol: Policy Press.

Stringer, Ernest T. 2014. *Action Research*, 4th Edition. Thousand Oaks, CA: Sage.

Thibault, Robert. E. 2007. Between Survival and Revolution: Another Community Development System Is Possible. *Antipode*, 39, 874–895.

Tierney, Kathleen. 2015. Resilience and the Neoliberal Project: Discourses, Critiques, Practices – and Katrina. *American Behavioral Scientist*, 59(10), 1327–1342.

Till, Jo. 2013. Icons of Toynbee Hall: Samuel Barnett. http://toynbeehall.brix.fatbeehive.com/data/files/samuel_barnett_spreads.pdf

Twells, Alison. 2008. Community History. https://archives.history.ac.uk/makinghistory/resources/articles/community_history.html

United Nations. 1955. *Social Progress through Community Development*. New York: United Nations Bureau of Social Affairs. https://babel.hathitrust.org/cgi/pt?id=mdp.39015015207007&view=1up&seq=16

Van den Berk-Clark, Carissa and Loretta Pyles. 2012. Deconstructing Neoliberal Community Development Approaches and a Case for the Solidarity Economy. *Journal of Progressive Human Services*, 23, 1–17.

van Kersbergen, Kees and Barbara Vis. 2013. *Comparative Welfare State Politics: Development, Opportunities, and Reform*. Cambridge: Cambridge University Press.

von Hoffman, Alexander. 2013. The Past, Present, and Future of Community Development in the United States. Shelterforce. https://shelterforce.org/2013/07/17/the_past_present_and_future_of_community_development/

Whyte, William Foote (Ed.). 1990. *Participatory Action Research*. Thousand Oaks, CA: Sage.

Willis, Katie. 2011. *Theories and Practices of Development*, 2nd Edition. New York: Routledge.

Yin, Jordan. 1998. The Community Development Industry System. *Journal of Urban Affairs*, 20(2), 137–157.

PART I

STRUCTURES AND PROCESSES FOR INTEGRATING PARTICIPATORY ACTION RESEARCH AND COMMUNITY DEVELOPMENT

2. Flipping the script: community-initiated urban research with the Liberal Arts Action Lab

Megan Brown, Jack Dougherty, and Jeff Partridge

At traditional academic research centers, faculty and graduate students make decisions on what topics to study. But the Liberal Arts Action Lab "flips the script" by empowering local residents of Hartford, Connecticut to drive this process. Prospective community partners from different neighborhood groups and non-profit organizations submit one-page proposals about real-world problems they wish to solve. All must agree to share their proposals on a public web page, designed to share – rather than hide – what different organizations are planning to work on. The Action Lab convenes a board of Hartford residents to review and prioritize these proposals based on city-wide needs. Teams of undergraduate students and faculty fellows are drawn from the two campuses that jointly run this program: Capital Community College and Trinity College. Working together for a semester, students learn action research methods as one large group and collaborate in smaller teams to collect and analyze qualitative and/ or quantitative data on the research project with their community partners. Depending on the needs of their partners, student teams produce solutions in a variety of formats, including educational materials, technological approaches, policy recommendations, and strategic shifts. The teams present their findings and proposed solutions at a public event and on the Action Lab website at http://action-lab.org.

From its launch in January 2018 through March 2020, the Action Lab has received 86 proposals from more than 70 different Hartford organizations, of which 27 have been selected to become teams, based on its capacity to staff training for undergraduate researchers. Community-initiated topics have included areas such as housing eviction, creative placemaking, and career advancement for food service workers. As one example, the North Hartford Promise Zone Mapping Project team worked with Community Solutions, a northeast Hartford community development corporation, to transform their block-by-block survey data into a series of story maps to illustrate the relationship between housing conditions and neighborhood health. Staff from this non-profit organization regularly attended classes with Action Lab students to learn GIS mapping skills, since their organization lacked this resource. As a result of the work, the organization added a residential strategy to their plans to redevelop an abandoned factory building. Also, the project sparked a larger collaboration on housing and health outcomes in all Hartford neighborhoods, funded by a 500 Cities Grant from the Urban Institute and the Robert Wood Johnson Foundation. Learn more about all of the projects at https://action-lab.org/projects.

This chapter offers a valuable opportunity to compile, analyze, and reflect on two years of data generated by Action Lab partnerships. Our research question is to what extent has the Action Lab model of promoting resident-initiated participatory action research influenced community development in the city of Hartford? In fall 2019, we conducted interviews with organizations that submitted proposals – both those that were and were not selected to become Action Lab teams – to evaluate the relative influence of our collaborations. How did the process of submitting their Action Lab proposals on a public website shape their organization's thinking? For those selected to become Action Lab projects, to what extent did the undergraduate research partnership influence their work?

The relationship between community-based participatory action research and community development outcomes is non-linear and often difficult to measure. Put another way, what counts as *action* in action-oriented research strains is undertheorized and under-researched (Stoecker, 2009). In most cases, when tasked with evaluating the broader impacts of community-based educational partnerships, researchers at academic institutions prefer to measure the effect on learning, student engagement, or the quantity of institutional partnerships, rather than investigate the ways in which student work may influence the broader work of the organizations and people with whom they work. In this chapter, we investigate, qualitatively, the variety of effects that we are able to identify in the first few years of Action Lab operation. While some effects are observable and concrete (such as contributing to the construction of a new park or center), most other effects are more amorphous (such as producing knowledge to help strategic planning). In a project like the Action Lab, in which organizations are asked to invest time and thought in crafting proposals with no guarantee that they will be included in a formal partnership, an additional question arises: what effects might we observe that accrue to the proposal process itself? Through our conversations with our past partners, we have identified five types of effects that may accompany community-based participatory research partnerships involving undergraduate students: reflective effect, process effect, discovery effect, applied effect, and strategic effect. By defining these types of effects using qualitative data from interviews with our partners, we aim to expand conceptions of what matters in community-based participatory research. In a field in which the most common outputs include organizing meetings or writing reports, it is important to investigate the significance behind these actions. In addition, we discuss the potential for longer-term impact in the building of the Action Lab itself, explaining the infrastructure required to promote participation and expand partnerships between organizations and institutions of higher education. In this chapter, we describe the theory and practice behind the Action Lab model, discuss how we use technology to increase participation in our project selection process, and provide a brief overview of the program itself. Then we define and discuss each of these forms of impact and how they contribute to the broader ecosystem of community development in Hartford, CT.

HOW DOES THE ACTION LAB DEVELOP COMMUNITIES?

The Action Lab is an educational partnership, first and foremost, between Capital Community College and Trinity College. Students from both institutions enroll in Action Lab courses and work on a semester-long project with a Hartford-based community partner, exploring and proposing solutions to the most intractable problems facing the city. We are committed to both high-quality learning and doing work that is important to the city of Hartford. Before turning to the ways that we define our effect on Hartford, we will begin by describing the conceptual underpinnings of the key programmatic components of the Action Lab, drawing on the literature surrounding community-based participatory research. First, we discuss the unique character of the educational partnership between two very different institutions. Then we discuss our techniques for encouraging community participation in our projects and remaining accountable to the broader communities to which we hold ourselves responsible.

Community-based participatory action research is a broad and diverse field, but the main innovation of the paradigm is centering the role of affected communities in knowledge production and using scholarship to actively combat oppression and marginalization (Cahill et al., 2010; Janes, 2015; Sherrod, 2006). Employing techniques designed to relocate epistemic authority from academic sites to affected communities, participatory research aims to democratize knowledge while also improving research (Cahill et al., 2004). By cultivating deep solidaristic relationships with affected communities, participatory methods practitioners strive to work *with* and not *for* people and places experiencing oppression and marginalization, knowing that these relationships are always contested and contextual, subject to reflection and mediation (Nagar and Sangtin Writers Collective, 2006; Albrecht et al., 1990; Cahill et al., 2010). In action-oriented strains of the tradition, research is tied directly to active engagement to change social conditions, especially feminist and anti-racist praxis (Bell, 2012; Smith, 1999). As Cahill et al. write, "more than studying a phenomenon, the research sets out to 'do something' within a context in which it is urgent" (2010: 407). The Action Lab was conceived in community-based participatory action methods, and while it remains a short-term, undergraduate-level, course-centered engagement, the questions posed by critical participatory research – namely how best to co-create knowledge alongside affected communities while working to remain accountable to broader forms of impact – are those that drive us.

Specifically, as we developed the Action Lab, we grappled with three questions, both practical and conceptual, that were posed by the goal of "flipping the script" of academic research: (1) conceptually, how should we define "affected communities" as we embark on several short-term projects in a semester?; (2) practically, using what democratic processes and what research techniques, how should we distribute decision-making authority among the participants?; and (3) by what standards will we know that we have "done something" of use or importance through our projects?

DEFINING AFFECTED COMMUNITIES – WITH WHOM DO WE WORK?

If centering the role of affected communities in research is a central component of participatory research, then defining the affected communities with whom we work is essential for new labs. The Action Lab takes its location in Hartford, CT as the starting point when defining the community to which we are responsible. The charter for the Lab states that we will work on projects that help to "strengthen the city and its role in the region, spark social innovation, and support civic engagement and sustainability" (www.action-lab.org). This breadth helps maintain the relevance of the Action Lab's work in the city, but it also creates specific programmatic closures that affect the direction of the work that we do.

While place-centric definitions of "community" are common, and indeed most attempts to define community include both "place-based" and "identity" components (Martin, 2003; Hoffmann, 2016), relying on the political boundaries of a city to provide a working definition of community runs contrary to current trends of community-based participatory research. Contrast our approach with projects like the Fed Up Honeys project in New York City (Cahill et al., 2004; Cahill, 2006) or the Mestizo Arts and Activism Collective in Salt Lake City (Cahill et al., 2010). These projects, like many others, define the communities to which projects are responsible using social categories such as race and gender, while geographic location serves as a container for activity. Other well-known projects, such as the Morris Justice Project in New York, take a hyper-local, neighborhood-level view of community, layering this geography with shared experiences of race, class, and gender (Stoudt and Torre, 2014). Indeed, in segregated United States (U.S.) cities, race and place are often conflated. In still other projects, communities are defined through shared circumstances, such as the Youth Action Hub, a participatory research project based in the Hartford area that employs youth with experiences of housing instability or homelessness in a long-term participatory research project (www.youthactionhub.org).

Keeping in mind the overlapping and intricate definitions of communities that drive many contemporary participatory projects, the Action Lab drew significant inspiration from an early example of participatory geographic scholarship: the Detroit Expedition. The Detroit Expedition was led by Gwendolyn Warren and Bill Bunge in the late 1960s and provided free college-level classes on geographic thought and empirical practices such as mapping and interviewing to residents of Detroit neighborhoods (D'Ignazio and Klein, 2020). As an education and research experiment that also sought to prove the usefulness of geographic thought to combating racial injustice, the Detroit Expedition combined college credit with impact-oriented scholarship designed to influence policy. Its groundbreaking book, *Fitzgerald: Geography of a Revolution*, was a detailed and critical analysis of its Detroit neighborhood, which the collective used to influence policymakers and neighborhood residents alike (Bunge, 2011). Like the Detroit Expedition, the Action Lab stays firmly embedded in its urban location, grappling with understanding and addressing problems relating to structural disinvestment, racial injustice, and poverty.

A NOTE ON HARTFORD

Hartford, Connecticut's state capital, is a small city of no more than 18 square miles. This city of 125,000 is home to a wide range of Latino residents (43 percent) from Puerto Rico and other Caribbean islands, Mexico, Central America, and South America; Black residents (39 percent); non-Latino White residents (15 percent), and Asian residents (3 percent). About one-third of Hartford residents identify as Puerto Rican, the second-highest concentration in the northeast, and the city also includes a vibrant West Indian community, with many who identify as Jamaican. Politically, Hartford was one of the first major cities in New England to elect a Black mayor (in 1981), a Black female mayor (in 1987), and a Latino mayor (in 2001).

During the Gilded Age of the late nineteenth century, Hartford was known as the "richest city" in the U.S. and as a center for banking, insurance, and manufacturing. But much of that wealth moved to the suburbs during the twentieth century. As a result, economic inequality defines metropolitan Hartford today. The median household income is about $34,000 in the city of Hartford versus $73,000 in the metropolitan area. Similarly, about 24 percent of the housing stock is owner-occupied in the city versus 67 percent in the metropolitan area. Trinity College adjoins three neighborhoods – Behind the Rocks, Frog Hollow, and Barry Square – with some of the highest concentrations of people living in poverty (34 to 40 percent) in the city of Hartford (U.S. Census Bureau, 2017; Data Haven, 2017). Hartford is also a city that is rich with institutions, home to a still healthy financial and insurance sector, and surrounded by substantial personal and family wealth. Despite these advantages, the city government struggles to bring in enough tax revenue to pay for the services it requires, largely because a majority of its landbase is owned by entities like the state of Connecticut and large non-profit institutions, which are not subject to property taxes. With all of its advantages, the city struggles to make needed investments in infrastructure, social services, and education.

Because we define our community based on the political boundaries of the city of Hartford, the next questions are with whom should we work, and how should we structure that work? Our decision to define our affected communities by using the scale of the city – even a small city like Hartford – creates some operational difficulties when designing the mechanisms through which we select projects and structure participation. While other participatory projects often identify and enroll individual community members, creating research collectives that live in various organizational settings, we work primarily with organizations in short-term collaborations. We have worked with small non-profits, city agencies, social entrepreneurs, community groups without non-profit status, and larger and more established non-profit organizations. Though the size and scope of the organizations are variable, it is important for us to have representatives to work closely with in our projects. Here we outline in more detail the digital infrastructure that we built and maintain in order to foster connections amongst organizations spanning the space of the city.

A STRATEGIC HIGHER EDUCATION PARTNERSHIP FOR HARTFORD

In investigating the effects of the first two years of Action Lab programming, it has become clear that the infrastructure created to sustain a partnership between two differently situated institutions of higher education is a crucial component of the lasting effect of the program. It also indelibly shapes the participatory nature of the work conducted at the Action Lab. An academic partnership between a private four-year liberal arts college and a public two-year community college is rare in the current higher education landscape. In fact, the Action Lab is the first significant curricular partnership that has been sustained between Trinity College and Capital Community College, despite the two institutions having shared the same small city for decades.

Trinity College is an internationally renowned liberal arts institution that draws from 45 states and 67 countries to make up its student body of 2,200. It is a residential campus of traditional college-aged students (i.e. 17–21), 44 percent of whom receive some form of financial aid and 18 percent of whom are people of color. As such, the average student joining the Action Lab from Trinity College is new to Hartford and does not identify experientially with the economic and ethnic make-up of the communities of Hartford. Capital Community College, by contrast, is a commuter college with an average student age of 29 and, like Hartford, is majority students of color, with 36 percent Black, 31 percent Hispanic, 5 percent Asian, and 9 percent self-identified as Other. Among the Black and Latinx populations, Jamaicans and Puerto Ricans predominate, which reflects the largest ethnic populations of Hartford itself. Like Trinity, Capital draws from students around the globe, with over 45 languages represented in its student body, but at Capital, only a handful of non-native students are true international students (i.e. students residing temporarily in the U.S. to obtain a degree), but rather are immigrants and refugees seeking to better their prospects in their new homeland.

Prior to the Action Lab's founding, both institutions were profiled by the *Hechinger Report* as pillars of opposite ends of educational privilege. In 2015, an article was published that the

Trinity College Communications Department simply refers to as the "flavored water" article. The author opens with the stark contrast between the dining hall at Trinity College and the campus of Capital Community College, one of the only other institutions of higher education located within the Hartford city limits.

> The main dining hall at Trinity College starts you off with a choice of infused water: lemon, pineapple, strawberry, melon. There are custom-made smoothies, all-day breakfasts, make-your-own waffles, and frozen yogurt, along with countless choices of entrees hovered over by white-jacketed chefs ... Across the city, off an exit from an elevated highway, other students dodge downtown traffic to squeeze into the sluggish elevators in time for the start of their classes at Capital Community College. This campus consists of a concrete parking garage and a onetime department store converted into classrooms and offices. (Marcus and Hacker, 2015)

Viewed through this singular lens, the two institutions are well positioned to reflect the staggering inequality in the higher education sphere. Yet both operate in the same city, and students, though not in large numbers, have attended both institutions. Two of these students currently serve on the Hartford Resident Advisory Board (HRAB) of the Action Lab. The Action Lab began as a partnership to create a curricular opportunity that was open to both Capital and Trinity students to learn about community-engaged scholarship and apply lessons to projects proposed by Hartford-based community partners.

At first glance, such a partnership may seem impractical. The connotations of the terms "private" and "public" suggest significant preparatory and class differences on the one hand; while significant practical differences surely loom on the other: residential versus commuter campuses, full-time versus part-time matriculation, traditional college age versus age diversity, and more. Such differences are real, and some of the challenges they pose will be briefly explored below. However, the Liberal Arts Action Lab was constructed around the expected benefits of such an unlikely partnership. In short, the strategy is intended to enhance the ontological groundedness and diversity of the research teams as they work with Hartford community partners in service of Hartford residents. Moreover, this strategy helps to bridge – and in some cases, demystify – perceived differences between these institutions and their students.

By joining forces with Hartford's community college, the Action Lab increases its experiential identification with the communities it seeks to serve and thereby increases its relevance and effectiveness. Although the Action Lab does tend to attract Trinity students who have already been exposed to Hartford through service learning and other Hartford-centric programs, it is rare for Trinity students to be from Hartford itself. Significantly, 71 percent of Capital's students are residents of Hartford and neighboring towns, with residents of Hartford proper making up 35 percent in 2019 and 50 percent in 2018. This ratio is mirrored in the Action Lab enrollment from Capital Community College. Each semester of its operation, the Action Lab has attracted a Hartford-resident percentage of 50 percent or higher from among its Capital cohort. In spring 2019, seven of the eight Capital students enrolled in the Action Lab were Hartford residents.

The strategy of partnering between these two institutions draws upon each institution's strengths. Trinity College has strong community-engaged research programming that encourages civic-mindedness among its students, a history of engagement with Hartford as a key anchor institution, and financial resources. Capital Community College has diverse and engaged students who both represent and identify with Hartford. Together they form an alliance that can collaborate with Hartford community organizations in their mission to address the problems facing Hartford and its residents.

The unique partnership influences the work it does in several important ways. First, Hartford community organizations are eager to work with blended teams of Capital and Trinity students. In the course of one-on-one discussions about the Action Lab, many potential partners have mentioned that they were drawn to the program because of the chance that some students would be local to Hartford and stay in Hartford after graduating. They also appreciated the fact that there would likely be students who came from the Hartford communities that their organizations represented or worked with: recent immigrants or migrants to the U.S., students who went through or worked in Hartford public schools, students who had experienced homelessness, Hartford residents who had lived in the neighborhood for 40+ years. In fact, each of these examples comes from a specific Action Lab project in which students paired with organizations had lived experience that was relevant to the project. As mentioned above, community-based participatory action research seeks to foster the deep involvement of affected communities in research. It is especially important to promote involvement that goes beyond data collection and includes designing the project and analyzing results. The Action Lab, by virtue of its partnership between Trinity College and Capital Community College, extends this commitment by building the institutional connections necessary to ensure that the student populations involved in all stages of these projects are likely to have relevant community ties.

In many cases, for example, Capital students had been long-term residents of the specific neighborhood in which a project was working. For one of these projects, a local parks organization, Riverfront Recapture, wanted to engage community input to help shape the development of the park they were planning for a north Hartford neighborhood. A long-term resident of the neighborhood was on the Action Lab team that took on the project. She was able to help connect the other students to important community locations, accompany them to the neighborhood to collect surveys, and identify important other neighborhood groups where she led the team to present its work. Without her presence the team would have had a harder time making inroads into the neighborhood to get and share relevant information.

Another example of the efficacy of this partnership can be found in the team formed for the Black Heritage project in Spring 2020. This project set the student team with the task of researching and promoting the historical significance of the Talcott Street Congregational Church, which was a center of emancipation, spiritual community, education, and Black resistance to white supremacy in the nineteenth century. The church existed a block from the Capital Community College and remains unmarked and un-memorialized. This project attracted four strong applicants, three from Capital, residents of Hartford, and one from Trinity, a resident of a Massachusetts city with many similarities to Hartford. All four of the students were attracted to this project because, as young Black scholars, they saw the erasure of this history as a personal affront. They reflected on their own schooling and were appalled that no one ever taught them about the Black community in nineteenth-century Hartford and the significant advances in resistance, education, and abolition that centered on this one site, now forgotten to nearly everyone. In the year following the completion of the Action Lab component of the Black Heritage project, the project itself has lived on. It was recently awarded a grant from the National Endowment of the Humanities to implement some of the recommendations made by the students and continue the development of the curriculum relating to these important historical sites.

DEMYSTIFYING DIFFERENCES

While the primary purpose of the partnership between these two very different institutions is strategic, the partnership has also helped shape a new narrative about their students. Community partners, staff and faculty of both institutions, and friends and family of the students come together at the end of each semester to view the digital poster presentations of each Action Lab group. Those who attend these sessions typically comment on the quality of the research and the professionalism of the presentations, and they call attention to the fact that the Trinity and Capital students, as one visitor put it, "stood shoulder-to-shoulder, you couldn't tell the difference." This comment not only attests to the impressiveness of the Action Lab teams, but it belies the implicit expectation that Trinity students would outperform Capital students.

For the Capital students, this demystification of the elite private college student is advantageous to their own progress in pursuing a four-year degree. Finding that they work as equals with Trinity students gives the Capital students confidence to aim high in life and believe in their own capabilities. By the same token, if any Trinity students entered with a low view of community college students, their experience in the Action Lab would likely explode their preconceptions and stereotypes.

While this demystification of difference clearly takes place in the Action Lab and is an important result of the partnership between Trinity and Capital, the process does not always come without a struggle. Student project teams are often confronted with real differences – like availability, levels of comfort in Hartford, and the digital divide (not just economic, but also age-based – several of the students from Capital have been senior citizens working on their college degrees). The more insidious differences, however, are the perceived ones. Common refrains from the students include "students from that college don't want to mix with us" and "we don't have as much time because our school work is more demanding" or "we don't have as much time because we have to work to pay for college." Undergirding all of these messages is the persistent refrain of group work, regardless of difference: "why do we have to pick up their slack?" Encountering and engaging with these power differentials, which are found between students from different colleges, between the academy and the community, and between teachers and students is the core of Action Lab work.

These differences, perceived and real, are the differences the students will continue to face throughout their working lives. The partnership between Capital and Trinity therefore allows students from both colleges to develop, under the guidance of their professor, real-life skills of teamwork and problem solving to meet an aim. In this respect, the Action Lab becomes a laboratory for learning teamwork and living democracy.

DESIGNING PARTICIPATION: WHAT TECHNIQUES DO WE USE TO DISTRIBUTE AUTHORITY?

Participatory research asks that affected communities be involved in each stage of a research project, from initiation, to data collection, to analysis, to write-up and dissemination. The methods used to structure this involvement vary substantially. Many thoughtful practitioners have noted that the persistent power imbalances between those in the academy and those on its fringes shape the quality and length of participation by affected communities (Janes, 2015).

When launching the Liberal Arts Action Lab in fall 2017, one of the key goals was to invert the regular routine of urban researchers by "flipping the script." Rather than asking academics what they wanted to study in the city, we invited Hartford community partners to define the problems and questions that they wanted to be answered, to help us attract and build teams of interested students and faculty from Capital Community College and Trinity College. The construction of the infrastructure used to encourage and structure participation in the process is a key outcome of Action Lab work in its first two years of operation. As we will outline below, the digital infrastructure, program policies and strategic investments in personnel are crucial to locating the Action Lab as a site for community-engaged research and action in Hartford.

As we developed the structure of the Action Lab, we deliberately designed programmatic and policy-oriented techniques to decenter the role of academic partners, whether students or faculty, during the project initiation phase of the research.[1] The Action Lab has removed our academic partners – faculty, staff, and students – from the project initiation phase of our research projects as much as possible. Twice a year, we solicit proposals using word-of-mouth advertising and targeted outreach to collect problem statements from a variety of organizations.

Every Action Lab team research project begins with a one-page proposal submitted by a Hartford community partner. Partners are broadly defined to include neighborhood groups, non-profit organizations, government agencies, social entrepreneurs, and others who seek to improve the city or its role in the metropolitan region. The Action Lab widely distributes an invitation for partners to submit proposals well in advance of the semester when projects will be completed, typically at the end of February for the fall semester, and the end of October for the spring semester. The online proposal asks for basic information about the community partner and their mission, along with three core questions:

- *Project*: What problem or question do you want an Action Lab team to help you solve? Up to one paragraph.
- *Research*: What type of information and research work will your project include? Up to one paragraph.
- *Products*: What products do you need (written, visual, web), and how will you use them? Up to one paragraph.

By design, the Action Lab minimizes barriers to entry by asking partners to write responses only to these core questions, which total up to about one page of writing. Since community partners and their organizations have different levels of funding and staffing, the Action Lab director tries to help everyone submit their best possible application by offering to meet with them in person to draft or revise their written proposals prior to the deadline. Furthermore, the Action Lab welcomes joint proposals from two or more partners, and our simple online form makes this relatively easy for partners to collaborate. Finally, we inform applicants that, if their proposal is selected, they must be available to meet with an Action Lab research team at least once a month during our project times (either Tuesday, Wednesday, or Thursday afternoons, or Wednesday evenings) at our downtown campus. We follow up with those who advance to the next round on their scheduling preferences.

During our initial start-up period, we often explained to prospective community partners that the Action Lab, as a joint partnership between two academic institutions, was best positioned to help them solve their "knowledge problems." For example, what kind of local data could our undergraduate teams help collect and analyze to answer a question about their work? Or how could we research different models of doing related work in other cities, and draw connections back to Hartford? We believed that "knowledge problems" needed to be distinguished from other types of problems that under-resourced organizations commonly face, such as "resource problems" (to obtain more funding for their work) and "political problems" (to build broader coalitions to support their work). It is not the mission of the Action Lab to directly distribute funds or lobby politicians on behalf of partner organizations, but the Action Lab emphasizes the power of education: by working together to gather research or interpret evidence to solve "knowledge problems," community partners certainly can become better equipped to make stronger pitches to prospective funders and political coalitions.

Unlike traditional applications that remain hidden behind closed doors, the Action Lab intentionally designed the application process to be online and open to the public. To submit an application on the website (http://action-lab.org/apply), a partner must check this box:

- *Public*: I grant permission for my proposal to be shared on the public web, after review by the Action Lab.

The Action Lab believes that making the application process public delivers important educational benefits to the broader community. When community partners can read each other's proposals, they learn more about each other's interests and plans for making positive change in the community, which increases the potential for cross-organizational collaboration. Furthermore, partners that are looking for ways to strengthen their written proposals can view all submissions online, and build on stronger examples that clearly identify the core problem or question and how a proposed Action Lab research team would work to address it. In our six proposal rounds, in which nearly 40 organizations submitted proposals, only one community partner expressed reservations about the public nature of the proposal process. When the proposal process is open, everyone has greater opportunities to learn.

Shortly after the deadline, all partner applications are compiled and reviewed by the HRAB. Its role is to ensure that community members make decisions on prioritizing proposals to receive support from Action Lab research teams, rather than granting this power to college administrators and faculty. HRAB consists of six city residents who are actively engaged in their communities and who are familiar with academic research, including what it can and cannot be expected to accomplish. HRAB members are nominated by the Action Lab director and the two faculty directors from each academic institution. Some members have been students at Capital Community College and/or Trinity College, which offers valuable insight to our undergraduate teaching mission and an opportunity for alumni to give back to their communities. The Action Lab director chairs the review meeting, where members are asked to discuss the merits of proposals on these criteria:

- Will this proposal lead to improving Hartford and/or its role in the metro region?
- Will this proposal lead to high-quality learning by a team of Capital/Trinity students?
- Have we prioritized proposals from a wide range of Hartford community groups?

These criteria reflect the Action Lab's continuous internal tension: weighing each community partner's institutional goals, versus the educational value to the students, versus the equitable distribution of academic research resources across the city. HRAB members address these issues during their hour-long discussion, and then submit their numerical rankings by secret ballot. The Action Lab director compiles the results to identify six top-priority projects to advance to the next round. Since HRAB members are not usually employed by Capital or

Trinity, the Action Lab provides a modest compensation for their valuable contribution in ensuring that Hartford residents are the key decision makers for research proposals involving the people of Hartford.

After HRAB has prioritized the community partners' top proposals, the next step is a "matching" exercise to recruit students and faculty fellows from Capital and Trinity to apply to join Action Lab research project teams in the upcoming semester. Since the launch three years ago, the average numbers each semester are now:

- 15–20 proposals submitted by Hartford community partners each semester.
- 6 top-ranked proposals by HRAB, and Action Lab recruits students and faculty to apply.
- 4–5 project teams matched by the Action Lab each semester, depending on faculty staffing and scheduling for all parties.

This "matching" exercise raised many logistical challenges. While it was crucial to our project to hold an open and community-driven process while identifying projects, the number of proposals and the variety of organizations presented logistical problems. How could we "match" all of these people without asking them to meet up in the same room at the same time, especially if it wasn't certain that a given project could move forward? Our solution relied on a creative lightweight open-source code addition to a typical online Google Form. When Hartford community partners submit proposals on the Google Form, their results appear in a Google Sheet, where the Action Lab director reviews content for clarity, adds a short project title, and checks a box to approve it. Approved proposals appear on the public Action Lab web page, thanks to a short JavaScript code extension written by Ilya Ilyankou, the Action Lab student software developer, which publishes the Google Form content online. (For details, see this open-source GitHub repository: https://github.com/Action-Lab/application-matching.)

The Action Lab seeks to democratize the knowledge process through a combination of newer web technology and old-fashioned face-to-face conversations. Both digital and human communication are essential: we could not relay all of these details to our partners, students, and faculty fellows without computers, but at the same time we could not persuade all of these people to participate in this public forum without personal support and assurance of mutual respect. The Action Lab depends on building relationships through transparency and trust.

ACTION LAB PROGRAMMING AND TEACHING

Once we have selected the projects that we work on and formed our project teams for the semester, Action Lab programming begins in earnest. Prior to the beginning of the semester, community partners, faculty fellows, and the Action Lab director meet to discuss the goals for the project, ironing out the details of the students' work and establishing expectations for the partnership. Each project is different, requiring the project teams to draw on tools from different disciplines, and the needs of a specific project may require tweaking the Action Lab curriculum to support the specific needs of the partner.

The students in the Action Lab enroll in two simultaneous courses, a survey course designed to introduce students to Action Research Methods and a project-based course. Our students are early career undergraduates, many of whom have not had prior coursework in research design or community-based projects. The survey course emphasizes ethical collaboration with diverse communities, including several weeks in which we critically reflect on the role of difference in knowledge production and collaboration.

The project-based course asks students to immediately apply what is being learned in the survey course to their collaboration with their community partner. Students work in teams to design a semester-long project, collect data, analyze data, and propose solutions to the problems they have been tasked with solving. Along the way, they meet regularly with their partner organization and with their faculty fellow to collaborate and debrief about the process. As the projects progress, students gain confidence in research skills. They also gain confidence in navigating differences within a team, fairly distributing work, holding team members accountable, reaching out to community members and community leaders for advice or interviews, navigating the city using public transportation, public-speaking skills, and incorporating a variety of conflicting perspectives in final products.

HOW DOES THE ACTION LAB PROCESS AFFECT HARTFORD COMMUNITY PARTNERS?

Since the Liberal Arts Action Lab announced its first call for proposals in September 2017, over 70 Hartford community partners have submitted a total of 86 proposals across a wide range of topics. Each semester the HRAB has prioritized six of these to advance to the student and faculty fellow recruiting stage. Based on the combination of Action Lab faculty staffing, as well as student interest and scheduling, either four or five research project teams have been created each semester, for a total of 27 during our first three years of operation (Table 2.1).

Table 2.1   *Community partner proposals to Liberal Arts Action Lab, 2018 to date*

Semester	Proposals submitted	Project teams created
2018 spring	11	5
2018 fall	10	4
2019 spring	21	4
2019 fall	14	4
2020 spring	15	5
2020 fall	15	5 (postponed due to COVID-19)
Total	86	27

Source: Action Lab application archives.

What effect has the Action Lab had on these Hartford community partners? Typically, when organizations (or their funders) discuss "direct impact," they often are seeking to answer the question of "How many people did you help?" But framing the question this way is too narrow. In this project, we interviewed community partners who have submitted proposals and/or worked with Action Lab teams to identify the ways that these partnerships have affected their organizations. Following these interviews, we analyzed the data using inductive methods to identify the forms of effect discussed by our partners. Based on this analysis, we believe it is more constructive to consider a broader framework to evaluate overall effect, and we suggest these five categories:

1. Reflective effect
2. Discovery effect
3. Process effect
4. Applied effect
5. Strategic effect

These five categories of effect emerged when we conducted an evaluation of Hartford community partners, based on emails and phone interviews with people who had submitted a proposal as of fall 2019. We reached out to all applicants, whether or not they had been selected to become a research team, to ask a series of open-ended questions about their experience, and what they gained (if anything) through the partnership.

At the outset it is important to state that "effect" here does not necessarily proceed in a straight line to more traditional evaluation-oriented searches for outputs, outcomes, and impacts. Our goal is to explore, through our qualitative interview data with our community partners, the different *types* of effects that may be observed during and after a short-term, research-based engagement between undergraduate students and community organizations. At the Action Lab, we are primarily engaged in knowledge production activities in collaboration with community organizations. We are not well suited to solving problems related to resources or funding, we are not direct service providers, and we are not able to engage in the long-term, deep relationship building necessary for community organizing work. Instead, we want to examine and explain the particular types of effects that may emerge from research and information-based work. Thinking in a new way about a problem (reflective), finding out new information (discovery), reconsidering a process used in ongoing work (process), using knowledge products in service of external communication with funders or the broader public (applied), or shifting a theoretical perspective or a core strategy of action (strategic) are all effects tied closely to research and information products. As a result, not all of these different kinds of effects directly result in a lasting edifice, be it a building or a formalized policy. Many of the observed effects that we discuss are still years in the making. That said, as educators and actors involved in community work, we argue that even amorphous and very long-term shifts in perspective, be they the result of being asked to reflect on a problem statement or upon the discovery of a new piece of information or issue framing, also represent an important location for change in community-based participatory action research.

Reflective Effect

We define "reflective effect" as the result generated by making time to think clearly and potentially reframe questions on a community development project. This is the most emergent form of effect that we identified in our interviews, and was described almost exclusively in conversations with organizations that proposed an Action Lab project but were not selected.

When Hartford community partners submitted proposals to the Action Lab, our application process asked them to write one-paragraph responses to questions such as: "What problem or question do you want an Action Lab team to help you solve?" and "What type of information and research work will your project include?" As we designed our proposal process, we explicitly tried to minimize the amount of time required of partners to produce and submit an

Action Lab proposal, but were still floored by the sheer number of proposals we were not able to accommodate, including those who went through multiple submissions. If we are to take seriously the labor that we ask of potential partners at all stages of a participatory project – including the precarious moments in which a partner's broader participation is not guaranteed – it is important to consider what (if any) effects might result from the application process. We found that regardless of whether or not their application advanced to the final round, several partners described that this stage made a "reflective effect" on their work, by setting aside some time to think about the day-to-day work facing their organization and reframing it in the form of a researchable question for a potential Action Lab project team, often with direct assistance from the Action Lab.

One example of reflective effect came from David Biklen and colleagues from Immanuel Congregational Church. They submitted their "$15 Minimum Wage" proposal to request an Action Lab team to interview Connecticut employers that had already chosen to pay more than the prevailing wage, to better understand their motivations, in order to persuade lower-paying employers to match them. Although this proposal did not advance to the next round, Biklen commented that the application process "Helped us think about what we might need regarding information and publicity" for their organization. Similarly, Richard Hollant and Zoe Chatfield from CoLab, a local design company whose leaders participate in the City of Hartford Commission on Cultural Affairs, submitted a "Public Arts" proposal that asked to research how other cities with related financial and organizational challenges have found successful ways to support arts and culture initiatives. This proposal did not advance to the next round, and when asked if the process of writing it up was helpful to their organization, the authors initially responded no, but then added: "It was helpful to return to the basis of the formation of the Commission, its duties as laid out in the ordinance, as well as reflecting on the changes in City funding and departments that have posed a challenge for the Commission moving forward with arts initiatives." In other words, while their proposal did not receive the acceptance they had desired, the application process did help them to reflect on how the problem arose within the institutional structures of city governance.

Also, Kathy Evans from the Southwest/Behind the Rocks Neighborhood Revitalization Zone (NRZ), one of the neighborhood advocacy organizations recognized by the city, submitted a "Neighborhood Needs" proposal to request an Action Lab team to assist them in conducting a community needs and assets survey in collaboration with other organizations. While their proposal did not advance, Evans explained how "the process of narrowing down our needs and discussing which ones might be interesting to Trinity College was useful for our members. This is the first project that the NRZ worked on with [another organization], so it was a good first step in forming our partnership."

We fully understand that, when the Action Lab asks unsuccessful applicants about the value of the process, their responses may emphasize positive aspects with the hope of future partnerships. Nevertheless, we believe that "reflective effect" is real and needs to be recognized, particularly in campus–community partnerships where education is the focus. Furthermore, some unsuccessful applicants above benefitted from time that the Action Lab director devoted to discussing and helping them to revise their draft proposals prior to submission. While people inside organizations are often pressured to focus solely on day-to-day activities, meaningful conversations with people outside their regular networks can help to reframe the fundamental questions facing them.

Discovery Effect

We define "discovery effect" as the result produced by answering research questions or uncovering knowledge for a community development project. When Hartford community partners submit proposals, a key component is to identify a problem or question that they want an Action Lab team to help them solve and the type of information or research work necessary to do so. While working together during the semester, teams and their community partners typically collaborate on qualitative interviewing projects or quantitative analysis of public datasets and share their analysis and findings through a public presentation and website. Since the Action Lab is supported by academic institutions, we value working with community partners to help them discover knowledge.

One example of the discovery effect emerged from our follow-up interview with Julie Geyer, the director of planning and market research at Capital Workforce Partners, a regional organization devoted to reducing employment barriers and closing gaps between skills and business needs in the Hartford area. Geyer and her colleagues submitted their "Opportunity Youth" proposal to collect and analyze local data on 16–24 year olds who are neither in school nor the labor market; the proposal was matched with an Action Lab research team in fall 2018. The team analyzed local demographic data from the American Community Survey and program data from five Hartford service providers and also conducted a focus group with eight Opportunity Youth program participants. Their findings focused on neighborhood differences (while most Opportunity Youth reside in Hartford's South End, most who currently receive services live in the North End) and also on the challenges these youth face due to criminal justice involvement and social service agency interventions. Geyer acknowledged that the Action Lab research process "got us thinking about different questions and different angles … so instead of making a preconceived notion about something, it helped us really delve further into it and ask more questions."

A similar response came from Violette Haldane, vice president of the West Indian Foundation, a non-profit organization focused on the needs of Caribbean migrants to the Hartford region. Their "Student Success" proposal was matched with an Action Lab team in spring 2019 to explore how local public schools integrate West Indian children and their families into the education system, given that most migrant programs are geared toward Latino students, whose needs differ from English-speaking West Indian students. The Action Lab team collaborated with the community partner to interview Hartford school administrators responsible for enrolling newly arriving students, examine the school district's "Welcome Center" for new families, and conduct surveys with parents who had emigrated from the West Indies. Their findings focused on structural and cultural differences between West Indian and U.S. schools, as well as a unique experience encountered by incoming West Indian children when they are placed a grade lower than they expected based on their educational attainment in Jamaica or other islands. Haldane summarized that the research project "let us see that there is a need to address how students are placed [in the school system], and to do it based on an individual's skills instead of only their birthdate." As a result of the Action Lab team's finding relating to the ways that incoming students are placed at a grade level, the West Indian Foundation has pursued collaborations with a variety of community groups in the area to address this issue with the local school board.

The discovery effect deserves mention as a specific category and should be distinguished from the application effect, described further below, where community partners incorporate findings into new work products.

Process Effect

We define "process effect" as the dynamic generated while people work together on a community development project. In the context of the Action Lab, this concept refers to collaborations between different groups of people involved in team projects: Hartford community partners and students from Capital Community College and Trinity College. While these groups do not ordinarily work together, in several instances the combined efforts of people with diverse perspectives and life experiences produced a richer outcome than would have happened if fewer viewpoints were represented.

One example of process effect arose in discussion with Lydia Velez Herrera, the chief executive officer and founder of Lilly Sin Barreras (translated as Lilly without Barriers). She submitted the "Hurricane Maria" proposal to research the lessons learned from efforts to integrate into the Hartford region Puerto Rican families displaced by the 2017 hurricane. Her proposal was matched with an Action Lab team in fall 2019. Together, they conducted retrospective research to investigate which sources of aid were most beneficial to displaced families, the obstacles that service providers faced when coordinating aid, and the challenges that families faced in accessing services. Based on the students' interviews with relocation agency representatives and displaced people, the team identified several barriers to low-cost housing, employment, and mental health, and the failure of a coordinated organizational response to this emergency. The team also identified successes, including the regional education council's welcome center, the sense of community cultivated in response to the tragedy, and the continuing education of displaced children. Speaking about their collaborative work, Velez Herrera explained, "I was so excited. It was three women … and there was diversity on the team," referring to the Latina, Black, and White students from Capital Community College and Trinity College. "The next generation after mine, and my daughter's and my granddaughter's, are so committed and passionate to find out what's happening in our communities."

Similar themes emerged in our discussions with Action Lab students about what they valued from their experience. Josephine Bensa, a Capital Community student on the "Creative Placemaking" research team in spring 2018, collaborated with her community partner, HartBeat Ensemble, a social change theater organization, to investigate strategies for leveraging the arts to serve the needs of Hartford's Asylum Hill neighborhood without gentrifying it. Bensa, a lifelong Hartford resident, emphasized how the Action Lab collaboration was "all about the process, the journey that it takes you on, to make a difference and be part of the community that you're in." Another student member of that team, Trinity College student Giana Moreno, who came to Hartford from the Chicago region, reflected on what Action Lab collaboration meant to her. "I'm really learning how to listen to my peers. We all come from different walks of life and places, so someone is always offering a different perspective … so I'm learning how to think about it in a different framework." Ordinarily, students in such different colleges probably would not have met one another, and definitely would not have collaborated on a research project with Hartford community partners, without a bridge-building entity such as the Action Lab.

Applied Effect

We define "applied effect" as instances when a community partner has incorporated findings from our research collaboration into newer work products for community development. To date, several Hartford community partners have applied knowledge or findings from past Action Lab research projects toward future efforts in program planning, grant funding, or future research.

One example of applied effect arose from discussion with Martha Conneely from Riverfront Recapture, a non-profit organization that connects people to the Connecticut River, a former pollution site that over time has become a reclaimed natural resource. Conneely and her colleagues submitted the "Cove Connection" proposal that asked for assistance in research-ing what residents in two neighborhoods – Hartford's North End and Windsor's Wilson area – desired in a revitalized riverfront park. They were matched with an Action Lab team in spring 2019, which surveyed residents in both neighborhoods and also attended public meetings to gather feedback. Most residents desired more park services for children, and emphasized restrooms as their highest priority. But the team also determined that Hartford and Windsor residents expressed different needs in other areas, such as intended usage and perceptions of safety. Months later, Conneely reported that her organization finally purchased the land and "we included the Action Lab survey in a grant proposal we sent to the EPA [U.S. Environmental Protection Agency] for cleanup of the property." Information gathered through the survey – such as a strong resident preference for actual bathrooms, not port-a-lets – "has had and will continue to have an effect on our plans for the park." Conneely valued her collaboration with the Action Lab because her organization did not have the capacity to conduct a community survey by itself, and rather than hiring a consultant to do it for them, "we really worked together on how to develop the survey" to produce "very meaningful" results. Furthermore, "funders want to know that we are reaching into the community" rather than "just claiming we plan to do it."

Another example of applied effect came from Fionnuala Darby-Hudgens, director of opera-tions at the Connecticut Fair Housing Center, a statewide advocate against housing discrimina-tion. Her organization submitted the "Eviction Project" proposal to investigate how Hartford residents came to face eviction, their experiences with the eviction process, and the immediate and long-term ramifications of evictions on their families; the proposal was matched with an Action Lab team in spring 2018. The research team designed a courthouse survey project that involved 22 people facing eviction in Hartford, inspired by sociologist Matthew Desmond's fieldwork in Milwaukee. Darby-Hudgens explained how "the Action Lab [team's] qualitative analysis helped us to ask better questions in a later analysis we conducted" for a project spon-sored by a local community foundation. Also, "we were able to use data from the Action Lab eviction interviews" in another grant proposal, since grant proposals often require applicants to demonstrate need through community participation.

In another example, a non-profit developer, Community Solutions, approached the Action Lab for help analyzing spatial data that they had collected during a neighborhood-wide housing survey. They were interested in making the case to funders that improving housing conditions – a key component of their work – was crucial to improving the health of neigh-borhoods, and asked the Action Lab whether their housing data showed any connection between housing conditions and health outcomes. Although the organization had access to an ArcGIS software license, they did not have anyone on staff with experience in GIS. During the semester, Action Lab students learned ArcGIS, cleaned and imported data, and conducted spatial analyses comparing housing conditions to health outcomes in the neighborhood. A representative from Community Solutions attended almost every project team meeting in order to learn ArcGIS alongside the students. Community Solutions' Esri account is the owner of the spatial data created during the Action Lab project, so they retain control over the story maps that are linked to the Action Lab project team website. After the project had concluded and the team had created a series of story maps to illustrate the results from the housing survey and the connection between housing conditions and health, this employee continued to edit and update the spatial data to make presentations for funders and better understand the underlying conditions of the housing market in their neighborhood. She even kept the Action Lab updated as she took more advanced coursework in ArcGIS. These maps continue to be updated for use in presentations and funding applications and remain linked on our website.

Strategic Effect

We define "strategic effect" as instances in which a community organization takes insights that were created or enriched by an Action Lab project and uses them to inform the broader strategic direction for the organization. A strategic effect implies a longer-term horizon than other effects, which might make this kind of effect more difficult to identify.

Given the nature of an Action Lab intervention, we might expect strategic effects to be relatively rare. However, we are already seeing glimpses of strategic effect in our partnerships. For example, in the fall of 2019, the Absentee Landlord Action Lab project worked with the Southside Institutions Neighborhood Alliance (SINA) to investigate the number of small multi-family homes in three South End neighborhoods that were owned by non-resident landlords. SINA had spent the last 30 years of its organizational history pursuing an acquisition strategy that focused on purchasing distressed and uninhabited properties. These vacant properties were typically distressed because of extreme deferred maintenance or because of financial insolvency leading to foreclosure. SINA rehabilitated these properties and created affordable rental housing or affordable home ownership opportunities for neighborhood residents. After the foreclosure crisis resolved in the neighborhood, policy makers and neighborhood residents began to notice an uptick in the number of investors purchasing small multi-family properties that had previously been owned and operated by owner occupants. Following up on this hunch, SINA asked the Action Lab team to investigate where the investor-owned properties were located in the area and to make a recommendation about whether changing its acquisition strategy to focus on occupied but investor-owned properties would be feasible. The team's work included data analysis and in-person occupancy tests, and the end results were shared at SINA's annual meeting, leading to a months-long discussion about the potential change.

CONCLUSION

The Action Lab is a unique educational partnership between two very different institutions, and its central goal is to work together with Hartford community organizations on the projects they have identified as most important to the work of the city. We have thought deeply about the mechanisms we use to "flip the script" during the project initiation phase, and remain committed to working on projects that have the capacity to contribute to the ongoing work of our partner organizations. With all that said, the question remains: what role do these educational partnerships play in the broader life of our city? How can we identify the effect of these short-term engagements in the broader institutional and communal landscape? By interviewing our previous partners – those who had completed a project with us and those who had proposed a project but had not been selected – we found five central forms of effect present in our work: reflective, discovery, applied, process, and strategic.

After the sum total of this effort for the first three years of Action Lab programming, can we say whether the Action Lab has helped Hartford? In a city facing big, thorny problems that are the result of decades of uneven development, disinvestment, and segregation, the effects of several short-term partnerships focused on research and action may seem like drops in the proverbial bucket. Regardless, it is important to tease out the potential for these collaborations – in a realistic way – and to dissect the contours of effects that are possible within these partnerships. Our discussions with our partners have suggested that the process of applying to work with the Action Lab has had emergent effects, such as the ability to think differently about a problem. Work with the Action Lab has also provided new information about a specific problem, or incorporated new diverse work processes and perspectives into ongoing collaborations. At the most concrete end of the spectrum, we found that our community partners have used Action Lab research projects to apply for funding, share plans with policy makers, and influence the direction of a specific project or organizational policy more generally. At times a new discovery leads directly (and quickly) to application; other times, the project confirms what is already known, but encourages a new strategic direction, the effects of which won't be measurable for years. Each of these possibilities represents seeds of influence and developing partnerships that may or may not fluoresce into more traditional outcomes or impacts.

All that said, another important, concrete, and lasting outcome of the Action Lab is the digital infrastructure of the lab itself, which we designed and constructed to open lines of communication between organizations (community groups and institutions of higher education) that often find it hard to talk effectively with each other. By taking the time to create an accessible and public application process, and by paying for the service of community board members to decide the projects the lab would work on, the Action Lab found ways to operationalize the democratization of research collaborations. None of these 15-week projects, taken in isolation, are intended to be a silver bullet, but the lasting impact of the infrastructure created to connect academic partners and community organizations should continue to produce work that matters to the overall health and well-being of the city. By continuing to reflect critically on both our process and our effect, we hope to contribute more to the well-being of Hartford and the communities that comprise it.

NOTE

1. Although this was not the inspiration for Action Lab program structure, a very similar model can be found in literature on "science shops." For a good outline of this model, see Chapter 3.

REFERENCES

Albrecht, Lisa Diane, Rose M. Brewer, and National Women's Studies Association. 1990. *Bridges of Power: Women's Multicultural Alliances*. Philadelphia, PA: New Society Publishers.

Bell, Ella Edmondson. 2012. "Infusing Race in the US Discourse on Action Research." In *The SAGE Handbook of Action Research*. London: SAGE.

Bunge, William. 2011. *Fitzgerald: Geography of a Revolution*. Athens, GA: University of Georgia Press.

Cahill, Caitlin. 2006. "'At Risk'? The Fed Up Honeys Re-Present the Gentrification of the Lower East Side." *Women's Studies Quarterly* 34(1/2): 334–363.

Cahill, Caitlin, E. Arenas, J. Contreras, N. Jiang, I. Rios-Moore, and T. Threatts. 2004. "Speaking Back: Voices of Young Urban Womyn of Color. Using Participatory Action Research to Challenge and Complicate Representations of Young Women." In *All About the Girl: Culture, Power, and Identity*. New York: Routledge, pp. 233–244.

Cahill, Caitlin, David Alberto Quijada Cerecer, and Matt Bradley. 2010. "'Dreaming of …': Reflections on Participatory Action Research as a Feminist Praxis of Critical Hope." *Affilia* 25(4): 406–416.

D'Ignazio, Catherine and Lauren F. Klein. 2020. "Data Feminism." MIT Press. https://data-feminism.mitpress.mit.edu/

Data Haven. 2017. Greater Hartford Community Wellbeing Index 2019. Retrieved from www.ctdatahaven.org/sites/ctdatahaven/files/DataHaven_Greater_Hartford_Index_2017_PrelimFinal.pdf

Hoffmann, Melody. 2016. *Bike Lanes Are White Lanes: Bicycle Advocacy and Urban Planning*. Lincoln, NE: University of Nebraska Press.

Janes, Julia E. 2015. "Democratic Encounters? Epistemic Privilege, Power, and Community-Based Participatory Action Research." *Action Research* 14(1): 72–87.

Marcus, Jon and Hacker, Holly. 2015. "The Rich-Poor Divide on America's College Campuses Is Getting Wider, Fast." *The Hechinger Report*. Accessed online: https://hechingerreport.org/the-socioeconomic-divide-on-americas-college-campuses-is-getting-wider-fast/

Martin, Deborah G. 2003. "'Place-Framing' as Place-Making: Constituting a Neighborhood for Organizing and Activism." *Annals of the Association of American Geographers* 93(3): 730–750.

Nagar, Richa and Sangtin Writers Collective. 2006. *Playing with Fire*. Minneapolis, MI: University of Minnesota Press.

Sherrod, Lonnie R. 2006. *Youth Activism: An International Encyclopedia*. Westport, CT: Greenwood Publishing Group.

Smith, Linda Tuhiwai. 1999. *Decolonizing Methodologies*. Chicago, IL: University of Chicago Press.

Stoecker, Randy. 2009. "Are we Talking the Walk of Community-Based Research?" *Action Research*, 7(4): 385–404.

Stoudt, Brett G. and María Elena Torre. 2014. *The Morris Justice Project: Participatory Action Research*. London: SAGE.

U.S. Census Bureau. 2017. 2013–2017 American Community Survey 5-Year Estimates. Retrieved from https://factfinder.census.gov/faces/nav/jsf/pages/searchresults.xhtml?refresh=t

3. Toward a community development science shop model: insights from Peterborough, Haliburton and the Kawartha Lakes

Randy Stoecker, Todd Barr, and Mark Skinner

One of the most glaring gaps in our knowledge of higher education engagement with communities is the kind of infrastructure we need to bring together participatory action research and community development for the actual improvement of a community rather than just its individuals. Instead we have focused on the projects themselves, and especially how academics and community members build "relationships" (Wang et al., 2017). But those relationships need a foundation to support them – a foundation that gathers resources and expertise (from academy and community) to sustain projects integrating participatory action research and community development.

This chapter focuses on a science shop model for such an infrastructure. A science shop is an organization dedicated to meeting a community's knowledge needs that can interface directly with community development efforts. This chapter will explore how three science shops in Ontario, Canada contributed to community development across an entire region, focusing on their integrated history, cumulative community effects, and lessons learned. Most of our focus will be on the historical trajectories of the science shops themselves, followed by a discussion of some of the participatory action research projects and how they linked to community development.

WHAT IS A SCIENCE SHOP?

The most common science shop process involves the science shop soliciting and intaking knowledge needs from community and other groups, working with those groups to turn their knowledge needs into researchable questions, doing a scan of existing knowledge both to find out what information currently exists and to inform research methods, finding researchers with the appropriate skillset and connecting them to the group seeking research, monitoring the progress of the research, facilitating presentation of the results, and supporting action (Mulder and de Bok, 2006). Mulder and de Bok (2006) argued that science shops can use both traditional science communication and more interactive or participatory methods. Many science shops, however, do emphasize participatory forms of research referred to by such labels as participatory action research, community-based research (CBR), and many others (Chandler and Torbert, 2003). When the science shop is university-based, Fokkink and Mulder (2004) noted that research projects can be attached to regular (thematic) courses or methods courses, or designed as senior undergraduate or graduate degree projects.

The science shop model overall emphasizes democratizing knowledge and fighting knowledge exclusion, with an emphasis on social and environmental justice questions (Farkas, 1999;

Leydesdorff and Ward, 2005). Science shops play an access role, mediating between researchers and those outside of universities seeking research services (Leydesdorff and Ward, 2005). They follow an ethic of serving groups who cannot pay for research, though they also do fee for service projects (Farkas, 1999).

This model began, and its name was coined, in the 1970s when activist students in Amsterdam, The Netherlands invented a form of higher education engagement with community to provide research for civil society groups. Many analysts agree that there have been four waves of science shops. The first two waves, in the 1970s and 1980s, were connected to social movements, and then to environmental movements spreading across Europe. In the 1990s the expansion of the internet shifted how we thought of knowledge and information, leading to a new wave of science shops, but also to the demise of many first- and second-wave organizations. The most recent wave saw an expansion of science shops in Eastern Europe (Fischer et al., 2004) and across the globe (Living Knowledge Network, n.d.a, n.d.b). Wachelder (2003) noted that there was at least one science shop in every Dutch University in 1987, but no longer in 2000, and that there had been a distinct cultural shift within the science shop movement from an ideological commitment to a professional research orientation.

In the most recent era, those who study science shops categorize them in various ways. Wachelder (2003) divided up science shops into four types: a non-profit service run by students; a fee for service model where professional researchers provide the service; a mixed model that engages both students and professional researchers; and a professional independent broker model that mediates between community groups and various research providers. Tryon and Ross (2012) distinguished between independent stand-alone organizations, university-based services, and hybrid organizations that are stand-alone but whose major funding comes from a university. Drilling down into the non-university model, Gnaiger and Martin (2001) divided the science shops field into non-profits with a university relationship, those with no relationship, and larger multi-mission non-profits that serve as incubators for smaller science shops. Raloff (1998) tried to argue that science shops are widespread in the United States (U.S.), but used examples that are actually single-issue advocacy research organizations. There is a lack of science shops in North America that approach the model developed in Europe where a university office or non-profit organization serves as a central intake for community groups' research questions and then finds skilled researchers to address those questions. Brown et al.'s chapter in this volume on the Liberal Arts Action Lab, combining the resources of Trinity College and Capital Community College, shows one example.

How well the model works remains as yet unknown. The same bias toward thinking about outcomes in terms of academic goals that dominates the service learning literature (Stoecker, 2016) also holds sway in the literature about science shops. Zaal and Leydesdorff (1987) studied the results of science shop projects, but only looked at follow-up research, methodological advances, and publications. Leydesdorff and Van Den Besselaar (1987) focused on research relationships – in their case between scientists and labor organizations – rather than the research outcomes. Of three science shop projects studied by Beunen et al. (2012), only one discussed community outcomes with the others concentrating on relationships. The two case histories presented by Mulder and de Bok (2006) stopped before any outcomes occurred. Others focused on student outcomes (Teodosiu and Căliman, 2002).

Part of the cause for this gap is probably the result of the higher education bias of the literature and its lack of connection with community development practice. This disconnect has likely been exacerbated by the permeation of neoliberal ideology in higher education, pushing the science shop model to veer away from its early activist roots and become "professional-ized," thus separating its models of research process from models of social change process. Without a strong theory of change, the science shop can only support research rather than social change.

We do not need to return to activist approaches nearly half a century old and rooted in a spe-cific European context to understand how the model can work today. Instead, in the context of the Canadian examples we will explore in this chapter, we need to understand community development models and how science shops can support them.

WHAT IS COMMUNITY DEVELOPMENT?

The practice of community development has followed a trajectory similar to that of science shops. Highly politicized in the 1960s and 1970s, this practice also became more professional-ized and more specialized in the 1980s, particularly with formalized community development corporation (CDC) models. The previous integration of community organizing and community development became split, particularly in the U.S. (Yin, 1998). Canadian scholars Boothroyd and Davis (1993) then distinguished three models of community economic development (CED), depending on whether "community," "economy," or "development" was the primary emphasis. Thus, cEd emphasizes forms of development that serve powerful economic actors; ceD focuses on forms of development that may not be fully capitalist but are still economic; and Ced concentrates on building community power to construct economies that serve all community members. In Canada, the federal government established the Community Futures Program in 1986 as a form of community economic development emphasizing the economy, with a network of 286 non-profits across the country in 2015 (Community Futures Network of Canada, 2015).

The term "community development" can be applied to everything from small informal grassroots community improvement activities to large-scale infrastructure and building projects. Our focus will be on the smaller-scale projects, designed and implemented using the same participatory democratic practices supported by science shops. For us, adapting Bhattacharyya (2004), community development refers to small scale community improvement projects in a geographically defined area, led by community-based groups and organizations though potentially including more powerful actors.

Community development is not about keeping things the same – it's not about charity ser-vices that maintain social problems at a certain level, such as a food bank that helps maintain an acceptable level of hunger. Community development is about changing a community to transform the conditions that lead to social problems, such as improving the local food system toward eliminating hunger. Good community development practice also does more than just complete isolated projects. In the process of doing such projects, it also engages community members, particularly those who are normally excluded from participation, helping them to understand the broader conditions affecting them, building their leadership capacity, and crea-tively using all available strategies (Community Development Society, 2018).

The connection between the participatory forms of research supported through science shops and the participatory forms of development supported through community development organizations might seem obvious. But the literature lacks any discussion of close working relationships between community development organizations and science shops, and that may explain the lack of literature on the impact of science shops. To address this gap, we will explore how science shops can connect with community development efforts to produce documentable community impacts.

CONTEXT AND RESEARCH METHODS

This is a story of three science shops in eastern Ontario, Canada: the Trent Centre for Community-Based Education (established 1996–1997 and later called the Trent Community Research Centre) in Peterborough, the U-Links Centre for Community-Based Research (established 1998) in Haliburton County, and the C-Links Centre for Community-Based Projects and Social Mapping (established 2009) in Kawartha Lakes.[1] All three organizations are, at least in part, examples of Wachelder's (2003) independent broker model of facilitating community–academy partnerships. All three are unique in being formally controlled outside of higher education institutions through non-profit structures.

The region served by these organizations is not historically wealthy, and has higher levels of poverty and unemployment than is typical in Canada. The city of Peterborough is a small historically industrial working-class city growing from about 70,000 to 80,000 people at the time this study covered, with another 50,000 or so in the metropolitan area. It suffered from the post-World War II deindustrialization that affected so much of industrial North America. But it is the home of Trent University, which has a unique history of being established with strong community and labor union involvement. It also has a relatively strong and innovative non-profit network that ranges from the arts to community services, and a surrounding agricultural and tourism base. Kawartha Lakes, west of Peterborough, is a city created by amalgamation so is county-sized and mostly rural. The city of Lindsay, population about 20,000, sits at the center, a community just large enough to have a small non-profit network. Lindsay is also the home of the Frost Campus of Fleming College. The college offers technical degrees in environmentally related fields. Haliburton County is north of Peterborough, above the rocky Canadian Shield in "cottage country," and is the most rural of the three areas. With only about 17,000 people at the time, its population density averaged a little over ten people per square mile. But it has an arts, entertainment, and culture scene far beyond what its population density and rurality would suggest, sustained by a strong voluntary civic culture making up for its lack of formal non-profit organizations. Haliburton County in particular has seen economic polarization as wealthy people from the Greater Toronto Area and others built mansions on the area's lakes, and it experiences all the stresses of tourist destinations. All three places are overwhelmingly white, with small immigrant and Aboriginal populations (Adams and Taylor, 2009; Bain and Marsh, 2012; Luka and Lister, 2012).

The data for these cases is drawn from oral history interviews with the leaders, organizers, and staff of all three science shops, conducted in 2015–2017. With approval from the Trent University Research Ethics Board and the participants' informed consent, the interviews were conducted either in small groups or one on one. Altogether, 28 individuals participated in interviews focused on the evolution of the organizations. Many of these individuals were leaders in the organizations, and in community groups that partnered on research projects. In addition, two unpublished histories of the Trent Centre and U-Links (Whillans and Wadland, 2014; Bowe, 2007) and independent research conducted by U-Links on the impacts of research projects were used to verify and supplement the information from the interviews.

This research employed a historical recovery form of participatory action research used when a group wants to preserve, learn from, and communicate their history and lessons. Leaders from the three organizations co-designed the project with Randy Stoecker, and reviewed and revised drafts. Because it is a historical recovery project, it is for the community as much as for a general audience, and thus contains names and details important to the community that may not have meaning for a general audience. Two of those participants agreed to be co-authors. Todd Barr is a former director of the Trent Centre and Mark Skinner is a dean at Trent University.

Our analysis follows an integrative approach, historically and geographically. Telling each organization's story is important, as each has a unique history. But together they have intersecting histories and serve a contiguous geographical region (Peterborough, Haliburton, Kawartha Lakes), making it challenging to tell their stories separate from one another. Thus, at times their stories will appear separately, and at other times together. C-Links, which began a decade and a half after the others, will appear much later in the discussion.

A HISTORY OF THREE SCIENCE SHOPS

We will begin by discussing the antecedents of community–academic partnerships in the region. Then we will trace the history of U-Links, the Trent Centre, and C-Links, showing their integration with community development organizations in their three communities. Later, we will briefly review the kinds of projects they supported and their community development consequences.

Origins and Impetus

The three science shops grew out of the efforts of natural science and history scholars and a community scholar. Most people attribute the origins to Trent University environmental scientist Tom Whillans and historian John Wadland and their Bioregionalism course. Haliburton and Peterborough Counties are linked and defined by the "bioregion" of the Trent-Severn waterway – a set of flowages that influence transportation, agriculture, commerce, and culture in the region (Adams and Taylor, 2009). Four influences shaped the course. First, the Brundtland report *Our Common Future* (1987) highlighted global and local sustainability. Second, Leopolda Dobrzensky, a prominent resident who had written a history of Dysart Township and Haliburton Village, influenced Whillans and Wadland (Dobrzensky, 1985). Third, Dr. Mary Northway, a prominent area resident, bequeathed the summer camp known as Windy Pine in Haliburton County to the Trent University Canadian studies program, allowing students in the course to be on site in a remote rural region. Finally, courses at Trent University were typically two terms long, allowing students much more time for research projects.

Tom and John approached the course through an ethic of CBR, before such an approach was commonly known, making an initial ten-year commitment to documenting the history, ecology, and social life of the bioregion guided by residents' interests. Each year they put an announcement in the local newspaper, recruiting residents to suggest and guide research projects the students could do. Professors, students, and residents met at the Haliburton Museum at the beginning of the fall term to design the projects. The students then spent the year working on the research projects, usually one student per project. In the spring everyone would reconvene at the museum where students presented their results. The museum stored the students' reports to be accessed the same way as any other book or article.

As all admitted, the students' work ranged from reports that still get cited to those that were immediately forgotten. The range of quality both brought out frustrations from some residents who were expecting more and ignited the imaginations of residents who were impressed by some of what was produced. Tom and John wisely invited both to get even more involved. A group of those residents would then go on to found U-Links.

The founding of the U-Links Centre for Community-Based Research

Part of the energy for U-Links came from an unsuccessful project. A group of residents[2] were brought together for a number of meetings by a graduate student who hoped to do a major community atlas project. The project never got funded but, rather than giving up, the group said "Well, why don't we just do this ourselves?" Tom Whillans and John Wadland encouraged them to try.

They began meeting in the upstairs space of the new wing of the Minden Hills municipal building, offered by Jeanne Anthon who was Reeve at the time, and which was vacant except for a stored collection of paintings by André Lapine, whose work would become prominent in one of the later research projects.[3] Their early vision included bringing adult education to Haliburton from a number of the higher education institutions in the broader region, drawing inspiration from the bioregionalism course projects.

These civically engaged residents were not just thinking about research. They were involved in numerous local issues, including violence against women, waste and recycling, and a desire for more local performance and visual artists in the county. About a year prior to creating U-Links the residents created the Haliburton County Community Co-operative in 1998. The Co-op was unique, organized to fund various community development initiatives, some of which would be incubated by the Co-op for a period and then become independent, and some of which would remain a Part[4] of the Co-op. A year later U-Links would become a permanent Co-op Part, with its own management committee providing it relative autonomy, but still reporting to the Co-op board.

The connection between the Co-op and U-Links created advantages for both organizations. Many new and potential Co-op Parts needed research to support their start-up planning, or inform their strategy choices. The Co-op and U-Links could also combine resources to support staff serving both. The Co-op connection helped keep U-Links' priorities focused on research supporting community development initiatives in the county. The choice for the generic "U" in the name was so the organization could partner with any higher education institution, not just Trent University, and to emphasize that their focus was on CBR.

The founding of the Trent Centre for Community-Based Education

Tom and John's work also influenced the Trent Centre. And, like in Haliburton, local community infrastructure – the Community Opportunity and Innovation Network (COIN, pronounced "coin"), led by Kevin Edwards, and the Peterborough Social Planning Council (PSPC), led by Jacqueline (Jackie) Powell – was crucial. COIN focused on inclusive community economic development in Peterborough, supporting what today would probably be called small social entrepreneurship startups. Some of the startups became arms of COIN, and others spun off to become their own entities. The Peterborough PSPC was part of a national network of organizations that combined research, policy development, and community engagement around various local, provincial, and national issues. The combination of COIN and the PSPC was already a powerful example of how to combine research and community development.

The Trent University Frost Centre for Canadian Studies and Indigenous Studies, directed by John Wadland, supplied much of the research support for PSPC. Another Trent University course, in this case a graduate course on community economic development offered by Professors Tom Whillans and Jim Struthers, provided research support. In 1995 and 1996 the course partnered with 14 Peterborough organizations.

The experience led the professors to create a new course designation called a Community Research Placement, allowing students to more easily do CBR for credit. And COIN and the PSPC began developing a system for gathering research needs from community groups and then connecting those needs with students. They developed some of their model from knowledge of the Dutch science shops. Trent University's Canadian studies program and the Frost Centre provided some initial funding. Kevin Edwards from COIN and Jackie Powell from PSPC did the bulk of the student project management work in these early years.[5]

Like in Haliburton, there was a conscious effort to make the process community-based rather than university-controlled. They also wanted to distinguish their approach from the co-op job training model gaining favor in universities at the time. So, they created a management committee, reporting to COIN, for the fledgling organization of four professors and four community group leaders. By the end of the century the professors had gotten support from university president Leonard Conolly, the faculty board, and the faculty senate for third- and fourth-year undergraduate students to take courses, including as independent studies, to serve community groups' research needs, as well as university office space. A job creation subsidy from Human Resources Development Canada to PSPC allowed them to hire their first staff, under the auspices of the PSPC. They also applied for one of the new Community–University Research Alliance (CURA) grants from the Social Sciences and Humanities Research Council but, even though CURA had been created after its designers had consulted with John and Tom, they were turned down.

The Trent Centre and U-Links together and separate
Even without the CURA grant, the Trent Centre, perhaps because of its proximity to Trent University and its more formal fiscal relationship with it, was fortunate to establish a strong funding base early on. The Canadian Imperial Bank of Commerce provided a substantial grant, matched by a private donor, for a total of $550,000 over five years. Trent University added $70,000 of funding. Within the next couple of years there was even more funding from a private donor wanting to promote community development in the region. With this new funding, the parties agreed that COIN had the most capacity to provide fiscal oversight, and the Trent Centre became a project of COIN. The Trent Centre then had much the same relationship with COIN that U-Links had with the Co-op.

Since COIN had supported projects in Haliburton County, and had relationships there, and John Wadland and Tom Whillans had been doing community-engaged scholarship in both places, the Trent Centre leaders agreed to share half the funds with U-links. Each organization then had an office and staff, two in the Trent Centre and one at U-Links initially. The money trail was complicated. Funds flowed from Trent University to COIN, who used half to fund the Trent Centre, and then sub-contracted with the Haliburton County Community Co-operative, who then used the funds for U-Links. Each organization agreed to run similar programs emphasizing community engagement with students, called community-based education, with broad local control over student projects.

The funding arrangement didn't exactly fit the distribution of work. Since the Trent Centre was located in Peterborough, on Trent University's in-town campus (the main campus was a few minutes' drive outside of the city), it was much more convenient for students to learn about, and troubleshoot, projects by going to the Trent Centre than contacting U-Links. Kate Hall, the U-Links director, would hold office hours at the Trent Centre regularly, but she still had limited contact with students and faculty. Consequently, Trent Centre staff managed most communications with students and faculty. This, of course, created some tensions about work-load and funding equity. To address this inequity the Trent Centre management committee created separate committees for Peterborough County and Haliburton County. The broader Trent Centre management committee then included two members of each county committee – a staff member and a management committee member from each organization. They restruc-tured the budget to create separate funding for the overall coordination work that the Trent Centre did, and split the rest between the Trent Centre and U-Links.

So geographic distance, the funding arrangement, and the fact that the municipality of Minden Hills (in Haliburton County) provided its office space all kept U-Links more separated from Trent University. The U-Links staff worked diligently to try to get other municipalities in the county to contribute, but only Minden Hills provided consistent support. The U-Links staff worked mostly with the bioregionalism course until the early 2000s, when they started to develop relationships with other faculty and courses.

As the initial funding cycle was reaching its end and the staff began to worry about future funding in the mid-2000s, the Trent Centre and U-Links got a multi-year McConnell Foundation grant, allowing U-Links to expand its staff to two people. This was just at the time that the Trent Centre became an independent non-profit organization, through the leadership of Jennifer Bowe, who had been involved with the Trent Centre first as a COIN board member and then as Trent Centre director. COIN had an incubator philosophy for new organizations, helping them to develop and then go off on their own. The Haliburton Co-op, in contrast, was more pragmatic, supporting organizations to either remain with the Co-op or become inde-pendent. U-Links stuck with the Co-op, and the new funding allowed for both new project staff and an administrative support position funded by both organizations and thus serving both.

By the mid-2000s, both U-Links and the Trent Centre had developed a similar "project cycle" mode of operation. They did project proposal intake over the summer, with staff helping organizations develop their project proposals. One intriguing innovation used by both the Trent Centre and U-Links was parsing out projects into a literature review stage and a local research stage. In some cases, all an organization actually needed was a report on the existing research literature about some intervention or program type. In other cases, the literature helped the organization make choices about what local research they needed. The staff did the bulk of the project shaping, but the U-Links management committee and the community-based education committee of the Trent Centre board did the overall project review work.

Because the projects were community-defined, it was challenging to find faculty who could fit them into their own work. Both organizations realized that students were their best advocates, and they recruited students through courses and sometimes independently, who then pressed their professors to mentor them through the projects. Eventually they got faculty to offer the projects to the students for credit in their regular courses, especially in geography, Canadian studies, and women's studies. Of course, not all projects would get chosen, and there was sometimes a gap between the more theoretical interests of the course professors and students, and the more practical interests of community groups, but that was not enough of a problem to break relationships. U-Links and Trent Centre staff would negotiate between the parties to assure that community groups got their practical research, even to the point of reviewing research reports to make sure they were written clearly and accessibly.

Managing the projects also required a set of processes. A project plan – which established outcomes, deliverables, timelines, and specified the responsibilities of all parties – guided the project management process. Trent Centre and U-Links staff monitored all the projects.

Increasing independence: U-Links

Gradually, the two organizations started developing their own styles. Haliburton County was experiencing an influx of wealthy property owners from the greater Toronto area, disrupting the area's class system, social networks, and infrastructure. In this context, U-Links went deeper into community development work, supporting research projects focused on establishing recycling, developing an art gallery, evaluating a small airport expansion, supporting active transportation options, and addressing other local development issues. They also were receiving more project proposals that exceeded the capacity of the average undergraduate student. Rural areas are often at a disadvantage in access to professional research and development support, and U-Links was looked upon by some for filling that gap. U-Links was getting invited to meetings across the county, not always because there was a clear research need, but sometimes because they were seen as an important general community development resource, making U-Links an important community connector.

As a consequence, U-Links began exploring fee-for-service activities, and in the 2010s they obtained a three-year Trillium grant to support that effort. Most such projects, such as with the Health Unit, only netted a few thousand dollars each. U-Links, with Heather Reid as director, began expanding its access to other universities in the region, particularly the University of Toronto, with the hiring of a new staff member.

The annual "Celebration of Research" in Haliburton County, begun with the bioregionalism project, continued to grow, with two dozen or more students presenting posters on their local research projects. This also served U-Links' community development mission, bringing people together to discuss the issues explored in the research, and creating lively civic conversation.

The important part of the U-Links model was linking research to specific development issues that community groups were working on. U-Links also increasingly used groups of students for single projects, allowing for strengths of different students to come together, and making the research even more usable. This was not often a quick process – it could take six or seven years from a research project to a group acting on the research to then having that action show results. Two past U-Links directors still live and work with community groups in the area, and became role models for linking research and action.

Increasing independence: Trent Centre

The Trent Centre was sitting pretty secure financially with the five-year $1.4 million McConnell grant supplemented by Trent University. They were also expanding their reach to other institutions, most notably Fleming College.

Under COIN, the Trent Centre was also oriented toward community development. With its new status as an independent non-profit in 2005 they began choosing their own path. Some made the distinction between the trailing phrases of the names for the U-Links Centre for

Community-Based *Research* and the Trent Centre for Community-Based *Education*. The "community-based education" part of its name allowed it to try other forms of student engagement. They did not stray too far into U.S.-style service learning or volunteerism, concentrating instead on a broader range of knowledge projects, working with organizations to do brochures, business plans, and other similar things.

Because it still served as a funding pass-through for U-Links, the Trent Centre structured its board to require a minimum of two board members from each region, like the management committee under COIN. But to be well grounded in Peterborough, they established *Community-Based Education Peterborough* – a community advisory board made up of Peterborough community members. They decided that their maximum capacity would be to manage 20 projects per full-time staff position.

In its more urban context, the Trent Centre was still an important network node, but perhaps less central than U-Links in Haliburton. With groups like COIN, PSPC, and large charity agency networks like the United Way, the Trent Centre was more in the mix, and as much a competitor for funds as a provider of resources. The Trent Centre also deployed a fee-for-service model for a time, but it was not looked upon as favorably as at U-Links.

The Founding of C-Links

C-Links had been on the minds of those behind the other two organizations from the very early days of U-Links and the Trent Centre. An organization in Kawartha Lakes, as well as a fourth one in Durham, much further west, were goals of the McConnell grant. But the community-based energy for a local CBR broker had never materialized in either place like it had in Haliburton and Peterborough. Todd Barr, then director of the Trent Centre, led the process of building an organization in Kawartha Lakes, about 45 minutes west of Peterborough, in the late 2000s. The Trent Centre had supported a few projects in the community, but the concept of community-based education was not widely known there.

Similar to the process that founded U-Links and the Trent Centre, Todd started by bringing together existing organizations that might sponsor such an effort, including the local United Way, Community Futures Development Corporation, and VCCS Employment Services, which would become the lead community agency and the fiscal home for C-Links. So, like U-Links, and the Trent Centre in its early days, C-Links had a steering committee rather than a board of directors. Both U-Links and the Trent Centre held membership on the steering committee, along with local community organizations like the Downtown Business Association and the Nature Center. C-Links was also represented on the Trent Centre board.

Lindsay, the municipal hub of Kawartha Lakes, was also the home of the Fleming College Frost campus that specialized in applied environmental and natural resource sciences. The Fleming College dean, Linda Skilton, took a particularly strong interest in C-Links, providing office space and other logistical support. The economic development department within the City of Kawartha Lakes was also very active in C-Links. The group applied for and received a three-year Trillium grant that allowed them to fund a staff person.

C-Links early on focused less on research projects and more on service projects than the other organizations. They recruited community groups desiring to work with students and then put 420 environmental leadership course students in small groups competing to write grant proposals for the groups. Each agency then got a small amount of seed money to work with the winning student group. In addition, some faculty at Fleming College, particularly

Josh Feltham, were attempting to organize a new program in applied CBR. And there were a few students doing much larger CBR-type projects with more of a community development orientation.

Hard Times for All

The rapid and deep recession of 2008–2009 and a majority right-wing federal government in 2011–2015 created a political and fiscal context that challenged all three organizations. Both Trent University and Fleming College were cutting their budgets. All three organizations also had fewer funding options in the philanthropic sector, having already tapped Trillium and McConnell. They were part of a grant from the Canadian Social Sciences and Humanities Research Council, but the grant's pie was divided so small it could not make up for the shortfall.

With no further funding after the three-year Trillium Grant, C-Links could not keep its staff person and tried to limp along with minimal administrative support provided through Fleming College and funded through Trent University. But it was insufficient to keep the momentum, and there was no local funding support forthcoming. By late 2016 they had ceased functioning.

The Trent Centre reduced its staff from a high of five down to two. In 2014 they went through intensive strategic planning, looking for a more sustainable path. They changed their name to the Trent Community Research Centre and changed their practice to emphasize larger, more research-intensive projects, which some would describe as more similar to the U-Links model. The Social Sciences and Humanities Research Council funding allowed them to hire graduate assistants to both conduct and mentor research, and they began experimenting with internships. The shift of Trent University from full-year to half-year courses also required adaptations in both the Trent Centre and community organizations. The Trent Centre was able to gradually patch their budget through a couple of long-term research contracts with a local organization and county government. But by 2018 the staff and board leadership of the Trent Centre agreed to be formally absorbed fully into Trent University, and the Centre was no longer an independent organization. Interestingly, a year earlier COIN, one of the organizations that had birthed the Trent Center and had served as its incubator in its first years, had closed its doors.

U-Links also went through a difficult period in this context of political and funding challenges, but they emerged pretty similar to how they entered. After a period of frequent staff turnovers, they found more stability in the mid-2010s. And in 2017 they began contracting directly with Trent University for their share of the funding that had previously passed through the Trent Centre. The university even increased its funding in exchange for U-Links providing engagement opportunities for more students. U-Links began experimenting with a service learning model to serve the requests they had been getting from local groups for volunteer labor power.

ACCOMPLISHMENTS FOR COMMUNITY DEVELOPMENT

The community development impacts of these organizations are substantial, though some are difficult to trace. For example, from the very early days of the bioregionalism course (and even before it with Leopolda Dobrzensky's (1985) work), some of the most important early research projects uncovered parts of the community history that held important lessons. A project by Andrew Hamilton called *Modernity, Metaphor and Maples: Landscape Created by the Wood Chemical Plant in Donald* [6] described the history of hardwood logging in the county and was widely read by residents. Another research project by Michèle Proulx exposed the problems left behind by the uranium industry in Haliburton County. But the community development impacts of those papers are difficult to document. The first research project with clear community development outcomes appears to be Sherry Feltham's paper, *Wilberforce Red Cross Outpost*, which told the history of the hospital and helped the Wilberforce Museum get it established as a national historic site.

U-Links built on the bioregionalism model to support research with profound community development influences that would not have otherwise occurred. Student research with a small community group called Rural Transportation Options helped establish a regional ride-share website, coordinating all the transportation providers in the community, hiring a navigator, and setting up a 1-800 number. In another case, three students interviewed the people impacted by the 2013 Minden Hills flood to assess the flood damage in the absence of any government study, and their results were cited by a provincial government review of flood prevention and response. Another student project inventoried vacant land that could be purchased for various kinds of development, assisting with municipality land use planning. Algonquin Highlands developed their recycling program from student research. When the U-Links organizing group first started meeting, it was in a spare room storing André Lapine's collection of paintings. Student research into the biography and importance of Lapine allowed the municipality of Minden Hills to get a grant that led to the construction of the Agnes Jamieson Gallery. The gallery became the home of the André Lapine collection, housed traveling exhibits, and provided community meeting space for speakers from wide and far.

In many cases, the student research helped a community group get funding that allowed them to take the next steps on a project. But in one case, a student assessment of public opinion surrounding the proposed expansion of a local airport became immersed in the controversy surrounding the expansion. The research itself may not have directly affected the ultimate outcome of the expansion proposal, but the research process may have lengthened the time needed for approval until a change in government stopped the project and made the question moot.

In some cases U-Links facilitated both the research and the community development efforts. When new provincial funding appeared for "active" or human-powered transportation, U-Links organized a coalition called Communities in Action to apply for funding, and then became the project manager. It supported research to assess who was already walking and biking, and then explored ways to expand active transportation that ultimately led to trail development around the area. It also helped create momentum for the Minden River Walk trail. In another coalition project, U-Links staff organized groups interested in local food that led to a food access mapping project done with a local environmental consultant and used for local food system planning. U-Links staff supported other projects, such as working with garlic growers to learn how to control the garlic leek moth. This was another funded research project led by U-Links staff using a citizen science process where the garlic growers collected data using pheromone traps.

The Trent Centre in Peterborough had an early list of community development accomplishments. When it was part of COIN, the Trent Centre organized students to provide student research support for various youth entrepreneurship projects, such as a solar energy business and a computer business called Nerds on Wheels. COIN also brought together an economic development opportunities brainstorming group including people from both Trent University and Fleming College, and students then did support research for many of those brainstormed ideas, including things like shared kitchens and co-operative car sharing. Other student research facilitated by the Trent Centre in those early days led to the creation of Sustainable Peterborough, which still exists as of the writing of this chapter.

There were also occasions when the target of research supported by the Trent Centre was Trent University itself. Tanya Roberts-Davis had a joint major in gender and women's studies and international development studies. She became involved in the "No Sweat" campaign to rid Trent University of sweatshop apparel, and her research ultimately informed Trent's apparel policy.

There were a wide variety of other projects that broadened the definition of research. One student worked with an organization supporting workers from an industrial plant who suffered from the toxins used there. The student created a pathway document that helped workers making health claims to navigate the system. A group of students produced a video for the YWCA women's shelter based on historical and policy research. The shelter wanted a video that would inform potential users of the shelter and help reduce the stigma that many women feel in considering the shelter's services. Another student did a project called "Planning for Great Streets" that researched bicycle- and pedestrian-friendly street design, used by the PSPC in its age-friendly city design campaign. Two other students surveyed seniors and non-profit organizations in Peterborough County on aging issues. Their research became part of the seniors' strategy of Peterborough County, which was a precursor for the region's success in becoming a World Health Organization-sanctioned age-friendly community.

When the Trent Centre changed its name to the Trent Community Research Centre, and refocused its mission on larger, more impactful projects, they rekindled their community development impacts. One of the more visible projects was with Lang Pioneer village, a nineteenth-century living history museum. Multiple groups of undergraduate and graduate students, over separate terms, did historical research to document the farm machinery and other artifacts of the museum. Student research with the Kawartha Turtle Trauma Center, which brings in injured turtles from Ontario's roads, used the research findings to help obtain a $30,000 grant to buy a generator. Another group of students produced informational material for the invasive plant council that was distributed across northern Ontario to help people identify and effectively dispose of invasive plants.

C-Links, even through its short existence, also achieved some notable accomplishments. Perhaps the largest project was an online social asset mapping project, mapping some 300 community agencies and transportation routes in Lindsay, supported by a Fleming College graduate. This project engaged the combined resources of the City of Kawartha Lakes, the United Way, and Fleming College. C-Links also supported a student from Trent University to evaluate the communication effectiveness of the United Way's Safe Communities project, helping improve the project. Another Trent student completed a trail-mapping project. The Gamiing Nature Centre was one of the organizations that participated in the Fleming research proposal competition and got a group of students who designed an environmental composting toilet building that is now in use. Other students did support research for the town of Fenton Falls to develop a pet waste management plan.

This is just a taste of the many projects facilitated by U-Links, the Trent Centre, and C-Links. Taken as a whole, it is possible to see the cumulative effects of these community development projects, and thus the cumulative effects of the research support. In Haliburton County, the projects listed have combined to influence transportation, waste management, land use planning, access to the arts, agriculture, health, and community services in the area. Similarly, in Peterborough, projects have combined to impact the local economy, aging culture, historical understanding, transportation, and many other aspects of the community. In Kawartha Lakes, the short life span of C-Links makes it more difficult to show cumulative impacts, but still shows the importance of the science shop infrastructure.

And that is the main takeaway. Aside from the importance of having competent research and good relationships, it is the support system that matters. At their best, the science shops helped community groups develop their understanding and use of research, and thus helped them engage in more informed community development. Science shop staff worked with community group staff and leaders to conceptualize projects, helped the groups find researchers, tracked and problem-solved the research process, reviewed and even edited reports to make them as accessible as possible, and managed communication between parties. Arguably, at least some of the community development visible in these communities today would not have happened without a strong science shop infrastructure in place.

ANALYSIS: INFORMING A COMMUNITY DEVELOPMENT SCIENCE SHOP MODEL

Understanding the overall model of these organizations is important. To varying degrees, they all worked from the basic science shop model where community groups propose research projects and then university and college students deliver the research. They also worked hard to build the capacity of community groups to propose research, receiving initial proposals from groups and then working with them to shape the proposals into projects that were appropriate for student skill levels and the academic calendar. Additionally, they closely monitored projects along the way, trouble-shooting when necessary, to maximize the chances that groups would get usable and high-quality research.

Within that basic model there was some variation. U-Links and the Trent Centre, perhaps because they began within organizations dedicated to community development, were the most focused on connecting research to community development. In other words, they organized research that fit into community problem solving and improvement strategies. U-Links hewed most closely to that community development approach, at times doing its own research without students because it prioritized the community development outcomes over the pedagogical outcomes, a prioritization more easily facilitated by a community-controlled organization. The Trent Centre emphasized community development support research most in its early years and later years, and nearly always with students. C-Links was also able to do some community development support research, even without having such a strong community development incubation, perhaps because it was well connected to city and non-profit groups with some community development focus.

There are also interesting differences in the contexts of the two organizations. The Trent Centre, in a more urban area with a larger number of non-profits, was structurally in a competitive milieu. The Centre in many cases competed for funding and attention with organizations it was serving. That background competitive structure was counter-balanced by the relationships of mutual aid between the groups in the city, though there was no entity that brought together all the other groups. In contrast, in Haliburton, a rural county of 17,000 residents, the Co-op brought together U-Links with nearly two dozen other groups in a county sparsely populated not just with people but also with organizations, overlaying relationships of cooperation on the relationships of mutual aid. In many ways, even though there are fewer people and they are more spread out in Haliburton, people's relationships are both tighter and more overlapping. That allows for less formality, more flexibility, and more trusting creativity in solving problems – research problems, community development problems, and others. As we have seen, community groups formed around issues, worked with U-Links to commission research, and then could act on the results to establish art galleries, recycling programs, and many other things. And C-Links was not only birthed at an historical time when the funding competition was even more intense, but did not survive long enough to become fully integrated with the other organizations in strong relationships of mutual aid.

The importance of research support for community development cannot be overstated. There is a severe lack of literature on higher education community engagement that results in actual community changes. For these organizations to facilitate research projects that can be directly tracked to such changes shows the power of their model. Much of that success can be understood as a result of each organization's relative independence from higher education institutions. To some extent, we can compare the three organizations and see that the connection to community development increases with distance from higher education. U-Links, through its history, had the most consistent integration of research and community development, as judged by those involved with both U-Links and the Trent Centre. It has been tied directly to community development activities as a Part of the Haliburton County Community Co-operative. U-Links also maintained a close relationship with the Haliburton County Development Corporation, allowing groups to get research support for projects that they could then take to them. And U-Links had the greatest independence from any single higher education institution. C-Links had the least integration, with a much closer relationship with Fleming College and much of its effort taken up by the internal college student proposal competition than on research projects with community groups. The Trent Centre was in-between, housed and funded by Trent University, but also a stand-alone non-profit that birthed through COIN and PSPC and always focused on serving community-generated projects. But it never developed as close a relationship with the area development corporation.

To what extent is this model, developed across three Canadian communities, viable? It is interesting that the one effort that has maintained its independence, in a strong and sustainable form, is U-Links. C-Links, with fiscal but not functional independence from Fleming College, only really lasted for the length of its founding grant. The Trent Centre, with no one to lean on in hard times, eventually gave up its remaining organizational independence and became part of Trent University. It is unknown at this point how much the Centre will change as a result, but those involved with the Centre before its assimilation into Trent University have been organizing to create a new independent organization. In contrast U-Links has always been a part of the Haliburton County Cooperative, which has both helped it stay the course of its mission and has helped it through tough fiscal times. So it is interesting to consider whether we are witnessing a "community development science shop" model in U-Links and the early years of the Trent Centre when it was a project of COIN. It is also interesting to consider the importance of rurality in the formation of these models, which were established by rural grassroots civic leaders aspiring to change their communities for the better, initially in Haliburton County via U-Links. To further expand our understanding of the benefits of community–academic partnerships, we advocate future research into other examples of community development science shops and the various contexts in which they might develop, for instance across the rural–urban metropolitan continuum in North America, Europe, and elsewhere.

ACKNOWLEDGMENTS

We wish to thank past and current staff and leaders of U-Links, C-Links, and the Trent Centre for Community-Based Education/Trent Community Research Centre for their time and generosity in contributing their memories and comments to this chapter. The research received support in the forms of travel funding from the University of Wisconsin-Madison and transcription funding from Communities First: Impacts of Community Engagement. We also thank Adrienne Falcón and Megan Brown for comments on an earlier draft of this chapter.

NOTES

1. The "U" in U-Links stands for "university" as the main higher education relationship at the founding of the organization was with Trent University. Similarly, for C-Links the main higher education relationship was with the Frost Campus of Fleming College, though some preferred to think of the C as standing for "community."
2. These included Jim Blake, Jeanne Anthon, Jack Brezina, Carolynn Coburn, Linnea Baynton, and Fay Martin.
3. André Lapine was a noted artist with connections to the area whose work has been exhibited at the 1939 World's Fair, among other places. This collection would become part of an early U-Links project.
4. This is both a descriptive and technical term. A Co-op Part acts like an independent organization in many cases, but it is still subject to the budgetary authority and operating policies of the Co-op. Thus, the Co-op is more than a fiscal agent for the Parts as the Co-op board still has ultimate decision making over the Parts.
5. Kevin Edwards, Jackie Powell, and Ruth Blishen also provided the early community leadership for this effort, along with Trent professors Tom Whillans, John Wadland, Sandy Lockhart, Jim Struthers, and Margaret Hobbs.
6. These reports were named by interviewees. Some are available from either the Trent Centre, U-Links, or the Haliburton Highlands Museum.

REFERENCES

Adams, Peter and Colin Taylor (Eds). 2009. *Peterborough and the Kawarthas*. 3rd edition. Peterborough, ON: Trent University.

Bain, Alison and John Marsh. 2012. "Peterborough: A Georegion in Transition?" In G. Nelson (Ed.) *Beyond the Global City: Understanding and Planning for the Diversity of Ontario*, pp. 151–168. Kingston: McGill-Queen's University Press.

Beunen, Raoul, Martin Duineveld, Roel During, G.H.M.B. Straver, and Albert Aalvanger. 2012. "Reflexivity in Performative Science Shop Projects." *Gateways: International Journal of Community Research and Engagement* 5(1): 135–151.

Bhattacharyya, Jnanabrata. 2004. "Theorizing Community Development." *Community Development Society Journal* 34(2): 5–34.

Boothroyd, Peter and H. Craig Davis. 1993. "Community Economic Development: Three Approaches." *Journal of Planning Education and Research* 12(3): 230–240.

Bowe, Jennifer. 2007. *Trent Centre for Community-Based Education: The First Decade.* Unpublished manuscript.

Brundtland Commission. 1987. *Our Common Future.* Oxford: Oxford University Press.

Chandler, Dawn and William R. Torbert. 2003. "Transforming Inquiry and Action: Interweaving 27 Flavors of Action Research." *Action Research* 1(2): 133–152.

Community Development Society. 2018. "Principles of Good Practice." www.comm-dev.org/about

Community Futures Network of Canada. 2015. Home Page. https://communityfuturescanada.ca/

Dobrzensky, Leopolda Z.L. 1985. *Fragments of a Dream: Pioneering in Dysart Township and Haliburton Village.* Haliburton, ON: Municipality of Dysart.

Farkas, Nicole. 1999. "Dutch Science Shops: Matching Community Needs with University R&D." *Science and Technology Studies* 12(2): 33–47.

Fischer, Corinna, Loet Leydesdorff, and Malte Schophaus. 2004. "Science Shops in Europe: The Public as Stakeholder." *Science and Public Policy* 31(3): 199–211.

Fokkink, Arie and Henk A.J. Mulder. 2004. "Curriculum Development through Science Shops." *Environmental Management and Engineering Journal* 3(3): 549–560.

Gnaiger, Andrea and Eileen Martin. 2001. "Science Shops: Operational Options – SCIPAS Report, 2001." www.livingknowledge.org/fileadmin/Dateien-Living-Knowledge/Library/Project_reports/ SCIPAS_report_nr._1_2001.pdf

Leydesdorff, Loet and Peter Van Den Besselaar. 1987. "What We Have Learned from the Amsterdam Science Shop." In S. Blume, J. Bunders, L. Leydesdorff, and R. Whitley (Eds) *The Social Direction of the Public Sciences: Sociology of the Sciences (A Yearbook).* Vol. 11. Dordrecht: Springer.

Leydesdorff, Loet and Janelle Ward. 2005. "Science Shops: A Kaleidoscope of Science–Society Collaborations in Europe." *Public Understanding of Science* 14(4): 353–372.

Living Knowledge Network. (n.d.a). European Partners. www.livingknowledge.org/contact/european -partners/

Living Knowledge Network. (n.d.b). Global Partners. www.livingknowledge.org/contact/global -partners/

Luka, Nik and Nina-Marie Lister. 2012. "Georgian Bay, Muskoka, and Haliburton: More Than Cottage Country?" In G. Nelson (Ed.) *Beyond the Global City: Understanding and Planning for the Diversity of Ontario,* pp. 169–200. Kingston: McGill-Queen's University Press.

Mulder, Henk. A.J. and Caspar F.M. de Bok. 2006. "Science Shops as University–Community Interfaces: An Interactive Approach in Science Communication." In D. Cheng, J. Metcalfe, and B. Schiele (Eds) *At the Human Scale: International Practices in Science Communication,* pp. 285–304. Beijing: Science Press.

Raloff, Janet. 1998. "Democratizing Science: Science Shops Are Tackling Research for and with Communities." *Science News* 154(19): 298–300.

Stoecker, Randy. 2016. *Liberating Service Learning, and the Rest of Higher Education Civic Engagement.* Philadelphia, PA: Temple University Press.

Teodosiu, Carmen and Anca Florentina Căliman. 2002. "Science Shop Contributions to Environmental Curriculum Development." *Environmental Engineering and Management Journal* 1(2): 283–293.

Tryon, Elizabeth and J. Ashleigh Ross. 2012. A Community–University Exchange Project Modeled after Europe's Science Shops. *Journal of Higher Education Outreach and Engagement,* 16(2): 197–211.

Wachelder, Joseph. 2003. "Democratizing Science: Various Routes and Visions of Dutch Science Shops." *Science, Technology, and Human Values* 28(2): 244–273.

Wang, Karen H., Natasha J. Ray, David N. Berg, Ann T. Greene, Georgina Lucas, Kenn Harris, Amy Carroll-Scott, Barbara Tinney, and Marjorie S. Rosenthala. 2017. "Using Community-Based Participatory Research and Organizational Diagnosis to Characterize Relationships between Community Leaders and Academic Researchers." *Preventive Medicine Reports* 7: 180–186.

Whillans, Tom and John Wadland. 2014. *Community-Based Education at Trent.* Unpublished manuscript.

Yin, Jordan. S. 1998. "The Community Development Industry System: A Case Study of Politics and Institutions in Cleveland, 1967–1997." *Journal of Urban Affairs* 20(2): 137–157.

Zaal, Rolf and Loet Leydesdorff. 1987. "Amsterdam Science Shop and its Influence on University Research: The Effects of Ten Years of Dealing with Non-Academic Questions." *Science and Public Policy* 14(6): 310–316.

4.   Elevating community voices

Jenice Meyer and Katelyn Baumann

This case study will show how community and academic partners leveraged participatory action research (PAR) to collectively examine the community from citizens' perspectives, asking: "What are the greatest needs and strengths of this community?" While a simple question, finding and articulating the answer was complex. A project team of community members came together and cultivated a process to create listening sessions and ultimately elevate community members' voices. This case study will serve as a guide for developing a listening sessions process, collecting community members' opinions, compiling qualitative data, and distributing findings.

Superior, Wisconsin has a population of just over 27,000, which has declined from more than 40,000 over the past century and is more than 90 percent white. The city is nestled on the northwestern tip of Lake Superior. Duluth, Minnesota and Superior make up what is known as the Twin Ports, a major international shipping port. The people that reside in greater Superior see themselves as proud, hard-working, resilient, friendly, and family-focused. Locally, the city has been known for its railroads, shipping yards, and a downtown nightlife area that supported such industries. In the last decade it has increasingly become known as a community in transition where a new identity is emerging. Heavy industries were key to defining the community in the past, but their decline has led to recreational opportunities emerging, as the area boasts the third largest municipal forest in the nation along with ample parks and noteworthy schools.

Like many other communities, Superior faces challenges that include limited affordable housing, high drug and alcohol abuse and use, low state Medicare reimbursement rates, a shortage of mental health services, and a lack of employment opportunities that provide a livable wage. The community has a working-class majority with, according to the United States Census Bureau (2019), a median annual household income of $44,916 and a poverty rate of 15 percent. Within the city of Superior itself different geographical neighborhoods provide a further sense of identity and belonging. It is not uncommon for people to ask in what part of the city one lives, referencing the differences between the North End, Central Park, East End, Billings Park, South End, and Allouez. Despite the differences in identity by neighborhood, residents still feel a strong sense of place for the broader city.

Superior also has a technical college and four-year institution of higher education located in the geographical heart of the community. The foundation of the PAR work that was accomplished in Superior, Wisconsin was based on University of Wisconsin-Superior and community partner collaboration. We write this chapter as members of the project team from the University of Wisconsin-Superior who helped organize this PAR project. Not all communities have an institution of higher education located within their boundaries; however, this is not necessary to pursue PAR. As you continue reading, consider if you might have access to an academic institution by way of college or university outreach offices or specialized programs that may increase your access to desired expertise and resources that can support any unique community need and can aid in defining community.

DEFINING COMMUNITY

While every community is unique, it is still possible to define community as a concept. Community can be defined as a "unified body of individuals," such as a group of people living in the same place or having a particular characteristic in common or a feeling of fellowship with others, as a result of sharing common attitudes, interests, and goals (Merriam-Webster, 2020).

Geographically, a village, city, state, or country can all provide arbitrary lines that ultimately create a geographical area or place. As described by Israel et al. (2005: 7), "Communities of identity may be geographically bounded, people in a particular physical neighborhood may form such a community."

The literature around community-based participatory research acknowledges that community can be defined as a unit of identity where people create and recreate their collective identity through social interactions (Israel et al., 2005). For example, a church can create a feeling of community as well as define a set of values and common beliefs amongst its members. The LGBTQA+ community has found strength, hope, advocacy, and a network through its common identity. In this case, the community may still have a main geographical area but the community itself extends beyond that area.

Typically, a person can identify with at least one community they find themselves in. And, each community is unique. Given this, no approach to working with a community will be "one size fits all." As this chapter walks through the process undertaken in Superior, it will highlight the successes and challenges of defining and working with a small, midwestern geographically located community.

DEFINING COMMUNITY DEVELOPMENT AND PARTICIPATORY ACTION RESEARCH

Community Development

From a higher education perspective, community engagement is defined as "the collaboration between institutions of higher education and their larger communities (local, regional/state, national, global) for the mutually beneficial exchange of knowledge and resources in a context of partnership and reciprocity" (Driscoll, 2008: 39). Community engagement has often involved students working with community non-profits and organizations, applying course learning to aid in addressing a community-identified need. In other instances, this can involve university faculty and staff working alongside community partners to conduct research and aid in bringing voice and momentum to a community's most pressing needs.

Related to the community engagement field is the concept of community development. According to Jnanabrata Bhattacharyya (2004: 5), "In community development projects are set up *with* the clients not *for* them." The author goes further, explaining that, in community development, "empowerment, capacity building, and similar 'buzz words' are not ends in themselves but means for the higher end of agency (Bhattacharyya, 2004:13)." Denise and Harris concluded (1990: 7), there are "numerous approaches to community development with differing values, beliefs, goals, purposes, and methods – all of which are concerned with improvement of the communities. The decade old social capital movement conveys the same meaning: networks, trust, and mutual obligations enabling people to take collective measures to address shared problems." Further Bhattacharyya argued (2004: 14), "this is also the argument for the public good. More practically, it implies a willingness to engage in collective effort to create and sustain a caring society."

Both community engagement and community development have a strong emphasis on reciprocity and sharing of resources in an effort to meet a community-identified and prioritized need. With community engagement a university, and often students, are involved. With community development, there is more of an emphasis on empowerment for longer-term change, ultimately creating a better and stronger society.

Participatory Action Research

PAR is still a relatively new model used to conduct research. In its essence, the research process intends to benefit the participants and the communities in which they reside or identify with.

As described by Blumenthal (2011), in PAR the research team enters into a partnership with the community and the community plans an equitable role in all stages of the research process. Bromley et al. (2015) had a similar perspective where the relationship dynamic in PAR can be characterized as shifting from the view of community as a research object to community as a partner. The process often entails academic researchers working with community representatives to address local concerns.

Community as agent of change assumes empowerment of the community as a change agent, and an egalitarian relationship between the community representatives and the researchers. The community partners are recognized as having expertise through their experiences and insider knowledge regarding the culture of the community, while researchers often possess research-related skills. Schalowitz et al. (2009) supported this in describing PAR as innovative because it harnesses community wisdom in an equal partnership with academic methodological rigor throughout the research process. Israel et al. (1998: 178) reviewed the PAR literature and identified core, evolving principles such as it is participatory; it is a co-learning process where there is a mutual exchange of expertise between partners, connecting different forms of knowledge; it involves building on the strengths of the community; it ensures all parties are disseminating the results; it entails implementing action based on the research findings; and it requires a long-term commitment by all partners.

What are the ways in which such a process can be beneficial to communities? To elevate local community voices, reciprocity as a key community engagement and community development approach were used for this PAR project. As is true with community engagement, the university played an important role in creating and developing an inclusive process, alongside the community, that led to determining the needs and priorities of the community. The collective wisdom of the community, by using PAR, identified what the community saw as its strengths to address its challenges, with the hope that it would lead to community change and ultimately play a part in creating a stronger society.

THE PROJECT

Lead-Up to the Project

In the fall of 2016, the University of Wisconsin-Superior administration created the Center for Community Engaged Learning (the Center). One primary focus of the Center was to deepen and expand the partnerships and impact of the work between the university and the community. This reflected and aligned with national trends and "The Wisconsin Idea," a public engagement philosophy championed for higher education in Wisconsin since the early 1900s (UW-Madison, 2021). The university aligned itself as an "anchor institution" and as an exemplar of "place-based organizations that persist in communities over generations, serving as social glue, economic engines, or both" (Cantor et al., 2013: 30). The university reflects an understanding that learning opportunities and expertise reside in both academic and non-academic settings. The Center was central to highlighting the current successes and bringing this recommitment back to life.

A critical first step in creating the Center was to broaden the understanding of partnerships based on learning the community's assets, challenges, and strengths. Through many conversations and research, the Center's director determined with community leaders and influencers that there was little information on the needs and strengths of Superior. Organizations across the region collected only limited data on specific slices of information or topics in the community. For example, the local county health department and hospital assessed the county's health outcomes. Within the Superior and Duluth area, a regional economic indicators forum provided fiscal health assessments and projections. Local school districts had specific strategic plans and goals focused primarily on students and not the broader community. These data sets did not serve our needs. The local Cooperative Extension office and United Way had collected some data a decade earlier, but it was now too outdated and there were no plans for new research.

As the discussion around the question grew, mostly led by Center staff, into a longer conversation spanning weeks and then months, the staff identified that capacity was a barrier to better understanding the community. For most community organizations, time is a valuable resource and must be used strategically (Fitzgerald et al., 2012; Lantz et al., 2001).

Creating the Project Team

Acknowledging this challenge, the Center brought together a group of community leaders, elected officials, and community members. Typically, PAR would include grassroots community members versus existing leaders, putting those whose voices are being elevated in charge of the overall research process. For this case study, due to the broad type of data being sought and the genuine commitment to hearing broad voices, the focus became ensuring different representatives from varied sectors were included. By design, this would help get results into multiple, powerful hands to produce the broadest impact from the results.

The mayor, a newly elected, ambitious, and visionary young leader, offered to help lead the process with the Center director. He was looking for data to better align Superior's budget allocations with community priorities, identify potential future projects, and inform policy. The cooperative extension director, based in the county where Superior resides, and the chief operating officer of the local hospital also joined the project team. A well-respected local public school teacher and former administrator on the project team brought a unique perspective on issues affecting youth that manifest in the schools. The chief executive officer from the Chamber of Commerce was important to the project team because of their role in local economic development and ability to direct investments. The university's Continuing Education and Institutional Research offices facilitated listening sessions and provided data expertise, respectively.

This group came together to discuss whether there was a need and commitment for a community-wide data set that could support community planning across multiple sectors. All agreed that having such information could support planning for their respective leadership roles as well as for the broader community. The group wanted a process inclusive of individuals from varied socioeconomic status and diverse populations throughout the city, being mindful that often decisions are made for people without their direct participation. Coming together and approaching the data collection and process in this way would result in strategic partnerships that are crucial foundation pieces of community development, and show how data across different sectors, industries, and community organizations and entities could build on each other.

This partnership had the potential to build alliances between organizations that may not usually work together and create more consistency across community approaches. When partners understand each other's organizational goals, they can contribute their own resources, skills, and assets to broaden organizational impact and access to new audiences (John Snow, Inc., 2012). Communities are interconnected, so understanding the priorities of different voices is central to the approach. Understanding the community more holistically also requires collaboration, planning, and connection. The next step was defining an inclusive process to obtain the information.

The project team committed to include all of the key principles and values detailed above. PAR assists with representing and elevating all community voices so that no single voice can be louder than the next. An underlying goal of this process was to build connection and pride in the community (Israel et al., 1998). PAR supports a methodology of facilitated dialogue, which the project team saw as more desirable than surveys. Dialogue allows people to connect to each other and the community and enables them to share more complete and complex thoughts and opinions. The PAR process would allow citizens to sit together and share their perceptions of the community and why they call it home. It would also provide an avenue for all partners in the process to contribute expertise and ownership of the process and outcomes. It's an approach that provides the opportunity to access a more holistic view of a community from their perspective.

The project team secured a small amount of funding from the local community foundation to purchase supplies, food, and childcare for the listening sessions. We also applied for, and received, a full-time AmeriCorps position. Without someone full time to manage all the pieces, this project would not have been possible.

Defining Questions for the Listening Sessions

Through preliminary work of the project team, three broad questions arose: What does the community see as Superior's strengths? What are the greatest challenges the community faces? And, what are the opportunities that Superior can pursue to further make the community a better place?

To keep the conversations general and non-leading, Center staff developed the three questions to ask of each listening session group. During the listening sessions, facilitators posed these questions in such a way to aid individuals to share their own opinions along with what they thought other people perceived.

1. What do you think people see as Superior's strengths?
2. What do you think people see as Superior's challenges?
3. What do you think people see as Superior's areas for improvement?

What do you think people see as Superior's strengths?
Learning about the community's perceptions of its strengths is an asset-based model for community development. An asset-based model for community development "recognizes that it is the capacities of local people and their associations that build powerful communities" (Mathie and Cunningham, 2003: 476). This approach differs from the common needs-based approach which, while well intentioned, can often present a negative or one-sided view. Research shows that often a community has the strengths within to address the concerns that it's facing (Mathie and Cunningham, 2003). PAR provides an opportunity for the community to recognize those strengths within themselves. After data is analyzed, communities can build on strengths to meet some of those identified challenges and opportunities. Asking about strengths is also a positive mental exercise to acknowledge the good things about a community and give participants the opportunity to feel pride in it.

What do you think people see as Superior's challenges?
Understanding the community's perception of its challenges gives more accurate information around community-wide challenges. As noted above, siloed data sets had been gathered throughout the community that focused on one issue or within one sector of the community. Asking about challenges, broadly, provided a space for community members to say what they saw as Superior's challenges from their unique standpoints. This process provided space to prioritize the challenges of the community, collectively, which no other data set at that time had accomplished.

What do you think people see as Superior's areas for improvement?
In addition to asking about the community's strengths and challenges, this question aimed to give participants the chance to speak about opportunities they see in the community. Although challenges and areas for improvement may seem similar, the project team expected that the information elicited from these questions would generate creative new ideas for moving the community forward. As the results below will show, participants in the sessions did in fact respond to this question differently than the challenges question.

Organizing the Process

The project team considered numerous data collection models, ultimately deciding that listening sessions, where people would gather with others and discuss specific assets and opportunities, would also generate a sense of pride within the community. The next step was to build an inclusive outreach strategy to invite participants to this process that we named "Embracing and Envisioning Superior." We hoped that using PAR would lead to "greater participation rates, increased external validity, decreased loss of follow-up, and increased individual and community capacity" (Viswanathan et al., 2004: 7). Center staff took the primary lead for designing the process in consultation with the project team.

Outreach strategies for participation in PAR can and should vary based on the community with which you are engaging. Superior is highly homogeneous and does not have a notable population of community members who speak languages other than English. Therefore, it was not necessary to facilitate any of the listening sessions in another language. However, other communities would certainly want to consider facilitating listening sessions in multiple different languages based on linguistic diversity. Being mindful of inclusion of the diversity of the demographics in the community one defines is important to include a broad understanding of the community's needs.

Project team members identified a variety of demographics within the community where inclusion was key, including people traditionally marginalized based on racial identity and socioeconomic factors. However, the group was somewhat stymied by the fact that 95 percent of our population identifies as white. So, the group shifted to considering age and socioeconomic status as the main demographics we would use. We recognized that younger middle school and high school students may see the community's strengths, challenges, and opportunities much more differently than senior citizens. Research has shown that involving youth can bring significant contributions to community development, while offering them the chance to gain valuable experience (Israel and Ilvento, 1995). We therefore created 12 listening session events at various times to draw in these broader groups.

Drumming up attendance at anything like this can be difficult. A core strategy that led to the success of the listening sessions was to build on existing connections and relationships and leverage the credibility and networks of various organizations. The project team members reached out to community contacts who worked with specific populations across the community. We partnered with local community groups and facilitated sessions as often as possible during already scheduled events at locations where the groups would typically meet. We provided food and childcare to limit barriers for people to attend.

To attract elementary-age children and families we created partnerships with the parent–teacher organization of the Superior School District. To optimize attendance, we scheduled the listening session during a monthly board meeting in the evening at one of the local elementary schools, and provided childcare. We recruited middle and high school-aged students by first contacting lead teachers at the middle and high school level. Facilitators met with the eighth-grade leaders group. Facilitators met over the lunch hour with students in a variety of classrooms across the high school. To gain perspective from college students, who make up nearly a tenth of the city's population, the University of Wisconsin-Superior student involvement office and the local technical college got involved. This event was held in the evening after most classes were completed. Center staff contacted two area young professional groups to tap into their perspectives. Facilitators attended a regular Jaycees meeting, and the young professionals' organization invited their members. The Retired Senior Volunteers Program hosted facilitators over their monthly lunch meeting in the basement of a local church.

We organized six other sessions around specific themes rather than demographics. The YMCA partnered in organizing a session at the university around the theme "Healthier Superior." The local national estuary and city environmental services offices partnered to provide a "Natural Resources" session. The Chamber of Commerce, with the local business development and business improvement districts, partnered to hold a "Business, Workforce, and Community Development Session." The local teacher education union partnered on a session held after a monthly union meeting. The United Way contacted their funded agencies to invite people who received services from these agencies to attend a session. Finally, the mayor's Commission on Communities of Color held a session entitled "Equity, Diversity, and Inclusion" in a local church basement where childcare was provided.

Listening session process
The listening session tables were arranged for participants to be seated at round tables to accommodate five to eight participants. Each table had a facilitator to support the process by guiding the discussion and assisting with questions. All the facilitators received basic training on the questions, intended goals of the sessions, and a few group facilitation practices for promoting discussion and recording answers. They also ensured all discussion points were accurately recorded, at times serving as the recorder themselves.

Although sessions occurred on different days, at varied times, sometimes on a "theme" to reach certain interest groups, and in unique spaces, the process was the same for each listening session.

Welcome and goals for the day
The mayor of Superior and director of the University Center welcomed participants. They discussed the goal of identifying the greatest needs, challenges, and strengths of the community. The mayor emphasized that summaries of the dialogue would elevate community voices to better inform community decision making by those holding power, citing future city budget proposals as an example. The Center director expressed gratitude for the participants and conveyed how the university would use the information. After a basic opening, the Center director provided an overview of the process for the day and invited the table facilitators to begin the discussion part of the session.

Introductions
When the discussion part of the session began, the table facilitator identified themselves before asking everyone at the table to introduce themselves. A simple introduction helped participants feel more comfortable with the group at their table. We considered using an ice breaker activity, but the 60-minute sessions did not allow it.

Designate a table recorder
Next, each table designated a participant to be a table recorder. Often, the table decided the facilitator could also be the recorder. The table recorder was responsible for ensuring that the points made during discussion would be recorded on the pieces of paper at each table, using a different, large, flip pad sheet for each question guiding the discussion.

Discuss questions
The table facilitator asked the table group to discuss one question at a time for 15 minutes each. As participants discussed the questions, the table facilitators helped to guide conversations without directing and asked clarifying questions if needed.

a.   What do you think people see as Superior's strengths?
b.   What do you think people see as Superior's challenges?
c.   What do you think people see as areas for improvement?

Display responses to questions

After each table had discussed a question, the facilitator took the large flip pad sheets that reflected the group's conversation and displayed them on a wall with the other tables' responses to that question. This strategy helped the participants immediately recognize trends and read discussion points that did not come up at their table.

Prioritizing

After the large flip pad papers were displayed, organized by each question on different walls yet inclusive of all recorded responses from every table, the Center Director invited all participants to read the recorded discussion points from each question. Each participant was then given five dots for each question (each question had a different color dot) and asked to place dots on the five discussion points that they believed were most important for each question. Participants could place all five dots or votes on the same discussion point or spread them out. This process was repeated for each question. The dot-voting strategy helped prioritize points quickly without lengthy discussion.

Participant questionnaire

Before leaving, Center staff thanked the participants for their time and asked them to complete an anonymous evaluation ranking the following statements from 1 (strongly disagree) to 7 (strongly agree):

● The input I contributed today will be heard and used in decision making.
● Attending today's session was a valuable use of my time.
● Participating in today's session increased my pride in my community.

Participants could also share their name and email address if they wanted future communication about the report published from the listening sessions and outcomes of the overall project.

Data Collection and Analysis

Ensuring the time and expertise to compile and distribute the results in a timely, responsive manner should be planned for before data gathering even begins. Center staff intended for the analysis to take one month. The time needed to compile the qualitative data was vastly underestimated. In total, it took four months to compile and analyze the data.

Just over 250 individuals participated in the sessions. Staff from the Center and the university's Institutional Research department, along with the full-time AmeriCorps member, reviewed the qualitative data for each session and then integrated it into a single spreadsheet, typing up the notes from the large poster sheets that listed discussion points along with the number of dots indicating participants' priorities. The data included demographics such as age and industry sector. A student assistant then compared the paper version and electronic version to ensure accuracy.

The project team initially planned to do a separate report for each listening session, as many were facilitated for distinct demographic groups, enabling them to assess each demographic group's view. However, given that the groups were small, there was not enough data to represent an entire demographic group in each listening session. This would have required a strategy such as sending out a broader survey to the community in order to provide more validity for specific demographic groups.

The Institutional Research office provided support to code the qualitative data into specific themes. For example, "Lake Superior" was noted numerous times as a strength in nearly every session at almost every table. In the coding, terms like "Lake Superior," "Our Great Lake," and "The Lake" were kept together to provide a proper weighting of the response. Many other judgments were necessary. For example, within strengths, we decided to separate outdoor recreation and natural resources. When a discussion point involved actively engaging with the outdoors, it was included in outdoor recreation. When a discussion point sounded more passive but was linked specifically to a place or a benefit enjoyed, it was recorded as natural resources. Further, Lake Superior could have been included within natural resources. However, there was so much emphasis by so many on Lake Superior independently, it became a strength independent of the Natural Resources category. Finally, Center staff, with support from the university's Office of Institutional Research, sorted the coded themes into top ten priorities for each of the three questions and created a report titled *Embracing and Envisioning Superior*, designed for any non-profit, school, business, elected official, community group, or governing body to use as a point of reference for their own work. The results discussed in that report appear below.

Results

Overall, participants in the listening sessions saw Superior's strengths in relation to outdoor recreational activities and community offerings; surrounded by natural resources and good schools, with a safe, small-town feel, and a low cost of living with big city access. Somewhat conflicting, the top challenge listed was lack of things to do. This spoke to common, ongoing types of access such as the lack of a theater or places to go and enjoyment across different seasons, in addition to the outdoor recreational activities that were available. This finding aligned with research by a group named Better Cities that was looking to create an indoor recreational and destination center in the city. Similarly, housing problems, lack of retail and shopping options, lack of health service options, and drug and alcohol use have been well documented by various city, county, and state reports. However, our listening sessions showed, for the first time, how these issues were ranked *in relation to each other*. Surprising to the author and others in the project team, identity emerged as something people wanted to see improve. This related to a challenge that people saw for Superior's relationship with Duluth. For many decades Superior has been seen as the lesser city of the Twin Ports, and citizens wanted to see this change. Relatedly, they wanted to build on community strengths, expressing a desire to further develop the parks and recreational opportunities. They wanted to reverse the declining retail challenge. With big box stores nationwide declining, a few small retail businesses in the downtown business district were beginning to emerge and show what could be a new opportunity for the community, which was reflected in our data.

Figure 4.1 summarizes the results. The graphics, created by Center personnel with support from the university's Communications Department, provides a visual of the listening session results. Figure 4.1 shows the top ten ranked strengths, challenges, and opportunities identified by citizens during the listening sessions. This provided a one-page, easy visual and handout to easily distribute the overall listening session results.

Source: Meyer and Burson (2018).

Figure 4.1   Summary of results

Strengths

When we asked listening session participants "what do you think people really like about Superior," the strengths of the city emerged. The categories in Figure 4.2 represent the strengths expressed in ranking order, from top left down, along with the most common examples described. For example, people ranked "Outdoor Recreation Activities" first, "Natural Resources" second, and "Lake Superior" sixth. Outdoor Recreation was voted for by 183 community members, 181 for Natural Resources, and 163 for Community Offerings. On the low end of the top 10 findings, 86 citizens voted for Small-Town Feel, 70 for Low Cost of Living, and 68 Small Community with Big City Access.

Outdoor Recreation Activities

- Paddling
- National forests
- Community parks
- Trails
- Hiking
- Biking
- Water

Lake Superior

- Swimming
- Landscape
- Public water access
- Near freshwater
- Economic development

Natural Resources

- Wisconsin Point
- Municipal Park
- State parks
- Local forests
- Clean air
- Water access
- High-quality Drinking water

Safe Community

- Police Department
- Fire Department
- Low violent crime rates
- Safe to bike and walk
- Improved park security

Community Offerings

- Skate park
- Billings Park
- Public library
- YMCA
- Museums
- Community events
- Farmer's market
- Cultural activities
- Senior Center

Small Town Feel
- Tight knit
- Size of the city
- Quiet place to live
- Population size
- Friendly and welcoming

K-12 Public Schools

- Athletics
- Great teachers
- Family events
- Scholarships
- Strong school system
- Modern buildings
- Multiple elementary schools

Small Community with Big City Access
- Close proximity to Twin Cities
- Mix of urban and rural
- Access to Duluth
- Convenient short lines

Higher Education

- Affordability
- Diversity
- Local higher education options
- Pride in local university
- Community education
- Event and meeting space

Low Cost of Living
- Lower sales tax
- Affordable housing

Source: Meyer and Burson (2018).

Figure 4.2   *Strengths*

Challenges

When we asked listening session participants "what do you think people see as Superior's challenges," people brought a diverse array of topics to the table. The response that resonated with community members most was a lack of things to do. The categories below represent the challenges expressed in ranking order, from top left down, along with the most common examples described. In Figure 4.3, participants ranked "Lack of Things to Do" first, followed by Housing, and ranked "Drugs and Alcohol" sixth. Citizens voted most for Lack of Things to Do and Promotion with 143 votes, followed by 117 for Housing Problems, with Retail and Shopping options following closely behind with 114 votes. On the lower end, Employment held 75 votes, followed by High Taxes with 60 votes, and City Planning with 59 votes.

Lack of Things to Do

- No theater
- No central event calendar
- Limited winter activities
- Lack of summer activities
- Not enough tourism
- Lack of after-school options for youth

Drugs and Alcohol

- Substance abuse
- Easy drug accessibility
- Drug education programs
- Need for residential drug treatment center
- Drunk drivers
- Link to health issues

Housing

- High rental costs
- Long wait for low-income and senior housing
- Lack of pet-friendly housing
- Access to affordable, high-quality rentals

Who We Are In Relation to Duluth

- Need to travel to Duluth often
- More money is spent in MN than WI
- Negative perception of Superior
- Superior overshadowed by Duluth

Retail and Shopping Options

- Need to travel to Duluth to meet retail needs
- No mall
- Limited shopping options
- Need longer business hours

Employment

- Need high quality, middle-class jobs
- Limited jobs for young people
- Attract and retain major employers
- Opportunities for professional growth

Health Services

- Access to public health services
- Mental health access for all ages
- Low-income access to dental care
- Need to travel to Duluth for care
- Low-reimbursement for services in WI
- High rate of chronic health problems

High Taxes

- High property taxes for current property values
- No free garbage

Retention of Small and Large Businesses

- Big business retention
- Lack of "Big Box" stores
- Lack of new employment
- More businesses to generate tax revenue

City Planning

- Airport capacity
- Intentional city development needed
- Lack of accessibility
- Communication and updates needed

Source: Meyer and Burson (2018).

Figure 4.3   Challenges

Opportunities

When we asked listening session participants "what do you think people see as Superior's opportunities," the attendees again brought a diverse array of topics to the table. The topic that resonated with community members most we themed as Identity. Like the other graphics, the categories in Figure 4.4 represent the opportunities in ranked order, from top left down, along with the most common examples described. For example, people ranked "Identity" first, followed by "Family-Friendly Activities," with "Attract Retail" sixth. Identity: Strengthen and Promote Brand had 147 votes, followed by Family-Friendly Activities: Expand and Promote, with 117 votes, and Parks and Recreation: Improve, Expand, and Promote had 102 total votes. Environmental and Natural Resources Planning had 64 votes, Sidewalks and Roads: Improve had 63 votes, and Employment: Improve Wages and Opportunities held 60 votes.

Identity

- Community organizing
- Positive promotion
- New attractions
- New brand/ marketing campaign
- Increased tourism ads

Attract Retail

- Access to shops
- More stores
- Upgraded mall
- Shopping district
- Movie theater

Family Friendly Activities

- Indoor recreation spaces
- Safe, positive programming for youth
- Family-friendly entertainment
- Options for teenagers

Community Support Services

- Access to child and senior care
- Service coordination
- Increased county service support
- Family Resource Center

Parks & Recreation

- Bike trail system
- Indoor spaces
- Trail maintenance
- Public lake access
- Camping

Environmental & Natural Resources Planning

- More dialogue around natural resources with diverse stakeholders
- Resiliency plan in preparation for impacts of climate change

Business Development

- Diversity
- Year-round sustainability
- Creative ideas
- Additional businesses to bars downtown

Sidewalks & Roads

- Maintenance to trails and sidewalks
- Increased active transportation
- Road and sidewalk snow removal
- More sidewalks

Modes of Transportation

- Infrastructure
- Modes of safe transportation
- High speed train to Minneapolis-St. Paul
- Bike-ability and walk-ability

Employment

- Jobs for teenagers
- Motivation for young professionals to stay here
- Increase job diversity
- Promote businesses that pay living wages
- More jobs

Source: Meyer and Burson (2018).

Figure 4.4   Opportunities

Distribution of the Results

Distribution of PAR results to participants and the general public is an ethical responsibility of researchers and a fundamental aspect of translational research. It is crucial to share information with the people whom the research ultimately aims to affect. And while dissemination through scientific publication is widespread, dissemination beyond scientific publication is occurring but can be improved. One study concludes that without an emphasis on dissemination of PAR results beyond scientific publication, the results and efforts cannot contribute to changes that can build up communities (Chen et al., 2010).

Distribution, if one continues to seek a collaborative, community-wide response and follow-through on the findings, is the truly heavy lift of such a process. The dissemination of results is an important part of the PAR process; yet it is a challenge for many who engage in it. It is important at the beginning of such a process to consider both how to collect the data and how to communicate the results and put them into action. We did not secure funding for disseminating results and supporting action on them. And just at that point in the project the AmeriCorps member grant ended. So, the data collection process was sound but, with no funding or a person dedicated to the project's continuation, little momentum was left to carry forward the intended dissemination plans.

Our circulation plan was thus not as robust as we had hoped. In the spring of 2019, the project team invited key partners for each of the listening session groups to hear the results. The director of the Center presented the data results. Participants offered feedback about how the content was presented, and we discussed how to best share the information.

In the summer of 2019, the project team compiled the data into an easily accessible report, which we distributed to the key constituencies involved in the process. We distributed the report to the university campus community and organized informational sessions for students considering undergraduate research projects in the fall semester of the 2019–2020 academic year. A small, new team of committed community members from the school district and city council, who had been involved with at least one listening session and were very interested in the results, came forth to determine the best ways to further distribute the results to specific groups and more broadly. We were planning to present the finding to the city council, school board, and county board, as well as other community service groups. Our plans for continued distribution and shared utilization, however, were completely upended in March 2020 by COVID-19. The last in-person meeting was days before the state of Wisconsin began the safer-at-home orders.

Even so, Center staff submitted a grant application to the local community foundation, on behalf of this new, smaller team, in April 2020. This grant would have built on the momentum created by the process and results of the Embracing and Envisioning Superior listening sessions. Termed *Phase Two: Moving Forward, Together*, we intended this next part of the process to facilitate learning and discussion of the published results, increase community pride, and inspire collective action to address challenges and opportunities identified by our community. The team intended to host a large, community-wide, very public dissemination of the results followed by a facilitated, small group-focused, world café process. The world café model is widely accepted as a powerful tool in helping with collaborative dialogue, engaging actively with each other and creating constructive possibilities for action (World Café Community Foundation, 2021). We intended for participants to connect, discuss the results of the listening sessions, and create action steps to address challenges and leverage opportunities. In addition, we wanted this event to create a broader understanding of existing efforts around the challenges and opportunities identified from the listening sessions, and collectively find gaps and new ways to address the community's greatest needs. At that time, it seemed an in-person option for such an event could have still been a possibility. And, if not, a virtual option could be a possibility.

Despite our best efforts, the grant was not funded. Soon after, the main staff member in the university's Center resigned. This, amidst the pandemic, brought the next steps for dissemination and coordinated utilization to a sharp stop. For months, our priorities were altered. With the pandemic and other related social justice and economic issues taking priority, we became concerned about how well the results still reflected citizens' voices. We thus began to explore hiring a new AmeriCorps member to pick up and facilitate the next steps in this process. Although the next specific steps have yet to be detailed, having staffing to provide the foundation support for such a project is key and a good first step.

Main Take-Aways

Successes of the project

It was encouraging and provided a sense of hope about the city of Superior's future to have so many people step forward to aid with data collection. We anticipated about 100 people attending the listening sessions, so to see over 250 people in attendance at such sessions was our first success. We attributed the attendance to how well the sessions were designed to meet people in their spaces, on their time, and to the project team's promotional efforts.

Also, numerous newspapers and local broadcasters covered the listening sessions. Early in the process, the *Superior Telegram* ran a front-page article about the listening session held at the high school which informed readers of future listening sessions and encouraged Superior residents to attend. Local news stations invited project team members and table facilitators for live morning broadcasts and local evening interviews. Local television stations also generated attention to the listening sessions by capturing interviews and live footage. Overall, the engagement with and coverage of the listening sessions far exceeded our initial intentions.

Bringing individuals together to share their perspective about their community created a sense of pride about the city of Superior for participants. In the compiled surveys, 80 percent of participants indicated that just by participating in the hour-long session their sense of pride about their community was enhanced. Further, a sense of possibility seemed to emerge. At each table, for each session, positive energy pervaded the room. Just being asked and able to engage in such a process seemed to create and build trust amongst attendees and facilitators. This energy also aided a sense of possibility for outcomes from the process. It seemed that many were excited about the possibility of change within the community that could come from the sessions.

For the project team, the findings and results provided data to inform strategies for addressing Superior's challenges, seizing its opportunities, and embracing its strengths. One hope we had for the findings and the report was to help answer the question: how can we use our combined expertise and passion across industries to facilitate collaborative macro-level solutions? In short, what can be accomplished if we work together?

The mayor has used the findings in the report as a valuable resource for talking points about the city's strengths and identity and for establishing budget priorities. As a part of his economic development team, the mayor decided to move forward with creating a new brand to address the identity opportunity identified in the report. The City of Superior, the Development Association, other development leaders, and the university have also worked diligently to improve branding of the community. A consultant was hired by the development association director, a new brand that was based on the strengths detailed in the listening sessions was created, and despite COVID, a strategy for rolling out the new identity, in a brand, is in process. The results were also referenced and aligned with the February 2020 yearly citizens' lobbying efforts by nearly 200 community members in the state capital, Madison. Although such efforts were canceled for February 2021, organizers have discussed how the report could be a central starting point for such efforts in the future.

For the Center, the findings and the report provided foundational information that has been used and referenced when seeking new partnerships for academic service-learning classes and other new partnerships. It has also prioritized time spent by Center staff on community committees. For other outreach offices, the report provided additional information for creating programming and continuing educational efforts. For students, the results helped spark ideas of what their undergraduate research projects could focus on for the greater good of the Superior community. For faculty and staff, the report spurred ideas for new, or modified, teaching and scholarship that begins with the community's priorities. The data is also directly tied to outcomes detailed in the five-year campus strategic plan for civic and community engagement, named the Civic Action Plan, that the Center provides leadership for.

Lessons learned from the project
As with any partnership or project, challenges and lessons emerged. We experienced challenges with the timeline, communication among project team members, data analysis, dissemination of the results, and working collaboratively.

Collaboration and partnership
True collaboration and partnership take time to develop, grow, and sustain. An advantage to working in a smaller community is many of the partners on this project were somewhat familiar with each other and some had even worked together on other projects. Even so, language barriers can exist within different sectors and organizations. In the future, writing down expectations of each part of the project at the beginning can help to ensure everyone at the table has the opportunity to clarify questions, expectations, a timeline, and outcomes for success. It can also ensure that all partners have provided in-depth feedback, not just about the data collection but also about the dissemination of results and work associated with the information after it is collected. It could also further ensure a more equitable distribution of the project needs.

Continued communication with team members
As with any project, communication is key. Throughout this process, the AmeriCorps member with the Center at the university was in contact with partners on a weekly, and at times daily, basis. The city's mayor also assumed more of a leadership role with this project. However, the project team as a collective only met twice – at the beginning of the process and 12 months later when the results were shared. In retrospect, the project team should have met together more frequently. This would have also helped ensure that disseminating and addressing the results could have been tackled collectively. Instead, with the AmeriCorps member's service year completed, that was delayed. The original intention of sharing the results a few months after the data was collected in 2018 did not occur and was held over into 2019.

Analysis of the qualitative data
A missed opportunity identified by the Center and their staff, after the results were compiled and ready for distribution, was engaging community partners in analyzing the data and interpreting the findings. The project team determined early on that the university would take on this part of the process. However, the time delay while the data was compiled led to a lack of ownership by the project team in distributing the data results. Cashman et al. (2008: 14–16) conclude that "given adequate time and with relevant modalities, engaging all partners in data analysis, interpretation of findings, or both, is doable and worth doing. By building on the trust and respect established in the earlier phases of research, PAR partners are uniquely positioned to take lead roles in data analysis and interpretation of findings." In retrospect, individuals from the project team should have been more involved in the data collection, data analysis, and interpretation of the results. This could have led to increased capacity building and commitment for the next stages of the result distribution and utilization of the results.

Sharing the results
Exploratory efforts began in 2016, the listening sessions took place in 2018, and in the fall of 2019 there was some small movement toward action related to the results. The project team experienced a challenge in continuing the momentum of the listening sessions when the report was published, especially in determining next steps. The findings in our case were complex and multi-faceted. Tackling them is a large effort to undertake. The question of investment and capacity available to do so comes up often.

As noted above, if the project team had met more regularly there likely would have been more momentum to disseminate the results. Without the AmeriCorps member, the infrastructure and time needed to share the final data was delayed. With the data being delayed, the creation of the report was delayed, thus, disseminating the results also took longer. Ensuring an ongoing project team, an accurate understanding of the time and people needed to complete each step of the project, and an agreed-upon dissemination process could have helped us stay on track with the original timeline and would have expedited the work before the pandemic took hold.

Community role outside of professional role
It is important to consider the dual nature of roles potentially played at any one time by those involved with a PAR project. A majority of the individuals involved with our project had grown up in the city we were assessing, with deeper and more complex ties to the community. Half of the project team had just recently stepped into community leadership roles. And, for a few project members, this work was made more personal coming from a disadvantaged upbringing. The complex layers of these relationships can be shared and discussed, leading to a deeper understanding of the commitment, passion, and desire for social change within the community. Further, doing so may help project team members to explore the complex nature of their potential privilege. It can also lead the group to ask early on: "Who is missing?"

Collaboratively working to meet goals prioritized in the listening sessions
Lastly, the sheer commitment from so many in the community to create a strong data set that was inclusive of many in the community was impressive. As described by Israel et al. (2005), what we have done is only the beginning of a truly effective PAR process. The time and commitment to see such a project through can be extensive, even with the work being shared by many. Some preliminary progress has started in relation to the results. However, much more can and needs to still be done (Israel et al., 2005).

CONCLUSION

Creating a cultural change in how decisions are made, and whose voices and opinions are included, is difficult, takes time, is layered, and needs leadership. Despite some of the challenges detailed as lessons learned, the overall process, collaboration, and feel during the process was in and of itself a change in the community. Of those who attended the sessions, 89 percent of attendees who filled out the brief exit survey strongly agreed or agreed that attending the session was a valuable use of their time. Further, 80 percent strongly agreed or agreed that just participating in the listening session increased their sense of pride in the community.

Although not perfect, progress was made. Creating one's own PAR project is worth the time and energy and can truly help provide data-driven priorities that can bring voice to the issues most needed for individuals and families within a community.

REFERENCES

Bhattacharyya, Jnanabrata. 2004. "Theorizing Community Development." *Journal of the Community Development Society* 34(2): 5–34.

Blumenthal, Daniel. 2011. "Is Community-Based Participatory Research Possible?" *American Journal of Preventative Medicine* 40(3): 386–389.

Bromley, Elizabeth, Lisa Mikesell, Felica Jones, and Dmitry Khodyakov. 2015. "From Subject to Participant: Ethics and the Evolving Role of Community in Health Research." *American Journal of Public Health* 105: 900–908. doi.org/10.2105/AJPH.2014.302403

Cantor, Nancy, Peter Englot, and Marilyn Higgins. 2013. "Making the Work of Anchor Institutions Stick: Building Coalitions and Collective Expertise." *Journal of Higher Education Outreach and Engagement* 17(3): 17–45.

Cashman, Suzanne B., Sarah Adeky, Alex J. Allen III, Jason Corburn, Barbara A. Israel, Jamie Montaño, Alvin Rafelito, Scott D. Rhodes, Samara Swanston, Nina Wallerstein, and Eugenia Eng. 2008. "The Power and the Promise: Working with Communities to Analyze Data, Interpret Findings, and Get to Outcomes." *American Journal of Public Health* 98(8): 1407–1417.

Chen, Peggy G., Nitza Diaz, Georgina Lucas, and Marjorie Rosenthal. 2010. "Dissemination of Results in Community-Based Participatory Research." *American Journal of Preventive Medicine* 39(4): 372–378.

Denise, Paul S. and Ian Harris. 1990. *Experiential Education for Community Development.* New York: Greenwood Press.

Driscoll, Amy. 2008. "Carnegie's Community Engagement Classification: Intentions and Insights." *Change: The Magazine of Higher Learning* 40(1): 38–41.

Fitzgerald, Hiram E., Karen Bruns, Steven T. Sonka, Andrew Furco, and Louis Swanson. 2012. "The Centrality of Engagement in Higher Education." *Journal of Higher Education Outreach and Engagement* 16(3): 7–27.

Israel, Barbara A., Amy J. Schultz, Edith A. Parker, and Adam B. Becker. 1998. "Review of Community-Based Research: Assessing Partnership Approaches to Improve Public Health." *Annual Review of Public Health* 19(1): 173–202.

Israel, Barbara A., Eugenia Eng, Amy J. Schulz, and Edith A. Parker. 2005. *Methods in Community-Based Participatory Research for Health.* San Francisco, CA: Jossey-Bass.

Israel, Glenn D. and Thomas W. Ilvento. 1995. "Everybody Wins: Involving Youth in Community Needs Assessment." *Journal of Extension* 33(2).

John Snow, Inc. 2012. "Engaging Your Community: A Toolkit for Partnership, Collaboration and Action."

Lantz, Paula M., Edna Viruell-Fuentes, Barbara A. Israel, Donald Softley, and Ricardo Guzman. 2001. "Can Communities and Academia Work Together on Public Health Research? Evaluation Results from a Community-Based Participatory Research Partnership in Detroit." *New York Academy of Medicine* 78(3): 495–507.

Mathie, Alison, and Gord Cunningham. 2003. "From Clients to Citizens: Asset-Based Community Development as a Strategy for Community-Driven Development." *Development in Practice* 13(5): 474–486.

Merriam-Webster. 2020. "Definition of Community." www.merriam-webster.com/dictionary/community.

Meyer, Jenice and Carly Burson. 2018. "2018 Community Listening Sessions Report, Embracing and Envisions Superior, Wisconsin." Superior, WI: University of Wisconsin- Superior.

Schalowitz, Madeleine U., Anothy Isacco, Nora Barquin, Elizabeth Clark-Kauffman, Patti Delger, Devon Nelson, Anthony Quinn, and Kimberly A. Wagenaar. 2009. "Community-Based Participatory

Research: A Review of the Literature with Strategies for Community Engagement." *Journal of Developmental and Behavioral Pediatrics* 30(4): 350–361.

United States Census Bureau. 2019. "QuickFacts Superior City, Wisconsin." www.census.gov/quickfacts/superiorcitywisconsin

UW-Madison. 2021. "The Wisconsin Idea." www.wisc.edu/wisconsin-idea/

Viswanathan, Meera, Alice Ammerman, Eugenia Eng, Gerald Garlehner, Kathleen Lohr, Derek Griffith, Scott Rhodes, Carmen Samuel-Hodge, Siobhan Maty, Linda Lux, Lucille Webb, Sonya F Sutton, Tammeka Swinson, Anne Jackman, and Lynn Whitener. 2004. "Community-Based Participatory Research: Assessing the Evidence: Summary." *Agency for Healthcare Research and Quality* 18(99): 1–8.

World Café Community Foundation. 2021. "The World Cafe: Shaping Our Futures through Conversations That Matter." www.theworldcafe.com/

5. Sociocultural intervention as a resource for social transformation in Cuban communities of the twenty-first century

Manuel Martínez Casanova and Adrienne Falcón

By successfully promoting participatory action research (PAR) over the past 20 years at the Universidad Central "Marta Abreu" de las Villas (UCLV) in Santa Clara, Cuba, the faculty and students in the sociocultural studies program have learned that transformative community development activity in a particular social context is not fully complete unless it has contributed to the development of the community in which it is involved. Our conclusion draws from lessons learned over time through the efforts at UCLV, which in 2008 was tasked with creating an interdisciplinary social sciences applied degree in sociocultural studies. While the degree was developed locally with a focus on the region of Santa Clara, this program then spread throughout the Cuban university system to address neighborhood aspirations and small community challenges across the island. In 2018, Manual Martínez Casanova, with other colleagues, redesigned the program and renamed it "Sociocultural Organizing for Development" (Licenciatura en Gestión Sociocultural para el Desarrollo).[1] This undergraduate program aims to "prepare a socially committed professional who is capable of being involved with and influencing the sociocultural aspects of social development projects, actions, and processes at the local and community levels using multiple tools drawn from diverse social sciences" (Ministerio de Educación Superior, 2016). By providing students with basic training in a range of social sciences, they are able to respond more effectively to local needs and possibilities and recognize when they need to bring in specialists to accomplish community goals.

To enact the mission, students and teachers were incorporated into numerous projects committed to accomplishing real transformation in local communities in Cuba. In addition to the practical or skill-based learning from these projects that students and faculty have gained, we also recognized the real potential of local communities, not only to participate in, but also to drive transformational processes and even to conceive and enact projects for their human and group development.

In simple terms, true community development is only possible if members of the community become the protagonists of the process. While the term protagonist does not translate well into English, it represents the vision for the core of UCLV's efforts and vision for the potential for community transformation. Protagonists are actors, community leaders, who understand that they are able to take action to enact their goals and how to do so. In the Weberian sense (Weber, 1978 [1922]), power is the capacity to act, and Protagonists act embracing their power. With community protagonism in the vanguard, the university can contribute social and informational resources and skills that are inevitably needed for community efforts, always doing so under the guidance of the full collective.

In order to achieve the goal of supporting community protagonists in their efforts, UCLV faculty and students have found it very effective to use PAR in the sociocultural collaborative projects. Over time, they recognize that their efforts have taught them much more than they taught participating community members or neighbors and other participants of the projects. Therefore faculty and students acknowledge and appreciate community and collaborators for their teaching. All the wisdom, experience, and academic resources would be worthless if the university members just took them to the communities to apply them. Without the faculty and students' commitment to making community members the leaders defining the issues, UCLV's efforts would remain a limited philanthropic endeavor that did not take into account the inhabitants of the community themselves, who really live there designing and carrying out the actions they seek, evaluating them and perfecting them.

THEORETICAL FRAMEWORK

In the Cuban context, community is frequently considered to be a place-based concept, the residents of a town or an urban neighborhood, even a small rural area. However, this understanding of a conglomeration of individuals is not enough to define a community. Instead, we consider communities to be groups of individuals who come together to share interests, develop collective actions, and share social practices. These actions lead individuals to feel a shared sense of identity, values, and collective memories.

Community development in the Cuban context emerges from social development, where success is measured by those who have the least. In general, development is a process, a pathway, that needs to be based in an integrated vision for the community and, through this vision, the steps to build community development will become clear.

At the same time, the development of a community has to be understood within the context of the community itself. For example, from the outside a hen house might look like a good community, with all the chickens fed and protected. Yet at the same time, a hen house is a community that is unknowingly headed towards its death as food for humans. When people of a particular group are led blindly by their environment, like the chickens, one can say that they are alienated. They are not really aware of their environment and are swayed by momentary interests or other brief pleasures such as drugs or fashion, with consumption led by market forces and the demagoguery of leaders who manipulate them. There is in these cases a failure of self-development.

In order to support community development, the university's sociocultural program promotes the use of PAR. In their approach to PAR, projects must include the community. This involvement includes not only the presence but also the participation of community members in identifying goals and objectives for projects: conducting initial diagnoses; designing transformative actions; and evaluating the processes (and not just the results) so that along the way successes and challenges are identified and celebrated or corrected. This is the only way in which community members can become the protagonists of their efforts. Furthermore with these efforts, participants develop their critical consciousness, not only of the problems they have, but also of how to participate in solutions, and to identify the limits to and possibilities for success which enable participants to seek partnerships and collaborations. This then becomes part of a process of community based dis-alienation, of liberation.

In their efforts to counteract alienation, the sociocultural studies program began from the approach that "social development in a particular social context is achieved as the result of a conscious projection that takes into account innumerable objective and subjective factors which are intrinsic to the system" (Martínez Casanova, 2018a, 29). Drawing upon social anthropology theory, the sociocultural studies program uses and teaches about the concepts of *etic* and *emic* as a way of focusing their approaches to get closer to a cultural reality other than that of the researcher.[2]

In brief, the *etic* approach, still frequently used in many anthropological studies, is characterized by interpretations about the situation from the perspective of the researchers. In the *etic* model, the researchers' actions are limited to "translating" the cultural system of others using as an interpretative framework the cultural system of the anthropologist. As a result of this translational approach, studies and projects may distort community realities, experiences, and aspirations. In its more problematic forms, *etic* approaches may lead to a manipulation of "facts" being studied (Martínez Casanova, 2003).

Unlike the *etic* approach, where the researcher remains external and translates for others, the anthropological *emic* approach aims to interpret the reality with which one interacts from within that sociocultural context. In other words, researchers in the *emic* tradition aim to discover and make coherent for the outside observer the dynamic sense that cultural processes have for the bearers of said culture. They locate their interpretations within the cultural framework rather than performing translational efforts. *Emic* practitioners seek to understand the internal logic of community members and situations rather than translating to interpret it using an outside logic.

For the most consequential transformative anthropology, the *emic* approach maintains the hermeneutical lens of anthropology which allows community-based PAR efforts to become not only an interpretive tool but also an active mechanism of social change. In PAR based in an *emic* approach, the presence of the community as an active collective subject seeking to transform themselves and their reality solves this academic challenge. Community members identify the questions, design the research process and tools, and interpret the results, all of which are then understood from within the *emic* perspective. Indeed, it is us, those from the academic world, who must change our focus and approach if we really want to understand what is happening and support actions that are in line with the interests of the community. This commitment and hermeneutical approach, along with the sociocultural studies program's efforts to become closer to the communities to contribute to their development, as they need and identify their goals, means that university labor should be reduced to what is strictly necessary. In these projects, the professional "researcher" who participates in community development efforts must become a facilitator, advisor, and active companion of the community members in their development process while the real protagonists (the ones making the action occur) remain community members.

But a "community" with an awareness of itself as such and as capable of acting is not achieved automatically. As a rule, individuals have co-existed outside decision-making processes that affect them in their daily lives, even those that are aimed at or which outsiders claim are promoting their development. Recognizing multiple forms of community was key for university collaborators in order to be able to fulfill their goal as an academic program and the role of being companions committed to the community's protagonism and its development projects. By recognizing and talking about different types or levels of capacity of the community in courses and projects, faculty and students developed the skills to partner with community members in their efforts to manage their development; to consider their ability to think of themselves as actors working together in order to understand the community's problems; and to support the development of community members' recognition that they need to and can act decisively to solve them.

Thus, we propose the existence of four types or levels of community awareness in their efforts to bring about their development projects:

- Level 1: Community as a place-based neighborhood
- Level 2: Community as a community (aware of a shared group identity)
- Level 3: Community for community (acting for itself)
- Level 4: Community engaged in emancipation[3]

Community as a neighborhood is a group of people who co-exist without having a vision of themselves as a community because they are not sufficiently integrated. As a result, they are not capable of taking on their problems or participating in a meaningful way in the solutions to these problems. The members are only neighbors who have the basic relationships of people who co-exist in a neighborhood, without understanding themselves as any kind of collective as such. As a result, members of this kind of community may potentially be alienated from each other and the larger systems and processes that shape their lives. They become easy to manipulate and because of this are unable to participate in the management/organizing of their own development as an intentional social collective.

The *community as a community* is one that recognizes itself as a shared collective; in other words, as a group of individuals who are in relationship to each other, and who realize that there are experiences or characteristics that identify them and that they share. Frequently, community members come to this awareness through differentiating themselves from others. As such, these kinds of communities emerge from a reactive state that then generates a certain identity, a sense of belonging, and even basic feelings of solidarity and cooperation among their membership.

The *community for itself* is a higher level of development to the extent that the social group that has been formed not only identifies as such but also takes on certain behaviors or projects for the benefit of the community itself. These efforts can then be concretized in actions of mutual help and collaboration in support of the larger whole. In so doing, the members respond to community members' requests and accomplish shared tasks and projects that go above and beyond the individual priorities of each of the participants. This form of community presupposes an awareness of common interests and seeks to attend to collectively defined needs and priorities and begin to act on them.

The *emancipatory community* offers a higher level of involvement and possibility to its members, because not only is the group identity visualized, or acted upon for collective benefit (as in the "community for itself" group), but also because its members share a critical awareness of the situation that affects everyone (Alonso et al., 2013). This critical awareness/commitment is achieved and expressed through the ways that members act. By aiming to resolve difficulties with a simultaneous goal of promoting growth and community self-development, the members and their institutions participate in active and effective ways that demonstrate and reinforce the protagonism of the community. Truly and effectively achieving community development becomes possible only when the community's development itself becomes an essential factor in accomplishing success. Once this has taken place, it becomes possible and even recommended to speak of "self-development," even if this is only an endogenous process.

This analysis of the community as emancipatory led us to the possibility of speaking of the communal as a key dimension of this form of community. The communal becomes the link in the social relations, enacted through interactions that are fundamentally symmetrical between members in the group. This permits and indeed facilitates sustained and effective participation, cooperation, critical consciousness, and collective projects (Author Collective, 2004). At this level of action and awareness, community members create the possibility of taking on the protagonist role in their own development. It is important to note that when this fourth level is achieved, community members possess significant social capacity to work on complex collective problems, including those which may be shared with other communities who may not immediately seem to have much in common with them.

Once researchers at the Universidad de Santa Clara began to conceive of their efforts through these categories of community, they also asked when and how communities move from one level of community to another. They found that when done properly, using PAR methodologies enables/supports the transition – which may not occur without difficulties or challenges – from one level of community consciousness and involvement to another. To accomplish the development of shared protagonism, the PAR approach must pay attention to sustaining a communal approach throughout, from defining the research question through to the analysis and final recommendations. In so doing, this form of research supports community members creating community development with projects that benefit their fellow neighbors and also the development of self-awareness of possibilities as possible goals.

In order to contribute to the development of the community, not only through particular project goals, but also in the transition to the fourth level of awareness and commitment, PAR projects must conceptually take into account both conceptual elements and sociostructural factors. While these projects can be launched through the initiative of community members, government authorities, college students, or faculty who are from or involved in those communities, the conceptual elements must include:

- Paying attention to the development/consolidation of a *critical awareness* among community members of what the real problems are that affect them.
- Promoting the *transfer of methods and procedures* based in the social sciences, and in particular sociocultural approaches, in order to support the development of *communal protagonism* as well as effective actions to seek to resolve problems that concern and affect them.

More concretely, elements of the social transformation of communities in processes of community development (including participation and self-determination) include the following components:

- Sociocultural organizers in and from the community.
- Mechanisms for exchange/interactions and consensus building.

In the Cuban context, sociocultural organizers (*gestores socioculturales*) contribute to establishing consensus or shared awareness and goals among community members. They share effective community engagement procedures and practices; educate about and help strengthen the values and concepts that promote social transformation; and support community development. These individuals may or may not be in/of the community but are involved in the community in a daily way. Furthermore, they can play this role independently of their awareness of it and of their level of professional development or education level (Martínez Casanova, 2015). Sociocultural organizers can be anyone who transcends from the individual to the collective in terms of their conceptions and actions. They are not necessarily leaders, although in their roles as organizers they engage others in concrete actions in which they also participate. Researchers – who do not intend to take over the protagonism of the community in its social development efforts – must take into account that their personal or academic opinions do not matter. In contrast, those of elders, who are activists, community leaders, and prestigious neighbors, will be listened to and respected, especially if their opinions demonstrate an awareness of the greater whole of the community. If the voices of the community members are honored (and *emic* knowledge validated) community members will see themselves as collectively responsible for the mindset, analysis, and actions of the community.

Mechanisms or processes for exchange and consensus building become essential for the success of any community-based effort that aims to be socially transformational. PAR cannot be separated from these community processes if it is really intended to bring about significant changes in the community and especially the self-development of the community. In smaller communities, holding systematic meetings where problems, concerns, and solutions are shared among participants creates a vehicle for exchange and community building. In these settings community members are able to reflect collectively on ways of acting and, above all, on how fundamental decisions are made. Through the experience at the Universidad de Santa Clara, faculty and students have learned that this form of organization cannot be carried out fully in larger social groups. As a result, we have explored alternatives and demonstrated that using a more organized and structured approach facilitates improved exchange and consensus building. To date, the most productive formula has been the formation of an organizing group.

Building an organizing team (*grupo gestor*) is a more complex but also highly effective resource that can support collective reflection and intra-community evaluation of actions that are carried out in the community and social development projects. A small group of 10–20 people who represent the community come together to improve their life conditions. As they share their experiences based on their roles in the processes that are organized, they play a key role in assessing the value of what is being attempted, correcting misguided points of view, and seeking and proposing new tasks that will be developed (Martínez Casanova, 2018b). Many, if not all, of the organizing group's members are sociocultural organizers whose ability to understand, express, and project ideas shared by the community is indispensable for the realization of community development projects and conceptions of self-development and collective consciousness. The organizing group functions as a constant presence seeking to identify the contradictions that slow down self-development, as well as creating space for the search for group cohesion and personal social transformation. Its presence enables community members to become the protagonists, and meaningfully engage in the work within the value system of the community. By participating in the organizing group, community members analyze existing contradictions and model a mechanism of dialogue, mediation, and consensus that allows them to engage in transformational processes that move them up levels of community awareness and commitment.

To understand these ideas in practice, the following sections will first explain the Cuban context and then provide three case studies to showcase elements of these theoretical concepts in action. The chapter will end with the conclusions that can be drawn from the three cases to inform future efforts and to share possible models for combining PAR and community development beyond Cuba.

CUBAN CONTEXT

The Cuban reality provides a particular context for examining these theoretical principles which emerge in and from the specific Cuban setting. In 1959 the nation was transformed under the leadership of Fidel Castro, who sought to transform all governmental institutions in order to make them of and for the people. After early years of idealism, in the 1990s with the collapse of the Soviet Union, which had been a major supporter of the economy in Cuba, the nation entered a time of significant hardship, known informally as *el Periodo Especial* – the special period. During this time, food and all resources were scarce. People developed creative approaches for meeting basic needs including creating urban gardens and even raising pigs in their bathtubs in cities. The people and the economy suffered during these challenging times. By the 2000s, tourism increased and life conditions improved. Now the nation has elected its third president and is again facing an economic downturn with increasingly limited resources because of new restrictions from former President Trump whose policies limited travel and resources that could be sent to Cuba, as well as the COVID-19 pandemic and the resultant dramatic drop in tourism. These economic ups and downs affect all the population, some sectors more than others. While there remains a commitment to improve the lives of all Cubans, there remain challenges to accomplishing this goal.

Currently there is a dense organizational infrastructure in Cuba and the government is very active at all levels. As such, boundaries between governmental efforts and community-based ones are not always clear. Citizens can become members of the Communist Party as well as campaign for government positions such as mayor or representative at local and national assemblies. People also join social organizations and place-based groups such as the Federación de Mujeres Cubanas (FMC), which is the branch of the government that is responsible for women's issues, or the Comités de Defensa de la Revolución (CDR), which are neighborhood groups organized to support the realization of revolutionary goals. The CDRs are the largest mass organization in the country and the majority in any community context. While they began as an organization dedicated to promoting the revolution and to helping meet social needs, the CDRs have become a way for communities to have a voice and to gather residents' opinions through their internal processes. In the projects described in this chapter, as well as collaborations with sociocultural studies projects in general, the community leaders who launch these projects and emerge as organic sociocultural organizers significantly overlap with the local CDR and FMC delegates and leaders.

To promote national development, plans are made in bureaucracies, such as the Ministry of Higher Education, which affect local communities. Local governments and organizations are tasked with implementing these national goals and also with contributing to defining them. Local governments which are elected by residents of these areas organize at least yearly public assemblies where they report on the progress in the communities. Local governments approve development projects that are either administrative or social where citizens can be involved even as the funding is provided from municipal government funds. In the case of community-based projects, the government is obligated to support them, especially with financial support and coordination with other institutions (state businesses and industries, professional organizations, schools and universities, and other centers that are connected with these projects) under the guidance of community-based leadership.

Higher education is also structured at multiple levels in Cuba with a centralized Ministry of Higher Education that oversees all undergraduate, masters, and doctoral programs as well as professional degrees. A few of the largest and oldest universities including UCLV are national in scope. These universities often develop new educational programs that support required civic engagement opportunities for all their students at both the local and national levels. Since 1959, in order to meet higher education needs, the government has provided a massive system of scholarships for college students in Cuba to attend university, at times bringing together students from across the island in particular universities and providing them with housing and food. For example, in the 1990s during the *periodo especial*, UCLV's student population numbered almost 9,000. As a result the university was the single largest food production site in Cuba, where lunch for 14,000 and dinner for 9,000 was cooked for students, faculty, and university workers. At the same time, in recent decades, the Ministry of Higher Education has built a significant number of smaller provincial universities such that there are now over 60 institutions of higher education in the country providing over 100,000 students annually with higher education opportunities.

In addition to the main university campuses, each institution of higher education also has Centros Universitarios Municipales (CUMs), which are small branches or extensions located in each municipality. Their role is to serve the needs of the local community through information sharing, college-going opportunities, and local hybrid education offerings. Since 2010 the sociocultural studies program originally developed by UCLV has spread to provincial schools and even many of the CUMs. Given that CUMs exist in part to offer local community members and organizations access to information, research, and analysis, depending upon what is needed to accomplish local projects, there is an easy fit with the sociocultural studies degree. To support place-based efforts, CUM professors and students, as well as students from those communities who are attending regional or national universities, can be brought in as part of their studies.

Every Cuban student has to do a community-engaged capstone to graduate, starting in their third year when students join place- or institution-based projects. These provide students with a way to contribute to their communities and the university to evaluate their knowledge and progress. University projects can be initiated either by government or other local institutions or by community leaders. Given the long history of the sociocultural studies degree and an associated *Centro de Estudios Comunitarios* (Center for Community Studies) at the University of Santa Clara, many requests come directly to them from municipal governments, students, or community members. They generally ask for a range of help, such as training, planning, or other technical support, to complete projects from the university on behalf of their local communities.

In addition to being engaged in their local communities through their studies, when university students in Cuba have graduated, they work in communities for several years at reduced wages as a way of repaying their education. This is a frequent pattern across Latin America where, for example, doctors provide years of service often in smaller rural communities. In the case of Cuba these experiences are designed to professionalize future workers and to pay the nation back for free higher education. Because of the combination of capstones and years of service, it can be challenging to identify the boundaries of community participation and leadership and higher education in the Cuban context.

While theoretical concepts are frequently valued in higher education in the universities, as well as in work sites including in schools, hospitals, and factories in Cuba, individuals need applied skills to become the best professionals that they can be. In general, the sociocultural studies programs offer not only learning opportunities for university professors and students but also training, advice, and accompaniment for all involved in the community. The following case studies provide examples of how this collaboration between community and university members can benefit neighborhood development.

CONCEPTS IN ACTION: FINDINGS FROM THREE CASE STUDIES

These three projects typify the trends, opportunities, and challenges that arise in the organizing of projects. They also offer sites to explore the potential of combining community development and PAR by showing when and how these efforts obtained the expected or desired results. They draw from Martínez Casanova's past 13 years of working on the ground. In general, compilations of efforts in different communities have led to the publication of six books on the experiences of communities engaging in their self-transformation collaborating with universities through the sociocultural studies departments. On average, projects usually last about a year and a half to two years to become autonomous and self-sustaining. At the same time, students and faculty from the university often continue to be involved to learn from communities. They are joined at times by residents of other communities who are facing their own struggles and can learn from their peers.

The three case studies span the geography and cultural diversity of the country, one in the far west (in an area known for its tobacco production) and the other two in the center in the province of Villa Clara where the university is located, one in a rural setting and the other urban. The first two were considered successful while the last reflects more conflict and struggle, which in turn allows for rich analysis.

In our descriptions, we will focus on the ideas and concepts that can inform other efforts. Our goal in so doing is to systematize the experiences, achievements, difficulties, and obstacles found in these collaborations. These are not ideal-type cases but specific lived ones. Therefore, to the extent that there can be no two communities that are socially identical, neither can the ways of acting or assessing the experiences be the same across communities. Instead, we will seek to critically reflect upon the examples with the goal of learning elements that lead to success both around projects and around efforts to transform community self-awareness.

Project 1: Economic and Community Development through the Arts: El Patio de Pelegrín, Puerta de Golpe, Pinar del Rio, Cuba

Pinar del Rio, the westernmost province of Cuba, is known for its natural resources, in particular as the land that produces "the best tobacco in the world." Nevertheless, for a long time this province was characterized by poverty and "the abandonment of its people." The region was nicknamed the "Cinderella of Cuba." Although this stereotype has been challenged by its residents and changed, the territory still faces environmental risks from hurricanes. As a result, the economic resources of the region – mainly based on the agricultural production of tobacco and tourism related to ecological beauty – systematically suffer the consequences of aggressive weather events which will only increase with climate change.

About 15 kilometers outside of the capital of the province sits a small town of a little under 8,000 residents named Puerta de Golpe. The town consists mainly of one long street that runs for about a kilometer and a half with only a few businesses. The main industries in the town are tobacco production and a tool-making factory. At the beginning of the twenty-first century, after a particularly violent hurricane, the residents of Puerta de Golpe faced the loss of their crops and the destruction of their few cultural and recreational facilities. Neighbors turned to one another, depending on each other. Only this solidarity made it possible to distribute what little was left so that everyone could cope with the disaster after the hurricane.

Mario Pelegrín Pozo, an artistic painter, whose home had a relatively large courtyard or *patio*, decided to do something to confront the challenges that his community was facing. Committed to interacting with others in a collaborative way – feeling solidarity with them, based in his experiences as an arts instructor and a culture promoter – he also demonstrated significant skills as a community sociocultural organizer. Pelegrín organized an informal cultural get-together in the courtyard of his home for his neighbors drawing upon local talents. Some folks sang, others recited poetry, and others performed short skits while community members sipped an infusion of guava leaf or sugar cane alcohol. The event was such a success that participants asked for more. What started as a one-time event became a regular cultural gathering, expanding as neighbors began making their contributions and integrating themselves into making numerous events happen. From this initial informal neighborhood gathering arose the Sociocultural Revitalization Project El Patio de Pelegrín. This name is now known by all across Cuba. Pelegrín played a key role in this community development effort by not only serving as the coordinator of the project itself, but also as the facilitator of the participation and protagonism of others and offering the courtyard of his home as a gathering space.

Over time, collaborative endeavors stretched far beyond the first dirt-filled courtyard. Community members took advantage of the availability of Pelegrín's patio and built concrete beds for flowers and medicinal plants. During the Special Period in Cuba, Cubans sought to grow their own food and developed new methods for urban gardening, *organoponicos*, where concrete beds are filled with soil and organic matter and then planted with a range of fruits and vegetables, using a crop rotation system and intensive care for high levels of production. The residents of Puerta de Golpe launched an *organoponico* in Pelegrín's courtyard, which over time expanded throughout his yard. Community members planted common and unusual fruit plants and trees. Over time, the gardening efforts spread. Plants were germinated, raised, and then seedlings were made available not just for use in the main garden but also offered to other community members for their use as they began to convert their courtyards and yards into fruit and vegetable production. The cultural-recreational projects were also maintained. Ideas were proposed and projects carried out, not just for the community as a whole, but also for subpopulations, such as the elderly, children, and young people with nights of dancing and music and other regular gatherings.

At a certain point, professors and students from the sociocultural studies major (that had expanded to the University of Pinar del Rio) became involved in the community endeavor which allowed both sides to benefit. On the one hand, collaborating with the community allowed the students to have professional training and development. On the other hand, the community could organize more projects including PAR. By incorporating PAR methodologies into their efforts, community members, with the support of the university students and faculty, strengthened the mechanisms for diagnosing and documenting their community development projects and their impacts. They focused on documenting and analyzing the needs, expectations, and satisfaction of those involved. This research served as the basis for subsequent collective discussions that contributed to the improvement of the projects and the community's sense of itself.

The community collaboration with the university involved everyone in Puerta de Golpe and included a wide range of development projects. For example, residents asked for lessons in traditional Cuban arts and crafts. In response, training workshops were developed for community members and visitors that drew upon the natural resources of the area such as sessions on wine, food conservation, drawing, dance, and music. Community leaders created a library composed mainly of donations from neighbors and community institutions. Building upon the *organoponico*, community members built a small canning factory to preserve the vegetables and fruits grown in their new garden beds. They also provided fresh food to a new organic restaurant on the grounds of the Patio de Pelegrín, contributing to the economic development of the area.

This community development project was created out of the good ideas and vision of a founder who valued the collective. At the same time, Pelegrín did not do this alone. Instead, as a natural sociocultural organizer, he built something that reflected and included the community by systematically organizing meetings with everyone from the community along the way. This collective process helped to contribute to consensus and legitimize the actions taken by participants to provide solutions to their problems. Not only has the project been successful locally, it has also garnered attention nationally and become a destination for tourists. Visitors enroll in workshops, eat in the restaurant, and learn about the community development experience while enjoying and partaking in cultural manifestations such as dance or music. Tourists are able to buy artistic products created there as souvenirs. Residents earn income from the visits, the restaurant, and the arts and crafts for sale, bringing much needed economic resources to the community.

Through their efforts to meet the initial needs of the residents of Puerta de Golpe after the hurricane, community members realized that they were able to also address other issues, such as emerging social fragmentation; neglect of the elderly who were numerous in the town; and a need for artistic expression. Over time, community members themselves became the bearers of new knowledge and skills. Sometimes they were joined in their efforts by university students or by activists and promoters of government organizations who sought to contribute to their community development efforts. However, Puerta de Golpe residents were the ones who acted in the community discussions and debates. At times, they became instructors, workshop facilitators, performers of individual and communal artistic creations, or guides who accompanied visitors wanting to learn about the community's endeavors. These experiences all contributed to strengthening the community, increasing creativity, participation, and shared identity among residents as individuals and as members of a larger social group. In other words, not only did community members become better neighbors to each other, they also became more and more interested in everyone's problems, sharing ideas and contributing to conceptualizing the future for the community. Through all this, cooperation and solidarity increased.

At first participants and leaders were amazed that such success could come from such a challenging start: an environmental disaster and a poorly integrated community. Does this mean that there are no problems and that everything has been transformed? No. But it is clear that thanks to the project El Patio de Pelegrín, the community is in a better position to face future crises and to be able to implement projects to improve their lives, because they have ceased to be a conglomerate of people who live close to each other and have shifted to a community that is conscious of itself as such. In other words, the community members of Puerta de Golpe have gone from level 1 of group consciousness (community as a result of living together) to level 4 (community aware of itself as a collective social subject, protagonists of their own destiny, aware of the forces impacting their town, and managers of their own development).

Project 2: Strengthening Identity and a Sense of Belonging, La Herradura, Manicaragua, Villa Clara, Cuba

The mountainous area of Escambray, located in the center of the island, is rich in history and known for complex social processes and conflicts. The mountains of the province of Santa Clara are known for their role in the Cuban Revolution in 1959. It was in the capital of the province of Santa Clara that the battle turned decisively for Fidel Castro. While the area is known for its ruggedness and isolation, in the mid-twentieth century inhabitants shifted from living independently to living in small communities. After the victory of Fidel Castro in 1959, the mountains proved effective not only for supporting Fidel's followers but also his opponents. Armed groups or "bands," formed by individuals hostile to the new government, persisted in their opposition with support from outside of Cuba. In the difficult mountainous terrain, from 1960 to 1965 the revolutionary forces sought to capture and eliminate these armed bands.

With the emergence of pockets of urbanization in a large rural geographic area, such as La Herradura, families who had been separated from each other came together and began to form new kinds of social connections. The new government was committed to a different kind of development and future for rural areas, so small communities in Santa Clara and elsewhere received significant improvements in housing and social services (new schools, medical posts, community centers, stores with a variety of goods, etc.). New agricultural investments sought to improve productive processes, especially with regards to coffee production, long a valued commodity from the Santa Clara region, as well as forestry and other forms of local food production. In addition to improving opportunities in communities, the new government sought to improve communication and access to larger towns with new highway construction and job creation, especially for women so that they could join the workforce and be compensated for their work and for the benefit of their families.

Yet these development efforts faced new obstacles when Cuba had to cope with the collapse of the "socialist camp" in the early 1990s and entered into the *periodo especial* of extreme economic hardship. Living conditions deteriorated substantially in communities across the country, including in La Herradura, a small town of about 700 located in the municipality of Manicaragua, south of Santa Clara. During this time, community members experienced and worried about higher levels of social disorder with increased rates of alcoholism, smoking, and domestic violence, along with other social problems. The lack of employment possibilities increased crime and deteriorated conditions for the daily lives of residents. As a result of these social and economic challenges, inhabitants lost their sense of belonging to a community. The decreased shared sense of community identity led to additional ruptures within the social fabric.

The municipal government working with the coffee industry sought to develop and strengthen the community. They formed a *grupo gestor*. Much like Pelegrín, Idaimi Díaz Nodal, another natural sociocultural promoter who was from the community, became involved and took on the role of a natural organizer. The first step in the community development project was to identify a shared goal for all and to develop a project that responded to the goal and encouraged community participation and commitment. To launch the project, local leaders decided to base their endeavors in a PAR project. They brought together a group of neighbors who began by identifying the design and initial areas of concern. The research projects were designed so that community members could take on the implementation, analysis, and reflection of the research project and findings. Through this, local leaders sought to develop an organizing group for the development efforts in the community, promoting not just informational findings but also protagonism among community members.

Through the PAR process, the *grupo gestor*'s members identified that residents were not fully aware of the natural wealth, both flora and fauna, of their surrounding environment, and that they also lacked a collective identity and sense of belonging. These deficiencies impeded the development of a community with a higher level of participation and critical consciousness about its opportunities and problems. In response, the community protagonists decided to launch a community development project with a cultural and natural resource focus to take advantage of the local environmental resources.

The PAR project also sought to identify community members who were interested in participating as amateurs in the cultural life of La Herradura. A number of people came forward who sought to learn more about and participate in diverse arts and cultural activities, including visual arts such as painting, drawing, sculpture, graphic design, and architecture as well as music and singing. In particular, respondents identified an interest in *repentismo* (which is the improvisational performance of a sung poem, of ten verses and eight syllables each, known as "tenth"). The sociocultural organizer Díaz Nodal took this information and aimed to boost the frequency of activities promoting the culture of the community. She organized cultural activities that celebrated social and cultural events in the community such as anniversaries of historical people and events, and recognition of the workers of the coffee company. These events included elements of fun and recreation to make them enjoyable for community members. Much like in the case of El Patio de Pelegrín, over time community members became involved in organizing events for themselves and joined the project management group. This led to the empowerment of community members in their daily social lives.

The effects of the community development project quickly became apparent. Community members created public art using local resources that showcased the beauty of the surrounding landscape. The first exhibits were displayed in the local school, in the community center, and even in the local coffee-processing factory. Singers and traditional folk dancers joined in performances surrounding the exhibits. The next step was the development of a yearly arts and culture festival which involved the artists and others interested in the culture of the region who lived in nearby villages. In the process, the municipal government collaborated with national cultural organizations to draw in national and international visitors who were intrigued by the massive mountainous zone in which the community was located.

These changes were not only expressed in outward artistic displays, but also within the community. Artistically, the creativity continues to flow. Residents joined in and appreciated the traditional popular cultural projects that were designed in the community. Socially, cooperation and solidarity increased among community members. Neighbors demonstrated a willingness to participate in organizing and contributing to collective projects or tasks. Finally, community members experienced an increase in the sense of belonging and self-identification with the community as well as an increased spiritual life and strengthened capacity for addressing the social problems that affected all of them. Today, the impact of these community development efforts has led to greater local employment opportunities for all, the improvement of the daily conditions of the inhabitants of the community, and the enrichment of cultural activities, all emerging from the original community-based creative activities, which still persist. With these projects, much like in the case of El Patio de Pelegrín, La Herradura has transitioned from a community struggling with social disorder to one which is aware of itself as a community and empowered to take action on behalf of its members.

This project not only demonstrates the success of the sociocultural organizing model, it also showcases the interconnection between the university and the local community. Díaz Nodal (2016), through becoming involved in this project, returned to the university to obtain a masters degree in sociocultural studies. As a result, not only did she bring her knowledge and skills to the community, she also advanced her own academic career, by writing her thesis on community development in the project. Through this work she also furthered the work of the community and contributed to moving their awareness of themselves to a level 4 of community protagonism.

Project 3: Learning from Failure, "Latin America," Santa Clara, Villa Clara, Cuba

The last case provides an example of community development in an urban setting in the city of Santa Clara, the capital of the province with the same name, where the University of Santa Clara is located. This community, called "Latin America," emerged in a shanty town, one of the many that existed in Cuban cities before 1959. After the triumph of the revolution, the new government created and built up a new neighborhood with a novel urban design that improved the living conditions of humble workers and people of diverse origins who were united in the original town. Much like in La Herradura, over time, and specifically during the Special Period after the collapse of the world socialist system that plunged the national economy into a deep crisis, neighborhood conditions of the hitherto flourishing neighborhood deteriorated, to the point where living conditions were affected and negative social behaviors (unemployment, disengagement of young people from school and work, dysfunctional families, social violence, an increase in criminal activities, etc.) began appearing among residents.

In response, a group of *cuentapropistas* (self-employed, small, private entrepreneurs, a new form of employment which emerged in response to the economic crisis) decided to launch a sociocultural community improvement project aimed at addressing the social problems that existed in the neighborhood. In so doing, they became informal sociocultural organizers. This group from the community realized that only by acting themselves would they be able to convince and engage with their neighbors and face the problems that had overwhelmed them. They began their modest efforts with a collective clean-up project of a site that was recognized as a shared problem facing all the residents: the elimination of a garbage dump that had formed spontaneously in the community. This dump affected everyone due to its bad smell and its negative public health risks as a breeding ground for rodents and other vectors for diseases. On the first day of their project, eight or nine neighbors showed up to help clean up the dump. Then in the days that followed more joined in. In a week they managed not only to eliminate the garbage, in part by using a freight truck that was contributed by one of the newly involved neighbors, but also to beautify the corner that had been a dangerous site and an eyesore.

With the successful clean-up as its starting point, community members began to consider other tasks for collective transformation. They realized that they needed a working group that would be representative of the community and that would follow up on the residents' identified needs, projects, and goals, coordinate them, and serve as a bridge between the different external factors that affected the life of the community (local government bodies, the school, the community health clinic, and more). The group began by trying to coordinate residents' interests – setting up meetings to debate priorities, organizing next projects, and nurturing reflection on the design and implementation of the projects or actions that residents took. In so doing, it ended up being a *grupo gestor* that the community development efforts needed and that created a way for other people to join in the efforts.

The next project that the group tackled was a small park (*plaza*) in the middle of the neighborhood, next to the local school, that was originally the social center of the community. With time and social deterioration the park had been lost. The majority of the trees had died off; the benches where neighbors rested weary feet and conversed had fallen into disrepair; and even the drainage system had clogged up. As a result, the park had become unusable, serving instead as a breeding ground for insects and wild plants or weeds, except for some neighbors who used it to graze animals. Unemployed individuals spent the day drinking alcohol and disturbing the neighborhood's tranquility. The challenge of rescuing the park was a much larger project than the garbage dump not only because it required much more work but also because it was more complex due to the potential for conflicts of interest. Some of the neighbors appreciated having grazing grounds for their horses or other animals or valued a place to imbibe, while others were apathetic due to the loss of the collective vision of a shared recreational space.

Nevertheless, the organizing group took the plaza project on, and soon miracles began to occur. Within a few days, more and more neighbors joined in and the results exceeded expectations. Community members chopped down the undergrowth, reseeded lost trees, planted flowers, and repaired the rainwater drainage system. It was beginning to be a community park again, even though some neighbors continued to use it to drink alcohol and others as a grazing ground. The organizing group members decided to visit each of the neighbors who could be blocking efforts to improve the plaza. With these conversations, which took time, one by one community members began to understand the importance of participating positively in the neighborhood's new efforts. To the extent that the battle to recover the park was won, the possibility of it as a space for socializing was also won. Elders began to sit on recovered benches every afternoon while taking fresh air. Children used it to play safely. One community member used his wages to set up an audio system to liven up the place by playing music that would meet with everyone's approval. With supplies donated by the *cuentapropistas*, residents painted the entire wall that separated the park from the school and with that added to the beauty of the project.

As the community development projects became more complex, the group that spontaneously took on new initiatives and group leadership on behalf of the community decided to ask for help from other leaders, including the head of the school, the police force, and other existing neighborhood organizations such as the CDR and FMC. They also reached out to UCLV and especially the Centro de Estudios Comunitarios led by Manuel Martínez Casanova, one of the authors of this chapter. Collaborating together, local leaders, university faculty, and students adopted a PAR methodology in their efforts. Community members were accompanied by UCLV collaborators in carrying out tasks and in the process learned new knowledge and procedures. In fact, there was an even further merger of university and community efforts when a recent graduate from UCLV in sociocultural studies who was from the community, Dudiexi Vasconcelos Ramírez, became involved. She could draw upon her recent studies to contribute to her neighbors' efforts. Throughout, Martínez Casanova and others from the university honored the protagonism of the residents. The initial goal of Vasconcelos Ramírez's project (which became her master's thesis) was to analyze and share this neighborhood experience as a paradigm or model for local authorities seeking to promote the self-development of local communities in the municipality of Santa Clara. As such, much like other cases in this degree tract, actual experiences inform students and faculty and in turn are brought out to the community in a dialectical process.

At first, everything was going well. The *grupo gestor* organized cultural activities which were well received as community members were already involved in neighborhood projects. The community appreciated the many changes they had been able to bring about, including the resources of the renovated park and other areas of the neighborhood. Craft workshops, physical exercises for senior citizens in the community, and commemorations of historical dates of common interest and collective birthday celebrations were all organized.

But then there was a moment of conflict that would bring the death of what had been a model sociocultural community development project. Disagreements began to occur with outside organizations who sought to become involved, including local government authorities, an evangelical church, and other individuals who sought to promote their individual agendas. These conflicts hindered the neighborhood's activities. The emergence of new leaders led to additional conflicts in the coordination between different community members and organizations. As a result, activities were poorly organized and run. Organizations from outside the community began to spread disinformation about local efforts. All of this led to a breakdown of the community-based and led approach which, until then, had been the cornerstone of the project.

The consequences of community conflict were dire. Some participants dropped out, the initiatives fell apart, and the organizing group stopped acting cohesively. The community and in particular the organizing group were unable to enact their projects and goals, or to facilitate the ongoing development of the community. In the end the project as it was initially envisioned ceased to be. Vasconcelos Ramírez (2016), along with her advisors, decided that the academic project could no longer focus on demonstrating the success of this community-led initiative. Instead of analyzing the accomplishments, they decided to assess the negative factors that had led to the failure of said project. The answer was straightforward – the inability of all involved to maintain cooperation between the community and the non-community bodies that facilitated the community development projects led to its demise. In this failure, the community ownership and drive for the project was lost.

Community members, who had felt that the project was theirs, ceased to believe in their capacity to act because of the acts of others and doubted their sense of community as such, in essence moving from a level 4 of community-engaged commitment to a lower level. Since then, projects have somewhat continued. Community members participate to a certain extent. Some problems are faced and solved collectively. There is still evidence of a greater capacity among neighbors to support each other and the practices of joining efforts to face common tasks together, but nothing has been the same. The protagonism of the community, its awareness of itself as a community acting to improve its lot with that self-awareness has been lost and the neighborhood has dropped in its level of commitment to participation and to bettering the lives of the residents through residents' protagonism. With more perspective, participants have realized that they did change the neighborhood and for the better. They are aware that they struggled with conflicts and challenges which led to a breakdown in unity and purpose, however, they appreciate that there has continued to be more active citizen participation. This demonstrates that even as projects move through cycles of possibility and challenge, the skills and sense of capacity that participants gain can persist and contribute to the development of future projects.

CONCLUSION

Summarizing the findings from these cases, we seek to highlight lessons learned that support the positive development of sociocultural development projects in specific communities, including:

- The most effective sociocultural projects aimed at community development are those that are able to take into account the needs, challenges, and possibilities of the communities themselves. These challenges and possibilities must be identified, not by external specialists but rather by using PAR methodologies which honor the *emic* approach. Allocating enough resources to enable the project to develop is also crucial even if these resources may entail significant investments because they will contribute to the transformation of the leadership potential of the community itself. This will be accomplished not only due to community members' actions, but also by incorporating their protagonism in the design and development of these efforts.
- Community-based protagonism enables the development of effective critical awareness and a sense of belonging among residents, including a community-based identity, solidarity, and intra-community cooperation. Developing this consciousness in turn promotes the consolidation of the community and its capacity for additional action.
- In brief, the key elements that lead to successful community development that we have identified through these cases and in our efforts in general include:
  - implementing actual social projects;
  - which are based on findings from PAR project experiences;
  - that involve the mobilization of the community;
  - through the creation of mechanisms of exchange and consensus; and
  - under the guidance of the sociocultural organizers (individual and collective) of the community, especially if there is an effective community-based organizing group.

In contrast to practices which promote community development and empowerment, others hinder or even lead to the failure of effective actions in sociocultural development projects. The presence of charismatic leaders or well-prepared activists is not enough. Nor is simply confronting the problems without efforts to develop the community itself for itself. Without prioritizing community building, community projects may benefit individual residents, but participants will remain the recipients of a service model whereby community members receive the beneficial actions without joining in the building of a new form of community. Over time, this leads community members to greater indifference and apathy. The loss of commitment to community protagonism, or leadership and ownership of their efforts in projects which are initially requested by and designed by them, can then end without as much success. While "development" projects may be initiated by outside actors, if they do not commit to a corresponding effort to develop the community awareness and ownership of their own future, to support the transition of community self-awareness to level 4 of consciousness, *community engaged in emancipation*, participants risk becoming indifferent and apathetic to certain possibilities and action, even those that could be important and beneficial to the community. We offer these insights to other practitioners of community development and participatory research in the hopes of spreading awareness about the Cuban model and inspiring other communities to engage in nurturing their own protagonism.

NOTES

1. One of the challenges and opportunities in co-authoring this work has been not only the translation of language but also of ideas across cultures. As an example, *gestión*, which is in the name of the degree, translates as management. However, through exchanges we have realized that the degree actually teaches the process of community organizing and hence from here on out we describe the community-based activities as organizing (with the implications of community ownership and activity) rather than management (with the implication of hierarchy). This example also demonstrates the value of collaborating across countries, where each of us can be deeply enriched by the other as we seek to truly understand different ways of being and thinking. The work from which this chapter draws was done in Cuba by Manuel Martínez Casanova and his colleagues and students. Adrienne remains deeply appreciative of Manolito's willingness to share his knowledge and experience while he appreciates her willingness to raise questions and share her perspective from similar kinds of efforts in the United States.
2. The conception of *etic* and *emic* was originally created by Kenneth Pike (1979) and then further developed by Gustavo Bueno (1990).
3. This model for community consciousness echoes and extends Marxist notions of class consciousness whereby members of different social classes may become conscious of and able to act on behalf of their class.

REFERENCES

Alonso, Joaquin., R. Pino, and Celia Rivera Vázquez. 2013. *Lo comunitario en la transformación emancipatoria de la sociedad*. Santa Clara: Editorial Feijoo.

Author Collective at the Universidad Central "Marta Abreu" de Las Villas. 2004. *Community Self-Development: Criticism of Recurrent Social Mediations for Human Emancipation*. Santa Clara: Editorial Feijoo.

Bueno, Gustavo. 1990. *Nostros y Ellos*. Oviedo: Pentalfa Editions.

Díaz Nodal, Idaimi. 2016. Sociocultural intervention to strengthen the community from the promotion of visual arts in the settlement La Herradura. Thesis, Universidad Central "Marta Abreu" de Las Villas.

Martínez Casanova, Manuel. 2003. La mítica y la mística del horror: "justificación" antropológica de la guerra. *ISLANDS* 137: 34–44.

Martínez Casanova, Manuel. 2015. The sociocultural manager as a factor of social transformation. In Manuel Martínez Casanova (Ed.). *Introduction to Sociocultural Management for Development*. Havana: Editorial Universitaria Felix Varela.

Martínez Casanova, Manuel. 2018a. Participation in sociocultural management processes for development. In Manuel Martínez Casanova (Ed.). *Sociocultural Management*. Havana: Editorial Universitaria Felix Varela.

Martínez Casanova, Manuel. 2018b. The methodology of community self-development. I: Martínez Casanova, Manuel (Ed.) Methodological aspects of sociocultural management. Havana: Editorial Universitaria Felix Varela: 150-154.

Ministerio de Educación Superior. 2016. Plan de Estudio "E" Carrera. Programa Universitario de Formación Profesional de Licenciatura en Gestión Sociocultural para el Desarrollo.

Pike, Kenneth. 1979. On the extension of the etic-emic anthropological methodology to referential units in context. *Lembaran Pengkajian Budaya* 3: 1–36.

Vasconcelos Ramírez, Dudiexi. 2016. The significance of the appropriate approach to the community in a sociocultural project: The failure of the sociocultural project "Latin America." Thesis, Universidad Central "Marta Abreu" de Las Villas, Santa Clara.

Weber, Max. 1978 [1922]. *Economy and Society*. Berkeley CA: University of California Press.

PART II

ORGANIZING COMMUNITIES

6. Community organizing for environmental change: integrating research in support of organized actions

Dadit G. Hidayat and Molly Schwebach

Participatory action research (PAR) practice is generally accepted as a process that involves communities. Some of the early academic advocates such as Lewin (1946) and Whyte (1991) incorporated a community participatory process in research. However, various forms of PAR still struggle to deconstruct power structures that benefit researchers more than communities. For example, researchers can determine parameters of the participatory process that leave community members as passive participants (Brown and Tandon 1983; Hidayat and Stoecker 2021). Another challenge is when researchers develop the actionable parameters when they are usually not going to participate in the action stage (Selener 1997; Noffke and Somekh 2009; UKEssays 2018).

This chapter will focus on an alternative practice of PAR. Instead of considering action as an ad hoc element that serves as an extension of the participatory process or the research, the research and the action are viewed as a package. Just as community members are an integral part of the team during the research phase, the researcher is an integral part of the team during the action phase. The team identifies immediate community issues and designs an initial plan for organized actions to create change. The research helps refine the plan by leveraging data from various sources. However, this commitment by the researcher to not only inform but also to engage in community action requires processes that can be contradictory due to the general expectation of maintaining independence and objectivity (Kock 2004). Negotiating these processes is the essence of community development (CD) about which PAR practitioners have talked but have struggled to walk the talk.

Part of the struggle is understanding the intersectionality of community actions in problem solving. When communities organize and work together towards change, they mobilize existing knowledge and generate new knowledge. As activities around knowledge mobilization and generation take place, CD occurs. Many of the principles of good CD practice are congruent with the ideals of PAR – including diverse voices, being open to diverse solutions, and empowering community members to know and act. Similarly, the key processes of community organizing (CO) are consistent with CD – listening to the people, clarifying common goals, framing strategies for action, helping build leaders, and mobilizing the community. In other words, CD happens all the time and naturally generates complex knowledge through a series of organized activities even without any formal research processes. Hence, CD helps mobilize PAR and CO, and at the same time both PAR and CO enrich the practice of CD.

The principles of good practice from the Community Development Society (2021) offer a foundation that can also support PAR:

- Promote active and representative participation toward enabling all community members to meaningfully influence the decisions that affect their lives.

- Engage community members in learning about and understanding community issues, and the economic, social, environmental, political, psychological, and other impacts associated with alternative courses of action.
- Incorporate the diverse interests and cultures of the community in the CD process; and disengage from support of any effort that is likely to adversely affect the disadvantaged members of a community.
- Work actively to enhance the leadership capacity of community members, leaders, and groups within the community.
- Be open to using the full range of action strategies to work toward the long-term sustainability and well-being of the community.

This chapter will discuss how to build the practice of PAR and CO on these CD principles, with the researcher closely involved in community action. The two case studies explore the key factors that diverse stakeholders need to negotiate and the conditions required for this integrated method to be successful. We will begin with some background on CO in connection with PAR and an overview of the case studies. This is followed by the historical trajectories of each case and then a comparison and analysis of the case studies and the role of PAR in each. Finally, we conclude with some strategies for getting started on a project that builds on CO principles with a research element integrated into it.

BEGIN AT THE END: THE "ACTION" OF PARTICIPATORY ACTION RESEARCH

To think about research from its conclusion contradicts the long-standing notion of its linear process. But to begin research at the end is a practical way to ensure that research is going to produce information that is relevant and useful to the actionable goal. And it is important to understand how the research process is built around CO principles.

Discussion about CO cannot be separated from Saul Alinksy (1971). Alinsky's model of organizing is about creating change in the public sphere that is rooted in local communities. The model helps community organizers to focus on the most important issues and put the issues in a larger context. Not only does CO help make sense of community issues but it also connects people to a network trying to create similar change. Through CO, community members determine the research end goals and inform the process of reaching those end goals. Using this model, PAR provides structure for the action at the same time it guides the research to inform those series of actions.

Our PAR model (Figure 6.1) requires clarity on the destination first. Understanding the destination will help us develop an operable plan, envision the bigger picture of the plan, and implement the plan. Moving backward from the destination provides a solid structure for planning and implementation.

Using a CO approach grounds PAR activities in a hyper-local focus. Neighbors discuss issues in homes, shops, community centers, or other common places. Those conversations lead to commitments to act, in turn supporting larger gatherings for a louder demand for change. Organizing amongst family and neighbors is the foundation upon which all other organizing builds (Stall and Stoecker 1998). "Community organizing seeks to teach people, through

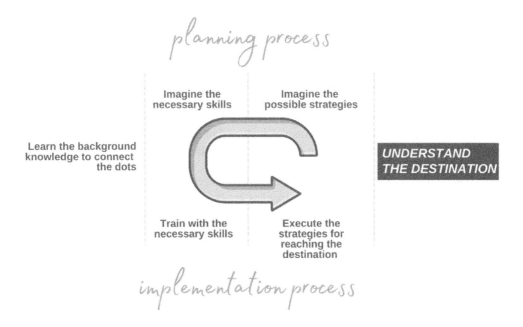

Figure 6.1   *The backward interaction of participatory action research and community organizing*

experience, that they can be effective in a larger and larger sphere – their own block, their own neighborhood, their city, their state, and so on" (Beckwith and Lopez 1997).

However, the adoption of CO principles into PAR may not seem natural to the researcher. Only PAR practitioners with experience being open and interactive (as in working collaboratively with non-credentialed researchers) are well prepared to negotiate the shared values in creating change. This process involves listening to people, clarifying common goals, framing strategies for actions, helping build leadership, and mobilizing the community. We have to ground any research in the people's understanding, with all of these principles informing each other to create social change.

Furthermore, grounding PAR in CO principles will guide researchers to carefully link the research steps backward from potential policy recommendations, data needs, and data collection methods to the eventual research questions. The inclusion of CO ensures that each research step is informed by the need to support practical actions. This is how our PAR differs from traditional research that is largely driven by a knowledge gap in the literature, not by the needs for societal change.

DEVELOP COMMUNITY: THE "RESEARCH" OF PARTICIPATORY ACTION RESEARCH

People do research every day through internet searches or casual conversations. But it is generally understood that research is what credentialed researchers do. Not only does this put day-to-day inquiries outside of the research realm, but it creates an ongoing dichotomy that inhibits meaningful collaboration between credentialed and non-credentialed researchers. Navigating the power balance between these two research practices in a partnership (one practice conducted by credentialed researchers and another by non-credentialed researchers) requires a contextualized understanding of why research is valuable in the first place.

Building on the CD practices in PAR empowers communities to influence decision making for their well-being. As members of a research team, community members are encouraged to teach each other and learn from each other to improve (Freire 1973). They will make better decisions to address community problems and analyze findings in ways that are relevant to their settings. It also helps build leadership capacity among community members as they become more familiar with navigating research environments and advocating for their communities. Often these layers of capacity building escape from research's reality due to the overwhelming focus on generating answers. The CD principles are necessary to ensure that research does much more than address a question, and it is also making sure that people can use the process with different community members to address future questions. This form of research often cites Paulo Freire's popular education process. It focuses on critical consciousness raising that liberates marginalized communities (Freire 1968). But people reference popular education in relation to social activism, so practitioners do not often consider it in the context of research.

A feature of popular education critical to PAR-CO is its ability to develop a foundation for social change (Hidayat and Stoecker 2021). The fundamental critique brought by popular education is about how knowledge is controlled, which largely contributes to the culture of silence among learners. Incorporating popular education in PAR-CO – i.e. by recognizing that community members have something to teach and that trained researchers still have something to learn – helps address the power inequalities between trained researchers and community members. Some critical influences of popular education include the Civil Rights Movement in the United States in the 1960s (Adams 1975; Horton et al. 1997), the Black Consciousness Movement in South Africa in the 1970s (Hirschmann 1990), and the Adult Learning Project in Scotland in 1977 (Kirkwood and Kirkwood 2011).

Recall the hyper-local focus of PAR-CO interaction. The research itself requires a process that will allow all individuals involved to grow. The project-based research model, which first "diagnoses" a community issue, then develops a "prescription" for addressing that issue, implements the prescription, and evaluates its effects (Stoecker 2013), has been tested to provide a research mechanism that is focused toward social change (Hidayat et al. 2014). The application of a project-based research model leverages the identified organizing needs. By putting these organizing needs in consequential steps of issue identification, strategy formulation, implementation, and then evaluation, we translate these needs into practical processes of social change (Stoecker 2013) through two case studies.

THE CASE STUDIES

Our two case studies include both social and environmental goals, pursued simultaneously. Local community members grappled with national, even global, issues like water pollution, the industrial food system, and mass incarceration. The community organizers brought their desire to work towards a better world while acting within their own spheres of influence – at the individual, neighborhood, and city levels. Navigating the tension between changing the world and taking personal or local actions added complexity to determining the end goals in each case study. PAR supported the changes over time as the scope of the communities' end goals narrowed and deepened. PAR also helped articulate the incremental steps required for progress towards those end goals.

These case studies were a part of a series of service-learning courses offered through the Nelson Institute for Environmental Studies at the University of Wisconsin-Madison. The authors played different roles in the various stages of the work. Overall, Dadit Hidayat was the lead researcher, community engagement practitioner, and instructor for the service-learning courses (working with a faculty supervisor in the first case, and a faculty supervisor and graduate teaching assistant in the second case). Molly Schwebach supported this work by developing administrative and funding resources and advocating for community-engaged work within the Nelson Institute administration.

Sustainable Monona: Refining Strategies for Environmental Action

The Natural Step Monona (TNS Monona) represented the collective efforts of Mononans (Monona residents) to promote a sustainable future (also see James and Lahti 2004). Monona, Wisconsin, is a predominantly white, middle-class, politically liberal city of approximately 7,500 residents (about 3,100 households based on the 2010 census). As a grassroots organization, TNS Monona organized a variety of educational events such as the Green Tuesday Lecture and Film Series and the eight-week study circles on sustainability, among others, during a little over a decade of operation (2007–2018). It also worked with the public library to establish a sustainability section. With a local farmers' market organizer, they secured a spot for rain barrel sales. Eventually they achieved broader, more coordinated action, and administered a year-long water conservation challenge among Monona households. At the government level, they also pushed the city to establish a sustainability committee to ensure strategic mobilization of the city's resources for Monona's local environment. The sustainability committee became a permanent committee of the city government after maintaining its ad hoc status for several years.

Unique to TNS Monona was the strong presence of self-interest among Mononans; they were aware of environmental issues and wanted to live more sustainably. TNS Monona had carefully engaged the self-interest of Mononans through various community-based events. They constantly looked for connections with other local organizations to broaden the engagement around environmental sustainability. Lastly, they strove for diversity in the conversations around sustainability actions in a way that was possible in a predominantly white, middle-class community. They believed in offering opportunities for residents to become involved in shared decision making on these local issues.

Listening to the people

The first step in CO is to listen to the people experiencing the problem. In this case, to listen is to understand TNS Monona in the context of Monona as a city. After 18 months of volunteering with TNS Monona, Dadit found a funding opportunity to support a more formal community–university partnership with the organization. Randy served as an initial instructor of record and provided advice on the course development. Molly, at the Nelson Institute for Environmental Studies at the University of Wisconsin-Madison, coordinated funding to graduate students to develop community partnerships and engage upper-level undergraduates in that work through a capstone course. Conscious that partnerships with universities tend to exploit the partnering communities (Stoecker and Tryon 2009), the project idea was carefully crafted so that the potential benefit would be the starting point. Dadit asked, "How would a semester-long project with a group of students benefit your organization and Monona community?" The question led TNS Monona to see the partnership as an opportunity for a pause from the dynamic and intense process of the organizing work. The partnership gave them time to reflect on their wins and losses and work toward more progress. They also realized they had achieved the "low-hanging fruit" and wanted to know how to engage harder-to-reach populations.

Clarifying common goals

TNS Monona had been quite successful in managing their members' interests and turning them into effective collection actions. But finding common goals for the project partnership was not straightforward. Five members of the TNS Monona project committee came up with various ideas for action in highly dynamic conversations. The researchers (Dadit and Randy) sometimes had to interject as a reminder not to jump ahead to action, but instead take the appropriate amount of time to explore the issues fully before eliminating some possibilities. Together, we mapped out all of the identified issues, connected, and then prioritized them. Through this process, we saw that a partnership between TNS Monona and the Nelson Institute was only one stage of many. The action delivered by the partnership was only a part of the larger picture of their sustainability activism.

After several planning meetings, we agreed on the key question: how could TNS Monona expand local sustainability actions? The objectives were to conduct an evaluation of the impact of the organization's first five years and to identify the sustainability issues Mononans cared about the most. TNS Monona wanted to take lessons from the past and refine their organizing strategies by focusing on the most engaging issues in Monona (Hidayat et al. 2014). We delivered on these two goals in a semester-long capstone course that conducted a community survey.

Framing strategies for action

The decision to focus on an evaluation and community interest survey provided a foundation for the PAR activities. Both were conducted through TNS Monona. With TNS Monona we carefully designed a city-wide survey on Mononans' engagement on local sustainability. We also developed a one-minute script for an engaging door conversation that everyone mastered through a role-play exercise. With 12 students, 12 Monona volunteers, one graduate teaching assistant, one professor, and one campus community engagement staff member, we canvassed the city, knocked doors, and distributed the survey in four afternoons. All of these preparations and activities were common in CO, and the inclusion in PAR was straightforward given project evaluation goals. Of the nearly 3,100 households, almost 21 percent responded to the study (Hidayat and Stoecker 2018). We then presented the survey findings in a community forum. In the forum, we reintroduced TNS Monona since some Mononans were unfamiliar with the organization. We shared findings around Mononans' participation in various civic events, local government, and then sustainability practices. This helped the team build an understanding on Mononans' areas of interest as well as their motivating factors in being involved in their communities. Most importantly, we designed several tables for facilitated conversations around the findings for any follow-up actions.

The study and community forum conversations showed that clean lakes and clean drinking water were the top two issues that Mononans wanted to address (Hidayat and Stoecker 2018). These issues were the foundation for a second capstone class; they also partially motivated the City of Monona to declare 2012 as the Year of Water to encourage broader city-wide engagement on water issues. We considered several engagement strategies that were new to TNS Monona and agreed on a *bloc recruitment* approach with the focus on water sustainability. The approach is common in CO when community organizers have limited outreach for expanding their work. Instead of recruiting individuals, community organizers recruit community-based organizations (CBOs) with aligned visions that would then coordinate individuals within their groups (Diani 2013). It served TNS Monona well. The new connection with local CBOs led to the use of shared resources for educating Mononans about water sustainability. With students, we identified over 30 CBOs and contacted them by email. Students made 14 presentations to CBOs who responded and secured a pledge to participate in a water-related project. After the conclusion of the capstone, TNS Monona followed up with those 14 pledges and provided resources to help plan their water conservation project. Seven CBOs eventually designed a water conservation project with their members and executed it.

The third capstone course was dedicated to conducting an evaluation study of the effectiveness of the engagement strategies. Initially, TNS Monona was unsure if the evaluation study would be helpful. As a non-profit organization, TNS Monona was certainly not alone in questioning the efficacy of evaluation for non-profit programming (MacNamara 1999; Theuvsen 2004; Campbell and Lambright 2017). They thought that we completed the project so we could move on to another. The cyclical project-based PAR process (Stoecker 2013) offers a reminder that the evaluation will inform the next actions, to get closer to the social change goals. Similarly, progression in CO takes place after community organizers evaluate their small wins. The evaluation revealed that TNS Monona volunteers burned out through the intensity of the first two capstone projects, and did not feel they had the energy to move to another project (Hidayat and Stoecker 2021). Table 6.1 illustrates how we set out the three capstone courses.

Table 6.1   Stages in TNS Monona project

Stage 1: Evaluation, diagnosis, prescription (spring 2011)	Stage 2: Implementation (fall 2011)	Stage 3: Evaluation (spring 2013)
Conducting a city-wide survey, organizing community forum	Following-up survey findings with organized actions with group-based engagement	Evaluating success of the group-based engagement

Helping build leaders

All of the capstone courses were meaningful and intense at the same time. They were integrated in a significant way to the work of TNS Monona. TNS Monona was involved in all of the key decisions including research decisions. TNS Monona experienced a reciprocal and interactive process connecting their CO initiatives to researchers. This process alone made everyone better including community leaders through the organizing activities and researchers working mostly in the community.

The first two capstone courses were successful in building a PAR project on TNS Monona's existing organizing work. Our partners indicated that, because of the PAR work, local environmentalism in Monona went in a direction that TNS Monona alone would never have done (Hidayat and Stoecker 2021). The impacts were clear, but the organizational consequences were also unavoidable. The amount of work directed toward the partnership, combined with the workload of administering the organization, overwhelmed this all-volunteer grassroots organization. TNS Monona itself, as an organization, had to close its doors in 2018 after years of struggling to regenerate its local leadership and power. Some of the work of the organization continues through the City of Monona Sustainability Committee.

Mobilizing the community
The application of PAR in this project reinforced the mobilization of Mononans for greater impacts. The city-wide survey identified the sustainability issues most important to Mononans. The community forum organized in the first capstone gave legitimacy for TNS Monona to launch broader organized collective actions. Through various community-based events, TNS Monona was successful in encouraging the public to think and live in a more sustainable way. Mononans increased the sustainable actions they took in their homes.

Reentry Services and Urban Agriculture: Establishing an Alternative Food Justice Narrative

The United States Department of Agriculture has designated South Madison as a food desert for decades. Like many other food desert communities, it is predominantly low-income and ethnically and culturally diverse. Additionally, statistics reveal that African Americans in Dane County (where the cities of Madison and Monona are located) experience one of the highest arrests and incarceration rates in the country (WCCF 2013). This amplified the challenge of employment among formerly incarcerated people in Dane County, where the general unemployment rate among African Americans has at times reached 25 percent (WCCF 2013).

In this context the South Madison Farmers' Market (SMFM) has served the south side of Madison since 2001 as a key alternative source for safe, affordable, and healthy food. SMFM, led by Robert Pierce, an African American resident who had been growing organic vegetables since 1984, had been struggling to attract enough vendors, a situation which became more obvious as the years progressed. SMFM engaged in collaborative program development called Farming After Incarceration Release (FAIR). Working with Dadit and two other local organizations focused on reentry services, FAIR wove together elements and ideas that showed the important benefits and co-benefits associated with the work of food justice.

Listening to the people
A key principle of this project was that the idea came from an individual who has deep knowledge of both reentry services and urban agriculture. As an urban farmer in a neighborhood with comparably high rates of incarcerated men, Robert saw an opportunity. He believed urban farming could offer a path forward for formerly incarcerated people in South Madison but he needed community support and partners to help operationalize the idea. Robert and Dadit looked for connections in the community who had a close understanding of the project idea, people with similar lived experience. We identified trusted partners to build the initial project alliance.

Dadit and Robert loosely started the partnership around food justice in South Madison. The Nelson Institute approved our proposal for capstone funding, leading to two courses in one full academic year. In the first capstone, Robert suggested holding conversations with farmers' market vendors in the neighboring farmers' markets on their thoughts about SMFM and their willingness to participate in SMFM. We had focus group interviews with 23 vendors. Data from the interviews supported Robert's concerns that vendors from outside the community were not primarily motivated by the idea of strengthening access to safe, affordable, and healthy food for the South Madison community. Robert started to float the idea of connecting reentry services with urban agriculture.

As soon as Dadit learned about SMFM's initial interest in connecting reentry services and urban agriculture, he reached out to the Nehemiah Center for Urban Leadership and Development (Nehemiah) that runs a reentry services program. Robert made the suggestion to contact Anthony Cooper, who at the time was the director of reentry services. A series of three-way conversations with SMFM and Nehemiah led to two aspirational thoughts. First, we believed that a farmers' market located in a low-income and multi-ethnic community could be more resilient and sustainable if supported by residents who shared a similar lived experience. Having local residents fully direct a localized food system from production, processing, distribution, to consumption would ensure a system that worked for them. Second, mass incarceration among African Americans had been at the center of social justice issues in South Madison. Reentry service initiatives were not adequately supported, causing ineffective reintegration. For formerly incarcerated people, securing stable employment to support themselves while meeting various court-ruled obligations remains a distant goal (Bazemore and Stinchcomb n.d.). Recidivism, job opportunities, and nutrition are significant issues that need to be addressed for individuals reentering society. Programs that focus on only one of the challenges these individuals face are insufficient. Former prisoners endure discrimination when seeking employment, and many also live in communities where healthy food options are scarce (Pierce 2014). We agreed that this partnership would tackle food injustice and issues of ineffective reentry services in one integrated program.

As a researcher, Dadit was comfortable with the work around sustainable agriculture. But the work around reentry services, the background, and the intersectionality of the issues were new to him. The conversations he had with Robert and Anthony helped him make the connections between food insecurity, racial equity, and reentry services.

Clarifying common goals
We agreed our focus would be the connections between food insecurity, reentry services, and racial equity. But we still needed the details of how the project would provide reliable access to safe, affordable, and healthy food in low-income, multi-ethnic communities and establish an effective reentry services program. The program needed to put formerly incarcerated people at the center and eventually address the larger South Madison community.

We looked closer at the needs and challenges that formerly incarcerated people have to navigate as they reenter society. The focus on employment (opportunities, readiness, retention, etc.) is still important. But the deficit model approach has not been supportive to the success of reentry services (Saleebey 2002; Urban Institute 2021). In addition to the focus on jobs in urban agriculture, we tried to be creative in improving the case management support system, including securing affordable housing, supporting mental health care, and attending to parole functions. We also wanted elements of the program to support formerly incarcerated people resettling within their families and communities. Hence, we wanted to be thoughtful that this program would help formerly incarcerated people as whole human beings reentering and resettling themselves in society.

The clarity on the goals of the partnership helped direct the next steps. We focused on three objectives: (1) establish a frame that interconnects food injustice and ineffective reentry services; (2) develop and run a pilot program; and (3) mobilize local organizations for expansion and sustainability. However, it is essential to note that we didn't know if we would have the resources to operate all of them. We agreed to move one step at a time while focused on the progression of the project. This is when the principles of CO become crucial as we laid out PAR processes of the partnership.

Framing strategies for action

We received Nelson Institute capstone service learning funding to support the first objective. In one year, we refined the project idea, communicated the narrative of urban agriculture and reentry services, and wrote grants to support the next steps. One semester was dedicated to course preparation, followed by a capstone course with 15 advanced undergraduates to execute the plan. In addition to SMFM and Nehemiah, we added other local organizations to leverage their expertise in criminal justice, reentry services, and case management, including Just Dane (formerly Madison-Area Urban Ministry), Madison Organizing in Strength, Equality and Solidarity (MOSES), and Breaking Barriers Mentoring. Through this loose coalition, we built collective knowledge on the interconnection of urban agriculture and reentry services. PAR facilitated the development of the collective ownership of the project. Students were engaged by SMFM, Nehemiah, and Just Dane, and participated in a group support program for formerly incarcerated people to learn about the complex processes of reentry services. They wrote about their experiential learning in blogs but most importantly used the newfound knowledge in practical writing assignments. One of them was a proposal for an internal university community engagement grant – the Baldwin Wisconsin Idea Endowment. The project was approved with $90,000 funding for two years of capstone service-learning instruction. The blogs written by students attracted attention from local media and a United States senator's office. Our community partners were contacted for a television interview and discussion. The aspirational idea was starting to generate concrete interest.

The two-year timeframe was broken down into a four-step process in four capstone service-learning courses – a total of 48 students and three graduate students were involved during these two years (Table 6.2). PAR facilitated the partnership to work on research, organizing, communications, and fundraising. They agreed that the FAIR program needed to be accommodated in a new non-profit entity. Students conducted research on how to establish a non-profit organization. They also worked to develop the curriculum for FAIR. These two separate investigations were driven by the programmatic needs from the community and used to inform the overall design for FAIR. Meanwhile, we continued to get individuals and groups organized to see an opportunity for FAIR to grow. We connected with a land trust organization that aspired to participate in the social justice realm. We also produced more blogs, worked on a 15-minute documentary film, held a community forum that discussed recidivism and food injustice, and wrote several grants for fundraising. In all of these initiatives, the role of community partners continued to be central. The community partners helped plan the syllabus, designed its semester-long project, and gave a guest lecture. The courses had become an avenue for mutual learning between community partners and students; they taught and learned from each other at the same time. In a classroom, Anthony encouraged students to share

Table 6.2   *Stages in the South Madison project*

Stage 1: Evaluation, diagnosis		Stage 2: Diagnosis, prescription	Stage 3: Prescription and implementation			
Fall 2013	Spring 2014	Spring 2015	Fall 2015	Spring 2016	Fall 2016	Spring 2017
Focus group with farmers' market vendors	Community-wide engagement	Developing initial narrative on urban agriculture and reentry services	Partnership building Communications (multiple platforms and audiences) Fund development Non-profit development Curriculum development			

their perspectives as white young adults in looking at the problems around reentry services. Students listened attentively about how Black leaders like Anthony tried to help their fellow Black men navigate reentry services.

Helping build leaders
The next step was establishing Neighborhood Food Solutions (NFS) as a new non-profit organization. After receiving legal counsel and recruiting South Madison residents to serve on the Board of Directors, we launched NFS to give a platform for a more socially just local food movement in South Madison with initial support from the local philanthropy, Bradshaw-Knight Foundation. NFS also secured CD funding from the City of Madison in 2017. Partnering with Nehemiah and Just Dane, NFS was ready to administer FAIR with five-year support from the city totaling $250,000.

The complexity of project implementation, the formation of a new non-profit organization, and the progression of the organizing effort created an intense dynamic for the partnership. The collaboration was able to address the power imbalance typically found in many community–university partnerships. The success from initial idea formulation, program development, and grassroots partnership development was evident. Conflicts and confrontations that took place between partners were a natural consequence, and often we were able to address them. As the project reached a level where funding and recognition was secured, the university took a step back to allow the dynamic of the community to take place more naturally. It was also an attempt to enable NFS to grow more independently without the university, building power from the ground up.

Mobilizing the community
PAR had facilitated the formation of a coalition in the intersectionality of reentry services. Our success in securing multiple funds was evidence of public acceptance of the innovative project idea. The fact that we could secure funds from an academic institution (theoretical-oriented) and a local government (practical-oriented) speaks volumes to the acceptability of our aspirational idea. We were pleased that in five years this project had evolved to engage various levels of community participants.

COMPARISON AND ANALYSIS

The case studies show two different strategies in community engagement. More than a superficial interaction between the project administrator and community members, the community engagement strategies build the capacity of the community to follow through on their immediate and long-term issues, understand those issues and collectively mobilize any available resources. It is about developing a whole community.

Following through from Initial Interests to Actionable Problems

In each case we began our work with a series of conversations on understanding the real problems and the factors driving them. The larger initial problems themselves were not necessarily actionable. PAR helped break them down into smaller actionable capstone projects. But we never considered the capstone course in and of itself as the action. We used the capstone courses to generate real and practical actions in the community such as responding to the city-wide survey, participating in the planning meeting to discuss project directions, and reviewing various grant narratives to secure project funds.

The issue selection stage was challenging in both projects. Unlike community organizers, issue development is not in the comfort zone of trained researchers. This is when the PAR-CO integration can fall apart if the community and the researcher are unable to find common ground. If done carefully, however, the collaborative team can become more solid and committed. In both our case studies, the researcher was involved in the issue selection process. We started with mapping all kinds of issues that were happening in the communities, prioritizing the select few and making the interconnections with and among the rest of them. We wanted to have a good understanding of the local issues, do something with the most important ones, and then leverage that initiative to address the other ones.

TNS Monona. TNS Monona existed to connect Mononans with personal interests in environmental sustainability. It successfully spurred sustainability actions. However, those actions had limited impact on the greater public because people committed to the actions in their private lives. The Alinksy model of organizing (Alinsky 1971) reminded us that, while we appreciated private actions, we wanted to bring people out of their homes to do more organized action in public for greater and more systemic change. Indeed, we designed the capstone courses with the goal of bringing people out of their homes to connect and collaborate. For example, the city-wide survey collected data and also facilitated active participation. Participants shared their voices about their sustainability practices, about their motivations that led to those practices, and about the most important community issues to them (Hidayat and Stoecker 2018). This was an attempt to narrow down the diverse self-interests to a few concrete and actionable issues. The community forum after the survey was designed for people to educate each other about the state of Monona's environmental sustainability and make a plan to follow up the survey results. The group decided to focus these collective actions around the issue of water conservation. The resulting plan informed the second capstone class work. We leveraged the resources of other local CBOs so they could lead their group members in collective environmental actions (Hidayat and Stoecker 2021).

SMFM. Going beyond "*what* are the initial interests?" to understand *why* and *how* these interests matter to the community can open up layers of contexts of oppression, exploitation, and exclusion. Elaborating on these questions requires a significant investment of time and energy. For SMFM, this involved wading through lived experiences of incarceration and reentry services without solid organizational back-up. Further, there was not any existing research that discussed the intersectionality of reentry services and urban agriculture. PAR played a significant role in both understanding the problems and translating them into practical strategies.

We designed the capstone partnership to further investigate the idea of combining reentry services with urban agriculture. Given the disproportionate numbers of Black men in Wisconsin's incarceration system (WCCF 2013; Quinn and Pawasarat 2014), understanding racism was central to our work. Being a researcher who had no experience being Black or incarcerated, Dadit was motivated to be even more careful when engaging community leaders and those who were in the reentry services program.

Training formerly incarcerated people in South Madison to do urban agriculture was never the only goal. The approval of the initial grant to support a capstone course partnership was a small win that allowed us to start to build a case through more traditional PAR actions by conducting a focus group. The focus group helped initiate thoughtful and reflective conversations around the provision of healthy foods in low-income neighborhoods. The idea of incorporating reentry services in the local food fabric in South Madison pushed the work even further by diversifying local food movement strategies and connecting with concrete social change goals (Fisher 2017). We wanted to create an urban agriculture program that would help address formerly incarcerated people's basic needs (i.e. food, housing, employment), build healthy relationships (find mentors, reunite families, and develop communities), and plan for the future (reflection on the past to build a constructive future). That makes FAIR not a straightforward job-training program.

Leveraging the Organizing Needs

CO is about creating systemic change. It is about mobilizing practical actions in a local community that can be a catalyst for a larger change. But a principle that is often forgotten is its cyclical process, the organizing never ends. It requires extensive energy and commitment to keep up with the constant changes. So when we think about organizing needs, not only do we think about addressing a problem but also about building people's capacity to work together effectively (Beckwith and Lopez 1997). By the same token, PAR not only generates accurate information for people to act on a set of problems but it also provides a framework so that the CO process can be more effective.

Educating the public and acting on the newfound knowledge in our two case studies required distinct CO strategies. Consequently, we applied two different PAR strategies to these projects.

TNS Monona. In Monona's case, the organizing needs centered around the eight-week study circles, a signature community-based learning program organized by TNS Monona. A concept that originated in Russia but was further developed in Sweden, the working-class and small farmers designed study circles to support popular movements (Oliver 1987). All participants in the study circles teach each other and learn from each other in a supportive learning environment (Barski-Carrow 2000; Moss 2008). As mentioned before, however, the emphasis on individual learning limited the actions to people's individual space. The idea of a local organization like TNS Monona to lead a small learning group was proven successful. The challenge was how it could offer greater and long-lasting impacts. That was when we considered a new learning design that would lead to a collaborative project outside of the home. The bloc recruitment approach acquired 14 pledges from local organizations with the hope that they would work with members within their organization around water conservation. Seven of them delivered the water conservation project of their own choice.

SMFM. The SMFM project's social justice element made it very sensitive to both the external dynamics of the changing national conversation about race as well as the internal dynamics of differing personalities, financial situations, and even the changing of the seasons. Combining reentry services and urban agriculture was a new idea from two community members with deep experience with these issues. SMFM alone didn't have the organizational infrastructure to widely communicate and develop the idea at the time. More work needed to be done to consolidate local resources and nurture shared interests with other groups. The series of conversations with Nehemiah, Just Dane, MOSES, and Breaking Barriers Mentoring opened new resources and opportunities. Most importantly, they helped elevate the conversation to a level that justifies the shared needs for such a program. The strategy was not without challenge. Within the team, we questioned if the project was too "exclusive" in working only with African American men. Partner selection was especially difficult and required a series of small conversations that slowed the pace of the project.

Viewing the Diversity

We addressed two completely different problems brought up by two organizations situated in two different community settings. Monona is a predominantly white, middle-class community while South Madison is a low-income, multi-ethnic community. We approached the projects with the same community engagement principles but enacted them differently.

TNS Monona. TNS Monona sought out an environmental topic that generated the most interest among the different civic, service, and environmental organizations in the community. Once they settled on the topic of "water" as the issue that could leverage the broadest number of supporters, they then began to explore how to connect people around that issue with even more diverse voices (for example, apartment dwellers) that led to further considerations about racial and socioeconomic representation in their work. It is important to note that the mainstream environmental movement was driven by the dominant cultural, economic, and political order (Perez et al. 2015). Given the white, middle-class demographic of Mononans, conversations about caring for the environment were not new though some residents resisted.

SMFM. SMFM is geographically situated in one of the most racially diverse neighborhoods in the region. SMFM could not help but be rooted in racial and ethnic diversity issues. From the public perception of the broader city and the university, South Madison is the flag bearer for all issues related to social inequity – health disparities, gentrification, racism, etc. SMFM's strategy was not focused on bringing in new diverse voices but instead on building partnerships with a small number of key collaborators, educating the public at large about a cornerstone issue for the Black community and ultimately creating an opportunity for formerly incarcerated members of the Black community to reengage with their neighborhood in a positive way.

The contrasting approaches could lead to the question of inclusivity versus exclusivity. On the one hand, TNS Monona expressed eagerness to listen to as many diverse voices as possible. On the other hand, SMFM and partners wanted the initial conversations to be limited so the project ideas could have a stronger foundation before including more voices with diverse and potential competing interests. But the case studies were consistent in one thing: they both followed community principles to start locally. The interconnection of PAR-CO offered flexible tools to navigate this dynamic and guide these local projects. These tools promote active and diverse participation toward a collective leadership that carefully manages all relevant community issues and organizes people for the long haul.

Implementing Project-Based Service Learning

Scholars and practitioners of higher education civic engagement have argued in favor of service-learning efficacy (Mitchell 2008). Others have argued for major deconstruction so the practice of service learning can better address community needs (Stoecker 2016). The case studies demonstrate how community needs, rather than students or research needs, were at the forefront of the partnership.

In both cases, with institutional support from Nelson Institute, Dadit led the customization of the service-learning capstone courses to allow for project progression. The capstone courses tried to incorporate more diverse interests beyond students and research, empower community leaders to direct course instruction, and leverage academic resources as part of the community-focused action strategies. Thus, the project-based approach allowed incorporating CD principles into the design. We finalized the goals for each capstone together with both community leaders and students, and the instructor's main responsibility was to facilitate their collaboration and project management. Most importantly, the four-step approach of diagnosis, prescription, implementation, and evaluation provided a framework that brought each course to a closure with a concrete plan for progression.

Recommended Strategies for Getting Started

Collaboration between researchers and community groups serves a good purpose. But, as in many other situations, collaboration tends to be easier said than done. Research has been perceived as an exclusive body of work done by credentialed experts and used as a form of oppression (McLaughlin 2012). As a result, communities distance themselves from research that lacks practical opportunities and takes uninformed actions (Nyden and Wiewal 1992). As illustrated in the case studies, PAR can be done, can be helpful, and can make a difference. Not only did the projects address social change, but they also built capacity in the community as a whole.

This chapter attempts to offer practical examples of conducting PAR in environmental organizations working towards social change. The theoretical supports built on the principles of CD help us understand how organized actions and research can support each other. Following the CD principles and basic steps of CO helps build a successful project from the ground up. However, in CO we often rush to action out of fear of not progressing. In contrast, unfortunately, researchers often start by conducting research with the hope that the intended outcomes will be produced through actions. Instead, framing research in support of organized actions through a social change process – the four steps of diagnosis, prescription, implementation, and evaluation – helps us think strategically. This allows research to begin with the intended action outcomes and move backward to research strategies to support the actions (Stoecker 2009).

Two important features were in place that allowed for this intense integration of PAR and community: institutional support and the lead researcher's identity.

Several key conditions at the institutional level made it possible to use this alternative version of PAR. First, the Nelson Institute was founded on a premise of interdisciplinarity. Within the unit, students and faculty maintain a wide range of academic homes across the physical, biological, and social sciences as well as the humanities. It is a logical setting for projects drawing on multiple areas of expertise. Second, undergraduate students were required to participate in a capstone experience that applies skills developed throughout the curriculum. These students were skilled and motivated to do work that could build community capacity and support community efforts. Finally, funding was available to support a researcher to spend a semester planning a community project before bringing undergraduate students into the work. The planning semester was intended to provide researchers with existing relationships in the community to develop a meaningful PAR activity directly connected to the community's end goals. Combined with an instructor's willingness to follow through the community's needs over several years, this funding availability offered long-term institutional support for a community-focused capstone experience. It was rare but did have precedence at the Nelson Institute. Dadit's role as a PhD student offered the flexibility that many professors or instructors do not usually have.

Dadit's identity as the lead researcher also gave a unique advantage. Managing the identity of the researcher and the associated power balance was important. Being a PAR practitioner as an international student could be challenging. For Dadit, however, the process of unlearning (Lee 2002; Bonchek 2016) as he entered the community and understood the context of the problems came naturally since he did not grow up as part of the community. He was more worried about being associated with the University of Wisconsin-Madison, which was often criticized for harmful community engagement approaches (Stoecker and Tryon 2009). Revisiting the literature on higher education civic engagement, this is not uncommon. Researchers conducting community-oriented work have not been as thoughtful on their power in directing research (see Foucault 1980; Horton and Freire 1990; Coben 1995). Academic training does not include learning how to work with non-credentialed experts in the community, let alone recognizing the expertise of the community.

It is our hope that this chapter can clearly demonstrate the practicality of PAR and its benefits in CD. Understanding the intricacy of CO and PAR helps us work on proactive sustainability movements, but also more broadly in support of any organized actions. Here are four fundamentals of how researchers and community groups will have to shift some practices by learning from each other.

1. *Researchers need to reflect on their privilege.* Reciprocity is a term we hear a lot in any collaborative work between researchers and community groups. It is meaningless. Researchers have to realize that they are among the privileged citizens and that the privilege itself can be manifested in various ways. Unnecessary tension arises from socially recognized expertise, differing communication styles, and decision-making processes. Credentials do not justify expertise, experience does. Being assertive when communicating – which sometimes slips into being aggressive – is not always a good thing. Because less-privileged groups have fewer opportunities to speak, researchers need to spend more time listening than talking. Privilege also extends to decision making. Let the community make decisions on the research direction. These power imbalances, often unrecognized by researchers, become forms of oppression and communities have little agency to change the dynamic.

2. *Community issues are interconnected, understand them all, really!* One of the most genuine forms of interdisciplinary practice takes place in the community. Community members interconnect issues on a daily basis. As most researchers are trained in a disciplinary way, it can be a struggle to practice interdisciplinary investigation. A common challenge to both community members and researchers is to make decisions on one or two highly important community issues among a dozen other almost equally important ones. This is when the issue selection process will make a difference. Researchers have to rely on the expertise of community leaders and their understanding of the issues they are experiencing. And then, only then, we can apply our analytical skills in contributing to project design, implementation, and evaluation.

3. *Groups need to spend time in deeper and theoretical thinking about their actions.* Community groups build knowledge and expertise through an experiential process. On the contrary, researchers build knowledge and expertise from a theoretical process. Encouraging community groups to shift from practical to theoretical thinking is a challenge that could undermine the value of lived experience. But theorizing will critically help community members to make a plan that goes beyond a crisis-driven action (for immediate impacts) that strategically considers the sustainability of the action (long-term impact). This is why Freire's popular education becomes essential. The process still recognizes communities as experts and facilitates conversation as an awareness-raising strategy (Freire 1968, 1973).

4. *Partners need to nurture collective excitement that goes beyond the partnership.* Ideally, it is not a one-time project. PAR generates new knowledge in support of community groups doing what they want to do. And sustaining the project for social change requires a collectivity of people outside of the project team. Building on the principles of popular education, the partnership has to find a way to excite the public to participate in the organized actions.

The way we interpret PAR in relation to CO is not about strategizing how to do better research. Rather, we want to build on the social change strategies that have been the foundation of CO. Consequently, we see research as a tool for community organizers so they can make informed decisions. The case studies presented in this chapter showcase how researchers and community groups interact in environmental projects built on social change strategies and supported by practical research. More documentation with other cases is needed to continue to inform a CO approach in PAR.

ACKNOWLEDGMENTS

We would like to thank the Nelson Institute for Environmental Studies at the University of Wisconsin-Madison that supported the work as reported in the case studies through its Charlotte Zieve Teaching Fellowship. The Baldwin Wisconsin Idea Endowment, also administered by the University of Wisconsin-Madison, provided funding support for two years of the South Madison project. Most importantly, we would like to thank Nelson Institute students who courageously joined in our 10 capstone service learning courses; Anthony Cooper Sr, Robert Pierce, and Monona friends for giving the opportunity for partnerships that led to this writing. We also thank Adrienne Falcón, Randy Stoecker, and Megan Brown for providing feedback to shape this chapter.

REFERENCES

Adams, Frank C. 1975. *Unearthing Seeds of Fire: The Idea of Highlander*. Durham, NC: John F. Blair Publishing.
Alinsky, Saul D. 1971. *Rules for Radicals: A Practical Primer for Realistic Radicals*. New York: Vintage Books.
Barski-Carrow, Barbara. 2000. "Using Study Circles in the Workplace as an Educational Method of Facilitating Readjustment after a Traumatic Life Experience." *Death Studies* 24(5): 421–439.
Bazemore, Gordon and Jeanne Stinchcomb. n.d. "A Civic Engagement Model of Reentry: Involving Community through Service and Restorative Justice." *Federal Probation: A Journal of Correctional Philosophy and Practice* 68(2). www.uscourts.gov/sites/default/files/68_2_4_0.pdf
Beckwith, David and Cristina Lopez. 1997. "Community Organizing: People Power from the Grassroots." COMM-ORG. https://comm-org.wisc.edu/papers97/beckwith.htm
Bonchek, Mark. 2016. "Why the Problem with Learning Is Unlearning." *Harvard Business Review*. https://hbr.org/2016/11/why-the-problem-with-learning-is-unlearning
Brown, L. David and Rajesh Tandon. 1983. "Ideology and Political Economy in Inquiry: Action Research and Participatory Research." *Journal of Applied Behavioral Science* 19: 277–294.
Campbell, David A. and Kristina T. Lambright. 2017. "Struggling to Get It Right." *Nonprofit Management and Leadership* 27(3): 335–351.
Coben, Diana. 1995. "Revisiting Gramsci." *Studies in the Education of Adults* 27(1): 36–51.
Community Development Society. 2021. *Principles of Good Practice*. Rochester, NY: Community Development Society. www.comm-dev.org/about/principles-of-good-practice
Diani, Mario. 2013. "Bloc Recruitment." In D. Snow et al (eds) *Wiley-Blackwell Encyclopedia of Social and Political Movements*. Oxford: Blackwell, pp. 149–150.
Fisher, Andrew. 2017. *Big Hunger: The Unholy Alliance between Corporate American and Anti-Hunger Groups*. Cambridge, MA: MIT Press.
Foucault, Michael. 1980. *Power/Knowledge: Selected Interviews and Other Writings 1972–1977*, edited by C. Gordon. New York: Pantheon Books.
Freire, Paulo. 1968. *Pedagogy of the Oppressed*. New York: Herder and Herder.
Freire, Paulo. 1973. *Extension or Communication*. New York: Seabury Press.
Hidayat, Dadit and Randy Stoecker. 2018. "Community-Based Organizations and Environmentalism: How Much Impact Can Small, Community-Based Organizations Working on Environmental Issues Have?" *Journal of Environmental Studies and Sciences* 8: 395–406.
Hidayat, Dadit and Randy Stoecker. 2021. "Collective Knowledge Mobilization through a Community-University Partnership." *Journal of Higher Education Outreach and Engagement* 25(2): 95–110.
Hidayat, Dadit, Randy Stoecker, and Heather Gates. 2014. "Promoting Community Environmental Sustainability Using a Project-Based Approach." In K.O. Korgen, Jonathan M. White, and Shelley K. White (Eds), *Sociologists in Action: Sociology, Social Change, and Social Justice*, 2nd Edition. Thousand Oaks, CA: SAGE, pp. 263–268.
Hirschmann, David. 1990. "The Black Consciousness Movement in South Africa." *Journal of Modern African Studies* 28(1): 1–22.
Horton, Myles and Paulo Freire. 1990. *We Make the Road by Walking: Conversations on Education and Social Change*. Philadelphia, PA: Temple University Press.
Horton, Myles, Judith Kohl, and Herbert Kohl. 1997. *The Long Haul: An Autobiography*. New York: Teachers College Press.
James, Sarah and Torbjörn Lahti. 2004. *The Natural Step for Communities: How Cities and Towns Can Change to Sustainable Practices*. Gabriola Island: New Society Publisher.
Kirkwood, Gerri and Colin Kirkwood. 2011. *Living Adult Education: Freire in Scotland*. Rotterdam: Sense Publishers.

Kock, Ned. 2004. "The Three Threats of Action Research: A Discussion of Methodological Antidotes in the Context of an Information Systems Study." *Decision Support Systems* 37: 265–286.

Lee, Virginia S. 2002. "Unlearning: A Critical Element in the Learning Process." *Essays on Teaching Excellence toward the Best in the Academy* 14(2). https://cft.vanderbilt.edu/wp-content/uploads/sites/59/vol14no2_unlearning.htm

Lewin, Kurt. 1946. *Action Research and Minority Problems*. In G.W. Lewin (Ed.), *Resolving Social Conflicts*. New York: Harper and Row.

MacNamara, Carter. 1999. "Basic Guide to Outcomes-Based Evaluation for Nonprofit Organizations with Very Limited Resources." https://managementhelp.org/evaluation/outcomes-evaluation-guide.htm

McLaughlin, Hugh. 2012. *Understanding Social Work Research*, 2nd Edition. Thousand Oaks, CA: SAGE.

Mitchell, Tania D. 2008. "Traditional vs. Critical Service-Learning: Engaging the Literature to Differentiate Two Models." *Michigan Journal of Community Service Learning* Spring: 50–65.

Moss, G. 2008. "Diversity Study Circles in Teacher Education Practice: An Experiential Learning Project." *Teaching and Teacher Education* 24(1): 216–224.

Noffke, Susan. E. and Bridget Somekh. 2009. *The SAGE Handbook of Educational Action Research*. New York: SAGE.

Nyden P. and Wiewal, W. 1992. "Collaborative Research: Harnessing the Tensions between Researcher and Practitioner." *The American Sociologist* 23: 43–55.

Oliver, L.P. 1987. *Study Circles: Coming Together for Personal Growth and Social Change*. Santa Ana, CA: Seven Locks Press.

Perez, Alejandro Colsa, Bernadette Grafton, Paul Mohai, Rebecca Hardin, Katy Hintzen, and Sara Orvis. 2015. "Evolution of the Environmental Justice Movement: Activism, Formalization and Differentiation." *Environmental Research Letters* 10: 105002. https://iopscience.iop.org/article/10.1088/1748-9326/10/10/105002

Pierce, Robert. 2014. Informal conversation.

Quinn, Lois M. and John Pawasarat. 2014. "Statewide Imprisonment of Black Men in Wisconsin." *ETI Publications* 7. https://dc.uwm.edu/eti_pubs/7

Saleebey, Dennis. 2002. "Introduction: Power in the People." In D. Saleebey (Ed.), *The Strengths Perspective in Social Work Practice*, 3rd Edition. London: Allyn and Bacon.

Selener, Daniel. 1997. *Participatory Action Research and Social Change*. Ithaca, NY: Cornell Participatory Action Research Network, Cornell University.

Stall, Susan and Randy Stoecker. 1998. "Community Organizing or Organizing Community? Gender and the Crafts of Empowerment." *Gender and Society* 12(6): 729–756.

Stoecker, Randy. 2009. "Are We Talking the Walk of Community-Based Research?" *Action Research* 7(4): 385–404.

Stoecker, Randy. 2013. *Research Methods for Community Change: A Project-Based Approach*. Thousand Oaks, CA: SAGE.

Stoecker, Randy. 2016. *Liberating Service Learning, and the Rest of Higher Education Civic Engagement*. Philadelphia, PA: Temple University Press.

Stoecker, Randy and Elizabeth Tryon. 2009. *The Unheard Voices: Community Organizations and Service Learning*. Philadelphia, PA: Temple University Press.

Theuvsen, Ludwig. 2004. "Doing Better While Doing Good: Motivational Aspects of Pay-for-Performance Effectiveness in Nonprofit Organizations." *Voluntas: International Journal of Voluntary and Nonprofit Organizations* 15: 117–136.

UKEssays. 2018. "Criticism of Action Research." UKEssays.com. www.ukessays.com/essays/education/research-methods-and-critique-action-research-in-education-education-essay.php?vref=1

Urban Institute. 2021. "Understanding the Challenges of Prisoner Reentry: Research Findings from the Urban Institute's Prisoner Reentry Portfolio." Washington DC: Urban Institute. www.urban.org/sites/default/files/publication/42981/411289-Understanding-the-Challenges-of-Prisoner-Reentry.PDF

WCCF (Wisconsin Council for Children and Families). 2013. "Race to Equity: A Baseline Report on the State of Racial Disparities in Dane County." Madison, WI: Wisconsin Council for Children and Families. http://racetoequity.net/wp-content/uploads/2016/11/WCCF-R2E-Report.pdf

Whyte, William. F. (Ed.). 1991. *Participatory Action Research*. Newbury Park, CA: SAGE.

7. The birth of a community of practice in Québec to support community organizations leading participatory action research as a tool for community development: what it teaches us

Lucie Gélineau, Sophie Dupéré, Marie-Jade Gagnon, Lyne Gilbert, Isabel Bernier, Nicole Bouchard, Julie Richard, and Marie-Hélène Deshaies

In the province of Québec, Canada,[1] community organizers (COs) have been, for the last 60 years, key players in community development. They are professionals, particularly social workers, based mainly in public health and social services centers (CLSCs) and, to a lesser degree, in community organizations. They have the mandate to support local communities in improving their living and health conditions when they are vulnerable, marginalized, excluded, impoverished, or devitalized. This practice stems from the social animators' tradition, inspired by American radicals such as Saul Alinsky or Latin American liberation theology (Baillergeau 2007).

COs can drive participatory action research (PAR) as a community development intervention strategy. While not academic researchers, they design and carry out research projects with other community stakeholders on their own. To our knowledge, this is a fringe practice with little scholarship (Gélineau et al. 2019), but full of potential. Using PAR in this way takes us to the heart of epistemic injustice debates: which knowledge takes precedence among the different groups involved in understanding a community reality – the communities directly concerned, the COs as social practitioners, or the scientists? Is scientific research an exclusive domain, or can anyone potentially become proficient in and consider themselves entitled to carry out such research or be inspired by it? Our experience tells us that communities of practice (CoPs) can provide answers to this debate. CoPs might represent a middle way, providing a learning space for scientific rigor and fundamentals in PAR while recognizing the value of practical and experiential input, supporting the development of an identity and a reflexive space for COs.

This chapter looks at a specific CO's PAR CoP, where COs support each other while having access to an academic researcher for methodological support and PAR fundamentals. We will first look at community organization in Québec and its relationship to PAR. We will then relate our CoP's story and examples of PAR by its members to develop a model of a PAR CoP. Then we will reflect on the challenges and opportunities of using PAR as a community development practice. Throughout, we will try to answer these questions: How can PAR led by COs, and the knowledge produced, be recognized? How do we give a place to non-academic knowledge? How do these knowledge production practices contribute to community development? By asking these questions, we wish to contribute to a greater understanding of how to support autonomous PAR carried out by and for local communities under the leadership of COs.

This "we" refers to members of the National Capital (Quebec City) Integrated University Health and Social Service Centre (CIUSSS-CN) COs PAR CoP. That is, five COs (Marie-Jade Gagnon, Lyne Gilbert, Isabel Bernier, Nicole Bouchard, and Andrée-Ann Roy Ross), two professional coordinators (Colette Lavoie and Manon Roy) and an academic researcher who accompanied them (Lucie Gélineau). The ideas presented partly stem from reflection that we have done since 2016. We presented the foundational ideas of this chapter at a *Midi*-RAP ("Lunchtime PAR"), a live forum for exchange between citizens, practitioners, and researchers involved in participatory research, in April 2019 (Gilbert et al. 2019). An enhanced presentation was then shared by the accompanying researcher with rural COs (Chaudière-Appalaches) (Gélineau 2019). A practitioner-researcher who is now a doctoral student (Julie Richard) and two researchers involved in accompaniment initiatives (Sophie Dupéré and Marie-Hélène Deshaies) have joined the writing adventure. At the practitioners' request, one of the researchers (Gélineau) agreed to hold the pen.

PARTICIPATORY ACTION RESEARCH FOR US

Our PAR draws from a broad research field including the work of Freire (1973a), Swantz (1975), Hall et al. (1982), Fals Borda and Rahman (1991), and Minkler and Wallerstein (2008). They refer to practices showing "a tendency to combine community participation in decision-making with methods of social investigation" (Hall et al. 1982: 21). There have also been parallel developments, particularly in the fields of feminist and post-colonial studies, as well as in health and community development in the Global North and Global South. We identified more than 40 designations for participatory research processes (Gélineau et al. 2019)! Participatory research questions the nature of knowledge production, the (in)validation of various forms of knowledge across Global North/Global South relations, class divisions, gender divisions, post-colonial relations, and the environment.

Our conception of PAR falls within the most politicized axis of this family of participatory research, where maximum attention is paid to its transformative and consciousness-raising scope as well as to the appropriation of the scientific research process by lay actors (Gélineau et al. 2012). In this sense, we are in this chapter not talking about research carried out by a team of university researchers, practitioners, and citizens, but rather led and carried out by practitioners and communities, with sometimes the support – as a methodological safety net – of university researchers who play an advisory role.

Gélineau et al. (2012) note how this strand of participatory research promotes four fundamental rights: (1) the right of lay actors to produce scientific knowledge; (2) the right of people who are experiencing exclusion, subordination, or marginalization to speak as real-life experts; (3) the right of lay actors to think, i.e., to be recognized for their analytical ability; and (4) the right of citizenship (*droit de cite*) i.e., to speak publicly based on the knowledge produced.

COMMUNITY ORGANIZATION AS A COMMUNITY DEVELOPMENT APPROACH IN THE PROVINCE OF QUÉBEC AND ITS RELATIONSHIP TO PARTICIPATORY ACTION RESEARCH

Who Are Community Organizers? And Where Are They Practicing?

Authors in Québec define community organizing as professional support intervention to geographic, identity, or interest communities who desire to improve their living conditions (Baillergeau 2007; Doré 1985; Lavoie and Panet-Raymond 2014; RQIIAC 2020). The interventions aim to consolidate spaces for citizen[2] participation and social change. The professional practices of COs emphasize communities most affected by situations of inequality, impoverishment, and exclusion (Lachapelle and RQIIAC 2010). They differ from other practitioners in health and social services by their collective rather than individual approach to social problems, and their willingness to act on the social determinants of health (Bourque and Lachapelle 2010; Lachapelle and RQIIAC 2010; Parent et al. 2012). They facilitate collaboration between public and community organizations, health and social services institutions, and socioeconomic partners (PDGA 2018).

COs worked initially through local CLSCs resulting from people's health clinics initiated by citizen mobilizations in the 1960s (Gay 2006). In 2021, they work for broader public health and social service systems (Baillergeau 2007) that have been in neoliberal reform turmoil (Hébert et al. 2017). Faced with structural transformations (but resisting despite everything!),

> Community organization is at the heart of paradoxes and contradictory logic. Indeed, on the one hand, it is expected to strengthen civil society and citizen participation. On the other hand, it is a stakeholder in an institution marked by the new public management based on public-private partnerships (PPP) and privatization. Similarly, it is supposed to act on the social determinants of health and the causes of social problems, whereas public action is only aimed at managing the consequences. (Bourque and Lachapelle 2010: 137)

Community Organizers' Roles and Use of Research

Community organizing bases its professional practice on a linkage strategy in the following fundamental dimensions: (1) analyzing; (2) raising awareness; (3) linking and mobilizing actors; (4) accompanying; (5) ensuring cohesion; (6) democratizing power relationships; and (7) making resources accessible (Lachapelle and RQIIAC 2010; Lachapelle 2017).

According to RQIIAC[3] (2020), the analysis process involves fostering a thorough understanding of the target object by identifying its various characteristics and placing it in its social, political, economic, cultural, and environmental context. The RQIIAC, in its reference framework, does not mention the CO as a potential leader of research in this analysis process. Still, it evokes its role in projects undertaken by professional researchers to participate in documenting the object of analysis: designing and helping using information-gathering tools; linking information; generating observations; and distributing knowledge through the creation of dissemination tools (RQIIAC 2020: 78).

We maintain that COs should do more than participate in professional researchers' projects. COs can use PAR as an intervention strategy in line with CO practice. PAR allows community members to take a more comprehensive and inclusive look at their issue (CO fundamentals:

analyzing), link stakeholders and mobilize partners around the issue (raising awareness, linking, mobilizing), and work on both structural and personal factors from a justice perspective (accompanying and ensuring cohesion) (Sen 2012). PAR is effective in these ways because it includes collective analysis strategies that combine various types of expertise (practical, lay, academic) in a rigorous framework that legitimizes the knowledge produced in the eyes of decision makers and the public (making resources accessible, here access to knowledge and the means to produce it). Thus, PAR encourages the involved agents (COs, stakeholders, and marginalized citizens) to be political actors (more than democratizing power relationships!).

Few academic texts address PAR as a social intervention strategy (Gélineau et al. 2019). There are results of empirical research carried out by practitioners or their organizations (e.g., Kingori and Ntulo 2011), as well as theoretical reflections by academics (e.g., Altpeter et al. 1999; Bortoletto 2017; Finn 1994; Hardwick and Worsley 2011; Healy 2001) and critical reflections by non-academic PAR practitioners (e.g., Gouin et al. 2011; Rahnema 1990; Sparr 1998). Methodological works are available to help organizations conduct their own research (e.g., Barnsley and Ellis 1992; McKinnon 2013; Stoecker 2005; Wadsworth 2016). Some scholarship highlights the kinship between social work and PAR: the interest in voices of people living in oppressive situations; the aims of empowerment and social change; and the care for realities on the ground (Branom 2012; Hick 1997; Sohng 1996). Some discuss whether research used as an intervention strategy is research (CIOMS in Snider and Stroup 1997) and consider its social and health benefits (Freudenberg et al. 2015).

Next let's see what CoPs developed around PAR and CO, the projects they carry out, and what they teach us.

CASE STUDIES

The Evolution of a Participatory Action Research Community of Practice for Community Organizers at the National Capital University Integrated Health and Social Services Centre

CIUSSS-CN[4] serves 750,000 citizens over 18,643 square kilometers and has more than 18,500 employees, amongst which, more or less, 40 are COs (CIUSSS de la Capitale Nationale 2021).

In 2016, Colette Lavoie, the CO's professional coordinator, invited L. Gélineau to present on PAR as a training activity offered to the COs. Around 15 COs attended. The subsequent interest of the COs led to the idea of setting up a CoP. Around ten COs have participated, plus the CO professional coordinator and an experienced academic researcher. To our knowledge, this PAR CoP is unique in the province of Québec.

There were a couple of reasons why a CoP for PAR was popular among the COs. First, one of the CLSCs was an affiliate university center. Thus, COs and social workers who wished to conduct research could request in-house CLSC researcher support. Lucie Gélineau was an in-house researcher. She encouraged the COs to undertake research independently, with her guidance instead of her being the professional researcher leading the research (Gélineau et al. 2009). C. Lavoie, the CoP's original professional coordinator, and Manon Roy, a later professional coordinator, were two of the COs developing PAR projects, independently or in an academic collaboration context. Additionally, the youngest members of this CoP received undergraduate training from researchers or former COs who practice PAR.

The COs in the CoP value PAR because it appeals to their community organization agenda and values, it can serve a strategic goal, and it facilitates outreach and collaboration.

In terms of the CO agenda and values, PAR makes it possible to move beyond a neoliberal New Public Management context (e.g., Bourque 2009), where public services must act like private enterprises, emphasizing efficiency, cost-effectiveness, and top-down decision making regarding work objectives and public health priorities. Managers encourage COs to work with local service organizations instead of being directly in touch with local community people carrying out community-driven projects with a social justice perspective. By promoting communities' involvement in its various steps, PAR provides opportunities to work more closely with marginalized citizens and rediscover the latter's surroundings through their eyes. It offers ways to develop more inclusive communities and work around marginalized citizens' agendas and knowledge. It allows COs to better understand local issues and co-develop sound critical actions.

The strategic goal addresses questions of perception and legitimacy of issues and responses. Despite the dawn of a post-factual era, evidence is still highly valued in the Québec government and administrative decision making. Unfortunately, at the same time, the voices of communities, citizens, and stakeholders can go unheard. Rigorous PAR helps lend credibility and legitimacy to local proposals, allowing COs, community members, and stakeholders to better influence policies and action plans in the public sphere.

PAR, as an inclusive approach, supports outreach efforts by allowing diverse stakeholders to meet and enter a conversation, thus increasing collective awareness, understanding, and ownership of local issues. It strengthens local expertise, whether based on experience or practice. It encourages skills development and empowerment while addressing local power imbalance. It empowers individuals, organizations, and social movements (Ninacs 2008).

Examples of Participatory Action Research Projects Related to the CIUSSS-CN Community of Practice

Since the beginning of the CoP in 2016, COs have completed three PAR projects: two on neighborhood community vitality and another on food security. As of 2020, four others were in progress. Let us have a look at two of the completed projects.

Co-creating a community environment that works for everyone: the Jean-Baptiste Duberger venue – a narrative from Lyne Gilbert

Duberger Sud is a local community of 4,300 inhabitants with a large African immigrant community mainly from Cameroon and composed mostly of university students. The area is bounded by a highway, a beautiful river, and a central boulevard. It is a part of a larger neighborhood called Duberger-Les Saules. There are two urban parks (without playgrounds for children ages five and under or sports fields), residential apartment buildings three to four stories high, some cooperative housing and municipal low-income housing for people ages 55 and over, two-family houses, and an industrial park. There are few nearby commercial services and no neighborhood organizations, but there is a local library with an adjacent community center, the Jean-Baptiste Duberger Venue.[5]

The Jean-Baptiste Duberger Venue is part of an engagement effort initiated in the fall of 2016 by the CIUSSS-CN in collaboration with partners of the Table de concertation Duberger-Les Saules (Duberger-Les Saules Consulting Group). This approach aims to:

- Coordinate the actions of community stakeholders to better respond to the needs and complex situations experienced by citizens.
- Improve the health and well-being of Duberger-Sud residents by facilitating access to health and social services.
- Facilitate the social, community, educational, and socioprofessional integration of residents.
- Improve the living conditions of residents, particularly in terms of housing, employment, food security, access to local resources, reception and integration of immigrants, and regional planning.

The community venue committee has been looking to encourage a sense of ownership of the Jean-Duberger Venue by residents through a process of consulting citizens. I formed a PAR task group (Figure 7.1) involving four women citizens from Duberger-Sud, a local outreach worker from the Centre d'action bénévole du Contrefort and a social work undergraduate student at the Université du Québec à Rimouski, Campus de Lévis. The co-researchers represent different life experiences in terms of age, migratory experiences, and education, some with young families and others living alone, and some with modest incomes or mobility issues. Our task group mandate was to think about and carry out this consultation. We wanted the approach to be rigorous so that public officials would pay attention to the results.

The question we chose to guide our work was "How to make the Jean-Baptiste Duberger Venue reflect the true colors of the citizens of Duberger Sud?" Wanting to share between us what we knew about Duberger Sud, we took exploratory walks, each of us guiding the others through the parts we knew better. We conducted eight group interviews with a diversity of residents, mostly in the library. Most of the participants had never been there before! They shared that they felt empowered by the committee recognizing their knowledge and understanding their community and realities. They felt secure that our task group would consider their experiences, seeing that local citizens were part of it. We collaboratively analyzed the data from the interview transcripts. Through our task group's 16 meetings we rediscovered the neighborhood, seeing it through other residents' eyes, combined with our perspectives as residents and long-term workers in the sector.

The results highlighted that the residents loved their local community and were emotionally attached to it. They were looking for space to meet informally and were concerned about integrating new residents, immigrants, and those who are more isolated such as elders or people with disabilities.

We identified ways to improve the local community, such as developing a housing action committee and information sessions on affordable housing access and tenants' rights; designing better bus schedules and routes to facilitate transportation to health and social services, daycare facilities, work, and schools; developing the park, outdoor sports infrastructure, and walkways for intergenerational use. We also made proposals for the Jean-Baptiste Duberger Venue, such as seeing the library as a community space for sharing activities (having tea, chatting, knitting; not only borrowing books!), developing an outdoor intergenerational program, art program, and financial literacy program; and harmonizing the Venue schedules to the residents' work schedules. We understood better the difficulties in accessing local health and

Source: Table de concertation Duberger-LesSaules.
Note: (right to left) Lyne Gilbert, community organizer, CIUSSS-CN; Sylvana Moussavoult, citizen; Marjolaine Trudel, citizen; Nathalie Belley, citizen; Kate McBrearty, social work student, Université du Québec à Rimouski – campus de Lévis; Marie-Pier Trudel, field worker, Centre d'action bénévole du Contrefort.

Figure 7.1   Members of the PAR task group

social services. We co-wrote the PAR report (Gilbert et al. 2017) and the consulting group put it online.

In 2017 our working group presented the results to the Table de concertation Duberger-Les Saules, whose mission is "to improve the quality of life of residents and create a sense of belonging in the neighborhood by fighting poverty and social exclusion in a concerted manner" (Table de concertation Duberger-Les Saules 2021). Twenty-nine organizations were part of it, mostly municipal, school, community or faith (Catholic) organizations, and provincial health and social programs or institutions. The presentation took place in an activity entitled "THERE ARE WONDERFUL MOMENTS!" After introducing a "living library activity" with the local citizens, we used a world café process to discuss and add their own experience and knowledge to the PAR results. This choice also made it easier for our task group members to speak. They felt more comfortable sharing the results in smaller groups than in front of a large audience! The community residents on the task group proudly hand-delivered the recommendations in personalized folders, carefully handmade and decorated, to each member of the consulting group as well as elected officials or their representatives from municipal, provincial, and federal government. They had strategically targeted and personalized recommendations for each official. I have been told that this personal contact was powerful.

Since the report's release, I have observed numerous positive effects from our work. Residents have been allocated a greater place in decision-making bodies such as the consulting group's Coordinating Committee and Members' Assembly meetings. The latter, which had been made up solely of organizations, now includes four places for community residents. The Table now also mobilizes citizens in planning and implementing activities. The Jean-Baptiste Duberger Venue has integrated the recommendations into their development and promotion action plan. These recommendations have also invigorated neighborhood life through, for example, a temporary summer square for picnics and neighborhood festivals benefiting families and single people. It has also led to activities proposed and run by community residents, including a writing workshop. The Venue has truly become their own!

The report also led to a taskforce addressing housing rights, under my leadership. Composed notably of citizens and a professional from the Fédération des Coopératives d'Habitation de Québec, Chaudière-Appalaches, this group obtained its community organization status in December 2020. The PAR task group has also inspired others: a CO from another CIUSSS drove 400 kilometers with members of their community to speak with us about doing PAR in their own neighborhood.

In my opinion, having done real rigorous scientific research, the Issue table has gained credibility with the city and other authorities, demonstrating our abilities to bring initiatives to fruition in a proper manner. It facilitated the realization of another PAR project led by Marie-Jade (CO and co-author) and Andrée-Anne (CO and collaborator) in another part of Duberger-Les Saules. These PAR projects helped secure subsequent funding.

To feel more skilled in using PAR as an intervention tool, I got involved in the CoP. The methodological support has allowed me, as a CO, to experience the challenges, stakes, and stimuli of such a project with citizens and other COs. Lucie's support as a researcher went beyond the CoP. She met once with our task group at my request so that we, as a collective, had a better understanding of the PAR process as only I was participating in the CoP. Lucie coached the student, as it was her first PAR contribution. At the task group's request, she participated in the world café activity, facilitating the methods breakout group, thus illustrating the CoP's presence. She also supported the writing process, particularly in terms of rigor and organization of the results. After the project, I continued my involvement with the CoP to support and encourage other COs' PAR projects based on my experience with tools that we used and tips and strategies to mobilize and support citizen participation.

My PAR experience helped me regain power in my practice from a critical and citizen perspective. If I hadn't retired, I would have liked to do more PAR. I am 100 percent convinced of its relevance to the practice of COs! It contributes to a detailed and contextualized analysis of the neighborhood, beyond statistics, by allowing a better understanding of the community through its residents' experience and life experiences. PAR allowed me to make connections that I didn't make before, even though I had worked in this neighborhood for over ten years! I gained a vision of what is meaningful to people and, as an OC, new priorities. It puts "eyes in front of the holes." For example, before, I was convinced that we needed to develop residents' sense of belonging to their neighborhood. With PAR, I found out that residents already have a sense of belonging. Many have chosen this environment. I used to see ugly buildings and the fact that the children didn't have a place to play even though there were beautiful trees. Well, the citizens have led me to find this neighborhood beautiful. More broadly through PAR I felt recognition for my work by the CIUSSS-CN and my colleagues. Experiencing a PAR project and publishing a scientific research report have helped promote value for our professional work as COs in the city's neighborhoods.

"From vegetable garden to plate: A solidarity network for Saint-Roch" – a narrative from Isabel Bernier, CIUSSS community organizer

The Saint-Roch neighborhood dates to the seventeenth century and covers 1.5 square kilometers.[6] As the first working-class suburb of Quebec City, it was a shipyard, then a manufacturing center. It declined in the 1960s with the development of the outskirts of town, shopping malls, globalization, and motorways that split the neighborhood in two. With an impoverished and marginalized population, community services developed. Then, an ambitious program of urban renovation and revitalization led by a municipal government created art cooperatives and studios, university faculties, high-tech companies, high-end restaurants and stores, condominiums, and tourist accommodations in the late 1990s–2000s. Through the process of gentrification, the neighborhood has become mixed. Amongst the 7,812 inhabitants, 37.5 percent report a gross income of less than $20,000, compared with 26 percent in Quebec City as a whole. Forty-four percent reported living alone, compared to 21.6 percent in Quebec City (Deschênes and Bernier 2019). This social gap raises issues for people living in poverty, both those who live there and service users.

In 2016, the neighborhood group and the CIUSSS-CN launched a neighborhood survey. We wanted to know what the neighborhood's priorities for the coming years should be. Food (in)security emerged as a main theme. A local food (in)security and follow-up committee was, therefore, created by L'Engrenage. It was composed of the Centre Le Bourg-Joie's collective kitchens, the Community Initiatives Office of the YMCAs of Québec, Moisson Québec (Harvest Quebec Foodbank), the CIUSSS-CN, the Table de quartier l'Engrenage de Saint-Roch, and one committed citizen (see Figure 7.2).

With my support, as a CO from the CIUSSS-CN, the committee designed a process of reflective thinking and action called "Food security in St-Roch: from individual to collective." The objectives were to provide a picture of food security services and needs in Saint-Roch; to provide a place for reflection and exchange for stakeholders and residents considering their knowledge of living in poverty; and to mobilize to develop and implement collective structuring projects for the neighborhood. Stakeholders were involved in three major meetings. These stakeholders included local service providers: meals on wheels, collective gardens, community fridge, food distribution, snack supply, soup kitchen, community meals, collective kitchens, educational workshops, mobile kitchen workshops, Christmas baskets, emergency assistance, and institutional, school, or private-sector partners and citizens.

During the first meeting, participants got to know each other. They debriefed around a committee's local food services status report, creating a map showing resources to access food in the neighborhood.

During the second meeting, the participants validated the map data and outlined a consultation to document neighborhood residents' reality and needs about food security. "Sticking to the scientific process" within the framework of a PAR project was seen by the follow-up committee as a strategy to bring more legitimacy to this consultation, particularly with potential donors for resulting projects. The committee set up public consultations through six meetings

Source: Véronique Demers.
Note: (right to left) Élise Groulx – Moisson Québec; Nathalie Lanctot – Cuisine Collective Le Bourg-Joie; Isabelle Bernier – community organizer, CIUSSS-CN; Olivier Martin – YMCA; Caroline Deschesne – Table de quartier l'Engrenage; Ginette Lewis – citizen.

Figure 7.2   Members of the follow-up committee

around food security, using the map of food resources to learn the places people used for food, challenges in accessing healthy food, and ideas for food security. We also used paper and web surveys. The different consultation methods reached 170 people. Of these, 94 attended local community services or lived in the Saint-Roch/Saint-Sauveur neighborhood and had an income of less than $20,000 per year. The committee considered only the latter responses for the consultation analysis.

The consultation identified challenges and barriers to food security (Deschênes and Bernier 2019) as well as various and numerous "dreams" for the neighborhood, such as:

- affordable local public market;
- more accessible collective kitchens;
- food surplus recovery programs;
- more accessible and affordable grocery stores and alternative grocery stores;
- more community gardens and urban agriculture;
- food-processing project to build skills and promote access to affordable meals;
- improved transportation and food delivery; and
- increased public awareness about healthy eating and food prejudices.

The third major meeting allowed participants to design a project for the Saint-Roch neighborhood and submit for funding to implement the proposed initiatives. The community received $225,000 over five years for urban agriculture and food-processing projects and a local market, as part of the Quebec Government's Action Plan for Economic Inclusion and Social Participation.

For me, the CIUSSS-CN CoP was a place to test ideas and "pre-chew reflections" before acting with the follow-up committee. It helped me to clarify who to consult by discussing participant profiles and challenges related to what would emerge from this community portrait; how to consult, by exploring the strengths and limitations of the intended strategies; and how to involve the community at the third major meeting to bring to light all relevant proposals, complementing my community organization strategies. The main issue was how to appropriately use the data from a web questionnaire put online by one committee member on their own initiative. To help me, the COs in the CoP then carefully thought about what data the committee should analyze and why. Lucie came with me to a sub-committee meeting to tackle the methodological rigor issue! Lucie also supervised an undergraduate social work student. The latter volunteered to help with the initial analysis of the consultation results, collaborating with me and the liaison officer for l'Engrenage. This assistance was much appreciated.

As a CO, I already had a concern for methodological rigor. My participation in the CoP has allowed me to develop a more refined knowledge and further develop my "critical eye," which now serves me in other projects, informing how I ask questions with an awareness of possible biases.

CIUSSS-CN COMMUNITY OF PRACTICE AS A MEANS OF SUPPORTING COMMUNITY ORGANIZATIONS USING PARTICIPATORY ACTION RESEARCH: A CONCEPTUAL MODEL

Based on the CIUSSS-CN case and a new CoP in the Chaudière-Appalaches region,[7] we identify the characteristics of CoPs that support PAR for intervention purposes.

Why a Community of Practice?

A CoP is a place where COs can share their PAR experiences and thus learn from and support each other. They discuss the challenges they encounter, the strengths they draw on, and the tips they develop. They talk about the reality of community organization practice within their organization. They ask each other questions and share advice on processes, tools for collecting and analyzing data, and participatory governance. They reflect on the strengths and limitations of their ongoing PAR projects. Some of us saw an analogy with co-development groups (Payette and Champagne 1997); others with CoPs or learning communities (Wenger 1998).

The idea is for the COs to formulate and bring forward their expertise, to see how PAR approaches feed into their community organization practices, rooted in a tradition of diagnosis, content analysis, community portraits, and evaluations. The idea is not to pretend to have the same methodological knowledge as a trained professional researcher. Instead, it is to acquire the tools to play a leadership role in a targeted PAR project. It is to produce knowledge through a scientific research process (or be inspired by it) that also draws on the community's experience and their own as interveners and is accepted as rigorous by decision makers and elected officials. In doing so, the CoP's participants put their finger on the knowledge they hold, create, or need to access, related to the social issue explored and research methods used (see Box 7.1).

BOX 7.1 OBJECTIVES OF A PARTICIPATORY ACTION RESEARCH COMMUNITY OF PRACTICE

- Creating a mutual desire to use PAR.
- Taking collective ownership of the scientific protocol associated with the research process.
- Developing approaches and tools specific to PAR and sharing them.
- Collectively researching solutions to difficulties encountered.
- Developing a CO's team or network of PAR expertise.
- Building bridges between community organizing and PAR practices.

Who Participates in a Participatory Action Research Community of Practice? Roles and Inputs

Although a PAR project involves many stakeholders and citizens, the CIUSSS-CN CoP targets COs as participants.

The PAR CoP expects the COs to be actively involved. It is not a place of passive training in research methodology, akin to "banking training" (Freire 1973b). Participants share their achievements and difficulties. They prepare questions and propose solutions to problems. The CoP is not there to provide a formula for success but rather help COs progress in their work while applying scientific rigor. As such, they help them identify the strengths and weaknesses of a PAR project from a CO perspective. This process helps better equip participants to defend their projects and present them to the public.

Two examples of exchanges come to mind: in discussing the food security project (see above), where several enthusiastic citizens participated in an online survey, someone asked the question: who were the people who participated, and are all those voices applicable? Since the aim was to consider the experience of people who lived in poverty, there followed an exchange on what it means to be "living in poverty." Who, in this community, lives in poverty? What would be the relevant level of income if we see poverty as a lack of money? What about households with children? Which voices should the PAR team consider – the ones coming from people living in the targeted area, or people passing through or using local community services organizations? At the end of the deliberation, participants proposed to include only people living or using community services in the neighborhood, with an income of $20,000 or less (i.e., a little higher than the market basket measure for a single person at that time) even if it meant excluding the responses, per se, of some living in poverty. The second example relates to exchange around the idea of developing a "sandwich-board questionnaire" as an initiative used to get people's attention (a PAR project facilitated by Marie-Jade Gagnon). A person would walk around the local parks, street parties, and commercial areas carrying a questionnaire on a sandwich board lit up by LED lamps. The ideas exchange was around the purpose of data collection. Could it serve to showcase different types of expertise and knowledge, in this case the manual skills of the citizens involved in the PAR team, who had proposed this idea and were willing to build the questionnaire board? What was the place of pleasure and play in research? Could it be a way to mobilize a diversity of people in the neighborhood and catch their interest? Could it be a way of initiating an exchange with the participants, as they would see the sum of answers? Is the aim of a questionnaire only to compile answers or also to provoke collective reflection? As the discussion unfolded, it became clear that gathering information is not merely a matter of using a conventional research process. It is also about mobilizing while taking rigor into account.

Many other questions raised in this CoP notably related to the nature of the citizen participation: which people – only those with first-hand experience of the phenomena explored or those interested in the improvement of their community, regardless of their status? How does this citizen participation manifest itself – as voices in data gathering, by involvement in the knowledge production process, in analysis, or in development of action plans resulting from projects? Lyne's project cited earlier is an excellent example of involvement as voices and in the PAR process, analysis, action plan development, and sharing results.

A professional researcher also participates in the CIUSSS-CN (Lucie Gélineau from 2016 to 2020; Marie-Helen Deshaies since then). She provides PAR clarifications if necessary and highlights the methodology's academic rigor. Because COs can rely on their experience, training, or professional skills in community analysis, diagnosis, and reports, her role is mainly to bridge PAR principles and COs' actions. She is a kind of methodology translator. Doing so, she accompanies COs and helps them become confident in PAR, clarifying the motives of using PAR as a tool for intervention and unveiling possibilities and opportunities through questioning: what is the issue here? What are they looking at, and for what purpose? Who is concerned by the matter that COs, a community, or stakeholders want to explore? How to listen or involve people in the process? How to deal with "inconvenient" data – when results go against what the PAR team expects or hopes? How can PAR be an extraordinary lever for citizen mobilization and community organization practice? How can the data be analyzed collectively? How to highlight the seriousness of a PAR endeavor? How to do research *with* people, and how to involve people in the process? The researcher helps the PAR CoP participants look at the strongest and weakest links of their project so they can defend, in the public arena, the results produced while maintaining PAR coherence with their practical community organization objectives. The professional researcher must embrace versatility because each PAR project is associated with a specific research question or hypothesis suggesting a particular approach and one or more methods. She relies on her expertise with PAR's foundations, the scientific realm, sampling, qualitative or quantitative approaches, data collection methods, ethics, analysis strategies, and writing angles. If necessary and requested, she advises on the processes, illustrating examples of projects carried out or supported over the years.

Sometimes, a particular PAR project needs extra support. L. Gélineau offered personalized coaching at crucial moments. She participated in follow-up PAR meetings, re-read tricky results, provided help in formulating the methodological elements of a report, helped with the collective analysis process, and assisted in answering methodological questions during presentations to key knowledge users.

Finally, the professional coordinator's role in the CIUSSS-CN experience (Colette Lavoie (2016–2019); Manon Roy since then) is vital because sessions occur in the workplace during working hours. They defend and promote the CoP as a positive force that widens the scope of social intervention work and contribute to COs' professional development, notably in senior management discussions. The coordinator is also key in mobilizing new members to participate.

In the new Chaudière-Appalaches CoP, experienced graduate students (here Julie Richard as co-author) and research professionals also participate with the researcher, as members of the Collectif de recherche participative sur la pauvreté en milieu rural. The idea is to form a pool of academic expertise for such support. At the participants' request, not only CIUSSS but also COs working in local community organization and other PAR project stakeholders or citizens are engaged in the Chaudière-Appalaches CoP. Participants discuss new issues, notably about power relationships. COs and stakeholders give careful thought to the decision process in PAR projects: should it be by consensus, consent ("I would have chosen otherwise, but as this decision corresponds to the values and intentions of the project, I do consent"), or majority vote? There is not a single answer here.

THE COMMUNITY OF PRACTICE: HOW DOES IT WORK?

The very first meeting of a CoP aims to set shared parameters, vocabulary, and guidelines (see Box 7.2). What is meant by PAR? How can it be a tool for community organization practice? In the CIUSSS-CN, if a new participant arrives, time is taken to recall these parameters at the beginning of their first session. The fact that all the COs are part of the same team with the same professional coordinator also helps share information. We video-recorded the Chaudière-Appalaches PAR CoP parameters for new attendees to view before beginning participation.

BOX 7.2   ELEVEN KEY FACTORS FOR A SUCCESSFUL PARTICIPATORY ACTION RESEARCH COMMUNITY OF PRACTICE

1. Build from a common base: jointly establish a broad outline of PAR.
2. Commit to participate for the long term.
3. Participate as necessary and when possible; flexibility is required.
4. Be actively engaged in a PAR process.
5. Use the support of the professional coordinator.
6. Ensure the CO's participation in the CoP is recognized by their institution as part of their workload.
7. Draw on other people's experience and what has been done before.
8. Realize that there is no one recipe for research success; the process is about deliberation in terms of rigor (trustworthiness).
9. Dare to share experience (positive and negative), questions, and doubts.
10. Have an academic researcher who is willing to recognize multiple knowledge forms and provide support.
11. Establish a collaboration/participation agreement.

Each session starts with everyone sitting in a circle, briefly sharing news and feelings that might influence their participation. This introduction helps us contextualize people's participation and offer space for emotions. Then, there is a swift identification of participants' needs and their urgency. Considering time limits to ensure equitable participation, the first person takes the floor, discussing how their PAR project is progressing. The other participants communicate their experiences and strategies they have developed to deal with similar challenges or raise questions to enrich the situation's analysis. The professional researcher highlights any issues around the PAR process or the research methodology or ethics, drawing on works such as Guba (1982), Lincoln (1995), or the Centre for Social Justice and Community Action and National Co-ordinating Centre for Public Engagement (2012). The facilitator invites each participant to present the status of their PAR work and ask any remaining questions before a closing round, where each person shares how they are now feeling, briefly evaluating the meeting if necessary.

Facilitating meetings is necessary. In some sessions of the CIUSSS-CN PAR CoP, the coordinator facilitated. Other times, participants rotated as facilitators. In the Chaudière-Appalaches CoP, it's the Collectif de recherche participative sur la pauvreté en milieu rural which provides facilitation.

The CoP is sought after, but attendance is limited to participants who have current or completed PAR projects. CIUSSS-CN participants attend in person,[8] in a meeting room of one of the many organizations facilities. However, in the Chaudière-Appalaches region, due to the size of the territory and its rural characteristics, a virtual community with video-conferencing is used, with occasional face-to-face meetings at the offices of one of the participating organizations.

The participants plan four to five meetings a year, or as needed. Attendance is not required at every meeting, allowing flexibility for practitioners' constraints. At the CIUSSS-CN CoP meetings, three to five COs (not always the same ones) attend, along with occasionally the professional coordinator and always a professional researcher. The Chaudière-Appalaches community has around eight to ten participants plus the facilitator. The meetings last two to three hours.

CHALLENGES AND OPPORTUNITIES USING PARTICIPATORY ACTION RESEARCH AS COMMUNITY ORGANIZATIONS

The CIUSSS-CN CoP allowed us to pinpoint challenges and issues using PAR as an intervention method in CO practice. We bring three of them to your attention.

Participatory Action Research and Epistemic Justice

For us, the PAR process used as CO practice is at the heart of epistemic justice debates. Epistemology refers to the relationship that human beings have with reality, and the way they name it, understand it, and thus produce knowledge. Epistemic justice questions that scientific research, especially when following the dominant patriarchal and colonial models developed in the Global North (i.e., Mies and Shiva 1993; Tandon 2000), is the benchmark of knowledge. Epistemic injustice "is a wrong done to someone specifically in their capacity as a knower. Testimonial injustice occurs when prejudice causes a hearer to give a deflated level of credibility to a speaker's world" (Fricker 2007: 1). In our own understanding, the search for greater epistemic justice thus requires a recognition of non-academic knowledge and expertise in this grasp of the world and different social realities. It should consider the experiential knowledge of the people concerned, practical know-how, indigenous knowledge, and even aesthetic knowledge, which can also teach us about the nature and intelligence of these realities (Gélineau and Mailloux 2002; Visvanathan 2016). In addition, "Hermeneutical injustice occurs at a prior stage, when a gap in collective interpretive resources puts someone at an unfair disadvantage when it comes to making sense of their social experience" (Fricker 2007: 1).

One way to ensure greater epistemic justice, for us, might be to democratize scientific production, i.e., that non-academic actors learn, use, and feed into the methods of scientific output and its vocabulary to be part of public debates and thus have their contributions recognized as legitimate. PAR in the broad sense might facilitate epistemic justice, mainly because it examines the control of knowledge production by university elites in the Global North and the need to break this monopoly (Hall et al. 1982). PAR is also open to other forms of knowledge, including WITH[9] research (Groupe de recherche Quart monde-Université 1999; Vaatavec 2014) involving as co-researcher those first concerned by the issues at stake. Another way to look at epistemic injustice might be to think about what is seen as worthwhile to be "researched." PAR as a CO practice allows for micro-research to deal with themes often overlooked by the academic community or targeted governmental scientific funding because they are too specific, micro-local, linked to a particular action, and thus judged as pointless. The search for greater epistemic justice thus requires us to rethink knowledge production modes. In this way, we can achieve a more richly informed understanding of the world.

However, as we continue our PAR CO CoP, we are now questioning how PAR can balance epistemic injustices. It might not be so simple! Our CoP highlights *a tension between the two forms of epistemic injustice: testimonial and hermeneutical*. Does addressing one form mean denying the other? On the one hand, the CoP makes it possible to appropriate scientific knowledge production methods. COs understand the basics, put them into practice, and involve citizens in the process. But in doing so, PAR should not make it appear that practical and people knowledge are invalid. How can these knowledges support and feed into the research question or hypothesis, offer tools, and, above all, strengthen the analysis and interpretation of the results? Mastering scientific tools helps to ensure a rigorous approach. It promotes the circulation of PAR results in a culture of evidence-informed decision making. Yet, it is also crucial to openly acknowledge that a PAR process and the results presented in the public arena incorporate a diversity of voices and knowledge sources. Therefore, we believe PAR CoPs must not value scientific knowledge to the detriment of other forms of expertise in these CoPs and should see different knowledge forms as complementary.

Instrumentalizing Participatory Action Research and Communities of Practice

Having access to professional researchers in a CoP might be seen as a calculated way to capture institutional stakeholders' interest, reassure financial partners, and give more credibility to the results when dealing with decision makers or elected officials. A fine line exists between developing people's capacity to produce significant and committed knowledge outside academia and instrumentalizing PAR to push a particular agenda in terms of political action, service provision, or public health objectives. Institutions might see PAR as a way to mobilize a community to reach predefined, institutional goals. Hence the importance of taking a critical and comprehensive look at PAR when using it as an intervention tool, particularly in the context of a CoP residing within a public health and social services institution. PAR is a powerful process because it shows ways to connect with people and mobilize their power of action. A PAR team must discern what the ultimate goal is and who is responsible for it. A CoP should address this issue.

The Blind Spots of Ethical Issues

We must also explore, document, and mark out *ethical issues* when COs use PAR and when academic researchers accompany them. Are we talking about intervention or research? Should PAR projects be submitted to the research ethics committee or the intervention ethics committee? Where does free and informed consent lie in intervention? Because the CIUSSS-CN COs use PAR for intervention purposes, they submit them only to intervention-related ethics committees when deemed relevant. At present, professional researchers who accompany the CIUSSS-CN CoP are not required to participate in their institution's ethics committee as they act only as support; the PAR projects are intervention-focused (Snider and Stroup 1997), funded and carried out by outside institutions. However, COs and their PAR team are by no means exempt from classic ethics considerations. PAR CoPs also raise issues around intellectual property and how to recognize the contribution of their members in the tools developed or analysis of data.

CONCLUSION

CoPs are a way for COs, who use PAR as an intervention strategy, to negotiate the tension between testimonial and hermeneutical epistemic injustices. The former refers to the lack of recognition by authorities of the value of non-academic knowledge. The latter relates to the informal ban, for community members who are not professional researchers, on using social research methods independently and of their own free will. COs find in a PAR CoP a safe space to question and master scientific modes of knowledge production so that they can autonomously explore issues of importance to them and their communities. A CoP also allows them to analyze and reaffirm the value of practical knowledge and life expertise in understanding complex social realities. Furthermore, the CoP facilitates reflection on how community organizations conduct community analyses, in particular, from the point of view of rigor, while at the same time giving shape to and calling on another form of knowledge.

Nevertheless, institutional CoPs do have their limitations. First, the risk of instrumentalization remains a reality in institutions where COs use PAR as an intervention practice. An institution's strategic aims might supersede the goals of giving voice to a community's concerns and making a real contribution to reducing social and epistemic inequalities. Second, institutional recognition of the value of these practices still falls short; however, CoP can play a role here, given that they are themselves institutional!

There are several ways to strengthen these practices. It would be interesting to observe these PAR CoPs in a variety of settings (e.g., other CIUSSSs in the province, urban versus rural settings, amongst autonomous community organizations) to address the following questions:

- How might we better understand the tension between recognizing the value of other knowledge (testimonial justice) and the appropriation of the means to produce scientific knowledge (hermeneutical justice), thus allowing us to enrich the theoretical framework empirically?
- In what way do CoPs contribute to knowledge production in more egalitarian relationships, and thus contribute to the theorization of autonomous PAR without professional researchers, as well as contribute to the theorization of critical community organization practices?

- In what way do CoPs support the emergence of hybrid criteria of rigor and ethical guidelines that integrate research and intervention, and thus contribute to the theorization of the co-production (or co-construction) of knowledge and CO practice?

Furthermore, CoP provides the impetus for consideration of upstream possibilities:

- How future COs could be trained in the use of PAR for interventions as part of their initial training (and what the advantage would be of doing so) – and thus contribute to the theorization of community organization intervention practices and training.
- How future researchers could be trained in a support role – and thus contribute to a reflection on the university's role in community service and communities' power in knowledge production.
- How to strengthen practical and academic environments to support PAR as an OC's intervention method, and thus contribute to the development of research culture in practice settings and community environments, and university recognition of other forms of knowledge.

ACKNOWLEDGMENTS

We want to acknowledge Andrée-Anne Roy-Ross (community organizer, CIUSSS-CN), Colette Lavoie and Manon Roy (professional coordinators and community organizers, CIUSSS-CN) for their participation in the first ideations, leading to the first communications at the origin of this chapter; the Université du Québec à Rimouski for their translation fund assistance; Helen Kinsella for her translation of the initial manuscript, and Louise G., Chantal B., Daniel B., Philippe L., and Annie M. for their kind hospitality.

NOTES

1. In Canada, health and social services are provincial jurisdictions. Each provincial health and social services system has distinctive characteristics and modes of operation.
2. The use of the term citizen aims to highlight people's capacity to act and take in hand their collective future, be it in terms of well-being or political actions, i.e., to work on structural dimensions promoting a "living together" (*un Vivre ensemble*).
3. "Since 1988, the Regroupement Québécois des Intervenantes et Intervenants en Action Communautaire (Grouping of community action workers) en CISSS et CIUSS (RQIIAC) has been bringing together, on a voluntary basis, community organization practitioners from health and social services institutions in all regions of Quebec" (RQIIAC 2021).
4. In French: Centre intégré universitaire de santé et de services sociaux de la capitale nationale.
5. For more details on results, methods, and processes, see Gilbert et al. (2017).
6. Some parts come from the consultation report Deschênes and Bernier (2019).
7. The Chaudière-Appalaches region is one of the territories served by the mission of the Université du Québec à Rimouski. It covers just over 15,000 square kilometers, with a population of nearly 429,000 inhabitants in a mainly rural territory, comprising 136 municipalities (Affaires municipales et habitation Québec 2020: 11). There are marked differences between the advantaged and disadvantaged areas, revealing an increase in social inequalities reflected in social health inequalities (CISSS-CA 2021).
8. In 2020–2021 the sessions were all virtual because of public health measures due to the COVID epidemic.

9.   People living in poverty are engaged in the research process as co-researchers. The research team recognizes them as "experts" regarding their experience of poverty, as bearers of a legitimate form of knowledge (in a perspective of epistemic justice). We usually capitalize it in French (la recherche AVEC), though, to clarify the notion, we made it an acronym in one of our research projects. It stands for: "Agir et Vivre Ensemble le Changement."

REFERENCES

Affaires municipales et habitation Québec. 2020. *Région Administrative 12: Chaudière-Appalaches*: 11.

Altpeter, Mary, Janice H. Schopler, Maeda J. Galinsky, and Joan Pennell. 1999. "Participatory Research as Social Work Practice." *Journal of Progressive Human Services* June. doi: 10.1300/J059v10n02_04.

Baillergeau, Évelyne. 2007. "Organisation Communautaire et Pratique Professionnelle au Québec. Nouveaux Défis, Nouvelles Problématiques." *Informations Sociales* 143(7): 98–107.

Barnsley, Jan and Diana Ellis. 1992. *Research for Change. Participatory Action Research for Community Groups*. Vancouver: Women's Research Centre.

Bortoletto, Nico. 2017. "Participatory Action Research in Local Development: An Opportunity for Social Work." *European Journal of Social Work* 20(4): 484–496.

Bourque, Denis. 2009. "La Création des CSSS et Certains de Ses Effets sur les Pratiques des Travailleuses Sociales." *Intervention, la revue de l'Ordre des travailleurs sociaux et des thérapeutes conjugaux et familiaux du Québec* 131: 161–171.

Bourque, Denis and René Lachapelle. 2010. *Service Public, Participation et Citoyenneté. L'organisation Communautaire en CSSS*. Québec: Presses de l'Université du Québec.

Branom, Christina. 2012. "Community-Based Participatory Research as a Social Work Research and Intervention Approach." *Journal of Community Practice* 20(3): 260–273.

Centre for Social Justice and Community Action and National Co-ordinating Centre for Public Engagement. 2012. *Community-Based Participatory Research: A Guide to Ethical Principles and Practice*. Bristol: Durham University, Centre for Social Justice and Community Action.

CISSS-CA (Centre intégré de santé et de services sociaux de Chaudière-Appalaches). 2021. *3e Caractérisation de nos communautés locales de Chaudière-Appalaches: chemin parcouru depuis 2006, Chaudière-Appalaches*. Ste-Marie: Direction santé publique. www.cisssca.com/accueil/

CIUSSS de la Capitale Nationale. 2021. "Organisation Communautaire." Québec. www.ciusss-capitalenationale.gouv.qc.ca/oc

Deschênes, Caroline and Isabel Bernier. 2019. "La Sécurité Alimentaire dans le Quartier Saint-Roch. De l'Individuel au Collectif ! Portrait de la Démarche en Sécurité Alimentaire, Portrait du Quartier Saint-Roch, Rapport des Consultations Citoyennes." Québec: Table de quartier l'Engrenage de Saint-Roch; CIUSSS de la Capitale-Nationale.

Doré, Gérald. 1985. "L'organisation Communautaire: Définition et Paradigme." *Service Social* 34(2–3): 210–223.

Engrenage St-Roch. 2021. "L'Engrenage, C'est Quoi?" Québec: Engrenage St-Roch. www.engrenagestroch.org/a-propos/

Fals Borda, Orlando and Muhammad Anisur Rahman. 1991. *Action and Knowledge: Breaking the Monopoly with Participatory Action Research*. New York: Rowman and Littlefield.

Finn, Janet L. 1994. "The Promise of Participatory Research." *Journal of Progressive Human Services* 5(2): 25–42.

Freire, Paulo. 1973a. "Research Methods: Excerpts from a Seminar Conducted at the Institute of Adult Education – University of Dar Es Salaam." Dar es Salaam: Institute of Adult Education, University of Dar es Salaam.

Freire, Paulo. 1973b. "Extension or Communication." In *Education for Critical Consciousness*. New York: Seabury Press, pp. 91–165.

Freudenberg, Nicholas, Emily Franzosa, Janice Chisholm, and Kimberly Libman. 2015. "New Approaches for Moving Upstream: How State and Local Health Departments Can Transform Practice to Reduce Health Inequalities." *Health Education and Behavior* 42(1S): 46S–56S.

Fricker, Miranda. 2007. *Epistemic Injustice: Power and the Ethics of Knowing*. Oxford: Oxford Scholarship.

Gay, Lorraine. 2006. "Les Fusions De CLSC: Chronique d'une Mort Annoncée – Marche Avant Vers le Passé." *Histoire du système de santé québécois*. Québec: Clinique communautaire de Pointe-Saint-Charles. https://ccpsc.qc.ca/fr/node/1814

Gélineau, Lucie. 2019. "Communauté de Pratique en Recherche Participative." St-Pierre de Broughton: Regroupement québécois des intervenantes et intervenants en action communautaire – RQIIAC-12 Chaudière-Appalaches.

Gélineau, Lucie and Carole Mailloux. 2002. "La Recherche Participative, Un Nouveau Lieu de Dialogue Interdisciplinaire ?" In *L'interdisciplinarité et la Recherche Sociale Appliquée, Réflexions sur des Expériences en Cours*, edited by Lucie Gélineau. Québec: Chaire d'étude Claire Bonenfant sur la condition des femmes.

Gélineau, Lucie, Ariane Vinet-Bonin, and Marie Gervais. 2009. "Quand Recherche et Proximité Se Conjuguent. Réflexions Autour de l'Émergence d'une Culture de Recherche dans les Organismes de Santé et de Services Sociaux." In *Proximités: Lien, Accompagnement et Soin*, edited by Michèle Clément, Lucie Gélineau, and Anaïs-Marie McKay. Québec: Presses de l'Université du Québec, pp. 303–314.

Gélineau, Lucie, Émilie Dufour, and Micheline Bélisle. 2012. "Quand Recherche-Action Participative et Pratiques AVEC Se Conjuguent: Enjeux de Définition et d'équilibre des Savoirs." *Recherches qualitatives, Hors-série "Les Actes"* 13: 35–54.

Gélineau, Lucie, Sophie Dupéré, Michael Rousseau, Julie Richard, and Simone Lavoie-Racine. 2019. "L'expérience d'Intervenant. E.S. Sociaux Qui Mènent des Recherches Participatives Comme Pratique d'Intervention Sociale: Une Revue de la Portée. Poster." Paper presented at the ACFTS, Vancouver.

Gilbert, Lyne, Nathalie Belley, Sylvana Moussavoult, Anne-Félicitée Ngueng-Nsasso, Marjolaine Trudel, Marie-Pier Trudel, and Kate Mc Brearty. 2017. "L'espace Jean-Baptiste Duberger Cœur De Duberger Sud: Ensemble, Créons un Milieu de Vie Qui Nous Ressemble!" https://numerique.banq.qc .ca/patrimoine/details/52327/3208409?docref=uzLzmOLwcVMpIHOLkJQmUQ

Gilbert, Lyne, Marie Jade Gagnon, Isabelle Bernier, Nathalie Bouchard, Andrée-Ann Roy-Ross, Colette Lavoie, and Lucie Gélineau. 2019. "Recherche-Action Participative et Organisation Communautaire: L'expérience d'une Communauté de Pratique au CIUSSS de la Capitale-Nationale." Lévis: Midi-Rap.

Gouin, Rachel R., Karen Cocq, and Samantha McGavin. 2011. "Feminist Participatory Research in a Social Justice Organization." *Action Research* 9(3): 261–281.

Groupe de recherche Quart monde-Université. 1999. *Le Croisement des Savoirs. Quand Le Quart Monde et L'université Pensent Ensemble*. Paris: Les éditions de l'atelier et Quart monde.

Guba, Egon G. 1982. "Criteria for Assessing the Trustworthiness of Naturalistic Inquiries." *ECTJ* 29(2): 75–91.

Hall, Budd, Arthur Gillette, and Rajesh Tandon, eds. 1982. *Creating Knowledge: A Monopoly?*, Vol. 1. New Delhi: PRIA – Society for Participatory Research in India.

Hardwick, Louise and Aidan Worsley. 2011. "The Invisibility of Practitioner Research." *Practice* 23(3): 135–146.

Healy, Karen. 2001. "Participatory Action Research and Social Work: A Critical Appraisal." *International Social Work* 44(1): 93–105.

Hébert, Guillaume, Jennie-Laure Sully, and Minh Nguyen. 2017. "Rapport de Recherche. L'allocation des Ressources pour la Santé et les Services Sociaux au Québec: État de la Situation et Propositions Alternatives." Montréal: Institut de recherche et d'informations socioéconomiques.

Hick, Steven. 1997. "Participatory Research: An Approach for Structural Social Workers." *Journal of Progressive Human Services* 8(2): 63–78.

Kingori, J. and C. Angela Ntulo. 2011. "Building Capacity of Local Governments, Service Users and Carers to Scale Up Provision for Community Mental Health Services in Africa: A Case Study of Kenya and Uganda." *Ethnicity and Inequalities in Health and Social Care* 4(2): 53–59.

Lachapelle, René. 2017. "Chapitre Vi. Travail Social et Métiers du Développement Territorial au Québec et en France." In *Les Nouvelles Dynamiques du Développement Social*. Nîmes: Champ social, pp. 159–185.

Lachapelle, René and RQIIAC. 2010. *Pratiques d'Organisation Communautaire en CSSS. Cadre de Référence du Rqiiac.* Québec: Presses de l'Université du Québec.

Lavoie, Jocelyne and Jean Panet-Raymond. 2014. *La Pratique de l'Action Communautaire.* Montréal: Presses de l'université du Québec.

Lincoln, Yvonna S. 1995. "Emerging Criteria for Quality in Qualitative and Interpretive Research." *Qualitative Inquiry* 1: 275–289.

McKinnon, Eddie. 2013. *Using Evidence for Advocacy and Resistance in Early Years Services: Exploring the Pen Green Research Approach.* London: Routledge.

Mies, Maria and Vandana Shiva. 1993. *Ecofeminism.* London: Zed Books.

Minkler, Meredith and Nina Wallerstein. 2008. *Community-Based Participatory Research for Health. From Process to Outcomes.* San Francisco: John Wiley and Sons.

Ninacs, William A. 2008. *Empowerment et Intervention. Développement de la Capacité D'agir et de la Solidarité.* Québec: Presses de l'Université Laval.

Parent, Andrée-Anne, Michel O'Neill, Bernard Roy, and Paule Simard. 2012. "Entre Santé Publique et Organisation Communautaire: Points de Convergence et de Divergence Autour du Développement des Communautés au Québec. Perspectives Interdisciplinaires sur la Santé et le Mieux-Être." 43(2): 67–90.

Payette, Adrien and Claude Champagne. 1997. *Le Groupe de Codéveloppement Professionnel.* Québec: PUQ.

PDGA. 2018. *Cadre de Référence en Organisation Communautaire du Centre Intégré Universitaire de Santé et de Services Sociaux de la Capitale-Nationale.*

Rahnema, Majid. 1990. "Participatory Action Research: The 'Last Temptation of Saint' Development." *Alternatives* 15(2): 199–226.

RQIIAC. 2020. *Pratiques d'Organisation Communautaire dans les Établissements de Santé et de Services Sociaux au Québec. Édition Actualisée. Cadre de Référence du RQIIAC.* Québec: Presses de l'Université du Québec.

RQIIAC. 2021. "Qu'Est-Ce Que le RQIIAC?" https://rqiiac.qc.ca/regroupement/

Sen, Amartya. 2012. *L'Idée De Justice.* Paris: Flammarion.

Snider, Dixie E., Jr. and Donna F. Stroup. 1997. "Defining Research When It Comes to Public Health." *Public Health Reports* 112(1): 29–32.

Sohng, Sung Sil Lee. 1996. "Participatory Research and Community Organizers." *Journal of Sociology and Social Welfare* 23(4): 77–97.

Sparr, Pamela. 1998. "Looking through the Telescope from Both Ends: Participatory Research and Action as a Feminist Political Practice." *Women's Studies Quarterly* 26(3/4): 68–76.

Stoecker, Randy. 2005. *Research Methods for Community Change.* Thousand Oaks, CA: Sage.

Swantz Bralup, Marja-Liisa. 1975. "The Role of Participant Research in Development." *Geografiska Annaler. Series B, Human Geography* 57(2): 119–127.

Table de concertation Duberger-Les Saules. 2021. "Qui Sommes-Nous ? Table de Concertation Duberger-Les Saules." Québec. https://concertationdls.com/qui-sommes-nous/

Tandon, Rajesh, ed. 2000. *Participatory Research: Revisiting the Roots.* New Delhi: Mosaic Books.

Vaatavec, Collectif. 2014. *L'AVEC, Pour Faire Ensemble. Un Guide de Pratiques, de Réflexions et d'outils.* Québec: Collectif pour un Québec sans pauvreté.

Visvanathan, Shiv. 2016. "La Quête De Justice Cognitive [The Search for Cognitive Justice]." In *Justice Cognitive, Libre Accès et Savoirs Locaux. Pour Une Science Ouverte Juste, au Service du Développement Local Durable*, edited by Florence Piron, Samuel Regulus, and Marie Sophie Dibounje Madiba. Québec: Éditions science et bien commun.

Wadsworth, Yoland. 2016. *Do It Yourself Social Research.* London: Routledge.

Wenger, Etienne. 1998. *Communities of Practice: Learning, Meaning, and Identity.* Cambridge: Cambridge University Press.

8. The centrality of storytelling at the nexus of academia and community organizing in rural Kentucky

Nicole Breazeale, Dana Beasley-Brown, Samantha Johnson, and Alexa Hatcher

To do lasting, impactful, critical community development (CD) work requires democratized knowledge production with those directly affected by and invested in the issues at hand. Community participatory action research (CPAR) can help with this. Similarly, for CPAR to be valuable and result in structural change, it needs to be embedded in critical CD work. These two practices need each other. But what methods and frameworks get us there? And is it possible to do this work in rural America, where open dialogue about structural inequality has been squashed? Feelings of rural invisibility and powerlessness in the wake of contemporary national conversations make the situation even more challenging. What spaces hold possibility for critical reflection and action? What partnerships are necessary to bring together the right people and knowledge bases? With what issues do we start? And how must our pedagogy and praxis be adapted to fit the rural American context of today?

This chapter highlights two cases of how teaching, research, and community organizing were combined at the nexus of CPAR and critical CD. Importantly, this work was done within the context of a regional college, where the boundary between "student" and "community member" disappears. The assumption that "college students" have privilege and the "community members" they partner with on PAR projects are marginalized also falls away here; many of the students at community colleges and regional public universities have marginalized identities. Thus, CPAR projects that involve collaborations between these students and organizers who are working to combat local community problems can be transformative – especially when narrative techniques are used to explore and build shared knowledge that motivates action (critical consciousness). Systemic change is possible when elements of popular education and organizing are combined over time.

Storytelling was key to our success in combining CPAR and critical CD, and it is also central to analyzing this work and writing this chapter. In what follows, we begin by describing the theoretical and pedagogical roots of the collaborative work, starting with our "origin story" of how we first came to understand, conceptualize, and practice CD and PAR. The chapter then describes the two academic-community projects and how they developed over time, moving between theory and practice to describe the approaches that came to define these partnerships as we worked towards long-term social change. We assess the community and individual impacts of each initiative, but also highlight the lessons learned and missed opportunities for making these projects even more impactful.

The chapter concludes by returning to the questions at the beginning of the introduction and lifting up six points: (1) CPAR and critical CD *can* be done in rural America and it is more important than ever that we try; (2) community colleges and regional universities are a crucial site for this collaborative work; (3) partnerships between social scientists, working-class "students," and organizers can lead to transformative change if the right skillsets are available; (4) addressing barriers to basic needs, such as food or housing, is a valuable starting point for such collaborations; (5) storytelling as a method and a social practice is key to bridging CPAR and critical CD; and (6) there is a need to redefine what constitutes "success" of such social change efforts in different contexts. In rural communities in the American South, effectively opening up civic spaces where people feel seen and can talk publicly about urgent social issues and learn to speak truth to power in ways that resonate *is* a noteworthy "success" in and of itself. It is also a critical precursor to growing the power and potential of rural organizing to change structural conditions of oppression over time.

BACKGROUND CONTEXT

While Kentucky ranks 48th in the nation for poverty, that is not the full story. In rural South Central Kentucky, there is a deep sense of connection and community pride. Multi-generational gatherings are common and neighbors watch out for each other's kids. When one family has been blessed with an abundance of green beans from their garden, they share – and if they notice someone is looking skinny, they are sure to be sent home with leftover pie. This strong sense of place and deep-rooted identity provide important protective factors.

This part of Kentucky has historically been an important agricultural and industrial hub, but as the state transitioned away from burley tobacco production and factories moved abroad, the rural economy changed in important ways. Overall, job growth in rural Kentucky has been stagnant, meaning labor force participation is much lower than the national average (Kentucky Center for Economic Policy 2018). Flat wages combine with inequities based on race and gender to make things particularly challenging for women and people of color who are living and working here (6 percent of the region's population are African American, 4 percent self-categorized as two or more races, and 2 percent are Hispanic (Bowling Green Area Chamber of Commerce 2021)).

As a result, many households struggle mightily to meet their basic needs. One in five children in Kentucky are food insecure, and rates in South Central Kentucky are slightly higher (Feeding America 2021). According to Bush (2018), 12 percent of the total housing stock is mobile homes, which is more than double the national average. Thirty-two percent of housing units are renter-occupied and affordability for these households has become a major issue since the recession of 2009–2012. Even before the COVID-19 pandemic, roughly half of renters paid more than 30 percent of their income on rent. Evidence also suggests that eviction rates are higher than national averages. Access to reliable transportation and quality health care are additional obstacles facing residents in South Central Kentucky.

Rural leaders try their best to address these sensitive and challenging issues. Rooted in values of community care, residents are strongly committed to rural prosperity. At the same time, deep polarization and long memories in tight-knit Kentucky communities discourage open dialogue while distrust and stereotypes of "outsiders" prevent authentic engagement with knowledge producers in the "big city," making it difficult to overcome knowledge and resource gaps.

Despite its moderate size and population, Kentucky has a rich tapestry of community colleges and regional comprehensive universities. There are 16 community colleges with 70 physical locations and six regional comprehensives, each of which has a handful of satellite locations – most in remote areas. Many of these are small campuses, with classes taught in a single building. The American Association of State Colleges and Universities (2002) argues that such institutions have an important role to play as "stewards of place." In other words, beyond their education and degree-granting function, they serve as anchor institutions that promote democratic values and utilize localized knowledge production to help communities confront their problems. Not all community colleges and regional comprehensives embrace this role, but there is significant potential for these institutions to help unlock public deliberation in rural America – and to develop generations of local leaders with the skills, knowledge, and motivation to address the root causes of local problems.

Western Kentucky University (Glasgow campus) is the institution of higher education featured in this chapter. Located in the heart of Barren County, Kentucky (population: 44,000), this commuter campus historically served 2,000 students. Most of the institution's students are non-traditional. Students often complete an entire BA degree by taking back-to-back classes (in three-hour blocks) on one or two days a week, working full-time jobs when they are not in class. Class sizes are small, ranging from 8 to 30 students, and students form close relationships with the handful of faculty who teach most of their classes. Few students leave their community after they complete their degrees.

THE ORIGIN STORY: THEORETICAL AND PEDAGOGICAL ROOTS OF NICOLE AND DANA'S COLLABORATIVE WORK

Our first case study describes how systemic change took place in Barren County as a result of Nicole and her regional college students partnering with Dana on a housing organizing project. Both Dana and Nicole had worked with other university/community partners in the past, but they agreed that this collaboration led to success in ways that were different. They committed to learn from each other and figure out what made this work successful and what could be replicated. In their individual stories, they each described how they came to understand and practice PAR and/or CD. At the point that they came together on this project, they each needed something: Dana was looking for specific CPAR skills and Nicole was seeking to assist with critical CD and learn how to make change happen. Together, they identified and discussed the key elements of the collaboration that led to success.

Dana Beasley-Brown's Story (Community Organizer and Leader, Housing and Homeless Coalition of South Central Kentucky)

I was blessed to grow up in the Beasley family. We drove around in a car too small for our family of eight. You could hear it coming from a mile away and smell it hours after we left. We went back-to-school shopping on our living room floor out of trash bags of clothing decades old. I spent too many nights shivering on top of a mattress from the side of the road under layers of sleeping bags, worrying about my family. As a little girl, I resolved that I would never dream big dreams, because poverty is a dream-stealer. To watch my dad work himself to the bone, day in and day out, only to see his dreams get crushed over and over again was too painful. But my mother's tears over her bible lit a fire in me that poverty could not put out. This fire turned into a passion and my life's work to empower our community to remove barriers that keep our families, neighborhoods, and city from thriving.

As a volunteer community organizer for Kentuckians for the Commonwealth (KFTC) in Bowling Green, Kentucky, I worked with families in neighborhoods that looked just like mine growing up. KFTC is a statewide organization that focuses on social change through leadership development of directly impacted people. I went door to door listening to the residents as they shared stories about landlord–tenant issues that were causing disruption in their families and the entire neighborhood. As we looked for solutions to these problems, we learned that in Kentucky, a community has to opt into the state landlord–tenant laws and without these protections your rights are whatever you agreed to in your lease. Slumlords took advantage of this power imbalance and wrote predatory provisions into their leases. To bring our community together, I worked with the neighborhood and other local non-profits and churches to form the Homeless and Housing Coalition of South Central Kentucky (HHCSCK). As the coalition advocated for our city to opt into the statewide protections, we also realized the need to educate tenants on how to identify leases that may lead to unfair evictions or how to avoid getting stuck in dangerous housing that is not up to code. The idea was to create a *Renter's Handbook* and accompanying community-based workshop to educate renters on how to protect themselves when the laws don't do it for them.

After a scan of community assets, we learned about WKU's Alive Center, which offered small grants to support faculty–community collaborations and research. The HHCSCK applied for a grant, which we received. This university grant was important because it provided money and resources to our group, but also because it helped legitimize the project and lend it credibility. Furthermore, it helped us identify other university partners to work with. We partnered with different faculty and students to illustrate and translate the *Handbook* and were eventually connected with Nicole, who was 45 minutes away at WKU-Glasgow.

In seeking to collaborate with Nicole, our PAR needs were very specific. We were looking for a critical sociologist or anthropologist with a deep understanding of structural inequality who knew how to do qualitative research and develop powerful educational curricula. We also needed a partner that had deep respect for the contributions of directly impacted people to inform social change. These values were non-negotiable because marginalized communities in the United States have been exploited and traumatized by faculty and students in the past. They are often wary of people from universities showing up in their spaces. Trust is a foundational principle of community organizing work.

Nicole Breazeale's Story (Sociology Professor, WKU-Glasgow)

As a child growing up in Kentucky, I lived in a stable home but befriended kids without one, raising all sorts of questions for me about social inequality and injustice. At Swarthmore College, I studied political science and education and began to explore these questions. I took a community development class with a "service-learning" assignment and volunteered at a non-profit that provided comprehensive services to homeless people in Philadelphia. I helped with parenting education classes. Borrowing language from the introductory chapter of this volume, this social service approach to homelessness might be characterized as a "low control," "low change" practice of contemporary CD. That same semester, I also volunteered with a second organization which was a collective of homeless people fighting for homeless rights (a "high control," "high change" CD strategy). I provided free babysitting services while members conducted strategy meetings. Through these experiences, I learned how empowering a community organizing (critical CD) model is for those who have been oppressed, excluded, or exploited – and saw how organizing can result in policy change that alters the rules of the game. It also clued me in to the importance of organizing around basic needs.

At the same time, I was also taking education classes and learning about the pedagogy of Brazilian educator Paulo Freire, who offered a critical approach to PAR (CPAR). I co-founded a summer program for adolescent girls and began to practice some of the popular education techniques that we were learning about (including storytelling) with this racially and socially diverse group of girls. Critically reflecting on their own social worlds, the girls designed and performed a community theater piece about what it means to be an adolescent girl. This experience taught me about the value of critical consciousness, or the ability to recognize one's positionality in a power-imbalanced world and take action to change that reality, as a gateway for academic motivation and community leadership development.

Ten years later, as a newly minted sociology PhD, I took my first job as a professor at WKU-Glasgow. I was interested in fostering community engagement in my classes and tried a traditional service-learning assignment, not much different from what I had been assigned in college. I asked my students to volunteer at a poverty-based organization for a few hours a week and then reflect on their experience in the classroom and through journals and assignments. In a class of ten students, two approached me after the introductory session. One was currently homeless and living out of her car; she couldn't fathom how she would pull off weekly volunteer hours. The other was a young, single mom who was receiving services from most of the organizations on my list. Both were extremely hesitant about the assignment.

Importantly, when designing this assignment, I had not considered the class background of my students – and how social class might mediate the experience of service learning (scholarly literature is just beginning to address this question – see Henry 2005; Lee 2005; Yeh 2010). I realized that I needed a different, more empowering approach that worked better for them, and that I needed to think differently about community engagement given that my students are also community members.

In fact, service-learning theory in the United States context does point out a major division between traditional versus critical approaches to the practice – or what is often distinguished as "charity" versus "change" (Morton 1995; Marullo and Edwards 2000). Most service learning in the United States follows a charity model. But even for those who promote a critical or change approach, the focus is on the students as change agents – while the community itself is reduced to an afterthought (Stoecker 2016: 23). To enhance the capacity of communities to affect change themselves, Stoecker argues that faculty and students need to be working alongside marginalized community members that are working to directly combat inequality. In his book, *Liberating Service Learning*, he offers two suggestions for how to proceed with these collaborations. First, Stoecker suggests that PAR be used to inform and support the action agendas of marginalized groups. Second, he highlights the importance of altering the social relations of knowledge production by validating and sharing expert and lay knowledge with all participants – particularly community members.

However, because I was finding that in my case the students were the impacted community members, a different recipe for success was called for. Indeed, PAR and CD, when done with and by students who are themselves members of the community, highlight the critical importance of capacity building and new leadership development within the classroom walls. Given my background and education, I knew I had the skills to train people in conducting rigorous research. I also knew how to use Freireian popular education methods, especially storytelling, to develop critical consciousness and to open people up to deeper social realities. Margaret Ledwith (2011: 63), in her textbook *Community Development: A Critical Approach*, notes the vital importance of Paulo Freire's work to the field of community development, "Storytelling is central to the process of community development, encouraging participation through listening and understanding. Belonging and confidence grow as people are listened to, valued and taken seriously. Autonomy and action gather strength in a collective process of change for equality and justice." In addition to these critical PAR skills, I had 15 weeks of structured class time with marginalized residents and access to space and university connections. I was willing to build an entire class around a project that could foster social change and believed that through this my students could meaningfully learn the content of a social inequalities class, but I wasn't sure how to make this happen.

Herein lies the magic of collaborating with community organizers. The job of a community organizer is to develop the leadership capacity of marginalized groups and to empower them to solve their own problems through collective action. Community organizers know how to "cut" important issues and how to strategize and pursue action that results in timely and important "wins." As I later learned in Szakos and Szakos's (2009) book, *Lessons from the Field*, rural community organizing looks different from its urban counterpart, but it shares the same end goal of capacity building. Many grassroots organizations have local leaders with the skillsets of a community organizer, but few academics bring students along to collaborate with organizers on knowledge-producing projects that further their capacity-building goals. Thus, students miss out on the opportunity to engage hard-to-reach populations in a deeper and more empowering way. Faculty miss out on the opportunity to deepen and improve their theorizing on development, change, and the sociopolitical world. And organizers and their marginalized constituents miss out on the resources and skills of higher education in their work towards a more democratic and just society.

Building on some of Stoecker's insights, my approach to developing PAR projects that contribute to CD reverses the usual order of priority. Rather than beginning with the question, what do students need to learn and how can I facilitate that through a volunteer assignment, I ask: What do *marginalized* groups in the community and their homegrown leaders need? I look for common experiences that many of my students share with these constituents before building a project and class around the collaboration. I then consider the broader community context and begin to layer on additional partners. I also follow the best practices of service learning, including multi-year projects and plenty of critical reflection.

Finally, I want to note that there are many ways of working with story to foster community change. Freire teaches us that public story sharing within marginalized groups is what unlocks critical dialogue and empowers new community leaders to work towards transformative change. I ask: can these same stories be reworked for the purposes of educating the broader public and mobilizing allies? In the collaborations described below, I also used a version of "leadership storytelling" adapted from the work of Marshall Ganz (2009). Ganz's leadership technique involves linking the story of self, the story of us, and the story of now in a way that helps people realize a pressing need and feel motivated to act on it. This is a difficult technique because there can be tremendous challenges associated with coaching this emotional dialogue. But when done correctly, it is very effective at breaking open real community dialogue about pressing local issues. Furthermore, when these stories are written and shared by those who have been historically oppressed, this "claiming of voice" can be transformative, setting people on a pathway for new leadership and lifelong civic engagement.

Adding to Ganz's model, I also bring the tools of a sociologist. I coach people in how to interview effectively and draw out other people's stories (as well as their own) to analyze the commonalities and differences across these stories, and to connect personal troubles to societal problems, just as C. Wright Mills (1959) challenged us to do. These sociological insights that illuminate the workings of power in society can then be integrated into the leadership story, which provides necessary context and helps a general audience develop a more critical understanding of the issues at hand as related to people's specific lived realities. This can advance critical CD because it contributes directly to movement building.

PARTNERSHIP AT THE NEXUS OF CRITICAL PARTICIPATORY ACTION RESEARCH AND COMMUNITY DEVELOPMENT: HOUSING INSECURITY

When Dana and Nicole met, they did so as professionals, but also as parents and care takers without enough time or resources to fully do the work they each dreamed of doing. Together, their community–university partnership overcame these limitations and opened the door for systemic change in Barren County. It was not a case of a class that learned about theories of PAR and CD, but rather a class that underwent a collective process of what Freire (1970/1993) calls *conscientization* (or critical consciousness) and put reflection into action to solve the issue of housing inequality in their own community.

After many conversations, Dana and Nicole agreed on a plan of work for the semester. Nicole's social inequalities class would interview a handful of local residents to gather their stories and their experience with housing insecurity. They would then develop and pilot a participatory community workshop that introduces residents to the *Renter's Handbook* and opens up a community conversation about positive solutions to this problem. Nicole's research methods class would develop a pre-test and post-test for the workshop participants to evaluate its impact and improve the curriculum.

Dana and Nicole built on their different skillsets to equip students to do research and develop and facilitate this type of workshop. The key PAR elements were as follows: Nicole taught the students about the structural roots of housing insecurity. She then taught them how to interview and they began collecting stories from local renters. When students revealed that they had firsthand experiences with housing insecurity, Nicole helped them construct their own public narratives that were also shared and analyzed with the class. This story-sharing process made it abundantly clear that this was not "their" problem, but rather "our" problem, a pressing issue that affected many of the students, their friends, and their families, which moved the students to engage deeply in critical reflection and action. Nicole also took the lead in teaching students how to evaluate a community workshop.

In addition to the research skills she contributed, Nicole's Freireian teaching pedagogy modeled a different kind of information flow inside the classroom that valued everyone's voice and fostered a participatory learning environment. This was important to Dana's organizing project because she wanted the community workshop to be a safe space for marginalized community members, a place where power inequalities between residents and students were minimized, and Nicole's class exemplified this.

Dana brought her critical CD skills to the collaboration. First, she brought in the context of local policies and solutions that might work given existing gaps. Together, the group discussed the banking model of education and how it is different from problem-based learning, in which people are encouraged to think and actively solve the problems before them. Dana helped students to understand the critical importance of providing a safe space for community members who are directly impacted by housing inequality to share their knowledge and solutions. The group learned about the "art of hosting," the importance of offering real-life examples of "what could be," and they considered how best to generate potential solutions and provide space for community members to carefully weigh each option (see National Issues Forums, www.nifi.org, for one way to do this). In addition to offering these essential CD skills, Dana also modeled the power of vulnerability and narrative when she shared her own personal story of economic insecurity on the first day of class, which resonated deeply with Nicole's students and set the tone for an educational experience that fostered critical consciousness.

The collaboration continued. The following year Nicole taught the social inequalities class again and this time the students facilitated several of the newly designed renters' workshops out in the community. Facilitating these workshops brought community members more deeply into the collaboration between organizer and university student, opening up space for a broader public conversation about this urgent social issue and providing a pathway for critical reflection and action. By way of example, the first workshop was with a grandparents' support group. These residents were raising their grandkids as their own children struggled with substance use disorders, incarceration, and other challenging situations. The workshop began with a student's personal story. They split into small groups and participants were asked to reflect on the story and what problems it revealed about housing insecurity in Barren County. We asked participants to share additional stories or examples. The grandmother sitting next to Nicole crossed her arms, remarking that she owned her own home and didn't know anything about housing insecurity. As the conversation continued, she realized that her daughter had, in fact, had some issues as a renter. She shared a few anecdotes, reflecting on what those experiences had meant for her grandson and how hard it had been.

Around the room, similar conversations were taking place. When the full group reconvened, a participant blurted out: "I had never thought about this issue before. Why do we have all these problems in Barren County?" The students shared some of what they had learned about housing policy. "That's just the way it is," one community member remarked. But is that true? Again, the students shared examples of what it was like in other communities and the workshop participants added their own anecdotes to add further fuel to the fire. The students shared the *Renter's Handbook* and then moved on to the final question: What can we do together to get to the root of the problem and improve the situation? For the next 30 minutes, they facilitated a spirited dialogue until ultimately arriving at a handful of "next steps." This process was repeated at additional venues. The class was taught one final time in the spring of 2017 with similar results.

The successes of this collaboration were surprising. After the semester ended, students (who are also community members) were so motivated that they kept collaborating with Dana. Several of the community members who attended the workshops did as well. As one collaborator noted, "I had not been in that kind of environment before, where people walked into the workshop not knowing anything about the issue and left being super energized and excited to work on that issue." Dana organized and built the capacity of this group of former students and community members. In essence, what started as a combination of CPAR and critical CD now became about fostering policy change through community organizing. Nicole was no longer involved, but we did identify some areas where CPAR could have been utilized.

First, Dana helped the group learn about the political process and how to get a law passed. Several of the former students and local residents had ties to local elected officials and they reached out to explain their work and talk strategy. They shared their stories and advocated for the passage of a local landlord tenant law (URLTA). They were so persuasive that they managed to convince their state representative to move the proposal to the statewide level and champion a bill. He whipped the votes and got URLTA through the state House of Representatives in 2016. The bill did not pass in the Senate because things had developed so quickly that none of the educational work had been done (this would have been a great place for PAR). Nonetheless, it was still an important "win." As Dana explains, "There had been people working on making URLTA statewide for years and years and they couldn't believe that these community members from Glasgow had managed to get it to pass in the House for the first time."

The group then turned its efforts to local policy change. Dana taught them about power mapping, which was used to inform their lobbying strategy. They reworked the local stories they had collected and sent them to their elected officials (note how this early PAR work was woven into so many aspects of the group's critical CD work). Then they worked with the county judge executive (himself a landlord) and brought URLTA to a vote in Barren County. The vote split and thus it did not pass, but the work continues in Barren County. Seven years later and the issue was still a point of debate at the 2019 local elections where it was discussed in a packed public forum.

Beyond policy change, an important accomplishment of this project was fostering community awareness and public deliberation about basic needs access. It also equipped individuals to protect themselves and those who are most vulnerable to rental abuse. The educational workshop has continued to be used by the Homeless and Housing Coalition all over South Central Kentucky, where it is helping renters to better protect themselves and landlords to improve their practices. Although the Housing Coalition did not use the workshop evaluation tool to measure impact, other data suggests the workshop is memorable and effective. Nicole's 2018 research methods class surveyed the students from her 2013 and 2015 classes who facilitated the workshop. Years later almost all the students reported that they continue to talk about the workshop and what they learned with family and friends. Across the classes, 50 percent felt they were better able to protect themselves as renters and 25 percent felt like they became better landlords because of it. Most of the students lived in their own homes and were neither renters nor landlords, so this was a surprising result.

Finally, a core component of the success of these efforts were the students themselves who went through a process of critical consciousness and became powerful new community leaders, committed to addressing local inequities through organizing. Research revealed an abundance of deep learning, personal empowerment, and increased civic engagement by most of the students involved in this collaboration. As one student explained:

> This service-learning project made a huge impact on not only me, but others as well. It taught me just how widespread poverty is, what challenges people in poverty face, many of which remain unseen by society and finally that we have a voice. The only way to stop the continuing cycle of poverty is to use that voice to raise awareness and to empower those in poverty to rise and be heard. As a result of completing this course, I changed. My thought processes became more critical and the issues that I once thought were beyond my control were brought out and addressed. In summary, I learned that

I have a voice and was empowered to use it to address and solve problems faced by people in poverty. (2013 student)

Analysis of the qualitative data revealed two specific components of the collaboration that were particularly consequential. First, students highlighted the importance of "putting a face to the problem." This is why they cared so much about the issue and why they felt so compelled to act on it. "Putting a face to the problem" included interviewing their neighbors and sharing their own stories, along with those they had collected, with other community members at the workshop. This is what facilitated the collective process of critical consciousness, whereby participants pushed past the stereotypes that keep us silent. Through the sharing of stories, they came to realize that housing insecurity affects a lot of good people that they know and care about – and that these problems are the result of structural issues, not personal deficiencies.

The students also emphasized the importance of working with a community organizer to do something about the problem. They discussed the participatory community workshop as a first step towards social change. As one student explained, "But then you go to the workshop and everybody else starts, like, chiming in, and you watch the process. You think in your mind, 'Holy shit! This is how change happens!'" It was important to the students – and the workshop participants – that they had an opportunity to continue to meet and work on the issue after the formal educational component concluded.

It was the combination of popular education, research, and community organizing that created the possibility for a different kind of project – one that led to systemic change, while also fostering open public dialogue and empowering new community leaders. Storytelling was the key practice that bridged the critical PAR and CD elements of this collaborative project and contributed to the success of the participatory workshops and the community action that followed.

STUDENTS BECOME COMMUNITY PARTNERS AND LEADERS

Many of Nicole's students who were involved in the housing organizing project experienced *conscientization* and continued forth with efforts to improve their communities, focusing on a wide range of issues. A handful of students also moved forward with Nicole's next project on food insecurity – some as students and some as community partners with an organizing mindset. To illustrate this, Samantha demonstrates the transition from student to CD leader.

The second case study describes how Nicole and her regional college students partnered with Samantha and the Barren County Detention Center on a sustainable food justice project. First, Samantha describes how she came to care about food insecurity and how she learned about the power and potential of critical consciousness and rural organizing. She explores the origin of Project Breaking Ground and what, as a new CD practitioner, she was hoping to gain through a partnership with Nicole and her classes.

For Nicole, this project was an attempt to continue work at the nexus of CPAR and critical CD, but to incorporate a broader array of marginalized community members into the heart of the knowledge production work. She moved her teaching into the jail facility and began teaching students and incarcerated women together to accomplish this goal. It was also an experiment in whether a collection of local leaders with an organizing mindset could carry the critical CD elements of the collaboration and achieve systemic change. Unlike the former collaboration where Nicole partnered directly with a community organizer who had a long-term action agenda and experience with leadership development and policy change, the "organizing" partners in this case were former students who had learned critical CD skills from Dana. Samantha and Nicole explore the key elements of PAR and CD that came together to achieve success and then describe the broader impacts of the collaboration.

Samantha Johnson's Story (Former WKU-Glasgow Student, Corrections Officer, and Community Leader)

In an early paper in my college career, I wrote my food story. It began:

> Some of my happiest childhood memories are of being on the farm. My mother and step-father raised hogs, tobacco, corn, hay, and a huge garden. We killed enough hogs to stock our freezer for the year and trade with neighbors for fresh beef. The only thing we bought at the grocery store was bread, milk, and things needed to cook with … Then, when I turned 14, everything changed. Within a year, my dad, my grandfather and my step-father suddenly passed away. It was a very dark time for my family. My mother was forced to move my brother and me to a two-bedroom apartment in town. No more garden, no more veggies. Food was no longer plentiful and enjoyable. It was scarce and considered a luxury. My mom worked full-time and now it was my job to cook. I resented having to cook processed foods, all that junk, and I began to hate everything about food.

I originally wrote this food story for Dr. B.'s agri-food systems class, but I shared it in front of legislators at the 2014 Kentucky Food Policy Council Forum in Frankfort. It was a very emotional moment for me to stand up and share that story publicly because I had a lot of guilt and shame about the way I had eaten for all those years after we no longer had access to fresh fruits and vegetables. When I was younger and a single mother, I would only shop at the grocery store. I had a budget I had to follow, and if I bought fruits and vegetables, there went 90 percent of my budget. It's not affordable for people like me who live off a fixed income to eat healthy.

But as part of Dr. B.'s class, we went to visit a farmer whose whole family was involved in producing food and it awakened in me a desire to eat those fresh foods again. Then, I went through a process of what Dr. B. calls "critical consciousness." When we were sharing our stories, I realized just how many other rural people like me are struggling to access fresh food. I decided it was important to use the opportunity and give voice to this hidden problem. After I shared my story in Frankfort, I was invited to be part of the Kentucky Food Council as a constituent, which shows how new voices can be brought into policy decisions when regional college students collaborate with organizers, as we did with the Community Farm Alliance (CFA). This was the start of my transition to community leader.

While at WKU-Glasgow, I also took Dr. B's social inequalities class where we worked on the housing project. I kept collaborating with Dana and the Housing and Homeless Coalition after the class was over and we worked towards policy change. That is how I learned skills in organizing. Community organizing is about finding a problem that affects people in your community and going out and addressing it with folks who are affected – getting them together for the common cause and making change. You bring like-minded people together and you reach out and touch your own resources and have everyone bring in their resources. You know you can do much more in a group than you can by yourself! Even though we weren't completely successful at changing policy, I'm proud of the work that we did because we made some noise.

We brought the issue to the attention of the people who needed to know about it and we got people talking.

At the time I was also working at the Barren County Detention Center as a corrections officer teaching basic life skills to inmates. Thinking about my own personal transformation at the intersection of PAR and CD, I wanted to bring that same experience of critical consciousness and empowerment to other oppressed populations – especially those who are incarcerated. So, using my new organizing skills, I started listening for what they wanted to work together to solve and what was feasible. One day people were talking about how bad the food was in the jail. They said to me, "They treat us like animals in here! They think we will eat whatever they throw into our cage." I took this concern back to Dr. B. and my friends at WKU-Glasgow and we decided that we could do something about it. My goal for the project wasn't just to solve the food problem (although that was important). I didn't want to organize a fresh food drive or put in a garden for them. Instead I sought out a CD strategy to build the capacity of inmates to solve their own problems by involving them in the process of making change happen. I wanted them to feel like their voice matters and give them courage to move forward in their lives – and I wanted to give them skills in food production so they would be more self-sufficient.

PARTNERSHIP AT THE NEXUS OF CRITICAL PARTICIPATORY ACTION RESEARCH AND COMMUNITY DEVELOPMENT: FOOD INSECURITY

"Project Breaking Ground: A Sustainable Jail Garden and Food Justice Project" (www .facebook.com/projectbreakinground/?fref=ts) was born in January 2016. As a result of this project, community development took place in Barren County. Most notably, a three-quarters of an acre permaculture garden was installed and maintained by incarcerated women and WKU-Glasgow students, which later morphed into a community-organizing campaign. Critical PAR went into the series of classes that were held at the facility. Story was again the center of critical consciousness development, which was essential for investments in CD to continue over time as new leaders continued to work towards expanding fresh food access for South Central Kentucky residents beyond the confines of this specific project. This section summarizes the project, highlighting the key elements of PAR and CD at work, and describes how the collaboration succeeded in fostering individual and community change (and where it fell short).

Over the winter break of 2015, Samantha, Nicole, and a handful of other former WKU-Glasgow students met with jail officials and staff, local farmers, WKU-Glasgow students, and incarcerated women. They developed a shared vision for the project and began implementation. Nicole taught her sociology of agriculture and food class at the jail that spring semester. The class was modeled after the Inside Out Prison Exchange program, meaning she had 15 undergraduates ("outside students") and five incarcerated women ("inside students") who took the class together and had the same readings and assignments.

For half of the class period, the group learned about the challenges of the contemporary food system and discussed emerging alternatives. Then, for the rest of the class period, local farmers instructed students in techniques of sustainable agricultural production, including composting, creating healthy soils, *hugelkultur* construction, and beekeeping. They then created a jail garden next to the facility using these techniques. Many other community partners provided critical resources and knowledge for this project.

The key PAR elements in this first component of the project included: (1) pedagogy – a participatory education process that equalized power dynamics and created opportunities for critical consciousness development and human connection across lines of difference; (2) theory – a critical theoretical perspective that taught students about the structural roots of social inequality in the food system; (3) research – an opportunity for students to learn how to gather and analyze secondary data to understand local dimensions of the "food" problem and identify potential solutions; and (4) legitimacy – the university's involvement brought a lot of credibility to the project, which was crucial for organizers and leaders who need to justify their work in a power-imbalanced world; it also made it easier to recruit a wide network of support. Nicole took the lead on these elements.

In turn, Samantha and other partners contributed the following CD elements: (1) strategy – what issue to work on at the jail and how to bring everyone on board and proceed; (2) relationships – localized knowledge and connections made it possible to recruit and convene diverse stakeholders to help with the effort, especially limited-resource farmers to instruct students in alternative agricultural practices, further democratizing the knowledge production process; (3) communication – community leaders taught students, faculty, inmates, deputies, farmers, and residents how to understand each other and work together effectively (this involved continuous explanation and translation); (4) financial resources – the jail had money for inmate programming that was not being utilized but could be accessed for this CD effort; and (5) marketing and promotion – community leaders worked effectively with local media to promote the effort and enhance public dialogue about this social issue.

For the first growing season, the garden provided several weekly meals to 200 inmates. The jailer established an official garden work program, and the farm manager offered weekly instruction to the incarcerated women who worked in it. Samantha was available to teach the food justice curriculum to subsequent groups of inmates. A year later the project was entirely passed off to the jail and continued for another two years. Unfortunately, it did not survive beyond that. In Kentucky, jailer is an elected position. The team had not considered that if leadership changed (as it did), they would want to differentiate themselves from the former jailer and shift focus.

This community development collaboration morphed in other directions, however. In the fall of 2016, Nicole taught a follow-up course at the jail, entitled "Food, Community, and Social Change." By this point, a number of "outside" students were trying to change their diets or garden at home. Their collective struggle to access fresh, affordable food brought the issue of food insecurity back to the forefront of the conversation, and they wanted to do something to address this issue in the wider community. Nicole introduced a new crop of "inside" and "outside" students to theories of social change, community-organizing techniques, and practices of leadership development, including how to reflect on and develop their own food stories (CPAR contributions).

The class provided a fresh meal using local ingredients at the neighboring soup kitchen (they cooked for 150). After the meal, they shared their food stories and hosted a community workshop to give voice to others who were also directly affected by the problem and to brainstorm positive solutions. They used the same methods for the participatory workshop on food injustice as they had for the housing work. Many of the students had seen these methods in action and knew they worked, so they taught each other these critical CD skills.

Importantly, staff from KFTC and CFA, who had previously worked with Nicole and her students on the housing project and agri-food system "learning journeys" class, tried to provide background support for this project. One of the benefits of working at the intersection of CPAR and critical CD is that once a faculty member has worked successfully to support a community partner, these partners are willing to bring their organizing skills to support future university–community initiatives, especially when spearheaded by community members. Their CD contributions included helping students develop strategy (the "fresh food for all" campaign) and learn how to run meetings with community members after the participatory workshop yielded intense passion and desire to address community food security. They were not able to provide long-term, continuous support, however, and a lack of local leadership meant the organizing campaign eventually ground to a halt.

Finally, there was one additional element of PAR that was critical to the project and its success. Nicole's 2016 research methods class investigated the impacts of Project Breaking Ground, which were used to help with planning and share the lessons learned. A handful of students continued to research the project over the next year. Our analysis revealed five broad impacts of the project in addition to deep individual learning.

First, the project shifted public perceptions of the jail. During its first year, the project was featured in 14 media reports. According to key informant interviews and comments on Facebook, the community response to the project was overwhelmingly positive. In a conservative, rural county where many people believe jails exist to "lock up offenders and throw away the key" or to provide "free labor," this widely publicized project provided a different way to think about the jail and its role in society. In the words of the chief deputy:

> When you are trying to provide programs and give [inmates] hope and tools to use to get out and not come back, that changes the public perception. They aren't just sitting in here and eating and sleeping and serving time. They are actually getting to be productive. And we're giving them tools to use.

Second, as outsiders began to see the jail differently, so too did those who worked there. In week 6, the jailer and chief deputy joined the students in filling the garden beds, setting a tone for appropriate interaction outside the facility. The rest of the deputies followed suit, leading to more positive social interactions between inmates and staff, with surprising humanizing effects. In the words of the jailer:

> I have been in law enforcement in Barren County for 25 years .... [This project] brought a different human aspect to things. You started calling them my "inside" and "outside" students and that stuck in my head. I think working in a jail, day in and day out, you kind of lose sight that they are still human and they won't be here forever and that they will be released back into society ... You see the human aspect to them and you can talk to them. We both know I am the jailer and they are an inmate. But for a few minutes, it gives you a chance to see a different side of them.

Third, this shift in perspective led to some interesting community developments. In addition to building a garden, developing a new work program, and improving the quality of the facility's food, leadership sought out other opportunities for inmates – and, for the first time, groups began to call on them for something other than free labor. In the jailer's words, "I think that once we had proven that Breaking Ground had worked, it opened up the possibility of new ideas as we are clearly open to collaboration!" In the past the jail had partnered with churches for prayer meetings and substance abuse programs, but now they layered on more ambitious and innovative collaborations. They became a key partner in local economic development efforts, helping former inmates transition into local jobs. They even partnered with KFTC on a voter registration drive.

Fourth, the project contributed to the expansion of community gardening in the region. In the wake of all the "community talk" the project elicited, Nicole, her students, and her community partners were awarded an EnviroHealth Link grant to host a community gardening workshop at the jail garden. Mini grants allowed for the creation and expansion of 11 community gardens throughout the region, including the G Town Soul Swales permaculture garden that was constructed behind the soup kitchen in Glasgow. Two of Nicole's students, having been trained by Dana in community organizing, used critical CD techniques to find and recruit marginalized groups and get them to the workshop, which was an important part of their success; the gardens were largely organized by poor and Black, Indigenous, and people of color-led groups.

Fifth, the soup kitchen organizing project from the fall 2016 class spawned a group that worked the land and expanded programming at the G Town Soul Swales garden. The group, which included former students, residents, and those who utilized the soup kitchen, also pursued the adoption of a "Fresh Food for All" city ordinance in Glasgow. They shared their stories with elected officials and advocated for more resources to expand community food security efforts and support area farmers. Grant funds were used to hire one of Nicole's students as a community organizer to support this work, along with a local farmer and community educator. A lot of community growth happened very quickly, demonstrating the long-term community development impact of regional campus students who go through these processes and continue to do organizing work, while also aspiring to foster critical consciousness. That said, their policy efforts were unsuccessful given the difficulty of sustaining organizing efforts without institutional support.

Finally, there were important individual-level outcomes, such as attitude changes. It was remarkable to witness how quickly the "inside" and "outside" students overcame deep-rooted stereotypes and became a tight-knit collective and how proud they were of their accomplishments. One WKU student explained, "Working with inmates to grow food for the jail is very rewarding, but more rewarding than anything is the hopefulness and empowerment to change the community and the world by working hard for equal rights to fresh food for everyone." This sentiment was echoed by a former inmate:

> I'm going to get really upset talking about this, but when you get booked, you become a number. Nothing you say matters. [The class] made me feel like I had a name again. I think a lot of it had to do with the material. This class had nothing to do with my shortcomings or my flaws or things I need to work on … It was about [food injustice], another kind of problem that I could help find a solution to … I felt pleased when I could offer something and others agreed … I was released with that momentum and now I can take control back of my life.

Many participants also reported changes in behavior, with important implications for community processes and social structures. From the beginning students began to garden and expand their use of composting and agroecological practices at home. One student from a traditional farming background explained:

> Many of the different techniques taught in class I plan on using to benefit our gardens at our farm. It showed me ways that we can change from using so much fertilizers and pesticides. Also taking the

trip to Barbour's farm opened my eyes to show me that we can finally stop growing tobacco on the farm; we can turn it into a huge, sustainable garden for our community to grow on.

Participants also mentioned a shift in what they chose to eat. A formerly incarcerated student explained:

My whole habits have changed … now I go to the farmer's market once a week and I stock up … I had never been to a farmer's market before in my entire life. I spend $50 a week for me and the lady I take care of. My stomach feels better, my whole being feels better … In the spring I am going to plant her a garden.

DISCUSSION AND CONCLUSION

These case studies offer important insights into the possibility of collaboration at the nexus of academia and community organizing in rural America, highlighting the importance of storytelling in enabling PAR and CD to work together effectively. Story is at the center of critical consciousness development. Without critical consciousness, investments in CD do not continue over time. Critical social scientists trained in popular education (CPAR) thus have an important skillset to offer as researchers and teachers – especially in the context of community colleges and regional public universities where students are also marginalized community members. That said, community-organizing skills and long-term support (critical CD) are also crucial for systemic change to occur. Organizers and community leaders who develop and utilize these skills and have the time and desire to invest in new leadership development and long-term policy change have a valuable skillset to offer likeminded academics and working-class students. In the discussion that follows, we unpack these points, analyze across the two cases, and speak to current scholarly debates. We also offer a handful of suggestions for academics and community organizers who are seeking the right "partner."

It is important to note that the literature on CPAR and critical CD in the United States is generally quite urban-focused. There is some research on southern Black organizations, but mainstream discussion would suggest that you otherwise cannot do critical PAR and CD in poor, white, rural places. What these stories reveal is that it is possible to do this kind of work in such contexts.

Place-based institutions of higher education are an important and largely untapped site for such collaborations to bloom. These are sites where critical thinking and democratic values are fostered. Furthermore, as some community colleges and regional comprehensives reposition themselves as anchor institutions that can foster development in the region, there may be increased support for faculty to partner with grassroots organizations to work on community problems while also developing local leaders. The students who attend these institutions are already deeply embedded in place, with long-standing and multi-stranded ties. That said, they are seldom students of privilege whose families have held political and economic power, but rather they are non-traditional and working-class students who rarely feel they have a voice in their community. Doing work at the nexus of critical PAR and CD with these kinds of students has the potential to transform the direction of students' lives – and, in turn, that of their rural communities.

In our case, developing CPAR projects around the research needs of local organizers was key to fostering a collective process of critical consciousness that motivated students to take action to solve local social problems. For these collaborations to develop, organizers and faculty must be able to find each other and develop trust. To find faculty who share the democratic values of organizers, we suggest that organizers may want to consider attending relevant on-campus events that are open to the public. Seek out the faculty and staff who care about social issues. These individuals can then make broader introductions around campus. A service-learning center or coordinator is another good place to start. Organizers should also be aware that faculty at public universities in the United States are not permitted to advocate for specific candidates running for office or otherwise engage in partisan politics on the job, thus role clarification at the outset of the project is extremely important. As knowledge producers, the strength of academics is their content knowledge, critical thinking skills, and teaching abilities. But universities also bring additional resources and legitimacy that is helpful to organizers, including access to marginalized students. Our case shows that faculty with backgrounds in popular education and/or the critical social sciences might be particularly valuable partners – as well as those who are willing to invest in long-term relationships and build entire classes around the collaboration.

For faculty interested in partnering with organizers on class projects, it is important to find the right collaborator. The knowledge production needs of a critical community developer are very different from their neoliberal counterparts. Many non-profits and community development organizations are asking universities for help with reporting, evaluation, and technical development, and this is usually where PAR fits in. Organizers, on the other hand, need help with base building, developing critical consciousness, and giving people language and skills to talk about public issues. Where does one find these types of CD partners? In rural Kentucky, such grassroots leaders may not have official titles or even call themselves "organizers." In fact, we recommend that faculty be cautious of leaders who call themselves "organizers" but who are not committed to new leadership development and power sharing. Consider asking: who is currently doing the real organizing work in the community? Is there a base of people who really support this person or organization? How large is it? Who is the person accountable to? Do they spend a lot of their time building up new leaders? Are the issues that this person or group is working on something that will truly resonate for students and other marginalized community members?

Faculty must also carefully consider the identities and class backgrounds of their students before engaging in such collaborations. Note that these kinds of projects may be especially risky for students who come from oppressed backgrounds. Take special care to center these students and their needs; check in frequently. In our case, it was especially helpful to have a critical mass of students who shared a common experience of marginalization. If there are only a few students from oppressed backgrounds in the class, an important ethical issue arises: can you protect these students and ensure that they have a positive experience with the project, knowing that the majority (who come from a place of privilege) may drive the conversation and struggle to relate or care about the work?

Once you have the right partners to combine CPAR and critical CD, what are the key elements that create the possibility for a different kind of project? We used storytelling (in the tradition of Freire) as a tool for validating knowledges that have been historically marginalized and delegitimized, and also as a tool for fostering critical reflection and mobilizing people to act. Students collected stories of marginalized community members who experienced food and housing insecurity, which they discussed and analyzed at length. Alongside their incarcerated peers, they also wrote their own stories of marginalization and exclusion, integrating what they were learning from scholarly texts. Notably, we used mostly ethnographies and documentaries in these classes, so narrative was also key to engaging with traditionally recognized knowledges. As "students" developed critical consciousness and gained confidence, some transformed their stories into public narratives using a version of Marshall Ganz's framework. These were shared at participatory community workshops that we collectively designed to elicit civic dialogue through story sharing and positive problem-solving processes. Fostering a "story of us" that bridges divides, highlights the commonality of lived experiences, and lifts up shared values was important in building community and establishing trust in all of these collaborations. We used story-based popular education techniques to achieve this. Nicole's research methods classes used a variety of methods (mostly qualitative, including interviews, focus groups, and narrative analysis of media coverage) to reflect on our processes and consequences of our actions. The "actions" we had developed were adjusted accordingly, in a continuous feedback loop.

Over the last year, with a global pandemic and our societal need to reckon with racial injustice, we have become even more convinced of the importance of authentic storytelling that allows for vulnerability and connection. Storytelling is such a powerful method to get to the heart of community issues. It can foster deep listening and empathy, minimize power inequalities, and bring people together. It can unlock new understandings and mobilize people to action around a shared vision. Given feelings of rural invisibility and powerlessness in this current historical moment, story-based methods are an especially valuable tool that can be utilized at the nexus of critical CD and PAR in these contexts.

Another important insight that can be gleaned from our case studies is the value of addressing basic needs as a part of the larger social change process. Scholars and activists often assume that if you are helping people to stay in their rental houses or access food, that this is charity, not part of a broader change effort. We argue that basic needs are an important part of critical CD as well. The Black Panthers were offering food, but also using it as an important mode of social action. Our case shows that a valuable starting point for fostering critical reflection and civic engagement is addressing the barriers to basic needs such as food and housing. This is especially important in rural areas where there is such a strong need to address these issues. These public problems also resonate with people in a different way. It's one thing if you are talking publicly about a coal boss, but something else altogether when you are sharing a story of trying to keep a roof over your head or feed your infant. Leadership stories framed around these basic needs issues help articulate the problem in a concrete way that helps others in the community to see and talk about them, opening up civic spaces that have otherwise been squashed in rural America. These public issues touch everyone in tight-knit communities in some way, thus we must engage with differentially positioned people, including jailers and those who eat at soup kitchens and county judge executives and grandparents raising school-aged kids.

Analyzing across the two case studies, we want to speak briefly to the question of "success." Stoecker (2016) notes that one indicator of success is whether the collaboration leads to notable "wins" that reduce power inequalities. In the first case, the entire project was built around a long-term community-organizing project that had already been identified as a local need, with significant resources and organizing support around it. These organizing resources meant that the project initiated a process that got much closer to fostering real policy change, given that the community organizer was able to maintain momentum after the classes finished.

In the second case, we learned from the success of partnering with a community organizer and built our critical PAR project around Samantha's "door-knocking" campaign that identified an important issue to organize around at the jail. We brought in KFTC and CFA to help scaffold on some formal community-organizing support for the fall 2016 class and secured grant funds to hire a community organizer over the summer to keep the momentum going. Ultimately, however, this scaffolding approach did not result in a sustainable effort. Because our work was not embedded in the action agenda of an existing community-organizing project, there was not a single person or organization committed to maintain the momentum around food insecurity in the same way that the Housing and Homeless Coalition has been able to with housing. Furthermore, the jail garden project, which temporarily changed the micro-structure of the facility's feeding operation, did not continue when the jail leadership changed hands.

That said, while the effort to get landlord-tenant law or a "fresh food all" ordinance passed might have failed, these projects did alter the social relationships of knowledge production in Barren County in significant ways. They validated students' and community members' knowledge and fostered the development of critical consciousness. This body of collaborative work propelled Nicole's non-traditional "students" towards meaningful careers, opening many doors along the way. Two of her former students are now employed full time as community organizers. Students talk about the projects in their applications to graduate school (one was even awarded a full scholarship because of it). They reference their experience with deep listening, interviewing, storytelling, and facilitation to successfully acquire local jobs in related fields such as social work and human resources. They have won university-wide awards related to these projects, including the Seneca Falls Personal Empowerment Award, the WKU Sustainability Award, a FUSE Award, Session Winner at the WKU Student Research Conference, among others. One of the students even ran for public office in Barren County!

Beyond individual recognition and opportunities, however, was the fact that we turned marginalized rural students into community change agents by investing in them as new leaders. Through our partnership, we taught them how to combine the knowledge and critical thinking skills they acquired from the university with experiential knowledge and feel empowered to participate in their community. This resulted in a collective process of leadership development. As waves of former students moved into informal leadership positions in the region and brought with them a commitment to civic dialogue and addressing structural inequality, they continue to shift the public discourse. Furthermore, as we brought our class out into the community and incorporated a broader array of marginalized "students" (e.g. incarcerated women) into the heart of the work, we further strengthened and expanded on this impact. In closing, in rural communities in the American South, we believe that effectively opening up civic spaces where people feel seen and can talk publicly about urgent social issues and learn to speak truth to power in ways that resonate *is* a noteworthy "success" in and of itself. It is also a critical precursor to growing the power and potential of rural organizing to change structural conditions of oppression over time.

ACKNOWLEDGMENTS

We would like to thank Adrienne Falcón, Randy Stoecker, Lucie Gélineau, Karen Rignall, Bleik Pickett, Krystal Carver, Ben Turner, Angela Briggs, and all the "students," community partners, and WKU faculty and staff who contributed to these projects and the writing of this manuscript. In memory of Phillip Ray Johnson II.

REFERENCES

American Association of State Colleges and Universities. 2002. "Stepping Forward as Stewards of Place." www.aascu.org/WorkArea/DownloadAsset.aspx?id=5458

Bowling Green Area Chamber of Commerce. 2021. "South Central Kentucky Demographics." www .southcentralky.com/demographics

Bush, A. 2018. "Affordable Housing Needs Assessment." Homeless and Housing Coalition of Kentucky. https://static1.squarespace.com/static/5bb6224ee66669232bc05751/t/5c1bc6be575d1feb99659aae/ 1545324223530/HHCK+Housing+Needs+Assessment+12202018.pdf

Feeding America. 2021. "Map the Meal Gap: Food insecurity in Kentucky before COVID-19." https:// map.feedingamerica.org/county/2019/overall/kentucky

Freire, Paulo. 1970/1993. *Pedagogy of the Oppressed*. New York: Continuum.

Ganz, Marshall. 2009. "Why Stories Matter: The Art and Craft of Social Change." *Sojourners*, March. https://sojo.net/magazine/march-2009/why-stories-matter

Henry, Sue Ellen. 2005. "'I Can Never Turn My Back on That': Liminality and the Impact of Class on Service-Learning Experience." In Dan Butin (Ed.), *Service-Learning in Higher Education*. New York: Palgrave MacMillan.

Kentucky Center for Economic Policy. 2018. "State of Working Kentucky 2018." https://kypolicy.org/ wp-content/uploads/2018/08/State-of-Working-KY-2018.pdf

Ledwith, Margaret. 2011. *Community Development: A Critical Approach* (2nd Ed.). Bristol: Policy Press.

Lee, Jenny. 2005. "Home away from Home or Foreign Territory? How Social Class Mediates Service-Learning Experiences." *NASPA Journal* 42(3): 310–325.

Marullo, Sam and Bob Edwards. 2000. "From Charity to Justice: The Potential of University-Community Collaboration for Social Change." *American Behavioral Scientist* 43: 895–912.

Mills, C. Wright. 1959. "The Promise." *The Sociological Imagination*. New York: Oxford University Press.

Morton, Keith. 1995. "The Irony of Service: Charity, Project and Social Change in Service Learning." *Michigan Journal of Community Service Learning* 2(1): 19–32.

Stoecker, Randy. 2016. *Liberating Service Learning and the Rest of Higher Education Civic Engagement*. Philadelphia, PA: Temple University Press.

Szakos, Joe and Kristin Layng Szakos. 2009. *Lessons from the Field: Organizing in Rural Communities*. New Orleans: American Institute for Social Justice.

Yeh, Theresa Ling. 2010. "Service-Learning and Persistence of Low-Income, First-Generation College Students: An Exploratory Study." *Michigan Journal of Community Service Learning* 16: 50–65.

PART III

BUILDING ORGANIZATIONS AND NEIGHBORHOODS

9. Putting theory into practice: leveraging community-based research to achieve community-based outcomes in DeLand, Florida

Maxwell Droznin, Kelsey Maglio, Asal M. Johnson, Cristian Cuevas, and Shilretha Dixon

For the past 15 years, Stetson University has developed extensive community engagement programs. Of those, few have proven as comprehensive and sustainable as those addressing public health needs within the Spring Hill community – a low-income, marginalized area of DeLand, Florida, located only a few miles from the university. A few details have set these initiatives apart, though none have been perfectly seamless: faculty-facilitated community-based research projects and needs assessments, student support through community-engaged learning courses, and equitable collaboration with community partners. The foundation for these initiatives was laid by the research conducted by Dr. Asal Johnson, assistant professor of public health, in conjunction with the Spring Hill Resource Center and Shilretha Dixon, the center's director. The use of participatory action research (PAR; also referred to as community-based research) created space for participation from faculty, students, and community members in a concrete and unified way. Moreover, the research prioritized health needs to be addressed in resulting initiatives, ensuring that programs and services are more relevant and effective for the community they serve. Overall, the trajectory of this project has created a model for the integration of research, university resources, and community programs that Stetson seeks to emulate in addressing other issue areas.

STETSON AND THE SPRING HILL COMMUNITY

Stetson University's relationship with its surrounding communities has a mixed history, as does the city of DeLand itself. This is particularly related to the fact that the city and region where Stetson is located have been resided by non-White residents as well as White communities who dominated power and wealth distribution in the region. Popular accounts of the city's founding often feature Henry DeLand's "orange fever" and establishment of a town centered on "education and culture," culminating in the establishment of the DeLand Academy, which would later become Stetson University (City of DeLand 2021). These stories which narrate a White history of a White city built by and for White people are depicted throughout the town murals. Recent accounts have included descriptions of Native American communities prior to Henry DeLand's arrival, yet few discuss social conflicts and inequalities that have persisted within the area. In particular, the Spring Hill area of DeLand was originally developed as a community for low-wage citrus harvesters. Generational poverty has been prevalent in this area since the late 1800s, especially since the vast majority of its residents come from histor-ically marginalized and disadvantaged backgrounds, due to racial and ethnic discrimination (Witek 2019). Partially due to decades of Jim Crow laws, most of Spring Hill was not incor-porated into the city of DeLand and remains unincorporated to this day (Cooper et al. 2019; Witek 2019).

Today, Spring Hill represents the geographic area of DeLand Southwest Census Designated Place, with only 260 of its 698 acres within the jurisdiction of the city of DeLand, barring the majority from access to city resources (U.S. Census Bureau 2018). Instead, the unincorporated areas must rely on well water, septic tanks, and county resources for fire and police depart-ments, often impacting the quality of these services (Johnson et al. 2016). Moreover, the area has a 27.8% poverty rate and a median household income of $21,662 (U.S. Census Bureau 2018). The five-year American Community Survey in 2018 estimated the area as having 1,004 residents, with 86% being non-White. The racial and ethnic composition of South West DeLand is 47% Black, 29% Hispanic/Latino, and 10% Asian. The remaining 14% are non-Hispanic White (U.S. Census Bureau 2018).

In 2004, the city of DeLand and the county of Volusia created the Spring Hill Community Redevelopment Agency (CRA) "to work jointly with the County Council in the completion of a redevelopment plan for the Spring Hill area in an effort to eliminate the blighted area of the Spring Hill community for the benefit of the residents therein and to offer the residents an improved quality of life" (City of DeLand 2020). As a result, the CRA established the Spring Hill Resource Center to help residents on items relating to employment, government benefits, and health programming. This organization has become a central hub for community programs, including those initiatives generated in partnership with Stetson.

Though Stetson University has put focused attention on meeting the needs of the Spring Hill community over the past ten years, it must be acknowledged that the university has certainly contributed to the marginalization of areas of DeLand throughout its history. For example, as the university sought to expand its student population and physical campus, it purchased buildings and residences that once were affordable to community residents, especially in "Red City," what was once the heart of DeLand's African American community (Witek 2019). Stetson itself did not begin to integrate and admit African American students until 1962, indicating that it has been a hostile place for those from racially and ethnically marginalized groups (Stetson University 2020). Much like the rest of north DeLand, Stetson University had been culpable in reinforcing segregation laws and traditions, such as black-face performances during the Jim Crow era (Ross 2017). Thus, understandably, the seemingly resource-laden university has long felt disconnected from the community in which it is situated, a problem that is not unique to Stetson. This can complicate community engagement programs initiated by universities since unequal power dynamics persist.

COMMUNITY ENGAGEMENT TRENDS

In response to this disconnect, as well as the mission to create civically minded students, higher education community engagement programs began in the 1980s and have resulted in the estab-lishment of designated university-led community engagement centers and high-impact service programs. Established in 2007, Stetson's Center for Community Engagement (CCE) was designed to be a central channel for the university's collaboration with community organizations and leaders ensuring that Stetson students, faculty, staff, and administration are conscientious and deeply engaged in their interactions with the broader DeLand and Volusia County communities. The CCE's mission – "Creating opportunities for student learning through community impact" – reinforces the equitable and mutually beneficial community partnership to which the university aspires, though frequently falling short. Because unequal power balances and distrust have permeated the university's relationship with its community since its 1883 founding, Stetson staff, faculty, and students must take particular care to empower the community's own voices and highlight its assets, rather than reinforcing colonialist notions of "saving" the community (Acheraïou 2008). As would become obvious later, maintaining equitable and collaborative relationships with community stakeholders would remain an ever present obstacle to successful community engagement work.

Though not all university-related community engagement work at Stetson is associated with the CCE, it has served as a central force for expanding opportunities for involvement with local organizations. The evolution of community engagement programs at Stetson has mirrored national trends in the field. Increasingly, the emphasis of these programs has shifted from extracurricular to now curricular and co-curricular activities. Thus, these initiatives are no longer seen as mere student volunteerism but are being integrated into faculty research and academic coursework. Additionally, the American Association of Colleges and Universities has included service learning among its list of "High-Impact Practices" (Association of American Colleges and Universities 2008). This trend towards academically rigorous community engagement work leverages the unique assets that universities provide – faculty members with a responsibility to generate and publish original content and students with formal academic requirements to further their personal, intellectual, and civic growth. Research-based projects also provide a solid ground upon which to begin developing and assessing community programs.

INTEGRATING PARTICIPATORY ACTION RESEARCH WITH COMMUNITY DEVELOPMENT

However, as noted by Stoecker and Falcón, the research frameworks used in academic settings have not always met the three necessary components of PAR shaped by and for community members. The research, or knowledge production process, has been the primary focus of institutions of higher education since this is the expertise of faculty and students. Though the higher education community engagement movement has increased the role of action – projects based on research aimed at tangible and meaningful community development – this part cannot be done well without participation. This condition means that the research process must be initiated and guided by community members, rather than having them merely play advisory roles or be participants in the research (Strand et al. 2003). In contrast to PAR practices developed in the global South, which have emphasized the mobilization of experiential knowledge within a community, universities have often favored researcher-led projects, as Stoecker and Falcón discuss in this volume. The latter model of PAR is external to the community and is aimed at incremental community development within a given system, rather than systemic changes. By focusing on the research aspect and its benefits for students and faculty, rather than principles for effective community development, these projects have been largely unsustainable. If universities are to continue progressing their community engagement programs, community development principles must be better integrated into the research process. This integration requires challenging the assumptions long built into the university's model for PAR about whose and what kind of knowledge is worth including in the process, placing community perspectives at the forefront (Gaventa and Cornwall 2001).

Community development efforts can be divided into four types, based on the amount of community involvement and the degree of social change (Beckwith and Lopez 1997). Beckwith describes social services as those with both low community involvement and low change. This is likely where most universities' programs would fit. Community organizing, on the other hand, features high community involvement and a high degree of change. Community development proper focuses on low change within a given social structure but emphasizes community ownership of the process. Meeting the criteria of community involvement is ultimately necessary to challenge the power differential between the university and the surrounding communities. Many of the struggles accompanying the community development process described in this chapter arose from the insufficiency of community involvement from the very beginning, especially during the research process.

Perhaps the most effective method to achieve the most change would have been to involve many more community members in the planning and inception of future programs, centered around sharing the results of the initial research. Planning through community forums, which had already generated strong community turn-out during the research phase, would have mobilized significant community resources and social capital. While greatly prolonging time to program implementation, such efforts would have mitigated many of the issues we encountered during program planning, development, and maintenance. Although we partnered with the Spring Hill Resource Center, there was little involvement from community members outside of the center's staff. Thus, we struggled consistently to create community "buy-in" for our projects. Nevertheless, these projects have been significant in shaping our understanding of PAR and its products.

In this chapter we present the story of four collaborations between Stetson University, Spring Hill community leaders, and various non-profit and government agencies to address community-identified needs. The collaborations are presented in a narrative, chronological manner meant to serve as case studies for others pursuing similar programming in their own communities. It is our hope that the successes and failures of each collaboration can serve to benefit community engagement activities at other colleges and universities.

NEEDS ASSESSMENT

Background

During the academic year of 2015–2016, the Florida Department of Health-Volusia County (DOH-VC) decided to address the prevalent environmental health concerns in the Spring Hill community through the Protocol for Assessing Community Excellence in Environmental Health (PACE EH). The methodology framed by PACE EH defines a stepwise process through which local health departments in collaboration with community partners generate action plans to set priorities to improve community environmental health (CDC 2000). Stetson's assessment of public health and community needs in Spring Hill began as a partnership between the DOH-VC and Stetson University's Department of Health Sciences. Stetson students are all required to complete a research thesis or project as part of the university curriculum, mentored and guided by Stetson faculty. In partnership with DOH-VC and the community of Spring Hill, particularly with the Spring Hill Resource Center, 11 students at Stetson University were involved in this project as part of their senior research.

Methods

Students participated in qualitative observational studies related to environmental health concerns. During this process, they conducted several walk-throughs of the community to document issues, such as decayed housing exterior, roof deterioration, trash, vacant lots covered by overgrown bushes, broken sidewalks, abandoned gas stations, and other issues. The results of the descriptive study were used by the DOH-VC and Stetson University to generate an asset map of Spring Hill's access to basic commodities and services – food, businesses, churches, hospitals, schools, and civic centers – which was later shared with the community. We created the asset map in response to the PACE EH process to identify "available resources, skills and capacities" in the community. This process also helps to build additional relationships with other possible community partners and organizations (Center for Community Health and Development 2020). The Spring Hill CRA boundaries were used as the community boundaries in part because the DOH-VC was interested in identifying environmental health issues within these boundaries.

In November 2015, DOH-VC organized a town hall meeting at the Spring Hill Boys and Girls Club. Prior to the meeting, DOH-VC staff and Dr. Johnson met with students to conduct a quick workshop instructing students how to listen and take notes during small group discussions. During this meeting, focus groups engaged in discussions about Spring Hill's strengths, weaknesses, opportunities, and threats and their community's public health issues. Each group had a moderator designated by DOH-VC and two student note takers – one to outline and summarize the discussion on group boards and one to transcribe discussions. Students then used responses from focus groups and observations from the descriptive study to generate a survey that could quantify concerns of Spring Hill residents regarding the community's environment and health, while the DOH-VC administered a separate survey focused on health and economy, mostly at the county level. Initial survey distribution was conducted by going door to door within Spring Hill, but this method did not yield a substantial amount of responses. Therefore, the data collection changed to a form of convenience sampling. Questionnaires were distributed to parishioners at worship houses and churches within the community. In total, 180 responses were collected, classified primarily by whether respondents indicated whether they lived in Spring Hill. Eighty-eight respondents identified as Spring Hill residents, 85 respondents identified as living outside of Spring Hill, and seven were unsure if their homes were in Spring Hill.

Results

The descriptive study conducted by students demonstrated a strong tight-knit sense of community identity in Spring Hill, embracing the neighborhood's historical heritage. In addition, community leaders have shown dedication to the positive development and empowerment of its youth. However, Spring Hill's overall health status seems to be hindered by high rates of unemployment and insufficient infrastructure.

The results of the Stetson survey found that Spring Hill respondents agreed that the community benefited from the Spring Hill Resource Center and the Boys and Girls Club. Spring Hill respondents were most concerned with their lack of access to fresh produce (90.5%). Only 11% of Spring Hill respondents agreed that they had access to exercise programs and felt safe in their community. Spring Hill respondents' top three health concerns were high blood pressure (73.9%), diabetes (71.6%), and HIV/AIDS (68.2%).

Participants who identified as residents of Spring Hill also expressed a high degree of dissatisfaction with sidewalks (67%) and streetlights (71.6%), feelings of safety from crime (75.0%), pleasantness of walking around the neighborhood (71.6%), and the maintenance of buildings (75.0%). Non-Spring Hill respondents possessed a more positive view of conditions in their community.

Participants were asked to rate their degree of concern for different socioeconomic and environmental aspects of their community. Drug/crime activity (84.1%), unemployment (78.4%), lack of jobs for those with prior convictions (78.4%), poverty (76.4%), land polluted with trash and illegal dumping (75.0%), lack of access to healthcare (73.9%), lack of affordable housing (70.5%), access to transportation (69.3%), and access to grocery stores (69.3%) were identified as problematic aspects of Spring Hill community. The lowest ranked items in relation to the concerns of residents were access to grocery stores and transportation options, approximately 69%, still a substantial proportion of respondents.

Priority Areas Identified

The findings of this survey were presented by Dr. Asal Johnson to the CRA in the summer of 2016. These findings suggested limited access to food and fresh produce, businesses, healthcare, schools, and civic centers for the community residents. During observational studies conducted as part of the assessment, it was noted that food options at the only corner store in the community lacked fresh fruit and vegetables, instead offering overpriced foods of little nutritional value. There seemed to be a direct correlation between respondents' concerns about cardiovascular health and diabetes and their responses regarding poverty, poor infrastructure, and lack of healthy food.

Based on aggregated community member responses and in consultation with community leaders, Dr. Johnson formulated the following recommendations and shared them with the City of DeLand, the Spring Hill CRA, and the DOH-VC (Johnson et al. 2016):

1. Expansion of the Spring Hill Resource Center.
2. Investment in the Spring Hill Boys and Girls Club.
3. Education and community outreach programs about the prevention and control of chronic and infectious diseases, such as diabetes, and HIV and other sexually transmitted diseases in the community.
4. Connecting residents with prior convictions to employment opportunities.
5. Reducing drug/crime activities in the area and restoring trust between police and the community.
6. Improving streetlights and sidewalks in the neighborhood.
7. Facilitating access to healthy food options for residents (for example through expanded and accessible community gardens).

Stetson's partnership with Spring Hill would soon begin to take shape in addressing the last recommendation – facilitating access to healthy food options – though resulting initiatives have branched off in many directions, due to the interconnected nature of these economic, health, and environmental concerns.

COMMUNITY GARDEN

Partnership Development

As results of the Public Health and Community Needs Assessment began to be circulated throughout Stetson University, the final year of the AmeriCorps VISTA program at the CCE was coming to an end. Following conversations with Stetson University administrators and staff at the Spring Hill Resource Center, Spring Hill leaders and CCE staff determined that the CCE would reapply for the VISTA grant with the next three-year project focused on addressing some of the priority areas identified in the needs assessment. With limited capacity of community members to devote themselves full time to the development of these new programs, the intention of the new VISTA would be to serve as an external community partner and advocate dedicated to addressing the needs of residents by leveraging Stetson University's resources to implement sustainable, community-led programs.

AmeriCorps VISTAs had previously been used by the CCE to develop a student-led grant-making organization focused on community development but having a VISTA work directly with community members on longitudinal community-based projects had not been done yet. Additionally, while the relationship between the university and Spring Hill leaders had made progress in the early 2000s, the past decade had seen a slow decline in programming and volunteering in the area. Again, a major challenge to the entrance of Stetson University to community development within Spring Hill was overcoming the trust barrier that could limit collaboration opportunities and community buy-in.

With nutritional insecurity, green spaces, and community gardens specifically identified as major unmet needs by Spring Hill residents, the development of a community garden to serve as a resource for the recreational and nutritional needs of residents was an evident priority. In an effort to develop programs from a Spring Hill and not Stetson lens, the first few weeks of the VISTA project were dedicated to learning about the community through assigned readings, independent research, and facilitated meetings with community leaders. Following these meetings, CCE staff together with Spring Hill leaders determined that food access, and specifically community gardening, was indeed the best first course of action that the VISTA should pursue.

While the Spring Hill Resource Center could help identify Spring Hill residents interested in community gardening, and the CCE could provide the volunteers to help build the garden, the project needed to add additional stakeholders to address the horticultural and engineering aspects of developing a community garden. Thankfully, within the United States, almost every county has an extension of a land grant institution that serves to support local agriculture and nutritional needs within that county (University of Florida 2020). In Florida, the extension is the University of Florida Institute of Food and Agricultural Sciences (IFAS). Reaching out to IFAS, the community garden project was able to gain eager interest from Master Gardeners, a group of IFAS-trained horticultural volunteers. Through their knowledge of community gardening best practices and central Florida vegetable growing cycles, they became invaluable partners by quickly filling knowledge gaps in the planning and development of the garden.

Around the same time as the IFAS partnership was beginning to develop, the VISTA was able to start building a partnership with a local United States Department of Agriculture (USDA) office. The conservationist there had volunteered with community gardens in the area, and like the Master Gardeners, was eager to lend his knowledge and expertise to help the project. Through the USDA the project was able to obtain garden blueprints, raised garden bed designs, a detailed irrigation system plan, and a cost estimation tool, all based on best practices. As a result of the active efforts of all partners, within four months the project had a garden plan, a group of interested Spring Hill gardeners, and a coalition of partners that included Stetson University, IFAS, and the USDA.

With a primary barrier to many public health initiatives being funding (Huang et al. 2011), CCE staff and Spring Hill community members worked together to identify potential funding sources both within and outside of the community. Following several weeks of research and inquiry, the most expedient funding source came from a Spring Hill-based non-profit called the Greater Union Life Center (GULC). Attached to the largest congregation in the greater Spring Hill area and led by prominent Spring Hill community members, GULC had recently received a donation for a farm-to-table project in the area and viewed the community garden proposal as a great fit for their new donation.

With the acquisition of local funding, the search for land in the area began. All project partners agreed that the goal was to build in the area where the greatest need was and where many people already congregated. Working with some officials from the City of DeLand, a vacant plot of land was identified between a city-sponsored community center, a church, and a community-based non-profit. It was not in Spring Hill where there was the most need, but it was in an area that was close and already had foot traffic moving past it. It was February 2017, and project team members were confident that construction could begin on site by April.

With word beginning to spread that a community garden was coming, others outside of the community began to find out about the project. Partially due to the fast pace of progress, the VISTA, who had taken on the role of facilitating conversation with outside partners, overlooked gaining buy-in from not just Spring Hill leaders, but from all necessary City of DeLand officials. Misconceptions about the intended purpose of the garden began to circulate in Spring Hill, and eventually reached staff at DeLand City Hall before the garden team had presented their case. Concerned about the sustainability, liability, and scope of the project, the City of DeLand Office of Parks and Recreation directed that all progress on the garden be halted immediately.

Over the next month, justifiably, Spring Hill partners viewed this action as another echo of the unfortunate relationship they share with the city. However, through leveraging Stetson's position as a large, influential community institution, project team members were able to establish back-channel communications with several city officials about how to remediate the directive and restore trust. Following a formal meeting with the city several weeks later, the miscommunications and misconceptions about the community garden were addressed, and the project was able to gain official approval. This is where the university partnership showed some of its greatest strengths: lobbying city officials to approve lasting change in Spring Hill, even if that meant starting with the approval of one vegetable garden.

FORMALIZING THE ORGANIZATION

Once official approval was obtained to start building a garden, project partners began to move forward with construction plans. While it may have been more beneficial to organize Spring Hill residents to participate in most of the construction to gain buy-in, project team members felt that the time sensitivity of the garden necessitated a more expedient approach. The CCE was able to recruit over 100 Stetson students to volunteer hundreds of hours, transforming an empty 4,800 square feet of space into a fully functioning community garden complete with automatic irrigation, in less than six weeks. Between the value of the grant, in-kind donations of expertise and materials, and monetized volunteer hours, the garden had gone from an idea to a very real $30,000 investment.

During the time that the garden was being constructed, project partners also began to formalize the garden into a community organization. Primarily through social networks established through the Spring Hill Resource Center, a board of Spring Hill residents interested in leading the garden was established. In addition to the community members, the VISTA and a long-time Stetson student volunteer with the project were selected to become part of the board of directors. Through Stetson University staff and faculty facilitation, a constitution and bylaws were written by the newly established committee, and the organization was formally incorporated as a non-profit called the Spring Hill Gardeners Association (SHGA).

The new non-profit focused its mission on providing accessibility to fresh produce, garden education, and a beautiful green space for Spring Hill residents. Based on best practices from IFAS, it was decided by the non-profit board that garden plots would be leased out at a rate of $20 per year, which included automatic irrigation, seeds, and weekly assistance from Master Gardener and Stetson student volunteers. Continuing to work closely with the Spring Hill Resource Center, CCE, IFAS, and USDA on programming and expansion, the SHGA began to market themselves within the community. As church affiliations are a foundational pillar of many social groups in Spring Hill, it was not surprising that the most effective recruitment of gardeners came not from pamphlets and infographics, but from interpersonal relationships with the newly inducted board members. By November 2017, most of the garden plots had been leased out with the rest of the plots being planted and made available to the community as free "U Pick" plots. By April 2018, two more grants had made possible the implementation of beautification projects, a community supplies storage space, and an external greenhouse on the IFAS extension grounds where Master Gardeners would raise seeds into potted plants and deliver them to the community garden.

Within a year, the garden had gone from an idea to a fully functioning non-profit organization. Most garden volunteers doing basic grounds maintenance were still Stetson students, but at this point the concern of the organization was to ensure that the garden remained a well-kept space to attract potential gardeners and community passersby. Outside of grounds keeping, to increase community engagement, festivals in collaboration with local businesses began to be planned several months out. The goal, of course, was to maximize the number of Spring Hill community members who are exposed to the garden and, eventually, make the garden feel like a safe, family-friendly community asset.

Part of the limiting factor to implementing the type of programming that the garden was hoping to put on was funding. While the SHGA had been able to acquire several capacity-building grants through collaborations with the CCE and IFAS, there was no source of income aside from the dues collected from plot leases. Identifying an opportunity to better utilize the U Pick plots, board members started approaching local businesses offering sponsorship packages where the business could "adopt" the U Pick plots and set up advertisements there. One such business owner jumped on the opportunity to increase their exposure in the community, and initially the new partnership went very well. The business owner, from north DeLand, seemed very passionate about the garden and took good care of their U Pick plots. However, it soon became apparent that the owner felt that since they were contributing financial resources to the garden, they should be part of organization decisions. Following several tense weeks, the relationship was dramatically severed when, while tending to their sponsored plot during an organized event which included community families with children, the owner started loudly verbally berating Stetson student volunteers and neighborhood kids who were mistakenly weeding one of the sponsored plots. In one Saturday afternoon, the perception of the garden as a community "safe space" was altered. While the board took quick action to terminate their relationship with the business owner and issue an apology to the community gardeners and those who witnessed the event, the damage had been done.

Over the next few weeks, several of the gardeners present during that day did not return, including some well-known Spring Hill community leaders. With the intolerably hot summer season rapidly approaching and with membership beginning to decline, the SHGA began to rely even more heavily on Stetson student volunteers to provide most of the maintenance around the garden. Formal student internships were developed through the CCE, and outside funding was acquired to help those student interns stay during the summer and work with the SHGA, but the basic issue of community engagement remained difficult to overcome.

While the VISTA board member of the SHGA served as the supervisor for the Stetson summer interns doing much of the work around the garden, the perception of the Spring Hill Community Garden as "Stetson's garden" began to take hold. While this had been an initial issue with the way in which the garden was constructed, the board of the SHGA thought the perception could be overcome through active plot owner engagement and making community members feel like the garden was meant for them. At this time, community passersby would see mostly Stetson student volunteers working in the garden and would understandably assume that the garden was for those students, not the Spring Hill community. The issue of community ownership, sustainability, and fiscal solvency of the organization further divided the board who began to move in divergent directions as to how to salvage the image of the garden.

BUILDING A COMMUNITY-FOCUSED ORGANIZATION

To address the concerns of community buy-in and the "Stetson's Garden" perception, the SHGA and the CCE agreed that the third year of the AmeriCorps VISTA project would be dedicated to a slow disengagement of the CCE from direct garden participation. While the rest of the board had been primarily made up of Spring Hill community members, the VISTA had served as a facilitator of the board meetings and championed many garden decisions, including the U Pick plot sponsorship idea. The third year of the VISTA project, as determined by the CCE and garden board leadership, would be dedicated to building up the garden volunteer infrastructure, while slowly reducing the need for Stetson volunteers in order to maintain the grounds.

During these discussions around eventual complete community ownership of the garden, the financial question continued to lurk. Board members had decided that potentially one of the best ways to solve the "Stetson's Garden" perception would be to hire a part-time grounds-keeper from the Spring Hill community. That, however, required far more financial resources than the garden had. With raising dues for garden beds out of the question and grant funding difficult to find, the board considered becoming acquired by a larger, more financially stable organization. Through discussions with GULC – the Spring Hill-based organization that provided the grant to build the garden – it was determined that the garden would be folded into the organizational structure as a sub-committee. Still able to retain their board structure, the garden transitioned from an independent organization to part of a larger organization in less than a day.

As the Stetson CCE VISTA position was ending, empowering the board and the Spring Hill community at large was of utmost priority. Shilretha Dixon, director of the Spring Hill Resource Center, was unanimously promoted to president of the SHGA. Stetson University – including the CCE and the VISTA member – took on advisory and support roles and left all major decision making and management to the SHGA board of directors. Specific Stetson volunteer groups and faculty-led classes continued to work in the community garden. However, all groundwork and volunteer management was supervised by a dedicated university IFAS Master Gardener, plot owners, and the SHGA.

Although the Spring Hill Community Garden is now firmly in the community's hands, the full transition away from Stetson University and the CCE has not been smooth. As discussed above, DeLand and Spring Hill have complicated, adversarial, and long-winding histories. Even within Spring Hill, relationships between various churches, community organizations, non-profits, and leaders can be volatile. As an example, the decision to make the SHGA a sub-committee of the GULC was not seen kindly by some board members of the SHGA, largely in part because of these volatile relationships. Tensions among board members were not uncommon, especially with controversial decisions on funding and from where it was derived.

Meanwhile, the lack of a comprehensive plan made with community members led to confusion about the extent of involvement the CCE was to have with the SHGA. While the goal of the CCE was always to empower the community, possible improvements could have been made in fostering stronger coalitions among community organizations, having stronger ownership and participation in developing the garden from the community at the foundational stages, and having a more collaborative rather than leadership role from the start.

In retrospect, it is easy to say that the garden should have started out as part of GULC and have had less CCE involvement in their day-to-day operations. However, these distinctions are difficult to identify without an explicit strategic plan leading the planning and development process. Even though the garden was identified by Spring Hill community members as an unmet need, more community input in developing such a plan, even if it meant a protracted timeline of implementation, proved to be essential for the long-term community-wide impact of the project.

FARMERS' MARKET

While the community garden was able to provide gardeners some produce, it was by no means a sustainable source of fresh produce for the entire Spring Hill community. The garden's true asset was its ability to serve as a community education and green space, bringing together people in the act of gardening and nutrition education, rather than providing them with sustained produce to take home. For that, a larger intervention was needed. Upon reviewing possible interventions, literature pointed to the potential use of the local farmers' market to address nutritional insecurities in low-income communities (Evans et al. 2012; Sadler 2016; Wetherill and Gray 2015).

Over the past two decades, farmers' markets have become associated in some communities with expensive, organic products catered towards a majority-White, middle-class clientele (Anguelovski 2015; Oths and Groves 2012; Slocum 2007). This led to the pricing out of more income-constrained customers, thus exacerbating the issues of food access (Anguelovski 2015; Oths and Groves 2012). To address this, programs through the 2008 and subsequent Farm Bills have aimed to make the farmers' market more accessible to low-income families, and particularly, to improve access to fresh produce (Markowitz 2010). As it turned out, the closest source of fresh produce to Spring Hill was a Friday night farmers' market on the south side of downtown DeLand, known as Artisan Alley. Only 1.5 miles from the center of Spring Hill, the CCE tasked the AmeriCorps VISTA with looking into how to potentially leverage this existing asset to focus on expanding produce access in Spring Hill.

The market had only recently started but had become a hit with the primarily White, middle-class demographic of north DeLand, attracting over 2,000 visitors each market day. The organizers of the farmers' market were very eager to help with improving access to fresh produce, and as farmers themselves, were also eager about the possibility of attracting additional clientele. Through preliminary conversations, it became clear that the initial barrier to individuals on a limited income from shopping there was the cash-only policy of the market vendors. For those on a limited income, most utilize the Supplemental Nutrition Assistance Program (SNAP) to purchase the majority of their food each month (Pomeranz and Chriqui 2015). Without an ability to accept their SNAP benefits, there was no reasonable way to expect Spring Hill residents to utilize the market. Upon further investigation, it was discovered that there was no farmers' market in the entirety of Volusia County that accepted SNAP. To the market organizers and staff at the CCE, it was very clear what had to be done first.

The process to accept SNAP included incorporating the farmers' market as a non-profit organization, developing a board of directors, becoming qualified to accept SNAP through the USDA, and receiving a grant for a card reader to process SNAP transactions. During this time, an additional grant source was identified through Florida Organic Growers, called Fresh Access Bucks (FAB). This grant would match dollar for dollar up to $40 what a customer at the market spent from their SNAP account. With the matching funds only eligible to be spent on produce grown in Florida, the goal was to simultaneously improve access to fresh produce to SNAP customers and to ensure that at least part of their funds were spent supporting local farmers. What became known as the non-profit Artisan Alley Farmers and Makers' Market opened their SNAP and FAB programs in November 2017, run by Stetson student interns supervised by the VISTA.

Located in the center of the market with a prominently labeled tent, market organizers and CCE staff members – who had been working closely with Spring Hill leaders to develop the community garden and had communicated the market updates to those leaders – were expecting the tent to be overwhelmed with families eager to maximize their SNAP benefits. The reality of the situation was significantly different. Several straight weeks of one or no SNAP customers made organizers realize they had missed the mark and severely underestimated barriers to accessing fresh produce.

To help elucidate these questions, two research projects were conducted concurrently in the Spring Hill community. One assessment was a questionnaire focusing on resident perceptions of the Artisan Alley market and SNAP program, developed by the CCE with input from Spring Hill leaders and administered through the Spring Hill Resource Center. Compiling data from 48 Spring Hill Resource Center visitors during the month of March 2018, CCE staff conducted analysis and reported these numbers to the board of directors of the Artisan Alley market. Like in the 2016 needs assessment, most Spring Hill residents reported that they wanted more access to fresh produce options (85%). Most SNAP recipients completing the questionnaire were familiar with the market (68%), were familiar with the SNAP program at the market (58%), and felt comfortable at the market (65%). According to the responses, the primary barriers were not knowledge of the program but physically accessing the market during its operating hours of Friday, 6pm–9pm. Only a small proportion of SNAP recipients reported being able to easily walk to the market (26%), and most indicated they would attend the market if there was a shuttle service (85%) (Sirutis and Droznin 2021). Being unable to change the location of the market, CCE staff wanted to further investigate the issue of walkability and transportation between the market and Spring Hill in the hope of utilizing the subsequent report to lobby for change to reduce the impacts of those barriers.

In March 2018, in collaboration with the Rollins College Master of Public Health program and DOH-VC, CCE staff and Stetson student volunteers systematically walked and analyzed all 192 streets in Spring Hill, utilizing ArcGIS for their walkability assessment. Public transit options were only found on three streets along the periphery of Spring Hill, only one street had a bicycle path, 47.3% of Spring Hill streets were found to have a trip hazard, and only 16.2% had a continuous sidewalk on at least one side of the road (Droznin et al. 2018). These results, of course, were of little surprise to Spring Hill residents, but they helped market board members and CCE staff better understand the barriers that residents faced in accessing basic needs outside of their community.

While neither the market board, CCE, or Spring Hill partner organizations had sufficient resources to develop the transportation or infrastructure improvements recommended by the assessments, those became crucial considerations in the strategic plan of the market moving forward. Results from both research projects indicated that the best actionable solutions would be to either set up a shuttle service to connect the market to Spring Hill or to open a satellite market in Spring Hill on another night. Additionally, while 65% of Spring Hill SNAP recipients were familiar with the market SNAP and FAB programs, there was an opportunity to bring awareness to the additional 35% (Sirutis and Droznin 2021).

As with the community garden, difficulties among the board, the vendors, and the volunteers were not uncommon. These issues became more apparent when market managers began to see some of the actions of the SNAP team – consistently checking in with vendors, influencing which farmers and vendors should come into the market – were intruding upon their own responsibilities. Eventually, these tensions made their way into the Artisan Alley non-profit board and unfortunately led to disbanding the board. Stetson volunteers and the VISTA who led them had to re-envision their path forward with the market, while also figuring out a way to mend broken relations. A more open dialogue among key stakeholders of the market should have been established early on to clarify the purpose, goal, and reach of the SNAP program and its Stetson volunteers.

With these issues coming to light, the SNAP volunteer team took time to refocus on its main goal of expanding access to fresh, local produce to all members of the community, no matter one's income. The VISTA worked to have an open, honest dialogue with the market managers, space owners, vendors, and volunteers with the hope that everyone could get on a similar page again. Eventually, relations among key stakeholders were repaired. One of the property owners donated office space for non-profit work and the team developed new ways to improve outreach for their programs, such as assisting with SNAP applications and collaborating with local non-profit organizations, food pantries, and churches, who all have similar visions regarding food access.

Overall, the market has been successful as a program in western Volusia County. Internal data collected by Stetson student volunteers – operating the tent through software made available by FAB – shows that, as of March 2020, the program had created SNAP access for 213 families, including 69 from 32720, the zip code that contains Spring Hill, facilitating the purchase of more than $12,600 worth of groceries from local farmers and food vendors since its November 2017 launch. While these numbers represent the program as a valuable asset in addressing nutritional insecurities, we believe that more Spring Hill community member involvement from the beginning would have yielded even greater results there.

THE WRIGHT BUILDING

Soon, Stetson and Spring Hill leaders would be given an opportunity to expand their efforts beyond addressing access to healthy foods. Partnering with GULC on the community garden opened the way for the organization to seek Stetson faculty and CCE staff assistance with the revitalization of what was once the cornerstone of DeLand's Black community, the Wright Building. This prospect would bring a vision for restoring a vibrant commercial district to Spring Hill, potentially meeting the economic and health needs of the area.

Economic Context

In 1920, around the height of Ku Klux Klan activity in Florida, a Black citrus pioneer by the name of James W. Wright built a two-story commercial building on the north end of the greater Spring Hill community (Witek 2019; Bullard 1998). James Wright was already a very respected member of the community, and as the owner of the largest Black-owned citrus business in the south, had served as a keynote speaker for a conference hosted by Booker T. Washington (Davis 1915). What became known as the Wright Building hosted a grocery store, a restaurant, medical offices, and other spaces that offered Black entrepreneurs a base to operate during one of the most oppressive times for Black communities in Florida. The concept was a success, resulting in greater Spring Hill community investment in the area and the development of a thriving Black business and arts district known as Wright's Corner (Witek 2019). Despite ever present Jim Crow laws and harassment from the Ku Klux Klan, Spring Hill and Wright's Corner thrived for several decades. As discussed in a recent oral history-gathering project conducted by Stetson University students and faculty, the Wright Building was viewed as a gathering place, not only vital to economic development but central to social life and a sense of community in Spring Hill (Seaver and Johnson 2019).

The good times, however, were not to last. Following the death of James W. Wright, competition with larger stores, combined with the 1970s heroin and 1980s crack epidemics that devastated Spring Hill and other Black communities across the United States, most businesses within and around the Wright Building permanently shuttered their doors (Witek 2019; Bourgois 2003). With the disappearance of activity around the Wright Building, so too went the strong sense of community vitality that was once felt by residents. For the next four decades, the Wright Building sat mostly vacant and in an ever worsening state of disrepair.

Revitalization Efforts

In 2016, as part of their efforts to revitalize the area, GULC purchased the Wright Building from the City of DeLand. At this point, the building was in such a dire state that there was significant danger of imminent structural collapse. Enlisting the help of the West Volusia Historical Society to host a community panel on the past and future of the building, Stetson University staff and faculty to do archival research on its historical significance, and CCE staff members to assist in strategic planning and resource development, GULC began to develop a plan for a revitalized Wright's Corner. While significantly more expensive, it was determined by GULC based on community sentiment that all modifications to the building were to be done in accordance with National Historic Preservation guidelines, with as much of the original building being preserved as possible.

Based on the 2016 Public Health Needs Assessment, the community panel, and the history of the building, GULC determined that the new Wright Building would serve as a source of fresh produce, economic development, and local history, much as it had 70 years before during its height. Working with CCE staff members, a floor plan was developed to host a grocery store, community cafe, and local museum space on the first floor, with a business incubator focusing on entrepreneurs from Spring Hill on the second floor. Seeing an opportunity to connect food access efforts at the Spring Hill Community Garden and Artisan Alley Market to a new community-gathering space, located only a few blocks from both, CCE and GULC staff members enlisted the help of IFAS and the Master Gardeners. The vision included cooking demonstrations, along with gardening and nutrition classes focused on produce that community members were most eager to learn about.

With stabilization of the building being the first priority, a local historic preservation expert and business owner volunteered to lead the restoration effort. Working closely with CCE and other Stetson staff, the team worked to identify funding sources to assist with the effort and apply for much needed historic preservation designations. Projects such as the effort by Stetson students to obtain oral histories of the building and Stetson faculty archival research ended up being vital to arguing the case of the structure's historical significance. The Wright Building was quickly added to a local list of historic buildings in need of repair, and an application to the National Register of Historic Places was submitted to ensure the building's legacy and purpose would not be forgotten.

By 2019, efforts to revitalize the Wright Building were making slow progress with most of the funding for emergency stabilization efforts primarily coming from donations by Spring Hill residents. While generous, without support of larger donations, it was feared that the Wright Building project may not be completed. In response to this need, CCE staff and Wright Building project team leaders began working on several grants utilizing local research from Stetson University, historic designations, and the revitalization plan to fund the transformation of the building. These efforts culminated in the successful receipt of over $120,000 for the project, including selection as one of 22 sites nationwide to receive support from the National

Trust for Historic Preservation's prestigious African American Cultural Heritage Action Fund (National Trust for Historic Preservation 2019).

Since the receipt of the grant from the National Trust for Historic Preservation, the Wright Building, and Spring Hill in general, have attracted significant local media attention. The City of DeLand allocated funding to support the Wright Building efforts, and what was once dismissed as a project not worthy of investment now has people in DeLand talking about its potential. In February 2021, following four years of careful and dedicated research by Stetson faculty, staff, students, and Spring Hill residents, the Wright Building was finally added to the National Register of Historic Places. The CCE and Stetson University are proud to be a part of this incredibly collaborative project and will continue to support the goals of the Wright Building, GULC, and Spring Hill as long as we are needed.

DISCUSSION

Research Can Empower Communities

As a result of the 2016 Public Health and Community Needs Assessment and subsequent community town hall, it was determined by the Spring Hill CRA, City of DeLand, and Volusia County Council to invest $750,000 into building a new Spring Hill Resource Center (Kustura 2019). The old center, while located in the heart of Spring Hill, had outgrown its space. Having long lobbied the city for such a larger resource center, residents reported feeling listened to and that such an investment was a breakthrough in the relationship between the communities. Utilizing the results from the 2016 assessment, residents organized meetings at the Spring Hill Resource Center to lobby the city and CRA to include access to health services as a central feature. With the groundbreaking ceremony taking place in April 2019, the new Dr. Joyce M. Cusack Resource Center will have both a dedicated health examination room and a full kitchen for cooking demonstrations with plans for the outdoor space surrounding the building to have fruit trees and an outdoor exercise pavilion for general health and wellness activities.

Aside from expansions of the programs developed in partnership between Stetson and Spring Hill, the Spring Hill Resource Center itself has expanded its programming to focus on health by developing a longitudinal chronic disease prevention and management course. The community response was very positive, and the course was so successful that organizations from around the east coast have flown down to meet with the program director and learn from its success.

Progress

Overall, the Spring Hill community response to programming resulting from the 2016 Public Health and Community Needs Assessment has been encouraging. Improvements to the community garden are continuously being made. As opposed to being directly involved in garden operations, Stetson and the CCE have taken a more supportive role. Several faculty members have worked with the SHGA to develop community-engaged learning courses focused around the garden, allowing students to participate in building a pollinator garden on the ground, as well as making the garden space accessible following the Americans with Disabilities Act. The Artisan Alley Farmers' Market continues to operate its SNAP and FAB programs through a dedicated group of Stetson student volunteers and interns at the original site. However, in response to the participatory action conducted on barriers to accessing the market from Spring Hill, plans are being made by Spring Hill leaders in collaboration with Artisan Alley and the CCE to open a satellite location of the market and SNAP and FAB programs in the heart of Spring Hill. The Wright Building is currently under construction and is both ahead of schedule and under budget, thanks to generous community contributions, recent grant funding, and in-kind donations of project team members. Stetson remains involved in continuing research projects to support further historic preservation and building development efforts.

Research has continued to play a central role in determining the direction of collaborative programs between the CCE and the Spring Hill community. As problems have arisen and adjustments to programs have needed to be made, the answers were made not on a hunch but by community-informed research. For programs such as SNAP at the farmers' market to successfully improve health outcomes for residents, it was necessary to determine the barriers residents faced to accessing these resources. Answers to these questions led to additional projects focusing on specific identified barriers, such as a lack of streetlights, bumpy or missing sidewalks, and a lack of public transportation. By clearly identifying infrastructure needs in the community, these assessments have created a space for dialogue with the people who can make change happen.

Between the Spring Hill Resource Center, the Spring Hill community garden, Artisan Alley Farmers' Market, and Wright Building, research projects have led to the investment of over $1 million into the Spring Hill community since 2016. Moving forward, the CCE will continue to work to assess and improve existing projects, while looking at closer collaborations between local, state, and federal agencies. The new spotlight on Spring Hill through large-scale projects like the new resource center and the Wright Building have created openings for collaborations with city and county officials, and hopefully the development of more comprehensive and systemic positive change in Spring Hill.

When interviewing a community leader involved in many of the programs described in this chapter, they identified this pathway for dialogue among Spring Hill residents, Stetson community members, and local government officials as the greatest success of these programs:

> Now, we have dialogue because of the needs assessments. We also have a community right here and a university that is willing to put pen to paper and make it happen for us when we didn't have the time to do it. You mobilized a group of people who were willing to come into our community and not just come in today and leave tomorrow, but to stay through the process and build friendships along the way …
>
> The needs assessment has cleared a pathway for us to have dialogue with the people who can make this happen; that's our city, our county, our local government. We're at the point now where we're at the table with them.

This statement is a powerful testimony to the impact of research that is centered around the community. It indicates that it is not enough to conduct research about the community. Rather, it is important to return to the community and discuss with them the results of research findings and take actions to reassure the findings are shared with important local decision makers and stakeholders. Universities and colleges have an important responsibility to prioritize the interests of community members in the way they structure community-focused learning outcomes. Student learning should be carefully integrated into a model of learning where the message to students should be "you are here to learn *from* the community" rather than "you are here to save the community."

Community Members Are Subject Matter Experts

As academics, we are taught to consult peer-reviewed evidence published by subject matter experts before drawing our own conclusions. While crucial to ensuring a degree of validity to the work we do, sometimes this attitude can minimize the voices of those who are already marginalized. As we learned through our work in Spring Hill, it is not enough to simply rely on the outcomes of research projects to guide the programming and development of community projects. To progress towards a more equitable relationship, universities must work to view community members as subject matter experts on themselves and their communities. In this way, large forums where community members gather to discuss issues can be thought of as its own form of peer review.

Reflecting on the successes and challenges of collaborative projects developed since 2016, there emerges a common theme. As representatives of the university, we did not take the time to gather enough community-informed evidence before forming conclusions on how to go about addressing the issues brought up in the needs assessment. The more the programs were out of our control, such as the progress on the Wright Building, the more successful they ended up becoming. This is not to say that we stood in the way of progress, but rather that the more community members could inform the decisions made on the projects themselves, the more successful and sustainable they were. Despite our early failures with the garden, we were able to maintain the trust of enough community leaders through our willingness to own up to our errors and our efforts to learn from those mistakes. Developing that community trust through taking the time to listen and learn, and the challenges and successes therein, can be the primary determining factor in the success of collaborative programming. From the perspective of the CCE, the three-year deadline to succeed by the AmeriCorps VISTA grant made the development of new programs like the community garden feel like they had to be completed and fully independent by the end of that project. In reality, the goals of the grant and the needs of the community were not totally aligned. In hindsight, it would have been beneficial to carefully plan, research, design, and recruit members to the garden utilizing the experience and social capital of Spring Hill residents themselves for most of the three years before implementing the program. When the needs felt so acute, and the solutions so tangibly at hand, the urge to rush into program development before thorough strategic planning proved too much to overcome. This line of action, however, missed a key aspect: that there are no tangible solutions without extensive community involvement. The Wright Building plan, while deeply frustrating to CCE staff members at times due to a lack of visible progress, was taken at the pace necessary for the long-term sustainability of the program. Stetson faculty and staff were able to conduct research and develop a strategic plan with building project leaders, while community members were engaged at forums, in their churches, and in conversations at home. This more protracted approach allowed Spring Hill residents time to give input and know their perspectives were valued and concerns validated.

Comparing these projects with the ideals of PAR, our projects needed community involvement from the very beginning to be successful. Even in the research process developing the health needs assessment, community members could have provided valuable input in shaping the questions asked. Furthermore, though the survey clearly identified the need for access to fresh produce, community members could have generated a wider range of potential projects to address these needs, perhaps avoiding some of the problems encountered with the garden and market. Community leadership throughout this process surely would have avoided the misconception of the garden as "Stetson's garden," while still utilizing the university's assets. Though we unsuccessfully tried to prioritize what we viewed as "efficiency" over community participation, these projects allowed us to build relationships in the community that led the GULC to involve us with the restoration of the Wright Building. Overall, we have strengthened the impact of these projects by returning to the foundational principle of community involvement and ownership, which will shape our approach to future research and community development efforts.

REFERENCES

Acheraïou, Amar. 2008. *Rethinking Postcolonialism: Colonialist Discourse in Modern Literatures and the Legacy of Classical Writers*. New York: Springer.

Anguelovski, Isabelle. 2015. "Alternative Food Provision Conflicts in Cities: Contesting Food Privilege, Injustice, and Whiteness in Jamaica Plain, Boston." *Geoforum* 58: 184 194.

Association of American Colleges and Universities. 2008. "High-Impact Educational Practices." www.aacu.org/leap/hips

Beckwith, Dave and Cristina Lopez. 1997. *Community Organizing: People Power from the Grassroots*. Washington, DC: Center for Community Change.

Bourgois, Philippe. 2003. "Crack and the Political Economy of Social Suffering." *Addiction Research and Theory* 11(1): 31–37.

Bullard, Sara. 1998. *The Ku Klux Klan: A History of Racism and Violence*. Collingdale, PA: Diane Publishing.

CDC. 2000. "Protocol for Assessing Community Excellence in Environmental Health." www.cdc.gov/nceh/ehs/docs/pace-eh-guidebook.pdf

Center for Community Health and Development. 2020. "PACE EH: Protocol for Assessing Community Excellence in Environmental Health." https://ctb.ku.edu/en/table-of-contents/overview/models-for-community-health-and-development/PACE-EH/main

City of DeLand. 2020. "Spring Hill Community Redevelopment Agency." www.deland.org/resources/spring-hill-community-redevelopment-agency

City of DeLand. 2021. "History of DeLand." www.deland.org/resources/history-of-deland

Cooper, Adam, Alexa Fortuna, and Satinder Ahuja. 2019. "Investigating the Missing Link: Effects of Noncompliance and Aging Private Infrastructure on Water-Quality Monitoring." *Separation Science and Technology* 11: 329–339.

Davis, William H. 1915. "National Negro Business League Annual Report of the Sixteenth Session and the Tenth Anniversary Convention." *National Negro Business League*. Boston, MA: African M. E. Sunday School Union, pp. 16–32.

Droznin, Maxwell, Keisha Nauth, Allen Johnson, and Valerie Feinberg. 2018. "Greater Spring Hill Community Walkability Assessment Report May 2018." www.stetson.edu/other/community-engagement/media/Walkability%20assessment%20final.pdf

Evans, Alexandra E., Rose Jennings, Andrew W. Smiley, Jose L. Medina, Shreela V. Sharma, Ronda Rutledge, Melissa H. Stigler, and Deanna M. Hoelscher. 2012. "Introduction of Farm Stands in Low-Income Communities Increases Fruit and Vegetable among Community Residents." *Health and Place* 18(5): 1137–1143.

Gaventa, J. and A. Cornwall. 2001. "Power and Knowledge." In *The SAGE Handbook of Action Research*, edited by P. Reason and H. Bradbury. London: SAGE, pp. 145–155.

Huang, Cunrui, Pavla Vaneckova, Xiaoming Wang, Gerry FitzGerald, Yuming Guo, and Shilu Tong. 2011. "Constraints and Barriers to Public Health Adaptation to Climate Change: A Review of the Literature." *American Journal of Preventive Medicine* 40(2): 183–190.

Johnson, Asal M., Emily Carey, Gregory Fernandez, Jacqueline Pollack, and Emma Shaefer. 2016. "Public Health and Community Needs Assessment Report of Spring Hill Community, 2015–2016." www.stetson.edu/other/community-engagement/media/Spring%20Hill%20Community%20Needs %20Assessment.pdf

Kustura, Katie. 2019. "DeLand, Volusia Break Ground on New Spring Hill Resource Center." *Daytona Beach News-Journal.*

Markowitz, Lisa. 2010. "Expanding Access and Alternatives: Building Farmers' Markets in Low-Income Communities." *Food and Foodways* 18(1–2): 66–80.

National Trust for Historic Preservation. 2019. "National Trust Awards $1.6 Million in Grants to Help Preserve African American History." https://savingplaces.org/stories/2019-action-fund-grant -recipients#.Xn0TVohKg2w

Oths, Kathryn S. and Katy M. Groves. 2012. "Chestnuts and Spring Chickens: Conflict and Change in Farmers Market Ideologies." *Ecology of Food and Nutrition* 51(2): 128–147.

Pomeranz, Jennifer L. and Jamie F. Chriqui. 2015. "The Supplemental Nutrition Assistance Program: Analysis of Program Administration and Food Law Definitions." *American Journal of Preventive Medicine* 49(3): 428–436.

Ross, Lawrence. 2017. *Blackballed: The Black and White Politics of Race on America's Campuses.* New York: Macmillan.

Sadler, Richard Casey. 2016. "Strengthening the Core, Improving Access: Bringing Healthy Food Downtown via a Farmers' Market Move." *Applied Geography* 67: 119–128.

Seaver, Chelsea and Asal M. Johnson. 2019. "The Wright Building Recognition Project." Paper presented at the Florida Undergraduate Research Conference Jacksonville, FL.

Sirutis, Douglas and Maxwell Droznin. 2021. "Assessing Fresh Produce Accessibility of a Low-Income Community in DeLand, Florida." *International Journal of Health, Wellness, and Society* 11(2): 41–58.

Slocum, Rachel. 2007. "Whiteness, Space and Alternative Food Practice." *Geoforum* 38(3): 520–533.

Stetson University. 2020. "History of Stetson University." www.stetson.edu/other/about/history.php

Strand, Kerry J., Nicholas Cutforth, Randy Stoecker, Sam Marullo, and Patrick Donohue. 2003. *Community-Based Research and Higher Education: Principles and Practices.* Chichester: John Wiley & Sons.

U.S. Census Bureau. 2018. "American Community Survey 5-Year Estimates." https://censusreporter .org/profiles/16000US1216937-deland-southwest-fl/

University of Florida. 2020. "State Extension Programs." https://sfyl.ifas.ufl.edu/who-we-are/state -extension-programs/

Wetherill, Marianna S. and Karen A. Gray. 2015. "Farmers' Markets and the Local Food Environment: Identifying Perceived Accessibility Barriers for Snap Consumers Receiving Temporary Assistance for Needy Families (Tanf) in an Urban Oklahoma Community." *Journal of Nutrition Education and Behavior* 47(2): 127–133.

Witek, Eli. 2019. "Spring Hill's Challenges Reflect Its History." *The West Volusia Beacon.*

10. From mission to praxis in neighborhood work: lessons learned from a three-year faculty/ community development initiative

Laura L. O'Toole, Nancy E. Gordon, and Jessica L. Walsh

This chapter presents the case study of a partnership between a resident-led neighborhood collaborative and the graduate leadership program of a local university, both in Newport, Rhode Island. A hybrid model of participatory action research (PAR) and community development (CD) grounded a two-year collaboration to develop a sustainability-focused strategic plan and to document the leadership/CD values and practices in use but not previously formalized or promoted in organizational publications or reports. The case study project assisted in securing funding to sustain resident mobilization and neighborhood development at the end of the collaborative's first five-year funding cycle, while illuminating the CD praxis that has made it a model of racial equity and inclusion among local organizations. We situate this project within a larger three-year grant-funded university initiative designed to facilitate transformation within institutional, pedagogical, and community/project interfaces by aligning the justice-based university mission and community-based collaborations between faculty and partner organizations.

The case we highlight is grounded in emergent models for partnership, transforming the locus of attention from university to neighborhood, while increasing civic engagement and involving students in ways that intentionally promote PAR and CD as important mechanisms for social change. Both community and campus outcomes demonstrate the ways in which centering neighborhood-identified needs and drawing on the experiences and skills of all stakeholders contributes to new knowledge and increases awareness of strategic practices.

The exemplary partnership between the Newport Health Equity Zone (HEZ), a grass-roots community and leadership development collaborative, and the holistic leadership graduate program in a small, Catholic university in the northeast United States is one of 18 projects developed within a larger initiative to shift the meanings, focus, and practice of campus–community partnership that characterized the university's traditional interpretation of its mission. Specifically, a cadre of faculty and community partners with administrative support and external funding studied and worked together to dislodge the dominant articulation of a *service-oriented* model in favor of a *justice-based* mission. The grant initiative foregrounded the Critical Concerns of the Religious Sisters of Mercy (RSM), the founding order of the institution in which two of us work, the academic literature on social change curricula, a critique of service learning most closely aligned with the "liberating service learning" model (Stoecker 2016), and a desire to learn with and from community partners and their constituents.

The authors of this chapter are two faculty members (undergraduate and graduate) of Salve Regina University, a university founded by the RSM and the executive director for the backbone organization that facilitates a federally and locally funded HEZ initiative in Newport, RI, the community in which we all work. The RSM have an ostensible founding mission to work in CD via the "spiritual and corporal works of mercy" as articulated by their founder, Catherine McAuley, in the late nineteenth-century class-stratified city of Dublin, Ireland. The "walking nuns" as they were known, were specifically focused on neighborhood-based work to develop the human capacity of – and provide hospitality to – the marginalized women and children who came to their house in the upper-class Baggot Street neighborhood for education and other critical resources.

More recently, the RSM International has committed to five global critical concerns: racism, women, the Earth (especially water), immigration, and non-violence (RSM of the Americas 2019). Salve Regina University, further, has a mission that references the central emphasis on *mercy* that undergirds these concerns and pledges to work for "universal justice." Yet, as is typical for many higher educational institutions, actualizing our mission in the community is largely operationalized through a discourse and orientation of service and includes a ten-hour community service requirement for undergraduates.

The three-year initiative, funded by a grant written by the first author, supported course development and prioritized building trust with our neighbors. It generated a new model for community-centric projects that pivot on facilitating relationships between faculty and community partners, with students as project team members. The defining characteristics of these projects are an essential focus on contributing to the "change work" of community partners, intentionality in embedding and scaffolding the projects in courses, and integration of the RSM charism. PAR principles ground our plans, particularly for those projects that involve data generation for CD applications. The initiative is cross-disciplinary, hence art- and co-education-based CD projects as well as PAR are mechanisms for our work with partners in the under-resourced neighborhoods in a town known for opulence and privilege. Although the university is not physically located in the neighborhoods where we worked, our town is small, and our intent is to align the spirit of the university mission with a contemporary understanding of resident-led CD and our capacity to support it.

Toward this end, three annual learning communities of six faculty fellows and two faculty principal investigators, and a second-year learning community of interested local partners, collaborated to build and implement a relational rather than transactional model of collaboration (see Ray 2016; Tryon et al. 2009) characterized by intentionality in developing praxis-based *knowledge projects* (Stoecker 2016) with local community-based organizations. The faculty participants embedded projects into courses with orientations toward civic engagement and problem solving across the university and at all course levels during the 2016–2019 academic years.

ELABORATING NEW MODELS FOR ACADEMIC COMMUNITY ENGAGEMENT

Beyond "Institutionalized Service Learning"

Contributing back to their local communities is a goal of most institutions of higher education, and service learning has been a component of that ethos for decades. More recently, efforts to augment traditional service learning by reinvigorating the civic engagement of universities and their constituents have been escalating. In 2010, the United States Department of Education constituted the National Task Force on Civic Learning and Democratic Engagement, subsequently facilitated by the American Association of Colleges and Universities. The task force report *A Crucible Moment* has been widely disseminated since as a "national call to action" to reinvigorate civic learning through civic engagement (National Task Force 2012). It emphasized the role of the liberal arts and sciences in educating engaged citizens who contribute to the common good. It also provided evidence that our current students generally want to be engaged in public work.

By now, civic and community-based learning is acknowledged as an educational priority to prepare students for lives as citizens in an increasingly diverse society; engaging with the larger community in the process is considered a high-impact practice that typically deepens student learning (Youniss 2011; Hurtado et al. 2012; Kuh 2009). Critical (Mitchell 2008) and social change (Stoecker 2016) models of campus/community collaboration, however, encourage interrogation of what Randy Stoecker calls *institutionalized service learning*, the most traditional form of "civic engagement" practice in college curricula.

For example, Stoecker's students, including co-editor Tryon, conducted research among community partners to learn their viewpoints toward service learning. Students discerned the extent to which university actors had not bothered to ask community partners about the efficacy of service learning and recorded a mix of both appreciation and frustration among respondents (2009). Stoecker's more recent critique flips both traditional and critical models by decentering the university and prioritizing collaborations that create knowledge for CD and social change – and where faculty and student learning are significant but subordinated to needs of communities, articulated *on their own terms*. Relationship and trust building among campus and community stakeholders, also elaborated in the work of Darby Ray (2016), are central aspects of collaborations.

When CD is part of a campus–community partnership, putting CD *outcome*s both at the center of engagement work and by extension curriculum design is critical. Indeed, numerous scholars have recognized that if community stakeholders are not at the table as co-designers of the work, civic engagement and service learning can reproduce the very bureaucratic control tendencies that have historically created tensions between universities and their extant communities as well as inflict other harms by exploiting the marginalized communities on which traditional research is typically focused (Blau 1999; Strand 1999; Stoecker and Tryon 2009; Stoecker 2016). Teaching students about the ways in which PAR and CD transform traditional community power relations is crucial.

A consensus is emerging among academics working with community organizations that relationships are foundational to engaged pedagogies and scholarship. Early cautionary voices, especially in the social sciences, suggest this realization has been a long time coming. Scholars observing through the lens of critical sociology, for example, have identified the ways in which service learning – and in particular, direct service provision – can reinforce individualist thinking among students (Strand 1999), reinforce traditional hierarchies (Blau 1999), and expose the limited knowledge both faculty and students have about local political and economic structures (Marullo et al. 2009).

Ray refers to the journey that she and other civic engagement practitioners have taken as one "from paternalism to partnership" (2016: 8). To refer to sites of engagement as community partners, she argues, imposes the weight of recognizing that *true* engagement as partners is relational, not transactional. Beyond any content knowledge students are expected to learn is a more fundamental lesson: that building relationships takes time, building trust is not easy, and that the privileged status of institutions in relation to many community agencies can manifest in bumps and potholes along the journey that must be owned and rectified, which can frequently require *rebuilding* relationships and trust.

Although it is likely that most faculty members who choose to participate in service learning/community engagement work envision it as a meaningful contribution to the public good, the focal concerns in developing projects must be led by community partners; modeling the often difficult work of building honest relationships that empower those on the deficit side of power imbalances is thus a crucial component of the work. Requiring faculty and students to participate in community work as obligations for such credentials as Carnegie's Community Engaged Campus designation can inadvertently contribute to resituating campuses at the center of engagement work and overwhelming partners with few staff and resources to accommodate projects (O'Toole 2017). Salve Regina University has thus far decided not to follow that path and to prioritize our relational and community work among our Newport neighbors.

Understanding the ways resource differentials affect campus–community partnerships is crucial. It requires that community partners feel empowered to critique current arrangements *and* that academics feel compelled to listen to their critiques. Listening and hearing as learned skills become critical – for both faculty practitioners who may be used to setting the terms of their own courses and for the students they send into the community or otherwise develop projects for community use. Faculty need to be present and collaborative, not in charge. Learning to share power over course content and assessments begins with talking less and listening more. Students must be trained for community work and to understand the stakes and stakeholders in the process. Therefore, structures for listening must be built and maintained for students and faculty (Ray 2016).

In many institutional settings, primary relationships are built between university staff in community service or civic engagement offices and agency representatives rather than with constituents of grass-roots community organizations (O'Toole 2017). Research suggests, however, that partners want "more direct communication with faculty" (Ray 2016: 10), an important observation that we foregrounded in developing our own model for transforming campus–community partnerships on the academic side of the house at Salve Regina University. But building relationships takes time and as Blau aptly suggests, service learning, and by extension civic engagement, is "not charity, but a two-way street" (1999: xiv).

Integrating Participatory Action Research, Community Development, and "Emergent Future" Co-leadership Models

Stoecker and Falcón in this volume advocate for the strategic necessity of integrating PAR *and* CD in collaborative work with partners, and this strategy is particularly salient to the community-based projects supported by our grant. We were mindful to intentionally integrate these practices throughout the three-year grant and, most specifically, within the HEZ–holistic leadership partnership where a hybrid approach to PAR and CD existed throughout the duration.

Clearly, then, one of the ways to move an institution beyond institutionalized service learning and toward truly collaborative and community-centered work is to define and ground that work in the literatures on PAR, CD, and emergent models of collaborative leadership – and to clarify that civic engagement involves citizen participation and not university-defined problems and methods. Stoecker suggests the common elements of participatory action approaches to research (which we extend to any course-based project) are focusing on being useful, incorporating diverse methods, and emphasizing collaboration (2013: 27). Maiter et al. correlate the central "principle and practice of reciprocity" (2008: 306) to a range of PAR outcomes, including the knowledge generated and its consequences. They also cite Bradbury and Reason's research (2003) that prioritizes "emergent developmental form, human flourishing, participation and democracy" as among the most important characteristics of PAR (Maiter et al. 2008: 306).

Fundamental among the challenges of PAR and CD is continuous and critical evaluation of the process, as well as the knowledge created, to identify potential reproduction of inequalities. There are risks of privileging those parties whose power is often so taken for granted as to become invisible to them, but not to their community partners (Smith et al. 2010; Maiter et al. 2008). Smith and her colleagues (2010) acknowledge the extent to which university researchers, who bring both limitations and value to community research, can become confused and feel "exposed" when episodes arise that illuminate such power differentials and require rearticulating the process. Their case studies demonstrate the extent to which idealism and reality often collide in the work; they provide important cautions that inform the work we undertake as members of a well-intentioned, but fairly traditional campus community. Situating ourselves as co-learners with our students and incorporating a redundant message that community members' lives are most affected by the outcomes of PAR (Minkler 2000) is incumbent among those of us who intend to transform our community partnerships as well as our pedagogies and scholarly work.

Introducing emergent relational models for partnered pedagogy (as is the case in the project we describe below) pushes faculty and students into interdisciplinary and transdisciplinary literatures about social, economic, and community change. Revisioning how faculty learn to share power with community partners in reciprocal ways and how university actors relearn ways to articulate and develop community partnerships are challenges in institutions with traditional models for community engagement. Creating approaches for training campus practitioners (students and faculty alike) in PAR and other methods for engaging in social change is also a new challenge for many. Shifting our focus, suspending judgment, and "leading into an emergent future" (Scharmer and Kaufer 2013: 3) are necessary for transforming institutional cultures as well as how faculty integrate engaged pedagogies into work that spans classroom and community. In some ways, shifting the mode of campus/community engagement work toward these principles is quite consistent with the relational processes and contingency management that community organizations like HEZ, of necessity, incorporate into their daily work.

Scharmer and Kaufer's ideas for recentering the privilege and power differentials from the university to the community and for redirecting the methods through which faculty train students to participate, shift the model from "ego-systems" characteristic of "pathological" (2013: 4) practices in public, private, and educational sectors to what they call "the co-creative eco-system model" or "from me to we" (Scharmer and Kaufer 2013: 16). Including the ecosystem perspective in training for CD work tightly aligns with processes for community change as it creates a transformative yet evolutionary focus that can help us think through the basics for revitalizing and recentering campus *and* community.

Student engagement in the PAR process also requires a unique set of skills beyond learning research methods that may be counterintuitive for many in an educational system that is centered around grade point averages, risk aversion, and individual achievement. Training in active listening, non-verbal and non-vocal conversational skills, as well as all facets of "helping relationship" responding skills (Schein 1999) are important. Schein (2013) outlines an active inquiry process called "humble inquiry" in which he suggests that "asking rather than telling" is a learned skill. He elucidates how to observe a social situation, how to adequately assess what is observed, and how to fully ground an understanding of complex social phenomena. He calls these processes "intervention in the service of learning": communication, deliberate feedback, and facilitative intervention techniques for individuals, groups, and larger systems (Schein 1999: 122–218).

The scope of the "Integrated Learning for Civic Engagement" initiative
Over the three-year grant cycle, 19 university faculty at both the undergraduate and graduate levels offered 23 civic engagement courses in which they collaborated as co-principal investigators with 14 different community organizations or agencies in Rhode Island. Five community partners worked with two or more faculty in multiple courses with unique projects and/or extensions of previous work over these three years. Projects focused on a variety of community-determined needs and included skills-based collaborations in data collection, data analysis, best practice research for program development, strategic planning, leadership development, public arts projects, environmental impact analyses, and archival development.

Over the course of the initiative, many faculty and community partners worked to "unlearn" the institutionalized service-learning model (Stoecker 2016) that privileges faculty as experts and student learning (and/or fulfilling a ten-hour graduation service requirement) as the primary outcome of the institution's community outreach. Those partners whose organizations are also built on service-oriented models were encouraged to "unlearn" their customary deference to the university, through which many student volunteer hours have been delivered over the years (see Mondloch 2009). Those partners with more formal, institutionalized organizational structures interrogated their own methods of engaging constituents and addressing community problems. Learning to listen, expecting to be held accountable as individuals and for institutional practices, and giving up some of the power invested in our pedagogies and practices were paramount commitments for faculty participants. Indeed, as one of the trustees of our funding institution noted, this project was simultaneously about faculty development, CD *and* organizational culture change.

Although we will include some concluding reflections from across the range of project evaluations, including focus groups with community partner representatives and a survey of student participants at the close of the grant cycle, we center our chapter on a case study that documents one project from the three-year relationship forged between numerous faculty fellows and the Newport HEZ. Over the life of the grant, the HEZ collaborated with five faculty in different disciplines on numerous projects including food access research, transgender health assessment and policy development, strategic planning, and an annual neighborhood Sidewalk Parade.

The evolution of the Sidewalk Parade is illustrative of the paradigm shift encouraged through this initiative: the parade is a response to PAR that HEZ staff and leadership conducted that uncovered, among many other community needs, a clear and demonstrable interest in access to public art. The Sidewalk Parade emerged from community meetings and faculty development consultations in the first year of the grant and has evolved into a fully community-led event where contributing partners such as the university are now in more supportive roles. Planning for the fourth year of the Sidewalk Parade was under way when the COVID-19 pandemic forced its cancellation for 2020 and the foreseeable future.

SITUATING THE CASE STUDY: THE NEWPORT HEALTH EQUITY ZONE

The Newport HEZ, one of Salve Regina University's primary community partners, is a collaborative initiative committed to innovative, resident-driven strategies that address health disparities and build resident leadership. The HEZ is a city-wide coalition mobilizing residents and resources of two city neighborhoods (Broadway and the North End) to make Newport a place where everyone can thrive. The HEZ envisions a city where:

- structural, financial, and environmental barriers to health and well-being are eliminated;
- public policy fosters the good health of all residents; and
- residents feel empowered to control the health of their families and community (Newport HEZ 2016).

The collaborative consists of 14 lead partners and over 15 contributing partners, as well as residents. The Women's Resource Center, the local domestic violence service organization, serves as the backbone organization for the project. Lead partners are (1) stipended for their engagement; (2) co-lead a working group; (3) provide technical assistance in their area of expertise to project staff and the collaborative as a whole; and (4) attend monthly HEZ local action team meetings, where strategic decisions about the project are made. Contributing partners are engaged in one or more working groups and/or support aspects of the project but are typically engaged at a lower intensity and don't have prescribed responsibilities. HEZ partners include direct service, health, arts-based, youth-focused, food sovereignty, environmental, land conservation, education, marketing, and violence prevention organizations.

Since the fall of 2015, the HEZ collaborative has organized residents and community partners to address structural determinants of health, environmental factors contributing to poor health in the HEZ neighborhoods. This collaboration is built on the racial justice analysis of the Racial Equity Institute; by acknowledging how power and racism operate within organizations and neighborhoods, the HEZ has intentionally built an inclusive collaborative infrastructure.

The Newport HEZ encompasses two census tracts with a total population of just under 8,800. This area contains the highest concentration of poverty in Newport. In addition to facing challenges commonly associated with poverty, significant geographic barriers isolate people in this district. For example, the ramps for the Newport Pell Bridge and the highway and rotary taking cars to and from the bridge divide the HEZ in half. There are limited sidewalks and crosswalks, making crossing the road dangerous. These barriers create challenges for building social cohesion within the district and limit access to downtown – with all its jobs, services, and cultural opportunities – for North End residents.

According to the 2017 American Community Survey, approximately 50% of the racially diverse North End of Newport identifies as non-Hispanic white, 27% as Hispanic or Latino, 7% as African American, 5% as Asian, 2% as Native American, and 7% as two or more races. 20% of the population living in the North End census tract speaks a language other than English. Median household income is $34,167, nearly half that of Newport as a whole. 22% of people are living below the federal poverty line. Youth under the age of 18 make up approximately 28% of the population. Approximately 38% of adults have only a high school diploma or less educational attainment (US Census Bureau 2018).

The second tract abuts the southeast corner of the North End. 72% of this second tract identifies as non-Hispanic white, 15% as Hispanic or Latino, 10% as African American, and 5%

as two or more races. A language other than English is spoken by nearly 17% of people living in this neighborhood. Youth under the age of 18 make up more than 13% of the population. The median household income of $62,149 is close to that of Newport as a whole. About 30% of adults have only a high school diploma or less educational attainment (US Census Bureau 2018).

Political and Economic Context

Residents of the HEZ, particularly the North End neighborhood, have historically been excluded from civic leadership and municipal decision-making structures. The Newport HEZ has made strides in shifting this culture of exclusion by building relationships with local decision makers, supporting residents with appointments to municipal boards and commissions, coordinating voter registration and get-out-to-vote initiatives, and supporting residents in establishing the North End Neighborhood Association. In the 2018 and 2020 elections, voters in Newport elected North End residents to City Council, unprecedented in recent history. The HEZ has very strong relationships with three of the seven councilors (at this writing) who regularly participate in HEZ initiatives and are strong champions for the work. At the state level, the HEZ has close working relationships with one sitting state senator and one sitting representative.

This progress is only a beginning, however, and there is a sense of urgency to increase HEZ residents' voice in decision making as the threat of gentrification is real. The city's economic development plan centers on development in the North End, an area that city officials have referred to as a "frontier" in public forums, despite the fact that more than 4,000 people already live there. At the same time, Section 8 housing developments will be exiting the conditions of their Housing and Urban Development (HUD) mortgages in the coming decade, and other tax credit financing of affordable housing will be expiring, opening those units up to market-rate rentals or sales. The first development met its HUD obligations in 2019, evicted many tenants, renovated, rebranded, and is no longer affordable for the people who formerly lived there. Preserving affordable housing is not a priority for decision makers who frequently cite the fact that Newport well exceeds the state's 10% affordable housing mandate, with 17% of its current housing stock classified as affordable housing. (However, even at 17%, the waiting list for the Newport Housing Authority consistently hovers around 10,000 applicants.)

Given these conditions, increasing civic engagement is the primary goal of the HEZ over the coming five years, with civic engagement strategies embedded throughout the work plan. In addition to the attitudinal barriers against affordable housing, the HEZ anticipates other barriers: public planning and permitting processes are opaque and hard for HEZ residents to navigate, and getting timely, accurate, and meaningful information about planning and development projects can be challenging, even when public disclosure requirements are in place. Moreover, the magnitude of the combined potential projects sited in the North End will require a comparable community response: mobilizing for an assessment of cumulative development impact (rather than project by project) as well as a community benefits agreement. The HEZ's approach is always to utilize champions to find answers, to systematically document processes, to advocate for more transparent processes, and to introduce tools (such as the Health Impact Assessment) that help to educate decision makers and the public on the health impacts of proposed policies and projects.

During Year 1 (2015) of the Newport HEZ project, staff and residents of the North End and Broadway neighborhoods that comprise the HEZ conducted an extensive needs assessment. Using a community-based participatory research approach, the assessment included a comprehensive community survey completed by over 500 residents and extensive qualitative assessments via focus groups, focused discussions, key informant interviews, and the collection of personal stories of residents. A highly organized interactive community-wide data giveback session – a Creativity Lab – attended by approximately 100 local residents and community-based organization staff provided a platform to share the data collected with the community. The assessment identified three core barriers to health among HEZ residents:

1. *Lack of transportation.* The lack of safe active transportation routes and frequent/widespread bus service is limiting access to food, healthcare, jobs, education, physical activity, arts and cultural opportunities, and parks and open spaces.
2. *Low social cohesion.* Perceived lack of community-based activities, particularly for kids and teens, is inhibiting social cohesion. Residents across the lifespan would like to see more opportunities for building neighborhood-level cohesion.
3. *Life stressors.* Adult residents identified life stressors such as lack of employment and raising a family on limited means as inhibiting their ability to be as healthy as they would like.

Based on lessons learned during the first five years of the project, the Newport HEZ identified the following components as necessary in all future assessments:

● Resident leadership: Processes that center resident leadership are vital. This commitment requires accounting for capacity-building needs when planning assessments.
● Empowerment evaluation model: An empowerment evaluation approach is highly compatible with resident-led assessment and evaluation (Fetterman 1994; Wandersman et al. 2005).
● Innovative methodologies: Mixed-method assessment design that incorporates non-traditional and interactive tools maximizes resident engagement with assessment processes.
● Built-in feedback loops: Incorporating opportunities to share assessment findings with the community and encourage collective solutions results in more innovative action plans and increased trust between the community and the Newport HEZ Collaborative.

The Newport HEZ uses a public health approach and data-to-action process in all its work. This cycle includes involving the HEZ Collaborative – and centering resident voice – in the process of defining community needs, developing approaches to addressing those needs, evaluating the processes and outcomes, feeding that information back to the stakeholders, and using stakeholder engagement to continue to define and refine its goals and implementation strategies. This is how CD is defined and practiced in the Newport HEZ. This CD approach is further manifested in the consistent attention to capacity building, hiring and promoting North End residents as fully paid staff members, and developing their expertise and leadership skills in areas of personal interest and community need.

Meaningful community engagement is the hallmark of the Newport HEZ. Residents have been included in the Newport HEZ Collaborative since the project's inception. Resident consultants are paid to represent resident interests at all levels of the HEZ project. Currently, between project staff, community health worker fellows, and resident consultants, 15 residents are working on the project. The HEZ also depends on the North End Neighborhood Association for resident input; in these situations, the HEZ provides incentives in the form of gift cards or meals to show its appreciation for their contributions. Finally, HEZ hosts an annual event inviting the broader community to hear about progress, provide feedback, and give guidance on future direction.

Our collective journey from mission to praxis with the HEZ began in the 2016–2017 academic year with several class projects developed by faculty members and the HEZ already in place after the first year of the university's project implementation grant. Those courses developed by both discipline-based and interdisciplinary faculty dovetailed with the university's Mercy mission and the HEZ mission, strategic principles, and one or more of its focus areas: food access, transportation, housing, greening urban spaces, arts and culture, civic engagement, maternal and child health, LGBTQ+ health, and the Collective of Phenomenal Women. The partnership with holistic leadership was established midway through the grant period. The case study project began in the second year of the grant and thus built on the foundation established in the first year and has influenced project development thereafter.

A CASE STUDY: APPLYING "THE HEZ WAY" TO STRATEGIC PLANNING, 2017–2018

As per Stoecker and Falcón's definition (this volume), the HEZ is "a place-based community led by community members." Integrating CD with PAR challenges the traditional notion of PAR because the focus for change, leadership, and practice are inverted. Coutu et al. state: "Change within the community context ... offers a different perspective for change, such as power and empowerment" (2010: 120–122).

Our focus here is on a collaborative project in which the university's holistic leadership graduate program formed a partnership with the Newport HEZ early in the fall of 2017. In keeping with the CD/PAR integration, HEZ executive director Walsh and professor Gordon met monthly prior to the start of the spring 2018 class to determine how the civic engagement class could best be of service to the HEZ at this point in its evolution. Through these discussions, Walsh determined that the most effective use of the partnership was to assist in the formalization of a sustainability plan to guide its work at the close of its initial four-year funding cycle.

According to Senge et al., "sustainability means capable of continuing indefinitely without depletion or diminished return" (2006: 44). Their definition informed the project and the approach to gathering data and enabled many fruitful discussions between the HEZ staff, residents, and leadership students. Sustainability became the topic of two summer retreats, which HEZ staff and Gordon co-designed and co-facilitated for the HEZ community partners and North End residents. Graduate students had the unique opportunity to observe the retreats and contribute observations on the process at the end of one of them.

While in planning mode, the December meeting between Walsh and Gordon also identified the second community engagement objective. Through a serendipitous conversation about process, Walsh remarked "we do things the HEZ way," after which Gordon asked, "*What is the HEZ Way?*" Of course, HEZ participants "knew" what it meant, but the processes and practices had never been formally identified. Thus, a seemingly tangential conversation led to the idea that Gordon and her class would observe the HEZ organizing process closely to identify the attributes of "the HEZ Way" as part of the larger sustainability project. During the project cycle, Walsh and Gordon met one-on-one for ten sessions, often over lunch; Walsh and one other staff member attended seven Gordon classes at Salve Regina; and Gordon alone and/or with students attended approximately 15 HEZ small staff meetings, monthly local action team meetings, workshops, retreats, and/or debriefs.

The strategic planning project that emerged from the planning process involved deep involvement with and providing deliverables to community members working on health and racial equity concerns at the same time that it provided excellent learning, training, and modeling for students to further understand effective community/university partner alliances and their potential impacts in the community. It also demonstrated the intentionality of our funded efforts to model how organizational processes work *outside* of the classroom (Schein 1999, 2013), while deeply integrating projects *within* grant-funded courses. Finally, this project fulfilled a mutual goal from the outset: to sustain the partnership between the university and the HEZ for as long as the HEZ specifies useful ways we can contribute "knowledge, power and action" to its social change efforts (Stoecker 2016: 101).

Articulating the Substantive Components of the Community Development Project

The HEZ leadership and sustainability project evolved during the second year of our grant in the academic year 2017–2018. Centrally integrated into three graduate-level holistic leadership classes, the project spanned a spring class, two summer classes, and tangentially a fourth class in the fall of the following academic year. The project involved several components falling into two goal areas: formally documenting the leadership and management practices that had become known among HEZ neighborhood constituents as "the HEZ Way" and supporting the development of a sustainability plan for the future of HEZ.

Over the course of several one-on-one meetings, HEZ executive director Walsh and course professor Gordon agreed to work together to meld the spring leadership class into a "working alliance" with the HEZ. Determining the shape of the partnership occurred over several brainstorming meetings, as stated above, and resulted in developing methods to facilitate the creation of a formal sustainability plan for the HEZ, a requirement of the HEZ's funder after initial funding from the state health department ended in March 2019. The spring 2018 "Introduction to the Holistic Leadership Perspectives" syllabus project description stated:

> The Health Equity Zone (The HEZ) is currently undergoing a transition due to the ending of its current funding cycle and the need to develop a large-scale sustainability plan. The instructor has committed to working with The HEZ to help with the sustainability design plan and its on-going development … As a class system, we will continue to form a collaborative leadership group to follow this project, become part of the team, and provide supportive help to The HEZ as identified and needed.

"The HEZ Way": A Circle Model

Gordon and Walsh determined that a key component of the sustainability plan would be to formally identify those processes and procedures that guide HEZ organizing and leadership development practices within the Newport community – those ways of going about business that staff and constituents often refer to as "the HEZ way." In its May 2018 newsletter, the HEZ describes our project as follows:

When we say that we do things "the HEZ Way," *what exactly do we mean*?

Dr. Nancy Gordon … and students of her Holistic Leadership class will be answering this question for us through observation, documentation, and discussion of our project and procedures. Students will interview team members and residents, sit in on meetings, create formal reports, and assist with retreats in an effort to better define and frame our work. Having our practices and processes documented will not only support our sustainability work but give us an opportunity to share our unique implementation with other projects and organizations. (Emphasis ours)

Documenting "the HEZ Way" reinforces the strategic necessity to integrate PAR/CD in real time because the design incorporates a mixed-methods approach to observing the HEZ, participating in its meetings, and assisting in, observing, and co-facilitating two actual HEZ/ community retreats. Gordon, during her fellowship year, along with several graduate students, utilized a formalized observation tool to observe and document practices at several small and large group meetings over the course of the spring and summer semesters. In addition, they conducted key informant interviews with several resident staff members of the HEZ. Gordon developed all instruments with input from Jessica Walsh on behalf of HEZ. Walsh and Gordon first pilot-tested the informant interview protocol in front of the 2018 spring holistic leadership class in February. Students supported the theming of these qualitative observations during a day-long class in summer 2018; Walsh and Gordon facilitated this in-class process jointly.

Ultimately, two students created a summative white paper document encapsulating "the HEZ Way" and the seven guiding principles that the HEZ Collaborative originally developed. The seven HEZ Way guiding principles, taken together, are emblematic of a CD model focused on resident-led "processes that build the bonds of community itself" (Stoecker and Falcón, this volume):

1. Community design: The community will design what the HEZ creates.
2. Equal voice: Everyone sits as equals when the HEZ convenes.
3. Disruption: Designing the HEZ will move beyond the comfort zone.
4. Open: The HEZ will pay attention and be open to the outcome.
5. Collective impact: The HEZ is one movement, with many participants.
6. Celebration: The HEZ will celebrate milestones of all sizes.
7. Sustainability: Shared power will sustain the HEZ. (Newport HEZ 2021)

The leadership class research team observed through five direct observations of HEZ monthly working group meetings that every member has an equal voice in all facets of the creation, development, and formation of policies, procedures, and programming. For example, the class observed that HEZ staff facilitated meetings, and innovatively structured each to include an opening check-in, a circle-structured seating arrangement, and a specific check-out process to close the meeting (Baldwin and Linnea 2010). They also confirmed that resident centering and capacity building is demonstrated through the intentional staffing of constituents in all capacities, including as trained community health workers situated in the neighborhoods.

"The HEZ Way," although not explicitly defined until the development of the class project, is (and was) embedded in all aspects of the HEZ collaborative process. The discernment of "the HEZ Way," then, illustrates the extent to which PAR helped illuminate the actual practice of CD deployed by the HEZ Collaborative. And that, in turn, has been used by the Newport HEZ to define their work more clearly for constituents, funders, and local policymakers with whom they engage in neighborhood change work (see Newport HEZ 2021). In this way, this project proved useful beyond typical strategic planning work: it is quite unusual for community groups to actually reflect upon their culture to develop compatible standards around which their work and accountability structures will be organized.

The class found that HEZ uniquely positions itself as (and actually practices) a model that centers neighborhood residents, utilizing the Model of Community Health Governance to guide the development of the collaborative's structure, processes, and practices. The collaborative change model deployed by the HEZ in their CD efforts outlines key characteristics essential to successful community-level health collaboratives and defines "special kinds of leadership and management" to ensure these characteristics are achieved (Lasker and Weiss 2003). Walsh and her team intentionally incorporate the leadership and management practices embedded in this model, which fall into four broad categories: promoting broad and active participation, assuring broad-based influence and control, facilitating productive group dynamics, and extending the scope of the process. The specific adaptation of these recommendations within the HEZ project constitute what is known within the community as "the HEZ Way." In this way, the PAR/CD integration in this organization's practice supports the observation that "place-based community development led by community members" is crucial (Stoecker and Falcón, this volume).

The case study demonstrates how this partnership with HEZ actualized the university's transformational priority to "create community engagements that empower our partners and ourselves" (Salve Regina University 2016). In addition to centering the community's priorities, the case also elucidates how the fit between partnership needs and syllabus-stated outcomes require dynamic balance, fluidity, and attention to emerging structures and content (Scharmer and Kaufer 2013).

Community Impact: Sustainability "the HEZ Way"

Gordon and Walsh conceived the original project to discover how to ensure sustainability of the HEZ collaborative and, in particular, develop resident leadership and ownership going forward. Anticipation of possible funding deficits, particularly, underscore the significance of this goal. Discovering "the HEZ Way" at the onset contributed to the emergent planning process to address organizational sustainability and the unique qualities embedded within the HEZ's structure and process that would guide the collaborative going forward.

In support of the development of the sustainability plan, students researched the sustainability literature for the HEZ and Gordon and staff co-facilitated retreats with the HEZ Collaborative. The Salve Regina research team provided technical assistance to Walsh leading up to, in between, and after the retreats on the components of the plan.

When this project began, the HEZ faced an uncertain future as the first round of funding came to a close and future funding was uncertain. At its conclusion, the initiative yielded concrete products that the HEZ could immediately use as it sought additional funding. Specifically, through the facilitated sustainability planning process, the HEZ Collaborative determined a five-year goal and associated indicators, along with prioritized strategy areas and a framework for an accompanying strategic plan. The two planning retreats in June and August identified the five-year goals, through which the HEZ staff shaped the funding proposal. In addition, the HEZ clarified and formalized its four key roles in the community and as a collaborative. Finally, the leadership and management practices that comprise "the HEZ Way" are clearly delineated on paper for the first time. Ultimately, this work contributed to the HEZ securing funding for an additional five years.

Course Impact: 2018

This experience was also new for the students. In the spring 2018 classroom, students learned to adjust to centering the needs of the HEZ community rather than focusing on their own learning needs, an essential lesson for preparing future professionals to engage in empowering CD work. Furthermore, the weekly teaching agenda always had to prioritize needs in service to the partnership. For example, when the HEZ asked for assistance in facilitating a June 2018 retreat on sustainability, nine out of ten summer class students wanted to attend and observe the process. To accomplish this, Gordon designed an observation handout with separate sections outlined for each segment of the day, and a detailed description of the role of participant as observer (Schein 1999; Schein 2013). Students observed a seven-hour retreat. Although some reacted negatively to sitting outside the retreat circle, as they are accustomed to being *in* the circle in class, other students saw themselves becoming part of something larger than their class.

The most significant learning occurred when the HEZ representatives and class members shared space and time in discussion, observation, and feedback. This happened over the course of approximately seven in-class and several more Gordon/student visits at the HEZ that occurred over several time frames in the following ways:

- The holistic leadership/HEZ Working Alliance began during the spring 2018 semester, where students began to observe HEZ meetings and pilot-tested an interview protocol for use over the spring and summer semesters.
- Several students observed two or more HEZ working group sessions and wrote about their observations in a final paper in both spring and summer classes.
- HEZ representative staff visited the spring 2018 class on four separate occasions, including the final videotaped class where students and HEZ staff shared ideas, feedback, and observations.
- An all-day Saturday session took place in the July summer session in which the HEZ project director and leadership professor facilitated a planning and design process dedicated to "the HEZ Way." Students had the opportunity to wrestle with actual data that would make a difference to the HEZ sustainability planning.
- Nine out of ten summer session students participated in two all-day retreats. Two students wrote a white paper on the HEZ principles that are integrated within the 2019 report. Others wrote up the observed group process as part of their mid-term reflective analysis.

Gordon's (2013) research on leadership and the texts chosen for three of the class periods helped shape an organic working alliance, introducing leadership principles to students, with the opportunity to experience first-hand research on "participant observer as participant." One student reflected in her final paper on the impact of the course(s); others reiterated these impacts in different ways in papers and course evaluations:

> When our class began involvement with the … Health Equity Zone, it was easy to see just how much more we would continue to learn from one another about each other in addition to leadership topics. Our class's involvement with the … HEZ not only inspired learning about leadership topics, but it also stimulated a leadership conversation concerning a topic close to home. Our class involvement offered the "perfect" environment to observe and ultimately practice what we were reading about in our texts. My personal involvement with the HEZ project included attending the Saturday morning event put on by the … HEZ and listening to several HEZ members speak about their experiences and

viewpoints in our classroom. Although I did not partake in the interview process, as did some of my classmates, I feel as though I was able to integrate course learning with what I was hearing from the HEZ members. (2018 spring class student)

The students began to see that they framed ideas based on their own experiences, whereas the HEZ staff members operate within a different context. Students started to appreciate that the many perspectives offered are all valid. For example, in one class session, students recognized the obvious differences in language and approach, frustrating to some students. In reviewing the experience, students reached a new level in their understanding of "letting go" of preconceived ideas about leadership engagement in an emerging partnership process.

This collaboration deeply impacted three separate semesters. Over the course of the partnership, Gordon revised reading assignments at least three times during one of the semesters and adjusted class sessions to facilitate meaningful, fruitful, and engaging visits with the HEZ staff. This meant having much less time to review readings and content, which most class participants understood and accepted as part of the emergent model so foundational to the project.

PRIVILEGING COMMUNITY OVER UNIVERSITY CONSTITUENTS

This project required a pedagogical flip from the classroom to the North End community. In this project and most others where faculty fully aligned with the model, we not only had to de-center the university in our change model (Stoecker 2016), we also had to de-center student-centered pedagogical models in our own classes. Building on the collaborative practice supported by our grant provided for a qualitatively different experience for the HEZ, a valued community partner. It diverged from typical service-learning engagement with students in the following ways:

1. *Professor engagement.* Grounding the partnership foundationally between the *professor* and the community partner meant that the HEZ leadership had access to an expert in the field as a thought partner as the project progressed. This relieved the HEZ from the challenge of managing the students throughout the project.
2. *Extended investment.* The HEZ identified a project that extended beyond the typical semester precisely because of the investment and commitment of the faculty partner to the project. This allowed the project to move at the pace that they needed it to move and eliminated any pressure on HEZ staff to figure out how to partition and parse out the project based on availability of support.
3. *Valuable support.* The HEZ could identify a meaningful piece of their existing work plan with which they needed support from advanced students and their instructor. They otherwise would not have had the resources to engage a consultant or other assistance to complete its sustainability plan.
4. *Partner-first mindset.* Designing the project first and foremost to meet the needs of the HEZ meant the professor took full responsibility for ensuring that the project met students' learning goals, adapting her syllabus and lectures to fit the needs of the project.
5. *Organic evolution.* All of the above factors translated into a project that evolved organically. As a genuine partnership, mutual investment between the professor and HEZ ensured the outcome as well as flexibility and adaptability to the needs of the community.

All stakeholders benefited from shifting expectations from funders, and the general unpredictability of thinly resourced, community-based work.

6. *Leadership studies, community transformation, and design thinking meshed in this project.* Timely course subjects, specifically leading change, sustainability, and citizen capacity building, reflect the current political and social climate. Community and campus participants reported that this project felt alive, organic, and based on the HEZ's sustainability concerns rather than centering predetermined pedagogical and/or student outcomes. HEZ needs, the process, the working alliance, and the assigned course materials all coalesced in an easy manner to demonstrate our specified model and provide a case for training future faculty cohorts as they develop civic engagement courses.

7. The strategic necessity to integrate PAR/CD occurred organically within this project because the HEZ was a highly developed community project that the holistic leadership program and class joined by invitation and with the specific focus to highlight HEZ processes and to assist in its strategic planning for sustainability. The HEZ had the information, expertise, and identified goals for the HEZ/holistic leadership alliance. The professor and class were able to provide PAR resources jointly and always when the HEZ requested and approved them. This eradicated the "outside expert" notion so often found in other similar partnerships.

LESSONS LEARNED FROM THE CAMPUS–COMMUNITY COLLABORATIONS: THE HEZ COLLABORATIONS AND BEYOND

The case study referenced above was a particularly innovative project among the many that faculty and their partners developed over the life of our grant. We learned that the experiences of faculty and partners who participated in these collaborations led to transformed relationships and that there is an energized commitment to CD work among our campus fellows. Evaluation of the overarching grant initiative also suggests new realizations about their community, the potential value of their work, and the learning process itself among student collaborators. Central among our lessons learned is how to more clearly identify and articulate a praxis that aligns with our organizational missions. For Salve Regina faculty fellows, it is a way of articulating and embedding the Mercy mission in relationship building, pedagogy, and generating knowledge with and for our neighbors. For the HEZ, the project with holistic leadership illuminated the praxis that constituents and staff had developed over four years of prioritizing racial equity and empowering residents as a necessary component of improving community health and development.

After consultation with our partners, we decided to share these lessons with other academics who aspire to engage in knowledge projects that incorporate PAR and CD to promote community change. During the final year of the university's grant, members of the HEZ community (residents and staff), two other community partners, and lead faculty (including the authors of this chapter) presented together at two academic conferences.

We presented at a national meeting of the American Association of Colleges and Universities and a Northeast Region meeting of Campus Compact to share challenges and rewards of our work together and lessons we are learning – and continue to learn – from the work. Both professional organizations are laser-focused on the importance of civic learning and democratic participation in establishing priorities, shaping discourses of practice, and theming gatherings. But rather than reproduce the scholars-as-experts model in academia, we centered the presentations on our partners' representations of their organizations and their collaborations with Salve Regina University faculty. They articulated their own perspectives on the efficacy of the partnership and the lessons learned along the way. Notwithstanding lively participation in our sessions, all of us noted the difficulty that some audience members had engaging directly with the community partners. Faculty tried their best to defer to our partners throughout the sessions.

As the grant period came to a close, Randy Stoecker, a co-editor of this volume, and principal investigator O'Toole facilitated four focus groups of community partners and faculty fellows and O'Toole designed and distributed a survey to capture the impacts of civic engagement courses more broadly among student participants in one or more classes developed under the auspices of the grant. We are particularly interested in the strength of our collaborative model for producing useful information for our neighbors, in students' experiences of being part of teams that often upended their ideas of how classes should be delivered, and in the uncertainties introduced by our focus on "emergent futures" in our community projects.

We share some of our findings here as a springboard for future conversations that readers may initiate in their own campuses and local communities. They are certainly shaping our own as we navigate our project's future with new senior administrators, past faculty fellows, and others who are interested to learn from our experiences – especially those of our partners.

First, not all faculty are cut out for the work (temperamentally, cognitively, pedagogically), as recognized by some partners and faculty themselves. This is fine; not everyone can or should be doing the work if they cannot fully embrace the model – particularly the need for collaboration, deference to partner expertise and contingencies, centering the project on the community, etc. Although some faculty, for various reasons, withdrew from future participation, many have been profoundly changed by the model of community involvement we piloted, and recognize the added benefit to students when their fallible humanity is evidenced in the classroom. For these faculty, modeling reciprocity and collaboration is important, as is intentionally illuminating the way responding to uncertainties is a facet of everyday life. Indeed, one of our faculty fellows is now the director of community engaged learning at Salve Regina, co-administering projects and funded by a recently secured grant from our initial funder. Students also observed their instructors' dedication to moving the university mission from theory to praxis.

Most community partners felt that students rose to the tasks of engagement and prioritizing community needs over their own. Being relieved of "supervisory" obligations in a model that squarely places student management on faculty is an important change that allows campus–community partnerships to function with fewer burdens on partner time and resources. Some partners articulated that decentering classes and student needs is still the most challenging component of the work for faculty at various points in time. In one example, a primary community need identified by HEZ residents – transportation – became an issue for a class with a large contingent of students without personal vehicles and with inadequate public transportation serving the North End. The staff member reminded the supervising faculty member who requested community members come to campus that this was *their own problem to solve* and that disrupting the organization's workflow and inconveniencing HEZ residents is never an option. We still have work to do.

After reviewing focus group data, it is clear that some partners struggle to leverage the knowledge power of partnerships with faculty and students in courses focused on subject areas and skill building that can contribute to their needs. The prevailing institutionalized service-learning model is hard to dislodge, especially when initiatives such as this exist in tension with university service requirements and staff whose training and focus is more traditional. Campuses and partners need to better develop the models of building relationships such that benefit is derived from both approaches. We also want to clarify our stance that PAR and CD-focused courses cannot supplant community needs for direct service and that we support our university's commitment to providing human resources for various projects that require them. Of course, student volunteers can also benefit greatly from engaging the literature that faculty fellows and community partners studied to situate themselves and their work within a critical perspective on neoliberalism and empowerment models of community change.

We also learned that, for many of our students, being involved in community projects is transformative. Both undergraduate and graduate respondents to surveys sent to participants in grant-funded courses rated their civic engagement courses far above traditional courses for learning course content and skills, and perhaps more significantly, wrote eloquently of the ways in which the work enhanced their sense of local citizenship, community expertise, and the power of the Mercy mission in action. For example, among 44 student respondents who participated in our survey, over 86% said they would be more likely to talk with other people about community issues, 77% would volunteer with a community organization, 61% would vote in a local or national election, and nearly 57% would work for systematic social change. 95% of respondents agreed that their community project aligned with the content of their course, with 85% agreeing that the project strengthened their understanding of course content and concepts and 90% agreeing that the project strengthened their capacity to apply skills learned in the class. 75% said that they learned more in their civic engagement classes than traditional lecture classes at our university.

Some typical responses to survey questions related to the impact of the course on their learning experience include: "I often reflect on my civic engagement course as one of the most important courses I have ever taken"; "My work within the CE classes at Salve was very influential for me as I chose my post graduate path in graduate school. I had always known that I wanted to help my community and those around me but I had never been given the tools for application until I became invested in these classes"; "This experience allowed for more in-depth learning of content but also instilled a deep desire and commitment to be involved in positive change in the community"; and "It felt more useful and meaningful to actually apply what we were talking about in class versus just reading/talking about principles of Mercy." Notwithstanding an online survey response rate of less than 15% of possible respondents, more comprehensive data from individual course assessments suggest these responses are valid overall as indicators of students' experiences with the initiative in the context of our university and its Mercy mission.

Regarding the HEZ, the impact that flows from this work into the community is not inconsequential. With a five-year goal of increasing civic engagement in the neighborhood, a commitment to centering residents throughout supported by documented, clearly defined practices, and a clear understanding of the strategies and roles that will ensure the goal is met, the HEZ is positioned to continue to make significant change at the neighborhood level to impact equity and quality of life.

A final note: we completed the first draft of this chapter as the COVID-19 pandemic exploded in the United States, disrupting both campus and community and requiring each of us to pivot to extraordinary measures to care for our various constituents and our families – and to meet our commitments to them. The final writing has been even more influenced by the effect the pandemic has had on neighborhoods in the HEZ and on building upon the relationships we have developed in the context of our work together. Collaborative writing under normal conditions can be challenging when it requires "integrative learning" from folks whose expertise is rooted in different knowledge systems. Writing under our current conditions once again illustrates the need for flexibility, reciprocity, patience, and embracing emergent models for collaborative work – in short, the challenges of this work over the long haul.

ACKNOWLEDGMENTS

The initiative described in this chapter, "Integrated Learning for Civic Engagement," was initially funded by a grant from the Davis Educational Foundation, a New England-based fund established by Stanton and Elizabeth Davis after Mr. Davis' retirement as chairman of Shaw's Supermarkets.

REFERENCES

Baldwin, Christina and Ann Linnea. 2010. *The Circle Way: A Leader in Every Chair*. San Francisco, CA: Berrett-Koehler, Publishers.

Blau, Judith. 1999. "Service Learning: Not Charity, But a Two-Way Street." In *Cultivating the Sociological Imagination: Concepts and Models for Service Learning in Sociology*, edited by James Ostrow, Garry Hesser, and Sandra Enos. Washington, DC: American Association for Higher Education, pp. ix–xv.

Bradbury, H. and P. Reason. 2003. "Issues and Choice Points for Improving the Quality of Action Research." In *Community-Based Participatory Research for Health*, edited by M. Winkler and N. Wallerstein. San Francisco, CA: Jossey Bass, pp. 201–222.

Coutu, R.A., S. Hippensteel Hall, and M. Goetz. 2010. "Community Change Context." In *Leading Change in Multiple Contexts: Concepts and Practices in Organizational, Community, Political, Social, and Global Change Settings*, edited by F.R. Hickman. Thousand Oaks, CA: Sage, pp. 121–149.

Fetterman, D.M. 1994. "Empowerment Evaluation." *Evaluation Practice*, 15(1): 1–15.

Gordon, Nancy. 2013. "Women and Leadership: An Integrative Focus on Equality." *Journal of Interdisciplinary Feminist Thought*. http://digitalcommons.salve.edu/jift/vol7/iss1/11

Hurtado, Sylvia, Adriana Ruiz, and Hannah Wang. 2012. "Advancing and Assessing Civic Learning: New Results from the Diverse Learning Environments Survey." *Diversity and Democracy*, 15: 10–12.

Kuh, George. 2009. *High-Impact Educational Practices: What They Are, Who Has Access to Them, and Why They Matter*. Washington, DC: American Association of Colleges and Universities.

Lasker, Roz D. and Elisa S. Weiss. 2003. "Broadening Participation in Community Problem Solving: A Multidisciplinary Model to Support Collaborative Practice and Research." *Journal of Urban Health: Bulletin of the New York Academy of Medicine*, 80(1): 14–47.

Maiter, Sarah, Laura Simich, Nora Jacobsen, and Julie Wise. 2008. "Reciprocity: An Ethic for Community-Based Participatory Action Research." *Action Research*, 6(3): 305–325.

Marullo, Sam, Roxanna Moayedi, and Deanna Cooke. 2009. "C. Wright Mills' Friendly Critique of Service Learning and an Innovative Response: Cross-Institutional Collaborations for Community-Based Research." *Teaching Sociology*, 37: 61–75.

Minkler, Meredith. 2000. "Using Participatory Action Research to Build Healthy Communities." *Public Health Reports*, 115: 191–196.

Mitchell, Tania D. 2008. "Traditional vs. Critical Service-Learning: Engaging the Literature to Differentiate Two Models." *Michigan Journal of Community Service Learning*, Spring: 50–65.

Mondloch, Amy S. 2009. "One Director's Voice." In *The Unheard Voices: Community Organizations and Service Learning*, edited by Randy Stoecker and Elizabeth Tryon. Philadelphia, PA: Temple University Press, pp. 136–146.

National Task Force on Civic Learning and Democratic Engagement, The. 2012. *A Crucible Moment: College Learning & Democracy's Future*. Washington, DC: Association of American Colleges and Universities.

Newport HEZ. 2016. "Ways to Improve Health and Well Being in the North End and Broadway: Final Needs Assessment." Newport, RI: Newport Health Equity Zone.

Newport HEZ. 2021. Homepage Newport, RI: Newport Health Equity Zone. https://newporthealthequity .com

O'Toole, Laura L. 2017. "Civic Engagement as Public Sociology: Considerations for Pedagogy and Practice." In *Community Engagement Best Practices across the Disciplines: Applying Course Content to Community Needs*, edited by Heather K. Evans. New York: Rowman and Littlefield, pp. 121–136.

Ray, Darby. 2016. "Campus–Community Partnership: A Stubborn Commitment to Reciprocal Relationships." *Diversity and Democracy* 19: 8–11.

Religious Sisters of Mercy (RSM) of the Americas. 2019. "Sisters of Mercy Social Justice Advocacy." www.sistersofmercy.org/what-we-do/social-justice-advocacy

Salve Regina University. 2016. "Salve Regina University Strategic Plan, 2016–2019." Newport, RI: Salve Regina University. https://salve.edu/sites/default/files/filesfield/documents/strategic%20plan %20external.pdf

Scharmer, Otto and Katrin Kaufer. 2013. *Leading from the Emerging Future: From Ego-System to Eco-System Economies*. San Francisco, CA: Berrett-Koehler Publishers.

Schein, Edgar H. 1999. *Process Consultation Revisited: Building the Helping Relationship*. Reading, MA: Addison-Wesley Publishing.

Schein, Edgar H. 2013. *Humble Inquiry: The Gentle Art of Asking Instead of Telling*. San Francisco, CA: Berrett-Koehler Publishers.

Senge, Peter, Joe Laur, Sara Schley, and Bryan Smith. 2006. *Learning for Sustainability*. Cambridge, MA: Society for Organizational Learning.

Smith, Laura, Lucinda Bratini, Debbie-Ann Chambers, Russell Vance Jensen, and LeLaina Romera. 2010. "Between Idealism and Reality: Meeting the Challenges of Participatory Action Research." *Action Research* 8(4): 407–425.

Stoecker, Randy. 2013. *Research Methods for Community Change: A Project-Based Approach*, 2nd edition. Los Angeles, CA: Sage.

Stoecker, Randy. 2016. *Liberating Service Learning and the Rest of Higher Education Civic Engagement*. Philadelphia, PA: Temple University Press.

Stoecker, Randy and Elizabeth A. Tryon. 2009. *The Unheard Voices: Community Organizations and Service Learning*. Philadelphia, PA: Temple University Press.

Strand, Kerry J. 1999. "Sociology and Service-Learning: A Critical Look." In *Cultivating the Sociological Imagination: Concepts and Models for Service Learning in Sociology*, edited by James Ostrow, Garry Hesser, and Sandra Enos. Washington, DC: American Association for Higher Education, pp. 29–38.

Tryon, Elizabeth, Amy Hilgendorf, and Ian Scott. 2009. "The Heart of Partnership: Communication and Relationships." In *The Unheard Voices: Community Organizations and Service Learning*, edited by Randy Stoecker and Elizabeth Tryon. Philadelphia, PA: Temple University Press, pp. 96–115.

US Census Bureau. 2018. "American Community Survey, 2017." Washington, DC: US Census Bureau. www.census.gov/programs-surveys/acs

Wandersman, A., J. Snell-Johns, B. Lentz, D.M. Fetterman, D.C. Keener, M. Livet, P.S. Imm, and P. Flaspohler. 2005. "The Principles of Empowerment Evaluation." In *Empowerment Evaluation Principles in Practice*, edited by D.M. Fetterman and A. Wandersman. New York: Guilford Publications, p. 25.

Youniss, James. 2011. "Service, Public Work and Respectful Public Citizens." *Liberal Education*, 97(2): 28–33.

11. Early childhood wellness through asset-based community development: a participatory evaluation of Communities Acting for Kids' Empowerment

Farrah Jacquez, Michael Topmiller, Jamie-Lee Morris, Alexander Shelton, Cynthia Wooten, Lakisha A. Best, Alan Dicken, Monica Arenas-Losacker, Giovanna Alvarez, Crystal Davis, and Shanah Cole

When positive policy changes and promising development projects come to cities in the United States (U.S.), inclusion in decision making and dispersion of benefits do not reach all neighborhoods equally. This includes efforts to increase access to early childhood education, where a substantial literature has documented quality disparities across income, race, and geographic space (Gordon and Chase-Lansdale 2001; Fuller and Strath 2001). For example, research from Georgia found that meaningful differences exist in access to quality preschool across communities, despite Georgia being one of the few states with universal preschool and being touted as a model (Bassok and Galdo 2016).

In Cincinnati, Ohio, a recent tax levy earmarked $15 million annually to make preschool available to every three and four year old in the city (Sparling and Huff 2016). Universal preschool has the potential to make an especially significant impact in this city because children from economically disadvantaged environments have been found to reap the most benefits from preschool (Phillips et al. 2017) and Cincinnati has one of the highest child poverty rates in the U.S. (U.S. Census Bureau 2012–2016). The Cincinnati preschool tax levy served as a catalyst for the creation of Communities Acting for Kids' Empowerment (CAKE), an 11-member community–academic partnership working to improve early childhood wellness in two underserved neighborhoods in northern Cincinnati. Broadly, CAKE aims to develop community capacity to enhance the wellbeing of young children in the neighborhoods of Carthage and Roselawn.

CAKE takes an approach to community development that is consistent with the principles of asset-based community development (ABCD), which calls for development that is (1) driven by what communities have rather than what they need; (2) identifies and mobilizes individual and community assets to make change; (3) is led by community voice; and (4) is fueled by relationships (Kretzmann 2010; Kretzmann and McKnight 1993; Mathie and Cunningham 2003; Stuart 2013). The foundational value of ABCD is public participation, which is effective and meaningful when community members "exercise influence over decisions and feel a sense of ownership toward the product" (Haines 2009: 64). One strategy to facilitate meaningful public participation is participatory research, the umbrella term we use for research designs, methods, and frameworks that use systematic inquiry in direct collaboration with those affected by the issue being studied for the purpose of action or change (Cargo and Mercer

2008). When integrating models of public participation into the research process, community–academic partnerships must make intentional choices about the methods and tools they use to share decision making in research (Vaughn and Jacquez 2020). As a community–academic partnership with the goal of community development with optimal public participation, CAKE intentionally used strategies that would maximize community voice.

Although often overlooked, evaluation is an essential component of successful ABCD (Haines 2009; McKnight and Russell 2018). In this chapter, we describe an approach to evaluation that integrates participatory research into the ABCD framework to understand CAKE's progress, community impact, and the degree to which our work together reflects our core values. We begin by briefly discussing the formation of CAKE, our neighborhoods (Carthage and Roselawn), and our preliminary activities. Next, we provide a description of our participatory evaluation process, methods, and results, after which we highlight the major themes that emerged from the process. Finally, we discuss how we used the results of the evaluation to guide our future work and ensure that project activities reflected the priorities of our two neighborhoods.

HISTORY AND POSITIONALITY OF COMMUNITIES ACTING FOR KIDS' EMPOWERMENT

In 2016, the first three authors of this chapter (two researchers, Farrah Jacquez and Michael Topmiller, and one community organizer, Jamie-Lee Morris) came together to develop a grant proposal focused on creating a community–academic partnership to carry out a place-based, participatory research project that was driven by community priorities. The Robert Wood Johnson Foundation funded the proposal and selected the three partners to be part of the first cohort of their Interdisciplinary Research Leaders (IRL) program, designed for teams of researchers and community partners working together to build a culture of health (Robert Wood Johnson Foundation 2018). The IRL program consisted of leadership training and support for our proposed early childhood wellness community-based research project that was to be place-based, asset-focused, action-oriented, and guided by the voice of those who live and work in two Cincinnati neighborhoods, Carthage and Roselawn. These neighborhoods were chosen by two of the IRL partners who had strong connections to community stakeholders in the area and noticed that neighborhood-based initiatives in Cincinnati tended to overlook these communities.

Carthage and Roselawn are both located in the northern part of Cincinnati and are somewhat isolated from local resources like universities, hospitals, and shopping areas. Demographically, Carthage is one of the most racially and ethnically diverse neighborhoods in the city; 34% of residents are White, 34% are Hispanic, and a quarter are Black. Roselawn's population is mostly Black (72%), with smaller representation by White (13%) and Hispanic (6%) residents. The median household income in both neighborhoods is lower than the city average. Carthage and Roselawn have many significant assets, including active neighborhood associations, more than a dozen early childhood care providers, and Su Casa, the largest Hispanic social service provider in the city. Churches are a particular resource in both communities, providing not only spiritual and social support but also community advocacy.

Working from the recognition of the church as a core community asset, the IRL partners approached the head pastor of a church in Roselawn (Pastor Damon Lynch III of New Prospect

Baptist Church) to ask if the church might serve as the funding home and primary community partner for the grant. Pastor Lynch was the ideal fit for our project because, in addition to his role as head pastor, he also served as part of the adjunct faculty network of the Asset-Based Community Development Institute at Northwestern University, facilitating workshops and seminars throughout the U.S. on the asset-based approach to problem solving and development. Pastor Lynch is an active community leader advocating for asset-based development in Cincinnati (Daudelin 2017) and agreed to partner on the condition that any research conducted concentrate on community assets rather than needs.

After identifying New Prospect Baptist Church as the funding home for the project and receiving research funding, the IRL partners immediately sought out individuals who could represent the diverse communities of Carthage and Roselawn and share decision making on all aspects of the project, ensuring that the group's actions would be truly informed by community voices. The IRL partners invited eight individuals to join the leadership team to represent specific types of professional and lived experience expertise, including community organizing, early childhood education, social service with Latino immigrants, and experience parenting young children in our target neighborhoods. After several meetings focused on building individual relationships, discussing project priorities, and developing protocols for meetings and projects, the 11 members brainstormed a name that reflected the group's mission and priorities. After generating lists of words that embody the work we aimed to do and our values, we collectively refined ideas until we decided on Communities Acting for Kids' Empowerment, or CAKE. We liked having an acronym that was easily understood and the symbolism of cake, where each member of the leadership team added an ingredient or a layer that combined to form something substantial and delicious. CAKE represents a diverse group of stakeholders whose positionality with the project varies widely, but share a passion for equity and justice for children and a motivation for change (see Table 11.1 for positionality statements from each of the CAKE leadership team members and co-authors of this chapter). CAKE members have multiple identities and represent multiple constituencies. In terms of profession, we include three community organizers, three individuals working in early childhood, two researchers, and two community organization leaders. Demographically, six CAKE members are Black, three are Latina, and Two are White men. Six of us were parents of children under five when CAKE started. Our personal and professional diversity allowed us to more easily work across sectors and neighborhoods, allowing us to overcome the silos that burden community development in Cincinnati.

COMMUNITIES ACTING FOR KIDS' EMPOWERMENT: GOALS, CORE VALUES, AND PRELIMINARY ACTIVITIES

CAKE uses an intentionally designed process reflecting the mutually identified core values of shared decision making, asset-based design, and real-world change. We have been working together in the Cincinnati neighborhoods of Carthage and Roselawn toward three goals: (1) to create a network of engaged stakeholders ready for action; (2) to develop a community-led intervention influencing several of the different systems that affect child health; and (3) to increase preschool awareness. For three years, we met monthly to develop plans, to connect resources, and to conduct research. We spent the early part of our partnership collectively developing our goals and values, then conducted research for community impact. We describe

Table 11.1   *Professional positions and positionality statements of CAKE members*

CAKE member professional position	Positionality statement
Farrah Jacquez, Ph.D., Professor, Psychology Department, University of Cincinnati	Farrah Jacquez works as a professor and engages in research with CAKE as part of her job. Her Latina identity and her personal experiences as a first-generation college student and a mother motivate her participation in the work, but she does not live in Carthage or Roselawn and does not have the lived experience expertise of raising children in these neighborhoods.
Michael Topmiller, Ph.D., Health GIS Research Specialist, American Academy of Family Physicians	Michael Topmiller is a researcher who helps lead CAKE as part of his job. He is motivated to do this work through his experiences seeing inequities and wanting that all kids have the same opportunities to succeed as his own children. Michael does not live in Carthage or Roselawn.
Jamie-Lee Morris, Community Organizer, New Prospect Baptist Church	Jamie-Lee Morris works as an educational programming coordinator at Elementz, a hip hop youth organization. As the community partner on the project, she uses her understanding of organizing to bring the community into the process of engagement. She aims to help the community interact with stakeholders regarding the educational issues that affect their families and neighborhoods as a whole.
Alexander Shelton, Co-Founder, The Green Store, Co-Founder, Heal n Build	Alexander Shelton serves as a community organizer that uses yoga and creative place making to create spaces that prioritize the mindfulness and illness of people of color. As a parent and an eco-activist, community matters, access matters, children matter. CAKE allows Alexander to continue the efforts of the Preschool Promise in a more localized way.
Cynthia Wooten, Center Director, Valley Early Learning Center, YMCA of Greater Cincinnati	Cynthia Wooten is a mother and grandmother with a purpose. She has worked in early childhood for over 40 years. As a director of an early childhood center, she sees the world as a window of opportunity for all, especially our children. She strives to be a voice for the voiceless, a hand to lift up when down. CAKE represents everything about who she is and has given her a renewed sense of hope that community matters.
Lakisha A. Best, Chief executive Officer/Operator, The Best Preschool Consulting Firm and Adult Education	Lakisha Best works in early child-care training, operates a consulting firm for preschools, and recently opened her own family child-care center. For eight years, she worked in a preschool that served the communities of Roselawn and Carthage. Lakisha is motivated by her passion to change impoverished children's view of the world by empowering the parents for a stronger foundation. She wants to be the advocate she never had in her childhood. Lakisha's motto is "Give children a childhood they do not have to recover from."
Rev. Alan Dicken, Pastor at Carthage Christian Church	Alan Dicken serves as the senior pastor at Carthage Christian Church. Part of his calling is service to the community and the needs of the neighborhood. He doesn't live in Carthage, but is involved with youth, parents, and community organizations that strive to improve the lives of those in that community.
Monica Arenas-Losacker, Bilingual Family Outreach Specialist, 4C for Children	Monica Arenas-Losacker is a social worker and community outreach specialist for a community agency that supports adults who care for young children. She has been working in Carthage and Roselawn since 2004. She is motivated to be a part of CAKE because her experience in these neighborhoods makes her confident that we can make change by working together for a common goal. In CAKE, she is a liaison for the Hispanic and immigrant communities.
Giovanna Alvarez, Director, Su Casa Hispanic Center, Catholic Charities Southwestern Ohio	Giovanna Alvarez works as the director of a non-profit organization that serves thousands of vulnerable international immigrants with focus on the Hispanic/Latino community. Giovanna is glad to participate in the CAKE initiative to be the voice of communities that are traditionally underrepresented. She strives for social justice for the most vulnerable in society.

CAKE member professional position	Positionality statement
Crystal Davis, Community Relations Developer, Entrepreneur, and Board Member of the Roselawn Community Council	Crystal Davis works as a community educator and mentor to students and families in Roselawn and throughout the city. As the mother of one daughter, she has found from her experience that if you just show genuine love and care to a child, he/she will respond by demonstrating how well he/she can behave, perform academically in school, and so on. CAKE not only enables her the opportunity to be surrounded by great people who serve the same purpose but also helps to broaden her view regarding children's health and education as she pursues her doctorate in leadership studies.
Shanah Cole, Parent, Valley Early Learning Center, YMCA of Greater Cincinnati	Shanah Cole is a parent of two children who attended the YMCA, Valley Early Learning Center in Roselawn over a five-year period. Shanah is passionate to take part in the CAKE initiative for parents' perspective. She strives for comprehensiveness and is an advocate for children with disabilities.

the structure of CAKE as a hybrid community advisory board–co-researcher model, where every member of CAKE has equal decision-making power and participates in research activities, but some community members play more active roles depending on the activity (Topmiller et al. 2021).

After collectively developing our values and goals, we decided to start our research process from what we saw as the beginning. Rather than assuming we knew how Carthage and Roselawn residents thought about early childhood wellness, we wanted to collect the current perspectives of diverse communities within our target neighborhoods. The research partners had experience using Group Level Assessment (GLA), a participatory method where data are collaboratively generated and interactively evaluated with relevant stakeholders leading to the development of participant-driven data and relevant action plans (Vaughn and Lohmueller 2014), so CAKE decided to use this tool to both collect data and begin activating a network of community partners.

We conducted GLAs in four sites in our target neighborhoods: a Catholic Church's Spanish-language mass, a Carthage community council meeting, a union meeting for providers of in-home child care, and a church serving a predominantly African American congregation. The participatory focus groups included more than 100 people across the four sites to identify community priorities for early childhood wellness. CAKE members were involved in every step of the GLA process – framing research questions, generating and refining prompts to be used in the GLAs, interpreting results across groups, and disseminating results. In our monthly CAKE meeting prior to our first GLA, one of the research partners of CAKE described the process for conducting GLAs and asked members to submit ideas for prompts based on our overall theme, which was "what do we need to have happy, healthy kids in our neighborhood?" All CAKE members also played an integral role in the data collection process. A few members took lead roles in planning the logistics (booking location, recruiting participants, organizing food and child care), while others helped facilitate the GLAs by clarifying questions about prompts and facilitating the small breakout groups.

As part of one monthly meeting, CAKE members participated in analyzing the data from the GLAs and interpreting the results. Using the overall themes from the GLAs, all CAKE members took part in a "pass the buck" exercise to generate priorities for CAKE moving forward and a list of potential questions for future surveys or interviews. In "pass the buck," small groups of CAKE members provided written responses to a prompt about priorities and then passed the paper to the next small group to add on additional responses. As a result of our collaborative data analysis, the 11-member CAKE team identified more specific priorities and goals across three levels, including (1) the community level – the need to connect with community partners already conducting successful youth programs to develop a youth arts and music program; (2) the child-care provider level – the need to capture the wisdom of the many successful neighborhood early childhood education providers, who range from small, in-home providers to large center-based programs; and (3) the parent/family level – the need to identify effective strategies to engage parents and families in school and community environments. We describe these activities and their results (which occurred after our evaluation) later in the chapter.

THE PARTICIPATORY EVALUATION

We conducted a participatory evaluation that examined our group's functioning and the extent to which our work adhered to our core values of shared decision making, asset focus, and research for real-world benefits. As a group, we aim for our work together to reflect the values of ABCD and will present the results of our participatory evaluation in that context (Kretzmann 2010; Kretzmann and McKnight 1993; Mathie and Cunningham 2003; Stuart 2013). Our hope is that by evaluating our functioning as a coalition through this lens, we can identify specific factors contributing to positive group functioning and transformative change in early childhood health and wellness.

Method

All 11 members of CAKE, the co-authors of this manuscript, collaborated on a plan to conduct a participatory evaluation of our first year as a collaborative. Participatory evaluation is an approach to evaluation that includes participants not just as data sources but as collaborators in the evaluation process (Cousins and Chouinard 2012; Whitmore 1998). Our approach was consistent with the goals of transformative participatory evaluation, which aims to empower individuals through the process of collaborative knowledge construction (Cousins and Whitmore 1998). Similar to other community–academic research partnerships (Sánchez et al. 2011), we wanted to use a structured process to understand the impact our work was having on our community and on ourselves as individuals. More specifically, we sought to determine how our work together has reflected our own values and encouraged transformative change in early childhood wellness. We all participated in semi-structured, in-depth interviews to assess views of group functioning and collaborative impact. All members attended the participatory evaluation meeting where data analysis and theme prioritization were conducted.

Research Design

We had two primary intentions with our participatory evaluation: to understand member perceptions of group functioning and to evaluate the extent to which CAKE collaborates using principles of ABCD in our work. To accomplish these aims with a strategy that would be most accessible to a large group of community partners, we used a general inductive framework approach to develop an interview guide and analyze the data. The inductive framework approach allowed research findings to emerge from the frequent, dominant, or significant themes in interviews (Thomas 2006). Using the protocol from an evaluation of another community-based participatory research team in our area as a model (Vaughn et al. 2018), we developed an interview guide to capture group functioning and our group process as a reflection of our core values. The interview protocol (see Appendix) included five prompts, with additional follow-up items included to elicit more information as needed. The five prompts elicited perspectives about:

- CAKE's current functioning and future impact.
- Group functioning in CAKE.
- Specific aspects of relationships and interactions within the CAKE team, including trust, shared decision making, voice, participation, and equitable collaboration.
- Community organizing to build leadership and power among the people of Carthage and Roselawn.
- Adherence to core values of CAKE: (1) shared decision making; (2) a focus on assets; and (3) a focus on real-world benefits.

To encourage open, honest reflection, CAKE decided that an external person should conduct the interviews. Given her access to students who could be paid for their time in research credit rather than funding, author Farrah Jacquez selected an interviewer who was well qualified academically, was a mature student with military service experience, and had no overlap with CAKE activities and was therefore unknown to all other members. Over the course of six weeks, the interviewer talked with each CAKE member by phone or in person for an average of 45 minutes. The interviewer recorded and transcribed responses.

Data Analysis

CAKE's two academic members (Jacquez and Topmiller) took the initial step of data analysis using an inductive framework approach. First, we independently used open coding to review the interview transcripts and identify initial themes. Next, we took the themes that were identified through open coding and presented them to the larger CAKE team. Over the course of a 90-minute meeting, we immersed ourselves in the data, using our own experiences as CAKE members to determine the most important aspects and patterns. At the end of our analysis meeting, we had a list of themes that we as a group agreed best represented our experiences and most accurately assessed our functioning. After the CAKE analysis meeting, the first author went back to the original interview transcriptions to assess for missing concepts or themes and to identify quotations that best represent identified themes.

Results

Themes are presented in Table 11.2. During the group analysis meeting, we found considerable overlap across themes and unanimously prioritized three specific points that universally applied, so we summarize themes in the table and in text according to CAKE-named categories.

"We hear our communities and our communities are heard"
The most salient theme from the interviews was that each member of CAKE feels heard during meetings and believes they have equal decision-making power on the team. We have the right people at the table to represent our communities, and those people are listened to and

Table 11.2   Summary of themes

	"We've formed the container, now let's fill it up."
We have created a structure that allows all CAKE members to feel heard	"CAKE is unlike other projects I've worked on in the past because the insights, ideas, thoughts, and feelings of the team dictate the direction of the work being done."
	"I feel confident that something I might have to say for myself or for my community will be heard."
Working with the right people is one of the most valuable functions of CAKE	"I love the diversity of the team and the respect that there is for each other's backgrounds, cultures, and professional expertise."
	"The most valuable benefit of CAKE has been networking and collaboration at our meetings."
We're still in a formational phase	"Haven't had a real impact yet, but we're doing a great job collecting the information we need to formulate what is next."
	"Right now, we have the POTENTIAL for impact, but we have to continue the movement, getting people to get involved and take on responsibilities."
We need to produce something concrete to keep residents engaged	"We're in the beginning stages so it is hard, but we will have an impact when something concrete is produced and given to the community."
	"People are encouraged by our requests for their input, but their interest won't last long if we don't provide some tangible result to the research."

respected. As stated by one CAKE member, "CAKE is unlike other projects I've worked on in the past because the insights, ideas, thoughts, and feelings of the team dictate the direction of the work being done." Another member said, "We are getting the right people in the room having conversations about community leadership in Carthage and Roselawn." Members especially appreciated the different perspectives represented on the team: "Diversity of people on the leadership team gives insight into communities that are often not included in the conversation (e.g., Latino community)." Although our team's diversity was valued, members identified areas where we needed to do better; for example, "We have got to involve Carthage more equally."

In addition to all members being heard, we have created infrastructure that allows the voice of community residents to guide our work. One member said, "This grant is really unique because it allows anyone to be engaged as much as they want to do so." Our first research activity (the GLAs) provided a powerful way for people in the community to get involved and to prioritize specific ways and places to intervene: "The GLAs created space for people to get involved and raise questions and concerns, which is very impactful." The complexity in analyzing results across diverse groups was acknowledged; one member noted that "Understanding dynamics between populations, like between our Jewish population and African American groups in Roselawn, is tough."

"Networking is our strength, but also our most important journey"

We found that networking and collaboration with other members has been the most valuable aspect of participating in the team. Several members noted that they especially appreciated the diversity of our team and how we work together in the spirit of recognizing and celebrating differences in backgrounds, cultures, and professional expertise. Although it has been challenging to build our reputation in the community from the ground up, we are beginning to engage with people and agencies outside of our leadership team. Members noted, "CAKE is growing in reputation so people in the community are jumping on board to collaborate" and "Outside organizations are seeking to work with CAKE specifically." Taking the next step in networking will be gaining the attention of policymakers and building collaborations with other organizations in Cincinnati doing similar work. Members acknowledge that "Building a reputation in the community from the ground up is really hard" and "trying to figure out how to engage established community organizations (e.g., School Board) can really be a struggle." Although networking is our strength, several members noted that we must work harder to avoid the silos that can plague our city. The demographic and professional diversity of CAKE members helps us to work through silos, but several members expressed concerns about how we can better connect the diverse populations (African American, White, Hispanic) in the neighborhoods that have unique needs and priorities.

"We've formed the container, now let's fill it up"
CAKE was built on three explicitly stated values that have guided the core functions of our group: shared decision making, focus on assets, and real-world benefit as the definition of success. We are an active, engaged group of community leaders who represent diverse communities and professional sectors. Members said they enjoyed being a part of CAKE as a group: "The most valuable benefit of CAKE has been networking and collaboration at our meetings." One member noted, "I love the diversity of the team and the respect that there is for each other's backgrounds, cultures, and professional expertise." We have successfully developed a structure that allows for equitable shared decision making. Members said, "CAKE is unlike other projects I've worked on in the past because the insights, ideas, thoughts, and feelings of the team dictate the direction of the work being done" and "I feel confident that something I might have to say for myself or for my community will be heard."

We have the potential for impact, and have made some progress in identifying and mapping community assets, but thus far we are still working toward real-world impact. One member described our stage as "Haven't had a real impact yet, but we're doing a great job collecting the information we need to formulating what is next." We are at a stage where we need to produce something tangible and concrete to keep residents engaged and to improve the health and wellbeing of young children in Carthage and Roselawn. Multiple members of the team eloquently expressed this crucial next step: "People are encouraged by our requests for their input, but their interest won't last long if we don't provide some tangible result to the research." A second member commented, "We're in the beginning stages so it is hard, but we will have an impact when something concrete is produced and given to the community." A third member said, "Right now, we have the POTENTIAL for impact, but we have to continue the movement, getting people to get involved and take on responsibilities." We collectively believed this consistent sentiment was best summarized by the words of one of our CAKE community members, "we have done a good job forming a really nice container, now is the time to start filling it up."

Discussion of Themes

As funding mechanisms, particularly the Robert Wood Johnson Foundation's Culture of Health programs, recognize the importance of collaborations between diverse community stakeholders and academic partners, an increasing number of community–academic partnerships are working to move the needle on health (Robert Wood Johnson Foundation 2018). There is a critical need to understand how these partnerships function in ways that center the voices and assets of communities through group processes that are relationship-based and change-focused. We conducted a participatory evaluation of CAKE's functioning to understand the degree to which we are adhering to our core values in our work and improving early childhood health. Through interviews with each member of the CAKE leadership team and group analysis and prioritization of themes, we identified three primary ways our community coalition functions: (1) being guided by the voice of our community; (2) constantly striving to build more comprehensive and productive networks; and (3) focusing on concrete, tangible results. Overall, our core values and collaboration for families in Carthage and Roselawn make us proud to be a part of CAKE and the infrastructure and network we have created, but also impatient for the real-world change that is our first priority.

The themes revealed in our participatory evaluation are consistent with the ABCD framework, which emphasizes solution-focused community development pursued by diverse stakeholder groups working together to identify and amplify place-based assets (Kretzmann and McKnight 1993; MacNeil et al. 2012). ABCD draws particular attention to social assets and the social capital that grows from relationships (Mathie and Cunningham 2003). We identified our relationships as the most valuable aspect of our work, yet also noted that developing relationships with other individuals outside of our group would be key to our sustained success. We also resonate deeply with the potential of ABCD to harness the *power within* individuals, *power with* communities as a whole to initiate collective action, and the need for *power to* communities through capacity building (Mathie et al. 2017). We are a team of 11 academic and community leaders representing diverse constituencies, but we share a unified commitment to representing the children and families in Carthage and Roselawn in our work by amplifying their voices and building capacity to replicate assets.

In addition to the ABCD context, the results of our participatory evaluation also highlighted several characteristics and core functions of CAKE that are well known in the community coalition literature to be associated with success, including community leadership, shared decision making, linkages with other organizations, and a positive organizational climate (Butterfoss et al. 1996). In particular, our most pervasive positive themes of valuable networking and shared decision making have been associated with effective health coalitions (Minkler et al 2008). The importance of collaborating with other organizations with overlapping missions to avoid silos is also well documented (Janosky et al. 2013; Center for Community Health and Development 2018). Our participatory evaluation contributes to the existing literature on community coalitions by framing these factors as not only positive for group functioning, but also central and essential to collaborating using an ABCD orientation to the work. From the perspectives of our diverse team of parents, social service providers, early childhood education specialists, and academics, there are three components that are required to ensure equitable collaboration: shared decision making guided by community voice, the consistent striving for comprehensive and productive networking, and the need for concrete, tangible impact. These factors represent coalition functioning and community-wide changes, two indicators of coalition effectiveness identified in the research literature (Zakocs and Edwards 2006), but our findings show that in the eyes of coalition participants, coalition effectiveness is intrinsically linked to shared decision making and authentically representing community perspective.

Limitations

We chose a participatory evaluation strategy to best fit our core values of shared decision making and asset-focused, action-oriented collaboration. The nature of participatory evaluation includes possible positive bias in interview responses. While having an outside, independent person conduct the interviews with CAKE members likely led to more open, honest responses, it is possible that members were reluctant to share negative impressions or critical feedback. Because we created the evaluation plan together, all members knew we would discuss survey responses together and might have wanted to avoid uncomfortable conversations.

Implications for Practice

CAKE was born through the funding and support of the Robert Wood Johnson Foundation's Interdisciplinary Research Leaders (IRL) program (https://interdisciplinaryresearch-leaders .org/), a unique leadership development initiative designed to use the power of applied research – informing and supporting critical work being done in communities – to accelerate that work and advance health and equity. The program requires partnership between academic and community leaders and places health equity and community representation at the forefront of training. We find it challenging to describe how deeply the values and training that the three IRL leaders (authors Farrah Jacquez, Jamie-Lee Morris, and Michael Topmiller) received in the program impacted CAKE's work. In addition to funding all of CAKE's activities, IRL leaders attended eight national conferences and weekly virtual meetings over three years where they received training in how to lead research toward creating a culture of health. Specifically, IRL trains leaders to develop skills in community organizing, equity and inclusion, interdisciplinary team science, and rigorous research methods for community impact. CAKE's approach to community development was rooted in ABCD and participatory research methods from its inception, but the continued support and training from the IRL program did a great deal to keep us accountable to our fundamental values.

Several concrete needs of community–academic partnerships emerged from our evaluation, including funding for community member participation, balance between relationship building and action, intentionally and consistently diverse teams made up of the right people, and avoiding silos.

Funding
While community coalitions often require community members to volunteer their time and expertise, we are fortunate because all members of CAKE are paid for their work through IRL funding. Given the increasing focus on community engagement in research, including funding through Clinical Translational Science Awards (National Institutes of Health 2018) and the Patient Centered Outcomes Research Institute (2018), future grant mechanisms should consider shared budgeting with community organizations and required funding for community members who live and work in communities that are the target for intervention. To reflect true value in community engagement, funding infrastructures must be equitable by financially benefiting not only academic and scientific expertise, but also the lived experience expertise needed to fight health disparities.

Representation in decision making
To make the biggest impact on early childhood wellness in our target communities, we needed representation from diverse racial and ethnic communities as well as from individuals with diverse forms of lived experience expertise. We initially invited five community members to be part of the collaborative, and relied on them to tell us who we were missing. We added parents of young children living in the neighborhood as well as key decision makers in faith-based organizations and social service agencies. To reflect our core values, it was important to have

our leadership team represent those who are living and working in our target communities as well as those who can influence policies affecting children in those communities. The diverse representation of our leadership team helps to ensure that the voice of the community is truly heard and we are placing community assets at the center of decision making.

Balancing relationship building and action

As is well documented in the community research literature, community–academic partnerships take time to develop and sustain and members can decide that the benefits do not outweigh the costs (Israel et al. 2006). Our results highlight two major facets of the time obstacle. On one hand, the networking and relationship development we have accomplished during our first year of functioning was identified as one of the most valuable assets of CAKE membership, suggesting the time we devoted to developing our team was well spent and worth it. Even the process of the participatory evaluation, which was a research endeavor but one conducted in ways that did not overtax CAKE members, was welcomed as a relationship-building exercise. On the other hand, in the evaluation CAKE team members expressed impatience for real action and transformative change to begin. Taken together, our evaluation suggests that ABCD coalitions should make intentional efforts to balance relationship building and action, being patient enough to take the time to form meaningful networks but identifying ways to accomplish specific tasks along the way.

Avoiding silos

A key challenge that remains for CAKE is advancing networking and building collaborations to avoid silos and replicated efforts. Although no other coalition exists in Cincinnati that specifically focuses on early childhood wellness in Carthage and Roselawn, many other education institutions and social service agencies are focused more broadly on overlapping community development issues. We are constantly striving to identify other activities that are happening in our neighborhoods that we could build upon to reach our goals, but we have struggled to form viable partnerships with other activities that have their own timelines, goals, and underlying values. This participatory evaluation has moved CAKE forward by allowing us to understand that working in silos means replicated efforts and wasted resources, which is anathema to the principles of ABCD. We have made silo busting a primary goal as we move forward toward dissemination efforts and action planning.

HOW THE EVALUATION INFORMED COMMUNITIES ACTING FOR KIDS' EMPOWERMENT MOVING FORWARD

After completing the evaluation it was evident that we needed to narrow our research focus and that the majority of CAKE members wanted a more action-oriented approach that leveraged existing community assets. The result was a series of activities on multiple levels where some CAKE members took more active roles based on their relationships to the neighborhoods, their areas of expertise, and their capacity to put more time into the project.

Community Level: Collaborating for Community Music and Arts Programs

One of the primary themes identified from the GLAs was a clear need for more community programs for kids, specifically around arts and music. We discussed at monthly meetings how CAKE could leverage community connections, networking, and skills to bring these programs to our neighborhoods. Members of CAKE were well connected to area churches conducting youth programs. We also discovered that the director of a local university school of music lived in one of our neighborhoods. CAKE facilitated a connection between the director and area churches, and collaborated to write (and be awarded) a local health grant to pilot-test summer and after-school community arts and music programs in the neighborhood churches.

Provider Level: Understanding and Addressing Barriers for Child-Care Providers

A second major theme of GLAs that was identified through the CAKE data analysis process was related to neighborhood early childhood providers, who reported a lack of support and several barriers for providing high-quality care. Several members of the CAKE team were neighborhood child-care providers or had connections to area providers. Discussion among the CAKE team also helped reveal that home-based child-care providers faced the most significant barriers, that some providers had more resources than others, and that CAKE should focus on understanding successful strategies for this group of providers. Next, one of the CAKE researchers, Michael Topmiller, had one-on-one meetings with an individual community member of CAKE, who is a home-based child-care provider. Through an iterative, collaborative process, the research and community member worked to create a final list of interview questions that better reflected the reality of neighborhood child-care providers. After completing several research methods and research ethics (Institutional Review Board-approved) training sessions, the community CAKE member went out and conducted 19 interviews over the course of three weeks.

The analysis and interpretation of the interview data also involved our home-based child-care expert community CAKE member. First, a CAKE researcher, Michael Topmiller, analyzed the 19 interviews, identified a few major themes, and then had a one-on-one meeting with the community CAKE member to help interpret the results and determine next steps. At the next monthly meeting, the researcher presented a brief write-up and summary to the rest of the CAKE team, which generated a list of results that included the need for more provider support and professional development workshops to help home-based providers achieve and maintain their Ohio state quality accreditation. Several members of the CAKE team then collectively determined the next steps of action, which included contacting connections at a local childhood service organization (4C for Children) to help organize professional development workshops in our neighborhoods.

Family/Parent Level: Concept Mapping for Parent Engagement (Ongoing)

Perhaps the most common theme from the GLAs involved parent engagement. The CAKE team used the ideas generated from the "pass the buck" exercise to develop questions for a concept-mapping survey. Several CAKE community members then went out and collected more than 300 surveys at local businesses, grocery stores, and child-care centers. This part of the project is still ongoing.

OVERALL LESSONS

Conducting the participatory evaluation of our community–academic partnership helped CAKE focus efforts on tangible projects that utilized existing assets. As a result, CAKE was able to (1) increase the likelihood of addressing questions that matter to people, (2) improve the quality and effectiveness of research activities and participant recruitment, and (3) ensure that research was leading directly to action.

First and foremost, the evaluation helped to ensure that research activities directly reflected community priorities. For example, an initial focus of our research was to highlight the value of early childhood education and help get more kids signed up for preschool. However, our collaborative process revealed that there was a lack of quality-rated options in our neighborhoods, and that we needed to focus our attention on neighborhood providers. We only did this because we had professional community experts in the room during our discussions to help frame research questions, conduct data analysis, and interpret results. For example, having a home-based early childhood provider and early learning center directors on our CAKE team helped to elucidate details that would not be known otherwise, as they highlighted differences between two groups of providers.

Our engaged research approach also improved the quality and effectiveness of recruitment. Because community leaders were also our primary data collectors, they were able to leverage previous relationships that allowed them to gain insights from key, hard-to-reach stakeholders (home-based providers). We initially attempted to have one of the researchers interview neighborhood providers, but quickly realized that this would not work due to a lack of trust. Another example involved the concept-mapping surveys, where several members of our CAKE team gathered more than 300 surveys. The CAKE research members initially dismissed the idea of doing surveys due to lack of time or budget to gather enough data. Our CAKE community colleagues knew better, as they were able to work collectively and use their standing in our community to collect the data over a few weeks.

A third key area where our engaged approach improved the quality of research includes our ability to immediately translate our research findings into action. This occurred because the CAKE community members were part of the data analysis and interpretation processes. For example, a key finding from the provider interviews was that training and workshops for quality improvement and professional development were not convenient because of irregular hours of home-based care. Thus, CAKE community members with knowledge of these and connections with local organizations helped to coordinate (and in some cases facilitate) neighborhood training which took place at neighborhood churches. The community arts and music programs were made possible by connections that were made through community CAKE members that identified an early childhood advocate who directed the community arts and music program at the University of Cincinnati. In addition, our formative data collection and analysis of the GLAs allowed us to secure funding for the programs.

REFERENCES

Bassok, Daphna and Eva Galdo. 2016. Inequality in Preschool Quality? Community-Level Disparities in Access to High-Quality Learning Environments. *Early Education and Development* 27(1): 128–144.
Butterfoss, Frances, Robert Goodman, and Abraham Wandersman. 1996. Community Coalitions for Prevention and Health Promotion. *Health Education Research* 8(3): 315–330.

Cargo, Margaret and Shawna L. Mercer. 2008. The Value and Challenges of Participatory Research: Strengthening Its Practice. *Annual Review of Public Health* 29: 325–350.

Center for Community Health and Development. 2018. Section 5: Coalition Building 1. Starting a Coalition. Community Tool Box. https://ctb.ku.edu/en/table-of-contents/assessment/promotion-strategies/start-a-coalition/main

Cousins, J. Bradley and Jill Anne Chouinard. 2012. *Participatory Evaluation Up Close: An Integration of Research-Based Knowledge*. Charlotte, NC: Information Age Publishing.

Cousins, J. Bradley and Elizabeth Whitmore. 1998. Framing Participatory Evaluation. *New Directions for Evaluation* 80: 5–23.

Daudelin, Drew. 2017. Interview with Pastor Damon Lynch, March 17. Retrieved from www.wfyi.org/news/articles/interview-with-pastor-damon-lynch

Fuller, Bruce and Annelie Strath. 2001. The Child-Care and Preschool Workforce: Demographics, Earnings, and Unequal Distribution. *Educational Evaluation and Policy Analysis* 23(1): 37.

Gordon, Rachel and P. Lindsay Chase-Lansdale. 2001. Availability of Child Care in the United States: A Description and Analysis of Data Sources. *Demography* 38(2): 299–316.

Haines, Anna. 2009. Asset-Based Community Development. In Rhonda Phillips and Robert Pittman (Eds) *An Introduction to Community Development*, 2nd edition. New York: Routledge, pp. 48–72.

Israel, Barbara, James Krieger, David Vlahov, Sandra Ciske, Mary Foley, Princess Fortin, J. Ricardo Guzman, Richard Lichtenstein, Robert McGranaghan, Ann-Gel Palermo, and Gary Tang. 2006. Challenges and Facilitating Factors in Sustaining Community-Based Participatory Research Partnerships: Lessons Learned from the Detroit, New York City and Seattle Urban Research Centers. *Journal of Urban Health* 83(6): 1022–1040.

Janosky, Janine, Erin Armoutliev, Anureet Benipal, Diana Kingsbury, Jennifer L. Teller, Karen Snyder, and Penny Riley. 2013. Coalitions for Impacting the Health of a Community: The Summit County, Ohio, Experience. *Population Health Management* 16(4): 246–254.

Kretzmann, John P. 2010. Asset-Based Strategies for Building Resilient Communities. In J.W. Reich, A. Zautra and J.S. Hall (Eds) *Handbook of Adult Resilience*. New York: Guilford Press.

Kretzmann, John P. and John McKnight. 1993. *Building Communities from the Inside Out: A Path toward Finding and Mobilizing a Community's Assets*. Evanston, IL: Center for Urban Affairs and Policy Research, Neighborhood Innovations Network.

MacNeil, Carole, Douglas Ragan, and Jon-Andreas Solberg. 2012. The State of the Field in Youth-Led Development: Through the Lens of the UN-Habitat's Urban Youth Fund. *Nairobi, Kenya: United Nations Human Settlements Program*.

Mathie, Alison and Gord Cunningham. 2003. From Clients to Citizens: Asset-Based Community Development as a Strategy for Community-Driven Development. *Development in Practice* 13(5): 474–486.

Mathie, Alison, Jenny Cameron, and Katherine Gibson. 2017. Asset-Based and Citizen-Led Development: Using a Diffracted Power Lens to Analyze the Possibilities and Challenges. *Progress in Development Studies* 17(1): 54–66.

McKnight, John and Cormac Russell. 2018. *The Four Essential Elements of Asset-Based Community Development Process*. www.centreforwelfarereform.org/uploads/attachment/626/4-essential-elements-of-abcd-process.pdf

Minkler, Meredith, Victoria Breckwich Vasquez, Mansoureh Tajik, and Dana Petersen. 2008. Promoting Environmental Justice through Community-Based Participatory Research: The Role of Community and Partnership Capacity. *Health Education and Behavior* 35(1): 119–137.

National Institutes of Health. 2018. Clinical and Translational Science Awards (CTSA) Program. Bethesda, MD. https://ncats.nih.gov/ctsa

Patient-Centered Outcomes Research Institute. 2018. PCORI: About Us. Washington, DC. www.pcori.org/about-us

Phillips, Deborah, Mark Lipsey, Kenneth Dodge, Ron Haskins, Daphna Bassok, Margaret Burchinal, Greg Duncan, Mark Dynarski, Katherine Magnuson, and Christina Weiland. 2017. Puzzling It Out: The Current State of Scientific Knowledge on Pre-Kindergarten Effects: A Consensus Statement. *Issues in Pre-Kindergarten Programs and Policy*: 19–30.

Robert Wood Johnson Foundation. 2018. Interdisciplinary Research Leaders: Collaborating to Advance Health Equity. http://interdisciplinaryresearch-leaders.org/

Sánchez, Victoria, Christina Carrillo, and Nina Wallerstein. 2011. From the Ground Up: Building a Participatory Evaluation Model. *Progress in Community Health Partnerships: Research, Education, and Action* 5(1): 45–52.

Sparling, Hannah and Rebecca Huff. 2016. School Levy Passes by Wide Margin. *Cincinnati Enquirer*, November 8. www.cincinnati.com/story/news/politics/2016/11/08/issue-44-school-levy-takes-strong-early-lead/93169434/

Stuart, Graeme. 2013. What Is Asset-Based Community Development? Blog post, August 15. https://sustainingcommunity.wordpress.com/2013/08/15/what-is-abcd/

Thomas, David R. 2006. A General Inductive Approach for Analyzing Qualitative Evaluation Data. *American Journal of Evaluation* 27(2): 237–246.

Topmiller, Michael, Jamie-Lee Morris, and Farrah Jacquez. 2021. A Place-Based Approach to Early Childhood Wellness in Cincinnati: Communities Acting for Kids' Empowerment (CAKE). In Farrah Jacquez and Lina Svedin (Eds) *Interdisciplinary Community-Engaged Research for Child Health*. Cincinnati, OH: University of Cincinnati Press.

U.S. Census Bureau. 2012–2016. *Selected Economic Characteristics, 2012–2016 American Community Survey 5-Year Estimates*. https://factfinder.census.gov/faces/tableservices/jsf/pages/productview.xhtml?pid=ACS_16_5YR_DP03andprodType=table

Vaughn, Lisa M. and Farrah Jacquez. 2020. Participatory Research Methods: Choice Points in the Research Process. *Journal of Participatory Research Methods* 1: 1–14.

Vaughn, Lisa M. and MaryAnn Lohmueller. 2014. Calling All Stakeholders: Group-Level Assessment (GLA): A Qualitative and Participatory Method for Large Groups. *Evaluation Review* 38(4): 336–355.

Vaughn, Lisa M., Farrah Jacquez, and Jenny Zhen-Duan. 2018. Perspectives of Community Co-Researchers about Group Dynamics and Equitable Partnership within a Community–Academic Research Team. *Health Education and Behavior* 45(5): 682–689.

Whitmore, Elizabeth. 1998. Understanding and Practicing Participatory Evaluation. *New Directions for Evaluation* 80: 1–104.

Zakocs, Ronda C. and Erika Edwards. 2006. What Explains Community Coalition Effectiveness? A Review of the Literature. *American Journal of Preventive Medicine* 30(4): 351–361.

APPENDIX: INTERVIEW PROTOCOL FOR PARTICIPATORY EVALUATION

1. Tell me about being part of CAKE.
   a.   First, can you tell me about how being part of the team affected you as a person?
   b.   What motivated you to want to be part of CAKE?
   c.   What parts of the process of working with CAKE stand out for you?
   d.   Tell me how you think this project has had an impact on Carthage and Roselawn.
   e.   Do you think CAKE has the potential to make a real impact on kids and families in Carthage and Roselawn – why or why not?
2. What has it been like working with the other members of CAKE? What have been the best parts? What has been difficult?
3. Now, let me ask you about some specific aspects of your relationships and interactions with other people within the CAKE team:
   a.   When it comes to trust among members of the CAKE team, how would you rate trust (5 being the highest amount of trust and 1 being the lowest amount of trust)?

   Tell me about why you gave that rating for trust.

   b.   When it comes to decision making among members of the CAKE team, how would you rate your involvement in decision making (5 being the highest amount of involvement in decision making and 1 being the lowest amount of involvement in decision making)?

   Tell me about why you gave that rating for your involvement in decision making.

   c.   When it comes to leadership among members of the CAKE team, how would you rate your level of leadership (5 being the highest amount of your leadership on the team and 1 being the lowest amount of your leadership on the team)?

   Tell me about why you gave that rating for your leadership.

   d.   When it comes to learning new skills and knowledge as part of the CAKE team, how would you rate your learning (5 being the highest amount of learning and 1 being the lowest amount of learning of new skills and knowledge)?

   Tell me about why you gave that rating for learning new skills and knowledge.

   e.   How much did the process of working with CAKE allow for your voice to be heard (5 being the highest amount of your voice heard and 1 being the lowest amount of your voice heard)?

   Tell me about why you gave that rating for your voice being heard.

   f.   When it comes to active participation within the CAKE team, how would you rate your active participation (5 being the highest amount of active participation and 1 being the lowest amount of participation)?

   Tell me about why you gave that rating for your active participation.

g.   To what degree did you feel like an "equal partner" in the CAKE team (5 is the highest amount of equal partner and 1 is the lowest amount of equal partner)?

Tell me why you gave this rating for equal partner.

h.   When it comes to working together and collaboration among the whole team of CAKE, how would you rate the level of collaboration and working together (5 being the highest amount of working together/collaboration and 1 being the lowest amount of working together/collaboration)?

Tell me about why you gave that rating for working together/collaboration.

4. We hope to use community organizing to build leadership and power among the people of Carthage and Roselawn. Can you identify examples of how we are doing this? Do you think it is working?
5. From the beginning, the three core values of CAKE have been (1) shared decision making; (2) a focus on assets; and (3) a focus on real-world benefits. Do you think our work and our time together has reflected these core values? Why or why not?

If you have not gotten a feel for the best and worst parts of CAKE membership, ask these last two questions:

6. Overall, what were the most challenging parts of being part of CAKE?
7. Overall, what were your favorite parts of being part of CAKE?

12. The complexities of participatory action research: a community development project in Bangladesh

Larry Stillman, Misita Anwar, Gillian Oliver, Viviane Frings-Hessami, Anindita Sarker, and Nova Ahmed

This chapter discusses how a university research group experienced participatory action research (PAR) with a major international non-governmental organization (NGO) in a community informatics and information and communications technology for development project. These projects typically focus on the appropriation of information and communication technologies (ICTs) and the design of information systems (hardware, software, people's activity) to meet the needs of communities, but in this case, we also tried to incorporate PAR.

Using Participatory Research and Ownership with Technology, Information and Change (PROTIC) – a five-year collaborative project between Monash University in Australia, Oxfam Australia, and Oxfam in Bangladesh – as a case study, we focus on what we understand to be the practice of PAR. We say "what was understood to be" because the international project team came to the problem from very different perspectives, cultures, and educational backgrounds, including that of Western university academics, local project staff in an international NGO, local staff in a remote NGO, and the villagers themselves in a hierarchical, traditional environment. These factors affected the type of PAR which was implemented. There were also geographical, institutional, and political issues that affected our activity, and we account for these.

Despite these limitations, we interpret the use of PAR in this context as a very positive intercultural exchange between partners, resulting in incremental, but still important changes in the lives of the women participants in the project. It changed how Oxfam thinks about technology in international development and how academics view PAR, and raised awareness and skills concerning ICTs on the ground in remote villages in Bangladesh.

Our observations may seem devoid of idealism or commitment to more radical social change principles proposed for PAR and community development. However, we think that we have a more realistic approach to developing change strategies in countries like Bangladesh where external players need to avoid research colonization (Bishop 2005), or enact an unwelcome intervention in a politically sensitive environment.

THEORIES BEHIND THE PROJECT

From a research perspective, it can be suggested that there is a "three-cornered" relationship between knowledge, international community development, and technology (Johnstone 2005: 10). However, the dynamics between these three points are not well understood, in part due to the use of ill-fitting conventional knowledge management models that do not consider the particular culture and activities of NGOs. Here we explore the three corners.

Community Development, Community and Development Informatics

Members of the team had worked in community development in Australia, or had undertaken projects and research with a community development dimension in countries such as Cambodia, Indonesia, New Zealand, South Africa, and Vietnam over past decades. However, it was only when writing this chapter that we realized the concept of community development had been largely unproblematized for PROTIC. Although literature such as Ife (2013), Rothman and Tropman (1970), and Wadsworth (2011) was known to some team members, there was no systematic attempt to raise the awareness of other team members to this core literature other than forwarding electronic copies of academic articles. The knowledge and expertise of the project leader in guiding the ideas were taken as a given.

Some PROTIC team members had also been part of an earlier research group at Monash which had a particular interest in the theory and practice of community informatics (Stillman and Linger 2009; Stillman et al. 2009, 2014). Members of this group had also had strong connections going back to the mid-1990s going back to the Community Informatics Research Network which had been meeting almost yearly at the Monash campus in Italy since 2003. For the Monash team, community informatics projects consider "lived-in and situated communities not as passive recipients of technological opportunities, but as actors engaged in the comprehension and 'doing' of community problem solving directed to social progress" (Stillman and Linger 2009: 256).

This long exposure to the practice of community informatics converged with an interest in development informatics, also known as information and communication technology for development, by the Monash team. International development which supports the technical dimension is regarded as a form of research and practice mediated by a "process of articulating knowledge and power through which particular concepts, theories, and practices for social change are created and reproduced" (Chae 2014: 145). If a scholar takes an activist perspective, a characteristic of development informatics is that it proposes "pro-poor" solutions with technology, rather than passive consumption of informational or technological systems. Additionally, the importance of collaboration with and participation of the people at the bottom has been highlighted as a critical success factor of interpretively oriented technology research (Heeks 2006; Walsham 2006).

Oxfam members of the project saw academic definitions of community development or international development as less important than practice. Community development is largely pragmatic and practice-oriented in a country which is regarded as an international development hub, and the focus is upon project management and implementation (Lewis 2016). This is not to say that international NGO workers lack academic skills. In this project, the Oxfam team held local qualifications in environmental science and anthropology at bachelor and master's level from prestigious Bangladeshi universities. All have worked in the field, some in other countries in international development. In the field, the local NGO workers also have academic training from regional universities or institutions, including Islamic studies, business, or agricultural science. However, due to resource constraints in the country and natural staff turnover, there can be gaps in institutional and sectoral knowledge of community development tools and techniques.

Gendering and feminization of production were central to this project and are central to international development in general (Ahmad 2014; Sen 1987). Thus, "one is not born but becomes a woman" (De Beauvoir 2014: 293). This "becoming" in traditional societies occurs in a situation of complex disadvantage and discrimination through the multiple intersectional limitations set upon gender *and* the structurally unequal conditions under which women live as compared to men (Crenshaw 1989, 1991; Murzacheva et al. 2020). Critically, Bangladeshi women "are defined by their relationships" (Arens 2014: 35). There are multiple and predominantly unequal relationships with the immediate family, relatives, and other parties, and these have a key influence on well-being (Moore 2010: 36). Thus, when applied to the case of land in Bangladeshi villages:

> [A] woman's decision on what she chooses, both the process and the outcome, is only partly determined by her agency, by how much power she has to negotiate with her brothers and make her own choices. Apart from women's agency, the decision is also determined by the gendered social structure with its patriarchal norm that women depend on men for their livelihood and e.g. that a family prefers to keep its ancestral lands intact (which may limit her freedom of choice). Besides these, the decision is determined by the class structure and other factors, such as a woman's own personality, her family background, and education. The social structure can constrain or enable a woman's agency, her freedom of choice. (Arens 2014: 32)

As an international community development project combined with a PAR methodology project, PROTIC aimed to have as much participation as possible from the women themselves in the development of localized content based on their highly localized information, indigenous knowledge, and needs, and this was seen as a means of giving them a voice in designing solutions to meet their needs.[1] A range of ideas and experiences had an influence on what the academic researchers thought this meant in practice.

Participatory Action Research

What did we intend by PAR? From a Monash perspective, early ideas were very much influenced by Wadsworth (1998, 2011), Stoecker's work on community-based research (Stoecker 2001, 2012; Stoecker and Stillman 2007), Kemmis and McTaggart (2005), and Tinkler (2010). Team members had written about PAR (Denison and Stillman 2012). In PROTIC program documentation, we proposed a four-stage cycle (diagnosis, prescription, implementation, evaluation), derived from Stoecker's work on community-based research, citing the following statement:

> [The] first goal of the overall participatory and action-oriented research process is to support action on a specific issue – the first form of social change … [The] second form of social change … is to transform the social relations of knowledge production so that people who have only been passive recipients of knowledge become participatory knowledge producers whose knowledge can inform action and build power. (Stoecker 2012: 91–92)

We were also aware that in Global South contexts, PAR is viewed as a decolonizing form of research, and it rejects uncritical approaches to knowledge and information production and technologies (Angeles 2011). The Monash team, while attempting to localize the project, also discovered a Bangladeshi version of PAR with published English-language literature going back some decades (Fals-Borda and Rahman 1991; Fugelsang and Chandler 1988;

Rahman 1994). The Bangladeshi ideal for PAR (*Gonogobeshona* in Bangla) closely matched the radical ideas present in some Western writing about community change (Arnstein 1969; Black 2007). However, PAR's popularity has declined over the years in the more controlled and neoliberal environment in which NGOs now work in Bangladesh (Barua 2009; Lewis 2016). Despite this, PAR remains an inspirational ideology in Bangladesh and India, taken up in other forums such as the Bangladesh Gonogobeshona Ecology Network, and in indigenous knowledge research in Bangladesh and elsewhere (Sillitoe 2006; Sillitoe et al. 2005).

The aspirational PAR model for the project is represented in Figure 12.1. What we hoped to do, in addition to working with community-based practices for problem diagnosis, solutions, and implementation of information and communication problems (Phases I–III), was to also engage in Phase IV evaluation with strong participation from communities throughout the life of the project.

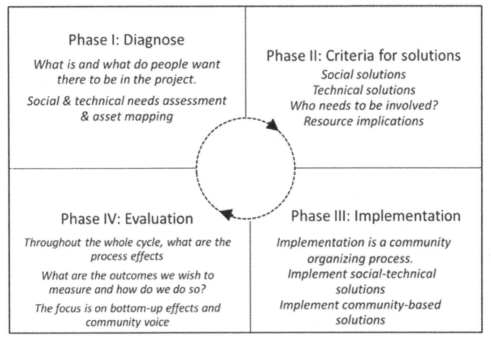

Source: Adapted from Stoecker (2001).

Figure 12.1   Stoecker's four-stage participatory action research process as for PROTIC

The practice of PAR changed during the course of the project in response to local conditions, once we saw that our expectations for full and robust local NGO and community-based evaluation were aiming too high, because of cultural, institutional, and logistical issues. This issue is discussed more fully in the case study.

BACKGROUND ON THE PROJECT

The Project Team

The academic research team itself was multicultural, with members from Australia, Bangladesh, Belgium, Indonesia, Italy, and New Zealand. The Oxfam Bangladesh staff in Dhaka were Bangla and English speaking and also had experience working across Asia. This interaction between different parties contributed to a rich mix of linguistic, textual, and cultural interactions in the process (see Sarrica et al. 2019). There were also five PhD students, four from Bangladesh, attached to the project. Communication among those involved was challenging. None of the Australia- or Italy-based researchers had more than basic Bangla (Bengali) language competency. Mostly, people used standard English, and what is known as "Banglish" – a locally emerging dialect of English, akin to Indian English – along with some Italian. At times, there were problems of meaning across Englishes in both face-to-face and video or voice communication, compounded by geographical distance and internet connectivity issues.

Consequently, many online meetings between Australia, Oxfam in Bangladesh, and Italy were inconclusive, with conversations being left to multiple emails and Skype or Facebook messages. The best work was done when the Monash team was in Bangladesh. But even then, the cross-cultural and language barriers were apparent; we deferred to Bangladeshi ways of doing and being and avoided research colonization by outsiders (Dutta and Islam 2016; Smith 1999).

In the target communities, the local NGOs had less facility with English. Most field workers, while understanding some English, did not speak English well enough to discuss the project in any detail. Some villagers knew basic greetings in English, but not enough to hold a conversation. Thus, variations in capacity or willingness to communicate in English (whether Oxfam staff, local NGOs, or villagers) prevented obtaining detailed and nuanced information. Additionally, project implementation was conducted in Bangla, with local dialects on the ground. Many meetings in Dhaka and in the field had to be interpreted by Oxfam staff for the English speakers, resulting in compression and filtering of information.

Additionally, for cultural and institutional reasons, NGO workers and managers wanted to present stories of successes rather than problems and failures to the foreign Monash team. Finally, the villages were two days or more away from Dhaka, via quite tiring journeys, and this also impacted the quality of interactions.

The Project Context

Bangladesh
About 80 percent of Bangladesh's population of 160 million live in villages. They engage in agriculture as well as pisciculture – fish and shellfish – for consumption and for local markets. Some products may also then be sold to wholesalers for trading in Dhaka and other markets. Villagers face environmental fragility including the effects of climate change and increasing salinization due to shrimp and crab cultivation. Many people cannot access fresh water anymore, and rivers are being lost due to climate change and the effects of human settlement and industrialization. Despite these problems, rural Bangladesh is spectacularly beautiful and "is not so much a land upon water as water upon a land" (Novak 2008: 22).

For social, economic, and cultural development, NGOs, whether large international or homegrown social enterprises, or locally based, are pervasive and involved in the delivery of a full range of services, subject to increasing government regulation and control. Their exact numbers are not known because many small local people-centered organizations (some based on religion) are not registered. Many villages are associated with several projects. It was estimated by the World Bank in the early 2000s that 20–35 percent of the Bangladeshi population received some form of service (education, credit, health) from an NGO representing a form of outsourced government. Anecdotally, the figure is probably much higher today, with the role of NGOs even more entrenched (Lewis 2011, 2016). By way of comparison, in India, it is thought that there is one NGO for every 400 people. Anecdotally, it is the same in Bangladesh. It is hard to think of a village without some sort of NGO relationship.

In this context, innovation with ICTs are important as a way to overcome the country's poor road and communications infrastructure which severely restricts travel, business, and access to core services such as hospitals. Most people appear to have cheap phones (as low as US$10), though increasing numbers buy cheap internet-enabled devices in village bazaars. At the same time digital divides replicating wealth and class divides affect access to ICTs (Rahman 2013). According to the Bangladesh Telecommunication Regulatory Commission, mobile phone users grew from 133 million in December 2015 to 162.5 million in August 2019,[2] though people may possess more than one phone or, conversely, may share devices. As of August 2019, the total number of internet users reached 98.1 million; 92.4 million of these used mobile phones.

The Bangladeshi government has a digital society policy agenda (popularly known as Vision 2021), but how to truly engage and connect with people in low-income communities, rather than expanding services for the middle class, business, government, and industry, remains problematic (Government of Bangladesh, Prime Minister's Office 2019).

Natural and humanitarian disasters and security
It was often difficult for our project to demand priority in the midst of frequent natural and humanitarian disasters that Bangladeshis face.

For example, when the Rohingya humanitarian emergency occurred in Bangladesh in 2018–2019, all Oxfam staff were pulled in to assist, including spending weeks in the camps, preventing Monash staff from working with the local NGOs (see Figure 12.2). The same problem occurred when there were floods in the country in August 2017 and July 2019. While the lead researcher was able to conduct some field trips in both periods, they were not in the mood to discuss how useful phones were to them even though we know they were filming and sharing footage of floods on Facebook.

From mid-2016 onward, the security situation worsened in Bangladesh. A terrorist attack on a café on 1 July 2016, the day that Larry Stillman and Mauro Sarrica arrived in the country, killed many foreigners. Foreigners and Bangladeshis alike were terrified. Security alerts resulted in ongoing lockdowns in hotels and alerts for foreigners, at times preventing field visits and even access to the project office in Dhaka.

CASE STUDY: THE PROTIC PROJECT

Background

The PROTIC project is a collaboration between Monash University, Australia, and Oxfam, through its affiliates in Australia and particularly Oxfam in Bangladesh. Key events in the project are highlighted in Figure 12.2 and taken up in the narrative. The acronym PROTIC fittingly means "sign" in Bangla. The first stage of PROTIC (2015–2019) tried to use a combination of community development and PAR to support and empower isolated village women with information and knowledge through the use of smartphones.

The kernel of the PROTIC project goes back to earlier desk research in 2012 and serendipitous discussions that took place with the then manager of Oxfam in Bangladesh projects in June 2013 during an Oxfam workshop.

After a series of field visits by Larry Stillman and online discussions over 2013–2014 the partners obtained funding (approximately US$3 million) from a private foundation for the PROTIC project for 2015–2019. A public launch was held in Bangladesh in June 2015. The project also received human ethics clearance from Monash University for activity in both the villages where smartphones were used and the control villages where phones were not distributed. In many ways, the PAR element was institutionalized within Oxfam and Monash University's ways of working. Both organizations are risk averse and concerned with their reputation. Projects still needed to go through the formalities of sign-off at the highest levels of the organization. Figure 12.2 shows a timeline for the project. A new project, focusing on different communities, but using the learnings from PROTIC, has been funded for 2019–2024, though COVID has created a new set of challenges.

Access to information and information rights are important to Oxfam, and this is reflected in the following statement from one of its key thinkers:

> Access to information is no abstract debate; it is an essential tool of citizenship. Knowledge expands horizons, allows people to make informed choices, and strengthens their ability to demand their rights. Ensuring access to knowledge and information is integral to enabling poor people to tackle the deep inequalities of power and voice that entrench inequality across the world. At a national level, the ability to absorb, adapt, and generate knowledge and turn it into technology increasingly determines an economy's prospects. (Green 2012: 43)

The significance of using PAR as a research method and transformational tool was highlighted in internal documents and proposals for the PROTIC project (Stillman 2014) as well as during extensive consultative meetings with other NGOs and visits to the field, and by thinkers in the formative period of the project in April and June 2015. This can be considered as part of Phase I activity in terms of Stoecker's model (see Figure 12.1). Oxfam emphasized that the importance of the project was its desire to build a relationship between Oxfam and its partners and leave behind knowledge and skills, in contrast to experience with other researchers who came, took, and left NGOs and communities behind. Consequently, as a continuation of Phase I, and resulting in Phase II, over a year was spent conceptualizing the project, and after funding was obtained, the middle of 2015 was spent in further consultation and negotiation between members of the Monash team and stakeholders in Bangladesh, including villagers, NGOs, and Oxfam, about the direction of the project.

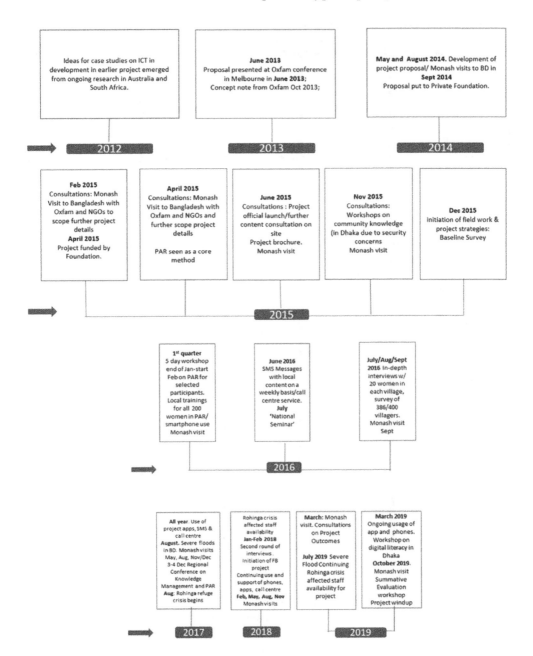

Figure 12.2   Timeline for PROTIC

An important outcome of these negotiations was the project brochure,[3] distributed at the PROTIC launch in June 2015, that reflected a consensus around language, concepts, and methods for the project. Local political and academic dignitaries attended the event. A table from the brochure appears in Figure 12.3.

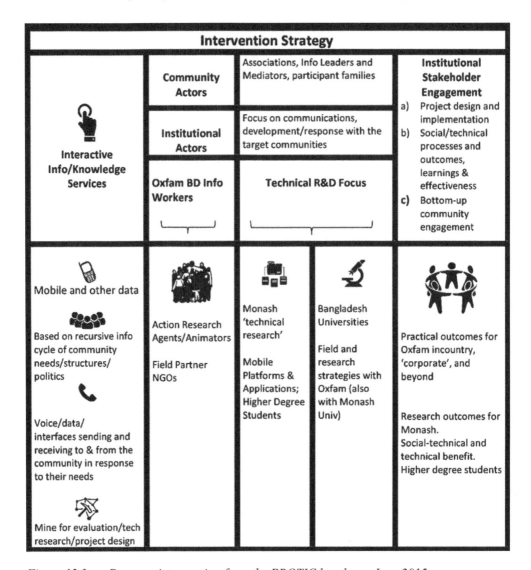

Figure 12.3   Program intervention from the PROTIC brochure, June 2015

Figure 12.3, from the brochure, represents the project as seen by Oxfam workers, local NGOs, Monash, and other academics. It shows key components of the intervention stage of the project, including actors, outcomes, and processes (see also Figure 12.1, Stage III).

Like the four-stage PAR cycle, this was an "ideal type" but was very useful as a reference peg for the project around which actions and conversations could take place, and upon which public presentations were made. Community actors – villagers – were deliberately placed at the top of the diagram in terms of the people involved. The benchmarking survey – to get more information about the community use of ICTs – took place in December 2015, though it was some months in the planning.

Through the process of negotiation between Oxfam and Monash, including input from village consultations during the program development stage, PROTIC's main goal was expressed in program documentation as: "To develop current, accurate, comprehensive, reliable and trustworthy Bengali-language interactive and localized information services and information provision skills for the community, particularly for women in agriculture, by providing access to information that enables them to act to improve their, and their communities' well-being and livelihoods."

The Project

For guidance in Bangladesh, Oxfam and Monash turned to Research Initiatives Bangladesh (RIB), which had a long history with Gonogobeshona or PAR (Research Initiatives Bangladesh 2014). Meghna Guhathakurta, its director, is a well-known Bangladeshi public intellectual, prominent writer on gender issues in the country and activist for community rights (Guhathakurta 2003; Guhathakurta and Van Schendel 2013). As Suraya Begum, who works with RIB, has said, "A central concept in Gonogobeshona is the premise that when it comes to knowledge and the ability to think, no group, class or community is more 'advanced' than the other" (Begum and Chakraborty 2017: 11). Thus, PAR is about breaking down barriers between groups, particularly between what she calls "the common people" who believe that the middle class are the experts. This is particularly the case in Bangladesh, where there is a culture of deference to authority.

Initial planning for local PAR implementation was conducted by Monash and Oxfam staff during December 2015–March 2016 when they participated in discussions and training with RIB. At the start of February 2016, another five-day intensive workshop was held where the participants learned about the process of self-inquiry and there were also field visits to other sites where PAR projects were in place. Over 30 participants were selected by Oxfam, including key villagers, representatives of the local NGOs, the contracted telco, and local universities. The aim was to develop a shared understanding of PAR/Gonogobeshona, its strengths and weaknesses particularly as related to bottom-up activity, and to focus specifically on the effects of gender on community action and the development of a community voice. Additionally, on 22 July 2016, what is known as a "national seminar" for policy makers, academics, and NGOs was held at the University of Dhaka, with speakers drawn from the project, academics, several of the villagers, as well as Larry Stillman by Skype (Begum and Chakraborty 2017).

Furthermore, during the first quarter of 2016, 200 women agriculturalists and pisciculturalists (100 each in two isolated villages in target regions) were provided with smartphones and phone credit by the project to enable them to access information on agricultural topics relevant to their everyday lives, and with PAR training. Additionally, there were control villages, already working with the local NGO on community development projects. They were not provided with phones by the project in order to compare the effects of the intervention.

The first community that worked with smartphones was in the far north-west of Bangladesh, on the river Teesta near the border with India. People in this area are heavily dependent on river flows for their crops. The second community lives in the ecologically fragile southern mangroves region, known as the Sundarbans. Its economy is based on aquaculture and small farming. A main problem in this area is the increase in salinity due to climate change and the spread of shrimping.[4] Oxfam staff used the term "animator" to describe their hopes for an activist role for the village women, based upon the language used by RIB. Suraya Begum from the research institute has said that "animators play a pivotal role in Gonogobeshona. Animators are the agents who can stimulate people into creative action" (Begum and Chakraborty 2017: 11). Oxfam believed that through PAR training the farming women would "animate" others to become engaged with smartphones.

Oxfam, with input from Monash, also contracted a telecommunications service (telco) with experience in providing information services to provide localized agricultural information about crops, poultry, livestock, vegetable gardening, fish and crab culture, and weather. Consultations by the telco with the women showed that they preferred very specific, localized information. The women were also very concerned that there would not be any ambiguous or unintentionally misleading information because the cost of error – no food production – was of critical importance to them.

Information was sent to the villagers via SMS and outbound dialing on a regular basis, usually weekly, beginning in 2016 until 2019 (see Figure 12.2), based on the experience of the telco with other information campaigns directed at cultivators. Information had to be carefully targeted and matched to the agricultural cycle and local needs, otherwise it was meaningless.

Messages included recommended planting times, or the need to treat plants for particular bugs. Follow-up calls could be made to the call center. In addition to this, the telco developed two mobile phone apps – one on maize production and the other on the government subsidies available to villagers for the project. The telco adapted one app from a beta version developed by a Monash University student for a summer project.

The local NGOs which were part of the project also hired local community development staff to provide ongoing smartphone training and support at the village level, including meetings with local government and extension services. We also know that some of the women began to innovate with the phones, using various apps for video calls to families outside of the village (for example in India). Others downloaded or obtained apps with hymns and prayers relevant to Hindus or Muslims. Some husbands used the smartphone to film sermons by religious speakers. Other women downloaded self-care and beauty apps. Others obtained movies. They often installed apps by Bluetooth from the tiny phone stalls in local villages rather than downloading them as that was too costly.

In November 2017, Oxfam produced a locally distributed report (in English and Bangla), about the effects of the project through the use of PAR during its pilot phase (Begum and Chakraborty 2017). The report concluded that there was increased interaction and precision in language to describe issues by the women, "which in turn has given them a sense of unity and improved their articulation [sic] as well and they have provided further feedback on the information they want. They are trying to identify their own problems. Their demands get more and more precise as the problem identification becomes sharper" (Auvi and Chakraborty 2017: 31). The women had also begun applying for various social benefits – something they had not had information about before. The point about becoming more articulate is quite an important one: we observed that women were using veterinary terminology quite freely, and despite supposed low levels of literacy, some were keeping organized notebooks (notebooks don't need recharging!) of information in Bangla, and developing wall charts for sharing with others, including phonetic spellings of medicine names. Their innovation in using written records is very important, low cost, and may in fact be a better solution in many cases than keeping vulnerable mobile phones as an information source (Frings-Hessami et al. 2020).

The government attempted to create a social support app, but it was considerably delayed due to changing government criteria. We had also hoped for a local university-linked research project to analyze call data and relate it to the distribution of text messages by the telco on particular topics. As all this was in Bangla (including call logs), it could only be done by a local researcher. Unfortunately, due to internal issues at the relevant university, in which we could not be involved, the project never went ahead, depriving us of a valuable longitudinal source of data which could have demonstrated causal effects for the SMS information campaign and its many different messages, as well as the calling habits of the women to the call center. The messaging of SMS information and the call center operation continued until mid-2019.

Once the villagers showed interest in doing new things with their phones, the project management group brainstormed a project using Facebook as an information medium during 2018. While there were initial thoughts by the team about developing a platform separate from Facebook, local staff believed we should go with what was already public. Many of the villagers had heard about Facebook, but had never used it, even though it was becoming very popular in the country.

The community development workers subsequently engaged in Facebook training with the women and encouraged them to make posts and upload photos and videos. However, the independent use of Facebook was not substantial, and tended to reflect what they were being taught by the community development workers. There was also a natural element of hesitation by some of the women to put themselves online because of the culture of shaming women who are seen to be too "open." The local NGOs and Oxfam also had concerns about community safety and privacy due to some instances of harassment. While this is a known problem for the urban middle class, it is clearly a new problem in other parts of the country.

The most effective means of obtaining evaluative information was the visits by Monash staff to Oxfam in Dhaka or to the field when we met face to face with Oxfam, NGOs, and sometimes the village women. We encouraged the women to speak out as much as possible either in Dhaka or in the natural setting of their village. During these meetings we used the classic white board, flip chart, or paper hung on walls and people charting out the data and assessing the value and worth of activity. Such activity was not new to them, as it is part and parcel of community development used by local NGOs. While most of the women were more inhibited in speaking to such audiences, a number were quite articulate and able to talk about community needs and responses. This produced naturalistic information on what had been done and provided information as a means of developing project direction (Guba and Lincoln 1981; Lincoln and Guba 1985). Oxfam then conveyed the results of these meetings to the local NGOs who also sought input from the local communities.

Additionally, several specific workshops on issues such as information literacy and cyber safety were held with the village women. In March 2019, a workshop in Dhaka brought together 12 leading project participants from the two locations to assess their information literacy. A participatory technique was used in the workshop, engaging the women in learning, sharing, and speaking out. The results gave important insight into participants' information seeking, evaluation practices, and preferred ways of preserving information, which were further discussed during focus groups the following month in one of the villages (Frings-Hessami et al. 2020). The workshop also gave insight into participants' understanding about cyber safety and how collective practices and other cultural norms contradicted what is generally emphasized for information privacy and cybersecurity.

The workshop showed that women understood their information needs and where to find information. While the concept of an information source was new to them, the participants were able to differentiate information needs and sources. Moreover, for some information, such as agricultural information, their search went beyond immediate needs to future needs like planning to increase production. This also revealed information format preferences such as the use of pictures and photos that were easier to use in conversation and learning when sharing with others.

The women were beginning to act as what Wadsworth has called a "critical reference group" to the project, and they were in fact regarded as such (Wadsworth 2011: 28). They were finding their voice, advocating on issues with their local councilors, becoming more comfortable with technology (for example, starting to use multimedia functionality to capture local data), or vaccinating their own animals and using a technical language to describe medicines that they used. They were able to assert their needs in a language that others understood.

Ultimately, however, fieldwork conditions and resource constraints were such that it proved impossible to implement an ongoing PAR evaluation process with the communities. We recognized that the ongoing PAR evaluation process in Figure 12.1, Phase IV, remained an ideal, and was impossible to achieve in practice due to the impacts of distance, resources, languages, security, and different approaches to the collection of data in the field. Despite these limitations, the ideal still helped to craft consciousness about PAR in the project and has influenced the development of the second stage of the project funded for 2019–2024.

REFLECTIONS

NGOs are very careful about how they act in Bangladesh, where government permission is required and political patronage essential. This is in addition to the traditional patriarchy and hierarchy found in villages, and the intersectional disadvantage experienced by women. NGOs also tend to operate in a more hierarchical and guiding fashion, rather than encouraging independence on the part of project "beneficiaries," the term commonly used to describe members of a target community. Local-level projects are the bread and butter of NGOs, and project control remains with them. Furthermore, in Bangladesh projects are usually designed by researchers or NGOs beforehand, signed off, and implemented under contract.

In contrast, in this project the multiple partners could query, reflect, correct, and alter the project as part of ongoing action research. In this spirit, the Monash staff endeavored to establish open and trusting relationships with Oxfam staff with frequent online conversations and physical presence. The Oxfam staff became quite excited by PAR possibilities, particularly at the grass roots.

However, collaboration was challenging. Between field visits, we were unable to always meet monthly online due to conflicting schedules and, at times, to the low quality of Skype or Zoom, or even phone connections. Email was not always adequate when discussing quite subtle matters, and there were problems in conveying issues in mutually intelligible English. But it needs to be stressed that none of this detracts from the overwhelming goodwill and trust which existed. We were just dealing with a complex project across distance.

The major participatory innovation for the project turned out to be the monthly meetings in the villages. Oxfam staff also attended a number of these meetings. We encouraged the meetings to be as open as possible, though this was not without difficulty, as the local NGO workers tended to take a leading role in discussion, rather than give women a free voice. Additionally, there was traditional deference to a few women leaders in the villages because of their recognized authority.

Despite this, Bangladeshi PhD students attached to the project, with their insider/outsider status, were particularly aware that the women in the project were subject to surveillance and monitoring by husbands, extended families, and the community at large, in line with local cultural practices. Reputation and being seen as a "good woman" are everything. The women's capacity to innovate with a smartphone can come into conflict with a culture of traditional restraint and constraint. Additionally, the NGO checked the women's Facebook pages to make sure that they were positive. Some husbands also checked the call history, SMS, and Facebook activities. While some phones had a password, it was likely to be shared among the family members so it was quite easy to get access to the apps in the phone including Facebook. From other data, we have the observation from one husband that:

> After coming back from work I checked my wife's phone every night. It is my duty to check it and keep her in the right way. NGO has given the phone but they will not take any responsibility if anything bad happened or if they respond to a trap. My respect, my family will be affected.

In fact, according to Anindita Sarker, some of the women engaged in a form of "display" to demonstrate their compliance, for example, deliberately NOT sharing their phones with other members of the family when NGO or Monash researchers were around. But some also engaged in non-compliance. Even though they were asked to display photos of themselves on their Facebook profiles by the NGO, some did not do so, out of reputational concern (Sarker 2021).

There were dropouts from the monthly meetings and dropouts from the project. Many women were simply too busy with their everyday family and farming responsibilities to take part. Dropouts and breakages of phones were not reported to us until many months later, compromising our research findings.

It was a matter of trial and error over some months until Monash, Oxfam, and the Italian researcher were able to develop a simple protocol to guide discussions. The original research questions relating to a theory of social-technical change were far too complex to implement (and easily translate) at such a geographic and cultural distance. NGO workers did not feel confident writing narrative reports, even though they sometimes made their own private notes (in Bangla). Their concept of reporting was something narrower, consisting of numeric and factual data according to prescribed reporting formats (for example, number of participants and hours spent in a particular training). They said that they were not sure what to write in a report or if they should write anything beyond the required structured information. As an example, they were unsure whether to include subjective impressions when visiting the participants, even though Monash researchers had emphasized the importance of this kind of observational data. There were also ongoing culture and translation issues: the field activity occurred in Bangla and had to be communicated to Monash researchers in English. Some field workers said that they were more comfortable sharing their findings verbally. However, they did not speak much English, and the simultaneous interpretation we thought we could get lacked detail, despite laudable attempts by our Bangladeshi colleagues. This resulted in an unanticipated strong filtering process and much was lost in transmission.

As a potential solution, we came up with the idea of recording the monthly meetings. We arranged for 36 recordings of meetings from mid-2017 to mid-2018 (several meetings were held in each village each month as the women were broken up into local community groups for community organization purposes). However, problems with the installation and the sharing of the database between our university and outsiders proved to be an irresolvable bureaucratic nightmare. In addition, some meetings were not recorded or forwarded to Oxfam in Dhaka. Additionally, trying to transcribe and translate was an impossibly large task. Ordinarily, such a quantity of group discussions – sometimes with people talking over each other – would be a treasure trove for a researcher, but we were in fact in real field-work conditions with limited skills and resources available to us at a distance. Only a selection of the recordings were consequently analyzed, and even then, the immediacy we were hoping to capture – the knowledge in them to be used as part of the ongoing research – was lost.

Despite such problems, the meetings were particularly useful in helping the women to identify many local problems that could be addressed by the project, including agricultural and fisheries issues, lack of electricity (many were reliant on solar panels or charging in village shops), restrictions on the movement of women due to traditional values, and the lack of job opportunities, which resulted in migration by men to other parts of the country (Auvi and Chakraborty 2017).

With these small steps toward a PAR framework, Stage IV (participatory evaluation) was never effectively achieved. While PAR evaluation as an ongoing process looked good in theory and in a brochure, its multilevel transformative potential remained theoretical and aspirational, mostly due to institutional and logistical constraints. In fact, in November 2019, the most practical thing to do was to bring key village women from the two villages to Dhaka, along with other stakeholders such as the local NGOs and academics, and workshop project findings with them in a summative fashion. The hard question is whether or not multileveled PAR across cultures, time zones, and distances is possible or even desirable. Having to spend two or more days from Dhaka traveling to a village site for a short, supervised visit does not amount to in-depth PAR. In the same way, are villagers coming to Dhaka under the aegis of an NGO really "free agents" in their participation? Who benefits from this?

Thus, while Oxfam organized meetings between Monash researchers and project partners as frequently as possible, they lacked a breakthrough PAR method from the bottom up for a project design and evaluation. Oxfam recognized that PAR was not quite working as it could be as an ongoing, transformative process. In an ideal PAR project, Monash and Oxfam would have spent months in the field working with the villagers in different parts of the country to design a project about mobile phones and let them take a direct role in crafting a solution. Institutionally, culturally, and logistically, this was not what took place. Perhaps the days of years-long village research, as found in older works about Bangladesh, are over, because of logistical, funding, and security challenges (Arens 2014; Hartmann and Boyce 1983).

In fact, it is clear that some of the women farmers (the animators) and the NGO field workers wanted a more top-to-bottom integration of PAR, and Oxfam staff said that "participants stressed that PAR was not sufficiently understood … and that there remained a lack of capacity in terms of facilitating PAR activities" (Chakraborty and Akter 2019: 9), but we were unable to bring about a strong change in direction.

Even with this problem at an institutional level, an unanticipated outcome of the project is that Oxfam has undergone a huge transformation in its own thinking about the role of technology in the work of an NGO, and about using participatory methods. Oxfam also now uses the PAR experience in PROTIC for its own advocacy of social justice issues with government and opinion makers in Bangladesh.

The project influenced Oxfam's thinking particularly because it was in accord with Oxfam's Asia region program which emphasized both more effective use of ICTs and more participatory approaches to development. They reported that PROTIC was:

> A breakthrough in Oxfam's work in Bangladesh, which also enriched the RECALL intervention [another major project] through ICT. Approaches like PAR have made this project "learning by doing" while involving multi-stakeholders in implementing in two hard-core vulnerable areas in Bangladesh. It is expected that a holistic approach will bring success in the long run with effective and timely intervention by all stakeholders involved and the evaluation will be a source of inspiration. (Chakraborty and Akter 2019: 9)

At the village level, the contrast between "life before PROTIC" and "life after PROTIC" can be summarized in the following statements from the field work with village women, drawn from the workshops and other more traditional interviews and research conducted in the project (Stillman et al. 2020a, 2020b).

Before PROTIC and the smartphone:

> I had no place in my family to give any opinion or suggestion for my own family development.

> I lost my legs when I was very young, which made me physically handicapped. I always have challenges to make my voice heard and challenging life in social circumstances.

> Our village is a very difficult place to cultivate crops, the land here is very salty. And the help for anything is far away from here.

> My husband used to have a feature phone, and I was scared to touch it as I feared what if I do something wrong.

After PROTIC and the smartphone:

> I get loads of information on agriculture, I share with my neighbors and use them on my own field too.

> I have built a library of eBooks that I have downloaded from Google and now I share those with my family members and friends.

> Protic Call center helped me to save my ducks, and previously it was very hard for me to get a doctor here, it used to take two days and 300 kilometers on average to bring a vet.

More broadly PROTIC has been featured on Bangla TV and in the English and Bangla press. Most recently, a color supplement, edited by the International Center for Climate Change and Development, appeared in the English-Language *Daily Tribune* in December 2019 (Ahmed and Mahmuda 2019).

CONCLUSIONS

In this project there were a host of factors at play beyond our desire to empower women with mobile phones. These inhibited the more aspirational aspects of the original PAR model that had been developed. Additionally, real-time and space differences between all players made coordination extremely difficult. Despite this, there were tangible changes at the grass roots and in Oxfam. Perhaps the academic researchers could have been more prescriptive in what they wanted of both Oxfam and its partners, but it was felt that this detracted from a more open, exploratory, and PAR approach. There was also a concern to avoid research colonization that would withhold research knowledge and skills from Oxfam, the local NGOs, and the villagers, rather than engaging them as much as possible in the act of knowledge production, difficult as that was.

The observations of the human computer interaction (HCI) researcher (Nova Ahmed) are particularly important, because they show a neat overlap between the aspirations for PAR in the project as expressed in Figure 12.2 and a progressive HCI agenda. HCI is at the software design end of things and struggles to recognize social and human diversity (including gender), particularly in the development world (Ahmed et al. 2016). From Ahmed's perspective, PROTIC can be critiqued in at least two ways. First, PROTIC was adopting existing technology tools for women in the community, rather than looking to develop a new "indigenous" tool. The project chose to look at smartphones, believing that this was the emergent technology of the time which would generate public interest.

In fact, as we saw in the project, some of the outcomes operated at a much simpler community level on the basis of a better understanding of community dynamics and information flows. The development of an "indigenous" tool would have required considerably more time spent in the design phase (and resources spent on it, on the ground), resulting in little time for implementation, observation, evaluation, and demonstration of effects, despite the deeper insights it could have provided. The community would have also had less time to just use the phones as they wished in the local setting.

From the Monash perspective, looking back, far more time and effort should have been spent cultivating more "critical reference group" activity before engaging in the broader intervention (Wadsworth 2011). In fact, it was only by accident, during the writing of this chapter, that we discovered that Wadsworth had also spoken and written about this issue to a PAR conference in Bangladesh. This knowledge only came about when a book that had been given to the first author in 2016 by the Research Institute Bangladesh was looked at again (Wadsworth 2004)! Hindsight is a wonderful thing.

Second, even though PROTIC did not achieve a fully structured PAR cycle as proposed (and outlined in Figure 12.1), the problematic situation of introducing an open technology like the smartphone in a sensitive community environment is also familiar in feminist HCI thinking which has a concern for appropriate methods and products in a country like Bangladesh (Bardzell 2010; Sultana et al. 2018). The development of suitable technology, content, and safe interfaces for women in Bangladesh has become a recognized problem, and will be considered in the next stage of the project (Sambasivan et al. 2019).

PAR thus provided the basis and guiding philosophy for this research project, but our experience demonstrates the essential need to consider the complexities of different cultural and resource contexts at the different levels of a project to achieve nuanced and appropriate outcomes. In the case of PROTIC, the cultural and resource complexities included the diverse backgrounds of all participants, including the research team. One significant but unintended consequence was the influence on our major NGO partner, Oxfam in Bangladesh. This suggests that evaluation of PAR impacts should use a broad view, including going beyond the boundaries of a particular project, its methods, and particular outcomes.

Furthermore, as the project progressed the ideal of "empowering" PAR, flavored with Western ideas about individualistic feminism, increasingly rang hollow for the Monash researchers. We were guest researchers in a gendered, patriarchal, and hierarchical society.

We learned that some women were reluctant to share stories about their experiences in an open environment, even with other women whom they knew. They didn't want to put their reputation or security at risk, including domestic violence or the new phenomenon of stalking and harassment online. PROTIC could not adopt change strategies which would have endangered women's safety.

And finally, everyone who participated from Monash has been deeply affected in their perception of not just Bangladesh and its people, but our views about the relationships between privileged researchers and people in the developing world. It has been a life-changing experience for us and will continue to be so in further stages of the project.

NOTES

1.   In this chapter we use the terms "information" and "knowledge" interchangeably, though knowledge tends to be interpreted as having more of an applied sense – "information-in-use."
2.   www.btrc.gov.bd/license-statistics.
3.   It is normal practice in Bangladesh to produce such materials in English as this is the working language of the international NGO sector.
4.   A third community in the north-east Sylhet region became involved at a later stage of the project with a similar number of women provided with phones but was not subject to the same field strategies or comparative research and is not discussed here.

REFERENCES

Ahmad, Fauzi Erfan. 2014. "Gender and Development in Bangladesh." In *Development Constraints and Realizations*, edited by M.K. Mujeri. Dhaka: UPL, pp. 307–326.

Ahmed, Syed Ishtiaque, Nova Ahmed, Faheem Hussain, and Neha Kumar. 2016. "Computing beyond Gender-Imposed Limits." In *Proceedings of the Second Workshop on Computing within Limits, LIMITS '16*. New York: Association for Computing Machinery.

Ahmed, Tania and Mity Mahmuda. 2019. "Bangladesh's Climate Champions." *Climate Tribune* 3(12).

Angeles, Leonora C. 2011. "Participatory Development." In *Encyclopedia of International Development*, edited by T. Forsyth. London: Routledge, pp. 506–511.

Arens, A.M.J. 2014. *Women, Land and Power in Bangladesh: Jhagrapur Revisited*. Dhaka: UPL.

Arnstein, S.R. 1969. "A Ladder of Citizen Participation." *Journal of the American Institute of Planners* 35(4): 216–224.

Auvi, Priodarshine and Tapas Chakraborty. 2017. *Community Resilience through ICT: At a Glance PROTIC*. Dhaka.

Bardzell, Shaowen. 2010. "Feminist HCI: Taking Stock and Outlining an Agenda for Design." *Proceedings of the SIGCHI Conference on Human Factors in Computing Systems, CHI '10*. New York: Association for Computing Machinery, pp. 1301–1310.

Barua, Bijoy P. 2009. "Participatory Research, NGOs, and Grassroots Development: Challenges in Rural Bangladesh." In *Education, Participatory Action Research, and Social Change: International Perspectives*, edited by D. Kapoor and S. Jordan. New York: Palgrave Macmillan, pp. 239–250.

Begum, Suraya and Tapas Chakraborty. 2017. *Participatory Research and Ownership with Technology, Information and Change (PROTIC). The Role of PAR*. Dhaka.

Bishop, Russell. 2005. "Freeing Ourselves from Neo-Colonial Domination in Research: A Kaupapa Māori Approach to Creating Knowledge." In *The SAGE Handbook of Qualitative Research*, edited by N.K. Denzin and Y.S. Lincoln. Thousand Oaks, CA: SAGE, pp. 109–138.

Black, Maggie. 2007. *The No-Nonsense Guide to International Development*. London: New Internationalist.

Chae, Young-Gil. 2014. "Development Discourse." *International Encyclopedia of Communication.* https://onlinelibrary.wiley.com/doi/book/10.1002/9781405186407

Chakraborty, Tapas and Pinash Akter. 2019. *A Journey towards Resilience: Lessons from PROTIC.* Dhaka.

Crenshaw, Kimberle. 1989. "Demarginalizing the Intersection of Race and Class: A Black Feminist Critique of Antidiscrimination Doctrine, Feminist Theory and Anti-Racist Policies." *University of Chicago Legal Forum.*

Crenshaw, Kimberle. 1991. "Mapping the Margins: Intersectionality, Identity Politics, and Violence against Women of Color." *Stanford Law Review* 43(6): 1241–1299.

De Beauvoir, Simone. 2014. *The Second Sex.* London: Vintage Books.

Denison, Tom and Larry Stillman. 2012. "Academic and Ethical Challenges in Participatory Models of Community Research." *Information, Communication and Society* 15(7): 1037–1054.

Dutta, Bipasha and Kazi Maruful Islam. 2016. "Role of Culture in Decision Making Approach in Bangladesh: An Analysis from the Four Cultural Dimensions of Hofstede." *Bangladesh E-Journal of Sociology* 13(6): 30–38.

Fals-Borda, Orlando and Muhammad Anisur Rahman. 1991. *Action and Knowledge: Breaking the Monopoly with Participatory Action-Research (PAR).* New York: Apex.

Frings-Hessami, Viviane, Anindita Sarker, Gillian Oliver, and Misita Anwar. 2020. "Documentation in a Community Informatics Project: The Creation and Sharing of Information by Women in Bangladesh." *Journal of Documentation* 76(2): 552–570.

Fugelsang, A. and D. Chandler. 1988. *Participation as Process.* Dhaka: Grameen Bank.

Government of Bangladesh, Prime Minister's Office. 2019. *Digital Bangladesh. Concept Note. Access to Information Programme.* Dhaka.

Green, Duncan. 2012. *From Poverty to Power. How Active Citizens and Effective States Can Change the World.* Rugby: Practical Action/Oxfam.

Guba, Egon G. and Yvonna S. Lincoln. 1981. *Effective Evaluation.* San Francisco, CA: Jossey-Bass.

Guhathakurta, Meghna. 2003. "Globalization, Class and Gender Relations: The Shrimp Industry in Southwestern Bangladesh." *Journal of Social Studies* 101: 1–15.

Guhathakurta, Meghna and Willem Van Schendel. 2013. *The Bangladesh Reader: History, Culture, Politics.* Durham, NC: Duke University Press.

Hartmann, Betsy and James K Boyce. 1983. *A Quiet Violence: View from a Bangladesh Village.* Dhaka: University Publishers.

Heeks, R. 2006. "Theorizing ICT4D Research." *Information Technologies and International Development* 3(3): 1–4.

Ife, Jim. 2013. *Community Development in an Uncertain World: Vision, Analysis and Practice.* Cambridge: Cambridge University Press.

Johnstone, J. 2005. *Knowledge, Development and Technology: Internet Use among Voluntary-Sector AIDS Organizations in KwaZulu-Natal.* PhD thesis, University of London.

Kemmis, Stephen and Robin McTaggart. 2005. "Participatory Action Research: Communicative Action and the Public Sphere." In *The SAGE Handbook of Qualitative Research,* edited by N.K. Denzin and Y.S. Lincoln. Thousand Oaks, CA: SAGE, p. 556–604.

Lewis, David. 2011. *Bangladesh. Politics, Economy, and Civil Society.* New Delhi: Cambridge University Press.

Lewis, David. 2016. "Non-Governmental Organizations and Civil Society." In *Routledge Handbook of Contemporary Bangladesh,* edited by A. Riaz and M. Rahman. London: Routledge, pp. 219–235.

Lincoln, Yvonna S. and Egon G. Guba. 1985. *Naturalistic Inquiry.* Beverly Hills, CA: SAGE.

Moore, Henrietta L. 2010. "Subjectivity, Sexuality and Social Inequalities." In *The International Handbook of Gender and Poverty,* edited by S. Chant. Cheltenham, UK and Northampton, MA, USA: Edward Elgar Publishing, pp. 35–40.

Murzacheva, Ekaterina, Sreevas Sahasranamam, and Jonathan Levie. 2020. "Doubly Disadvantaged: Gender, Spatially Concentrated Deprivation and Nascent Entrepreneurial Activity." *European Management Review* 17(3): 669–685.

Novak, James. 2008. *Bangladesh. Reflections on the Water.* Dhaka: University Press.

Rahman, Atiqur. 2013. "ICT Impact on Socio-Economic Conditions of Rural Bangladesh." *Journal of World Economic Research* 2(1): 1–8.

Rahman, Muhammad Anisur. 1994. *People's Self Development.* Dhaka: University Press.

Rothman, Jack and John E. Tropman. 1970. "Models of Community Organization and Macro Practice Perspectives: Their Mixing and Phasing." In *Strategies of Community Organization*, edited by F.M. Cox. Itasca, IL: FE Peacock, pp. 3–26.

Sambasivan, Nithya, Amna Batool, Nova Ahmed, Gaytán-Lugo, Laura Sanely, David Nemer, Kurt Thomas, Tara Matthews, Elie Bursztein, Elizabeth Churchill, and Sunny Consolvo. 2019. "'They Don't Leave Us Alone Anywhere We Go': Gender and Digital Abuse in South Asia." *CHI Conference on Human Factors in Computing Systems Proceedings*, May 4–9, Glasgow, pp. 1–14.

Sarker, Anindita. 2021. *ICT for Women's Empowerment in Rural Bangladesh.* PhD thesis, Monash University, Melbourne.

Sarrica, Mauro, Larry Stillman, Tom Denison, Tapas Chakraborty, and Priodarshine Auvi. 2019. "'What Do Others Think?' An Emic Approach to Participatory Action Research in Bangladesh." *AI and Society* 34(3): 495–508.

Sen, A. 1987. "Gender and Cooperative Conflicts (Family Poverty)." *Working Papers – World Institute for Development Economics Research*, Helsinki.

Sillitoe, Paul. 2006. "Introduction: Indigenous Knowledge in Development." *Anthropology in Action* 13(3): 1–12.

Sillitoe, Paul, P. Dixon, and J. Barr. 2005. *Indigenous Knowledge Inquiries: A Methodologies Manual for Development.* Dhaka: UPL.

Smith, Linda Tuhiwai. 1999. *Decolonizing Methodologies: Research and Indigenous Peoples.* London: Zed Books.

Stillman, Larry. 2014. *Empowering Community Voices Project: Research Studies from South Africa and Bangladesh.* Melbourne: Monash University.

Stillman, Larry and Henry Linger. 2009. "Community Informatics and Information Systems: How Can They Be Better Connected?" *The Information Society* 25(4): 1–10.

Stillman, Larry, Graeme Johanson, and Rebecca French. 2009. *Communities in Action: Papers in Community Informatics.* Newcastle upon Tyne: Cambridge Scholars.

Stillman, Larry, Tom Denison, and Mauro Sarrica. 2014. *Theory, Practices and Examples for Community and Social Informatics.* Clayton: Monash University Publishing.

Stillman, Larry, Mauro Sarrica, Tom Denison, and Anindita Sarker. 2020a. "After the Smartphone Has Arrived in the Village. How Practices and Proto-Practices Emerged in an ICT4D Project – Evolving Perspectives on ICTs in Global Souths." In *Evolving Perspectives on ICTs in Global Souths. 11th International Development Informatics Association Conference, IDIA 2020, Macau, China, March 25–27, 2020, Proceedings. CCIS 1236*, edited by D.R. Junio and C. Koopman. Cham: Springer, pp. 81–94.

Stillman, Larry, Mauro Sarrica, Manuela Farinosi, Misita Anwar, and Anindita Sarker. 2020b. "Sociotechnical Transformative Effects of an ICT Project in Rural Bangladesh." *American Behavioural Scientist* 64(13): 1871–1888.

Stoecker, Randy. 2001. "Community-Based Research: The Next New Thing." July 11. http://coserver.sa .utoledo.edu/drafts/cbrreportb.htm

Stoecker, Randy. 2012. "Community-Based Research and Two Forms of Social Change." *Journal of Rural Social Sciences* 27(2): 83–98.

Stoecker, Randy and Larry Stillman. 2007. "Who Leads, Who Remembers, Who Speaks?" In *Constructing and Sharing Memory: Community Informatics, Identity and Empowerment*, edited by L. Stillman and G. Johanson. Prato: Cambridge Scholars, pp. 262–274.

Sultana, S., F. Guimbretière, P. Sengers, and N. Dell. 2018. "Design within a Patriarchal Society: Opportunities and Challenges in Designing for Rural Women in Bangladesh." *Proceedings of the 2018 CHI Conference on Human Factors in Computing Systems. Paper 536*, pp. 1–13.

Tinkler, Barri. 2010. "Reaching for a Radical Community-Based Research Model: Two Community-Based Research Experiences Lead to a Conceptual Model That Puts Control in the Hands of the Community." *Journal of Community Engagement and Scholarship* 3(2).

Wadsworth, Yolanda. 1998. "Paper 2. What Is Participatory Action Research?" *Action Research International*, November.

Wadsworth, Yolanda. 2004. "How Can Professionals Help? Groups Do Their Own Action Research." In *Participatory Action Research Perceptions and Practice. Papers and Proceedings of the International*

Workshop, edited by Research Initiatives Bangladesh. Dhaka: Research Initiatives Bangladesh, pp. 91–138.

Wadsworth, Yolanda. 2011. *Everyday Evaluation on the Run*, 3rd ed, edited by Y. Wadsworth. Walnut Creek, CA: Left Coast Press.

Walsham, Geoff. 2006. "Doing Interpretive Research." *European Journal of Information Systems* 15: 320–330.

PART IV

GROWING YOUTH POWER

13. Youth participatory action research as an approach to developing community-level responses to youth homelessness in the United States: learning from Advocates for Richmond Youth

M. Alex Wagaman, Kimberly S. Compton, Tiffany S. Haynes, Jae Lange, Elaine G. Williams, and Rae Caballero Obejero

Ending youth homelessness (ages 14 to 24) is a federal priority in the United States (USICH 2013), prompting many states and local communities to develop coordinated plans to address this complex issue. While research has identified successful interventions with youth experiencing homelessness, a great deal is still unknown, particularly with regard to community- and system-level responses.

In any community, youth homelessness involves people across all identities, multiple stakeholders, and several systems. Such complexity requires that communities employ innovative and collaborative approaches. Based on national data and best practices, successful responses to youth homelessness must consider the following:

- Youth from specific subpopulations experience greater risk for homelessness (i.e. LGBTQ youth, youth aging out of foster care, youth who are parenting and youth of color, particularly Black youth), and although the demographic makeup of youth experiencing homelessness may differ across communities, addressing their specific needs is essential (Choi et al. 2015; Côté and Blais 2019; Cray et al. 2013; Dworsky et al. 2013; Hadland et al. 2016).
- Youth homelessness looks different from adult homelessness, and successful interventions must attend to the similarities and differences in youth and adults (Gaetz et al. 2019; National Child Traumatic Stress Network n.d.; Tompsett et al. 2009).
- The way that youth homelessness looks and feels varies by context; so best practices require community context to guide successful interventions (Esparza 2009; Gharabaghi and Stuart 2010; Skott-Myhre et al. 2008). Building a contextually relevant, community-level response requires a community infrastructure with networks of stakeholders coming together around a common goal.

Youth participatory action research (YPAR) and community development (CD), when used together, take into account these specific needs. In this chapter, we present the history, mechanisms, and impact of Advocates for Richmond Youth, a YPAR team that we designed to develop and implement youth-directed, community-level solutions to address youth homelessness in Richmond, Virginia, and what lessons we can learn about YPAR and CD as a result.

YOUTH PARTICIPATORY ACTION RESEARCH AND COMMUNITY DEVELOPMENT

What Is Youth Participatory Action Research?

YPAR is both a philosophy and methodology that comes from the traditions of critical youth studies and participatory action research (Akom et al. 2008). Cammarota and Fine describe YPAR as "a formal resistance that leads to transformation" (2008: 2). YPAR requires iterative cycles of praxis, or reflection, action, and reflection again (Freire 2003), where "research is done not just for the sake of it but to inform solutions to problems that young people themselves care about" (University of California, Berkeley and San Francisco Peer Resources 2015). YPAR centers the experiences of youth most directly affected by the focal issue and assumes that research about youth is better understood from the position of youth (Bautista et al. 2013; Cammarota and Fine 2008; University of California, Berkeley and San Francisco Peer Resources 2015).

YPAR has the capacity to create transformation at the individual, group, and community levels (Wagaman 2015). Transformation refers to change that is systemic, gets at the root of the issue, and can be sustained over time, as opposed to incremental change which aims to tinker with existing systems without questioning or shifting the very foundation upon which they are built. At the individual level, transformation supports people to put their personal experiences into a systemic or structural context; to understand their own power and the ways in which that power has been systematically limited or repressed.

Not only is YPAR transformational, but it also is a mechanism for sustainable CD: "for these initiatives to have sustained impact … communities must play a major role in identifying the issues facing residents and suggesting solutions which will tackle the causes rather than symptoms of disadvantage" (Gilchrist 2003: 18). In YPAR groups, youth use their experiences to develop questions and then critically investigate the root of the social issues that they face (Bautista et al. 2013; Freire 2003; University of California, Berkeley and San Francisco Peer Resources 2015). YPAR opens the possibility that the world is changeable by encouraging young people to critically question social systems – the status quo (Cammarota and Fine 2008) – and use the evidence they collect through research to inform action for social change (Powers and Tiffany 2006).

When youth lead and adults support them in solving problems, changes can be more transformative and sustainable (Anyon et al. 2018). Youth who have experienced homelessness have experiential expertise with homeless services which, when meaningfully incorporated into problem solving and solution building, benefits other youth, agencies, providers, and homeless service systems by improving service delivery and interactions between service providers and youth (Altena et al. 2014; Ferguson et al. 2011; Gharabaghi and Stuart 2010).

YPAR has been used to successfully engage young people in change work related to homelessness (Garcia et al. 2014; Schoenfeld et al. 2019). Meaningful youth engagement is key for systems change work that positively impacts the lives of young people (Iwasaki 2012), and YPAR provides the CD tools to create change by effectively addressing the complex and contextual nature of this issue.

We chose a YPAR approach because it centers the voices and expertise of people who have experience with the issue under study and especially those of young people. YPAR problematizes *adultism*, which devalues youth's experiences and knowledge because of the privilege and power dynamics taken as inherent in adult–child relations (Flasher 1978; True Colors Fund 2017). Youth receive contradictory messages – on one hand they are expected to grow up quickly and function as adults at age 18, and on the other hand they are told implicitly and explicitly that they are not equipped to make decisions for themselves. YPAR offers a different way where those with experiential expertise are the experts, and youth voices are respected and acted upon.

Community Development-Informed Approach

CD emphasizes the need for sustainable solutions developed with community members, supported through the development of social capital, local capacity building, and collective action skills (Gilchrist 2003; Smith 2017; Taylor 2000). A CD response to addressing issues like youth homelessness requires a systemic approach, where "communities … should be included in decision-making about things that affect them" (Gilchrist 2003: 18). The CD approach offers a flexible response to the causes, consequences, barriers, and complexities outlined previously, while providing a sustained and community-led approach to solving youth homelessness.

Any solutions to youth homelessness must address the interwoven issues that are both causes and consequences of youth homelessness to holistically prevent and interrupt recurrence of homelessness (Slesnick et al. 2009). Perhaps most importantly, youth with direct experiences with homelessness can lead the work; bringing valuable expertise, insight, and a passion for innovation to overcome existing barriers faced for decades by stakeholders and service providers seeking to end youth homelessness.

The Value of Youth Direction in Community Development

Although youth advisory boards have existed since the 1980s in the United States, youth-directed initiatives like Advocates for Richmond Youth go beyond having youth share their opinions on issues that affect them. Youth-directed CD puts youth at the center of decision making and developing plans for action on issues that affect them (O'Donoghue et al. 2002; Schoenfeld et al. 2019). When youth-directed CD goes beyond soliciting feedback, it can lead to sustained change and a greater perception of youth ownership over program outcomes, better trust building between providers and youth, and an increased sense of community overall (Ferguson et al. 2011; Schoenfeld et al. 2019).

CD has historically been contextualized as a government-sponsored response (Smith 2017), subject to co-optation. Ideas like *community participation, community-engagement,* and *capacity building* can be enticing buzzwords that have a spectrum of values attached to them. For example, the United States Department of Housing and Urban Development (HUD) has been encouraging communities to engage young people to address and end youth homelessness, including the design and implementation of point-in-time counts (HUD Exchange 2016). However, these government-led efforts lean in the direction of being youth-informed – where young people are asked to advise or contribute ideas to an already existing framework or service system (i.e. HUD Exchange 2016). When *participation* is conceptualized as *input*, it can give youth's voices only equal or even less weight than others who have not experienced homelessness, failing to embrace youth-directed approaches.

YPAR offers a youth-led alternative, which embodies the spirit of CD, while allowing the freedom and necessity to call any and all institutions and systems to account and into "the work." Youth-directed CD centers the expertise of directly affected young people at the beginning of and throughout solution identification and implementation, pushing CD into deeper and deeper levels of participation and control over decision making (*à la* Arnstein 1969).

Sustainability through the Practice of Iteration

YPAR and CD both are grounded sustainable solutions. YPAR can embody and expand on the best hoped for outcomes of CD, especially when it comes to the authentic participation and the sustained engagement that is needed from community members who are directly affected by the issues at hand to ensure long-lasting, community-led solutions. As the case of Advocates for Richmond Youth will demonstrate, iterations of praxis – reflect and act, research and act, develop solution and implement – provide the mechanism for sustainable CD through YPAR. According to Stringer (2013), action research has three phases: look and learn about the issue from one another and through data collection; reflect on what is observed and the insight it provides for creating change; and act on the findings to create social change. Every part of this process is an opportunity for learning and growth, even failure. "If we release the framework of failure, we can realize we are in iterative cycles, and we can keep asking ourselves – how do I learn from this?" (brown 2017: 105). When one phase is completed, another begins or has already begun. Youth researchers, in this case, are led to look, think, and act again – transforming in response to new information or new contextual facilitators and challenges.

The case of Advocates for Richmond Youth provides invaluable lessons learned and we hope that by sharing these, it will encourage and enable other communities to use YPAR to guide sustained CD efforts where youth are centered in developing a community-level response to youth homelessness.

ADVOCATES FOR RICHMOND YOUTH: INCEPTION STOR(IES)

Advocates for Richmond Youth is a YPAR team that started in 2014 to respond to a lack of action around youth homelessness in a mid-size, urban, southeastern United States city – Richmond, Virginia. The inception happened between Alex Wagaman, faculty in Virginia Commonwealth University's School of Social Work, and a homeless service provider who connected around a shared commitment to centering the voices of youth directly affected by homelessness before making important decisions about how best to address youth homelessness. A shared commitment led to funding to ensure that YPAR participants would receive stipends and support to engage in the research team. Alex and the service provider brought a group of community stakeholders to the table to discuss launching such an initiative. From the beginning, Alex and the service provider decided that a YPAR team addressing youth homelessness would need to represent the subpopulations most impacted by youth homelessness. We invited adult stakeholders to participate in supporting the launch of a YPAR initiative because they had connections to one or more of these subpopulations through service provision and/or advocacy work. We asked adult stakeholders to commit to supporting the YPAR team in other ways. Youth would need a circle of community support to assist with making resource connections and referrals as needed for individual youth, and to uphold the value of youth voice in other contexts where people were making decisions about how best to address the issue of youth homelessness.

The stakeholders who committed to assist with recruitment and support at the beginning included the local school system, a program for youth who had aged out of foster care, homeless service providers, a mentoring/support program for youth experiencing homelessness while in high school, and a legal aid organization. Engaging key stakeholders was important to establish the infrastructure that would grow over time. The commitment to supporting young people was at the core of the connection, and soon became a commitment to a specific group of young people with names and stories and important things to teach the community. Alex primarily supported and hosted the YPAR effort, however, it was not linked in any formal way to a specific organization or program. A research assistant, Rae Obejero, who was within the same age range as the target population, developed recruitment materials. Alex and Rae also recruited participants through social media and places where young people spend their time, including community centers, coffee shops, and local homeless service organizations. Youth who expressed interest in joining were scheduled for an initial meeting with Alex or Rae to collect basic demographics, ensure they fit the criteria for involvement (age and experience with housing instability), identify any barriers to participation that we could help overcome, and discuss the project. These initial meetings were important to establishing connections and relationships early in the project. During the recruitment process, Alex spoke to a local youth support program for students experiencing housing instability and met Elaine Williams, who was immediately interested in the idea of a youth-led effort to conduct research for change. Elaine was planning to transfer to Virginia Commonwealth University and joined the project as a research assistant upon enrolling.

Following the initial recruitment, Alex and Rae held an information session open to any young person interested. At the information session, they gave a brief overview of YPAR, including how it has been used in other communities, the focus of this effort, and what participation would look like for this six-month project. Young people made their own decisions about committing to the project over this timeframe and identified any barriers that could be reduced to support their participation. Alex, Rae, and Elaine incorporated this feedback into a process for ensuring stipends, meals at the weekly meetings, child-care assistance, and transportation support.

Becoming the Advocates for Richmond Youth

The founding members of what would become Advocates for Richmond Youth – 12 young people between the ages of 18 and 24 with direct experience of homelessness – began meeting weekly. Alex, Rae, and Elaine served as facilitators. Between meetings the facilitators contacted each young person to remind them about upcoming meetings and generally check in with them. The facilitators debriefed immediately following each meeting, reflecting on team process and dynamics, and identifying issues to address in the coming week.

During the weekly team meetings, the young people established their norms and guidelines for working together and developed a "problem map" using their own expertise on youth homelessness, which included causes, symptoms, and areas for solutions. The team also constructed an identity as an advocacy group. They chose a name, Advocates for Richmond Youth, developed a purpose statement, and chose a logo designed by a friend of a team member. Identifying a lack of common language as a primary barrier to the community's ability to collectively resolve the issue, they also developed a definition of homelessness based on their own experiences.

Those Who Experience the Problem Know the Problem

The young people sought out data on youth homelessness in Richmond and, finding none, identified research questions. The team implemented a qualitative study guided by these questions, including data collection, analysis, and preparation of dissemination materials. They then developed a set of community recommendations based on their research and work together which they presented with the research findings in several community forums they organized. The recommendations included specific housing programs, policy recommendations (such as tenant rights), and structural changes they saw as essential to the work going forward (such as a changed definition of homelessness for determining service eligibility and formation of a permanent youth advisory board).

Inward and Outward Iterations

Since the initial study, the YPAR team has gone through four additional iterations of the participatory action research process. Each iteration included (1) observing/discussing how youth homelessness impacts the community, (2) identifying what knowledge the team and/ or community need to be compelled and informed to act, (3) designing and implementing research to fill this knowledge gap, (4) using the research findings to inform action and educate others for planning and advocacy, and (5) reflecting on how those efforts impacted the team and the community. Each iteration lasted approximately a year – some shorter, some longer, depending upon the goals, funding, and complexity of the research design.

During each iteration, both the YPAR team and the broader community would be transformed. After each iteration, the team paused to identify anyone who wanted to stop participation and add new participants. In each iteration the team also restarted its process of establishing norms, being trained in how to run a meeting and conduct research, and developing a sense of community. Each time, the process differed based on the young people involved, the purpose of the work at hand, an assessment of key stakeholders who could be leveraged to support change, and the socio-political context within which the team was working.

INWARD- AND OUTWARD-FOCUSED ITERATIONS: WEAVING TOGETHER YOUTH PARTICIPATORY ACTION RESEARCH AND COMMUNITY DEVELOPMENT

The iterations of the work have flowed back and forth between an inward focus and an outward focus. Community change and development emerge from a team that is solid at its core and committed to addressing root causes. This inward strengthening comes through knowledge building and is vital to the team's ability to face and push through resistance to the work, including adultism, racism, transphobia, and other institutional barriers, and ultimately is a catalyst for community change. In the sections that follow, we describe what we have learned about the process of building and maintaining a strong core (inward focus) and what youth-informed CD looks like (outward focus) in the context of ending youth homelessness in our community.

This work is neither easy nor always palatable. The team and the adult researchers have met a lot of resistance. YPAR and CD approaches are desired until it becomes clear how much of "how we do things" needs to shift in order to be youth-led. System-level change means that systems have to change. The systems of youth homelessness have been stagnant and inefficient for decades. Can you imagine the kind of adultist resistance youth would receive for having the audacity to believe that they have the power to revision youth homelessness systems?

Iterating Inward: Building Knowledge and Power

We have done a lot of intentional reflective practice to tease out the lessons learned from engaging in a YPAR effort over multiple years of sustained work, focusing on the inward facing labor. We build this into our work – during and between iterations – and have employed research methods, such as case study and autoethnographic methods, to identify the inward-focused mechanisms that are presented below. Given the potential for pushback when confronting long-standing service systems, it's important to create a team that has the knowledge and emotional strength to withstand blowback and continue to move forward towards long-term and sustainable community change. Based on the experience of Advocates for Richmond Youth, (1) *space* – both physical and emotional, (2) *roles* – particularly those that promote growth while honoring the expertise of youth, and (3) *relationships* – among youth researchers as well as between the adult researchers and youth researchers are all important to building a strong team that can engage in youth-directed work for community change and development. These factors are intricately interconnected and, working through the lens of *purpose*, create the opportunity necessary for youth to center themselves in community-based solutions.

Purpose

The *purpose* of the Advocates for Richmond Youth is central. It is through the lens of purpose that all other factors are decided. For example, Alex and the service provider with whom she worked predetermined the purpose of the group before we had a team. They organized and funded the group to look at youth homelessness. They determined that young people who had been directly affected by youth homelessness should be meaningfully involved. And they identified research as a tool for developing a better understanding of the issue. Beyond that, however, the team shaped the purpose during meetings and before events. The team consistently revisits the purpose and how their activities fit that purpose (or not). The purpose is also emergent and iterative based on the time, place, and context.

Some key elements of purpose that the team has defined are (1) focusing on community change, (2) having hope, (3) teaching and learning, and (4) using differences as a strength. The focus on *community change* is a particularly important draw for team members, keeping young people coming back to the team week after week, year after year.

Feeling loved and like I do have a purpose to help people. When you feel like you are actually doing something to help make a change in someone's life, or you're important enough to make a change and help, and feel like what you are doing is very needed, who wouldn't want to keep doing it? Who wouldn't want to?

Hope is also a key factor that is reflected in our team's purpose – hope for change and for eventually being able to prevent and end youth homelessness. By laying claim to the possibility of ending youth homelessness, hope is built into our team's purpose in a way that is owned within the team and projected into the community.

Another part of the purpose is *to teach and to learn.* Early on, we learned that the differences among us were greater than we imagined. This showed up, for example, through interactions between transgender team members and team members who held biases about transgender people. Interactions that reflected these biases, such as misgendering, caused conflicts. Transgender team members talked about the boundaries they needed to set in order to stay with the team. This example happened over months and years, and it was full of messiness and challenges. And deeply ingrained beliefs did not just disappear once a team member shared that they were harmful. But the capacity of the team to keep trying – on both the teaching and learning side of things – and to stay invested meant that the ability to show up in the community for one another was built on a firm foundation that was hard to crack. We were strong enough to withstand the resistance we experienced when we challenged community stakeholders and systems.

This, and similar moments, established opportunities for each team member to be a teacher and a learner. Team members educated each other about their unique experiences and identities in the context of youth homelessness, creating learning opportunities for the team as a whole. The differences in experience and identity among team members became an important part of the purpose – to hold the community accountable to meeting the needs of *all* young people experiencing homelessness. Team members learned how to use *differences as strength* for achieving our purpose and not to let differences pull the team apart. *The purpose of the work [holds us together]. We agree to disagree.* Team members use the purpose to move through intra-team conflict. *Knowing no matter what happened in the past, once we entered this room [meeting room] it's not about us, it's not about our friendship, it's about the research we're doing and the homeless teens we're trying to help.* Purpose is also used to refocus after outside groups attempt to co-opt or redirect the team's work. *We know the work we are doing is positive, for a purpose, we're passionate, so we're not going to stop just because someone's trying to take credit for our work.* The purpose of the group, as redefined throughout the process, continues to be an important focal point to move the team past barriers and onwards towards successful change.

Each team member articulates and recognizes our own and each other's individual purposes for participating in the team. We also recognize the team's purpose as being bigger than any of us individually and that we need one another to succeed. The purpose is intimately connected to team members' lived experiences, and thus provides connection for each of us to a mission, a sense of contribution to something larger than ourselves, and offers something to focus time and energy on. Many team members identify the opportunity to use our own experiences and stories to make things better for other youth as deeply connecting us to the purpose of the group. *I wanted to join because I wanted to bring awareness to the issue ... I'm a part of the team to show youth who experience homelessness that their experience matters and that you can make change through utilizing your story.*

The purpose creates an opportunity space that allows young people to believe in and lay claim to what is possible, as opposed to settling for the status quo. In relationship to the broader community of stakeholders, the purpose creates both a boundary between what young people should be asked to settle for and a collective vision of how young people and youth homelessness should be addressed. For example, over time the team embraced a "nothing about us without us" mentality. This kind of demand, however, from a Black-led group of youth, often causes adult community leaders to frame the team as angry or unreasonable or unaware of how the system really works. But through the lens of purpose and possibility, the team can contextualize these responses as resistance to change that is rooted in racism and adultism. We are centered by our purpose, which functions as a public declaration: *That [homelessness] never should have happened to me and I want to let the community know that we shouldn't ever let it happen to another young person.*

Being accessible and consistent: physical and emotional space setting

Space, as it is used here, refers both to *physical* space and *emotional* space and is a requirement for building a strong team that can affect community change. For our team, the physical space is at the university. The room itself is set up conference-style so that everyone can see everyone else, which is important for trust and rapport. The university is centrally located in the city, on the bus line, and the building is open and accessible, which reduces barriers to attending and participating. Most importantly, it is a consistent space. When other things in life are inconsistent, the space our team's work occupies maintains consistency. The team has developed a sense of ownership over the space. In fact, one team member described feeling disrespected when a university staff member came through the room during a meeting to get to her office.

Emotional space refers to the norms and boundaries that we establish and maintain when we are together. The emotional space has been iterative – shifting to meet the needs of the team at the time. The team first established our emotional space by generating a list of norms on a big piece of paper. This has transformed over time into a creed that summarizes the norms and is repeated together during meetings. *The creed is how we are able to learn each other's comfort zones, each other's boundaries and spaces, because we were able to openly share our opinions and feelings about things and create a [creed] that is a combination of everyone's stuff.* As team members change, team members revisit, revise, and reinforce the emotional space and the norms that uphold it.

The physical and emotional space signals what all those who enter should expect. *As soon as someone walks in, it's like the room lights up. No matter who you are, if you're known or not, everyone stops what they're doing and openly invites whoever you are into the room. No one [in other spaces] really does that anymore ... You need a space that allows youth to be vulnerable, open, to share their frustrations, to be able to talk about their past and help them through it.* As our team learns how to work together, the space shifts and changes based on the needs of the individuals in it. The essence of both the physical and emotional space, which does not shift, is that it is accessible and consistent.

The team also carries this emotional space into different physical spaces that they occupy, modeling the inward process into outward CD work. For example, we designed and delivered a day-long training for service providers and advocates in the region. At the beginning team members asked all of the training attendees to recite together a creed (Box 13.1) that the team wrote specifically for the space and people in it. This tool helped the team set boundaries with people at the training, and set up collective accountability for maintaining the emotional space. This creed was necessary because our youth team members' lived experiences in spaces with adults made them concerned that the team would be treated as children – minimized and patronized. We had worked hard to establish our team members as experts of their own experience, which took time for our team to believe. We needed to set clear boundaries with the training participants about what our team needed in order to share that expertise with them.

BOX 13.1 TRAINING CREED

I am an advocate for youth. I am the voice of those who depend on my work. I am part of a partnership that depends on trust, respect, and honesty. As an advocate I vow to listen to others' expert opinions regarding their individual experiences and identities. I vow to trust those around me and in return be trustworthy. I will honor the trust I am given by returning discretion. I vow to honor my time and the time that has been put into this training. I am here to learn and to teach. To be vulnerable and to appreciate vulnerability from others. I am here because I am an advocate for youth, and through my voice their voices must be heard.

Getting things done: defining and redefining roles

In the beginning, our team discussed specific roles and tasks that needed to happen in order to achieve our purpose (a.k.a. getting things done), such as notetaking or timekeeping or facilitation. Over time, the team expanded these task-oriented roles to include process-oriented roles as well. The role of a team member is to *be there. Be present. Let us know where you are. We have people who are the ones to hug. We have people that want to check up on you. We have people that's the mom.* Roles and how they emerge will be unique for each team and even each iteration of the same team, depending upon the individuals involved, the context, and the specific task at hand. Roles give each team member an individual way to contribute to the purpose of the team's work. Roles manifest the transformational aspect of YPAR rather than focusing solely on transactional relationships.

Roles can be both limiting and empowering. In some instances, team members fill a role that they have become known to fill. Alex, the research assistants who worked with the team, and other team members cross-trained young people on different roles, and they often had favorites. However, the longer the team was together the more that roles emerged and were shaped by combinations of strengths and talents, areas that team members wanted to grow in, or roles they took on based on comfort level. For example, team members who are less vocal in meetings and like to observe process would often take on the timekeeping role. Team members might encourage one another to step away from the role that they always fill and try something new. When team members have opportunities to reflect on and express their interest in certain areas of growth, then other team members can offer support and encouragement. Willingness to try new roles seems to coincide with the level of trust established among team members and collective experiences of successes and failures. For example, facilitating inside the team – where our team member will be built up and supported – is often a precursor to facilitating outside of the team at a community event or meeting. We try to build in opportunities for trying on new skills and when ego gets in the way, we name it. It can be easy to lean on a more outgoing team member who demonstrates lots of confidence. But when we don't make space for others to grow, then we are limiting our power as a team.

The team itself also has a clear role in the community as a research and advocacy group of directly affected young people. *People around the table who have actually experienced homelessness* are needed to make an impact in a team like this. Advocates for Richmond Youth is a team of directly affected young people who are in the role of expert in a way that has not existed before in this community context. That, in and of itself, creates a sense of possibility that did not previously exist and a sense of accountability that it can be replicated and reinforced in other spaces.

During periods of reflection, the team often asks itself, "What role does Advocates for Richmond Youth play in this community?" The team positions itself in the role of researchers and advocates for the issue and for other young people experiencing homelessness. *We speak for people who are afraid to speak.* Being aware of this role and keeping it centered is particularly important as community stakeholders – often who are adults – begin to tell the team what role they should play.

This became very clear after conducting training for service providers, program directors, and policy makers, when several agencies asked the team to do training for their organizations. Our team felt affirmed by this request. We must have done a good job. However, after reflection, the team determined that training could consume all of our time and take away from our role as a research and advocacy group for community- and system-level change. This is not to suggest that the role of the team could not shift. However, upon reflection the team realized that this kind of role would not be meeting our current purpose and could actually distract from the structural shifts that we know are needed to end youth homelessness.

Advocates for Richmond Youth have used visual mapping exercises as a tool for reflection on our team's role in the broader community and to ensure a sense of connection between team purpose and personal purpose. To do the visual mapping exercise, the team starts by drawing a wheel. At the center of the wheel is the collective purpose and role of the research team. Each team member is represented as a spoke on the wheel. This is where personal goals and purposes can be articulated and a discussion can be facilitated about how the work of the team can support or hinder individual goal achievement. An activity like this one generates valuable reflection on the connections between individual and collective roles.

Building mutual love and respect: prioritizing relationship building

In addition to space and roles, the inner strength of the team requires mutual love and respect. Relationships refers to the ways team members interact with one another both inside and outside of the team environment. Relationships are central to the group's ability to function as a team. *If you're going to have a team, they need to be able to work together. And in order to be able to work together successfully, and be in the same space and all be cordial, you need to have at least some sort of personal relationship ... or you're not going to want to open up or going to want to take time out of your day to be with this person.*

Relationships include spoken and unspoken ways of being with one another, expressing or demonstrating value for one another, and actively committing to one another in the context of the work. Relationships are not always positive; they include conflict and negative interactions as well. *It's like brothers and sisters. You might hate each other's guts, but that's still your brother, still people you care about at the end of the day. It's still your family. We're like a little family.*

Relationships require consistent care and attention. This was evident during a community presentation. Team members had not been intentionally nurtured and solidified relationships prior to the presentation, because the team had gotten out of its regular weekly meeting schedule. This caused team members to question if they would or could support one another during the presentation (which had been discussed and agreed upon in prior presentations).

This uncertainty magnified team members' normal anxiety about public speaking and created conflicts, all of which had to be debriefed and reflected upon before moving forward to the next project.

Similar to roles, deep relationships require acknowledging and recognizing that no team member has all of the qualities and skills necessary to achieve the purpose. *We all have flaws, but we're able to work together. That may be an asset that people may see that we're not perfect – we try to have positive attitudes – we all fall short, but us together, we can keep things going, keep things positive, keep a sense of humor. Everyone's personalities keep people wanting to come – contrasting personalities.*

Similar to space, team members' relationships are consistent even during times of struggle for individuals. *I go through a lot of emotional things, so I distance myself from the team. But the team has always been a big support and love group. No matter what, we're still there trying to support each other and love each other.*

One tool the team has used to facilitate relationship building is storytelling. Storytelling has helped team members share experiences of homelessness in a way that puts them in control of their story, reduces the stigma associated with their experience, and fosters a sense of connection with one another. Each person can share their story when it feels right for them. Through storytelling, each team member has an opportunity to see the issue from that person's vantage point, find connections and differences between their stories, and ultimately build trust with one another through vulnerability and understanding. Storytelling also enhances our analysis of the issue we are working to change. By understanding the issue from multiple perspectives, we can more effectively identify solutions and change strategies reflecting the diversity and complexity of experience.

Another tool is mediation techniques adapted to the needs and interests of team members. The team begins each new project by discussing that conflict can be expected and how preparing for it is important. Team members identify various ways that conflict can be addressed when it arises, including having a "safe" mediator available upon request. Alex, the university researcher, often fills this role, but so do trusted peer co-researchers, especially team members who have been doing the work longer and have built mediation skills.

Iterating Outward: Developing Community Capacity for Ending Youth Homelessness

Iterations between building inner strength and focusing outward on CD created capacity in the community to end youth homelessness. Time spent on inward knowledge sharing fortified team members with skills and confidence to lead community capacity-building efforts. Through these iterations of inward and outward, more stakeholders became engaged in the work. This reflected a movement-building approach to CD that was more about depth of connection than urgent or broad-based engagement, which led to intentional engagement and collaboration across sectors of the community that are needed to facilitate transformative, system-level change rather than incremental change. It also allowed for deep reflection on how traditional partnership methods can reinforce adultism, white dominance, and other forms of oppression.

The youth and young adult members of our team developed the community's capacity for change in four primary ways: (1) building a broad base of connections, (2) reimagining systems instead of being bound to incremental changes within existing systems, (3) engaging in program development, and (4) developing a workforce of young people who could move into paid positions focused on ending youth homelessness. As with the inward-focused section, each form of community capacity building will be described using a specific example.

Building a broad base of connections

The team built a broad base of connections by starting with their immediate spheres of access and influence to bring in stakeholders who were dedicated to addressing youth homelessness. As the work iterated between inward knowledge building and outward CD, each iteration brought in additional stakeholders with different interests and skills; connecting them to those already at the table and extending the reach to the new networks. These ripples out were always led by the youth who had been directly affected.

After the team conducted our first research study, we engaged in several community forums and training to share the results. These events became critical for building knowledge and buy-in from stakeholders and thus for CD. For example, one participant group in the original research study was direct service providers. Some of these participants attended the forums to hear the research findings and then asked how they could help move the recommendations forward. Additionally, two community organizations decided to partner with the young people to design and deliver training on youth homelessness.

As the team designed this day-long, youth-led training, it became clear that the goal was bigger than educating people. It needed to be about connecting people – connecting providers and other stakeholders with young people in different ways (beyond the client/worker relationship), connecting stakeholders with one another, and helping attendees see their connection to the work of ending youth homelessness – building common purpose. With the additional goals in mind, the team conducted a focus group with providers to hear about ways to deliver the training that would most support them in their job roles.

The team used a visual map to capture the connections between attendees at the training. The young people put up a large piece of paper on the wall with youth homelessness in the middle and various community sectors that would be represented at the training around it. The young people then asked each participant to place themselves and their organizations onto the map and draw lines to connect them to the sectors they felt that they brought to the table. Kimberly Compton (a graduate research assistant from the university) digitized the map and shared it with participants after the training along with contact information and other resource-related information about what they could provide to/for a young person experiencing homelessness. Digitizing and distributing the map meant that both youth and service providers could access it and find resources after the training. At the time, there were very few services specifically developed to serve youth experiencing homelessness, but many providers nonetheless served youth experiencing homelessness. This mechanism helped providers and other stakeholders to see how they were connected to one another and to the issue of youth homelessness, and to see some of the gaps in engagement and resources.

Reimagining systems to address youth homelessness

More connections, buy-in and skills meant that youth had created an informal collection of stakeholders with the strength to reimagine systems to respond to the unique needs of young people experiencing homelessness or housing instability. Now, instead of just internally researching and building knowledge, youth, along with community stakeholders, were beginning to shift their thinking about the existing systems' ability to end youth homelessness.

Outsiders – both those who had begun to partner and those who had not yet gotten involved in the work – encouraged Advocates for Richmond Youth to work within the existing homeless service systems to address the needs of youth. However, the existing system had little experience in equalizing power between service providers and people directly impacted by homelessness. Those within the existing system of services resisted this new way of thinking about and doing the work. The existing system of services has limited resources to achieve its purpose with adults and some community stakeholders had little trust in the existing system's ability or willingness to address its capacity to harm populations that already faced added barriers, such as LGBTQ people.

Setting a new table
Tensions and system resistance came to a head in a meeting when providers who ran the homeless service system in the community walked through a complex structure of governance and decision making in the existing system. Providers envisioned plugging youth leadership in via a subcommittee within the existing structure, which would inform one small piece of the larger system. Advocates for Richmond Youth realized that their vision for transformational shifts in decision making were not going to happen in the existing system at that time. The team decided to set a *new table* that started with the youth and built in other stakeholders around them in a coalition. With this in mind the team began exploring how to imagine and create a new system to end youth homelessness rather than accepting incremental changes controlled or granted by adults in the existing system.

Building a coalition
Because the team had already established a body of research and connections across stakeholder groups, the initial coalition was fairly easy to organize. Advocates for Richmond Youth were at the table as equal partners and leaders the whole way. The young people knew from their inward-focused work that relationships matter, and relationships had been broken between stakeholders who had not committed to common values and principles. The coalition began by focusing on relationships, establishing guiding principles (e.g. to be LGBTQ-affirming and anti-racist) supporting the relationships, and setting a framework for knowledge and skill building for coalition members to fulfill their commitment to one another. The coalition established a framework with eight areas of focus to holistically meet the needs of young people, along with identifying community stakeholders in each area or sector who could be coalition members (Figure 13.1).

After recruiting representatives for each area, the team held a three-day planning summit. During the summit, the coalition met with funders to encourage them to anticipate more opportunities to invest in the work of youth homelessness; facilitated youth leadership training with 25 directly affected young people from across the community; and brought together 75 additional community stakeholders and coalition members to set goals and objectives in each of the eight areas. The coalition further developed these goals and objectives over the following six months, resulting in a comprehensive community-wide plan to end youth housing instability. The plan served as a blueprint for the coalition going forward.

By *setting a new table* and establishing core principles that connected the coalition members to one another through commitment and relationship, the stakeholders and young people could begin to reimagine a new system offering program responses that functioned outside of existing systems while continuing to hold those systems accountable. The dual emphasis on process

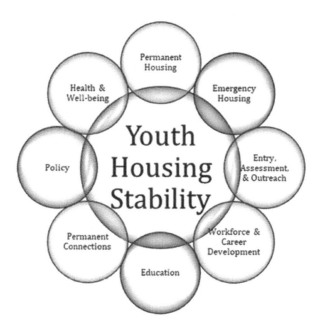

Figure 13.1   Framework for plan

and product – how we achieve our goals is just as important as the outcome – created shifts in power and the community capacity to strive beyond what was originally believed possible in a community response to youth homelessness. It also allowed the young people and their supporters to reimagine the role of young people in those programs and systems, which was something that had been lacking.

Program development with youth as decision makers
Advocates for Richmond Youth team members felt strongly from team inception that there needed to be direct, tangible results of our work that youth would be able to benefit from. *Youth are in need of services and housing support now and we need to be helping them.* The team's next outward iteration led to the development of programs to serve youth in the community who are experiencing housing instability. Our team viewed the system-building work and the efforts to train others to serve young people as an effort to help the community develop the capacity to respond. Seeing and filling gaps in resources is another part of that effort.

Advocates for Richmond Youth had established a solid knowledge base and confidence in our expertise to contribute to the development of effective programs and began to put it into practice; however, valuing lived experience as expertise required a paradigm shift among adults who had been working in these spaces for years. The Advocates strategically partnered with organizations that demonstrated their commitment to this shift in thinking and lived into sustainable CD values. The partner organizations – all of which primarily serve the LGBTQ+ community – supported the payment of youth with lived experience as planning team members, centered intention over urgency and the needs of LGBTQ+ young people who have multiple marginalized identities, and resisted *business as usual*. The result was a housing program that addressed both prevention and intervention – a shift in a system that primarily does crisis response. This program also had a peer navigation component, which established an expectation that young people with direct experiences of homelessness should be hired as program staff – a true shift in thinking around what equips someone to do the work of service provision!

Designing a program to serve youth experiencing homelessness produced a tangible increase in available services and resources and provided an opportunity for young people and community organizations to practice engaging together in work that is often deemed as specialized or requiring professional training. Similar to the community capacity established through service provider training, the partnerships formed through program development and implementation built optimism for what can be accomplished when young people are centered in decision making. This effort also provided evidence for the fourth form of CD – workforce development among young people doing the work of ending youth homelessness.

Workforce development

As a result of the team's work to share research, build stakeholder engagement, and guide paradigmatic shifts on the roles of young people, organizations began hiring youth as full-time workers in positions focused on ending youth homelessness. We have emphasized these positions being prioritized and funded in partnerships on grants and projects that the team has been involved with. At the time of this writing, there are four positions in the community that employ young people with lived experience to work with youth experiencing homelessness. This signals an important and lasting shift indicative of sustainable change: the community is committed to centering young people at the table, and the young people are also developing further skills to step into roles as hired experts.

This new iteration of the work opens up possibilities and challenges that the community and Advocates for Richmond Youth continue to grapple with. Much of what our team does to build capacity among youth with lived experience to step into paid positions seems to be within the team's control. However, there is much unpredictability in the community and more opportunities to build trust. For example, what does it mean to hire someone with lived experience expertise without shifting anything else about the organizational culture? What does it look like to truly embrace the value of lived experience *as* expertise, rather than as the lowest paid frontline worker? As we explore the value in this kind of positioning of youth as paid workers, how does it both increase and decrease their power to create systemic change? What is the value of a young person seeing themselves reflected in the person paid to support them through a program? Can we ever really know?

Indicators of Success and Meaningful Youth Engagement

Team members view specific accomplishments including research, training, presentations, and requests to give advice or input to other communities or groups as indicators of their success in creating community-level change around the work of ending youth homelessness. However, we offer three primary indicators of success that are less product-focused and that could be transferable to other communities as they seek to develop a strong YPAR team that aims to create community-level change around youth homelessness in a way that centers young people. These include youth visibility, feeling heard and valued by external stakeholders, and the ability to overcome internal conflicts.

Youth visibility looks like youth being prioritized in discussions around ending homelessness, and being physically present during discussions that directly reference and impact them. Feeling heard and valued by external stakeholders includes being sought out for input and *them actually listening to us*. Young people are used to being treated by adults as not having anything of value to contribute. When young people invite community stakeholders to attend their forums and presentations, they are aware that people show up for things that they value. Maintaining a strong, cohesive team that can weather challenges and stay focused on the purpose is an important indicator of success and vital to the relationship between YPAR and CD. Young people see other community groups rendered ineffective by unaddressed internal problems. A team's ability to prevent that provides a sense of power.

LESSONS LEARNED AND IMPLICATIONS FOR PRACTICE

We have learned many lessons through the work of Advocates for Richmond Youth that could be valuable to earnest communities considering how to sustainably address long-standing, systemic issues affecting youth populations. We have highlighted the following among many lessons learned over the years.

1. Adult stakeholders need to be supportive and be able to step out of the way. Adult stakeholders must demonstrate a capacity to center youth voice and fight adultism to build trust with a youth team.
2. Fluidity is key in a team like this. A flexible and fluid approach to youth membership, roles and relationships, and even solution building reduces barriers for youth and allows for emergence and iteration to take shape organically. Such an approach leads to more innovative solutions that are relevant to the local context. This is where spaces that support transformation are created in communities.
3. Along with fluidity, focusing on purpose and having tangible team products provides invaluable benchmarks indicating success – defined as movement toward the purpose – and provides meaningful evidence of impact that supports sustained engagement among youth and other stakeholders.
4. A university social work program primarily supported and hosted this YPAR effort. However, it was not linked in any formal way to a specific organization or program. This positioning became important, retrospectively, to preserving the autonomy and control of the young people over the direction of their research and subsequent action. Whether or not it is the best organizational structure for the next phase of the work is yet to be determined.
5. The iterating process between inward and outward development is essential. Without the development and maintenance of a strong team and core body of knowledge, team members would be less prepared to weather the anticipated challenges that come when doing work that seeks system transformation while also battling racism, adultism, transphobia, and other forms of oppression that are built into existing structures. The outward work of CD does not happen without the inward work of the YPAR team.
6. This work is powerful and worth doing right. With the support of the community, this team of directly affected young people has been positioned in the role of expert in a way that has not been done before in this community context, or many others.

7. Research is a valuable tool for shifting power. It gives youth the capacity to speak with authority based on data they have collected and analyzed. It gives them the power to ask the questions that they believe need to be asked. And it positions them as knowledge experts.

The iterative relationship between YPAR and CD in the experiences of Advocates for Richmond Youth highlight the power and potential of using these two approaches in concert to tackle deeply rooted community issues while centering the voices of those most impacted by the issue. The result is meaningful change; paradigmatic change; change in how people with lived experience see themselves and one another; change in how decision-making tables are set; and change in how solutions are designed and implemented.

In traditional human service spaces, young people are engaged in a program and then they leave when they finish the predetermined curriculum or outcome. In YPAR, engagement is about deep knowledge building and long-term investment in young people that builds capacity in individuals and in communities, iteratively, to systematically end youth homelessness. Similarly, if we learn by building a base of knowledge, confidence, and skills that can then be applied in action with others, reflected upon, and adapted as needed, then YPAR's iterations with CD have the ability to build a solid core of young people that can continue to ripple out over time – moving into other decision-making tables, jobs, and positions of leadership.

If we want to make meaningful and long-lasting change, then entire communities need to invest in work centering experience as expertise. Using YPAR and CD as a framework, we can develop a model of change that works and, like a fractal, replicate that model with more people across all spaces until it becomes the way of being and working together. The levels of confidence and skill established over time among young people who have experienced home-lessness, through multiple iterations of YPAR and CD, support the team's capacity to hold the community accountable to higher and higher levels of justice and compassion. In turn, the community's increasing confidence in being led by young people with lived experience comes when the knowledge and capacity of young people have been established as the starting place. This is what helps us to end a systemic social issue like youth homelessness.

REFERENCES

Akom, A. A., Julio Cammarota, and Shawn Ginwright. 2008. "Youthtopias: Towards a New Paradigm of Critical Youth Studies." *Youth Media Reporter* 2(1–6): 108–129.

Altena, Astrid M., Mariëlle D. Beijersbergen, and Judith R. L. M. Wolf. 2014. "Homeless Youth's Experiences with Shelter and Community Care Services: Differences between Service Types and the Relationship to Overall Service Quality." *Children and Youth Services Review* 46: 195–202.

Anyon, Yolanda., Kimberly Bender, Heather Kennedy, and Jonah Dechants. 2018. "A Systematic Review of Youth Participatory Action Research (YPAR) in the United States: Methodologies, Youth Outcomes, and Future Directions." *Health Education & Behavior* 45(6): 865–878.

Arnstein, Sherry R. 1969. "A Ladder of Citizen Participation." *Journal of the American Institute of Planners* 35(4): 216–224.

Bautista, Mark. A., Melanie Bertrand, Ernest Morrell, D'artagnan Scorza, and Corey Matthews. 2013. "Participatory Action Research and City Youth: Methodological Insights from the Council of Youth Research." *Teachers College Record* 115(10): 1–23.

brown, a. m. 2017. *Emergent Strategy: Shaping Change, Changing Worlds.* Oakland, CA: AK Press.

Cammarota, Julio, and Michelle Fine. 2008. *Revolutionizing Education: Youth Participatory Action Research in Motion.* New York: Routledge.

Choi, Soon Kyu, Bianca D. Wilson, Jama Shelton, and Gary J. Gates. 2015. *Serving Our Youth 2015: The Needs and Experiences of Lesbian, Gay, Bisexual, Transgender, and Questioning Youth Experiencing Homelessness*. Los Angeles: The Williams Institute with True Colors Fund.

Côté, Philippe-Benoit, and Martin Blais. 2019. "Between Resignation, Resistance and Recognition: A Qualitative Analysis of LGBTQ Youth Profiles of Homelessness Agencies Utilization." *Children and Youth Services Review* 100: 437–443.

Cray, Andrew, Katie Miller, and Laura E. Durso. 2013. *Seeking Shelter: The Experiences and Unmet Needs of LGBT Homeless Youth*. Washington, DC: Center for American Progress.

Dworsky, Amy, Laura Napolitano, and Mark Courtney. 2013. "Homelessness during the Transition from Foster Care to Adulthood." *American Journal of Public Health* 2(S2): 318–323.

Esparza, Nicole. 2009. "Community Factors Influencing the Prevalence of Homeless Youth Services." *Children and Youth Services Review* 31(12): 1321–1329.

Ferguson, Kristin M., Min Ah Kim, and Stacy McCoy. 2011. "Enhancing Empowerment and Leadership among Homeless Youth in Agency and Community Settings: A Grounded Theory Approach." *Child and Adolescent Social Work Journal: C & A* 28(1): 1–22.

Flasher, Jack. 1978. "Adultism." *Adolescence* 13(51): 517–523.

Freire, P. 2003. *Pedagogy of the Oppressed*. New York: Continuum.

Gaetz, Stephen, Ashley Ward, and Lauren Kimura. 2019. "Youth Homelessness and Housing Stability: What Outcomes Should We Be Looking For?" *Healthcare Management Forum* 32(2): 73–77.

Garcia, Analilia P., Meredith Minkler, Zelenne Cardenas, Cheryl Grills, and Charles Porter. 2014. "Engaging Homeless Youth in Community-Based Participatory Research: A Case Study from Skid Row, Los Angeles." *Health Promotion Practice* 15(1): 18–27.

Gharabaghi, Kiaras, and Carol Stuart. 2010. "Voices from the Periphery: Prospects and Challenges for the Homeless Youth Service Sector." *Children and Youth Services Review* 32(12): 1683–1689.

Gilchrist, Alison. 2003. "Community Development in the UK: Possibilities and Paradoxes." *Community Development Journal* 38(1): 16–25.

Hadland, Scott E., Baligh R. Yehia, and Harvey J. Makadon. 2016. "Caring for Lesbian, Gay, Bisexual, Transgender, and Questioning Youth in Inclusive and Affirmative Environments." *Pediatric Clinics of North America* 63(6): 955–969.

HUD Exchange. 2016. "Ending Youth Homelessness – Guidebook Series: System Planning." www .hudexchange.info/resources/documents/Ending-Youth-Homelessness-System-Planning.pdf

Iwasaki, Yoshitaka. 2012. "Reflection on Learnings from Engaging and Working with High-Risk." *Marginalized Youth* 27(4): 24–36.

National Child Traumatic Stress Network. (n.d.). "Impact of Complex Trauma." www.nctsn.org/sites/ default/files/assets/pdfs/impact_of_complex_trauma_final.pdf

O'Donoghue, Jennifer L., Benjamin Kirshner, and Milbrey Mclaughlin. 2002. "Introduction: Moving Youth Participation Forward." *New Directions for Youth Development* 96: 15–26.

Powers, Jane L., and Jennifer S. Tiffany. 2006. "Engaging Youth in Participatory Research and Evaluation." *Journal of Public Health Management and Practice* 12: S79–S87.

Schoenfeld, Elizabeth A., Kate Bennett, Katy Manganella, and Gage Kemp. 2019. "More Than Just a Seat at the Table: The Power of Youth Voice in Ending Youth Homelessness in the United States." *Child Care in Practice* 25(1): 112–125.

Skott-Myhre, Hans A., Rebecca Raby, and Jamie Nikolaou. 2008. "Towards a Delivery System of Services for Rural Homeless Youth: A Literature Review and Case Study." *Child and Youth Care Forum* 37(2): 87–102.

Slesnick, Natasha, Pushpanjali Dashora, Amber Letcher, Gizem Erdem, and Julianne Serovich. 2009. "A Review of Services and Interventions for Runaway and Homeless Youth: Moving Forward." *Children and Youth Services Review* 31(7): 732–742.

Smith, M. K. 2017. "What Is Community Development?" In *The Short Guide to Community Development*, 2nd Edition. Bristol: Policy Press, pp. 9–28.

Stringer, Ernest T. 2013. *Action Research*. New York: Sage.

Taylor, Marilyn. 2000. "Communities in the Lead: Power, Organisational Capacity and Social Capital." *Urban Studies* 37(5–6).

Tompsett, Carolyn J., Patrick J. Fowler, and Paul A. Toro. 2009. "Age Differences among Homeless Individuals: Adolescence through Adulthood." *Journal of Prevention and Intervention in the Community* 37(2): 86–99.

True Colors Fund. 2017. "Youth Collaboration Toolkit." http://learn.truecolorsunited.org/wp-content/uploads/sites/2/2016/08/Youth-Collaboration-Toolkit.pdf

University of California, Berkeley and San Francisco Peer Resources. 2015. "YPAR Hub." http://yparhub.berkeley.edu/learn-about-ypar/

USICH (United States Interagency Council on Homelessness). 2013. "Framework to End Youth Homelessness: A Resource Text for Dialogue and Action." February. www.usich.gov/resources/uploads/asset_library/USICH_Youth_Framework__FINAL_02_13_131.pdf

Wagaman, Mary A. 2015. "Changing Ourselves, Changing the World: Assessing the Value of Participatory Action Research as an Empowerment-Based Research and Service Approach with LGBTQ Young People." *Child and Youth Services* 36(2): 124–149.

14. Volunteerism as a vehicle for civil society development in Ukraine: a community-based project to develop youth volunteerism in a Ukrainian community

Danielle Stevens, Tetiana Kidruk, and Oleh Petrus

Ukraine has been independent since 1991 and the country's 30-year journey with autonomy has not been a smooth one. Political and economic instability contribute to their continual struggle to stabilize post-independence, and inhibit a thriving civil society. The lack of a volunteer culture is characteristic of weak civil society in Ukraine, and research indicates a relationship between developing volunteerism and increasing civic capacity. There are opportunities to use volunteerism in youth development activities and influence the long-term likelihood of civic engagement in Ukrainian communities. Additionally, participatory action research (PAR) as a methodology for mobilizing communities holds promise for engaging Ukrainian citizens long term. In this chapter we discuss how PAR supported implementing youth development projects in Rivne, Ukraine, and created space to build a foundation of youth volunteer leaders dedicated to community-based work.

AT A GLANCE: UKRAINIAN HISTORY AFTER INDEPENDENCE

Ukraine has endured two significant political revolutions – the Orange Revolution in 2005 and the Revolution of Dignity, or Euromaidan, in 2015 (Afineevsky 2015; Bunce and Wolchik 2006; D'Anieri 2003; Hale 2006; Katchanovski 2008; Nalbandov 2014; Shveda and Park 2016; Stepan 2005; Watch 2018). A primary provocation for the revolutions was corruption (Afineevsky 2015; Shveda and Park 2016), which 41.5 percent of surveyed Ukrainians indicated encountering in their personal lives (Koriukalov 2019). Despite the two political revolutions, engaging the Ukrainian people with civic activities remains a challenge. Although Ukrainians generally believe that their nation's overall situation is terrible, there is the conflicting sentiment that their individual communities are perfect (Dashchakivska 2019). Compounding this "perception" challenge are local media sources persistently focusing on issues of corruption and other factors contributing to distrust, which has desensitized people and reinforced a culture that inhibits civil society from really flourishing (Koriukalov 2019).

Although momentum from the Orange Revolution ultimately dissipated, the mobilization that resulted from Euromaidan continued after the revolution concluded, which is an encouraging result that may hold promise for long-term mobilization and perhaps overcoming culture themes.[1] Citizens, specifically younger people, dedicated their time and lives volunteering for the war effort in the Donbass, a region in eastern Ukraine where conflict with Russia began in 2014.[2] According to Gatskova and Gatskov (2015), the Orange Revolution failed to influence any long-term change because there was no clear direction or well-defined set of principles.

Less than a decade later, continued corruption provoked Euromaidan, which was far more violent and initiated sweeping government reform, and motivated people – particularly young people – to mobilize for the revolution itself and volunteer in the Donbass war. The question remains whether Euromaidan's momentum will survive and how to take advantage of opportunities to carry forward the ideals for which protesters fought.

COMMUNITY BUILDING: MOVING FORWARD IN A POST-EUROMAIDAN UKRAINE

According to DeFilippis and Saegert (2012: 6), community development is broadly defined by efforts to "1) provide for everyday needs of adults and children; 2) create institutions that more fairly and democratically allocate goods and resources; and 3) cultivate relationships among people that promote human and cultural development, effective citizenship, and political will." This third principle is reminiscent of civil society and minding it requires bridging social divides. Social trust and social capital are the pillars of a well-functioning civil society (Gatskova and Gatskov 2015; Putnam 2000) and bridging gaps in social capital is considered a tenet of community building and necessary for increasing civic engagement (Putnam 1993, 2000; Saegert 2006). Social capital is the network of social resources that individuals have at their disposal (Putnam 2000).[3] Putnam (2000) emphasizes that social capital is the act of doing things *with* other people. Considering Ukrainians are typically distrustful of their fellow citizens due to early learned behaviors and persistent corruption (Eckstein 1988; Putnam 2000), it is not too far-fetched to ascertain that Ukrainians might have lower social capital given low levels of trust. There is a symbiotic relationship between honesty, civic engagement, and social trust (Putnam 2000). Trust is an essential ingredient for fostering greater social capital and building community at the local level, and "Place based 'community' starts with a single relationship of trust and mutual benefit that one resident or stakeholder shares with another. It is the aggregate of those relationships, along with the loose connections that bind a diversity of them together, that forms the structural framework for community" (Traynor 2012: 216).

Peer-to-peer relationships are vital building blocks for the pillars of functioning civil society. Focusing on the micro level and nurturing those individual connections fosters a stronger network that is the fabric of a community's thriving civil society. Despite low levels of general social trust, Ukrainians have vibrant informal communication networks (e.g. word of mouth) through which they share information with people in their social circles (Bugaric and Kuhelj 2015; Gatskova and Gatskov 2015; Stevens 2019). Lutsevych (2013: 17) posits that to maintain momentum from revolutions like Euromaidan over time, "democracy promoters and local activists need to focus on civil society itself. Active and empowered citizens, not the expertise and capacity of a few NGOs [non-governmental organizations], are the indicators of civil society's strength." Ukrainians' informal networks are a form of social capital and are the structural framework for the community, but they have not been consistently leveraged to build community in a manner that would increase wider social trust and encourage greater civic participation, thereby strengthening civil society.

Given existing social capital but a lack of wider social trust, there is room to explore how community building can be used in Ukraine as a catalyst for enhancing those informal networks, and connecting them to build civil society. According to Saegert (2006), a community-building approach assumes the following:

1. Community members collectively solve problems.
2. Community members have a shared purpose and action agenda for solving those problems.
3. Community members support individual leadership development, and enhance the organizational skills of individuals and groups so that there is more capacity for solving problems.
4. Community members sustain their dedication to solving problems through shared goals.

Community building can establish an environment for civic engagement to thrive by consolidating individual relationships into a robust network of connections that share a vision and are engaged in collective action – i.e. bridging social capital (Saegert 2006). Additionally, there is a correlation between increasing involvement in community life and decreasing rates of corrupt behavior (Putnam 2000). In the case of Ukraine, building communities from this grassroots, community-driven approach could not only build civil society, but also decrease the very behavior that perpetuates social distrust and inhibits civil society development.

Volunteerism: A Mode for Building Community

A useful strategy for building community is to encourage voluntary work, which can lead to greater civic capacity (Putnam 1993, 2000; Saegert 2006). A non-vibrant culture of volunteerism is characteristic of the "third challenge" of developing civil societies in post-Soviet space. In Ukraine, "Over all the years of [the] country's independence, the share of respondents who declared to belong to a political movement, social organization, or club remained almost unchanged – around 17%" (Gatskova and Gatskov 2015: 675). In a study focused on six post-Soviet countries, Kamerāde et al. (2016) posited that an increase in civil liberties should lead to a rise in voluntary work. Prior to the Orange Revolution, Ukraine was partially free and the 2005 protests ushered in a new wave of civil liberties; yet a decrease in volunteerism followed, demonstrating that more civil liberties do not always result in more voluntary work. However, this reality is not entirely perplexing when considering (1) that Ukraine's departure from the Soviet Union was mostly circumstantial rather than publicly motivated; and (2) that voluntary work in the Soviet Union was compulsory (Dekker and Halman 2003; Gatskova and Gatskov 2015), illustrating that perceptions of "voluntary work" are perhaps culture themes (Eckstein 1988; Metraux and Mead 1954) resulting from the non-voluntary nature of how volunteerism looked in the Soviet Union. According to Howard (2002: 27), participation in any sort of organization "was based mainly on obligation, obedience, and external conformity, rather than internal and voluntary initiatives." Yet, developing a culture of volunteerism is a community-building strategy and can lead to greater civic capacity (Putnam 1993, 2000; Saegert 2006).

Motives for volunteering are rarely altruistic. There are many reasons why individuals choose to volunteer; perhaps for an opportunity to learn, social benefits, personal values, career development, personal enhancement, or protective inclination (Bales 1996; Clary et al. 1998; Dekker and Halman 2003). According to Bales (1996), the fourth dimension of a volunteerism-activism attitude is a sense of effectiveness for addressing social problems. Such a motive makes establishing a culture of volunteerism a useful strategy for bridging social capital in Ukraine (Dekker and Halman 2003; Putnam 1993, 2000; Saegert 2006), for knitting together the existing informal networks and engaging people in a shared vision for their communities, and fostering a desire to act and solve problems in their communities. Indeed, "social networks foster norms of reciprocity that encourage attention to others' welfare" (Putnam 2000: 117). Volunteerism could be the structural framework for restoring public trust and building social capital between Ukrainians, which could ultimately result in the "harmonization of relations between authorities and the public" (Tkach and Tkach 2019: 56). Volunteerism has the capacity to close the chasm that often exists between average citizens and the institutions that affect their everyday lives (Putnam 2000; Tkach and Tkach 2019).

Volunteerism: A Mode for Engaging the Younger Ukrainian Generations

Developing a culture of volunteerism requires focusing on a specific demographic, so that initiatives are appropriately targeted to engage the population. According to Bales (1996), survey results indicated that younger respondents received high scores as potential volunteers.[4] Research also shows that "adult volunteers and givers are particularly distinguished by their civic involvement as youth" (Putnam 2000: 121–122). Engaging youth in a nation like Ukraine, which has survived political instability for decades, could have particular significance for influencing the long-term trajectory of civil society development.

The United Nations Working Group on Youth released an analytical report in 2019 detailing the situation for youth in Ukraine. More than half of Ukrainian youth reported that they were ready to participate in community-based volunteerism, and nearly just as many young people believed that each youth citizen has an individual responsibility to participate in defining solutions for problems affecting youth in their country. Ukraine's tradition of collective action and vast informal networks make successful volunteer mobilization more possible. However, despite youth comprising the majority of volunteers in Ukraine, the country's youth volunteerism rates continue to lag behind the majority of Europe. According to the United Nations Working Group on Youth (2019: 61):

> Young Ukrainians still have low awareness of volunteerism. Despite the concepts of "volunteer organization," "volunteerism," "volunteer movement" becoming more widely known in Ukraine, indicating their importance to society, there is still a degree of ambiguity regarding people's understanding of what these terms mean. Consequently, many young Ukrainians are already engaged in volunteer activities without realizing it.

Young Ukrainians may not have a clear understanding of where volunteer opportunities exist in their communities, partially due to the aforementioned low awareness, but also because volunteer opportunities are not easily found outside the country's largest cities of Kyiv, Kharkiv, and Lviv. Additionally, the country's decentralization reform plans that resulted from Euromaidan do not detail how the government can engage youth at the local level, despite the existence of a national ministry dedicated to youth opportunity.

The projects that are the focus of this chapter occurred in the urban community of Rivne, Rivenens'ka Oblast – a small city of approximately 247,000 people in western Ukraine. It is the administrative center of a region consisting of more than 1 million people. According to a community profile published by the city of Rivne in 2016, youth comprised 21.3 percent of the city population that year. When we implemented this project, there were few organizations in the community dedicated to youth, and none to developing youth volunteerism. Considering that one-fifth of the city's population is youth, there was an opportunity to increase the capacity of organizations wanting to deliver youth development services. The community-based projects detailed in this chapter focused on the following recommendations from the United Nations for increasing youth participation in public life and developing volunteerism (United Nations Working Group on Youth 2019):

- Create opportunities for adolescents and youth to participate in settings and areas of practice that they experience on a regular, day-to-day basis, including at schools and in their communities (54);
- Develop the capacity of Ukrainian organizations to diversify their approaches to mobilizing, facilitating, and managing youth volunteers and align these with international best practices (62);
- Create opportunities for youth to volunteer on a regular basis in their communities (62); and
- Empower youth volunteer activists and representatives of the youth volunteer movements to further promote the culture of volunteerism among their peers (62).

The Leadership, Engagement, and Activism Program (LEAP) is the primary project discussed in this chapter and PAR was the primary method for development and implementation. This title was chosen in part for how it encompasses the project goals, and also for flexibility in marketing (e.g. LEAP into action!). This acronym does not translate directly in Ukrainian. An unofficial LEAP project goal was to support English-language learning, and we decided this title without PAR; in hindsight we could have consulted project participants and allowed them to name it, which may have contributed to greater feelings of participant ownership. That said, LEAP utilized PAR tools to discern community needs and interests, incorporated sustainable development practices, and maintained focus on the aforementioned United Nations' recommendations for increasing youth participation in public life through volunteerism.

PARTICIPATORY ACTION RESEARCH: PURPOSE AND METHODOLOGY

A challenge associated with research focused on community development efforts is that direct participants (i.e. those who are affected by these endeavors) are not always intimately involved with the development, implementation, and evaluation of projects – if they are involved at all. This imbalanced reality can result in outcomes that may be skewed toward the researcher's bias. PAR is inherently participant-driven and establishes a horizontal structure in which the researcher and the researched are equally important to and have an active role in the entire development process (Arnstein 1969; Baum et al. 2006; Greenwood et al. 1993; Rodriguez and Brown 2009; Rowe and Frewer 2005).

Community-based projects are interventions, actions taken to influence a section of the community over a period of time. When PAR is utilized as the primary research methodology in the project process, participants share the role of "researcher" with professionals, and determine how these interventions might affect them and their communities in the long term (Rodriguez and Brown 2009). This approach is relevant when considering that international development workers can negatively impact communities by knowingly or unknowingly projecting exceptionalism (Harvard Crimson 1968; Rothmyer 2011). PAR is an active approach to balance these power relationships that may otherwise subjugate participants to the researcher's bias or agenda. A core assumption of PAR is that locals are the absolute experts on their community dynamics (Córdova 2004), and according to Rodriguez and Brown (2009: 23), "PAR validates the knowledge of local communities as well as their authority to determine the truth." Just as professionally trained researchers are experts in their field, so are participants experts in what their communities need (Greenwood et al. 1993), and they offer perspective that contributes to intervention relevancy (Rodriguez and Brown 2009). There are multiple advantages to utilizing PAR, including local expertise, informed decision making and out-comes, a holistic understanding of community dynamics, capacity-building opportunities, and access to opportunity for engaging in the community development process (Arnstein 1969; Rowe and Frewer 2005).

In its purest form, PAR is a democratic and reflexive process that continually adapts to changing attitudes, knowledge, and expertise (Arnstein 1969; Rowe and Frewer 2005). Research is intentionally pursued and "the reflective process is directly linked to action, influenced by understanding of history, culture, and local context and embedded in social relationships" (Baum et al. 2006). The pillars of PAR include collaboration, consideration, and inclusion of local knowledge, diversity, case orientation, adaptation, and action (Greenwood et al. 1993). According to Tandon (1990: 99), "partnership requires sharing of visions, dreams, hopes, fears, aspirations, and frustrations among members of the project constituencies." When utilizing PAR in the project process, participants are partners to the researchers, co-sharing responsibility for setting goals and direction, for establishing parameters in the process, and for evaluating success (Baum et al. 2006; Greenwood et al. 1993). The opportunity for partic-ipants to critically evaluate initiatives in their individual communities, and identify solutions for gaps, reveals pathways for social development through research–participant partnerships, ultimately promoting long-term sustainability (Tandon 1990).

PAR is also a methodology that relies on quantitative *and* qualitative measures (Baum et al. 2006), meaning that characteristics difficult to quantify (e.g. self-reliance) are equally as important as hard data (Garaycochea 1990). The nature of PAR necessitates that processes be consistently observed and interpreted, so that co-researchers (professional researchers and participants) can adapt them as needed over time. According to Greenwood et al. (1993), PAR projects are case-oriented – i.e. specific project methods are not predetermined and are dependent on current circumstances in a given community. However, methodology is not just tailored for each community – it is customized for *every project* because circumstances change between and within interventions (Garaycochea 1990). These continuously evolving targets make the direction of PAR projects somewhat unpredictable and impact may not be entirely clear until well into the future. However, not achieving initial goals does not necessarily con-stitute project failure (Garaycochea 1990).

Youth Participatory Action Research

PAR has been utilized in youth-focused projects to elicit their perspective and engage them with solving community challenges. Youths are commonly dismissed from decision-making arenas and consequently do not always have a voice in determining how interventions will impact their lives. Using youth participatory action research (YPAR) is an opportunity to not only give youths a voice, but also to create spaces for youths to have agency with identifying problems, implementing solutions, and evaluating the results (Ginwright 2008). Collaborating with youths through YPAR is a paradigm shift, given that the methodology requires adult–

youth partnerships as part of the process (Foster-Fishman et al. 2010). According to Kuhn (1962), such paradigm shifts inform new thinking and are an opportunity for youths to exercise critical thinking skills, which may inspire action (Gaventa and Cornwall 2007).

Successful YPAR requires that communities be genuinely interested in how youths experience their everyday lives (Foster-Fishman et al. 2010). It's crucial to note that lack of access to civic engagement opportunities is not the same as lack of motive – youths cannot civically participate if spaces do not exist for them to do so (Fox et al. 2010). As mentioned previously, volunteer opportunities in Ukraine are mostly concentrated in the metropolises of Kyiv, Kharkiv, and Lviv, and volunteer participation rates are relatively low compared with other European nations (United Nations Working Group on Youth 2019). Considering this, lack of access in addition to cultural standards may explain low participation, rather than lack of motive. According to Fox et al. (2010), youth leadership, youth organizing, and YPAR intersect in what they term *critical youth engagement*, which is the manifestation of how youths translate inquiry (e.g. questioning community challenges) into social action. As a methodology, YPAR has the potential to engage youths and prompt them to be civically engaged adults. While critically questioning why challenges exist in their communities, "youth learn how to study problems and find solutions to them" (Cammarota and Fine 2008: 6).

The literature illustrates that soliciting youth participation in community-based work positively impacts civic engagement (Hamilton and Zeldin 1987; Melchior 1998). Camino (2000: 13) posited that "Youth participation helps build strong communities, building healthy communities contributes to youth development, and adults' negative attitudes about youth can be overcome when adults work with youth to address community concerns." Research also illustrates that soliciting youth participation at a decision-making level increases "critical thinking, teamwork, social capital, an enhanced sense of group belonging and commitment to service when they are actively involved in collaborative decision making" (Zeldin et al. 2008: 263; Catalano et al. 1998; Scheve et al. 2006). Additionally, Scheve et al. (2006) stress the value of adults supporting youth in decision making, and that youth have the opportunity to do meaningful work and learn new skills. Focusing on youth development initiatives to promote volunteerism could positively impact civic engagement in the Rivne community – thereby strengthening civil society – and would also contribute to establishing more amicable relationships between adults and youth.

Tools in This Study

We utilized a United States Peace Corps-published handbook for volunteers working in their communities of service, known as the *Participatory Analysis for Community Action* (PACA) *Field Guide*, to identify tools for project design, implementation, and evaluation. We chose the *PACA Field Guide* for three reasons: (1) it is replete with participatory tools for engaging community members in the project process; (2) all of the project leaders, including Tetiana Kidruk and Oleh Petrus, were trained with this field guide; and (3) we wanted to experiment with the effectiveness of the *PACA Field Guide* when it is actively used. Theoretically, the purpose of this handbook aligns well with the core elements of PAR – collaboration, participants-as-researchers, power balance, capacity building – but may not always be true to PAR in practice. LEAP is a case study for implementing the *PACA Field Guide*. Additionally, the *PACA Field Guide* and PAR as a methodology are people-centered and directly reflect the goals of community building as posited by Saegert (2006), which are that community members collectively solve problems; community members have a shared purpose and action agenda for solving those problems; community members support individual leadership development, and enhance the organizational skills of individuals and groups so that there is more capacity for solving problems; and community members sustain their dedication to solving problems through shared goals.

THE AUTHORS AND THE ROLE OF PEACE CORPS

We started working together on projects after Danielle Stevens was placed in Rivne as a United States Peace Corps volunteer. The Peace Corps consistently emphasizes that volunteers are placed to develop people, not things, and the projects discussed in this chapter have a multifaceted design targeted at a charitable organization and Ukrainian youth. It is important to mention that projects with which Peace Corps volunteers are involved vary widely in scope, focus, and sustainability. We were fortunate that we all are especially interested in opportunities for youth, and we brought community development experience and a well-rounded understanding of grassroots, community-driven projects. We approached our work from a community-based perspective and the evolution of these efforts was primarily participant-driven. Additionally, we introduced various project design and management tools to the sponsoring organization, and advocated for sustainable practices that would create opportunities for long-term impact. Due to the decades-long instability in Ukraine, organizations often exhibit the effects of such prolonged uncertainty, such as not planning for the long term and not establishing strategic direction for an organization. However, these characteristics also represent cultural differences that need to be respected.

President John F. Kennedy established the United States Peace Corps in 1961, and although it continues to operate in more than 70 countries, we would be remiss to not acknowledge that questions loom around whether the institution is a neocolonial beacon of soft power. As early as 1968, returned Peace Corps volunteers lamented that the organization did not espouse the values as idealized by President Kennedy, but rather was "arrogant and colonialist in the same way as the government of which it is part" (Harvard Crimson 1968). More recently, Rothmyer (2011) questioned whether the Peace Corps was ever a necessary creation and why it exists today, when work conducted by Peace Corps volunteers would be well suited for locals. In his poetic discourse on colonialism, Césaire (2000 [1955]: 42) opined that "colonization = thingification," arguing that Western development efforts on an international scale dehumanize indigenous peoples; that "societies are drained of their essence, cultures trampled underfoot, institutions undermined, lands confiscated, religions smashed, magnificent artistic creations destroyed, extraordinary *possibilities* wiped out" (43). It is not uncommon for international volunteers to project exceptionalism and white saviorism, whether consciously or unconsciously (Harvard Crimson 1968; Rothmyer 2011). Therefore, it was imperative that we were cognizant of frustrations that presented actual barriers to project success, as opposed to frustrations that were due to cultural differences and were not necessarily inhibitive. A unified definition of "community development" was helpful for mitigating some of these colonial tendencies. We had a common understanding that community development should be centered on people – from an organizational level down to individual constituents – and that development processes should elicit participation from stakeholders across sectors so that communities reflect the needs of all people living in them, rather than a few with the loudest voices or most resources. Our unified understanding of community development places affected persons at the center of all interventions. This approach is a pillar of PAR and research indicates it can precipitate improved civic engagement among community participants – specifically individuals who become involved at a young age (Cammarota and Fine 2008; Foster-Fishman et al. 2010; Fox et al. 2010; Ginwright 2008).

PROJECT DESIGN, IMPLEMENTATION, AND EVALUATION

Designing the Leadership, Engagement, and Activism Program

As a Peace Corps volunteer, Stevens focused on establishing connections in order to identify organizations with which to partner for community projects. It was through this process that she became aware that Kidruk, her Ukrainian-language tutor and friend, had an existing relationship with a charitable organization in the community that could possibly be nurtured into a partnership for implementing community-driven projects. Sertse Dityam Ukrainy (SDU) is well rooted in the Rivne community and has been an innovative leader advocating for marginalized children across Ukraine since 2006. Historically, they have helped at-risk children and families who do not have access to basic needs or are socially insecure, improved conditions for orphans, and supported the development of children's institutions. After operating these services for more than a decade, the organization determined that they wanted to expand programming and possibly impact a wider youth population. They expressed this desire to Kidruk, who then initiated the collaborative process with Stevens and Petrus. When we started working on community projects with SDU, there were four youth development-focused organizations in Rivne that were mostly inactive, creating inconsistency and an even greater services deficiency for youth. This – coupled with SDU's interest in branching out – provided an opportunity to focus on this demographic. This was the impetus behind focusing on youth development and initiating smaller projects in the community, which ultimately led to LEAP.[5]

SDU pursued a grant through Peace Corps and the United States Agency for International Development with our assistance. We tried to engage the organization in the grant-writing process, but they could not dedicate the time to learning this skill. However, Kidruk did not have prior grant-writing experience and it was a valuable learning process for her.[6] These types of grants require that projects focus on organizational capacity development. SDU did not have the human capital to drive youth development projects and determined that developing volunteerism would be an ideal strategy for building capacity. It was important that we did not aimlessly develop volunteerism, so we and SDU determined that youth development initiatives could be the strategic focus area in which volunteers would spend their time.

LEAP was born out of this desire to combine organizational capacity development with community youth development opportunities. SDU was granted funding to implement a project with the established goals of (1) developing the organization's volunteer capacity in the Rivne community and (2) providing practical skills application for the organization's trained volunteers. We planned for trained volunteers to design, implement, and evaluate two youth development seminars in Rivne as the practical application component. We established objectives to recruit and train at least ten volunteer leaders for SDU, a target determined by using the number of people who expressed interest in volunteering at the seminars that SDU sponsored prior to LEAP. Given that volunteers are unpaid and have no real obligation to commit, we initially targeted volunteer recruitment at a wide age group, predicting that we would be able to determine which demographic was most interested in committing as volunteers for the life of the project, and then focus our efforts on those who were especially engaged. Following the initial project announcement, 17 volunteers aged 14 to 43 applied for the training activities and agreed to dedicate time to post-training project development and implementation, including two staff members from SDU.

LEAP began in March 2019 and was projected to close in August 2019. After recruiting volunteers, we engaged them in a participatory process to identify training needs. We facilitated *brainstorming* sessions with the purpose of identifying topics they felt were necessary to successfully implement youth development seminars. SDU engaged in this session as a participant, whereas we facilitated the discussion. Ultimately, participants indicated that training in sustainable project design and management practices; leading interactive seminars for youth; finding resources, developing partnerships, and attracting funding; and social media management would be the most relevant training topics for implementing youth development seminars.

Our next step was to conduct *community mapping* and create a *people and connections map* to define existing community resources that might be leveraged for the training of trainers. Participants drafted maps (drawings, lists, webs) of Rivne that included all the resources of which they were aware and with whom we might connect throughout LEAP; including libraries, businesses, NGOs, and schools. Recruited volunteers then identified individuals and organizations with content expertise in the decided training topics – some were local to Rivne, some not, but all identified connections were Ukrainian. Completing this participatory analysis helped us, SDU, and participants to conceptualize possible strategies for pulling together content experts from this resource pool. We recruited trainers from the *people and connections map* who led the training-of-trainers seminars.

We collaborated with SDU on a *risk assessment* so we could conceptualize all possible problems that might arise through the project lifecycle and identify action steps to take in each of those scenarios. We did not involve recruited volunteers in this process because this task would likely be completed by the organization in the future, and we wanted to ensure they adequately considered all possible angles where a project could go awry (e.g. injured youth, failure of trainers to show, more participants than expected, etc.). The risk assessment was particularly important for planning with the organization to ensure that they can implement projects with or without outside funding, and this participatory analysis drew upon the *community mapping* and *people and connections maps* to maximize a backup plan if they are not able to procure funding for future projects.

After identifying lesson topics, recruiting content experts, and evaluating possible risks, volunteers completed a week of training focused on sustainable project design and management practices; leading interactive seminars for youth; finding resources, developing partnerships, and attracting funding; and social media management. To supplement the training content and ensure LEAP remained on track, we facilitated conversations with SDU and volunteers to brainstorm potential youth seminar topics after their formal training concluded. We established baseline criteria for seminar ideas to streamline the process, which included that ideas must be specific, measurable, actionable, realistic, and time-bound (Peace Corps 2018); have enough content to fill two or three days; and be relevant for the target age group (youth ages 13 to 17). We used *problem trees* as a participatory tool to facilitate conversation about barriers for youth in the community – volunteers considered the symptoms of these obstacles by filling in the leaves of the trees, and considered what the causes of these might be by completing the tree roots. For example, (symptom = cause), youth are unsure of what they want to pursue in adulthood = lack of access to developmental opportunities outside of the traditional academic system; youth have low self-esteem = not enough exposure to mental health-oriented experiences; and stray dogs roaming the streets of Rivne = not enough animal shelters in the community. When this discussion concluded, the volunteers contextualized their problem trees with the criteria we established for seminar topics and identified focus areas for two youth seminars – careers and developing soft skills, and personal health management.

Implementing the Careers Youth Seminar

Once trained volunteers identified the seminar topics, we focused on recruiting youth participants for the first seminar. We were the primary driving force behind marketing in this first round – SDU again did not have the time or desire – and we felt too pressed for time to adequately engage volunteers. The target age group for LEAP (ages 13–17) was highly active on social media networks, and we determined that using these platforms would be the most effective way to encourage new youth participation, while also marketing to local schools and encouraging word-of-mouth promotion. We determined participant goals based on youth seminars that SDU implemented prior to LEAP, and decided that 30 participants were a reasonable goal for each of the LEAP seminars. However, we received more than 65 applications for the seminar over less than a week of open registration and were forced to close the application process earlier than intended. Due to funding restrictions, we had to limit participants and accepted 30. Although we were not able to accept all applicants, we saved information for all interested persons so that we could inform them about future events.

The first seminar focused on developing skills that are indispensable to a young career seeker. We planned this initial LEAP event in collaboration with the volunteer leaders – adult and youth – who participated in the training-of-trainers events. Youth volunteer leaders were especially helpful for identifying human resources in the community that could be accessed for seminar implementation – specifically for leading lessons. The lesson topics that volunteers identified while planning the seminar included teamwork and leadership, writing resumes and motivation letters, making a personal elevator pitch and successful interviewing, and volunteerism as an introduction to careers. Most of the sessions were conducted by professional trainers identified through the organization and adult/youth volunteer leader *people and connections maps*. However, some were co-led by an adult–youth partnership and some were led by youth who were comfortable leading sessions on their own. We partnered all youth who co-led a lesson with an adult volunteer so they could create their sessions together, during which the volunteers collaborated on their lesson plans and determined who would lead each component. This was an excellent opportunity for adult volunteer leaders to teach youth skills related to successfully facilitating group lessons.

Adult and youth volunteer leaders decided to invite professionals from different sectors in the Rivne community to present about their professions. The youth volunteer leaders provided input on the sectors that should be included in a survey, which we distributed during the planning process to youth participants who registered for the seminar, so we could define the sectors that most intrigued them. From there, youth volunteer leaders used their personal connections to identify guest speakers in sectors including acting, culinary arts, writing, human resources, law enforcement, and teaching. This speaker session was inspiring, and this description does not adequately capture the energy we could feel from youth during the speaker series. The session lasted longer than planned and youth sought out the speakers who were experts in professions they liked to inquire more about schooling and how to gain experience. Despite being difficult to quantify, the motivation and enthusiasm in the room were palpable and illustrated that this participant-driven session was a success.

While planning the careers seminar, our volunteer base started to break down, primarily because trained adult volunteers dropped out of the project. SDU's staff actively participated in the training of trainers but they were not motivated to implement the seminars that were the practical application component for training, which was a surprise for us. Other adult volunteers unassociated with SDU also were not engaged with implementing the seminars, partially due to our project description lacking clarity. Although we specified in the project objectives that training would be for volunteers aged 18 and older, it was convenient that we ultimately decided not to limit participation based on age because we heavily relied on youth volunteers to complete LEAP. We were not deep in the planning process for the careers seminar before our volunteer base was primarily youth, with just two or three trained adults who participated depending on their availability. Most of the volunteers who helped with the careers seminar were recruited after the training of trainers through existing volunteer leaders and did not have existing knowledge of the topics we offered in training, but we used it as an opportunity to teach them while implementing the events.

Personal Health Management Seminar

After working collaboratively with youth in the careers seminar, and witnessing their responsibility and care while leading lessons, we determined that youth volunteer leaders should have more authority over the next seminar's design and implementation. However, SDU did not welcome this idea because they did not trust youth volunteer leaders, and they wanted professionals to handle everything. They did not view youth volunteer leaders as an asset but rather as a manual workforce capable of doing only simple tasks related to event management; and although SDU wanted professionals to lead the seminars, as an organization they were largely non-existent for every step in the process of planning and implementing them. We felt discouraged with this obstacle but referred to the goals of LEAP – (1) develop the organization's volunteer capacity in the Rivne community and (2) provide practical skills application for the organization's trained volunteers – and decided how to move forward. Given the second goal's emphasis on providing experience for volunteers, we determined that giving youth more autonomy was within the project scope.

After success with involving youth volunteer leaders in planning the initial seminar, we delegated more responsibility to them for planning the next event on personal health management. The application rate for this seminar again exceeded participant targets and six new youth volunteer leaders joined the team as well – all of whom were participants in the previous careers seminar. We relied on previously active volunteer leaders to train the newcomers and provide a peer-to-peer learning experience. We delegated full marketing responsibility to youth, and their intimate knowledge of social media platforms elevated our advertising to new heights. Youth volunteer leaders identified the content areas that they felt were most relevant for personal health management. Youth volunteer leaders decided on lesson topics to address self-esteem, self-confidence, emotional intelligence, positive body image, stereotypes, public speaking, the bystander effect, individuality versus conformity, media literacy, manipulation, and diversity and tolerance. Considering the success of co-creation sessions in the first event, we determined that youth volunteer leaders should have more freedom with developing and delivering lessons. We divided them into youth teaching teams, and they created their own lessons and taught participants in the personal health management seminar. The focus of this second event necessitated fostering an environment of trust for participants' wellbeing, and we hypothesized that this could be achieved through youth volunteer leaders teaching the lessons because they were the participants' peers. We reached this hypothesis by observing lessons in the careers seminar and witnessing greater enthusiasm when youth volunteer leaders were teaching, and by asking youth volunteer leaders if they would be interested in full teaching responsibility.

DISCUSSION

Leadership, Engagement, and Activism Program Outcomes

The end of the second seminar marked the termination of the project's active phases. We reached or overachieved the project goals established for LEAP, which were to (1) develop the organization's volunteer capacity in the Rivne community and (2) provide practical skills application for the organization's trained volunteers. Seminar participant numbers were difficult to increase given our budget, but the application volume – more than 100 percent of projected participant goals – illustrated that there was significant community interest in opportunities like LEAP. In total, we and SDU were able to implement official training for eight adult volunteer leaders aged 18+ years old and four youth volunteer leaders aged 14–17 years old in the areas of project design and management; social media management, finding resources, fundraising, and developing partnerships; implementing interactive seminars for youth; lesson planning; creative problem solving; time management; and communication. Four of SDU's staff members also learned more about managing large groups of people, how to keep youth engaged, managing crises, and developing partnerships with people and organizations in the community. In addition, the volunteer team, with our guidance, successfully planned and implemented two interactive youth seminars on the topics of careers and personal health management that directly impacted 60 youth. By consistently monitoring the project, we determined that youth are more likely than adults to engage in volunteerism and LEAP was tailored according to their needs. The result is a capable and interested youth volunteer leader group for SDU.

The seminars implemented as part of this grant were so popular among youth in Rivne that youth volunteer leaders insisted on organizing one more event. We consulted with them about the potential challenges of implementing an unfunded project and on a short timeline, a discussion which helped us decide that conducting a Model United Nations (MUN) seminar would be the most feasible because many resources already existed. This participatory process also allowed us to reflect back on LEAP's *risk assessment* and use it to develop the MUN seminar with youth volunteer leaders. We were able to connect with a regional United Nations representative, who led a session on the Sustainable Development Goals with youth participants and expressed interest in continuing to work with SDU on youth development projects.

As a result of LEAP, SDU planned to develop a new strategic direction dedicated to youth development, with the hope that community outreach through smaller youth projects would make them a more recognizable and trusted organization in the community. Staff at SDU collaborated with trained volunteers to implement a short-term (less than one year) program to introduce youth to various professions and help them build skills that would be valuable in the workplace. It was called Job Test-Drive (direct translation from Ukrainian) and we strongly encouraged SDU to collaborate with youth volunteer leaders in all phases of the project and give them autonomy to determine how it would look. SDU implemented this program in partnership with a community school that offers alternative education for children. Additionally, they intended to partner with the Department of Education in Rivne to focus on engaging school children in volunteering and community activism, with the goal of creating youth volunteer communities led by students in schools around the city – building on the youth volunteer leader base developed through LEAP. We all left the Rivne community before SDU could implement any of these ideas, so we are mostly unaware of which concepts were successful, and to what level they engaged youth volunteer leaders and partners in the project process.

Although SDU struggled to entrust youths with higher-level tasks, this did not inhibit youth volunteer leaders from organizing their own projects independent of the organization after LEAP concluded, in addition to the MUN seminar. Youth volunteer leaders developed and implemented three seminars for other youth in the community after LEAP concluded. Although COVID-19 significantly impacted the extent to which these types of projects could continue, youth volunteer leaders adapted their ideas to online platforms. While we are unaware of participation rates for those seminars, the act of planning and implementing represents success with utilizing PAR in LEAP, and demonstrates that engaging youth in volunteer leadership may impact their long-term participation in volunteerism.

As of June 2021, Tetiana Kidruk (the current director of SDU) is partnering with a local library in Rivne to build a youth center. The city's youth ministry was awarded funding from the International Research and Exchanges Board, which will partially fund the project. Other funders include SDU, Rivne City, and other community stakeholders. The design process is under way and construction is scheduled to begin in September 2021, with an anticipated completion date in mid-2022. LEAP was the impetus behind this cooperative agreement between the government, an international organization, and NGOs. LEAP was successful in motivating youth and their civic engagement is now visible at a community level.

Participatory Action Research: Lessons Learned

LEAP combined PAR focused on adult and youth participants, more out of organic project evolution than intentional planning – even though we used the *PACA Field Guide*, the project's natural process drove our selection of PAR tools more than rigid planning; and although not every aspect of the project was participatory, it was an appropriate methodology to utilize with LEAP and we gleaned vital knowledge regarding the potential for volunteer development in Rivne, Ukraine. PAR provided the theoretical foundation that allowed us to shift direction with LEAP as needed. If we didn't use this methodology, we may not have been so ready to pivot when we realized that adults were not engaged with the project, and LEAP could have been dead on the vine. Volunteers set the project parameters by demonstrating engagement – while moving through the participation process (Greenwood et al. 1993), youth established that they were the volunteer base most willing to follow through with the initial project goals and objectives, and were therefore the volunteers with whom we and SDU should spend the most effort. Conversely, adult volunteers illustrated early in the project that our focus should be elsewhere. We did not need to establish a rigid structure for LEAP because collaborating with volunteers created space for the project to form itself.

Utilizing PAR also taught us how to recognize the difference between when a project may not be feasible and when external forces apply pressure to mold the intervention in a way that is not participant-driven. For example, when we attempted to persuade SDU to fully collaborate with youth volunteer leaders, their response was autocratic. When we made no progress with them, we realized that LEAP was at a crucial defining moment. Despite the temptation to concede, we determined that it was our responsibility to continue with the project because there was clear demand for it, and to incorporate everything we had learned through PAR up to that point. SDU's stance was an interesting contrast to our participatory methods – we placed emphasis on the value of lived experience, local expertise, and individual experience, and yet the organization seeking greater capacity refused to acknowledge the value of youth perspective. This dichotomy reinforced the stereotype that adults know more, and is another example of why implementing YPAR can be incredibly challenging (Foster-Fishman et al. 2010).

Results indicating increased youth engagement when utilizing YPAR reflect existing literature on the benefits of including younger people as partners in the project process. We documented multiple instances of improved participation as we increased our use of YPAR. One of LEAP's greatest achievements is the level of youth engagement in volunteerism, which we attribute to utilizing YPAR whenever feasible. While planning the careers seminar, we started hosting weekly volunteer meetings as a forum for keeping youth volunteer leaders on track; and while planning the second seminar, when we delegated more responsibility to youth volunteer leaders, new faces appeared at each gathering. We noticed that new volunteers were not only coming from previously held events – they also heard about the initiative on social media platforms, from friends, and from their parents. Trusting youth volunteer leaders improved their engagement level and desire to participate. They willingly accepted challenges and expressed desire to co-facilitate sessions and teach their peers. After all of the seminars (careers, personal health management, and MUN), even more youth expressed interest in volunteering and organizing events for their peers. It was especially rewarding to watch their self-confidence grow over time and see them develop friendships with other volunteers. One volunteer leader generally struggled to make friends but throughout the course of LEAP they succeeded in establishing relationships with others, elected to co-facilitate sessions, and organized several volunteer gatherings independent of any project-related meetings. In total, after LEAP concluded we had a list of 37 youth who wanted to be involved with designing and implementing future projects – a substantial increase from the four youth volunteers who signed up for training when the project started. YPAR has the ability to revolutionize how youth conceptualize their place in society and inspire them to take action.

Recommendations for PAR Methodology

These recommendations are based on the successes and limitations we encountered with LEAP, and are not an exhaustive list for how PAR can be more effective. These strategies would likely improve our project outcomes if we implemented a similar project in the Rivne community, and they are replicable.

1. When seeking external funding to implement a project, be as vague as possible when setting project goals. Research indicates that donor expectations can inhibit the efficacy of

PAR because external bias influences what should be a natural evolution. We were fortunate that broad goals were acceptable for the grant we received – otherwise, pivoting when necessary might have been difficult. We did not establish a target age group when setting our goals; and if we had, it would have been hard to justify shifting demographic focus.

2. If implementing a project in a community where the primary spoken language is not your native tongue, solicit project partners who speak the language and whose content expertise complements your own. Many community development/community-building concepts do not directly translate from English to Ukrainian, and my two Ukrainian co-authors and project partners were crucial for accurately communicating this vital information to SDU and volunteer leaders. As a foreigner, successfully implementing a project of LEAP's scale as a solo effort would have been highly improbable.

3. Limit your expectations and allow the process to move as PAR dictates it should. It is incredibly difficult to not instill your own agenda in a project's process, but doing so is the absolute antithesis of what researchers using PAR seek to achieve.

4. If collaborating on a PAR project with an established organization, be prepared for pushback and find ways to navigate it that are culturally respectful, are cognizant of community needs, and allow for continued use of participatory action (if appropriate).

5. Remain mindful of multiple project phases and that, according to the principles of PAR (Greenwood et al. 1993), participants should be actively involved as partners in every stage. Excluding them from any of these steps limits their opportunity to have agency, and according to Baum et al. (2006), human agency constructs reality.

Leadership, Engagement, and Activism Program Limitations

Despite in-depth planning and incorporating PAR in the development process, we still encountered implementation challenges ranging from communication issues to cultural barriers. While these obstacles brought frustration and sometimes hostility between us and SDU, some of the limitations ultimately evolved into strengths because we adapted our project to changing circumstances. These potential limitations should still be considered when pursuing similar interventions in other communities, but they are not necessarily a be-all-and-end-all to project success – rather, teams can adapt to these challenges and look for new ways to move forward.

We did not adequately communicate the purpose and scope of the project, and during the training of trainers participants had some different ideas about why they were there. A common sentiment was that they would get to work exclusively with Peace Corps volunteers to implement English-language projects, or that they might be able to obtain a Peace Corps volunteer for their for-profit organizations. Not everyone understood that the purpose of LEAP was to develop volunteer capacity for SDU. We also failed to include volunteer leaders in all project phases, especially the data analysis phase, which is the most commonly excluded stage when working with youth participants (Foster-Fishman et al. 2010).

Since the project rapidly evolved and grew, we also faced challenges with identifying steps forward after LEAP terminated. When trying to identify the scope for future activities and vision for the youth development direction in the organization, there was resistance to new ideas due to the organizational culture of SDU. Their autocratic management style made it difficult for unpaid volunteers to work with them. It seemed that the organization was merely looking for performers, not partners, in the project process. While they seemed to consider some of our advice for their future endeavors, we do not know if they actually heeded it.

Implications for Civil Society Development in Ukraine

The development of civil society – and increasing civic engagement by building a democratic society through active participation in the identification and resolution of community issues – requires mobilizing persons who are interested in community problem solving and identifying solutions. Through encouraging and promoting youth volunteerism, and organizing projects led by active youth, we foresee local youth leadership development and increased youth volunteer capacity focused on problem solving in Rivne. Braiding knowledge transfer with application allowed volunteers to see beyond the theoretical and conceptualize how content knowledge could be applied in real time. This tactic aligned well with recommendations from the United Nations Working Group on Youth (2019) and LEAP pursued each recommendation in the following ways:

1. "Create opportunities for adolescents and youth to participate in settings and areas of prac-tice that they experience on a regular, day-to-day basis, including at schools and in their communities" (54): The focus on Rivne proper and the greater metropolitan area allowed us to singularly devote resources towards creating spaces for youth engagement in this area and have a more refined approach to project development. Implementing the seminars during the summer months also provided learning opportunities when the academic school year concluded, mitigating possible regression students might experience from being out of school for several months. SDU's plans to partner with the Department of Education and alternative schools also align with the United Nations' recommendations for engaging youth. Bringing the concept of volunteerism into the traditional academic learning space has long-term potential for influencing youth motivation to civically participate in their community.
2. "Develop the capacity of Ukrainian organizations to diversify their approaches to mobi-lizing, facilitating, and managing youth volunteers and align these with international best practices" (62): SDU staff and volunteers acquired content knowledge for various strate-gies that can effectively engage youth volunteers. This training provided a well-rounded foundation for developing sustainable projects. A significant aspect of LEAP was people management, specifically managing youth volunteers, and we attempted to engage SDU in working with this valuable resource base.
3. "Create opportunities for youth to volunteer on a regular basis in their communities" (62): LEAP engaged youth in volunteerism by including them in the design, planning, and implementation phases of the project, and by delegating responsibility to youth in order to increase accountability. All of the activities in this chapter were enacted in Rivne and attracted youth from the city and smaller surrounding communities. Facilitating regular volunteer meetings contributed to ongoing interest in the project, even when there was a slight lull in seminar activities. Volunteer numbers increased over the project's life and the interventions were so popular that volunteers pushed for organizing a third event that was not part of the original project idea. Facilitating regular volunteer meetings also pro-vided opportunities for volunteers to establish close friendships, which will have lasting impact and reflect the literature exploring social capital and civil society development.
4. "Empower youth volunteer activists and representatives of the youth volunteer movements to further promote the culture of volunteerism among their peers" (62): The increase in volunteerism while conducting LEAP can be attributed to youth seeing their peers in these

leadership roles. This peer-to-peer learning allowed youth volunteers to be perceived as role models with agency, which other youth wanted to emulate; and this mechanism was the vehicle for showing youth that they are capable of engaging in such activities and of being community leaders. However, organizations supporting youth development initiatives could be more open to the value of youth–adult partnerships in community-based projects, and actively support decision-making opportunities for youth.

Despite limitations with LEAP and challenges engaging SDU to promote participatory youth initiatives, project outcomes illustrate the possibility for youth volunteerism to drive civil society development. PAR revealed that youth were far more likely to participate in Rivne volunteer activities than adults, which is consistent with the report that the United Nations Working Group on Youth (2019) released. Additionally, opportunities for youth to organize and solve problems correlate with a higher likelihood that those individuals will remain civically active adults (Fox et al. 2010). LEAP exhibited that increased access to decision-making power influenced youth engagement in volunteering for project interventions. There is room to explore the potential for participatory action to find natural pathways for civil society development; and future research in Ukraine and other nations with developing civil society could utilize YPAR as a method for engaging youth at all levels of community project design, implementation, and evaluation.

CONCLUSION

LEAP was fairly successful given its timeline, goals, and challenges. The attention paid to PAR and responding to community needs undeniably impacted the project's trajectory. The real challenge now presented to SDU – and other organizations seeking to develop civically engaged youth – is whether they will continue to utilize the best practices of YPAR methodology. Losing LEAP's volunteer base could negatively impact the potential for a culture of volunteerism in Rivne, considering that SDU would be just another organization that did not meet community needs. Despite the challenges that SDU is likely to experience, LEAP arguably engaged youth in Rivne on a level they had never before experienced. Their motivation and interest in solving community problems illustrates that Ukrainian youth are willing to tackle the most pressing social issues in their communities. The major hurdle is whether they will be provided opportunities to cultivate those skills and confidence in themselves so that they can become future change agents in Ukraine.

NOTES

1. If we situate Ukraine's reality in the context of culturalist theory (Eckstein 1988) and use this as a lens for explaining political change – or lack thereof – it is possible that Ukraine's slow civil society development is the result of learned behavior patterns established early in life. These patterns are called "orientations" and are dictated by culture. When these orientations occur across populations, they are known as "culture themes" and determine actions and reactions for people in that culture (Metraux and Mead 1954). We can think of culture themes as influencing perceptions of dichotomies such as trust–distrust, hierarchy–equality, and coercion–liberty (Pye and Verba 2015). Ukrainians' learned perceptions of national corruption may significantly influence how quickly or effectively civil society can develop. Culture themes are tenacious and difficult to reform because

they are learned early in life, when human development has particular permanence (Eckstein 1988; Putnam 2000).

2.   With more than 14,000 casualties, the Donbass war has not only claimed thousands of lives but also reinforced the "us versus them" mentality between Ukraine and Russia (Dixon and Gryvnyak 2020). Separatist sentiments fueled Russia's invasion in the Donbass "to support breakaway enclaves" (Kramer 2020). The war is not especially visible in most of the country – indeed, as a Peace Corps volunteer living in western Ukraine, Danielle Stevens' primary association with the conflict was knowing people with loved ones who perished in the war. Throughout most of the country, it isn't obvious that they are dealing with an armed conflict. The *New York Times* compared this conflict to the Berlin Wall – it is a 280-mile long trench across which Ukrainians and Russians/separatists throw "mortar and artillery fire at one another" (Kramer 2020).

3.   People with high levels of social capital will likely have a vast network of people with whom to connect for a variety of reasons – whether professional, personal, social, or otherwise; while those with lower levels of social capital may not have as strong a network foundation, which could impact opportunities over a lifetime.

4.   If we situate volunteerism in culturalist theory (Eckstein 1988) and consider the effects of early learned behavior, it stands to reason that engaging youth as volunteers holds promise for steadfast volunteerism in adulthood.

5.   Prior to LEAP, Sertse Dityam Ukrainy sponsored the development and execution of two youth seminars, which the team implemented between July and October 2018. Although the organization provided in-kind donations for the two events, the organization itself did not want to be involved in the planning, design, and implementation process. Overall, we reached 53 youth participants through these two seminars. Sixteen youth attended both events and there were ten new participants for the seminar in October 2018. There was a 62 percent retention rate from youth attending the first to second event, and a 37 percent new recruitment success rate for the second seminar. This success rate helped us justify implementing a larger, longer-term youth development project in Rivne, which led us to LEAP.

6.   After LEAP, Kidruk wrote grants and successfully secured funding for SDU. As of May 2020, she is the director of SDU.

REFERENCES

Afineevsky, Evgeny. 2015. *Winter on Fire*. Motion picture.

Arnstein, Sherry R. 1969. "A Ladder of Citizen Participation." *Journal of the American Institute of Planners* 35(4): 216–224.

Bales, Kevin. 1996. "Measuring the Propensity to Volunteer." *Social Policy and Administration* 30(3): 206–226.

Baum, Fran, Colin MacDougall, and Danielle Smith. 2006. "Participatory Action Research." *Journal of Epidemiology and Community Health* 60(10): 854.

Bugaric, Bojan and Alenka Kuhelj. 2015. "Slovenia in Crisis: A Tale of Unfinished Democratization." *Communist and Post-Communist Studies* 48: 273–279.

Bunce, Valerie J. and Sharon L. Wolchik. 2006. "International Diffusion and Postcommunist Electoral Revolutions." *Communist and Post-Communist Studies* 39(3): 283–304.

Camino, Linda A. 2000. "Youth–Adult Partnerships: Entering New Territory in Community Work and Research." *Applied Developmental Science* 4(1): 11–20.

Cammarota, Julio and Michelle Fine. 2008. *Revolutionizing Education: Youth Participatory Action Research in Motion*. New York: Routledge.

Catalano, Richard F., Lisa Berglund, Jean A. Ryan et. al. 1998. "Positive Youth Development in the United States: Research Findings on Evaluations of Positive Youth Development Programs." *Annals of the American Academy of Political Science* 591(1): 98–124.

Césaire, Aimé. 2000 [1955]. *Discourse on Colonialism*. New York: Monthly Review Press.

Clary, E. Gil, Mark Snyder, Robert D. Ridge, John Copeland, Arthur A. Stukas, Julie Haugen, and Peter Miene. 1998. "Understanding and Assessing the Motivations of Volunteers: A Functional Approach." *Journal of Personality and Social Psychology* 74(6): 1516–1530.

Córdova, Teresa. 2004. "Plugging the Brain Drain: Bringing Our Education Back Home." In *Latino Social Policy: A Participatory Research Model*, edited by David R. Diaz and Juana M. Mora: 22–53. New York: Harworth Press.

D'Anieri, Paul. 2003. "Leonid Kuchma and the Personalization of Ukrainian Presidency." *Problems of Postcommunism* 50(5): 58–65.

Dashchakivska, Olena. 2019. Participatory Government – It Isn't Just Open City. *Peace Corps Ukraine Local Government Retreat*. Interviewer. March 2.

DeFilippis, James and Susan Saegert. 2012. "Communities Develop: The Question Is, How?" In *The Community Development Reader*, edited by James DeFilippis and Susan Saegert: 1–7. New York: Routledge.

Dekker, Paul and Loek Halman. 2003. "Volunteering and Values." In *The Values of Volunteering*, edited by Paul Dekker and Loek Halman: 1–17. Boston, MA: Springer.

Dixon, Robyn and Natalie Gryvnyak. 2020. "Ukraine's Zelensky Wants to End a War in the East. His Problem: No One Agrees How to Do It." *Washington Post*. www.washingtonpost.com/world/europe/ ukraines-zelensky-wants-to-end-a-war-in-the-east-his-problem-no-one-agrees-how-to-do-it/2020/03/ 19/ae653cbc-6399-11ea-8a8e-5c5336b32760_story.html

Eckstein, Harry. 1988. "A Culturalist Theory of Political Change." *American Political Science Review* 82(3): 789–804.

Foster-Fishman, Pennie G., Kristen M. Law, Lauren F. Lichty, and Christina Aoun. 2010. "Youth ReACT for Social Change: A Method for Youth Participatory Action Research." *American Journal of Community Psychology* 46: 67–83.

Fox, Madeline, Kavitha Mediratte, Jessica Ruglis, Brett Stoudt, Seema Shah, and Michelle Fine. 2010. "Critical Youth Engagement: Participatory Action Research and Organizing." In *Handbook of Research on Civic Engagement in Youth*, edited by Constance Flanagan and Judith Torney-Purta: 621–649. Hoboken, NJ: Wiley Press.

Garaycochea, Ignacio. 1990. "The Methodology of Social Development Evaluation." In *Evaluating Social Development Projects*, edited by David Marsden, Peter Oakley, and Brian Pratt: 66–75. Oxford: Oxfam.

Gatskova, Kseniia and Maxim Gatskov. 2015. "Third Sector in Ukraine: Civic Engagement before and after 'Euromaidan.'" *Voluntas* 27: 673–694.

Gaventa, John and Andrea Cornwall. 2007. "Power and Knowledge." In *The SAGE Handbook of Action Research: Participative Inquiry and Practice 2*, edited by Peter Reason and Hilary Bradbury: 172–189. New York: SAGE.

Ginwright, Shawn. 2008. "Collective Radical Imagination: Youth Participatory Action Research and the Art of Emancipatory Knowledge." In *Revolutionizing Education: Youth Participatory Action Research in Motion*, edited by Julio Cammarota and Michelle Fine: 13–22. New York: Routledge.

Greenwood, Davydd J., William Foote Whyte, and Ira Harkavy. 1993. "Participatory Action Research as a Process and as a Goal." *Human Relations* 46(2): 175–192.

Hale, Henry E. 2006. "Democracy or Autocracy on the March? The Colored Revolutions as Normal Dynamics of Patronal Presidentialism." *Communist and Post-Communist Studies* 39(3): 305–329.

Hamilton, Stephen F. and R. Shepherd Zeldin. 1987. "Learning Civics in the Community." *Curriculum Inquiry* 4: 407–420.

Harvard Crimson. 1968. "Its' Arrogance of Power Must End if Peace Corps Hopes to Survive, Ex-Volunteers Contend in Critique." *The Peace Corps: An Indictment*. www.thecrimson.com/article/ 1968/1/17/the-peace-corps-an-indictment-pwe/

Howard, Marc Morjie. 2002. "The Weakness of Postcommunist Civil Society." *Journal of Democracy* 13(1): 157–169.

Kamerāde, Daija, Jo Crotty, and Sergej Ljubownikow. 2016. "Civil Liberties and Volunteering in Six Former Soviet Union Countries." *Nonprofit and Voluntary Sector Quarterly* 45(6): 1150–1168.

Katchanovski, Ivan. 2008. "The Orange Evolution? The 'Orange Revolution' and Political Changes in Ukraine." *Post-Soviet Affairs* 24(4): 351–382.

Koriukalov, Maksim. 2019. "Community Perceptions of Corruption." *Peace Corps Ukraine Local Government Retreat*. Interviewer, March 3.

Kramer, Andrew E. 2020. "With Trump Fading, Ukraine's President Looks to a Reset with the U.S." *New York Times*. www.nytimes.com/2020/12/19/world/europe/trump-zelensky-biden-ukraine.html

Kuhn, Thomas. 1962. *The Structure of Scientific Revolutions*. Chicago, IL: University of Chicago Press.

Lutsevych, Orysia. 2013. "How to Finish a Revolution: Civil Society and Democracy in Georgia, Moldova, and Ukraine." Royal Institute of International Affairs, Chatham House. www.chathamhouse.org/publications/papers/view/188407#

Melchior, Alan. 1998. *National Evaluation of Learn and Serve American School and Community-Based Programs*. Waltham, MA: Boston University, Center for Human Resources.

Metraux, Rhoda and Margaret Mead. 1954. *Themes in French Culture*. Stanford, CA: Stanford University Press.

Nalbandov, Robert. 2014. "Current Politics of Russia, Eastern and Central Europe." *Strategic Studies Institute and U.S. Army War College Press*.

Peace Corps. 2018. "The Participatory Analysis for Community Action (PACA) Field Guide for Volunteers." *Office of Overseas Programming and Training Support*. Washington, DC: Paul D. Coverdell Peace Corps Headquarters.

Putnam, Robert D. 1993. *Making Democracy Work: Civic Traditions in Modern Italy*. Princeton, NJ: Princeton University Press.

Putnam, Robert D. 2000. *Bowling Alone: The Collapse and Revival of American Community*. New York: Simon and Schuster.

Pye, Lucian W. and Sidney Verba. 2015. *Political Culture and Political Development*. Princeton, NJ: Princeton University Press.

Rodriguez, Louie F. and Tara M. Brown. 2009. "From Voice to Agency: Guiding Principles for Participatory Action Research with Youth." *New Directions for Youth Development* 123: 19–34.

Rothmyer, Karen. 2011. "The Nation: A Radical Alternative to Peace Corps." *NPR*. www.npr.org/2011/03/02/134194082/the-nation-a-radical-alternative-to-peace-corps

Rowe, Gene and Lynn J. Frewer. 2005. "A Typology of Public Engagement Mechanisms." *Science, Technology, and Human Values* 30(2): 251–290.

Saegert, Susan. 2006. "Building Civic Capacity in Urban Neighborhoods: An Empirically Grounded Anatomy." *Journal of Urban Affairs* 28: 275–294.

Scheve, Julie A., Daniel F. Perkins, and Claudia C. Mincemoyer. 2006. "Fostering Youth Engagement on Community Teams." *Journal of Youth Development* 1(1). www.ncbi.nlm.nih.gov/pmc/articles/PMC3297413/

Shveda, Yuriy and Joung Ho Park. 2016. "Ukraine's Revolution of Dignity: The Dynamics of Euromaidan." *Journal of Eurasian Studies* 7(1): 85–91.

Stepan, A. 2005. "Ukraine: Improbably Democratic 'Nation-State' But Possible Democratic 'State-Nation'?" *Post-Soviet Affairs* 21(4): 279–308.

Stevens, Danielle. 2019. "Reform and Democratization in Ukraine: My Service as a Peace Corps Volunteer with an Ukrainian Local Government Organization." Department of Politics and Government, Stevens Center for Community and Economic Development: Illinois State University. https://ir.library.illinoisstate.edu/cppg/33/

Tandon, Rajesh. 1990. "Partnership in Social Development Evaluation." In *Evaluating Social Development Projects*, edited by David Marsden, Peter Oakley, and Brian Pratt: 96–101. Oxford: Oxfam.

Tkach, Anatoly and Olga Tkach. 2019. "Volunteer Movement in Ukraine in the Situation of External Aggression." *Ukrainian Policymaker* 4: 52–61.

Traynor, B. 2012. "Community Building: Limitations and Promise." In *The Community Development Reader*, edited by James DeFilippis and Susan Saegert: 209–219. New York: Routledge.

United Nations Working Group on Youth. 2019. "The State of Youth in Ukraine: Analytical Report Compiled by the UN Working Group on Youth." United Nations Ukraine. https://ukraine.un.org/sites/default/files/2020-06/THE%20STATE%20OF%20YOUTH%20IN%20UKRAINE%20report.pdf

Watch, C. 2018. *Ukraine: Country Review*. Country Watch, August 20. www.countrywatch.com/Intelligence/CountryReviews?CountryId=179

Zeldin, Shepherd, Jule Petrokubi, and Carole MacNeil. 2008. "Youth–Adult Partnerships in Decision-Making: Disseminating and Implementing an Innovative Idea into Established Organizations and Communities." *American Journal of Community Psychology* 41: 262–277.

15. Design Your Neighborhood: the evolution of a city-wide urban design learning initiative in Nashville, Tennessee

Kathryn Y. Morgan, Brian D. Christens, and Melody Gibson

As cities grow and change rapidly, youth participation in local decision making is crucial for building equitable urban spaces. Although they are often excluded from decision making, youth have a stake in their neighborhoods and can exert influence when effectively engaged (Checkoway 1998, 2013). They are particularly well positioned to take action in their communities when presented with avenues for participating in local civic processes. Through participatory action research, political advocacy, and community organizing, youth gain skills and knowledge rooted in sustainable community development and the equitable design of local built environments.

This chapter describes the creation, goals, and target outcomes of Design Your Neighborhood (DYN), a place-based action civics curriculum that teaches urban design as a tool for engaging youth in community development processes. The curriculum addresses the need for affordable housing and public transit in Nashville, Tennessee. Youth study places as "texts" (Demarest 2014) by determining how disparities in access to housing and transit have impacted vulnerable communities in Nashville. They then use community development concepts/theory and participatory action research to critically reimagine spaces with more possibilities (Taylor and Hall 2013).

Through this case study, we trace the development of the DYN curriculum to offer a framework for engaging in participatory action research on community development with youth. Drawing on theories of positive youth development, empowerment, and participation, we describe engagement in the civic design process as a method for bringing youth voice into community development practice and decreasing disparity in the built environment. We conclude with a reflection on the modalities of participation that were made possible or foreclosed in each phase of the development of DYN. The ladder of youth participation (Hart 1992) offers a useful conceptual framework for understanding the degree to which adults offer youth opportunities for meaningful participation in processes that they have historically been left out of. This model is widely taken up by youth-serving professionals to address the importance of authentic youth participation in a range of settings and projects of real importance. It emerged from writing on participatory urban design (Arnstein 1969) and is therefore particularly useful for considering the participant identities that youth enact while engaged in youth participatory action research (YPAR) and community development.

PLACE-BASED YOUTH PARTICIPATORY ACTION RESEARCH

The DYN curriculum approaches community development through engaging middle school students in YPAR, a research modality through which youth engage in critical inquiry, undertake collective action, and disrupt social inequity (Cammarota and Fine 2008). Through YPAR, youth identify pressing social issues and conduct research to understand the nature of these problems. Insights from these analyses are positioned to illuminate struggles for power and improve social conditions. Youth then use their research to advocate for change (Bertrand et al. 2020; Ozer 2016).

YPAR relies upon qualitative, quantitative, and critical methods such as participatory mapping and design charrettes to expose and resist oppression (Bautista et al. 2013; Ozer 2016). This methodological pluralism allows youth to approach issues of local importance in ways that are responsive to a range of audiences. Through YPAR, youth can draw on local knowledge to imagine alternative futures and challenge power imbalances. As a pedagogical practice, school-based YPAR can offer a space for learning and development among youth and adult facilitators (Fine 2008; Morrell 2008). YPAR processes can bring youth, educators, and neighborhood residents together as co-investigators (Fine 2008; Tuck and Guishard 2013). Intergenerational YPAR further necessitates that youth and adults engage in ongoing conversation and reflection toward the creation of shared knowledge. This intergenerational knowledge construction is akin to Freire's (2018) description of praxis as critical action/reflection undertaken by youth and adults.

The YPAR literature identifies several key processes that support the development of youth–adult partnerships towards collective inquiry. These include integrating research and action, training students in research skills, offering opportunities for practice, and intentionally sharing power with youth (Caraballo and Lyiscott 2018; Kornbluh et al. 2015; Ozer et al. 2010). This final process, power sharing, is an element of YPAR processes through which the status quo can be challenged and new ways of knowing can be privileged through the dissemination of youth-generated counternarratives (Cammarota 2017).

In YPAR, students are supported in efforts to question the status quo and enact change. Although research is just one of many interventions that youth can leverage toward change in their neighborhoods (Tuck and Yang 2014), YPAR has implications for community well-being and can serve as a powerful policy tool (Dolan et al. 2015; Fine 2008). Opportunities for authentic participation in planning and civic design processes abound in YPAR because youth are experts over their own experiences (Hart 2013). When rooted in local concerns, YPAR has been found to contribute to a range of positive outcomes for youth, including sociopolitical development, feelings of belonging, and sense of agency (Anyon et al. 2018).

YOUTH PARTICIPATORY ACTION RESEARCH AND COMMUNITY DEVELOPMENT

Community development theory and practice center on collective action and its interplay with other social, political, and economic forces that shape local communities (Matarrita-Cascante and Brennan 2012). Critical and participatory approaches to community development often seek the involvement and leadership of those most impacted by local issues in constructing more equitable solutions to local issues (Ledwith 2015). Involving youth in community development recognizes youths' potential as change agents and encourages active participation for all members of a community (Fletcher 2020). Youth–adult partnerships are common across a variety of approaches to community development. Through these partnerships, youth can be supported as active agents in communities, rather than as passive recipients of community resources.

Evidence suggests that place-based YPAR has a stronger action orientation than projects that do not contextualize social issues locally (Buckley-Marudas and Soltis 2019). Schools are natural settings for place-based YPAR. Projects that are facilitated in schools sometimes benefit from additional resources and connections that allow for research to translate into action (Ozer et al. 2010), however, school contexts can sometimes constrain issue selection and action steps (Kornbluh et al. 2015). Variability in school settings and contexts offers a space for exploring differences in outcomes, as spatially oriented investigations draw on youths' rich knowledge of their communities. This process can provide opportunities for youth to be at the forefront of acting on issues that directly impact their lives and neighborhoods, effectively creating avenues for participatory community development. Place-based YPAR can therefore function as a community development process through which youth examine material conditions in their neighborhood in order to improve them.

YPAR and participatory community development can be important approaches for involving youth in neighborhood design and development (Checkoway 1998). Both seek to engage youth in ongoing local change efforts led through governmental organizations (e.g., youth councils, city planning department participation) (Derr et al. 2013), community organizing (Zeldin et al. 2013), and neighborhood coalitions (Morrell 2008). Each of these approaches can create settings in which youth build power and expertise to influence the design and development of their own neighborhoods.

Still, involving youth in the neighborhood design is at odds with prevalent sensibilities about urban development. Many decisions about urban development are driven primarily by elite political actors, landowners, and real estate developers with access to substantial financial capital. Elite actors' disproportionate influence on decision-making processes are insulated by layers of bureaucracy and legal and financial complexities. The notion, therefore, that neighborhood residents can and should influence the design and development of their neighborhoods remains radical even when residents are property owners of legal voting age. Meaningful youth involvement in neighborhood design decisions adds another dimension of resistance to prevailing assumptions about whose voices should matter in local decision making. For these reasons, youth involvement in participatory urban design has great potential as a multifaceted form of participatory community development practice. Yet it is also a challenging practice since it starkly contrasts many existing arrangements that benefit local elites.

NASHVILLE CONTEXT

The DYN curriculum centers on an investigation into the impact of Nashville's urban design and built environment on its residents. Nashville is the capital of the American state of Tennessee. The city had an estimated 687,488 residents in 2019 and the larger metropolitan area had an estimated 1.96 million residents (U.S. Census Bureau 2019a, 2019b). Over the last several decades, Nashville has been experiencing rapid growth and change in its built environment. Growth accelerated in particular during the 2010s, as the city gained greater prominence as a tourist destination and an expansion or relocation site for residents and corporations. For instance, a *New York Times* article in 2013 labeled Nashville as the "It City" (Severson 2013), both recognizing and helping to drive growth in tourism to Nashville.

Tourist visits have increased from 10 million per year in 2010 to 16.2 million per year in 2019 (Nashville Convention and Visitors Corporation 2020). Alongside residential population growth of around 100 new residents per day in the metropolitan area, this has sparked levels of real estate investment, development, and speculation without precedent in the city's history. Many once-affordable neighborhoods are now experiencing rapid gentrification, with the construction of luxury housing, some specifically designed as short-term rentals. Some of these neighborhoods have long histories as communities of color. As these neighborhoods gentrify, residents with fewer resources are displaced, often relocating to more affordable (typically more suburban/remote) areas. Long-standing social and institutional networks are disrupted, as the changes to the built environment in some Nashville neighborhoods accumulate to the point that they are nearly unrecognizable to their former residents.

The city's rapid growth and change has not been matched by investments in its transportation system. In fact, in recent years, citizens overwhelmingly rejected a transit referendum that would have increased investment in light rail and bus rapid transit, the city bus system has been privatized, and several key bus routes in communities with fewer resources have been cut. Furthermore, the city substantially lags peer cities in infrastructure for other non-automotive forms of transportation. For instance, the city continues to set new records for pedestrian deaths due to a woefully deficient system of sidewalks (Ong 2020). Nashville is currently a Bronze-Level Bicycle Friendly Community according to the League of American Bicyclists (2015). To reach the average levels of Silver-Level cities (such as nearby cities Louisville, KY and Chattanooga, TN), Nashville would need to approximately triple its bicycle network mileage and increase daily ridership levels by more than 1000 percent.

Metro Nashville Public Schools

Despite Nashville's economic growth, the city's school district continues to face barriers rooted in race and class inequities. Legacies of Jim Crow-era school and neighborhood segregation followed by out-migration of White, affluent students to suburban school districts have profoundly impacted the city's educational landscape (Erickson 2016). Metro Nashville Public Schools (MNPS) is therefore surrounded by suburban county-run school districts that are generally better resourced and have higher average standardized measures of student achievement. Although problems in school and neighborhood environments are interrelated, attempts at reform have largely centered on interventions aimed at individual school personnel (e.g., teachers, administrators) rather than the underlying systems and practices that have resulted in educational inequity (Nation et al., 2020).

MNPS currently serves over 86,000 students across 550 square miles throughout Davidson County. The district serves a high poverty population, with 71.4 percent of students considered economically disadvantaged. MNPS is highly diverse, with students representing nearly 140 countries and speaking over 120 different languages (Gonzales 2015). Teacher shortages in the district have grown substantially in the past five years, with many teachers citing disproportionately low wages and diminishing morale as their catalyst for leaving the district or the profession (Garcia and Weiss 2019). Teachers who remain struggle to afford housing in the city where they teach.

Nashville has used zoning and school choice policies to achieve within-school diversity and socioeconomic balance since forced bussing began in the 1970s (Wadhwani and Gonzales 2019a). These policies have important implications for students' connection to their school neighborhood, as MNPS parents can send their children to schools they are not zoned to attend as long as there are openings and they can provide their own transportation. The choice model gained traction as a mechanism for allowing families agency in determining the learning environment that best fit their child's needs. MNPS offers an academy model in which several specialty high schools offer distinct career pathways that encourage students to choose a school based on vocational interests instead of proximity. During the 2019–2020 school year, more than one in three MNPS students commuted to a public school outside of their neighborhood zone (Wadhwani and Gonzales 2019b), which has deleterious impacts on neighborhood schools both in terms of funding and fostering school connection (Wadhwani and Gonzales 2019b). Zoned schools in neighborhoods facing gentrification face dwindling enrollment, as long-time residents are displaced and newer, more affluent residents are choosing to send their children to schools outside of their neighborhoods. Coronavirus has further impacted enrollment in Nashville's public schools, exacerbating budget concerns (Mangrum 2020). Given Nashville's limited public transit availability, school choice is inaccessible for some families in racially and socioeconomically isolated areas of the city. These dynamics leave the district with challenges in getting parents to choose their neighborhood schools again.

Civic Design Center

In the 1990s, a group of residents, including many professionals involved in architecture and design, organized in opposition to a proposal for a new limited-access highway running through the southern end of Nashville's downtown. Through informational events and advocacy, the group was eventually successful in transforming what would have been a highway built to move traffic through the city into an urban boulevard, complete with cycling and pedestrian infrastructure, a median, and street trees (now called Korean Veterans Blvd.).

This successful grassroots urbanist action created an echo of similar efforts in other cities, such as when residents of Manhattan (including Jane Jacobs) organized to prevent the construction of the Cross-Manhattan Expressway, preserving miles of dense mixed-use urban blocks in Lower Manhattan. In Nashville's case, however, the land surrounding the proposed highway had not yet been densely developed but had the potential to be given the city's rapid growth. The group of residents that had organized to stop the highway formed an organization to continue with education and advocacy of this sort, called the Urban Design Forum. A candidate for mayor, Bill Purcell, promised that if elected, he would support further institutionalization of this group.

In 2001, following Purcell's election as mayor, the Civic Design Center was founded as a non-profit with pledged supports from multiple city agencies (e.g., planning department, housing and development agency, and historic commission) as well as philanthropic support and several university partnerships (most importantly, a partnership with the University of Tennessee's College of Architecture and Design). Some of the staff and board members at the new Civic Design Center had been involved with the Urban Design Forum, which has since been officially hosted by the Civic Design Center.

The fledgling Civic Design Center began working with neighborhood groups to generate community-based urban designs, and within several years took on a more ambitious project called the *Plan of Nashville* (Gaston and Kreyling 2015; Kreyling 2005). Inspired by Daniel Burnham's *Plan of Chicago* a century earlier, the Civic Design Center set out to create a 50-year plan to guide design and development decisions in the city. Unlike many earlier plans – and in keeping with its grassroots origins – the *Plan of Nashville* was a deeply participatory process, involving hundreds of urban Nashville residents in design charrettes. Yet the participatory urban design processes that the Civic Design Center created only involved adults.

Ten years after the *Plan of Nashville* was published, 22 percent of Nashville's residents were estimated to be 18 or younger. The Civic Design Center saw the importance of engaging youth in developing equitable cities and again looked to the *Plan of Chicago* as a model. Burnham's plan had been adapted into an eighth-grade civics textbook called *Wacker's Manual* and was taught as a standard curriculum in all Chicago schools for two decades (Baker 2010; Moody and Wacker 1916). The Civic Design Center hoped to similarly integrate the *Plan of Nashville* into the public school system to be adopted and supported by residents. This inspired the launch of the DYN curriculum. DYN draws on principles of equitable urban design outlined in the *Plan of Nashville* to contextualize local issues rooted in histories of structural inequity that youth see occurring in Nashville, including access to transit and housing. A very brief urban design education provided at the outset of the curriculum offers a shared language to describe central issues (e.g., displacement, gentrification, redlining) and responses/solutions (e.g., placekeeping, community land trusts, tenant protections) that underlie Nashville's housing and transit crises. This becomes a lens through which youth can deepen their community development and YPAR work to engage with issues of local importance. The rest of the curriculum centers on community development and YPAR strategies that offer youth a way into collaborative local decision-making processes that address the structural barriers entrenched in Nashville's built environment and support the creation of a more equitable city.

The Design Your Neighborhood Team

To develop DYN, the Civic Design Center combined the expertise of design and education professionals. The Civic Design Center's education director, Melody Gibson (third author), led the development of the curriculum and accompanying programming. Melody has a Bachelor of Architecture, Master of Arts in Curriculum and Instruction, and seven years of teaching experience. With expert knowledge in urban planning and education, Melody was uniquely positioned to develop DYN into a program that would engage youth in city planning and urban design. Additionally, the research team members and their institution, Vanderbilt University, have long-standing active collaborations with both the Civic Design Center and the MNPS. The first and second authors have collaborated with the Civic Design Center since 2016 and 2002, respectively, and have been involved with the curriculum since its inception. This project therefore benefits from and builds on a long-standing community–academic partnership.

DESIGN YOUR NEIGHBORHOOD CASE STUDY

Nashville has a robust history of grassroots community organizing, particularly in addressing disparities in access to affordable housing and transit. However, there are few opportunities for youth engagement or leadership in these efforts. DYN is a scalable intervention with the ability to bring youth voices from around the city into policy conversations regarding these topics. This case study addresses the tension between impact and scale when doing participatory action research and community development with youth. We see the evolution of DYN as having three distinct phases. In the first phase, we facilitated participatory action research-informed community development projects with a small group of youth from across the city, which had a positive impact on a smaller group of young people and the communities where they focused their work but did not achieve systemic change in schools. In the second phase, we scaled our programming to 3000+ youth, but the community development component of the work suffered as we shifted our focus to saturating the school district with a place-based action civics curriculum. This prompted the DYN team to move into the current phase of the work, in which we are engaging students through in-school and out-of-school programming simultaneously.

We recognize that this case study does not contain every element of community development and participatory action research. There are limitations of the DYN initiative that we describe as we trace the program's history. However, DYN is interesting due to several aspects of its local context. First, Nashville's urban environment is changing very quickly as the city's population and levels of tourism increase (Plazas 2018). Second, innovative work is being done by the Civic Design Center in collaboration with MNPS, providing middle school students with opportunities for engaged learning about community development. Finally, the approach taken by the DYN curriculum fuses several promising pedagogical practices, including place-based education (Demarest 2014; Gruenewald and Smith 2007), experiential learning (Dewey 2013; Hildreth 2012), and action civics (Levine and Kawashima-Ginsberg 2017; Rebell 2018). We discuss the possibilities and challenges of doing participatory action research and community development across a range of contexts and settings, the limits of each approach without the other, and the barriers and opportunities that come with bringing the program to scale across a city and within a school system.

Phase 1: Community-Based Design Your Neighborhood Pilot 2017–2018

The Civic Design Center began laying the groundwork in 2017 for programming that would bring youth voice into the urban design process, with the goal that every young person in Nashville would engage with the *Plan of Nashville* at some point before graduating from high school. This began with writing the *Community Design 101* curriculum (Civic Design Center 2016). *Community Design 101* features a series of hands-on activities that engage youth with the basics of neighborhood design, then introduces community development and participatory action research strategies that can be leveraged to understand and address social problems that manifest in built environment disparity.

To pilot the curriculum, we held four-week paid summer DYN internships for groups of 16 youth entering the 10th–12th grades in the summers of 2017 and 2018. We marketed the DYN internship to students interested in working toward social change in Nashville through community organizing, activism, art, and design. We then interviewed applicants and selected a cohort of interns who were diverse in terms of race/ethnicity, gender, high school/neighborhood, and preferred approaches to social change. The pilot internships followed a similar format each summer. The internship began by introducing principles of urban design. Interns learned about six factors in the built environment – transportation, walkability, food resources, neighborhood identity, parks and open spaces, and buildings. These factors offered a framework for exploring how the form and characteristics of a neighborhood impacted individuals' lived experience. Through the curriculum, interns evaluated Nashville's built environment using a multistep process that incorporated participatory action research and community development strategies. First, interns analyzed health-promoting and health-defeating physical features in the built environment and interrogated dominant narratives about their neighborhoods. This helped interns develop a rich sense of the assets, challenges, and opportunities present in the built environment. Interns then traveled around the city to see successful local community development efforts firsthand. They worked with design professionals to address the feasibility of spaces in their neighborhoods as sites for community development efforts and generated potential target locations for intervention. Finally, interns designed interventions for their communities and developed the advocacy and funding strategies needed to implement their designs. After the implementation of their projects, interns held a community exhibition to share their work with stakeholders.

The summer internship model allowed interns to carry out grant-funded community development efforts in the city. Members of Nashville City Council, Tennessee Department of Transportation, Metro Planning Department, and other design professionals consulted with interns to share community development strategies that interns could leverage in their work. In 2017, the first cohort of interns collaborated with city leaders to activate an underutilized park. Interns were tasked with developing plans for a park at the historic Amqui Station in Madison, TN. This park would serve as a multigenerational public and play space on a site surrounded by active edges with a diversity of potential users, located behind the public library branch and adjacent to a historic train station and senior community center. Interns collected community feedback from Madison residents and then used that feedback to inform a site plan. They shared their concept plans with city leaders for feedback, revised them, and gave the revised plans to landscape architects to develop the site. Interns collaborated with a team of architects and landscape engineers hired by the city to generate a community-informed masterplan of the space to draw in new visitors through adding lighting, furniture, recreational equipment, seating, green space, and community events. The Metro Parks Department of Nashville then executed the interns' plan.

The following summer, the second cohort of interns enhanced pedestrian safety along a major corridor. They were tasked with making improvements that would serve the "Little Kurdistan" neighborhood of Nashville, home of the Salahadeen Center of Nashville (a mosque and community center), Middle Eastern food markets, and several other popular restaurants, businesses, and residences. Interns collected data from residents and business owners and generated short- and long-term recommended improvements for the Little Kurdistan area. Interns carried out the short-term design improvement projects and long-term project recommendations were collected in a report and shared with local stakeholders and city leaders. Interns worked alongside Civic Design Center staff and design professionals on a tactical urbanism design/build aimed at installing temporary traffic-calming measures and concurrently worked to advocate for funds to provide permanent crosswalks. In both years of the DYN summer internship, interns concluded their experience by hosting a Youth Town Hall where they invited the greater Nashville community to learn about their design work and support their ongoing efforts to improve the built environment.

Each year, the internship also included training in research methods to prepare interns to leverage YPAR as a mechanism for enhancing community development. Youth learned how to administer and analyze survey data, how to conduct interviews, and how to collect unobtrusive observational data through neighborhood audits. YPAR allowed interns to better understand how space was being used in their target intervention sites. For example, in the park design project, interns organized a "Play Day at the Park," promoted the event on social media, and activated the space with games, music, and food. They then interviewed attendees to learn about their use of and hopes for the park. In 2018 when the target intervention was a major corridor that had seen several pedestrian accidents due to insufficient sidewalks, crosswalks, and lighting, interns took a different research approach, administering a survey to residents and conducting observations at peak traffic hours to assess walkability and safety. In both cases, interns analyzed these results, represented them graphically, and developed summaries to share with stakeholders who could help them leverage design and community development strategies to improve conditions in the built environment.

Challenges with community-based Design Your Neighborhood
DYN summer internships followed locally specific grants, which made it difficult for interns to remain engaged after their time in the program ended. This meant that partnerships formed in communities with youth-serving organizations, neighborhood associations, city council members, and residents were often not sustained beyond a single grant cycle. Additionally, logistical issues concerning the time it takes for permanent infrastructure change to occur were difficult for interns to navigate during their short experience. Interns would graduate high school and leave Nashville before their work came to fruition, particularly if it involved a prolonged policy campaign or permanent infrastructure adjustment.

Through the internship experience, the DYN team acknowledged that summer programming would never reach the scale that we hoped to achieve through DYN when we conceptualized it as the Nashville equivalent of Chicago's pervasive *Wacker Manual*, which every young person engaged with during their secondary education. While the internship model helped the DYN team refine the curriculum, we concluded the summer of 2017 eager to pilot the DYN initiative in schools.

Phase 2: School-Based Design Your Neighborhood, 2017–Present

In the summer of 2017, we hosted free training to introduce middle and high school teachers to the *Community Design 101* curriculum. Teachers from a variety of content areas and grade levels attended. The training sought to familiarize teachers with the basics of urban design, facilitate an understanding of how design plays a role in equitable communities, and prepare teachers to lead their classes in addressing a community issue through community development and YPAR strategies.

Teachers began implementing *Community Design 101* in the fall of 2017, and we were encouraged by how students took up the work in their classrooms. For example, one freshman seminar course used the curriculum to launch a Ninth Grade Civic Design Showcase that focused on gentrification and the displacement of low-income residents in their neighborhood. In matching t-shirts with the logo "Respect the Locals," students led a workshop on how to combat displacement, an environmentally sustainable design demonstration, a walkability tour to point out areas of inaccessibility near their school, a gallery of oral histories they had collected about changes in the neighborhood, and an interactive art showcase. These projects were largely focused on raising awareness of issues impacting students, but some students became deeply committed and continued to advance their community development work after the curriculum concluded. For example, one group of students formed "Panel up the 'Ville" while engaging in the curriculum and went on to advance the use of solar-powered sidewalks in high-traffic areas around the city. Another group successfully lobbied their City Council member about dangerous holes in the street caused by missing storm drain covers.

Many pilot schools faced barriers to implementation. Teachers of enrichment and elective courses often adopted the curriculum, but only high-achieving students had access to these classes while their peers took courses aimed at improving their standardized test scores. Some schools were not able to implement the final project due to time constraints and pressure to align instruction to testable material, thus leaving out the critical community action portion of the curriculum altogether. Overall, barriers to implementation that emerged in the pilot projects were rooted in concerns over school accountability and standardized testing, a reality in United States schools that we felt could be mitigated through drawing explicit links between curricular standards and authentic, place-based action civics education. The DYN team took what we learned from our pilot program and set out to produce standards-aligned, place-based action civics curricula for core courses that could be brought to scale across the school district.

In spring 2018, the DYN team began meeting with MNPS district officials to discuss ways to formally partner with them to bring the DYN curriculum into all 33 MNPS middle schools. The district helped us assemble a team of high-impact teachers who had a history of engaging their students in project-based learning and social justice-oriented curricula. We hired these teachers to co-write the curriculum with us during the summer months. We began the writing process by giving teachers an introduction to urban design and the built environment so that they were prepared to write curriculum outside of their realm of expertise. We then crafted three-week cross-curricular units for seventh- and eighth-grade social studies, English, science, and visual arts classes. Our writing team designed each unit to be aligned to grade-level academic standards. All units address an urban design issue that has exacerbated inequality in Nashville, with seventh graders focusing on transportation and eighth graders focusing on affordable housing.

Our teacher-led curriculum team developed a suite of projects that students could complete in their classes that were actionable within the confines of a school but had implications for addressing disparity in the built environment. The curriculum is cross-disciplinary, and each core subject took a different approach to decreasing disparity in the city's urban policies, systems, and environments. For instance, in English language arts classes students created a podcast in which they introduced these built environment issues to other youth by interviewing neighbors, reaching out to government officials for comment on their position, and spotlighting community organizations that focus on these issues. Projects in social studies classes included generating a policy and advocacy campaign, conducting power mapping, community research, and a social media strategy, and putting pressure on local officials to address an issue related to housing or transit in their neighborhood. Art and science classes focused on community development processes and design. Projects for these subjects included designing sustainable micro units to address housing affordability, leveraging knowledge of their neighborhoods to locate spaces that could accommodate affordable housing infill. Students also worked with the local transit authority to locate, design, build, and install bus stops based on results from community surveys. The bus stops feature student artwork on public transit infrastructure that is illustrative of the culture of their school's neighborhood.

To prepare teachers to engage their students in this curriculum, the DYN team led professional development sessions open to all middle school teachers in MNPS during the fall of

2018. This allowed us to introduce urban design and the built environment as critical topics of classroom conversation for all teachers, focusing on the impact that sociohistorical inequities have on schools and students. These sessions are a crash course in Nashville's history of neighborhood displacement, White flight, redlining, blockbusting, systemic disinvestment in public transit, highway construction, pollution within historically Black neighborhoods, and school bussing policies (Erickson 2016). We hoped that even if teachers chose not to adopt DYN in their classrooms, they would leave feeling more prepared to talk to their students about the ways that inequity manifests in the built environment.

For teachers who opted in to teaching the DYN curriculum, we provided all teaching materials and follow-up planning support. We also offered DYN teachers access to volunteers to assist with curriculum implementation in their classrooms. We recruited professionals from a range of fields related to community development to serve as volunteers, including architects, urban planners, community organizers, engineers, government officials, and artists. The Civic Design Center's history of engaging adults interested in design and community development meant that we had access to an extensive network of professionals who consulted with students and teachers during the intensive design portions of the projects. The DYN team trained the volunteers on best practices for working with middle school students and providing scaffolded learning experiences that acknowledge students as budding neighborhood experts with cultural knowledge and skills (Gauvain 2001). Bringing volunteers into the classroom allowed intergenerational partnerships to form between professionals – many of whom have influence in shaping Nashville's neighborhoods – and students who will inherit the impacts of their decisions. We hoped that engaging in partnerships with professionals who occupied positions in the design/development field would encourage students to consider similar career trajectories. This would be a step toward correcting the underrepresentation of students from low-income neighborhoods and marginalized groups in careers that can address built environment disparity (Griffin and Yang 2015).

In May 2019, DYN hosted a Youth Design Exhibition to showcase student projects. As part of the curriculum, students invited community stakeholders (e.g., business leaders, school and government officials, community organizers, design professionals) to attend the exhibition to engage them in addressing local issues through urban design. At the exhibition, students set up stations to share their community development projects with attendees and led a panel discussion to address topics relevant to the curriculum. Attendees circulated between groups of students to learn about their projects, offer feedback and next steps for their work, and support students' ongoing efforts toward improvement of the built environment.

DYN concluded the 2018–2019 school year with 31 teachers partnering to engage around 2,000 students across 18 MNPS middle schools. By the beginning of the 2019–2020 school year, we had once again doubled our scale, with 63 teachers in 23 middle schools signed up to teach DYN. In March 2020, Nashville was hit by a tornado that devasted many of our students' communities and schools. Weeks later, the coronavirus pandemic shuttered schools across the city indefinitely. We immediately began restructuring the curriculum to work in a virtual learning environment, altering the focus of the work to not only address the way that the pandemic was impacting access to public transit and affordable housing but also giving students space to consider how to build and maintain community when we must be physically distanced from one another.

While the pandemic disrupted our ability to engage students in completing design builds or meeting in person to showcase their work, it presented new avenues for community development and YPAR. For example, we created a virtual mapping process that allowed classes to spatially share their experiences of the pandemic, thus creating a sense of community during a period of separation. We drew from a mapping exercise from the DYN curriculum in which students collaborated to conduct an audit of their schools' neighborhood. They would first walk the school grounds to identify assets, opportunities, and challenges present in the built environment, then plot these features on a physical map of their school's neighborhood. Virtually, students worked independently to map features of their own neighborhood in a shared map with their peers. This included mapping spaces that students were still able to access during the pandemic, mapping spaces that they were not able to access and missed, reflecting on what their home and neighborhood meant to them in these new times, and commenting on each other's contributions to ease the anxiety of isolation.

As a result of the pandemic and the tornado, transportation and affordable housing resources in Nashville became even more precarious than when we began the school-based DYN in 2018. It was therefore increasingly crucial for schools to offer young people opportunities to stay engaged in their communities and advocate for their needs. By the start of the 2020–2021 school year, our curriculum team had refined our virtual curriculum to support students as they resumed online learning. We chose to reenter schools virtually to scale our impact, which was ultimately successful even in the face of a global pandemic largely because of our partner teachers' dedication. They chose to engage their students in a curriculum that was relatively untested twice; first when we entered schools in 2018 and again when we went virtual in 2020. This has required teachers to learn about topics beyond the scope of their disciplines and shifted power to define learning outcomes to their students.

Challenges with school-based Design Your Neighborhood
Beyond the unprecedented obstacles that the pandemic presented to our work, we experienced a range of tensions and challenges in doing community development and participatory action research in schools that emerged early in the process that we will continue to navigate when schools resume in-person. For example, we noticed while writing the school-based DYN curriculum that teachers in our writing group who taught in neighborhood schools could connect urban design features in the school community with potential interventions that their classes might choose to take on, but teachers in magnet schools or schools with many students who were bussed in from other areas of the city struggled to do the same. Teachers in neighborhood schools might acknowledge that their students walked to school on the side of the road because there was no sidewalk or share that they lose many students during each school year due to rising property values in the neighborhood. However, teachers working outside of neighborhood schools were challenged with bringing the curriculum to bear in ways that would incorporate the many spaces that students occupied. They were also confronted with the possibility that students might not feel connected to the neighborhood that their school was nested within.

There were also sociopolitical factors that limited the effectiveness of the curriculum that are rooted in the same inequitable policies and practices that our work aims to educate students about. This includes the way that school choice policies leave many students without a connection to the neighborhood their school is nested in. We also found that the districts' disproportionately low teacher pay created barriers to a sense of belonging in school neighborhoods among participating teachers. Many of our teachers commuted from outside of Nashville and reported that they had been priced out of the communities where they work (Shaw 2020). When teachers did not live in the neighborhoods that they taught in or felt disconnected from the history of their school neighborhood, they faced added barriers to engaging students in place-based curriculum (Demarest 2014).

We also faced additional unforeseen obstacles rooted in ever evolving education policy and practice. Schools face many competing requirements that can require teachers to abandon the curriculum to fulfill mandates from their principal or district. For instance, science, technology, engineering, art, and math (STEAM), project-based learning, and socioemotional learning have all been considered at one time to be the top district priority during the two years that DYN has been a school-based initiative. As district politics shift priorities, the DYN team attempts to respond to support our teachers in making the case for keeping this curriculum in their classrooms. In practice, this has involved the DYN team writing socioemotional learning competencies for each lesson in the curriculum, making explicit the way that the curriculum aligns with project-based learning legislation the state mandated mid-year in 2018, aligning the curriculum to new STEAM standards, writing curriculum for virtual learning, adding supplemental materials to respond to local events, or simply tailoring the way we present the curriculum to administrators as their needs and priorities shift.

Additionally, we struggled to offer all students opportunities to apply community development strategies they learned from the curriculum given the increase in the program's scale. For example, before we began doing school-based programming, we were able to connect former DYN interns with new opportunities to remain active in aspects of community development work that were of the most interest to them. This ranged from connecting a student who was passionate about advocacy and activism to a community-organizing group that focused on housing and affordability to supporting a student who was a talented artist as she built a portfolio and prepared for architecture school. These connections were natural for DYN to provide when it functioned as an internship but required relationships with students that became very difficult to cultivate when DYN started operating as a curriculum provider. Now that we have scaled up from working with 16 students to around 3,500 students annually, our ability to support students' ongoing engagement in community development efforts has been impacted. We can facilitate spaces like the Youth Design Exhibition, which serve an important role in bringing city stakeholders to the table to promote students' voice and their ideas, but providing these spaces is certainly not enough to shift power to students in unequitable planning processes (Arnstein 1969). This led the DYN team to the realization that improving our programming requires making sure that students have more than a deepened conceptual understanding of built environment disparity and have opportunities beyond sharing ideas at a design exhibition. Students need opportunities for putting their plans into action. To do this at a city-wide scale requires being in schools to offer comprehensive education about the built environment, but the work must also extend back into the community to achieve the greatest impact.

Phase 3: The Nashville Youth Design Team 2020–Present

After operating both as a community- and school-based program in previous iterations, we have come to realize that both elements are crucial to support youth as agents of change in the built environment. Having a wide-reaching school-based component of our work will eventually allow every young person in Nashville to learn about the role that the built environment plays in creating and sustaining a thriving city. However, school-based work has an eight-month lifespan and does not allow for prolonged engagement in community development or YPAR.

Students move on to new grade levels and new schools each year. To ensure that this work has implications for communities it cannot function exclusively in a school building, and instead needs concurrent, synergistic, developmentally appropriate out-of-school programming.

Connecting students to other ways to pursue this work is one way to address the gap that was left after we discontinued DYN community-based programming and moved into schools. In practice, this involves letting our teachers know about opportunities for students to join the youth transit board or speak at a convening on affordable housing. We found that existing community groups were coming to us to help them connect to youth, and we were not well positioned to do that without the help of teachers, as increasing the scale of the program had made it difficult for us to form relationships with youth and their families that would allow us to match students to opportunities for engagement.

We also found that interest in this work far outpaces opportunities for youth involvement. For instance, the Metro Nashville Mayor's Office, Metro Planning Department, WeGo Public Transit Department, and other stakeholders in this work have expressed a desire to have youth involved in their work. However, engaging youth in participatory planning processes is relatively novel in Nashville, and as a result we have more students who are interested in remaining engaged after completing the DYN curriculum than we can connect to ongoing efforts.

To that end, we have begun leveraging the reach of the school-based work to engage "graduates" of the curriculum in participatory action research and community development through our own out-of-school programming. In June 2020, we reimagined the DYN out-of-school internship to be a YPAR and community development collective known as the Nashville Youth Design Team (NYDT). Through NYDT, we can keep youth engaged in ongoing urban design and planning efforts in the city after they have completed the DYN curriculum. DYN students who express interest in community development and YPAR as a modality for social change are invited to join the NYDT to build upon experiences in their classrooms and school communities and apply their knowledge to broader urban design issues in the city. This idea stemmed from focus groups with students who had completed the curriculum. They expressed that as many students as possible need exposure to design education, but students who are passionate about urban design and community development needed more opportunities than what was possible in the classroom. Teachers shared this sentiment, noting that they observed that YPAR and community development as a method for social change resonated with many students in each of their classes, but without avenues for continued participation their passion for the work would dwindle.

The first cohort of 14 NYDT members were chosen from a pool of applicants in June 2020. We selected one team member from each school in the city to facilitate geographic diversity. Team members are paid for their time and meet virtually to carry out projects that draw on YPAR and community development strategies. For example, the team is currently creating a "Nashville Youth Wellness Map" in ArcGIS to spatially represent factors in the built and natural environment that contribute to youth wellbeing. They created interview and survey instruments that they used to ask other youth about how their neighborhoods contribute to their wellbeing. They had respondents rank themselves on a scale of 1–10 on a range of dimensions of wellness (e.g., physical, social, intellectual) and identify spaces that contribute to or detract from their wellness. NYDT members add each contributor's responses to the map, which they will use to drive their design, policy, and advocacy work. NYDT plans to continue crowdsourcing their virtual map and analyzing the resulting data until it is once again safe to engage in face-to-face community development work, at which point they will have a rich dataset to use to pinpoint areas with the highest need of ground-truthed design solutions to support youth wellness.

Simultaneous programming happening in classrooms through the DYN curriculum and out of classrooms through the NYDT positions school as the catalyst for learning that informs the community development and participatory action research that team members do in their communities as members of the NYDT. It will also allow the DYN team to keep team members involved in this work as they progress through high school, where they can choose to take on bigger roles on the team with increased autonomy and opportunities for leadership. We envision this model developing into a youth-led organization in which team members graduate high school with five to six years of community development and participatory action research experience that has allowed them to see projects of deep local importance through from beginning to end.

DISCUSSION

The three phases of DYN implementation described in this chapter include a range of shifts, tensions, and tradeoffs that arise when combining community development and participatory action research. This includes changes in scale across phases as we increased the breadth of the program from serving a handful of students annually in Phase 1 to thousands in Phase 2 before adding a supplemental program in Phase 3. Phase 1 allowed a small group of students to have meaningful community development and YPAR experiences. This pilot phase brought revisions to our curriculum and helped us develop relationships with design professionals who remained involved as volunteers and classroom fiscal sponsors when we entered schools. The transition to Phase 2 required increased organizational capacity as we coordinated with hundreds of teachers, administrators, and volunteers. Through prioritizing scale, we are introducing a generation of students to place-based action civics and experiential learning about equitable urban design in Nashville. In doing so, we temporarily sacrificed opportunities for authentic youth participation in order to deliver a curriculum that could be executed within the logistical, temporal, and political boundaries of a school district. Adding Phase 3 as a supplemental extension to our school-based work revives and extends opportunities for prolonged engagement in community development and YPAR that were disrupted when we transitioned out of the community and into schools.

Critical ingredients for the success of the program at each stage include (1) recognition of youth expertise, (2) locally rooted collaborative curriculum development, (3) scaffolded experiential learning about urban design, (4) YPAR, and (5) partnership between youth and adult volunteers. Applying these critical ingredients in a more concentrated way (e.g., smaller number of students and/or lengthier timeframe) is likely to enhance community development outcomes. The partnership with public schools has enabled a much broader reach and larger number of students to participate in DYN. However, this larger scale also likely results in variance in the quality of implementation, spreads resources (e.g., Civic Design Center staff members, community volunteers) thinner, and necessitates curricular adaptations to forces within this broader environment (e.g., frequent educational policy shifts). Our phases of implementation represent attempts to realize the benefits of different scales at different points in the project's evolution. For instance, starting small enabled more collaborative and locally rooted curriculum development to take place, and provided intensive exposure to place-based action civics that resulted in a "proof of concept." Subsequently, scaling up through partnership with MNPS has enabled a much larger portion of Nashville's young people to gain experience with place-based action civics. This broader visibility has resulted in new partnerships (e.g., with WeGo Public Transit) that are helping the project to sustain this broader scale, while also pursuing new avenues for enhancing community development and youth development impacts through more intensive smaller-scale efforts, such as the NYDT. The DYN project therefore points to the value of flexibility and adaptability over time with regard to scale when combining community development and participatory action research.

CONCLUSION

DYN offers one model for sustained youth engagement that brings youth voice into community development practice. Foundational to this model is that youth need opportunities for prolonged participation in community development and YPAR, and these opportunities need to be scaffolded as youth build confidence and competence in carrying out the work with increased independence. The DYN team has found Hart's (1992) ladder of youth participation to be a useful conceptual model for understanding the evolution of our work as it relates to supporting and sustaining more meaningful community development and YPAR opportunities. The ladder outlines eight increasing levels of decision making, agency, and power that youth can enact when engaged in spheres that are typically controlled by adults. At the lowest levels of Hart's (1992) ladder, youth participate in traditionally adult work in ways that are tokenistic and performative, and their voices are co-opted to support an adult agenda. Towards the middle of the ladder, youth are assigned tasks within adult spaces and are consulted by adults to gain their perspective, but ultimate power firmly belongs to adults. At the top of the ladder, participation is youth-initiated, youth are integral to the direction of the work, and decision making is shared with adults.

There are several elements of the ladder of youth participation (Hart 1992) that align with our vision of meaningful engagement in participatory action research and community development among youth. First, we view learning as situated and socially produced. DYN offers critical forms of participatory learning that supports youth capacity building towards authentic leadership roles in community development. To that end, youth are not responsible for initiating all projects as a part of DYN and the NYDT; they are often responding to local needs and being called upon by groups like the city government, the transit authority, or the parks department because they have important funds of knowledge and a unique perspective that they bring in to collective, intergenerational work with important city stakeholders. In this way, the role of adults who partner with DYN is to do more than boost youth closer to the most participatory rungs of the ladder (Hart 2008). We want youth to develop competencies needed to take on leadership roles within community development, but we see this as a non-linear process predicated on youth feeling empowered to name and critique the disparity they see in their neighborhoods and to imagine new realities for their community (Taylor and Hall 2013). We are taking a range of approaches as we try to support youth to act on what they learn from the curriculum, from the community, and from one another as our program scales out. This includes connecting youth with out-of-school opportunities to engage with the Civic Design Center and other youth-serving non-profits. This also includes work with local government to ensure they're prioritizing youth voice in their processes, connecting youth and schools with these opportunities, and equipping volunteers to provide youth with opportunities for further growth through internships.

Second, adult engagement is always a factor in the ladder of youth participation, even at its highest levels (Hart 1992). DYN is situated in a history of attempts in both the community development and positive youth development fields to bring youth voice into otherwise adult spaces. Many of these attempts have not offered meaningful opportunities for participation and contribute to tokenizing youth (Hart 1992). This often looks like having one youth member (often without voting power) on the board of a youth-serving organization or having one student presenting with a group of adults about a topic that centers youth (Hart 2008). We attempt to combat this history by fostering shared decision making and the promotion of youth–adult partnerships, particularly in ways that bring community members and professionals together and aid youth in making sense of their role and responsibilities within the larger practice of community development (Akiva and Petrokubi 2016).

As we move the program forward, we are engaged in a larger discourse among professionals in the field about the spaces where conversations about city planning and design are typically taking place. This includes questions of representation, both in terms of fostering authentic community engagement during the process of planning to mitigate the harmful impacts of gentrification and bringing more people of color and people from low-income communities into the design and planning professions (Griffin and Yang 2015). However, fostering these spaces will have real impacts in urban design and city-planning processes only to the extent that adults reorient their professional identities to make room for youths' knowledge and their local expertise (Ishimaru 2019).

Since 2016, we have aimed to create opportunities that allow youth to access higher rungs of the ladder of youth participation. We believe that through DYN and the NYDT we are moving closer to sustaining youth–adult partnerships in community development and participatory action research that acknowledge the sociopolitical realities that limit youth power (Prilleltensky and Fox 2007). This mediates several barriers to participatory community development for youth, including participation without redistribution of power (Arnstein 1969), tokenizing participation (Hart 2008), and participation based on neoliberal logics that position youth through consumerist lenses (Rosen 2019). Our programming acknowledges the collective contributions of youth, design professionals, and neighborhood residents in this work, even as DYN scales and evolves to be more youth-initiated.

REFERENCES

Akiva, Thomas, and Julie Petrokubi. 2016. "Growing with Youth: A Lifewide and Lifelong Perspective on Youth–Adult Partnership in Youth Programs." *Children and Youth Services Review* 14: 248–258.

Anyon, Yolanda, Kimberly Bender, Heather Kennedy, and Jonah Dechants. 2018. "A Systematic Review of Youth Participatory Action Research (YPAR) in the United States: Methodologies, Youth Outcomes, and Future Directions." *Health Education and Behavior* 45(6): 865–878.

Arnstein, Sherry. 1969. "A Ladder of Citizen Participation." *Journal of the American Institute of Planners* 35(4): 216–224.

Baker, Laura. 2010. "Civic Ideals, Mass Culture, and the Public: Reconsidering the 1909 Plan of Chicago." *Journal of Urban History* 36(6): 747–770.

Bautista, Mark A., Melanie Bertrand, Ernest Morrell, D'artagnan Scorza, and Corey Matthews. 2013. "Participatory Action Research and City Youth: Methodological Insights from the Council of Youth Research." *Teachers College Record* 115(10): 1–23.

Bertrand, Melanie, Sarah M. Salinas, Dawn Demps, Roberto Rentería, and E. Sybil Durand. 2020. "'It's Everybody's Job': Youth and Adult Constructions of Responsibility to Take Action for School Change through PAR." *The Urban Review* 52(2): 392–414.

Buckley-Marudas, Mary Frances, and Samantha Soltis. 2019. "What Youth Care About: Exploring Topic Identification for Youth-Led Research in School." *The Urban Review*: 1–20.

Cammarota, Julio. 2017. "Youth Participatory Action Research: A Pedagogy of Transformational Resistance for Critical Youth Studies." *Journal of Critical Education Policy Studies* 15(2): 188–213.

Cammarota, Julio, and Michelle Fine, Eds. 2008. *Revolutionizing Education: Youth Participatory Action Research in Motion*. New York: Routledge.

Caraballo, Limarys, and Jamila Lyiscott. 2018. "Collaborative Inquiry: Youth, Social Action, and Critical Qualitative Research." *Action Research* 18(2): 194–211.

Checkoway, Barry. 1998. "Involving Youth in Neighborhood Development." *Children and Youth Services Review* 20(9–10): 765–795.

Checkoway, Barry. 2013. "Education for Democracy by Youth in Community-Based Organizations." *Youth and Society* 45(3): 389–403.

Civic Design Center. 2016. "Design Your Neighborhood Curriculum." https://designyourneighborhood.org/curriculum

Demarest, Amy B. 2014. *Place-Based Curriculum Design: Exceeding Standards through Local Investigations*. New York: Routledge.

Derr, Victoria, Louise Chawla, Mara Mintzer, Debra Flanders Cushing, and Willem Van Vliet. 2013. "A City for All Citizens: Integrating Children and Youth from Marginalized Populations into City Planning." *Buildings* 3(3): 482–505.

Dewey, John. 2013. *The School and Society and the Child and the Curriculum*. Chicago, IL: University of Chicago Press.

Dolan, Tom, Brian D. Christens, and Cynthia Lin. 2015. "Combining Youth Organizing and Youth Participatory Action Research to Strengthen Student Voice in Education Reform." *Teachers College Record* 117(13): 153–170.

Erickson, Ansley T. 2016. *Making the Unequal Metropolis: School Desegregation and Its Limits*. Chicago, IL: University of Chicago Press.

Fine, Michelle. 2008. "An Epilogue, of Sorts." In Julio Cammarota and Michelle Fine (Eds), *Revolutionizing Education: Youth Participatory Action Research in Motion* (pp. 213–234). New York: Routledge.

Fletcher, Adam. 2020. "The Youth Industrial Complex." Freechild Institute. https://freechild.org/fletcher_the-youth-industrial-complex-2/

Freire, Paulo. 2018. *Pedagogy of the Oppressed*. New York: Bloomsbury Publishing.

Garcia, Emma, and Elaine Weiss. 2019. "The Teacher Shortage Is Real, Large and Growing, and Worse Than We Thought. *Economic Policy Institute*. www.epi.org/publication/the-teacher-shortage-is-real-large-and-growing-and-worse-than-we-thought-the-first-report-in-the-perfect-storm-in-the-teacher-labor-market-series/

Gaston, Gary, and Kristine Kreyling. 2015. *Shaping the Healthy Community: The Nashville Plan*. Nashville, TN: Vanderbilt University Press.

Gauvain, Mary. 2001. "Cultural Tools, Social Interaction and the Development of Thinking." *Human Development* 44(2–3): 126–143.

Gonzales, Jason. 2015. "Nashville Schools Have More Than 120 Languages." *The Tennessean*. https://eu.tennessean.com/picture-gallery/news/2015/11/13/nashville-schools-have-more-than-120-languages/75664508/

Griffin, Toni., and Esther Yang. 2015. "Inclusion in Architecture Report." New York: City College of New York. https://ssa.ccny.cuny.edu/blog/2015/12/15/inclusion-in-architecture-report-2015/

Gruenewald, David A., and Gregory A. Smith, Eds. 2007. *Place-Based Education in the Global Age: Local Diversity*. New York: Routledge.

Hart, Roger A. 1992. "Children's Participation: From Tokenism to Citizenship." *UNICEF Essays* 92(6): 1–12.

Hart, Roger A. 2008. "Stepping Back from 'The Ladder': Reflections on A Model of Participatory Work with Children." In Alan Reid, Bjarne Bruun Jensen, Jutta Nikel, and Venka Simovska

(Eds), *Participation and Learning, Developing Perspectives on Education and the Environment, Health and Sustainability* (pp. 19–31). New York: Springer.

Hart, Roger A. 2013. *Children's Participation: The Theory and Practice of Involving Young Citizens in Community Development and Environmental Care*. New York: Routledge.

Hildreth, Robert W. 2012. "John Dewey on Experience: A Critical Resource for the Theory and Practice of Youth Civic Engagement." *Citizenship Studies* 16(7): 919–935.

Ishimaru, Ann M. 2019. *Just Schools: Building Equitable Collaborations with Families and Communities*. New York: Teachers College Press.

Kornbluh, Mariah, Emily J. Ozer, Carrie D. Allen, and Ben Kirshner. 2015. "Youth Participatory Action Research as an Approach to Sociopolitical Development and the New Academic Standards: Considerations for Educators." *The Urban Review* 47(5): 868–892.

Kreyling, Kristine. 2005. *The Plan of Nashville: Avenues to A Great City*. Nashville, TN: Vanderbilt University Press.

League of American Bicyclists. 2015. "Bicycle Friendly Community Report Card: Nashville, TN." https://bikeleague.org/bfa/search/map?bfaq=37212&centroid=001G000000w8yLCIAY

Ledwith, Margaret. 2015. *Community Development in Action: Putting Freire into Practice*. Bristol: Policy Press.

Levine, Peter, and Kei Kawashima-Ginsberg. 2017. "The Republic Is (Still) at Risk – and Civics Is Part of the Solution." Medford, MA: Jonathan M. Tisch College of Civic Life, Tufts University.

Mangrum, Meghan. 2020. "Coronavirus Concerns Could Have $11M Impact on Metro Nashville Public Schools Funding Next Year." *The Tennessean*. https://eu.tennessean.com/story/news/education/2020/10/05/nashville-public-school-students-enrollment-decline-budget/3586609001/

Matarrita-Cascante, David, and Mark A. Brennan. 2012. "Conceptualizing community development in the twenty-first century." *Community Development* 43(3): 293–305.

Moody, Walter Dwight, and Wacker, Charles. 1916. *Wacker's Manual of the Plan of Chicago*. Edina, MN: Calumet Publishing Company.

Morrell, Ernest. 2008. "Six Summers of YPAR: Learning, Action, and Change in Urban Education." In J. Cammarota and M. Fine (Eds), *Revolutionizing Education: Youth Participatory Action Research in Motion* (pp. 154–188). New York: Routledge.

Nashville Convention and Visitors Corporation. 2020. "Research and Hospitality Stats." www.visitmusiccity.com/research

Nation, Maury, Brian D. Christens, Kimberly D. Bess, Marybeth Shinn, Douglas D. Perkins, and Paul W. Speer. 2020. "Addressing the Problems of Urban Education: An Ecological Systems Perspective." *Journal of Urban Affairs*: 1–16.

Ong, Linda. 2020. "Special Sidewalk Committee Calls for Urgent Changes, Dedicated Funding." WKRN. www.wkrn.com/news/local-news/special-sidewalk-committee-calls-for-urgent-changes-dedicated-funding/

Ozer, Emily J. 2016. "Youth-Led Participatory Action Research: Developmental and Equity Perspectives." *Advances in Child Development and Behavior* 50: 189–207.

Ozer, Emily J., Miranda L. Ritterman, and Maggie G. Wanis. 2010. "Participatory Action Research (PAR) in Middle School: Opportunities, Constraints, and Key Processes." *American Journal of Community Psychology* 46(1–2): 152–166.

Plazas, David. 2018. "The Costs of Growth and Change in Nashville." *The Tennessean*. www.tennessean.com/Story/Opinion/Columnists/David-Plazas/2017/01/29/Costs-Growth-And-Change-Nashville/97064252

Prilleltensky, Isaac, and Dennis R. Fox. 2007. "Psychopolitical Literacy for Wellness and Justice." *Journal of Community Psychology* 35(6): 793–805.

Rebell, Michael A. 2018. *Flunking Democracy: Schools, Courts, and Civic Participation*. Chicago, IL: University of Chicago Press.

Rosen, Sonia M. 2019. "'So Much of My Very Soul': How Youth Organizers' Identity Projects Pave Agentive Pathways for Civic Engagement." *American Educational Research Journal* 56(3): 1033–1063.

Severson, Kim. 2013. "Nashville's Latest Hit Could Be the City Itself." *New York Times*. www.nytimes.com/2013/01/09/us/nashville-takes-its-turn-in-the-spotlight.html#:~:text=%22Nashville%2C%22a%20song%2D,Texas%20city%20in%20the%20'80s

Shaw, Randy. 2020. *Generation Priced Out: Who Gets to Live in the New Urban America, with a New Preface*. Berkeley, CA: University of California Press.

Taylor, Katie Headrick, and Rogers Hall. 2013. "Counter-Mapping the Neighborhood on Bicycles: Mobilizing Youth to Reimagine the City." *Technology, Knowledge and Learning* 18(1–2): 65–93.

Tuck, Eve, and K. Wayne Yang. 2014. "R-Words: Refusing Research." *Humanizing Research: Decolonizing Qualitative Inquiry with Youth and Communities*: 223–248.

Tuck, Eve, and Monique Guishard. 2013. "Uncollapsing Ethics: Racialized Sciencism, Settler Coloniality, and an Ethical Framework of Decolonial Participatory Action Research." In Tricia M. Kress, Curry Malott, & Brad J. Porfilio (Eds), *Challenging Status Quo Retrenchment: New Directions in Critical Qualitative Research* (pp. 3–27). Charlotte, NC: Information Age Publishing.

U.S. Census Bureau. 2019a. "State and County Quick Facts – Davison County, TN." www.census.gov/quickfacts/davidsoncountytennessee

U.S. Census Bureau. 2019b. "ACS Demographic and Housing Estimates – 2019." www.census.gov/newsroom/press-kits/2020/acs-1year.html

Wadhwani, Anita, and Gonzales, Jason. 2019b. "The Power of Choice: 1 in 3 Nashville Public School Students Opt Out of Neighborhood Schools." *The Tennessean*. https://eu.tennessean.com/story/news/education/dismissed/2019/11/07/nashville-school-choice-zoned-neighborhoods/1981731001/

Wadhwani, Anita, and Gonzales, Jason. 2019a. "Nashville's School Choice System Can Be Complicated. Here's What You Need to Know." *The Tennessean*. https://eu.tennessean.com/story/news/education/dismissed/2019/11/07/nashville-school-choice-system-what-you-need-know/3974720002/

Zeldin, Shepherd, Brian D. Christens, and Jane L. Powers. 2013. "The Psychology and Practice of Youth–Adult Partnership: Bridging Generations for Youth Development and Community Change." *American Journal of Community Psychology* 51(3–4): 385–397.

PART V

RESPONDING TO CRISIS

16. Rethinking participatory development in the context of a strong state

Ming Hu

Participatory development (PD) has gained prominence in the world of development since the 1990s (Chambers 1994; Kapoor 2002). Due to its assumptions of traditional communities as isolated, homogeneous, and relatively free of power relations (Mansuri and Rao 2004; Williams 2004), and a weak state unable to address development needs around health care, transportation, food, and education (Bratton 1989; Puplampu and Tettey 2000), PD puts development agencies (usually international development institutions and domestic non-governmental organizations (NGOs)) at the center of the community development process (Kapoor 2002; Korten 1987). Additionally, PD has increasingly emphasized participatory governance – primarily in democratic states – as an important piece of it (Fung and Wright 2001; Gaventa 2004).

The PD literature, however, has neglected how the model may work in the context of a *strong* authoritarian state such as China. How does the strong state context challenge the assumptions about traditional communities, the centrality of development agencies, and the goal of a participatory state? How do development agencies promoting participatory governance respond to the strong state context?

This chapter explores PD in a community stricken by the 2008 Sichuan earthquake in China where NGOs and the state engaged in post-disaster reconstruction. The study, taking the participatory action research (PAR) strategy, finds that the disaster relief context generated *invited space* (Gaventa 2004) where development agencies had relatively greater room to operate and engage residents in reconstruction. The temporary weakening of state control at the neighborhood level allowed community-based participation to create a fleeting *claimed space* (Gaventa 2004) that residents created and managed themselves. But, as basic services were restored, strong state control was also reestablished, marginalizing development agencies. Still, the newly gained power of NGOs and community organizations partly sustained the invited space, laying a foundation for possible participatory local governance. By virtue of PAR, this study contributes to the understanding of the dynamics of community-level power relations and to the search of development alternatives in a strong state context.

LITERATURE REVIEW

The Challenges and Progress in Participatory Development

PD was developed in the context of international aid, Third World development, and poverty alleviation (World Bank 2000). Owing to limited state capacity to control territory or provide core services at the community level in the developing world context – the "weak state" (Hanlon 2011) – many host communities for PD programs are seen as "traditional communities" with specific characteristics. The first characteristic is clear rather than fluid or overlapping boundaries and thus memberships (Williams 2004). Second is isolation from the broader social context. PD typically deals with impoverished traditional communities, and imagines community development as an isolated social process confined within a spatially bounded region (Kesby 2005; Williams 2004). Third, PD understands community as a homogeneous and harmonious social unit (Mansuri and Rao 2004; Mohan and Stokke 2000). Consequently, tensions in the community power structure and the reproduction of power relationships are ignored or underemphasized, as if participation promoted by aid organizations is exempt from conflict within the existing power structure (Crewe and Harrison 1998; Kesby 2005). Finally, classical PD theories assume that community administration is closed and relatively independent of the state because of the latter's weak local presence (e.g., Bratton 1989).

The localism of PD is based on this model. It assumes that a community will be stuck in poverty and/or inequality if its residents do not "own" the development agenda and development agencies do not respect local culture and knowledge. Therefore, the primary foci of PD are to "empower" the disadvantaged by strengthening their participation in local decision making, and engage civil society to achieve community-owned development (Chambers 1983).

But the model is imperfectly applied. As "experts" in charge of scarce external resources, development agencies often assume a dominant role in agenda setting and policy execution in development programs (Botes and Rensburg 2000; Kesby 2005). This dominance can expand into other community affairs. In extreme cases, development agencies act like a shadow government (e.g., Zanotti 2010).

The assumptions of a weak state and a traditional community have incurred criticism. Nelson and Wright (1995) noted that the "community" concept is often used by governments and NGOs rather than by the people themselves, and connotes a sense of consensus and collective needs that are actually set by outsiders. Fine (1999) argued that, in an increasingly globalized era, broader processes and institutions frame local development problems. Development agencies are criticized for focusing on depoliticized technocratic issues and beneficiaries' participation while failing to change the broader sociopolitical environment constituting the root cause of underdevelopment (Green 2000; Hickey and Mohan 2005).

Nonetheless, the lack of development capacity in weak states has popularized NGO-led community participation as an optimal alternative to state-directed development (Korten 1987), and this idea is promoted by the World Bank and other international development institutions (Nelson 1995). But inadequate state capacity may still undermine the effectiveness of PD (Burde 2004; Jütting et al. 2005), and the relationships between NGOs and the state are not clear-cut (Clarke 1998). NGOs' (and in a broader sense, civil society's) values of voluntarism and solidarity challenge the state's authority (Atack 1999), and may incur its hostility. However, the state may support NGOs' involvement from a utilitarian perspective, specifically when the state cannot meet development goals or is under international pressure (Bratton 1989; Puplampu and Tettey 2000).

As awareness of the state's role in development grew along with the knowledge of the potential and risks of engaging with NGOs, researchers developed the concept of "participatory governance" to pursue transformative change for deepening democracy and improving public administration (Cornwall 2002; Fung and Wright 2001; Gaventa 2004). Emphasizing government decentralization and civil society engagement, participatory governance can widen people's participation beyond the community/project level while improving governments' responsiveness and accountability. This approach was most promoted at the local level in states with democratic tendencies such as the United States, Brazil, the Philippines, India, and post-apartheid South Africa (Gaventa 2004; Heller 2001).

However, many PD programs occur in strong state contexts, which "derive the power to rule from competent institutions of coercion" (Hanlon 2011: 5). Though they "vary in their ability to provide core functions and in their legitimacy" (Hanlon 2011: 5), strong states maintain dominance over community and thus community development. Some authoritarian regimes build rigorous political and social control systems to suppress civil society and see any independent effort to mobilize citizen participation as a threat to the regime (Bratton 1989; Clarke 1998). On the other hand, consolidating state legitimacy requires controllable public participation (Midgley 1986), which is difficult to accomplish. Strong states may allow service NGOs to embark on relief and welfare aid, but it is unclear how they deal with NGOs emphasizing "empowerment" (Korten 1987), particularly in relation to community development.

The State, Non-Governmental Organizations, and Community Development in China

China provides a case study for examining the relationship between national/local state, community, and NGOs in the strong state context. Oi (1992, 1995) labels the Chinese state, in relation to development, as "local state corporatism," and argues that the local state is responsible for managing much of the economic development (and community development) in China. But it does so via a strong authoritarian state that nonetheless integrates market reforms. This goes beyond the older local state literature that relegated the local state's role to managing the social reproduction side of capitalism rather than capitalist production itself (Cockburn 1977; Gottdiener 1987). In China, then, the local state is still accountable to the national state that influences economic development and social welfare. This formulation has important implications for the role of NGOs.

Chinese NGOs are non-profit and voluntary organizations that operate outside the state apparatus in pursuit of public or community interests (Ma 2006). Though there are three legal forms for NGOs, including *jijinhui* (foundation), *shehui tuanti* (association), and *minban feiqiye* (private non-enterprise),[1] a large proportion of NGOs are not registered with the government and risk being regarded as illegal organizations. Originating in rural poverty alleviation in the early 1990s, Chinese NGOs have multiplied strikingly in number, capability, and foci in the past decades (Huang et al. 2013). This increase has been occurring at the same time that the state has imposed rigorous regulations on NGOs in terms of registration, work area, fundraising, and general operations in fear of their threat to state legitimacy, and in the face of severe punishment of NGOs engaged in rights issues concerning democracy, labor, environment, LGBT, and so forth. Contrastingly, the state has recently supported service-oriented NGOs in social service provision at the local and community levels by lifting registration restrictions and funding their programs, while still reinforcing ideological and operational control over them (Kang 2018; Spires 2011; Teets 2013).

Consequently, community development became a niche field for Chinese NGOs. While extending its formal system to the township level, the government began to promote "community self-governance" in the late 1980s at the neighborhood level. A neighborhood branch of the ruling Chinese Communist Party and a residents' committee elected by neighborhood residents (or Party members) serve as the major self-governing bodies of the neighborhood under government supervision. But their self-governance is often nominal and limited to service and welfare delivery (Bray 2006). The state, in the early 2000s, launched the "Community Building" campaign to improve social welfare and reinforce state legitimacy at the grassroots level by expanding community services and the social-political apparatus (Bray 2006; Yan and Gao 2005).

Introduced by international development agencies, PD has been well accepted by Chinese NGOs since the 1990s. Chinese scholarship explores PD's performance at the community level (e.g., Guo 2010; Yang 2010), but few studies question PD theories in China's specific strong state context. Presenting the experience of an NGO-conducted PD program in a community hit by the 2008 Sichuan earthquake in west China (Zhu and Hu 2011), this study aims to explore how state strength varied between the moment of the earthquake and the ultimate reconstruction of the area and how PD (and its related participatory governance) was able to make inroads at certain times and under certain conditions during the community reconstruction process. Our findings challenge the traditional assumptions of PD and add texture to PD theory in the strong state context.

THE COMMUNITY

The Bai neighborhood, with 1,500 registered residents, is located in Long Town, a rural part of greater Chengdu. In the 1950s the central government founded a state-owned mining firm in the town and recruited workers from around the country. At its peak, the firm employed 3,000 workers, whose families constituted the majority of Bai's population. When the firm went bankrupt in 2002, all workers were laid off and fell into poverty. The elderly and children became the majority of residents when young and middle-aged people had to work outside the town. About one fourth of the residents sold their houses and moved to cities. Some city residents bought the houses for summer leave use and became seasonal residents. The firm was transformed into an administrative unit and incorporated into the town government system after its bankruptcy, but disagreements over layoff benefits and the distribution of the firm's residual assets created conflict and distrust between residents and the town government. A deserted community, Bai had no theatre, gym, museum, or organization to provide services.

On May 12, 2008, an 8.0 magnitude earthquake struck west China, leading to 69,227 deaths and 17,923 missing people. Over 40,000 rural and urban neighborhoods were destroyed. The earthquake ruined Bai, killing 14 people and destroying over 95 percent of the houses. The drinking water system was severely damaged and the power supply destroyed. Residents lost all of their possessions. They lived in crowded tents and received limited food, clothes, and other everyday provisions from the government. Without house insurance or employment opportunities, they were faced with a dim future in terms of community reconstruction.

Two months after the earthquake, the author, who represented a non-profit research institute, arrived in Bai along with professionals from three other NGOs. The four NGOs, including three *minban feiqiye* and one *shehui tuanti*, launched a community-based recovery program, the New Hometown Plan (NHP), to help survivors recover from the disaster and reach sustainable reconstruction and redevelopment. Unlike most PD programs, NHP's office was located in the neighborhood and staffed by volunteers recruited from outside the town and employees who lived part time in the neighborhood to work closely with survivors.

METHODS AND DATA

This study used PAR, a process of research, education, and action committed to working with members of communities that have traditionally been oppressed or exploited, in order to pursue positive social change (Brydon-Miller 1997). By integrating academic rigor and practical relevance, PAR supported NHP's primary purpose of assisting earthquake survivors and secondary purpose of exploring how to adapt PD approaches in the context of strong state intervention.

Research was incorporated into NHP's operational system, rigorously following the three-phase cycle of PAR: partnership building, research design and implementation, and shared reflection and reexamination of research contexts (Maguire 1987). A research team led the research, but nearly all NHP members were involved in producing knowledge about community practice, using various research activities such as surveys, interviews, group discussions, program reviews, and document analysis. NHP developed information management instruments to record the PAR process. For example, NHP produced group diaries every workday to keep notes of important events in the program and in the neighborhood, and kept minutes for every group meeting. Photographing and videotaping were also widely used.

Data analyzed in this study include participant observation, qualitative interviews, and document analysis. The author served as NHP's on-site coordinator twice between August 2008 and July 2011 and as program consultant the rest of the time. He could thus observe, from the inside, the interplay between local governments, NGOs, survivors, media, and the public. He took regular and timely field notes to track progress in practice and research. He also conducted unstructured interviews between July 2008 and December 2012 with 85 interviewees, including 16 NGO professionals and volunteers, four government officials, five neighborhood cadres, and 58 residents. Some were interviewed multiple times. Sixty-five percent of interviewees were female, and all but one interviewee were 18 years of age or older. In addition, he collected documentary data between July 2008 and December 2012, which included NHP's archives, government documents, neighborhood archives, and news coverage.

Given the high ethical requirements of disaster settings, the author rigidly followed the five principles presented by O'Mathúna (2010): appreciating vulnerability among research participants, balancing benefit and burden, avoiding coercion, taking no rush to research, and protecting research participants as the first priority. Pseudonyms are used to stand for the neighborhood and town for privacy's sake. Measures taken to ensure scientific validity included strategically selecting research participants, engaging participants in data collection and analysis, triangulating data reliability with different stakeholders, and making long-term observations (Gelling and Munn-Giddings 2011).

COMMUNITY RECONSTRUCTION: THE STATE, SURVIVORS, AND NON-GOVERNMENTAL ORGANIZATIONS

From NHP's entry into Bai in July 2008 to its withdrawal in May 2012, NHP's PD efforts experienced three phases: organizing the community, piloting participatory governance, and confronting community politics (and finally leaving the community).

The central government responded quickly to the disaster. A company of soldiers arrived in Bai to help rescue victims and provide emergency aid such as food, water, clothes, and emergency shelters the second day after the primary earthquake. They stayed for three months to assist in public security and delivery of material relief. The central government offered each survivor ¥300 ($46 in an exchange rate of 6.5:1) and 15 kg of rice per month for three months. A state-owned construction company was assigned to build temporary housing for survivors and repair/rebuild public facilities like highways, schools, hospitals, police stations, and so forth. These quick and effective measures earned the central government great honor and trust, as survivors very often exclaimed "Thank the central government for helping us!" or "Thank our People's Liberation Army soldiers!" during our interviews.

Phase 1: Organizing the Community (July–December 2008)

In contrast, lower-level governments (primarily the Long Town government) seemed much less effective. First, they had to strictly follow policies made by upper-level governments due to the top-down centralized government in China. Second, the town government itself suffered severe losses in the earthquake: its office building was ruined and several officials injured. With no disaster management system, the weakened local government failed to launch effective relief measures of their own. Their major responsibility was to assist in implementing the upper government's policies such as collecting loss information, distributing aid, and communicating among aid agencies. The local government's ineffectiveness led to discontent and distrust among survivors who often complained in private gatherings observed by researchers.

NHP chose to assist Bai for three reasons. First, Bai was heavily stricken and thus in most need of assistance. Despite the central government's relief measures, the 1,200 or so earthquake survivors still experienced numerous difficulties, including aftershocks, public hygiene risks, shortage of shelter, unreliable food supply, and mental health challenges. About 400 seniors and children had no one to care for them. Deprived of all possessions, survivors had to share crowded tents with other families. Blocked transportation routes and closed stores limited survivors' access to food and other daily life supplies. About one fourth of the survivors left the town, frustrated with life there. Second, the town government welcomed NGOs, hoping that NGOs could help assuage survivors' grief and assist in community reconstruction. Third, one NGO had previously collaborated with the local primary school and developed good relations with government officials, teachers, and students.

Soon after arriving in Bai, NHP conducted a two-month participatory assessment that engaged about 90 survivors and ten neighborhood cadres (in other words, nearly one fifth of residents and all cadres remaining in Bai) to identify community needs, resources, and possible solutions. Focus groups, interviews, and surveys were conducted along with the application of popular PD instruments such as resource mapping, historical mapping, and SWOT analysis. This research found short-term primary needs – daily living supplies, child care, elderly health, public hygiene, and social life – and long-term needs including elderly care, housing, and employment. With limited fundraising capacity, NHP decided to focus on delivering services and fostering community organization rather than funding housing and public facilities. The decision was accepted by the resident participants appreciating that NHP had limited capacity in resource mobilization as staffed by volunteers and grassroots NGOs.

NHP then developed a three-step PD strategy by consulting some cadres and survivors: first, NHP would lead community recovery initiatives and meanwhile empower survivors; second, when community capacity grew, NHP would co-lead community initiatives; third, when the community was fully prepared, NHP would transfer all leadership responsibilities and exit.

The strategy was carefully communicated with all the survivors. Aware of NHP's commitment to helping them and its planned exit in the future, they proved to appreciate NHP's support, work closely with us, and seek to enhance their self-reliance during NHP's operations in Bai.

Following this PD strategy, NHP established a volunteer station to provide child care, public hygiene, elderly care, and daily living supplies for all 900 plus survivors in the first months after the earthquake. It recruited about ten volunteers to staff the station, who each served three to six months. The major activities included summer classes for children (such as painting, English, hand crafts), a temporary community bookroom, a tea house equipped with televisions and DVD players, and frequent visits to the elderly who had no offspring living nearby. Volunteers also took responsibility for disinfection and firefighting in public facilities. A great deal of relief materials were raised through NHP's social networks to help with survivors' daily needs. These efforts generated social space for residents to communicate with and help each other. Survivors often met at the community center and exchanged their post-disaster life experience and their viewpoints about reconstruction policies. Such efforts also enhanced their trust in NHP and engaged them in the community. For example, about 50 residents volunteered to assist the NHP staff in performing disinfection, helping maintain NHP's office utilities, and organizing neighborhood events. Some residents would show up to help without any recruitment.

NHP's staff was alert to political risks. They avoided public discussion of local government's failure in disaster recovery, investigation of earthquake loss, and religious issues, all of which were regarded as politically sensitive by the state (Lin 2012). Seeing that NHP's efforts helped meet survivors' needs and caused no trouble for them, the town government expressed their satisfaction with NHP, gave support when asked, and did not interfere with its projects.

Phase 2: Piloting Community Self-Governance (all of 2009)

Four months after the earthquake, the central government issued the Sichuan Earthquake Reconstruction Master Plan (State Council of PRC 2008b), including a ¥10 trillion investment in reconstruction over three years. State-owned media likened the earthquake response to a "war." The reconstruction policy emphasized centralized decision making, intensive investment of resources, and quick solutions. The state employed top-down planning and market intervention to fulfill its plan.

Governments of all levels created reconstruction plans focusing on land and natural resources, housing and public facilities, business and manufacturing, public service delivery, and the establishment of government and community organizations (State Council of PRC 2008a). But there were clear hierarchies of authority as the plans of lower-level governments were accountable to higher government levels. The reconstruction planning was thus also a process through which control over basic resource allocation was centralized upward.

A few months after the release of the Master Plan, the Long Town government, which was required to take the ultimate responsibility for the town's reconstruction, publicized its draft reconstruction plan. In this plan, the 900 or more current residents would be resettled to a nearby government-owned riverbank. The neighborhood's current land would be redeveloped into a business district to boost local tourism, consistent with a 2006 plan not yet implemented. Though the State Council required that the municipal or county government "should engage relevant institutions and experts and fully hear the opinions of earthquake-affected masses when making rehabilitation and reconstruction plans" (State Council of PRC 2008a), the township government bypassed the affected people during plan formulation, partly due to the three-year time frame of post-earthquake reconstruction set by the central government. It did not hold any public meetings or conduct any formal surveys to collect residents' opinions when developing the plan. The plan was posted on placards in the downtown and on the publicity columns at government buildings to allow for residents' comments. Little informed of the plan's details and the channels for feedback, survivors were in all practicality excluded from the planning process.

The government equipped their administrative instruments with legislative force by approving them through government-controlled legislation. For example, when some residents asked to rebuild their houses on their land that would be developed for the planned new business district, the mayor answered: "No, you cannot do that. The prerequisite of rebuilding houses is that you must observe the plan, this is, the downtown reconstruction plan … As long as your project matches it, the government will never stop you."

After the state reinforced its control of basic resources through top-down planning, it engaged the market to convert them into economic forces. The government employed market-oriented measures such as attracting private investors, giving interest subsidies and tax reductions for enterprises, and advancing the trading of land for construction (State Council of PRC 2008a). In Bai, the township government asked the construction firm to advance the expenses of building new housing and public facilities, guaranteeing they would repay the firm with proceeds from selling the neighborhood land. The next step would be to move the residents to the new location, and use the saved land to attract private investors. The state even conducted direct market interventions by setting quotas for producing construction materials and regulating prices to reduce survivors' financial burden in home rebuilding (Chengdu Municipal Government 2008).

As the government created the plan, the community was temporarily free from direct government control. This created room for NGO intervention in community recovery. Five months after the earthquake, survivors moved from tents to temporary housing built and allocated by the local government. NHP's volunteer station moved with them. The move marked the end of emergency relief and the beginning of temporary settlement as survivors had reliable access to electricity, transportation, health care, food, and shelter.

NHP shifted from providing services to empowering residents through three strategies. The first was promoting public services and the public sphere. With the assistance of neighborhood cadres and resident volunteers, NHP built a community center with a hall, training classroom, public shower room, tea house, community library, and internet café. Run by a team of NHP volunteers and residents, the center became a hub for residents' social life where they exercised, read, enjoyed entertainment, and made friends, with 20–40 visitors on an average day. Nearly 60 percent of all residents visited the center during its existence, and the center's services reached 80 percent of the community residents. The second strategy was advancing community organizations and volunteerism. NHP encouraged and funded residents to meet their needs in arts, culture, and community service by volunteering and establishing self-help groups. About 200 residents got involved in activities. Some residents launched public projects such as repairing the drainage system, reconstructing a trail, and establishing a dancing club. With NHP's managerial support, they established steering committees to manage projects, organize other residents to participate, and disclose financial information in the neighborhood. The third strategy was improving resident participation in decision making and enhancing government–resident communication. NHP had regular meetings with the town government to communicate residents' concerns and suggestions for improving survivor assistance and community reconstruction, and helped the community launch a regular assembly where all residents were encouraged to discuss public projects they needed, directly involving about 100 residents. Meanwhile, a special council composed of resident representatives, NHP representatives, and neighborhood cadres (elected by residents but affiliated to the government) was established to conduct the assembly's decisions. NHP also convened a community recovery conference in the town at the second anniversary of the earthquake with more than 80 representatives from survivors, NGOs, researchers, and local governments.

When residents' self-help and self-management abilities were well developed, NHP volunteers' roles shifted from service delivery to giving advice on developing a community agenda, mobilizing resources, organizing meetings, supervising finance management, and settling conflicts.

NHP's PD approach seemed very successful during this period. Waiting on the government reconstruction plan as standers-by, survivors otherwise actively participated in NHP's community empowerment strategy of self-help and self-management. NHP's success made it a model program in NGO circles and attracted numerous visitors from outside Bai. Knowing that other local governments in affected areas had expelled external NGOs and restricted local ones to prevent NGO-supported collective action that might conflict with governmental plans and deadlines for community reconstruction set by upper governments, NHP decided to avoid direct involvement in the planning process but focus on capacity building for survivors and community organizations. The township government in turn continued its support for NHP's projects. For example, government officials regularly communicated with NHP about survivors' needs, NHP's work plan, and long-term neighborhood recovery, attended NHP-hosted events, and even offered NHP free office space.

Phase 3: Confronting Community Politics (Early 2010–May 2012)

When the local government finished planning reconstruction and then rebuilding public facilities (such as highways, schools, and hospitals) in early 2010, it focused on housing for survivors. However, local government became entangled in a great deal of tension with survivors when it could no longer exclude them from decision making as they did in the planning process.

According to the plan, Bai survivors had to join the government-sponsored housing project or leave town. Leaving would net them only a small payment (￥25,000 for each household) from the central government. Joining the government project required an extra co-pay amount of ￥22,750–45,250 varying by house size, in addition to giving up the previous homestead land and the replacement allowance. But, because of the Property Law of 2007, the town government was required to obtain the homeowner's written consent before they could act on any private property. Many people, especially the elderly, did not want to move out of their bungalows to five-story buildings without elevators. They also thought they should get new domiciles for free as their current housing land was close to the downtown area and had high market value. But the town government, faced with the peaceful and timely rebuilding of affected neighborhoods required by upper governments, insisted on the conditions and urged neighborhood cadres to perform "ideological mobilization in the masses." Cadres then visited residents to persuade them to accept the government's proposal. An old woman described her experience in one interview:

> The *juweihui* [Residents' Committee] members and other cadres attended those governmental meetings on ideological mobilization. Sometimes when they came back, I asked what happened. They said, "I don't know. I was just asked to persuade you to accept the government's proposition, to fill out these forms, to give up your homestead land to save land (by constructing high buildings rather than bungalows). Your personal housing plan should give way to the governmental plan."

Considering that they had no money to independently rebuild their houses and that all the neighborhood land had been "planned" by the town government, many survivors accepted the plan. However, a dozen households in Bai refused to join the government-controlled reconstruction project and painted warnings on their damaged houses like "No moving my private property without consent." Some residents demanded the right to share profits from future land appreciation and organized several collective negotiations with the township government, though to no avail.

Conflict broke out when the town government sent two bulldozers to a street corner one night, intending to tear down some unoccupied damaged houses. About 20 residents living nearby noticed them and organized to prevent them from continuing. The next day, a dozen residents and one chief negotiator elected by them came to the local government and asked to negotiate with officials about how to finance the house rebuilding project. A representative said:

> Before the government and residents reach an agreement on house financing, the government cannot tear down those damaged houses. It may lead to "disharmony" [Note: a euphemism for resident protest] and do harm to both you and us. We think you should leave those houses intact. When the financial situation becomes better in the future, we request the government to provide our laid off workers with more patronage. Then we can remove them based on an agreement by both sides.

Although the action did not produce a more favorable solution for residents, it forced the town government to publicly acknowledge that their behavior was inappropriate and to promise that they would never do that again, in fear of more group protests by residents.

When the town government began implementing its survivor resettlement plan, NHP soon ran into internally and externally induced difficulties, making the third step of NPH's strategy, community-led recovery, almost impracticable. Internally, residents' self-management was still vulnerable without the NHP staff's presence. For example, during the 2010 Spring Festival NHP asked station volunteers to leave Bai to enjoy the holidays and transferred all remaining work to local residents. Almost all of the community center services then stopped due to poor coordination among resident volunteers. In addition, the principles of transparency and participation in decision making and finance management, which NHP had always exemplified and advocated through its community efforts, were not substantially adopted by neighborhood cadres or government officials. Resident influence was limited to the community center in which NHP was directly involved. Furthermore, with survivors' gradual return to a more normal everyday life, and with the start of government-sponsored reconstruction projects, resident participation in NHP's projects declined by 60 percent or more. Due to many members' absence, NHP could not convene the assembly and council as effectively as previously, which NHP had regarded as the stepping stone for community self-government.

Externally, the intensified conflict between the local government and survivors inevitably involved NHP. The survivors expected NHP to speak for their housing interests during their negotiation with the government, considering NHP's survivor-centered efforts in the community. But the government hoped NHP would persuade survivors to accept the government's proposal, or at least not support survivors. NHP finally chose to take a neutral position on housing reconstruction issues, based on NHP's risk assessment: supporting survivors risked NHP's relationship with the local government and consequently an immediate exile from Bai, like NGOs exiled in other earthquake-affected regions; but supporting the government could cost NHP its foothold in the community.

Other circumstances also prevented NHP from becoming more involved in the housing conflicts. For one thing, NHP had long suffered from internal challenges concerning funding, human resources, and legal status, which significantly damaged its performance in the community. Its initial funding was limited to private contributions collected through volunteers and their personal networks. During the second and third years NHP received grants of only around ￥800,000 from three foundations, which made it impossible to finance survivors' house rebuilding. Because of the funding shortage, NHP began as a volunteer organization staffed by volunteers and employees from founding organizations. Nearly one year later, it became able to hire two volunteer-turned-employees with foundation grants. But low salaries led to high staff turnover in the following two years.

Another difficulty was lack of an independent legal status. Because NHP was not a legal entity, local government could declare it illegal. To ensure NHP's legitimacy, four NGOs signed an agreement to entrust all legal affairs to one local partner that registered with the government. But this complicated decision making by multiplying communication costs among partners. To solve this problem, another partner mobilized its social network and registered NHP as an independent NGO (specifically, a private non-enterprise). Later, NHP established a supervisory committee consisting of representatives from the founder NGOs and formed a new work team staffed by full-time employees.

Realizing the impracticability of advancing community self-governance during neighborhood displacement, NHP then decided to step back to maintain basic service delivery but suspend community-organizing projects after communicating with cadres and residents. The purpose was to endure the displacement period, a politically sensitive period, and transfer its program to the rebuilt community in the future, when NHP could help residents reconstruct public life and reactivate community organizations to pursue sustainable development. The government appreciated NHP's decision and did not interfere in its projects. However, NHP still paid the price through a decline in survivors' trust that undermined its capacity in community organizing. A former employee commented (Zhu and Hu 2011: 18):

> In the past, we did not face the tension between residents and the government. Residents were most concerned about their new houses. When we avoided this problem, or told them that we were unable to give help, they said they understood our situation. But when they had more complaints against government (and were going to protest), they excluded us from their plans (considering our helplessness).

After the Bai neighborhood was relocated in early 2012, a bit behind the central government's schedule, the town government did not expect NHP to move with survivors to the new neighborhood. They seemed to fear that NHP's community efforts might encourage survivors in organizing against the government, as exhibited by their self-organized group negotiations during the displacement process. Officials found several excuses (saying, for instance, that Bai had limited office space and would have no staff to support NHP's work) to turn down NHP's proposal to launch new initiatives there. Instead, they invited NHP to work in neighboring communities where residents were more satisfied with the town government's reconstruction performance, and offered to continue their support as usual. Considering the challenging relationship with the government and the difficulty of raising money for its future work in Bai, NHP decided to withdraw from Bai after three and a half years of PD efforts in May 2012. This decision was communicated with residents who accepted it and showed their great gratitude for NHP's long-term service. Shortly after, the community center, resident assembly, and community council were dissolved. Only the dancing club remained active.

REFLECTIONS ON PARTICIPATORY DEVELOPMENT IN COMMUNITY RECONSTRUCTION

Rethinking Community and Participatory Development

This analysis shows that traditional PD theories confront a series of challenges in the context of a strong state like China. First, far from homogeneous and harmonious, Bai was fragmented by the rapid transition to a market economy. Though Bai has relatively clear geographic boundaries, the emigration of laid-off workers and influx of seasonal visitors/residents blurred community identity. Seasonal visitors, especially those who bought houses in the community, were usually middle-class people from cities and had little community participation. The earthquake further split the community through displacement, discriminatory subsidies based on household registration, and resettlement. Such internal divisions negatively affected the community's capacity to organize. In addition, rather than being isolated, the community was shaped by contextual changes. The market economy destroyed Bai's planned economy and created a community of laid-off workers. The rise of tourism in the early 2000s had improved employment and the local economy but was disrupted by the huge disaster of 2008. Residents' everyday lives were intertwined with the broader context, embodied in the high incidence of cell phone and internet use, social networks beyond the community, intervention by NGOs, connections with mass media, and involvement of private investors.

Second, the state as a whole remained a primary economic, political, and sociocultural force in the community. The Chinese strong state operates at the central, regional, and local levels (Oi 1995). Even in a centralized government system, the different levels allow for variation in administrative authority, interests, and policy preferences. This system of multiple levels with different interests created interstitial spaces for NGOs to operate in.

The central and local levels of the government played critical roles in Bai's response to the Sichuan earthquake. The central government took the lead in emergency relief and post-disaster reconstruction by developing policies and general plans, mobilizing resources, coordinating intergovernmental relations, and then later in funding and overseeing redevelopment. The local government, especially the town government, was in charge of specific community reconstruction projects at the neighborhood level. These functional differences influenced their different responses to civil society engagement in the three phases.

The state's unpreparedness for such a huge disaster opened space for volunteers and NGOs to provide emergency relief (Lin 2012), which was initially supported by both the central and local governments. The state's acceptance allowed NHP to create *invited space* (Gaventa 2004; Sinwell 2012) for civil society engagement. Mobilizing the invited space, NGOs such as NHP promoted the generation of "claimed space" in the temporary resettlement phase by organizing survivors to address community needs through collective action. But such claimed space was temporary, existing when the town government was preoccupied with reconstruction planning. It declined as the local government launched its reconstruction program, except for brief acts of resistance. Having recovered from the earthquake, the local government felt no more necessity for NGO support in meeting survivors' needs and instead faced the risk of uncontained community participation. The invited space for NGO engagement then narrowed. Some trusted NGOs were kept but limited to service delivery while others were exiled. The space of engagement might expand again after permanent resettlement due to the decline of earthquake-related political risks and the needs of long-term community redevelopment.

Similar to its role in local economic development, the local government was important in determining the space of civil society engagement. With only some basic central government policies regulating NGOs, local governments had discretion in determining whether and to what extent NGOs could engage in community reconstruction. Local government needed community members' participation during the recovery phase, as it was unable to meet all the needs on its own. NGOs provided the capacity and infrastructure to engage and coordinate community participation. However, the specific forms of participation and their effectiveness were dependent on power relations among the actors: government, NGOs, and community (Cornwall 2002; Gaventa 2004; Sneddon and Fox 2007).

This and other research about NGO participation in locale-based social service provision (e.g., Teets 2013; Yang 2001) show potential for participatory governance in China where the strong state has developed decentralization institutions especially in the domains of economic development and public services even while maintaining the centralized political system (Oi 1992, 1995). However, the missing critical precondition (Heller 2001) is a well-developed civil society capable of participating in local governance, voicing community needs, and nurturing participation among grassroots organizations and individuals. The NHP example showcased this weakness, echoing what is found in extant literature (e.g., Spires 2011; Teets 2009). Additionally, the Chinese strong state is structured so that accountability derives from upper levels of government rather than from the citizenry. So participatory governance cannot function as it does in the democratic states, in terms of interest representation and decision making (Heller 2001). Rather than becoming institutionalized, Chinese NGO participation is still subject to change in government policy, as seen in the fluctuating NGO sector after the Sichuan earthquake (Kang 2018).

Suggestions for Practicing Participatory Development

This case shows that, under specific conditions, aspects of PD and its related formulas such as participatory governance have the potential for transformative change in a strong state context at the community level. There are three ways that NGOs can tap this potential.

First, NGOs can identify and take advantage of opportunities for expanded invited space to institutionalize community participation. Invited space can be created when the strong state is temporarily weakened or distracted by external events such as disasters, public service crises, or new policy initiatives that require local state restructuring and may show the benefit of inviting NGOs into local governance (Fung and Wright 2001; Sinwell 2012). The challenge is to then widen and regularize the invited space which is still dominated by the government. One way to do this is for NGOs to adopt a consultative partnership with the local government as it has the advantage of supporting the expansion of relatively autonomous civil society in an authoritarian state without seeming to threaten general state control (Teets 2013).

The Bai case shows that a consultative partnership where the government acted as leader, and NGOs as facilitators, is possible in a strong state context. In this partnership, NGOs play three roles. One role they can play is *social service provider* to compensate for government gaps in providing for the public good. The community services organized by NHP were significant in meeting earthquake survivors' various needs in public health, child care, elderly care, culture, and education. A second role they can fill is *facilitator of dialogue*. NGOs can improve communications between government and community by assessing community needs and collecting residents' viewpoints, organizing multilateral dialogues, and developing public events that can reduce misunderstanding and improve trust. NHP, for example, convened policy forums that brought together government officials and earthquake survivors to exchange their concerns and ideas concerning community recovery. NHP also had regular meetings with the town government to communicate NHP's observations and suggestions for improving government practice in the community. A third role the NGOs can fill is *facilitator of resident organization*. As most resident organizations are not fully developed, they have difficulty expressing collective opinions and organizing collective actions. NGOs can support their capacity building in terms of research, internal management, and communicating skills. For example, NHP facilitated the establishment of several community organizations like the dancing club, the community council, and a financial management committee.

The strong state's (especially the local state's) political will to accept power sharing is the precondition for this consultative partnership (see Gibson and Woolcock 2008). It is possible to nurture this will in a strong state by understanding the limits created by a strong state structure. For one thing, the increasingly rationalized government will accept civil society engagement in local governance when it sees advantages such as cost efficiency and accountability sharing (Salamon 1995) and does not see the engagement as undermining the state's legitimacy (Spires 2011; Teets 2013). Additionally, the state–civil society partnership can be strengthened and institutionalized as partners build trust in locale-based practice (Teets 2009).

A second way NGOs can tap this potential is by incorporating development intervention into the community's everyday life and promoting community leadership. A typical PD project aims at outputs rather than impact. This output-oriented mode often allows for only superficial participation, creates dependence on development agencies, and increases inequality (Guo 2010; Lyons et al. 2001). Instead, NGOs can engage more with residents' civic life to promote active and representative participation and enhance the leadership capacity of community members. For example, NGOs can organize residents to design and implement projects to ensure that they are practical, understandable, and appropriate for residents' needs, just as NHP did in Bai. NHP also established a local NGO and other voluntary associations that were based in the community and served community members.

The third way is to improve civil society capacity by enhancing partnerships among civil society actors. NGOs, community organizations, independent media, and other voluntary associations need to partner with each other to form a more collaborative and autonomous third sector. In NHP's case, local NGOs developed close partnerships with outside NGOs for collecting resources and recruiting volunteers, kept frequent contact with local media to promote NHP's projects, fostered community organizations, and even attempted to collaborate with social enterprises to boost the local economy. Strong civil society partnerships can support consultative partnerships with government that can expand participatory governance (Gaventa 2004; Heller 2001). However, we know little about how to effectively enhance partnerships within the civil society in a strong state context where the state exerts discriminative control over civil society organizations (Kang and Han 2008) and thus sets obstacles to cross-organizational partnership.

Lessons Learned about the PAR Practice

This study also reveals the dynamics of conducting PAR in a community reconstruction setting. First, the partnership structure (and behind the partnership the power relations) in PAR varied in different reconstruction phases. During emergency relief, NHP partnered with survivors, neighborhood cadres, and town officials for the common objective of meeting survivors' pressing and basic needs. When temporary resettlement began, government officials moved to be peripheral in the partnership by shifting to emphasize social stability and reconstruction planning. Some cadres who were earthquake survivors stayed in the partnership but also worked closely with government officials. In the neighborhood relocation phase, survivors become half-detached from their partnership with NHP, realizing the limited help they could receive from the relationship in terms of their primary concern of house rebuilding. This fluidity of partnership often broached the questions for researchers during the PAR process: Who were "we" as the subject of collaborative inquiry? With whom should we work in the community? And for whom? Action researchers had to reassess and readjust partnership strategy in different phases until the termination of the partnership.

Second, power relationships are at the center of PAR (Greenwood and Levin 2007) for they define both the social problem and the solution to it. As the community reconstruction unfolded, the power relationships in the community changed. The government was not the only holder of power. NHP had power due to its professional capacity and external connections. Usually regarded as powerless, survivors also could build power by learning about change making together with NHP and taking collective actions, as seen in group protests and public goods provision. Thus, participatory action researchers should be aware of the power dynamics in the community to which they are subject and adapt their problem identification and solution development accordingly.

Third, being a core part of PAR, research should keep in balance with action. In addition to working closely with local participants in community action, researchers need to document both the investigative processes and conclusions in sufficient detail so that other interested parties can also evaluate them for the sake of research validity (Greenwood and Levin 2007). NHP exemplified an integration of PAR in the PD practice. Information management was made a top priority in NHP, which received wide support from internal and external research participants such as NGO professionals, volunteers, survivors, and cadres. In addition to the participatory needs assessment, NHP also engaged all major stakeholders in conducting two mid-term evaluations and a final program evaluation to find program outcomes, challenges, and lessons learned and to track the change sought. Admittedly, however, the co-generation of knowledge primarily relied on the NHP staff due to the fluidity of partnership with other stakeholders. That may lead to bias in knowledge production and constrain knowledge sharing.

There should be wide use of PAR in PD programs. As demonstrated in the NHP case, PAR can enhance community practice by bringing NGOs and local stakeholders together to make community change, by empowering local stakeholders (particularly the vulnerable groups), and by combining action and reflection for continual community improvements. It also contributes to knowledge production by linking community practice with a broader social context and energizing the ongoing dialogue between practice and theory (Greenwood and Levin 2007). NGOs and their grantmakers should invest more in the building of research capacity in NGO professionals, better integrate research activities in PD programs to support well-informed action and reflection, and improve the communication of practice-based knowledge through partnerships with academia, media, government, and other stakeholders.

CONCLUSIONS

Through a four-year combined PAR and PD process of community reconstruction in an earthquake-stricken neighborhood in west China, this research finds that, different from their traditional counterparts, China's modern communities are greatly impacted by external social processes such as urbanization, marketization, and state control. In the context of a strong state, both development agencies and communities can be marginalized while the state dominates community development. However, this state-directed community development model still makes room for the growth of real community participation owing to the state's inability to practice absolute control in a disaster context and its need for administrative effectiveness and legitimacy. Finally, this study offers suggestions for NGOs in using PD in a strong state context in addition to its lessons about conducting PAR.

ACKNOWLEDGMENTS

I thank Randy Stoecker for his thoughtful suggestions and very helpful editorial support. I also thank Jiangang Zhu, Constance Flanagan, and Larry Stillman: the chapter benefited from my discussions with them.

NOTE

1. *jijinhui* is a non-profit organization that uses donated assets to undertake charitable or social welfare causes typically by making grants. *shehui tuanti* is another type of non-profit organization that is composed of individual and/or organizational members for a joint purpose. The third type of non-profit organization, *minban feiqiye*, provides social services but is not membership-based and usually makes no grant. See Ma (2006) about their similarities and differences in detail.

REFERENCES

Atack, Iain. 1999. "Four Criteria of Development NGO Legitimacy." *World Development* 27: 855–864.
Botes, Lucius and Dingie Van Rensburg. 2000. "Community Participation in Development: Nine Plagues and Twelve Commandments." *Community Development Journal* 35: 41–58.
Bratton, Michael. 1989. "The Politics of Government–NGO Relations in Africa." *World Development* 17: 569–587.
Bray, David. 2006. "Building 'Community': New Strategies of Governance in Urban China." *Economy and Society 35*(4): 530–549.
Brydon-Miller, Mary. 1997. "Participatory Action Research: Psychology and Social Change." *Social Issues* 53: 657–666.
Burde, Dana. 2004. "Weak State, Strong Community? Promoting Community Participation in Post-Conflict Countries." *Current Issues in Comparative Education* 6: 73–87.

Chambers, Robert. 1983. *Rural Development: Putting the First Last*. Harlow: Longman.

Chambers, Robert. 1994. "Participatory Rural Appraisal (PRA): Analysis of Experience." *World Development* 22: 1253–1268.

Chengdu Municipal Government. 2008. *Guanyu jiakuai zaihou chengxiang zhufang chongjian gongzuo de shishi yijian [Measures for Accelerating House Reconstruction in Disaster-Affected Areas]*. Chengdu.

Clarke, Gerard. 1998. "Non-Governmental Organizations (NGOs) and Politics in the Developing World." *Political Studies* 46(1): 36–52.

Cockburn, Cynthia. 1977. *The Local State: Management of Cities and People*. London: Pluto Press.

Cornwall, Andrea. 2002. "Locating Citizen Participation." *IDS Bulletin* 33(2): 49–58.

Crewe, Emma and Elizabeth Harrison. 1998. *Whose Development?* London: Zed Books.

Fine, Ben. 1999. "The Developmental State Is Dead-Long Live Social Capital?" *Development and Change* 30: 1–19.

Fung, Archon and Erik Olin Wright. 2001. "Deepening Democracy: Innovations in Empowered Participatory Governance." *Politics and Society* 29(1): 5–41.

Gaventa, John. 2004. "Towards Participatory Governance: Assessing the Transformative Possibilities." In *Participation: From Tyranny to Transformation? Exploring New Approaches to Participation in Development*, edited by Samuel Hickey and Giles Mohan. London: Zed Books, pp. 25–41.

Gelling, Leslie and Carol Munn-Giddings. 2011. "Ethical Review of Action Research: The Challenges for Researchers and Research Ethics Committees." *Research Ethics* 7: 100–106.

Gibson, Christopher and Michael Woolcock. 2008. "Empowerment, Deliberative Development, and Local-Level Politics in Indonesia: Participatory Projects as a Source of Countervailing Power." *Studies in Comparative International Development* 43: 151–180.

Gottdiener, Mark. 1987. *The Decline of Urban Politics: Political Theory and the Crisis of the Local State*, Volume 30. Thousand Oaks, CA: Sage.

Green, Maia. 2000. "Participatory Development and the Appropriation of Agency in Southern Tanzania." *Critique of Anthropology* 20: 67–89.

Greenwood, Davydd J. and Morten Levin. 2007. *Introduction to Action Research: Social Research for Social Change*. Thousand Oaks, CA: Sage.

Guo, Zhanfeng. 2010. "zouchu canyushi fazhan de biaoxiang [Beyond the Surface of Participatory Development]." *Open Times* 28: 130–139.

Hanlon, Querine. 2011. *State Actors in the 21st Century Security Environment*. National Strategy Information Center.

Heller, Patrick. 2001. "Moving the State: The Politics of Democratic Decentralization in Kerala, South Africa, and Porto Alegre." *Politics and Society* 29(1): 131–163.

Hickey, Sam and Giles Mohan. 2005. "Relocating Participation within a Radical Politics of Development." *Development and Change* 36(2): 237–262.

Huang, Chien- Chung, Deng Guosheng, Wang Zhengyao, and Richard L. Edwards, eds. 2013. *China's Nonprofit Sector: Progress and Challenges*. New Brunswick, NJ: Transaction Publishers.

Jütting, Johannes, Elena Corsi, Celine Kauffmann, Ida McDonnell, Holger Osterrieder, Nicolas Pinaud, and Lucia Wegner. 2005. "What Makes Decentralisation in Developing Countries Pro-Poor?" *European Journal of Development Research* 17(4): 626–648.

Kang, Xiaoguang. 2018. "Moving toward Neo-Totalitarianism: A Political-Sociological Analysis of the Administrative Policies in the Chinese Nonprofit Sector." *Nonprofit Policy Forum*. https://doi.org/10.1515/npf-2017-0026

Kang, Xiaoguang and Han Heng. 2008. "Graduated Controls: The State–Society Relationship in Contemporary China." *Modern China* 34: 36–55.

Kapoor, Ilan. 2002. "The Devil's in the Theory: A Critical Assessment of Robert Chambers' Work on Participatory Development." *Third World Quarterly* 23(1): 101–117.

Kesby, Mike. 2005. "Retheorizing Empowerment-through-Participation as a Performance in Space: Beyond Tyranny to Transformation." *Signs* 30: 2037–2065.

Korten, David C. 1987. "Third Generation NGO Strategies: A Key to People-Centered Development." *World Development* 15: 145–159.

Lin, Thung-hong. 2012. "The Politics of Reconstruction: A Comparative Study of Earthquake Relief Efforts in China and Taiw." *Taiwan She Hui Xue Kan* 50: 57–110.

Lyons, Michal, Carin Smuts, and Anthea Stephens. 2001. "The Changing Role of the State in Participatory Development: From the Reconstruction and Development Program to Growth, Employment and Redistribution." *Community Development Journal* 36: 273–288.

Ma, Qiusha. 2006. *Non-Governmental Organizations in Contemporary China: Paving the Way to Civil Society?* New York: Routledge.

Maguire, Patricia. 1987. *Doing Participatory Research: A Feminist Approach.* Boston, MA: University of Massachusetts Center for International Education.

Mansuri, Ghazala and Vijayendra Rao. 2004. "Community-Based and-Driven Development: A Critical Review." *World Bank Research Observer* 19: 1–39.

Midgley, James. 1986. "Introduction: Social Development, the State, and Participation." In *Community Participation, Social Development and the State*, edited by Anthony Hall, Margaret Hardiman, and Dhanpaul Narine. London: Methuen, pp. 1–11.

Mohan, Giles and Kristian Stokke. 2000. "Participatory Development and Empowerment: The Dangers of Localism." *Third World Quarterly* 21: 247–268.

Nelson, Nici and Susan Wright. 1995. *Power and Participatory Development: Theory and Practice.* London: Intermediate Technology Publications.

Nelson, Paul. 1995. *The World Bank and Non-Governmental Organizations: The Limits of Apolitical Development.* London: Macmillan.

O'Mathúna, Dónal P. 2010. Conducting Research in the Aftermath of Disasters: Ethical Considerations. *Journal of Evidence-Based Medicine*, 3(2): 65–75.

Oi, Jean. C. 1992. "Fiscal Reform and the Economic Foundations of Local State Corporatism in China." *World Politics* 45(1): 99–126.

Oi, Jean C. 1995. "The Role of the Local State in China's Transitional Economy." *The China Quarterly* 144: 1132–1149.

Puplampu, Korbla P. and Wisdom J. Tettey. 2000. "State–NGO Relations in an Era of Globalisation: The Implications for Agricultural Development in Africa." *Review of African Political Economy* 27(84): 251–272.

Salamon, Lester M. 1995. *Partners in Public Service: Government–Nonprofit Relations in the Modern Welfare State.* Baltimore, MD: Johns Hopkins University Press.

Sinwell, Luke. 2012. "Transformative Left-Wing Parties' and Grassroots Organizations: Unpacking the Politics of 'Top-Down' and 'Bottom-Up' Development." *Geoforum* 43(2): 190–198.

Sneddon, Chris and Coleen Fox. 2007. "Power, Development, and Institutional Change: Participatory Governance in the Lower Mekong Basin." *World Development* 35(12): 2161–2181.

Spires, Anthony J. 2011. "Contingent Symbiosis and Civil Society in an Authoritarian State: Understanding the Survival of China's Grassroots NGOs." *American Journal of Sociology* 117: 1–45.

State Council of PRC. 2008a. *Wenchuan dizhen zaihou huifu chongjian tiaoli [Regulations on Post-Wenchuan Earthquake Rehabilitation and Reconstruction].* www.lawinfochina.com/display .aspx?lib=lawandid=6851andCGid

State Council of PRC. 2008b. *Wenchuan dizhen zaihou huifu chongjian zongti guihua [The Sichuan Earthquake Reconstruction Master Plan].* www.gov.cn/zwgk/2008-06/09/content_1010710.htm

Teets, Jessica C. 2009. "Post-Earthquake Relief and Reconstruction Efforts: The Emergence of Civil Society in China?" *The China Quarterly* 198: 330–347.

Teets, Jessica C. 2013. "Let Many Civil Societies Bloom: The Rise of Consultative Authoritarianism in China." *The China Quarterly* 213: 19–38.

Williams, Glyn. 2004. "Evaluating Participatory Development: Tyranny, Power and (Re)Politicization." *Third World Quarterly* 25: 557–578.

World Bank. 2000. *The World Development Report 2000: Attacking Poverty.* Washington, DC and Oxford: World Bank and Oxford University Press.

Yan, Miu Chung and Gao Jianguo. 2005. "Social Engineering of Community Building: Examination of Policy Process and Characteristics of Community Construction in China." *Community Development Journal* 42(2): 222–236.

Yang, Tuan. 2001. "Tuijin shequ gonggong fuwu de jingyan yanjiu: daoru xinzhidu yinsu de liangzhong fangshi [An Empirical Study of Enhancing Community-Based Public Service: Two Fashions to Introduce New Institutional Factors]." *Guanli Shijie* 4: 24–35.

Yang, Xiaoliu. 2010. "Canyushi fupin de zhongguo shijian he xueshu fansi [Reflection on Participatory Poverty Reduction Practice in China]." *Si Xiang Zhan Xian* 36: 103–107.

Zanotti, Laura. 2010. "Cacophonies of Aid, Failed State Building and NGOs in Haiti: Setting the Stage for Disaster, Envisioning the Future." *Third World Quarterly* 31: 755–771.

Zhu, Jiangang and Hu Ming. 2011. "Duoyuan gongzhi: dui zaihou shequ chongjian zhong canyushi fazhan lilun de fansi [Pluralistic Governance: Reflecting on Participatory Development Theory in Post-Disaster Community Reconstruction]." *Kaifang Shidai* 10: 5–25.

17. Tracing power from within: learning from participatory action research and community development projects in food systems during the COVID-19 pandemic

Laura Jessee Livingston

Starting in spring 2020, COVID-19 spread across the United States, causing disruptions in many systems including the educational and agricultural systems. The spread of COVID-19 shaped the way we interact with each other and with our food systems. Community-engaged projects, whether research- or development-oriented, faced novel obstacles and opportunities. Community-engaged projects in food systems faced additional strain, as COVID-19 laid bare inadequacies in the food system. Consumers saw changes in food availability, farmers pivoted from selling to restaurants to farmers' markets, and marginalized communities faced the greatest hurdles in accessing healthy and affordable food. Academic researchers navigated university protocols for travel and gatherings. In this chapter, I investigate how COVID-19 shaped community-engaged projects by interviewing community and university members from two community-engaged projects in the upper Midwest.

WHAT IS A FOOD SYSTEM?

The food system is broad and complex; community-engaged projects in food systems span across disciplines and address environmental, social, and economic issues. The food system includes food production, processing, the distribution of, and access to food (Phillips and Wharton 2016). Environmental drivers, such as climate, water, and soil, and socioeconomic drivers such as demographics, culture, and economy shape the food system (Ericksen 2008).

Community-engaged food systems projects address many issues, such as climate change, social inequality, and environmental degradation. The cases for this chapter include collaborations around economic and social systems as well as farming systems. Although the cases focus on different areas of the food system, both community-engaged projects are working towards supporting local and regional food systems and community-engaged agriculture.

To frame the community-engaged projects I will cover in this chapter, I have outlined the history of participatory action research (PAR) and community development (CD) in food systems.

Participatory Action Research in Food Systems

The positivist paradigm dominated early food system research, directly informing research practice as the dominant theory of knowledge. The positivist paradigm, which originated in the Enlightenment period, asserts the existence of one absolute physical-material reality from which there are no variations (Patton 1980). Chambers (1983) notes the unequal privileging of modern scientific knowledge over traditional ecological knowledge and lived experience. Agricultural researchers presumed knowledge to flow in one direction, which serves to strengthen and reproduce power relations (Foucault and Gordon 1980). Epistemologically, positivists see researchers as independent from the subject being studied and aim to reduce bias and subjectivity in research. Ritzer and Gindoff (1992) argued that positivist arguments privilege scientific methods and knowledge too strongly, reducing the relevance of local context and ignoring a systems approach to understanding complex problems (Šūmane et al. 2018).

Over time, food systems research developed into a multiparadigm field incorporating disciplinarily distinct epistemologies that incorporate and interrogate political, cultural, social, and contextual aspects of the food system. Constructivist, interpretivist, and critical scholars see reality as relative, multiple, and socially constructed. Epistemologically, these scholars rely on the relationship between the researcher and the phenomena, and the inquiry process is subjective and interactive. Additionally, context (sociopolitical, environmental, and economic) impacts research outcomes. They view the values of investigators as shaping and influencing research, as values shape what researchers define as a problem and how they choose to investigate it (Stocking 1993).

As epistemologies broadened, researchers realized that the complexity and uncertainty of real-world problems in food systems required the knowledge and perspectives of stakeholders outside of academia (Pretty 1995) and PAR evolved within the academic field. As a methodological approach, PAR seeks to generate liberating knowledge that is rooted in popular knowledge (Fals-Borda and Rahman 1991). This popular knowledge is used to inform social change and increase political power.

In food systems research, PAR began with the questioning of extension and non-farmer-led training systems to modernize agricultural systems (Freire 1970). In the 1980s, food systems researchers began involving stakeholders in research design and participation (Bruges and Smith 2007). From the mid-1990s onward, PAR in food systems became more institutionalized, although not uniformly across research institutions. PAR has been used in agriculture to promote technological change while improving ecological sustainability of farming systems (Chambers 1994a, 1994b).

PAR still makes up a small portion of food systems research, with traditional or non-participatory research dominating the field, and it faces challenges in combining the depth of participatory approaches achievable at a small scale with the necessary outreach needed to include as many stakeholders as possible to make change within food systems (Neef et al. 2013). In their 2001 book, *Participation: The New Tyranny?*, Cooke and Kothari (2001) compile and build on critiques of participatory practices, specifically the concept that participation is unequivocally good. The authors suggest that participation, while often masked in liberation rhetoric, can actually maintain existing power relationships. Other authors have outlined challenges to participatory processes in PAR, including different levels of participation from stakeholders, issues of power imbalances, and requiring sometimes impractical levels of resources and time from participants (Bentley 1994; Selener 1997; Voinov and Bousquet 2010). These critiques reaffirm the importance of being attuned to and addressing power differentials during the PAR process.

Through the critiques, PAR has flourished in sustainable food systems and agricultural research (Bruges and Smith 2007), where farmers, farm workers, and other members of the food system provide local wisdom and drive research questions. Bruges and Smith (2007) note that the contextually complex nature of sustainable food systems research requires locally specific and participatory research methods. A bottom-up approach to food systems research allows for the integration of local knowledge into the research process (Fraser et al. 2006; Montoya and Kent 2011). Badstue et al. (2012) recommend that food systems researchers help identify solutions to problems that influence participants' livelihoods and collaboratively share and learn specialist knowledge with participants throughout the research process.

Community Development in Food Systems

CD has a longer history within the food system than PAR. CD is both a process and an outcome, evolving from social action around tenement housing and infrastructure improvement within the Progressive Movement of the late 1800s. Originating as a transdisciplinary process, CD historically has been more community-led and interdisciplinary than traditional food systems research projects. Contemporary practitioners draw on models like those of Freire (1970) and Fals-Borda and Rahman (1991), opposing "top-down" approaches of institutions and instead promoting power sharing and incorporating perspectives of those impacted in decision-making processes. Phillips and Pittman (2015: 6) define the process as "developing and enhancing the ability to act collectively" and the outcome as "taking collective action and the results of that action." In CD projects, community members define, analyze, and address their own problems (Warner and Hansi 1987).

Although CD can deal with physical and economic development, it also focuses on the soft side of development – issues of equity and other social dimensions – and relies on the resources and knowledge of community members (Phillips and Pittman 2015). Similar to PAR, authors have critiqued how power is operationalized in collective processes and how local knowledge is valued. Cooke and Kothari's (2001) critical view of participation can also be applied to CD. The authors question the degree to which these participatory methods enact change or benefit participants. Furthermore, Cooke and Kothari (2001) note the dominance of funders and institutions within CD and the suppression of local power differentials. To address these critiques, Mosse (2001) and Cleaver (2001) argue that CD practitioners must attend to the social relationships which develop local knowledge and power differentials.

CD and food systems connect deeply around improving community well-being and sustainable livelihoods. CD practitioners work in rural and urban food systems and their work can be applied broadly to both small- and large-scale activities. In food systems, CD issues may center around issues of food production, including land use and access and statewide funding for conservation practices. On the consumption end of the food system, CD initiatives may address issues of food access and food justice. Additionally, CD projects address priorities around labor and food distribution.

There are many examples of food systems CD. As early as 1860, farmers organized a farmers' institute movement, so they could learn from each other (FAO 2017). The first Community Support Agricultural program began in the 1960s when Japanese women, who were concerned with the increase in imported foods, asked local farmers to grow vegetables and fruit for them. Farmers in turn agreed, but only if the families committed themselves to supporting the farmers for a full season (Van En 1995). These types of community-driven collaborative CD projects have elements of social interactions and civic empowerment (Phillips and Pittman 2015). Such projects connect individuals and groups, creating social networks of reciprocity and trustworthiness, known as social capital (Putnam 2000).

Universities have played a role in CD in food systems, with efforts as early as the nineteenth century when President Theodore Roosevelt's Country Life Commission urged land grant colleges to play a more active role in the development of rural communities (Summers 1996). The Morrill Act of 1862 established land grant colleges on 10.7 million acres taken from nearly 350 indigenous nations through more than 160 violence-backed land cessions.[1] This appropriation of indigenous land allowed states to create and fund colleges of agriculture and the mechanic arts. The Country Life Commission also urged for the establishment of a national extension workforce to provide agricultural resources and knowledge to stakeholders in each state. Before the national extension workforce was established, Booker T. Washington, founder of the Tuskegee Institute, traveled to communities of black farmers with "A Moveable School" called the "Jesup Wagon" taking an innovative and community-based approach to improving local food systems in 1906 (James 1971). Nearly a decade later, the Cooperative Extension service was created as a joint endeavor of the United States Department of Agriculture and state land grant colleges with matching federal and state funding through the Smith-Lever Act of 1914. Even at the fundamental stages of Cooperative Extension white voices and farmers were centered, whereas black farmers were actively discriminated against (Harris 2008) and Extension activities with Indigenous farmers focused on assimilation to European farming practices (Brewer and Stock 2015). By the 1950s, the University of Missouri had created one of the first CD programs for rural development. CD continued to grow, with more than 60 colleges and universities offering majors in CD (Cary 1976). Land grant universities carry out CD extension work, however, federal support for these programs has not been consistent (Rasmussen 1989).

Currently, many CD projects work toward building community-based sustainable food systems, connecting regional food production and CD. CD projects rely on networks to engage citizens in political participation and social change (Putnam 2000). Similar to PAR in many ways, CD networks build social capital and address community concerns. However, there is little discussion in the literature about the relationships between collaborations that engage with both CD and PAR, and especially how those collaborations were impacted by the COVID-19 pandemic.

COVID-19 PANDEMIC AND IMPACT ON COMMUNITY ENGAGEMENT

The disruptions caused by the COVID-19 pandemic may have dramatically shifted power and participation in PAR and CD. Reardon et al. (2009), Bolin and Stanford (1998), and Mashiko et al. (2018) have all documented participatory efforts in planning and development after a disaster occurred, but we do not yet have studies on what happens to PAR and CD during COVID-19, when communities faced extreme disruption and uncertainty. As the rippling effects of COVID-19 have evidenced, systemic shock through disasters that both create and lay bare vulnerabilities in our food system (Bande 2020; International Panel of Experts on Sustainable Food Systems 2020; Poppick 2020) and people have shown great creativity and agency in addressing these vulnerabilities. Understanding how systemic shocks impact relationships and power relations is important, as collaborators will have to consider a greater range of shock events when planning future community-engaged projects in food systems.

Systemic shocks, or disasters, are widespread and severe events causing disruptions in regional and global systems. Examples of systemic shocks include weather-related shocks (Rosenzweig et al. 2002), nuclear war (Helfand 2013), and epidemics (McCloskey et al. 2014). Future uncertainty and disturbances could destabilize various aspects of our regional and global systems, likely impacting community-engaged projects into the future. PAR and CD in food systems are vulnerable to these systemic shocks, as even localized disruptions to the food system can have sizable impacts (Bailey et al. 2015). Even before the 2020 COVID-19 pandemic, we were living in a period of environmental change with considerable instability and uncertainty.

REFLEXIVITY STATEMENT

I experienced the impacts of COVID-19 on my community-engaged research projects first-hand, which inspired this inquiry. I began my community-based food systems research at the University of Wisconsin-Madison in 2018 aiming to learn from my community partners and co-create participatory evaluation tools that could be used to improve agricultural education programming and address systemic and cultural inequalities. I partnered with three agricultural education programs: the Wisconsin Organic Vegetable Farm Manager Apprenticeship Program, Gompers Grows, and MoringaConnect.

When COVID-19 spread across the United States during 2020, I watched firsthand as each participatory evaluation took a different path. I worked with Gompers Grows, a food systems education program at Gompers Elementary in Madison, Wisconsin, to begin co-piloting participatory evaluation tools during March 2020 in the classrooms. As the school district closed due to COVID-19, we pivoted to create "Gompers Grows Kits" to meet the priorities of the families during the pandemic. Community members voiced other priorities as a response to food insecurity during the pandemic, causing us to pause the initial Gompers Grows participatory evaluation. My second case study was with MoringaConnect, a social enterprise supporting Moringa farmers in Ghana. My community partners at MoringaConnect and I have postponed the participatory evaluation until international travel is allowed. MoringaConnect partners did not have the capacity or desire to conduct the evaluation virtually. My final partnership was with the Organic Farm Manager Apprenticeship Program in Wisconsin. This also stalled due to the demands on the staff members who were supporting farmers to learn about online and reduced-contact direct marketing, labor and personal safety, government support programs, and liability issues during the pandemic. The diversity of impacts from COVID-19 led me to wonder how community-based research projects are structured and how relationships and power relations may allow for projects to continue and adapt while others stall during times of systemic shock.

METHODOLOGY

Institutional Ethnography

While some qualitative research focuses on studying people or systems from an institutional perspective, I would like to understand how institutional and power relations shape practices and norms of practice from the standpoint of people within PAR and CD projects. By doing this, I am asserting that people are the experts of their lived experience and that the research process should start from the perspective of these partners. Institutional ethnography (IE) is an ideal method for this approach, as IE offers opportunities for finely grained and situated understandings of institutional processes.

IE is a critical theory, research strategy, and methodology, focusing on people's everyday lives and how their lives are organized and coordinated by institutional forces (Campbell and Gregor 2004; Smith 1987, 2005; Taber 2010). Dorothy Smith first discussed this "feminist research strategy" in her 1987 book, *The Everyday World as Problematic: A Feminist Sociology*. Smith (2005) created IE as an alternative to the objectified subject of knowledge centered in social science discourse. She contrasts IE with "mainstream sociology" by noting that IE does not reify or posit social theory as existing over and above people. Smith (2005) states that an ontological and epistemological paradigm shift is required to understand that knowledge is an extension of ordinary ways in which we know in our everyday world.

IE studies reveal how power is built into the way institutions are organized to accomplish particular goals, as opposed to the individuals who do the organizational work (Foucault 1978), and material conditions that inform how and what people can produce (Marx and Engels 1932). In this chapter, I detail how power is built into participatory research and development projects and how COVID-19 reinforced and/or changed these power structures. By understanding people's everyday experiences, I trace where partners experience changes in power during the spread of the pandemic. Using a multicase approach, I compare how relationships and power relations shaped the ways that PAR and CD partnerships changed as a result of COVID-19 in two distinct case studies using multicase IE as the framework and method for inquiry. Each case, or partnership, creates a window from a different angle into the generalizing ruling relations that shape collaborative work.

Methods

I recruited informants through disciplinary specific listservs and by using snowball sampling procedures to form a "networking sample" (Werner and Schoepfle 1987). Using dimensional selection (Arnold 1970), I chose informants who were collaborating on projects with both academic and community participants. I selected projects with principal investigators (PIs) from both within and outside of academia (i.e. graduate student, post-doctoral student, faculty member, community member, etc.). For the purpose of this chapter, I will discuss one project led by a community member and one project led by a faculty member.

I drew data for the two cases analyzed in this chapter from 12 interviews conducted over Zoom video conferencing with seven informants. These individuals included a restaurant owner, a farmer, an independent plant breeder, a faculty member, a research staff member, a chef, and a graduate student. I used open-ended questions to collaboratively explore power relations within and beyond the project partnerships during each 60–90-minute interview.

Each informant played a different role in these collaborations and provided a unique standpoint to understand the impacts of COVID-19 in community-engaged work. I also observed one virtual project meeting per research group, taking deidentified notes on how participation was actualized. I asked each group to provide institutional forms or texts, including grant applications, sub-award agreements, university-sanctioned paperwork, and material transfer documents. I analyzed these documents by mapping how these forms connected to the informants reported actions and decisions.

While analyzing these various sources of data, I used specific techniques to embed data in the local context. Categorizing or counting events, themes, and languages can distort and obscure the relations at the core of the IE approach (Campbell and Gregor 2004). I used mapping, indexing, and writing accounts in my analysis. While indexing, I organized data into linked practices to support an analytic view into the institution. I also mapped power relations to bring a visual coherence to my findings (Rankin 2017). By mapping and indexing, I cross-referenced across cases while continuing to highlight particularities from each case. Writing an account entails selecting an instance of activity from the IE data and describing how it is socially organized (Rankin 2017). This reassembling of data relies less on reinterpretation from an outsider theoretical frame (Smith 2005). These techniques were used to produce the below cases and analysis.

CASES

In this chapter, I will discuss two cases of collaborative projects in food systems taking place in the upper Midwest during the spread of COVID-19. Each of these collaborations has elements of PAR and CD, though the scale and scope of those elements varies dramatically. In one project, the PI is a faculty member at a public research institution in a medium-sized city and in the other, the PI is a restaurant owner in a rural town. The project with a faculty PI has been collaborating for over six years, while the community-led collaboration began because of the food system impacts of COVID-19.

Participatory Research with Farmers: Farm to Table Initiative

The Farm to Table Initiative (FTI) started as a conversation between one chef and two university researchers about breeding vegetables for other characteristics besides productivity, including flavor. Inspired by this first conversation in 2015, Marie,[2] at the time an untenured professor, grew a program that would come to incorporate hundreds of stakeholders, including farmers, plant breeders, seed companies, university researchers, and chefs. This collaborative project is rooted in the idea that academic research in plant breeding should be informed and shaped by people in all positions of the food system. Located in a medium-sized city in the upper Midwest, the FTI meets the unique needs of farmers cultivating organic vegetables in a climate different from the coastal environments where their seeds are produced. Using a PAR approach, collaborators in this initiative share a commitment to meeting the priorities of local food systems by producing food sustainably. Marie and a staff researcher, Kye, grew this network through conversations at conferences and other events and by plugging into established participatory trials at the university.

In a typical year, the program collects data on vegetable varieties through on-farm trials by farmers and through research station trials by students and researchers. Farmers and university researchers (including undergraduate, graduate, faculty, and research staff) plant seeds of different vegetable varieties and measure their productivity as well as disease and pest presence. Farmers also send photographs and provide qualitative details about markets and overall variety performance. Although research design is primarily driven by the university team, other stakeholders make decisions that shape the trials. Participating seed companies and plant breeders decide which seeds to provide for the variety trials. Farmers select which classes they would like to trial and ultimately decide what varieties from those market classes they will plant for the season. For example, Casey, an independent tomato breeder, selects tomatoes with specific flavors and genes of interest to trial.

Marie and her research team of staff and students trial more varieties than any one farmer and they communicate what market classes (cucumbers, tomatoes, melon, squash, etc.) are available for trialing each year. Marie's team also conducts tasting panels within the lab, on campus, with the public, and with local chefs. Data from this collaboration are made public on the lab's website. Farmers, plant breeders, and chefs utilize these data to make decisions about what they grow and who they might want to collaborate with from the FTI network.

In addition to university-led research, farmers and plant breeders are reading literature reviews and applying for funding for their own independent research trials based on their priorities and interests. For example, Katya, a diversified vegetable farmer, trials carrots on her farm to address unpredictability in the seed market. Varieties of vegetables that she likes to grow may not be sold in future years because of disease or pest pressure in the regions where the seeds are grown (which is not often in the Midwest). Some of these community partner-led research projects influence the direction for FTI research questions and priorities. Kye and Katya have written grants together about issues they have identified in the food and seed system. Different collaborators in the project – including farmers, seed companies, chefs, and university researchers – collaborate on other research and production projects sparked by FTI. Furthermore, some of the farmers generate more frequent and specific data on their own trials than the research team expects from farmers participating in FTI.

Consistent in-person and remote communication is required to maintain this collaboration. Marie, Kye, and graduate students send emails and call farmers to learn their priorities, what vegetables they would like to trial, challenges they face during the season, and recommendations for improvements to the program. Marie also communicates remotely with seed companies and independent breeders to learn about their priorities and what seeds they would like to provide for the trials. As the project grows, Marie hopes to utilize app-based communication to streamline communication and data collection. Noting a tension in the process Marie states,

> The more you streamline it, the less personalized it becomes, and the less committed people are to something that they don't feel like they have a personal connection to. So I don't want to streamline it too much, but I do need to make it more efficient so that I can actually get the data back to people in time to have it make a difference.

During the current trialing phase of this app, Katya (farmer) and Casey (plant breeder) noted the difficulty of using the phone-based app with limited broadband connection and the preference towards relationship-based communication in collaborative projects.

The current FTI model works as a spoke and hub, with the university remaining central in the communication and decision-making process, facilitating the participation of over 100 stakeholders. Prior to the pandemic, Marie and her research team hosted meetings and field days in multiple locations across the state to engage with farmers, chefs, plant breeders, and seed companies to set priorities and make changes to the overall structure and activities of FTI. Marie and Kye also hosted conference sessions and roundtables to learn the priorities of farmers and guide future vegetable trials. All the informants from the FTI program spoke to the importance of the informal and generative conversations that are elicited during farm visits and conferences.

Once the communication and priorities have been aligned and organized, Marie, Kye, as well as other staff and students aggregate seed orders and send the seeds to farmers. Under Marie's guidance, the research team starts seedlings in their greenhouses and farmers do the same with the facilities they have available to them. Additionally, Marie and Kye train farmers in how to plant randomized trials and how to observe their crops. After the varieties are planted in the field, the farmers and research team generate data. The research team generates more robust and frequent data than is expected from the farmers. Farmers report back data through a phone-based app or by Excel spreadsheets. At the end of the season, Marie analyzes the data and makes them accessible to others in the collaboration through their website and by direct email.

Challenges for the Farm to Table Initiative

This large collaboration has not always been smooth sailing. In the early days Marie faced several bureaucratic challenges. When applying to the Institutional Review Board (IRB), she had difficulty explaining the collaborative approach and the roles that chefs and farmers in particular play in the research. For example, the IRB suggested that if farmers and chefs were considered co-researchers, they should also take the Collaborative Institutional Training Initiative training (required for conducting research with human subjects), although the data they were generating were not about human subjects. Additionally, as the program grew, administrators became concerned about seed distribution and requested that each farmer sign a Materials Transfer Agreement form for each variety they were growing, which would be onerous for both the farmers and the research team. Two other more senior faculty members outside of this collaborative successfully advocated for this requirement to be waived, as it was not normally required for on-farm trials. This led to reduced paperwork which helped to increase farmer participation.

With those two barriers resolved, Marie identified paying community partners as the largest bureaucratic barrier. In order to be compensated for their time and expertise, farmers, seed companies, and chefs must provide invoices and W-9s. The processing time can be extensive with many farms, and often draws questions from administrative staff higher up in the university administration who are not familiar with the program, which leads to a greater administrative load on department and program staff.

COVID-19 impacts on the Farm to Table Initiative

With the spread of COVID-19, the types of work and who was able to work changed dramatically. In mid-March 2020, when the university campus closed to undergraduates, the research team had not completed packing and sending seeds to farmer participants. Marie spoke about the rush:

> Which meant that Kye, the lab manager, and I spent like 18-hour days finishing that. The lab manager, I think, pulled more than one all-nighter. I remember coming into my office at like four in the morning. I was trying to get an early start on the day, and I found this note in the box and it's like "I finished this off, I didn't send an email because I didn't want you to see the timestamp."

The university put a hold on research processes conducted by students or employees on or off campus. To request research permissions, the university required Marie to submit individual travel request forms for each staff member and for each location they were traveling to as well as an extensive adapted Continuity of Operations Plan.

Marie followed these guidelines and after conversations with administrative and research staff, submitted requests to continue only about 25 percent of the research station trials – primarily projects that supported graduate student graduation timelines and avoided loss of genetic material or long-term project data. But importantly, as the on-farm trial varieties were already sent out, 100 percent of the on-farm trials received the materials to start their trials. Marie communicated with stakeholders via email and phone calls about the changes to the FTI research process. She also created organization and communication protocols for these research processes.

Katya reported that she was understaffed on her farm and faced challenges such as navigating new markets and ensuring that their families and staff members could live and work safely. Although challenged by the COVID-19 pandemic in a myriad of ways, Katya continued to conduct FTI research and her own independent research projects. Casey also continued his breeding projects and research independent of FTI. He noted barriers, like losing access to a shared greenhouse for starting seedlings, but research was not as stalled as with his university partners. Seed companies were impacted by an increased demand for seeds at both a commercial and recreational level. However, they had already provided seeds to the SKC trial before the spread of COVID-19 closed the university campus.

Although the on-farm trials were able to start, the farmers' response rate fell from 60–70 percent on an average year to 50 percent. Marie, Kye, and other research team members were not able to visit farms or host field days, which is where researchers build relationships with other stakeholders and informally generate collaborative research ideas. This engagement is important for all members of the collaborative team, with Katya reporting that she was more likely to return data on projects where she had a personal connection: "Those relationships are really important for how I put in effort, like how I think about those relationships too has to do with how much I also get back from them." Kye also noted:

> That's something that I really miss. Just being able to have those, those very open-ended conversations with farmers and to have the opportunity to look beyond that specific piece of work that we decided to do together and see what else is happening on the farm. And make those associations you might not make until you are actually there, taking it all in and seeing the farm as a system ... You, you get to see the, the equipment that they have, the machinery that they're using. And you get to know people as persons a little bit as, as people.

Fortunately, more transactional communication systems, email, and phone calls were already in place to sustain the functioning of the collaboration.

The pandemic was not the only reason for reduced participation. Katya noted that the difficulty in participation in the research process came from the difficulty of reporting the data using the data-reporting app while she worked in the field because of her limited access to broadband. Marie recognizes this limitation and provides spreadsheets for trial participants to enter data. Yet data aggregation is still a barrier for Katya, who said, "I meticulously collect my data and then I don't want to type it into a sheet because that is the worst." Casey also noted the difficulty of using app-based reporting systems, although to a lesser degree than Katya.

COVID-19 also impacted the tasting component of the collaboration dramatically. Marie cancelled all chef-tasting and public-tasting events. Marie notes the tension she felt with maintaining communication with chefs who were greatly impacted by the pandemic and her desire to sustain their relationship, stating "I also don't want them to feel like they're pressured to do something that they really don't have time to do. But I need to get back in touch with them relatively soon because I also don't want them to think that OK, things are complicated, and [the university] just disappears." Marie and Kye both mentioned the desire to not burden stakeholders with research activities during the spread of COVID-19. Although the chef and public tastings were put on hold, Marie and her research team adapted crew-tasting protocols to allow for remote tastings. This transition used an online survey platform licensed by the university which saved time in data collection, yet required additional labor for preparing and transporting individualized trays.

Once the 2020 growing season ended, Marie aggregated and analyzed data, although there was less data than in previous years. Marie and Kye also organized virtual conference presentations and roundtables to continue engaging with stakeholders. Many farmers attended these virtual events, yet there was less opportunity for informal conversations and relationship building than during in-person conferences.

Community Development in Food Systems: Community Food Hub

When COVID-19 spread, disruptions in the supply chain impacted the food system dramatically. Andrew co-owns a farm-to-table restaurant and community venue with his wife in a small city in the Midwest. Together they source food and beverages from local farmers, producers, and secondary food processors (cheese makers, breweries, etc.). When COVID-19 started to spread in the state, Andrew cancelled events and paused all restaurant activities due to the uncertainty of how people transmit COVID-19 and his desire not to be a vector in his community. He decided to close the restaurant in the early hours of the morning while tossing in his bed after working at the restaurant. His decision was based on a gut feeling – there had been no state- or county-wide mandates to close restaurants at that point. Andrew communicated with his staff in the morning, announced the closure on social media, and put up a sign on the door of the restaurant.

Andrew and Elise quickly recognized the community need for accessible, local food. Within one day of closing the restaurant they pivoted their farm-to-table restaurant to a farm-to-grocery and no-contact delivery operation. The owners saw multiple needs within their community from the spread of COVID-19, including (1) a need for farmers to shift markets as institutions closed, (2) a need for people to safely purchase food, and (3) a need for local employment. Within a day of closing the restaurant, Andrew designed a website for food ordering. Utilizing their previously established network of local farms, Andrew purchased smaller packaged quantities of food and posted these options on the website. Prior to the pandemic, the restaurant sourced 75 percent of their food from farms or local secondary distributors. Andrew packed orders in boxes from their restaurants and delivered them in his own car. Over 30 people placed orders during the first week of the restaurant's pivot and within a month

Andrew received over 150 orders per week. As the number of orders grew, the number of local farms and secondary processors that he sourced from also grew.

As Andrew and Elise were adapting their restaurant to meet community priorities, they also began applying for funding to sustain this pivot. Andrew decided to apply for a federal grant program that supports local food businesses. To increase their credibility in the grant award process, they invited a current employee and doctoral student to join their collaboration. Andrew met Charlie overseas in 2013. In fact, it was Andrew who first told Charlie about the master's program at the university where she is pursuing her PhD. Throughout her studies, Charlie has worked at Andrew's restaurant. She had taken the first steps in her dissertation project with farmers in another state when the pandemic started and decided to pause that project until the impact of the pandemic was more certain. As the pandemic wore on, Charlie kept her out-of-state research on hold, even as her academic advisors advised her to try virtual engagement.

Andrew recruited Charlie to join the Community Food Hub (CFH) project during the grant-writing process. She agreed to join this project during the pandemic partially because of the positive relationship she had with Andrew and Elise. Her role in the project, as outlined in the grant proposal, is to lead educational and outreach events and evaluate the grant activities and overall goals. She plans to use the data from this collaboration to write her dissertation instead of her out-of-state collaborative project. Underscoring the importance of relationships, Charlie said, "I think something could have come out of it even with the pandemic happening if I had had the relationships in place first and I just didn't feel like I had that [with the out-of-state research project]."

The specific funding program that the CFH team applied to does not fund research. Andrew and Charlie had to be very explicit in the grant application about her role and her outreach and evaluation contributions. Additionally, they worked closely with grant administrators and the university to separate Charlie's role as a project evaluator from her unfunded dissertation research. Andrew and Charlie also included Charlie's advisor on the academic team. Additionally, Andrew sought out a collaboration with a local videography team and included two other employees from his restaurant. The team also included a farm, which left the partnership during the grant-writing process, with the final number of collaborators totaling eight.

Andrew led the communication between the collaborators during the grant-writing process meeting with the academic team. Towards the beginning of the grant-writing process, most of the communication happened via email. However, Andrew also met with the academic team virtually and with the videography team and employees in-person following CDC guidelines. Andrew would listen to the collaborators, glean ideas from their conversations, and then piece the ideas together for the collaborators to provide feedback. The videography team had less experience with writing grants. With experience in grant writing through his master's degree and prior job experience, Andrew coached them through the sub-award and budget creation process. The academic team (Charlie and her advisor) utilized university resources, such as administrative staff and sub-award templates. These resources are not without a cost: the university requires payment in the form of indirect grant costs, calculated at 55–55.5 percent as Modified Total Direct Costs for federal grants. This equated to 28.38 percent of the university sub-award while there was no indirect cost for the videography team sub-award.

The funder awarded the CFH team a sizable grant in the fall of 2020 with the university and videography teams written into the grant as sub-awardees. The academic partners also created a Memorandum of Understanding to solidify the expectations of both parties. The eight collaborators take a decentralized approach to decision making within their project. On the academic side, Charlie and her advisor wrote and submitted the IRB application for the research and evaluation component of the grant.

While the CFH team is not hosting in-person events to engage community members, Andrew asks Charlie to support and assess community engagement virtually. These activities include auditing the farm-to-table purchases to assess what percentage of restaurant purchasing comes directly from their local community. She will use this data as an evaluative starting point and share content on a community-facing blog. Charlie also creates education and outreach content for the restaurant's website including interactive maps. Utilizing surveys and interviews, Charlie collects data on whether these educational and outreach initiatives are impacting how community members interact with their food system, including whether they are purchasing more local food or supporting farm-to-table establishments. This data collection has multiple purposes. Andrew and Elise will use the evaluative data to make iterative programmatic decisions and guide future CD initiatives. In her dissertation, Charlie will include this data in an ethnographic inquiry on how resiliency and community are actualized in food systems.

The videography team produces video content featuring farmers and local food programming for the restaurant website and focuses on telling the narrative of the restaurant and the local food system as a part of their education and outreach strategy. These products (blog posts, videos) are sent back and forth by email to get feedback from other team members. During 2020 and early into 2021, the restaurant team worked to expand their market and purchase food from local farmers and sell directly to local consumers either through pick-up or delivery, although the number of deliveries has decreased substantially over the past year. Monthly virtual meetings provide space for the team to talk over their shared goals and objectives.

Challenges to the Community Food Hub
The largest barriers to this project are the rigidity and lack of communication from the funder. With issues related to COVID-19, the funding program provided limited communication and had significant delays in invoice payments. As a small restaurant and business owner during the pandemic, the delays in funding were a dire situation as Andrew's restaurant was paying salaries for members of the academic and videography teams. Andrew spends time communicating with the funding staff and working on the administrative components of the grant. The change in demand in grocery deliveries has been slightly problematic for the collaborative team, as the grant they were awarded requires meticulous measurement of where and how funds were spent while allowing for little deviation from the awarded proposal. With the rigidity of the grant funding, Andrew noted that they cannot pivot as quickly as they could to meet changing community needs and priorities. He described his frustration, "It's like, oh, we have to do all this paperwork just to change one staff member. Where normally as a business you can be like, all right, we're going to have you do something different than what you'd normally do, or you don't have to jump through a bunch of hoops to make any tiny change." Although still in the beginning stages of their three-year grant, this barrier looms large.

Andrew also acknowledged the lack of informal conversations and relationship building because of virtual collaboration. He specifically mentioned a reduction in creativity, "Like we're in a meeting right now, we have to be formal. Before and after you get all that informal, kind of jazzier time when there is more creativity or interesting conversations." Charlie also noticed this tension, stating that with in-person collaboration, "I feel like I would feel maybe more part of the community. I already do to some extent because I worked there. But it would be more like I was not just coming in, like Zooming in from the university."

ANALYSIS

These two community-engaged projects provide a lens to analyze the institutional forces and power relations of collaborative projects in food systems during the COVID-19 pandemic. The spread of COVID-19 laid bare the inequities in our systems and the relationships that sustain new and old initiatives.

Relational Practices

Relational practices are foundational for building trust and creating shared research goals. Interviewees from the two projects described relational practice as including being present and listening to informal discussions between farmers at conferences, touring farmers' fields, and holding informal discussions over a meal or drink after a meeting. This type of work is not often compensated in grants, rewarded through tenure, or accounted for in institutionally imposed timelines, yet it was described as vital in both the FTI and CFH cases. Both projects reported a reduction in ability to engage in relational practices during COVID-19, either because of travel or gathering restrictions.

No matter what stage a project was in, whether a few months into conception or seven years, researchers and community partners noted the decrease in lingering post-meeting conversations and moments of shared experiences during the pandemic. Interviewees noted that these moments in between the research allow for us to recognize the humanity of collaboration partners, be innovative and expansive with research and development ideas, and build trust to navigate difficult moments. Yet, for both projects, collaborators relied on already established relationships to continue activities despite the spread of COVID-19 and limits on in-person farm visits, meetings, field days, and other events where relational practices are likely to occur.

University and Community-Led Initiatives

For the FTI project, the initial conversations were between faculty, farmers, and chefs, yet the project itself has been university-led. In comparison, CFH was a community-led project that invited university partners to join. This difference was reflected in how projects responded to COVID-19. Although the spread of COVID-19 temporarily stalled typical restaurant and event activities, CFH responded dynamically and adapted quickly to meet community priorities as the food system was impacted by COVID-19, utilizing community resources and networks. As the research component is secondary to the CD goals, the CFH project responded to community priorities that were not research-based.

The university-led project, FTI, maintained participatory research processes, but faced more insurmountable challenges to research work as university resources such as research stations and undergraduate labor became less accessible. Additionally, farmer, chef, and other stakeholder priorities shifted during the pandemic, decreasing the overall stakeholder participation in FTI research processes and overwhelmingly reducing overall participation of chefs in the collaboration. FTI's primary objective is to generate data with stakeholders and therefore was not equipped to support the emerging needs of stakeholders due to COVID-19. Marie, the faculty lead for FTI, also had to obtain approval of research processes and steps through the university for research projects to continue. However, CFH makes decisions about project activities through discussions within the project team. The power to decide what project activities can continue ultimately exists within the PI of CFH whereas with FTI the power lies in the hands of the university administrators. This lack of control is a potential weakness in university-led collaborative projects, especially during disruptive moments like the COVID-19 pandemic.

Integration of Community Development and Participatory Action Research

The level of integration of CD and PAR varied within these projects. For the CFH, the collaboration began with CD to meet community needs and priorities during the pandemic, while the research for CFH is defined and shaped by the CD action. The research component was integrated into the project to understand the impact and effectiveness of the CD. This connectedness allows for CFH to take a nimble approach to addressing pertinent issues in the food system caused by COVID-19 utilizing both CD and PAR approaches. As the CD component adapts to community needs, Charlie is able to shift the evaluative research questions following the lead of the CD action.

FTI utilizes a very participatory research model. But, in contrast to CFH, the research goals drive the collaboration. The CD component is a result of the connections formed through the research and relational activities offered by FTI. These relationships bolstered the success of PAR during the pandemic, yet the FTI was not able to be as nimble as CFH because of the emphasis on research goals. The action component of FTI is limited to the decision individuals in the collective make based on the data analysis and experience in the trials. The action is not only more individualized, but it is also dependent on the research component. FTI's model of collaboration was in part shaped by the institutional forces of the university. Marie's university tenure committee approved her tenure because of the large research network she created and the quantities of data that farmers contributed, along with her more traditional research station vegetable trials. Marie noted that her tenure-mentoring committee had cautioned her against participatory data collection, let alone developing CD components or emphasizing action in PAR. The constraints of the tenure process narrowly define what a successful collaboration looks like, which limits what can be accomplished during times of disruption like the COVID-19 pandemic.

Project Scale

FTI started with a grassroots approach. But as the number of participants in FTI grew, the project became more of a spoke-and-hub model to manage large-scale participation and data collection. Katya described the difference between the early stages where she had more influence over the varieties and seeds she received, to now where FTI acts more "like a machine" to allow for increased farmer participation and data generation. Marie also noted that she was less able to spend time building new or sustaining old relationships as the project grew. Institutionally, faculty conducting applied research are expected to have large data sets and are warned against participatory research because of the potential for having fewer data points. Multiple informants highlighted the tension between growing research projects to meet university tenure evaluation standards and maintaining relational practices that are vital to community engagement.

The larger size decreased opportunities for relational practices. The more campus-centered, hub-and-spoke model succeeded during COVID-19 because farmers took the initiative to continue generating and reporting data while university-led research faced different institutional challenges. Because FTI already utilizes community assets, like farmer knowledge and fields, they continued generating data during the spread of COVID-19. With the research station trials stalled by COVID-19, the bulk of the FTI data came from the farmers and their on-farm trials. This highlights a strength of this PAR approach compared to primarily research station-based trials and exemplifies how decentralization of research activities can strengthen project resiliency during instability.

Although CFH is not nearly as large as FTI, the CFH team has grown over the COVID-19 pandemic. CFH initially began as an individual business engaging in CD to support themselves and their community. As they applied for funding, they invited academic and videography partners into the grant-writing process and the project team doubled in size. Andrew, the project lead, continues to act as the central point of communication, which works for their eight-person team. Andrew's management style allows for the three teams (restaurant, videography, and academic) to maintain autonomy of their specific projects while capitalizing on their unique strengths in community organizing, video creation, and data generation. However, the largest obstacle in expanding the project came when they were awarded a federal grant.

Funding

Andrew and his team applied for the federal funding because of the COVID-19 pandemic, seeing this as an opportunity to expand their CD initiatives and add a PAR component. This funding allowed CFH to officially bring on the videography and academic teams into the project and expand their project goals. When writing the grant, Andrew cited their use of "agile management" with monthly development cycles to allow for iterative improvements and adjustments to the different components of the project. However, their specific funder fiercely audits expenditures and grant activities. This oversight reduced CFH's ability to be nimble and react to changes in the food system and community priorities during the continued spread of COVID-19. Although customers' purchasing patterns have changed during the pandemic, they have not been altering grant activities for fear of the time and effort to have those changes approved.

FTI is funded by Marie's university appointment and through various grants supporting different components and extensions of the project. Similar to CFH, FTI's grants require FTI faculty and staff to certify effort and deliver grant outcomes. Marie pays a small part (10 percent) of Kye's salary through unrestricted funding from her department and has a fee-for-service account which can be used more flexibly to support Kye's grant-writing and relational practices. This flexibility allows for Kye to commit time to relationship building. However, Marie noted that with the negative economic impacts of COVID-19 on the university, this flexible funding could be cut for the next fiscal year which could negatively impact the FTI team's ability to build and sustain relationships. Even with the current flexibility afforded by this funding structure, Marie notes that she and her research staff are often working more than 40 hours a week to incorporate and improve relational practices in addition to other funder expectations as required grant deliverables tend to focus on quantitative metrics.

DISCUSSION

These issues of power, relationships, and participation in academia are not novel. However, understanding how they impact collaborative projects during times of uncertainty and change is. CFH began as a CD initiative and added a PAR component to meet their goals. They pivoted to meet community priorities and needs during the COVID-19 pandemic but this adaptability has been slowed by inflexible funding restrictions. FTI had a stronger PAR component and limited CD. Stakeholders continued to generate research during the pandemic because of the strength of the participatory approach.

Yet, both projects faced barriers. In CFH the largest barriers were due to issues with funding. FTI's barriers were institutional and related to scale. Scaling up projects is important for addressing watershed-level or regional food systems issues. To sustain project growth, scaling up should also mean scaling out, forging partnerships with organizations outside of the university. Partnering with other organizations may also foster opportunities for CD initiatives that complement or guide PAR goals. Universities and funders should see and reward the strength of collaborations that incorporate community assets. Tenure and promotion committees should place equal value on CD components of collaborative projects. Projects that incorporate both PAR and CD can be more resilient to systemic shocks by not relying as heavily on one institution or university's resources or relying on PAR to the detriment of CD.

There are ways that collaborators from PAR and CD projects can mitigate the impacts of systemic shocks. These cases underscore the importance of relationship building during the early stages of project development and sustaining relationships that can withstand disturbances like the COVID-19 pandemic. Furthermore, when applying for funding opportunities, applicants should write in relational practices as grant activities, highlight prior relational practices, and justify funding for relational practices within the grant proposal. It is also important to critically think about which partner, whether university or community, applies for the funding. Especially for novice researchers or researchers with limited-term positions, it might be advantageous to join community-led projects that align with one's research interests, as these projects have the advantage of building on community assets and priorities.

During times of systemic shock, collaborations should adapt their priorities and mechanisms to support participation and maintain relevance to stakeholders. With larger collaborations, this type of maneuvering will be difficult. Additionally, altering priorities can be more difficult during different times of the year, like during farming season or after receiving grant funding. Integrating a strong CD component in the foundations of a collaborative PAR project could allow for more dynamic responses to systemic shocks.

From both cases, we can see the importance of relational practices and flexible funding during times of disturbance and reactive stability. COVID-19 also made visible gaps in the PAR approach. The large, research-oriented models of collaboration privileged by academic tenure and promotion processes may not be as adaptable as projects guided by CD goals. Universities and funders should support collaborative projects during times of disruption by recognizing both financially and institutionally the importance of relational practices and CD before disruptions take place. The outputs of CD-guided projects will be different than PAR-led projects, and this difference should be accounted for in tenure and promotion committees and graduate school program graduation requirements. Funders and research departments should also allow for flexibility and fund CD approaches so collaborative projects can adapt to changing contexts over time. By changing the institutional and funding requirements along with departmental evaluation criteria, academic collaborations will be more resilient to pandemic-sized shocks and smaller disruptions to local systems.

NOTES

1. In the last decade, the idyllic narrative of the 1862 Morrill Act has been disrupted by activists and scholars who have laid bare the exploitative origins of higher education (Lee and Ahtone 2020). To learn more visit the Land Grab Universities project website: https://www.landgrabu.org/.
2. All names are pseudonyms.

REFERENCES

Arnold, David O. 1970. "Dimensional Sampling: An Approach for Studying a Small Number of Cases." *American Sociologist* 5: 147–150.

Badstue, A. Lone B., Jon Hellin, and Julien Berthaud. 2012. "Re-Orienting Participatory Plant Breeding for Wider Impact." *African Journal of Agricultural Research* 7(4): 523–533.

Bailey, Rob, Tim G. Benton, Andrew J. Challinor, Joshua Elliott, David I. Gustafson, Bradley Hiller, … and D.H. Wuebbles. 2015. "Extreme Weather and Resilience of the Global Food System." Synthesis report from the Global Food Security Taskforce. www.researchgate.net/publication/281029049 _Extreme_weather_and_resilience_of_the_global_food_system_-_Synthesis_Report

Bande, Tijjani Muhammad. 2020. "The Impact of COVID-19 on Global Food Security and Nutrition: Preventing a Health Crisis from Becoming a Food Crisis." General Assembly of the United Nations. www.un.org/pga/74/2020/04/17/the-impact-of-covid-19-on-global-food-security-and-nutrition -preventing-a-health-crisis-from-becoming-a-food-crisis/

Bentley, Jeffrey W. 1994. "Facts, Fantasies, and Failures of Farmer Participatory Research." *Agriculture and Human Values* 11: 140–150.

Bolin, R. and L. Stanford. 1998. "The Northridge Earthquake: Community-Based Approaches to Unmet Recovery Needs." *Disasters* 22(1): 21–38.

Brewer, Joseph P. and Paul V. Stock. 2015. "Beyond Extension: Strengthening the Federally Recognized Tribal Extension Program (FRTEP)." *Journal of Agriculture, Food Systems, and Community Development*, 6(3): 91–102.

Bruges, Murray and Willie Smith. 2007. "Participatory Approaches for Sustainable Agriculture: A Contradiction in Terms?" *Agriculture and Human Values* 25(1): 13–23.

Campbell, Marie Louise and Frances Mary Gregor. 2004. *Mapping Social Relations: A Primer in Doing Institutional Ethnography*. Lanham, MD: Rowman Altamira.

Cary, Lee J. 1976. *Community Development Education and Training Programs throughout the World*. Colombia, MO: Community Development Society.

Chambers, Robert. 1983. *Rural Development: Putting the Last First*. New York: Longman.

Chambers, Robert. 1994a. "Participatory Rural Appraisal (PRA): Challenges, Potentials and Paradigm." *World Development, Elsevier*, 22(10): 1437–1454.

Chambers, Robert. 1994b. "Participatory Rural Appraisal (PRA): Analysis of Experience." *World Development, Elsevier*, 22(9): 1253–1268.

Cleaver, Frances. 2001. "Institutions, Agency, and the Limitations of Participatory Approach to Development." In *Participation: The New Tyranny?*, edited by Cooke, Bill, and Uma Kothari. London: Zed Books, pp. 36–55.

Cooke, Bill and Uma Kothari. 2001. *Participation: The New Tyranny?* London: Zed Books.

Ericksen, Polly J. 2008. "Conceptualizing Food Systems for Global Environmental Change Research." *Global Environmental Change* 18(1): 234–245.

Fals-Borda, Orlando and Mohammad Anisur Rahman. 1991. *Action and Knowledge: Breaking the Monopoly with Participatory Action Research*. London: Intermediate Technology Publications.

FAO, ed. 2017. *Leveraging Food Systems for Inclusive Rural Transformation*. Rome: Food and Agriculture Organization of the United Nations.

Foucault, Michel. 1978. *The History of Sexuality*. New York: Vintage.

Foucault, Michel and Colin Gordon. 1980. *Power/Knowledge: Selected Interviews and Other Writings, 1972–1977*. New York: Pantheon Books.

Fraser, Evan D.G., Andrew J. Dougill, Warren E. Mabee, Mark Reed, and Patrick McAlpine. 2006. "Bottom up and Top down: Analysis of Participatory Processes for Sustainability Indicator Identification as a Pathway to Community Empowerment and Sustainable Environmental Management." *Journal of Environmental Management* 78(2): 114–127.

Freire, Pablo. 1970. *Pedagogy of the Oppressed*. New York: Continuum.

Harris, Carmen V. 2008. "'The Extension Service Is Not an Integration Agency': The Idea of Race in the Cooperative Extension Service." *Agricultural History* 82(2): 193–219.

Helfand, Ira. 2013. "Nuclear Famine: Two Billion People at Risk." International Physicians for the Prevention of Nuclear War. www.ippnw.org/pdf/nuclear-famine-two-billion-at-risk2013.pdf

International Panel of Experts on Sustainable Food Systems. 2020. "COVID-19 and the Crisis in Food Systems: Symptoms, Causes and Potential Solutions." www.ipes-food.org/_img/upload/files/COVID -19_CommuniqueEN.pdf

James, Felix. 1971. "The Tuskegee Institute Movable School, 1906–1923." *Agricultural History* 45(3): 201–209.

Lee, Robert and Tristan Ahtone. 2020. "Land-Grab Universities." *High Country News*. www.hcn.org/ issues/52.4/indigenous-affairs-education-land-grab-universities

Marx, Karl and Friedrich Engels. 1932. *The German Ideology*. London: Lawrence & Wishart.

Mashiko, Tomoyuki, Monia Guarino, Gianfranco Franz, and Shigeru Satoh. 2018. "Collaborative Planning for Post-Disaster Reconstruction in Italy: Community Participation in Four Small Towns, Focusing on Novi Di Modena." *International Planning History Society Proceedings* 18(1).

McCloskey, Brian, Osman Dar, Alimuddin Zumla, and David L. Heymann. 2014. "Emerging Infectious Diseases and Pandemic Potential: Status Quo and Reducing Risk of Global Spread." *The Lancet: Infectious Diseases* 14(10): 1001–1010.

Montoya, Michael J. and Erin E. Kent. 2011. "Dialogical Action: Moving from Community-Based to Community-Driven Participatory Research." *Qualitative Health Research* 21(7): 1000–1011.

Mosse, David. 2001. "'People's Knowledge', Participation, and Patronage: Operations and Representations in Rural Development." In *Participation: The New Tyranny?*, edited by Bill Cooke and Uma Kothari. London: Zed Books, pp. 16–35.

Neef, Andreas, Benchaphun Ekasingh, Rupert Friederichsen, Nicolas Becu, Melvin Lippe, Chapika Sangkapitux, Oliver Frör, Varaporn Punyawadee, Iven Schad, Pakakrong M. Williams, Pepijn Schreinemachers, Dieter Neubert, Franz Heidhues, Georg Cadisch, Nguyen The Dang, Phrek Gypmantasiri, and Volker Hoffmann. 2013. "Participatory Approaches to Research and Development in the Southeast Asian Uplands: Potential and Challenges." In *Sustainable Land Use and Rural Development in Southeast Asia: Innovations and Policies for Mountainous Areas*, edited by H.L. Fröhlich, P. Schreinemachers, K. Stahr, and G. Clemens. Berlin: Springer, pp. 321–365.

Patton, Michael Quinn. 1980. *Qualitative Evaluation Methods*. Newbury Park, CA: Sage.

Pretty, Jules N. 1995. "Participatory Learning for Sustainable Agriculture." *World Development* 23(8): 1247–1263.

Phillips, Rhonda and Robert Pittman. 2015. *An Introduction to Community Development*. New York: Routledge.

Phillips, Rhonda and Chris Wharton. 2016. *Growing Livelihoods: Local Food Systems and Community Development*. Abingdon: Taylor and Francis.

Poppick, Laura. 2020. "The Effects of COVID-19 Will Ripple through the Food System." *Scientific American*. www.scientificamerican.com/article/the-effects-of-covid-19-will-ripple-through-food -systems/

Putnam, Robert D. 2000. *Bowling Alone: The Collapse and Revival of American Community*. New York: Simon & Schuster.

Rankin, Janet. 2017. "Conducting Analysis in Institutional Ethnography: Guidance and Cautions." *International Journal of Qualitative Methods* December.

Rasmussen, Wayne D. 1989. *Taking the University to the People: Seventy-Five Years of Cooperative Extension*. Ames, IA: Iowa State University Press.

Reardon, Kenneth M., Rebekah Green, Lisa K. Bates, and Richard C. Kiely. 2009. "Commentary: Overcoming the Challenges of Post-Disaster Planning in New Orleans: Lessons from the ACORN Housing/University Collaborative." *Journal of Planning Education and Research*, 28(3): 391–400.

Ritzer, George and Pamela Gindoff. 1992. "Methodological Relationism: Lessons for and from Social Psychology." *Social Psychology Quarterly* 55(2): 128–140.

Rosenzweig, Cynthia, Francesco N. Tubiello, Richard Goldberg, Evan Mills, and Janine Bloomfield. 2002. "Increased Crop Damage in the US from Excess Precipitation under Climate Change." *Global Environmental Change* 12(3): 197–202.

Selener, Daniel. 1997. *Participatory Action Research and Social Change*. Ithaca, NY: Cornell University Press.

Smith, Dorothy E. 1987. *The Everyday World as Problematic: A Feminist Sociology*. Boston, MA: Northeastern University Press.

Smith, Dorothy E. 2005. *Institutional Ethnography: A Sociology for People*. Walnut Creek, CA: AltaMira Press.

Stocking, Michael. 1993. "Soil Erosion in Developing Countries: Where Geomorphology Fears to Tread!" School of Development Studies, University of East Anglia.

Šūmane, Sandra, Ilona Kunda, Karlheinz Knickel, Agnes Strauss, Talis Tisenkopfs, Ignacio Rios, Maria Rivera, Tzruya Calvão Chebach, Amit Ashkenazy, and Ignacio De Los Rios. 2018. "Local and Farmers' Knowledge Matters! How Integrating Informal and Formal Knowledge Enhances Sustainable and Resilient Agriculture." *Journal of Rural Studies* 59: 232–241.

Summers, Mary. 1996. "Putting Populism Back In: Rethinking Agricultural Politics and Policy." *Agricultural History* 70(2): 202–215.

Taber, Nancy. 2010. "Institutional Ethnography, Autoethnography, and Narrative: An Argument for Incorporating Multiple Methodologies." *Qualitative Research* 10(1): 5–25.

Van En, Robyn. 1995. "Eating for Your Community: Towards Agriculture Supported Community." *Context Institute*, 42(Fall): 29–31.

Voinov, Alexey, and Francois Bousquet. 2010. "Modelling with Stakeholders." *Environmental Modelling AND Software* 25(11): 1268–1281.

Warner, Sam Bass, Jr. and Hansi Durlach. 1987. *To Dwell is to Garden: A History of Boston's Community Gardens*. Boston, MA: Northeastern University Press.

Werner, Oswald J. and G. Mark Schoepfle. 1987. *Systematic Fieldwork: Foundations of Ethnography and Interviewing*. Newbury Park, CA: Sage.

18. The information and knowledge landscapes of mutual aid: how librarians can use participatory action research to support social movements in community development

Alessandra Seiter

In March 2020, as COVID-19 began to rock the foundations of human existence, my library colleagues and I were finishing a mass digitization campaign of all the not-yet-digital course materials assigned to students at our university. With the reality of quarantine and remote education looming, we realized the importance of ensuring that students could complete their coursework in a fully online environment. Apart from a few hiccups due to copyright restrictions and human error, we succeeded.

As academic librarians operating in a global pandemic, my team understood our role in supporting students' informational needs. But as a longtime United States (U.S.)-based activist who came to the field of library and information science (LIS) with the goal of supporting the information and knowledge landscapes of leftist social movements, I was much more confused. How to meet the immediate, material needs of ordinary people – especially those least able to leave their homes because of coronavirus? How to do that while also exerting pressure against the decades of neoliberal austerity measures, attacks on social services, and dismantling of workplace protections that disproportionately exacerbated the pandemic's effects on those most marginalized? How to combat the virus-related and public health misinformation spewing forth from the Trump Administration, other authoritarian governments, and right-wing movements? And how, if at all, to offer my personal and professional expertise to these efforts – was it even relevant in this moment, and could I do it in a non-patronizing way?

With these questions swirling, I – like tens of thousands of others around the world – joined my neighborhood's newly formed and virtually organized mutual aid group. The folks next door, turns out, were trying to answer many of the same questions through trial and error. They were learning from similar groups cropping up worldwide, and digging up the long history of mutual aid grounded in North American Black, LGBTQ, and anarchist communities. As I played my small part by bike-delivering groceries and personal protective equipment, organizing virtual game nights with neighbors, and offering minor technical assistance on data collection and digital cartography, I started to realize just how much information management was necessary to coordinate the complex logistics of mutual aid. Simultaneously, and rather uncomfortably, I also began to understand how much my "non-expert" neighbors and their counterparts worldwide were teaching me about grassroots, justice-focused information management and knowledge production in a sociopolitical moment of acute crisis,[1] and about the role librarians could play in supporting leftist social movements beyond the COVID-19 pandemic.

I eventually came to see these lessons through the lens of participatory action research (PAR), realizing that the epistemic frameworks of the social movements I had been involved with since 2011 were just as useful, if not more so, than my master's degree in LIS – at least in terms of determining how best to leverage my professional expertise to support those movements.

This chapter is an effort to synthesize these lessons and make practical recommendations to other librarians and knowledge professionals. Mutual aid – including and beyond the COVID-19 pandemic – is a case study in how social movements can facilitate transformative community development (CD) through grassroots knowledge production, reliant on information management. The approach aligns with PAR, which can provide a framework for librarians and other knowledge professionals to support the social movements in their communities by leveraging relevant expertise in solidarity-minded ways.

THEORETICAL FOUNDATIONS

Social Movements

A social movement is a group of people publicly expressing unified goals for social change against dominant powers, and doing so over a sustained period of time (Stoecker 2020). Through this work, social movements produce knowledge that challenges status quo understandings of societal phenomena. Social movements are often able to do so thanks to participation and leadership from people who have directly experienced oppression and exploitation. For example, in the U.S. social movements have recently been at the forefront of shifting dominant frameworks about how and for whom the police function (Black Lives Matter), the conditions necessary for the rise of fascism (Antifa), the inequities intrinsic to capitalism (Occupy), the urgent threat of climate change and its disproportionate effects on marginalized peoples (#NoDAPL, Sunrise, Extinction Rebellion), and the imperialist agenda at the heart of the national security apparatus (immigrant rights and anti-war movements). Historically, U.S. social movements have played critical roles in dismantling normative assumptions about who deserved voter enfranchisement (Civil Rights and Women's Suffrage movements), economic independence (second-wave feminist movement), autonomy over one's own body (reproductive rights movement), and freedom from "anti-Communist" intervention (movement against the Vietnam War).

Chesters (2012) popularized the theory of social movements as knowledge producers. He argued that advanced industrial democracies have assimilated social movements into normative ontologies of political participation, thus rendering them "commodifiable objects" for the academic to create knowledge *about* rather than *with*. A number of Chesters' contemporaries have heeded his call, identifying social movements as knowledge co-creators in their collaborative, independent research processes (Halvorsen 2015), "uniquely self-reflexive nature" (Lewis 2012), internal ability for critique and analysis (Dawson and Sinwell 2012; Arribas Lozano 2018), critical application of non-dominant theories of social change (Atton 2003), and visionary ideas and goals of societal transformation (Castells and Graham 2004).

Community Development

Through their work as grassroots knowledge producers, social movements can function as critical nodes of CD. For marginalized peoples, CD tends to happen through the formation of "counterpublics" – sociopolitical spaces that challenge Habermas' "bourgeois conception of the public sphere" by explicitly centering the needs of marginalized peoples. Social movements can create counterpublics by legitimizing, mobilizing, and sustaining marginalized communities in disrupting and eventually shifting the status quo (Jackson and Foucault Welles 2015). This liberatory view aligns with McCrea et al.'s (2017) definition of CD as a process of "provid[ing] legitimacy for educational engagement that seeks to make power visible and to consider the tactics by which it can be reclaimed, negotiated, or resisted." Here, social movements' knowledge-production capacities are crucial to CD, especially given CD's "ambivalent story" wherein governments have harnessed CD rhetoric to respond to structural crises in superficial and disempowering ways. In contrast, social movements – by targeting the structural underpinnings of oppression in order to eliminate their material and ideological bases – provide the non-dominant forms of knowledge necessary to guide CD towards its transformative potential.

Library and Information Science

While social movements are well positioned to lead transformative CD work, they don't have unlimited capacity to do so. Though their power hierarchies are often horizontally organized, social movement activities are usually vertically integrated. Social movements are frequently responsible for simultaneously fulfilling the material and emotional needs of their communities, coordinating protest and direct action, applying pressure to elected officials, and recruiting and integrating new activists. Community members can alleviate the pressures on social movements by offering existing relevant expertise.

One area of expertise relevant to social movements' knowledge production processes is information management. As "fundamentally communicative" formations (Bennett and Segerberg 2015), social movements locate, collect, curate, disseminate, and preserve information to advance their causes. Social movements are often the only ones managing certain information in explicitly political and transformative ways, and thus cannot always depend on other more traditional informational entities. Especially with the ubiquity of internet-based information and communications technology (ICT), including social media, information management is crucial in facilitating the interpersonal and communal connections necessary to social movement organizing.

Information management and ICT-based knowledge production can facilitate CD by alleviating feelings of social isolation in the wake of disaster (Glasgow et al. 2016), maintaining informal social networks ready to mobilize in moments of crisis (Loudon 2010), building individual and communal resiliency (Semaan 2019), and creating a sense of stability (Semaan and Mark 2011). Marginalized communities have also wielded ICT to strengthen diasporic bonds (Everett 2002; Riedel 2019), facilitate transnational solidarity (Everett 2002), and collaboratively reconceptualize their own identities (Bonilla and Rosa 2015).

In geographically defined communities, librarians serve as people-centered experts on information management. Librarians have expertise in many areas relevant to social movement activity, including protecting privacy, evaluating reputable sources, managing and preserving organizational records, democratically communicating information across demographics, working with data, conducting qualitative and quantitative research, evaluating projects based on community outcomes, and leveraging ICT (ALA Council 2009). Critically, librarians aim to make their expertise as accessible as possible throughout their communities, prioritizing collective benefit over profit. This goal is unique within the neoliberal public sphere, and necessary for the survival of society's most socioeconomically precarious (Drabinski 2006). Based on these qualities, U.S. librarians have largely earned the trust of their communities (Horrigan 2016). Librarians are thus uniquely positioned to support social movements in their knowledge production processes.

Participatory Action Research

As a methodology of communal and grassroots knowledge production, PAR provides an ethically and politically vibrant framework for librarians and other knowledge professionals to pursue co-creative work with social movements. PAR recognizes that a small group of people – namely, white Western capitalists and the academics working at their behest – are responsible for the majority of sociopolitically legitimized knowledge, which upholds their monopoly on power. This recognition traces back to Marxist philosophy, which encourages the "proletariat" to "create their own history" instead of passively inheriting the "science of the bourgeoisie" (Rahman 2008). Colombian sociologist Orlando Fals Borda has observed the potential for PAR practitioners to impose their own notions of what this creation looks like on marginalized communities (Rahman 2008), which has encouraged PAR practitioners to critically assess how to co-create knowledge with non-academic collective actors in useful and sustainable ways. To this end, Stoecker (2014) has highlighted the popular education movement advanced primarily by Brazilian educator Paulo Freire and U.S. labor and civil rights activist Myles Horton. Popular education as a method gathers members of a marginalized community and facilitates dialogue between these community members on their common experiences. Through this process, community members can identify the systemic roots of their experiences and develop collective strategies for addressing them (Stoecker 2014) – directly mirroring how social movements function.

Halvorsen (2015) and Lewis (2012) take PAR a step further, advocating a practice of "militant research" that aims to "pus[h] the movement forward" through "committed and intense process[es] of internal reflection from within particular struggle(s)" (Halvorsen 2015). To do so effectively and ethically, Halvorsen (2015) argues that militant researchers must "tak[e] seriously the ontologies and epistemologies of social movements themselves" by defining their positionality "from within a movement" rather than from their work in academia. In other words, militant researchers must understand themselves first as having a vested interest in the movement's goals in order to genuinely contribute to its knowledge production processes. This movement-first positionality applies to librarians and other knowledge professionals who wish to support the social movements in their communities.

MUTUAL AID DURING AND BEYOND COVID-19

Within weeks of COVID-19's initial global spread, a vast network of grassroots groups coalesced under the banner of "mutual aid" thanks to rapid coordination by longtime and first-time community organizers (Town Hall Project 2021). In a time of necessary physical isolation, these virtually organized groups were paying close attention to the needs of the most medically and socioeconomically vulnerable members of their hyperlocal communities. They were recognizing the difficulty that elderly and immunocompromised people would have obtaining basic supplies, and developing practical methods of confronting the disproportionate impacts of the virus on poor people and people of color (Science for the People 2020). On a structural level, these groups were filling the enormous gap in state-run social services and people-centered policy that had long left millions of people in chronic crisis due to lack of adequate healthcare, income, housing, and socioeconomic mobility.

Mutual aid groups soon began coordinating volunteers to deliver groceries, medication, and other essentials to homebound community members (Adler-Bell 2020); making face masks and organizing their distribution to hospitals and to those without means of procuring their own; providing free lunches for food-insecure kids facing school closures and for people experiencing houselessness (Goodman et al. 2020); pressuring local lawmakers to enact immediate moratoriums on rent collections and evictions (Rent Strike 2020); and raising bail funds for people in prison, where some of the most severe COVID-19 outbreaks were taking place (Goodman et al. 2020). A few months later, as police officers and white vigilantes carried out a spate of racist murders against Black people including Ahmaud Arbery, Breonna Taylor, and George Floyd, many mutual aid groups expanded their activities to draw attention to the U.S.'s centuries-long legacy of white supremacist violence; support Black Lives Matter protestors with water, food, and first aid; and lobby municipal governments to defund their police departments.

A Brief History of Mutual Aid in the United States: 1787–2021

Though "mutual aid" was a term of relative obscurity in North America until the pandemic began (Solnit 2020), it has existed in name for over a century and recorded practice for over 200 years. Russian anarchist Pëtr Kropotkin first coined the phrase in his 1902 book, *Mutual Aid: A Factor of Evolution*, describing mutual aid as the ideal state of human affairs wherein society is organized through collective means. He argued that the state sees mutual aid as a threat to its dominance, and sows individualism in ideology and material reality. Within Kropotkin's framework, mutual aid is a necessary strategy of working-class survival and ultimate liberation from state-based society.

Kropotkin was describing a phenomenon that Black communities in the eastern U.S. had been carrying out since at least 1787, when two Philadelphia ministers founded the Free African Society that would soon take primary responsibility in caring for the sick, orphaned, and dead during a yellow fever epidemic (Aberg-Riger 2020). In the early 1800s, as more Black people self-emancipated and migrated north, mutual aid societies proliferated to challenge slave-catchers, offer legal defense, and provide for the basic needs of formerly enslaved peoples (National Humanities Center 2007). These efforts continued into the late nineteenth century, when 15 percent of Black men and 52 percent of Black women in New York City belonged to a mutual aid society (Aberg-Riger 2020). At the turn of the century, Chinese, Jewish, and Mexican immigrants formed similar groups to care for their own amidst rampant racism (Aberg-Riger 2020). Two decades later during the Spanish Flu, women-led mutual aid groups recruited volunteer nurses and ran soup kitchens for patients (Stoecker 2020). Mutual aid activities declined after the Great Depression, but returned in full force by the late 1960s when the Black Panther Party launched a free breakfast program in Oakland that quickly grew to serve over 50,000 children across the country. The Panthers also provided armed community self-defense from racist police, and liberatory education on the history of U.S. white supremacy. This organizing prompted the FBI under Herbert Hoover to infiltrate the Panthers in a mass undercover campaign known as COINTELPRO (Aberg-Riger 2020; Pien 2010). Despite state efforts, marginalized communities throughout the U.S. continued to pursue mutual aid activities for decades to come. In the early 1970s, the Puerto Rican Young Lords in New York City won municipal services for their previously neglected neighborhood. In the 1980s and 1990s, the Chicken Soup Brigade in Seattle supported people living with AIDS (PWA) in their daily tasks (Aberg-Riger 2020). In 2005, Mutual Aid Disaster Relief covered the basic needs of New Orleans residents after Hurricane Katrina while the federal government demonized the city's predominantly Black population (Milstein 2020). And in 2012, Occupy Sandy built on the anti-capitalist Occupy Wall Street movement to provide politically vocal relief for those affected by Hurricane Sandy (Soden 2020).

Mutual aid in the U.S. has sometimes manifested as a key strategy within a broader social movement, and other times as a social movement itself. Given its centrality to pandemic response among marginalized communities, especially as much other movement activity slowed due to physical distancing measures, I consider COVID-19 mutual aid to be a social movement itself.

As did their predecessors, COVID-19 mutual aid groups represent a wide range of political analyses. Some are explicitly anti-state, others view their work as a temporary necessity until a more responsible state structure is built, some are intentionally apolitical, and still others are part of the state itself (Stoecker 2020). But two principles tend to dominate among them. First, they recognize that ordinary people experience precarity not because of personal failure, but because of systemic processes that foster poverty and inequity. Summed up by the slogan "solidarity not charity" (Big Door Brigade n.d.), mutual aid groups prioritize those most affected by crisis by trusting them as experts in their own needs. This model contrasts that of state agencies and non-profit organizations, whose interests may not align with the communities they purport to serve (Goodman et al. 2020). It also mirrors PAR's methodologies for co-created knowledge.

Second, mutual aid groups enact "prefigurative politics," meaning they try to build models for a liberatory society within existing structures – often through communal modes of living and service. Many groups view prefigurative politics as a necessary step toward societal transformation because it can meet marginalized peoples' basic needs and facilitate their disruptive efforts, while others see it as itself a disruptive effort. PAR is built on a recognition of the short- and long-term transformative potential of prefigurative efforts.

Community Development through the Information and Knowledge Landscapes of Mutual Aid

Mutual aid throughout history has involved information management, done by and for communities who wouldn't otherwise have access to its processes or potentials. COVID-19 mutual aid groups are no exception, given the necessity of correcting the misleading and often dangerous virus-related information spouted by right-wing governments and their supporters worldwide. A collective of Chinese anti-statist organizers has even called COVID-19 mutual aid groups "crucial nodes for the distribution of information and goods" (COVID-19 Mutual Aid Seattle and PARISOL 2020). Globally, these groups have compiled spreadsheets and maps on social services and the availability of personal protective equipment, testing locations, protest locations and safety tactics, mental health resources, and beyond. They've curated digital handbooks for fellow organizers on launching websites, facilitating meetings, and exerting pressure on elected officials (MAAMA 2020a, 2020b; MAMAS 2020). They've collected and analyzed data that states and corporations have refused to release (Adler-Bell 2020). They've developed virtual communication spaces via Facebook, Zoom, WhatsApp, and Slack for their neighbors and fellow organizers to coordinate aid and alleviate loneliness. Some of them have explicitly described their work under the banner of LIS, such as the *Coronavirus Tech Handbook* maintained by a team of volunteer librarians (Newspeak House n.d.) and Mutual Aid Arlington in Massachusetts which provides virtual reference through their website (MAAMA 2020b).

Grassroots information management like that practiced by COVID-19 mutual aid groups is critical in mediating crisis outcomes. Indeed, during COVID-19 some researchers have identified "any global health crises [as] also *information* crises that require serious attention" (Xie et al. 2020, emphasis in original). The field of crisis informatics – which studies the ways ICT shapes societal relationships to various types of disaster (Soden 2020) – emphasizes the importance of reliable, up-to-date information in shaping crisis response. Traditional media sources, however, are often unable to provide real-time updates to constantly changing situations due to limited access to crisis zones and lack of familiarity with local conditions (Chernobrov 2018). Additionally, policymakers can hoard information and communicate it publicly in ways that deny the gravity or nuance of a situation, reducing the social trust necessary for successful crisis response (Clarke and Chess 2008). At the beginning of the COVID-19 pandemic, for example, many health experts inaccurately claimed that masks were ineffective. Though they probably intended to preserve masks for healthcare workers, their messages likely stoked virus denialism (Tufecki 2020). These shortcomings combined with the internet's overloaded information landscape can lead to rumors and conspiracy theories that tend to undermine public health efforts (Kou et al. 2017). This phenomenon has appeared during COVID-19 with the pervasive spread of lies about the origin of the virus, its severity, and its treatment.

To prevent the potential consequences described above, some crisis informatics researchers have suggested the "first communicator" as an informational first responder (Chernobrov 2018; Palen et al. 2020; Reuter et al. 2013). As members of communities directly affected by crises, first communicators can augment formal emergency response with experiential knowledge by monitoring social media, verifying official information, creating and updating digital maps (Palen et al. 2020), collecting information on missing people (Kaufhold and Reuter 2016), and producing journalistic content (Chernobrov 2018). These contributions can drastically increase the likelihood that the public will make "informed decisions that protect their health" (Parmer et al. 2016). Radio announcer Genie Chance provided this kind of information-focused mutual aid in the immediate aftermath of the massive 1964 Alaska earthquake, when she broadcast an endless stream of messages from city employees and civilian volunteers to paint the most reliable picture available of who was safe, who was missing, and where aid was needed (Meigs 2020). The widespread availability of ICT today has opened up new and more accessible volunteer opportunities (Chernobrov 2018), with "risk communication for crises now commonly occurring in online spaces, especially social media" (Palen et al. 2020). The concept of first communicators shares a foundation with mutual aid by centering the experiential knowledge of ordinary people as experts on their own communities and needs, and facilitating that work through information management and ICT use.

Where crises introduce pain and hardship, they also introduce opportunity. COVID-19 mutual aid has taken advantage of the opportunities introduced during the pandemic to unify previously atomized individuals, recognize common experiences of systemic oppression, and form strategies to overcome the symptoms and foundation of those structures. While during COVID-19 some leftists have expressed doubt that traditional movement organizations can absorb thousands of newly engaged activists (Adler-Bell 2020), others have voiced their hopes that the networks of solidarity developed through COVID-19 mutual aid can be leveraged for long-term movement organizing (Tolentino 2020). These hopes seem viable, considering that many COVID-19 mutual aid groups rose up out of the Black Lives Matter, prison abolition, anti-colonization, disability justice, and Occupy Wall Street movements (Goodman et al. 2020; Holder 2020; Soden 2020). Following the worst of the COVID-19 crisis, it seems well within the realm of possibility that these movements could return to less circumscribed modes of organizing with an even greater number of participants.

An historical realization of a similar possibility is instructive. The information-focused mutual aid undertaken during the U.S. AIDS activist movement highlights the transformative CD potential of such efforts. McKinney (2018) details the Philadelphia-based organization Critical Path, spearheaded by Kiyoshi Kuromiya, a Japanese-American civil rights and anti-war activist and co-founder of the Gay Liberation Front. In the 1980s, Critical Path produced a print newsletter for PWA based on the latest health research, which at that time was shared through novel ICT to which many PWA didn't have access. Critical Path augmented this research with firsthand "information on support groups, organizational schedules, experimental AIDS medications and protocols, alternative therapies ... and direct services available to PWA" – which "was otherwise unavailable through mainstream media and public-health agencies." By distilling this information in a physical newsletter distributed to the most vulnerable PWA – including intravenous drug users, those in prison, and those experiencing houselessness – Critical Path exponentially increased the likelihood that PWA would access treatment and community. Critical Path continued its work throughout the 1990s, becoming a free internet service provider for PWA and AIDS service organizations. Critical Path's practices of community-focused information management were essential to ACT UP, whose AIDS activism expanded the U.S. Center for Disease Control's definition of the virus, broadened and accelerated the National Institutes of Health's AIDS research, and destigmatized the virus and queer identity. Through their savvy wielding of ICT grounded in firsthand knowledge of the virus and its impacts, AIDS activists "improve[d] PWA's lives and ultimately [found] a cure by bridging community knowledge with medical research." Mutual aid during the AIDS crisis thus played a huge role in sustaining queer communities, building strategies, and legitimizing epistemologies that would continue to transform queer folks' lives in the U.S. for decades to come.

PARTICIPATORY ACTION RESEARCH, LIBRARIANS, AND MUTUAL AID

Librarians are information experts, trusted community anchors, and service providers for socioeconomically precarious community members. They are therefore well positioned to support mutual aid and other social movements' information management and knowledge production, in service of transformative CD. Jessamyn West (2020) has even described U.S. librarians as long-standing providers of mutual aid. We can look to recent examples during COVID-19 like the Columbia University librarian who leveraged her 3D printing expertise to produce a face shield design, a printing guide, and hundreds of prototypes in collaboration with healthcare providers around New York City (Morrow 2020); and the University of Colorado research working group pursuing qualitative and quantitative data analysis in collaboration with U.S. mutual aid groups (Soden 2020).

Historically, though, librarians' own mutual aid efforts are exemplified perhaps most notably in Radical Reference (RR). RR was a non-hierarchical group of hundreds of volunteer library workers who throughout the early 2000s "support[ed] activist communities, progressive organizations, and independent journalists by providing professional research support, education and access to information" (Brant and Yanek 2009). RR emerged from the recognition that "most adults do not have the affiliations with colleges and universities that allow them access to the rich print and electronic collections of academic libraries," leaving social movements particularly hindered (Morrone and Friedman 2009). RR would deploy "street librarians" equipped with "ready reference kits" to protests and demonstrations, offering reliable information to activists where they most needed it. RR also provided timely, multilingual online reference to activists worldwide on topics ranging from mass incarceration in the U.S. to anarchism in Czechia (Friedman and Morrone 2008). RR's educational outreach included presentations on archival processes for movement documentation (Edel et al. 2010; Cuellar et al. 2009); strategies for getting radical and independent media sources into library collections (Freedman and Ross 2009); and research methodologies (Freedman and Thelen 2008). RR volunteers also participated in social movements, recognizing themselves as "part of the activist communities they serve" (Friedman and Morrone 2008). Though in late 2017 RR announced a hiatus due to their increasingly limited capacities, RR's mutual aid efforts sustained leftist social movements by collecting and disseminating radically minded information based on the needs and feedback of activist communities.

While there is a robust history of radical librarianship in line with RR's work,[2] two dominant frameworks of LIS in the U.S. prevent librarians from effectively supporting the mutual aid groups and other social movements in our communities in widespread ways. The first is an implicit paternalism that pervades the historical discourse of library outreach, framing librarians as bestowers of services upon "those in need" rather than as fellow community members with similar liberatory interests. This paternalism directly opposes the trust that mutual aid and PAR vest in the expertise of community members, including mutual aid and social movement participants. It dates back to the late seventeenth and early eighteenth centuries, when the Anglo-Saxon Protestant colonizers who founded U.S. librarianship "viewed librarians like missionaries" (Brady and Abbott 2015) who could promote "good" books in order to cultivate "moral character" among the indigenous people and immigrants in their midst (Wiegand 1989). Similarly patronizing attitudes continued through the 1970s, when public libraries used federal grant money from the Library Services and Construction Act to initiate outreach projects for the "disadvantaged" without the direct input of the marginalized communities they purported to serve – some librarians at the time even saw "citizen participation [as] a radical incursion" (Owens 1987). Today, library discourse tends to prioritize outreach as a means of justifying to patrons why libraries are relevant, saying little about community impact. For example, public library leaders interviewed by Scott (2011) made such assertions as "the challenge is how we inform the public how we are meeting the challenge of serving the public," and "[d]oing what we can to build strong communities through libraries will enable libraries to thrive in the future." But acting as constructive participants in our communities should be an end in and of itself for librarians. If our communities do not see us as relevant to their information needs, then – in the spirit of mutual aid and PAR – we should focus on collaborating with fellow community members to fill service and structural gaps.

The second dominant LIS framework is political neutrality, codified in the profession's core ethical guidelines which assert the need to "distinguish between our personal convictions and professional duties" (American Library Association 2008). This mandate is based on the notion that those who hold strong political views are "censorial" and therefore in defiance of the guiding principles of intellectual freedom in LIS (Shockey 2015). Of course, this assumption fails to acknowledge that the U.S. status quo – inclusive of neoliberalism, structural white supremacy, and imperial power – is itself a strong political view that has rendered necessary the direct care and visionary organization of mutual aid and other social movements. Gibson et al. (2017) highlight the consequences of so-called political neutrality in their paper on the responsibilities libraries have to "engage with and support communities of color as they challenge systemic racism, engage in the political process, and exercise their right to free speech." The authors argue that librarians have "ignored the Black Lives Matter (BLM) movement," and in doing so "actively elect[ed] not to support the information and service needs of a service population" and "allow[ed] inequality to persist as the status quo." The question of how to facilitate CD through information management and knowledge production is an inherently political one, as mutual aid groups and PAR practitioners have shown. In order to effectively answer it, librarians must define explicitly political professional principles and practices instead of hollow ones easily manipulated to serve oppressive power structures and their foot soldiers.

TOWARD NEW MODELS

PAR offers a framework for developing an explicitly political praxis of librarianship. At its core, PAR is a methodology of knowledge production undertaken by knowledge professionals in close collaboration with groups of marginalized actors who seek to enact structural sociopolitical change (Rahman 2008). As fellow knowledge professionals, librarians can look to PAR's unabashedly political and community-led efforts for models of supporting the mutual aid groups and other social movements active in our communities.

Librarians Mehra and Braquet (2007) and Phillips et al. (2019) have employed PAR in, respectively, campus LGBTQ solidarity efforts and union contract negotiations. Excitingly, their work only scratches the surface of the PAR-informed efforts librarians can pursue to support the CD work of mutual aid and other social movements. As a starting point, librarians can use Fals Borda's four informational techniques for building community power: pursuing collective research, recovering critical history, valuing and applying "folk" culture, and disseminating new knowledge (Rahman 2008).

Based on these techniques, below are some of my own concrete suggestions for how librarians can support the social movements, including mutual aid, in their communities:

- Hire new staff or rework existing outreach-focused positions to serve as mutual aid- and/ or movement-embedded librarians. Precedent for such positions already exists in academic libraries which employ subject-specific or disciplinary liaisons. Similar to these liaisons, movement-embedded librarians would need movement experience and theoretical expertise.

- Work with mutual aid groups and other movement actors to identify archival techniques most relevant to the cultural artifacts they're producing. Depending on librarian and organizer capacities, either offer workshops on those techniques to groups so they can continually document their own knowledge production practices, or take on those documentation processes as movement-embedded librarians. Create physical and digital repositories to house and preserve this documentation, determining how to provision access based on movement needs and privacy concerns.

- Maintain a directory of local, non-institutional community organizations and activist groups, built through voluntary registrations and the experiential knowledge of mutual aid groups. Such a directory could provide a jumping-off point for community members not yet involved but interested in mutual aid and other social movement activity, as well as a resource for existing groups to find and pursue collaborative efforts with others working on similar issues.

- Maintain a directory of local PAR practitioners and community facilitators (Mackewn 2008) whom mutual aid groups and other movement actors can contact for assistance with conducting independent research projects, running meetings, creating designated spaces for political assessment and internal reflection, and pursuing conflict resolution and accountability strategies for organizers who have experienced harm in the course of their work. Establish library grant programs so these collaborations don't have to depend on either free labor or the constraints of academic research protocols. Establish program evaluation practices that allow groups to assess the efficacy of their work with these practitioners, and collaborate with practitioners to improve their work based on this feedback.

- Open up library makerspaces for mutual aid groups and other movement actors to make posters, signs, and banners in preparation for upcoming protests and demonstrations.

- Open up library meeting spaces for mutual aid groups and other movement actors to host meetings, lectures, and other in-person educational and organizational pursuits.

- Offer multimedia creation and editing hardware and software for checkout or use in library computer labs. Work with mutual aid groups and other movement actors to facilitate workshops on the use of these materials for independent media production.

- Offer consultations with mutual aid groups and other movement actors wishing to publish their own writing. These consultations could include information on independent publishing platform possibilities, strategies for establishing editorial boards, advice around copyright and open access, and networking with local publishers of newspapers and other independent media outlets.

- Negotiate with vendors or pursue grant funding to offer mutual aid groups and other social movements access to subscription-based journals and databases relevant to their work.

- Work with local digital and data privacy groups to advise mutual aid groups and other movement actors on internet security best practices and social media protocol, both in general and surrounding specific protests or mobilizations.

- Establish an ongoing oral history project that invites past and present mutual aid groups and other movement actors to give spoken testimonies of their work and the lessons they've learned. Organize these testimonies and provision access to them based on movement needs and privacy concerns.

- Work with union representatives or colleagues to pass resolutions or policy documents affirming the rights of librarians to support and engage directly in mutual aid and other movement activity. Include in these documents explicit guarantees that the library will come to the defense of these librarians if they are targeted by the state, law enforcement, or counterprotest groups.

It's critical to unambiguously delineate the groups and movements librarians should actively exclude from their support work. There have long existed in the U.S. movements of white supremacists, fascists, and neo-Nazis. The Ku Klux Klan is a classic example, but we need not look as far back as their founding in the mid-1800s to find evidence of organized groups that romanticize and seek to harness the nationalism, racism, xenophobia, and indigenous genocide that has pervaded U.S. history. Embedded in these goals are the reactionary hopes of maintaining the "purity" of a narrowly defined white nation under "threat" by Black people, immigrants, Muslims, the LGBTQ community, and organized leftists (Miller and Graves 2020). Since Donald Trump's election in 2016 the U.S. has seen a surge in far-right activity – including 125 rallies, marches, and protests nationwide – and the growth of extremist hate groups (Miller and Graves 2020). Such groups include the Atomwaffen Division, a coalition of terror cells working toward civilizational collapse; The Base, a similar coalition seeking societal collapse specifically in order to establish a white ethnostate; Vanguard America, a neo-Nazi group whose membership includes James Alex Fields, Jr., the young man accused of murdering anti-racist protestor Heather Heyer with his car at the "Unite the Right" rally in Charlottesville, Virginia on August 12, 2017; and Proud Boys, who helped to organize the aforementioned rally and spread white nationalist, anti-Muslim, and misogynistic rhetoric online (SPLC n.d.a, n.d.b, n.d.c, n.d.d). These groups are already responsible for multiple civilian deaths, including most recently at the insurrectionary occupation of the U.S. Capitol building on January 6, 2021 (Healy 2021). Such movements often persuasively wield the identity-based and pro-free speech rhetoric of left-leaning collective actors, claiming that they merely want to celebrate their white identity and honor U.S. history through such supposedly benign acts as the maintenance of Confederate memorials (Miller and Graves 2020).

Historians and scholars of fascism have warned us about the need to treat these movements as a serious threat to the functioning of a liberatory society (Ádám et al. 2020). They have similarly warned us about the potential for otherwise well-meaning civilians of relatively unthreatened socioeconomic standing to pave the way for these movements to achieve state power, such as when the majority of German voters elected Hitler to power (Evans and Alexandra n.d.; King et al. 2008; Mayer 1997; Snyder 2016). Librarians, like all U.S. residents, have a responsibility to actively decry and challenge the rise of these movements. Unfortunately, there is precedent for librarians to implicitly support them, such as in 2018 when the ALA Office of Intellectual Freedom issued an amendment to the Library Bill of Rights that defended the rights of hate groups to organize in library meeting rooms (ALA Council 2019). The amendment was later revised due to organized opposition by rank-and-file librarians (Schaub 2018), but it made clear how easy it is to fail to act in solidarity with the marginalized members of our communities targeted by the groups in question. Instead of defending these groups and the movements under which they organize, librarians must expose them for their cooptation of "free speech" as a cover for organizing hatred and bigotry in order to carry out violence (Seiter 2018). Our profession took an explicitly anti-fascist stance in 1938 as Hitler's dictatorship was coming to power (Robbins 1996). We must do so again today if we are to support transformative CD efforts like those of mutual aid groups and other leftist social movements, for such work hinges on preventing the rise of nationalistic authoritarianism that promises the violent intensification and expansion of widespread socioeconomic vulnerability.

CONCLUSION

The transformative CD work undertaken by mutual aid groups throughout history is truly impressive. During COVID-19 alone, mutual aid has allowed community members to keep a roof over their heads, food on the table, and a sense of social isolation at bay. Librarians and researchers have supported these efforts, but COVID-19 mutual aid groups didn't *need* us in order for their work to function successfully. On the contrary, they have become their own experts on community information management and knowledge production. Where knowledge professionals have most effectively strengthened COVID-19 mutual aid and other social movements, we've done so as fellow community members with additional expertise to lend. In other words, we've invested in the health of the community and its members first, and have tried to figure out – in close collaboration with our neighbors – where our professional expertise might be relevant second. While the professional expertise of individual knowledge professionals can be quite useful for social movements, the social and material resources offered through access to an established institution are also numerous. Some of these resources are immediately useful, such as internet access and meeting space. In a broader sense, though, these institutions lend epistemological legitimization that can popularize movement activity and politics, contradicting state and corporate claims that they constitute fringe elements of society. Our institutionally backed work around information management and knowledge co-production can be another tool in the social movement toolkit – and not the other way around.

NOTES

1. Unless explicitly noted, when I refer to "crisis," I mean acute and temporally bounded instances of crisis (such as aftermaths of environmental disasters), as well as chronic modes of social crisis (such as structural racism).
2. See, for example, Joan C. Durrance's 1984 book *Armed for Action: Library Response to Citizen Information Needs*.

REFERENCES

Aberg-Riger, Ariel. 2020. "'Solidarity, Not Charity': A Visual History of Mutual Aid." *Bloomberg CityLab*. www.bloomberg.com/news/features/2020-12-22/a-visual-history-of-mutual-aid

Ádám, Zoltán, Giulia Albanese, Anjali Arondekar et al. 2020. "How to Keep the Lights On in Democracies: An Open Letter of Concern by Scholars of Authoritarianism." *The New Fascism Syllabus*. http://newfascismsyllabus.com/news-and-announcements/an-open-letter-of-concern-by -scholars-of-authoritarianism/

Adler-Bell, Sam. 2020. "Coronavirus Has Given the Left a Historic Opportunity: Can They Seize It?" *The Intercept*, April 14.

ALA Council. 2009. "ALA's Core Competencies of Librarianship." American Library Association. www.ala.org/educationcareers/sites/ala.org.educationcareers/files/content/careers/corecomp/ corecompetences/finalcorecompstat09.pdf

ALA Council. 2019. "Meeting Rooms: An Interpretation of the Library Bill of Rights." American Library Association. www.ala.org/advocacy/intfreedom/librarybill/interpretations/meetingrooms

American Library Association. 2008. "Code of Ethics (COE)."

Arribas Lozano, Alberto. 2018. "Knowledge Co-Production with Social Movement Networks. Redefining Grassroots Politics, Rethinking Research." *Social Movement Studies* 17(4): 451–463.

Atton, Chris. 2003. "Reshaping Social Movement Media for a New Millennium." *Social Movement Studies* 2(1): 3–15.

Bennett, W. Lance, and Alexandra Segerberg. 2015. "Communication in Movements." In *The Oxford Handbook of Social Movements*, edited by D. Della Porta and M. Diani. Oxford: Oxford University Press.

Big Door Brigade. n.d. "What Is Mutual Aid?" *Big Door Brigade*. https://bigdoorbrigade.com/what-is-mutual-aid/

Bonilla, Yarimar, and Jonathan Rosa. 2015. "#Ferguson: Digital Protest, Hashtag Ethnography, and the Racial Politics of Social Media in the United States: #Ferguson." *American Ethnologist* 42(1): 4–17.

Brady, Hillary, and Franky Abbott. 2015. *A History of US Public Libraries*. Digital Public Library of America.

Brant, Natalie, and Cheryl Yanek. 2009. "Radical Reference: Using Technology to Improve Access for All." Presented at the Special Libraries Association Annual Conference, June 19.

Castells, Manuel, and Stephen Graham. 2004. "Space of Flows, Space of Places: Materials for a Theory of Urbanism in the Information Age." In *The Cybercities Reader*. London: Routledge, pp. 82–93.

Chernobrov, Dmitry. 2018. "Digital Volunteer Networks and Humanitarian Crisis Reporting." *Digital Journalism* 6(7): 928–944.

Chesters, Graeme. 2012. "Social Movements and the Ethics of Knowledge Production." *Social Movement Studies* 11(2): 145–160.

Clarke, Lee, and Caron Chess. 2008. "Elites and Panic: More to Fear Than Fear Itself." *Social Forces* 87(2): 993–1014.

COVID-19 Mutual Aid Seattle and PARISOL. 2020. *Self-Organization in Times of Pandemic: How the Masses Are Reconstructing Society – Part 1.*

Cuellar, Jillian, Nicole Martin, and Nick Gilla. 2009. "Radical Reference Presents: Do It Yourself Archives." Presented at the 2009 NYC Anarchist Book Fair, New York, April 11.

Dawson, Marcelle, and Luke Sinwell. 2012. "Ethical and Political Challenges of Participatory Action Research in the Academy: Reflections on Social Movements and Knowledge Production in South Africa." *Social Movement Studies* 11(2): 177–191.

Drabinski, Emily. 2006. "Librarians and the Patriot Act." *Radical Teacher* (77): 12–14, 44.

Durrance, Joan C. 1984. *Armed for Action: Library Response to Citizen Information Needs*. New York: Neal-Schuman.

Edel, Deborah, Matt Metzgar, and Alan Ginsberg. 2010. "Documenting Struggle Redux: Radical New York City Archives." Presented at the Brecht Forum, New York, April 26.

Evans, Robert, and Sofiya Alexandra. n.d. "Part One: How Nice, Normal People Made the Holocaust Possible." Podcast.

Everett, Anna. 2002. "The Revolution Will Be Digitized: Afrocentricity and the Digital Public Sphere." *Social Text* 20(2): 125–146.

Freedman, Jenna, and Jess Ross. 2009. "Radical Reference Unpanel: Alternative Materials in Libraries." Presented at the Grassroots Media Conference, New York, May 30.

Freedman, Jenna, and Lana Thelen. 2008. "FACT-UP: Fact Check, Research, and Thinking Critically like a Radical Librarian." Presented at the Women and Media Conference, Massachusetts Institute of Technology, March 28.

Friedman, Lia, and Melissa Morrone. 2008. "The Sidewalk Is Our Reference Desk: When Librarians Take to the Streets." In *Simultaneous Interpretation: Reference and Information Services*. Quebec.

Gibson, Amelia, Renate Chancellor, Nicole Cooke, Sarah Park Dahlen, and Shari Lee. 2017. "Libraries on the Frontlines: Neutrality and Social Justice." *Equality, Diversity and Inclusion: An International Journal* 36(8): 751–766.

Glasgow, Kimberly, Jessica Vitak, Yla Tausczik, and Clay Fink. 2016. "Grieving in the 21st Century: Social Media's Role in Facilitating Supportive Exchanges Following Community-Level Traumatic Events." In *Proceedings of the 7th 2016 International Conference on Social Media and Society – SMSociety '16*. London: ACM Press, pp. 1–10.

Goodman, Amy, Mariame Kaba, and Dean Spade. 2020. "Solidarity Not Charity: Mutual Aid and How to Organize in the Age of Coronavirus." *Democracy Now!*

Halvorsen, Sam. 2015. "Militant Research against-and-beyond Itself: Critical Perspectives from the University and Occupy London: Militant Research against-and-beyond Itself." *Area* 47(4): 466–472.

Healy, Jack. 2021. "These Are the 5 People Who Died in the Capitol Riot." *New York Times*, January 16.

Holder, Sarah. 2020. "The Many Protests of the Coronavirus Pandemic." *Bloomberg CityLab*. www .bloomberg.com/news/articles/2020-04-27/the-many-protests-of-the-coronavirus-pandemic

Horrigan, John. 2016. *Libraries 2016*. Washington, DC: Pew Research Center.

Jackson, Sarah J., and Brooke Foucault Welles. 2015. "Hijacking #myNYPD: Social Media Dissent and Networked Counterpublics: Hijacking #myNYPD." *Journal of Communication* 65(6): 932–952.

Kaufhold, Marc-André, and Christian Reuter. 2016. "The Self-Organization of Digital Volunteers across Social Media: The Case of the 2013 European Floods in Germany." *Journal of Homeland Security and Emergency Management* 13(1).

King, Gary, Ori Rosen, Martin Tanner, and Alexander F. Wagner. 2008. "Ordinary Economic Voting Behavior in the Extraordinary Election of Adolf Hitler." *Journal of Economic History* 68(4): 951–996.

Kou, Yubo, Xinning Gui, Yunan Chen, and Kathleen Pine. 2017. "Conspiracy Talk on Social Media: Collective Sensemaking during a Public Health Crisis." *Proceedings of the ACM on Human-Computer Interaction* 1(CSCW): 1–21. doi: 10.1145/3134696

Kropotkin, Pëtr. 1902. *Mutual Aid: A Factor of Evolution*. New York: McClure Phillips & Co.

Lewis, Adam Gary. 2012. "Ethics, Activism and the Anti-Colonial: Social Movement Research as Resistance." *Social Movement Studies* 11(2): 227–240.

Loudon, Melissa. 2010. "ICTs as Opportunity Structure in Southern Social Movements: A Case Study of the Treatment Action Campaign in South Africa." *Information, Communication and Society* 13(8): 1069–1098.

MAAMA. 2020a. "How to Set Up a Mutual Aid Website." Mutual Aid Arlington, MA. https:// mutualaidarlington.org/setup/

MAAMA. 2020b. "How to Set Up Library Help Chat on a Site." Mutual Aid Arlington, MA. https:// mutualaidarlington.org/setup/chat/

Mackewn, Jenny. 2008. "Facilitation as Action Research in the Moment." In *The SAGE Handbook of Action Research*. London: SAGE, pp. 615–628.

MAMAS. 2020. "Neighborhood Pods How-To." https://vspot.s3.amazonaws.com/sign-up/Article+ Graphics/Trends-Fads/How+to+Neighborhood+Pod.pdf

Mayer, Milton. 1997. *They Thought They Were Free: The Germans 1933–1945*. Chicago, IL: University of Chicago Press.

McCrea, Niamh, Rosie R. Meade, and Mae Shaw. 2017. "Practising Solidarity: Challenges for Community Development and Social Movements in the 21st Century." *Community Development Journal* 52(3): 379–384.

McKinney, Cait. 2018. "Printing the Network: AIDS Activism and Online Access in the 1980s." *Continuum* 32(1): 7–17.

Mehra, Bharat, and Donna Braquet. 2007. "Library and Information Science Professionals as Community Action Researchers in an Academic Setting: Top Ten Directions to Further Institutional Change for People of Diverse Sexual Orientations and Gender Identities." *Library Trends* 56(2).

Meigs, James. 2020. "Elite Panic vs. the Resilient Populace." *Commentary*. www.commentarymagazine .com/articles/james-meigs/elite-panic-vs-the-resilient-populace/

Miller, Cassie, and Howard Graves. 2020. "When the 'Alt-Right' Hit the Streets: Far-Right Political Rallies in the Trump Era." *Southern Poverty Law Center*. www.splcenter.org/20200810/when-alt -right-hit-streets-far-right-political-rallies-trump-era

Milstein, Cindy. 2020. "Collective Care Is Our Best Weapon against COVID-19 and Other Disasters." *Mutual Aid Disaster Relief*. https://mutualaiddisasterrelief.org/collective-care/

Morrone, Melissa, and Lia Friedman. 2009. "Radical Reference: Socially Responsible Librarianship Collaborating with Community." *The Reference Librarian* 50(4): 371–396.

Morrow, Allison. 2020. "Columbia University Librarians Producing 3D-Printed Protective Face Shields." *Columbia University Libraries Spotlight Blog*. https://blogs.cul.columbia.edu/spotlights/ 2020/03/23/columbia-university-librarians-provide-guide-and-design-for-3d-printable-face-shields/

National Humanities Center. 2007. "Mutual Benefit." *The Making of African American Identity, Volume I: 1500–1865*. http://nationalhumanitiescenter.org/pds/maai/community/text5/text5read.htm

Newspeak House. n.d. "Coronavirus Tech Handbook."

Owens, Major. 1987. "The War on Poverty and Community Outreach." In *Activism in American Librarianship, 1962–1973, Contributions in Librarianship and Information Science*, edited by M.L. Bundy and F.J. Stielow. New York: Greenwood Press.

Palen, Leysia, Jennings Anderson, Melissa Bica et al. 2020. "Crisis Informatics: Human-Centered Research on Tech and Crises: A Guided Bibliography Developed by Crisis Informatics Researchers." www.researchgate.net/publication/344310469_Crisis_informatics_Human-centered_research_on_tech_crises_A_guided_bibliography_developed_by_crisis_informatics_researchers

Parmer, John, Cynthia Baur, Dogan Eroglu, Keri Lubell, Christine Prue, Barbara Reynolds, and James Weaver. 2016. "Crisis and Emergency Risk Messaging in Mass Media News Stories: Is the Public Getting the Information They Need to Protect Their Health?" *Health Communication* 31(10): 1215–1222.

Phillips, Margaret, David Eifler, and Tiffany Linton Page. 2019. "Democratizing the Union at UC Berkeley: Lecturers and Librarians in Solidarity." *Library Trends* 68(2).

Pien, Diane. 2010. "Black Panther Party's Free Breakfast Program (1969–1980)." *BlackPast.* www.blackpast.org/african-american-history/black-panther-partys-free-breakfast-program-1969-1980/

Rahman, Md. Anisur. 2008. "Some Trends in the Praxis of Participatory Action Research." In *The SAGE Handbook of Action Research.* 1 Oliver's Yard, 55 City Road, London England EC1Y 1SP United Kingdom: SAGE, pp. 49–63.

Rent Strike 2020. 2020. "Organizing Toolkit."

Reuter, Christian, Oliver Heger, and Volkmar Pipek. 2013. "Combining Real and Virtual Volunteers through Social Media." *Proceedings of the Information Systems for Crisis Response and Management* January: 780–790.

Riedel, Samantha. 2019. "What a Viral Twitch Stream for Trans Charity Says about Modern Activism." *Them.* www.them.us/story/hbomberguy-twitch-stream-trans-charity

Robbins, Louise. 1996. "Champions of a Cause: American Librarians and the Library Bill of Rights in the 1950s." *Library Trends* 45(1): 28–49.

Schaub, Michael. 2018. "Policy Allowing Hate Groups to Meet at Libraries Comes under Fire." *Los Angeles Times*, July 11.

Science for the People – Mutual Aid Working Group. 2020. "Mutual Aid Narrative." *Science for the People.* https://scienceforthepeople.org/mutual-aid-narrative/

Scott, Rachel. 2011. "The Role of Public Libraries in Community Building." *Public Library Quarterly* 30(3): 191–227. doi: 10.1080/01616846.2011.599283

Seiter, Alessandra. 2018. "Libraries Can't Afford to Welcome Hate." *Socialist Worker.* https://socialistworker.org/2018/07/13/libraries-cant-afford-to-welcome-hate

Semaan, Bryan. 2019. "'Routine Infrastructuring' as 'Building Everyday Resilience with Technology': When Disruption Becomes Ordinary." *Proceedings of the ACM on Human-Computer Interaction* 3(CSCW): 1–24. doi: 10.1145/3359175

Semaan, Bryan, and Gloria Mark. 2011. "Creating a Context of Trust with ICTs: Restoring a Sense of Normalcy in the Environment." *Proceedings of the ACM 2011 conference on Computer Supported Cooperative Work – CSCW '11.* Hangzhou, China: ACM Press, p. 255.

Shockey, Kyle. 2015. "Intellectual Freedom Is Not Social Justice: The Symbolic Capital of Intellectual Freedom in ALA Accreditation and LIS Curricula." *Progressive Librarian* 44: 101–10.

Snyder, Timothy. 2016. *Black Earth: The Holocaust as History and Warning.* New York: Tim Duggan Books.

Soden, Robert. 2020. "Crisis Informatics and Mutual Aid during the Coronavirus Pandemic: A Research Agenda." *Items: Insights from Social Sciences.* https://items.ssrc.org/covid-19-and-the-social-sciences/disaster-studies/crisis-informatics-and-mutual-aid-during-the-coronavirus-pandemic-a-research-agenda/

Solnit, Rebecca. 2020. "'The Way We Get through This Is Together': The Rise of Mutual Aid under Coronavirus." *The Guardian*, May 14.

Southern Poverty Law Center (SPLC). n.d.a. "Atomwaffen Division." *Southern Poverty Law Center.* www.splcenter.org/fighting-hate/extremist-files/group/atomwaffen-division

Southern Poverty Law Center (SPLC). n.d.b. "The Base." *Southern Poverty Law Center.* www.splcenter.org/fighting-hate/extremist-files/group/base

Southern Poverty Law Center (SPLC). n.d.c. "Patriot Front." *Southern Poverty Law Center*. www .splcenter.org/fighting-hate/extremist-files/group/patriot-front

Southern Poverty Law Center (SPLC). n.d.d. "Proud Boys." *Southern Poverty Law Center*. www .splcenter.org/fighting-hate/extremist-files/group/proud-boys

Stoecker, Randy. 2014. "What If?" *All Ireland Journal of Higher Education* 6(1).

Stoecker, Randy. 2020."Mutual Aid during COVID-19." Presented at the CIRN Community Informatics Seminar Series, November.

Tolentino, Jia. 2020. "What Can Mutual Aid Do During a Pandemic." *The New Yorker*, May 11.

Town Hall Project. 2021. "Mutual Aid Hub." www.mutualaidhub.org/

Tufecki, Zeynep. 2020. "Why Telling People They Don't Need Masks Backfired." *New York Times*, March 17.

West, Jessamyn. 2020."Libraries as Longstanding Mutual Aid Community Anchors." Presented at the CIRN Community Informatics Seminar Series, November.

Wiegand, Wayne. 1989. "The Development of Librarianship in the United States." *Libraries and Culture* 24(1): 99–109.

Xie, Bo, Daqing He, Tim Mercer, Youfa Wang, Dan Wu, Kenneth R. Fleischmann, Yan Zhang, Linda H. Yoder, Keri K. Stephens, Michael Mackert, and Min Kyung Lee. 2020. "Global Health Crises Are Also Information Crises: A Call to Action." *Journal of the Association for Information Science and Technology* 71(12): 1419–1423.

PART VI

EXPANDING OUR THINKING

19. Be and build the city: an experience of sociopraxis in Cuenca, Ecuador

Ana Elisa Astudillo and Ana Cecilia Salazar

This chapter systematizes the theoretical and practical learnings of the citizen collective *Cuenca Ciudad Para Vivir* (Cuenca City to Live (CCCV), www.cccv.ec), which was founded to promote active citizen participation and a culture of *covivencia* (living together in community, collaboration, and coexistence) to guide the development of the city of Cuenca, our home.[1] CCCV does this through an approach that is based in citizen co-responsibility and participatory action research (PAR). CCCV claims that taking on our citizenship responsibility in constructing (not only physically but also socially and culturally) the city is part of the political and social commitment of the city's residents. To accomplish its goals, both citizen participation and organizational structure are fundamental to enable active political and civic engagement with an understanding of politics not only as related to parties or electoral endeavors, but also as a part of our daily lives, in all the decisions and interactions in our community.

Cuenca's experience is located within the Ecuadorian national development approach of *Sumak Alli Kawsay*, a cultural paradigm based in the philosophy and culture of the indigenous peoples and nationalities seeking to recover the Good Life (which is the translation of *Sumak Alli Kawsay* from Quichua to English). *Sumak Alli Kawsay* offers alternatives to the current capitalistic, neoliberal hegemonic systems and envisions new forms of relations between people and with the environment. The CCCV's theoretical foundations are in line with "Right to the City" proposals (Lefebvre 1996; Brenner et al. 2012), which represent our ideals about community development. Methodologically, participatory research enables the transformation of the political culture through engaging in collective reflection-action processes. Throughout, we realize that it is necessary to recognize the city as a disputed space, inhabited by diverse individuals with their own ways of life, who come together as community (and in fact many small communities in one larger urban setting) despite all their differences.

Since 2010 CCCV has brought together people from many walks of life, including academics, activists, and residents to discuss urban conflicts and concerns from their particular experiences in order to envision a new future for the city. The aim of the CCCV is to contribute to the construction of Cuenca as a public good and an ethical project promoting citizen deliberation about the present and future of Cuenca. In this framework, participatory methodologies (PM) generate spaces for reflection, self-criticism, and construction so as to transform reality and lead to new forms of community development.

LATIN AMERICAN URBAN CONTEXT

Urbanization in Latin America during the twentieth century was characterized by a scarcity of food, adequate and safe housing, and other basic goods as well as an informal economic sector which did not protect workers. Urbanization processes were based in the commodification and commercialization of land, along with built structures that reproduced asymmetry and segregation between inhabitants. In fact, South America is the most urbanized (United Nations 2016) and unequal region in the world (CEPAL 2016). Conditions of poverty and social exclusion in both the city and the countryside demonstrate the limits of current urban models. As a result, a regime of multiple inequalities dominates which leads to living conditions that create a permanent incubator of social and environmental crises.

The limits of modern human settlements, and of the western model of neoliberal cities (Theodore et al. 2011) are demonstrated by the unsustainability of the risks generated by ways of living that perpetuate relationships of power and domination among people and with the natural world (Lander 2010; Svampa 2016) and the irreversibility of the effects caused by fossil fuel dependencies and extractive economic systems which have led to the climate crisis. In this context, the COVID-19 pandemic serves as a problematic symptom that shines light on the limited capacity that rotating governments have to respond, such as in the case of Ecuador.

In sum, urban management in Latin American cities is challenged by global dynamics like climate change, international markets, massive tourism, migration (Pérez and Tenze 2018) and currently the COVID-19 pandemic. In Cuenca the local conditions include an economic recession, an outdated urban planning model, unemployment, a lack of essential services, and a decontextualized heritage and cultural management model. Moreover, the public management of the city is suffering from a crisis of credibility and high levels of corruption. In this context, the organization of civil society is indispensable for the construction of the city as a socioculturally, economically, and environmentally diverse community that sustains life, beyond its simple materialistic needs.

Given these larger national and global constraints and dynamics, CCCV focuses upon developing their vision of the city as a public good and an ethical project based on new forms of cooperation between citizens, local government, and public and private actors. CCCV endeavors to contribute to larger urban debates and to promote community development from the perspectives of active citizens. An analysis of CCCV's experiences demonstrates that promoting citizen participation through active research can be an effective strategy to support building the city in response to local claims and problems. A sustainable territorial management model incorporates values like diversity, social and environmental justice, and equity. It is grounded in greater public participation in decision making, as well as new forms of democratic practice. Lessons learned along the way include that urban planning and management must embrace a holistic approach to the territory, addressing local demands within the global context by developing context-based solutions through articulated social-political, economic, cultural, and infrastructure dimensions.

CCCV does not promote predetermined models. Instead, it takes into account differences of opinion, disagreements, and inequalities when defining the goals and ways of doing citizen politics. On the one hand, CCCV envisions PAR as a way to create and exercise citizenship based on dialogue between diverse people to generate meaningful knowledge that democratizes decision making. On the other hand, CCCV believes that it is fundamental to establish a shared vision of the city's future and its aspirations, starting with community development and strengthening the social organization in/of the city. Importantly, the authors recognize and value that the information presented in this article has been created through a process of collective construction of knowledge – both from the internal reflections of the CCCV as well as from the active citizen participation encouraged by the CCCV for the past ten years.

In what follows, the first section will outline CCCV's conceptual framework, including the shared understandings of its members and the principles that guide the actions of the collective's members. The second section will lay out CCCV's practical experiences of citizen participation. Finally, the third section will briefly summarize the lessons and reflections on using PAR and PM and the collective construction of objectives and knowledge.

CONCEPTUAL FRAMEWORK

CCCV conceives of the city as a sociopolitical reality (Lefebvre 1996). To inhabit a city is an eminently political act, since by inhabiting we are participants in the production of space. The city as a sociospatial reality is reproduced by and has continuity in the daily life of its citizens, in all of us. CCCV understands the political dimension of the city as a field of action that is concretized or made real in the daily practices of the inhabitants. Within this framework, CCCV focuses more on community organization than on community development (Stoecker 2003). That is to say, we dedicate ourselves to strengthening civil society and organization and its ability to influence and advocate for the Right to the City, which can be understood as a call to its constituents' power to demand the common good. Stoecker (2003) explains how this works:

> Community organization is the process of building a constituency that can go on to create a move-ment, and it occurs at a level between the micro-mobilization of individuals (Snow, Rochford, Worden, & Benford, 1986) and the political process of the broader social system (McAdam, 1982). Community organizing is not just a means to win issues, but also to build powerful community organizations, in the process of which community relationships are rebuilt and individuals are empowered. (Stoecker 2003: 494)

In this framework, CCCV is committing to a new form of politics, an antipolitics of sorts based in emancipatory praxis wherein the responsibility for the Other, for the neighbor, is a way of doing and being community (Dussel 2001). This new politics is a call to the active constituent, to the insurgent capacity of civil society, and, in the words of Holloway (2003), to the transformation of the world without taking power.

The work of CCCV is resignifying (in other words giving new meaning to) local politics, from our personal experiences as the inhabitants of Cuenca as well as taking on the daily dialectic. That is to say, we take into account that the reality in which we act will be displaced historically and spatially (Dussel 2011). In this approach, with the ethos of liberation (Holloway 2003), the ethical-political proposal of the CCCV is to free ourselves from the mercantile model of modernizing urbanism allied with current governmental structures through social and community organizing and through the citizen collectives that propose a new way of living. This requires unlearning the way in which things have always been done and decisions have always been made. Transformative political praxis emerges in the relations between different actors, each one with diverse demands, positions, and visions (Holloway 2003). PAR and PM enable the possibility of these encounters which reinvent the exercise of politics through the relational. CCCV incorporates PAR and PM drawing from the contributions of Orlando Fals Borda (1985), which is to say that they engage in investigations from and for the citizens and the transformation of the city.

Participatory Action Research and Political Influence

PAR is one of the most important contributions by thinkers, academics, and activists from the 1970s to the 1990s who were committed to social struggles and who advocated for the generation of critical and transformative knowledge. PAR incorporates concepts from the ontological turn that challenged the typical dichotomies of Euro-American thought (Del Campo 2017). "A basic tenet of modernist epistemology has become the opposition between the world as the totality of things and the multiple worlds of experienced reality" (Descola 2014: 336). This ontological turn created a space to analyze the dynamics of power and emergent movements (Adams et al. 2015).

One of the basic principles of the ontological turn that incorporates PAR is to interrupt the relations of "subject investigator – object investigated." PAR considers that the collectives – communities of people – are active subjects in the research processes and not only the objects of investigation. In this approach, PAR is connected in many ways with the pedagogy of the oppressed (Freire 1993), liberation philosophy (Dussel 1994), liberation theology, and the arts (Boal 1974), including lessons learned from feminist, environmental, and territorial struggles for the recognition of other narratives based on local historical memory. "This constituted a wide-ranging, pervasive body of thought in Latin America" (Robles and Rappaport 2018: 600).

PAR "pays close attention to social class, and forging relationships with organized popular sectors of society" (Robles and Rappaport 2018: 600) in their specified historic context. Within this perspective, "social agents are considered historicity condensers and agents of possible futures" (Zemelman and Valencia Garcia 1990: 90). Generation of knowledge is socially structured based on the particular experiences of each territory. Hence PAR generates a situated knowledge which comes from a complex system of practices, beliefs, and internal relations in a particular space, that which Boaventura de Sousa (2014) names an "ecology of wisdoms." As a consequence, it is impossible to outline a universal PAR methodology (Robles and Rappaport 2018). Even more so, the epistemological grounding of PAR focuses the participants on understanding and learning from their contexts which are shaped in part by dominant capitalistic global agendas. "PAR positions itself as an alternative to traditional research models. It is an action focused on local and regional problems involving emancipatory educational, cultural, and political processes" (Fals Borda 2001: 27).

Unlike traditional social movement approaches seeking to take static, detached, and explanatory snap-shots of collective action, PAR attempts to contribute to critical reflection from within movements or collectives. The best way to develop people's consciousness about their surroundings and their understanding of reality is to start by collectively analyzing with participants the causes of their problems and their consequences for their lives. Therefore, CCCV believes that reflexivity must be included in and through all the elements of PAR. This means that even as we do the work, we question ourselves about where we are building the world from and how our relationships networks are established. "Self-reflexivity is intended to help us to 'articulate our own value systems, our multiple identities and locations of power and privilege, and how these understandings influence our interactions with others'"(Lake and Wendland 2018: 27). In brief, we analyze who is involved and how we are advocating for change. In general, PAR requires a high level of sensitivity to others and acknowledgment that knowledge production is grounded in the emotional experiences of people. Finally, PAR entails significant attention to the material and political conditions of the collaborative process since the stories and information shared may arouse strong emotions, "because the goals of the grassroots organizations involved are articulated through sentiments related to land, family, and community" (Robles and Rappaport 2018: 607).

As a result of reflexivity and network analysis, PM within PAR unravel the relationships, problematics, and strengths of a community (Villasante and Gutiérrez 2006). Consequently, these methodologies enable us to problematize everyday issues and acknowledge lived knowledge. In other words, dialogues between different people raise awareness about the varied conditions, inequalities, and lifestyles of the people who live in our community and city. Collective problems can then be identified and grounded in this knowledge created through the process of sharing. Utilizing this framework, CCCV believes that dialogues are not necessarily enriched by mass participation but rather more importantly by diversity, which shows that the city is made up of different realities.

The problematization resulting from participative dialogue must be systematized and constantly fed by new perceptions from others who encounter it. "The 'systematization' is an incompletely defined set of collaborative procedures for collecting and analyzing research materials, both in their historical contexts and in the context of relationships" (Robles and Rappaport 2018: 607). Once the dynamics and contradictions of a network are visible in the problematization, PAR participants using PM proceed to diagnose, negotiate, co-construct, and propose changes based on small-scale initiatives. They also seek to establish bridges between citizen initiatives and public administration. PAR is not a linear process, instead it entails incorporating constant multistakeholder feedback. Once the results are systematized, they are returned to the participants, so together, we can define the possibilities for intervention and transformation of reality. For example, developing the capacity to auto-diagnose (to reflect on their particular reality to understand it) with a community or a neighborhood allows members to discover the forces that coexist in social systems and the struggles over what should or should not be done to resolve their problems. The consensus among participants is built from a deliberative process to decide how to intervene in the transformation of their reality.

In general, CCCV considers that it speaks for itself. It does not intend to interpret social reality, but rather to make visible the concrete conditions and positions of citizens and communities since these do not always correspond to the discourse of the decision makers. By using PAR and PM, CCCV operationalizes its aims and ideals. Moreover, over time, this methodology continues to enable new sociopolitical dialogues and social struggles. In that way CCCV contributes to the larger efforts of participatory research grounded in civil society movements and organizational knowledge and demands. In order to articulate their social struggles and valuable learnings, CCCV embraces PAR and PM because these approaches build bridges between diverse and even opposing actors, enabling the circulation of information and dialogue as the basis for collective agreements.

With these methodological and ethical commitments, CCCV has taken actions such as hosting citizen forums (*Foros Ciudadanos*) and open workshops or popular assemblies (*Cátedras Abiertas*) on themes of shared interest using methodologies that problematize local realities. By coming together, participants define the citizen demands that benefit the common good rather than the individual. Debates, plenaries, and conversations allow information to be shared across sectors. These organized spaces allow for opposing positions to be shared and for people to enter into tension with each other and even conflict at times. Then through dialogue and deliberation they can create potential imaginations of the desired community development. These kinds of activities enable the identification not only of areas of agreement, but also of tensions where agreements and solutions that are focused on inclusion, solidarity, and democracy are worked out. Both the *Foros Ciudadanos* and the *Cátedras Abiertas* are spaces where constant feedback guarantees reflexivity on the situation in which we find ourselves as citizens and as political subjects connected through a heterogeneous network.

Even with this approach, CCCV believes that it is necessary to take a retrospective and critical look at how PAR has been applied and by whom. We acknowledge that over the years, PAR has been "partially alienated from its radical roots by the appropriation of research techniques by multilateral aid agencies and governments, pilloried by Fals Borda as 'developmentalists, experts, academicians and entrepreneurs'" (Fals Borda in Robles and Rappaport 2018: 589). In the case of Ecuador, starting with the law of citizen participation that was passed in 2010, participatory processes have been used as part of the dominant political discourse. Populist political leaders manipulate the expectations of the people and disable the organizational processes of the masses. When politicians say that they will do the public projects that a community needs in exchange for votes in the next elections, they convert citizens into receivers of favors and not citizens with rights. One could even say that the state has co-opted the discourse of participation to the degree that it has not been duly used.

Faced with this situation, the promotion of participatory processes implies restoring the credibility of and explaining the meaning of participatory initiatives, which is a complex task. Because of this CCCV does not offer prefabricated solutions or standardized recipes, but instead commits to constant reflection and the resignification of these processes, taking into account sociopraxis contributions (Villasante 1998). In order to avoid the institutional cooptation of the practices and create truly communally constructed results, it is necessary to critique our own social processes. CCCV takes the position that, to strengthen the organization of civil society as a central goal, one must continuously ask why and for whom projects are being done.

Sociopraxis combines various methodologies in order to create approaches to problems based on interactive, theoretical, practical, but above all people-centered dialogue about knowledge and the strengthening of organization and collective action. "It is not about contributing to the final solutions to the problems we have. But rather [developing] ways and styles of approaching them … these styles are positions to face life … as the result of the learning processes of the social movements themselves" (Villasante 2006: 22). In this sense, sociopraxis as social change is essentially dialectical, complex, and continuous (Villasante 1998), which enables it to overcome the tension between "to be" and "could be." As we often say in CCCV, "building on what is built," which means that we must acknowledge previous experiences, and what has already been established. This guarantees that proposals will recognize and respond to their context. For this reason, we also look for new creative ways of being and doing.

Within this framework, CCCV's actions have followed PAR principles such as the collective, contextualized, and relational construction of knowledge, the encounter with diverse perspectives, the recognition of gaps, power relations, and inequalities, and the creation of proposals based in experiences and local demands. These principles assume that the city is made up of a network of social-spatial relations that operate according to the logic illustrated in Figure 19.1. This figure also summarizes our vision of PAR in action to promote transformative community development.

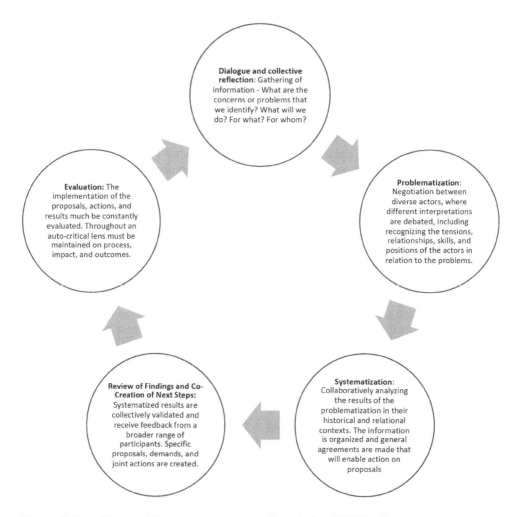

Figure 19.1   The participatory action research cycle for CCCV in Cuenca

CCCV KEY CONCEPTS

CCCV was born from the need to reflect on the problems of Cuenca and on the capacity of its people to participate in decision-making processes. Dialogue is the fundamental act for CCCV in order to rethink what we understand as political ethics and practice as well as the fundamental principle that must guide citizenship. We are also dedicated to promoting collective actions that motivate citizen organization, and discussions that challenge citizen habits generated by unsustainable and inequitable urban models. The principles which emerged from our work include the following.

Co-responsibility

Being aware that coexistence generates reciprocal relationships in the community in which we live is the first step towards understanding that the city belongs to all of us and that it is necessary to take on collective responses to the problems of our natural and social surroundings. Hence, people must embrace active participation in the design and implementation of public policies as well as in their daily practices. To be co-responsible is to contribute to the construction of the city, developing a synergetic social network that is committed to collective well-being. For CCCV, co-responsibility implies an openness to creative cooperation between civil society, local governments, and diverse actors from the public and private sectors and between actors and institutions. This cooperation is a continuous process of negotiations that demands ethically responsible communication to democratize the decision-making process. Active co-responsibility is rooted in dynamics that allow us to feel like co-authors or co-creators of what is happening around us.

Active Citizenship

The participation of civil society in the construction of the city creates an inclusive space that is environmentally sustainable, where through deliberative democracy, socioeconomic gaps are overcome and equality of opportunity is generated for diverse individuals and the collective (CCCV 2012). With this approach, CCCV understands participation as instituting collaborative practices to identify creative solutions to problems. These processes have as a goal the transformation of place. Participative practices also make possible collective spaces for diverse actors where they can feel mutually involved and collectively responsible. They generate equality of opportunities to contribute to the identification, treatment, and solution of common problems and goals. Active citizenship and participation have to incorporate diverse perspectives and face the gaps between the actors in the specific context of each community. Active citizenship is not through a set model or goal, but rather consists of practices which open new possibilities (Villasante 2014). For CCCV, citizen participation is a right and a medium through which we are encouraged to develop a conscious and autonomous practice in the construction of the city as a public good and an ethical project, conceived from the perspective of a non-state public space (CCCV 2020).

The City as a Public Good and Ethical Project

Cities are spaces of multiple human transactions, of individual and social projects in permanent construction and transformation. They are not spontaneous phenomena, natural or external to ourselves. The social construction of the city is built through relations of co-living, in order to construct spaces where most of the population enjoys an adequate quality of life. Every person is responsible for transforming the social, political, cultural, and urban architectures of the city. Coming together to act makes possible a cohesive and organized community that works for the sake of common interests and even more for vulnerable populations. For CCCV, the city as a *public good* should be built by and for the citizens. In so doing, the city also becomes an *ethical project*, since it must articulate and negotiate the tensions and power relationships to overcome the significant economic and social gaps between people. At the same time, we must resignify equity, dignity, and justice, considering the diversities that make up the community that we seek to inhabit without privileges or exclusions. We question who determines what is ethical or fair. In the complex reality of cities, we cannot take such ambiguous concepts for granted.

In sum, the CCCV advocates a civic ethic that involves the action of people who know that they are part of a network or collective. To change political culture requires overcoming individualism and isolation, and developing a sense of belonging and shared concern for public space. The CCCV claims for civic ethics are based on empathy with the Other, caring for the Other, and seeing ourselves as part of a community. More than community development per se, the aspiration of CCCV is the social organization and strengthening of the sense of community between neighbors. For us, the meaning of public is not only a space but also a quality of shared living and of making the city an entity that distributes opportunities and services, both in terms of quality and quantity, and not a system that perpetuates and consecrates social fractures (CCCV 2020). For the CCCV, social organization is the only entity that can promote an equitable distribution of goods and services, spatial justice, and equal opportunities, which can also be understood as community development.

Paradigm of Care and the Right to the City

CCCV's claims to re-envision the city as a public good and an ethical project demand a shift in the values and ethos of our political culture. But where could and should this shift lead? To answer this, CCCV takes into account two ethical-political proposals. First, a paradigm of care – co-responsibility, empathy, and reciprocity – enables the existence of networks that weave the community together in the face of a culture which promotes individual rights. The ethic of care focuses on strengthening relations of proximity, of knowing and of acting for the well-being of those who surround us; in other words care for the ecology that makes life possible (Boff 2009). This paradigm upholds the commitment of caring for the Other to take care of ourselves. Components of this care include: care for the world, care for language, care for things, care for nature, care for wisdoms, care for institutions, care for the multitudes, care for the economy, care for the anomaly, care for politics, care for dreams, and care especially for the desire and the power to persist in ways of being that are caring (Ferrán 2020). For CCCV, community development implies promoting coexistence with respect, cooperation, and harmony with the other residents of the planet which is articulated through the emancipation that is connected to the claims of justice for all (Gattino 2013).

Second, CCCV incorporates the concept of Right to the City of Lefebvre and Harvey who propose that the city that we love cannot be separated from the type of people that we seek to be, from the type of social relations that we seek to have, from the relationships with nature that we appreciate, the style of life that we desire, and the ethical values that we respect (Harvey 2012). The Right to the City is therefore much more than the right of individual access to urban benefits. Instead, it implies a right to change and reinvent the city, which inevitably depends upon the exercise of collective power in the urbanization processes (Harvey 2012).

Ecuador is one of the few countries in Latin America that includes the Right to the City in its constitution with the following statute: "the guarantee of equitable access to the benefits of living in a city, the possibility of participatively building that city, and the full array of human rights for those who live in her" (Article 31). This therefore includes all of the economic, social, cultural, environmental, civil, and political rights that are regulated through the international human rights treaties. The national legal framework, which sought to provide citizens' constitutional rights, established people's rights including: a safe and healthy abode, an adequate experience of life with dignity, citizen participation, and property in all its forms. Ecuador enshrines in its constitutional framework the human right to the city which includes:

(a) The full exercise of citizenship to ensure the dignity and collective well-being of the inhabitants of the city under conditions of equality and justice. (b) Democratic management of cities through direct and representative forms of democratic participation in the planning and management of cities, including mechanisms for public information, transparency and accountability. (c) The social and environmental approach to property that puts the general interest before the particular and guarantees the right to a safe and healthy habitat. (Ciudadana and Pleno 2016)

The Right to the City and the Paradigm of Care propose that community development is a process that allows inhabitants to make decisions about their surroundings, strengthens the organizational fabric, and resignifies the principles of coexistence and political action. While the Right to the City challenges linear conceptions of urban development, the paradigm of care calls into question the community development approach based in international cooperation. The paradigm of care centers the importance of strengthening people's agency in the sectors organized to participate in decision making in and for the construction of public policies for the collective benefit.

The Imagined City

"Every city is always imagined because nobody can have a total vision of it" (CCCV 2012: 4). Imagining the city is part of our creative capacity which enables us to build not only an ideal representation of the space in which we want to live, but also aspirational ways of inter-action and coexistence. Imagining the city is an attitude and a practice. With this creativity and commitment, cities can become a dream-created reality at every moment, as long as their inhabitants exercise their citizen power consciously and with empathy.

Using this conceptual framework, CCCV proposed the following workplan that operational-izes these principles in the context of Cuenca:

1. To generate information on the current situation of the city and its aspirations for public decision making in the service of local actors: citizens, local governments, and academia.
2. To strengthen the capacities of local actors to act on issues related to the city.
3. To promote the connections between and organization of various social actors to contribute to the construction of the city as a public good and an ethical project.
4. To promote spaces for deliberation, reflection, and citizen actions around a common interest.

CASE STUDY: THE EXPERIENCE OF CCCV

Cuenca is located in a valley in the Ecuadorian Andean Highlands. The city displays its postcolonial heritage in several historical layers. As people walk the streets of the city, they encounter the legacies of Spanish colonialism, Incan occupation, and the original Cañari people. Over time the territory has been known by at least three names corresponding to each of these eras: Guapondelig for the Cañaris, Tomebamba for the Incas, and Cuenca for the

Spanish. Currently, Cuenca is the third most populated city in the country. Since the 1950s, Cuenca's inhabitants have experienced an urban transformation due to its accelerated urban growth (Hermida et al. 2015). This has brought about cultural changes, in the use of space as well as the socioeconomic structure of the city. The more recent local governments have embraced a logic of neoliberal urbanism (Theodore et al. 2011), which involves prioritizing global agendas and external investors influencing the planning and urban growth of Cuenca over local demands.

In 1999, UNESCO recognized the historic center of Cuenca as a world heritage site for Cuenca's "remarkable example of a planned inland Spanish town" in colonial America.[2] "Cuenca is at the forefront of a growing list of intermediate-sized cities whose landowning classes have prioritized developing competitive tourism industries as a means of increasing revenues generated from urban space" (Hayes 2020: 5). The public administration used this declaration as an opportunity to launch successful global marketing campaigns, earning high rankings in international ratings of cities. This has affected the city's morphology and its social fabric, promoting urban displacement processes in the last 20 years (Cabrera and Reino 2020).

On November 3, 2020, Cuenca commemorated the bicentennial of its colonial independence from the Spaniards. Within these celebrations, various citizen organizations and higher education institutions promoted critical reflection on the history and future of the city, succeeding in interrupting the traditional imaginaries of the *cuencano* identity by making visible the contributions of workers, indigenous people, women, and countercultural movements. This has caused us to question what we have overcome and what we have maintained from the colonial heritage and how we have revalued and recuperated/retrieved other stories.

CCCV, as an organization, also recognized the necessity of doing a retrospective and sharing lessons learned from our ten years of experience. This provided us the opportunity to take on the challenge of systematizing CCCV's experience as a social agent that seeks to contribute to the improvement of the political culture and sense of social responsibility in Cuenca.

Political Context and Birth of the CCCV

CCCV emerged from and was configured in response to the last ten years of the national political context. From 1995 to 2006 Ecuador was characterized by significant political instability including nine presidents. This instability affected the legitimacy and credibility of the national political system, not only the political parties but also the state itself as well as the prevailing system of representative democracy. Then, in 2007, the government called for a constitutional process through a referendum and for the election of assembly representatives to develop the new constitution.

The national process led to heated debates, a reformulation of the responsibilities of the state, and a recognition of the need for citizen participation. In 2008, in a historical milestone, the new constitution was approved by 64 percent of the voters. The Ecuadorian constitution is one of the most advanced in the world in terms of the rights of nature, indigenous claims, participation, and recognition of diversities (Lalander and Ospina 2012).

The new political-legal framework of the 2008 constitution demanded the establishment of new laws, regulations, and ordinances to guarantee active and legitimate citizen involvement by strengthening mechanisms of social participation at all levels of society. For example, the Organic Law of Citizen Participation and Social Control establishes that: "social organizations have the right to make claims, propose works, formulate public policy proposals or debate budgets" (Article 97).

The new constitution also acknowledged the need to guarantee a dignified and equitably just life based in positive relationships between people and with the environment. Accordingly, the incorporation of the Right to the City and the principles of the indigenous cosmovision known as *Sumak Kawsay* or Good Living as collective rights in the Ecuadorian constitution created the possibility of advocating for a new way of understanding life in community, as a space of coexistence and respect for the interests and needs of all, including respect for nature (Constitución del Ecuador 2008, Article 275). Implementing this framework has involved rethinking the development model – including the production and energy systems, and human interactions with each other and nature – that has been based in a free market economy that has subsisted historically on an extractivist economy.

In this historical context, characterized by a crisis of representative democracy, the diminished credibility of political parties, and the national transformation due to the 2008 Constitution, a group of people in Cuenca who were involved in local social movements and the universities began to reimagine citizen participation for the city. This first core group of citizens organized a series of conversations on how to re-establish public ethics and motivate deliberative processes about what citizens should do. These initial efforts led to the founding of CCCV in 2009 to overcome the traditional delegitimized forms of political organization, transform the political culture, and strengthen deliberation and participation by civic society. Its members recognize themselves as self-representing, autonomous from government institutions, and without electoral interests, constituting CCCV as a space based on dialogue and consensus within the framework of deliberative democracy.

After more than a decade, despite the constitution's mandate at the national level to promote citizen participation, the results are far from what was expected. Increasingly, participating citizens have experienced their efforts being distorted and undermined as government officials appropriated terms such as citizenship, rights, and participation. These core concepts were stolen from citizens' efforts and transferred to a set of public apparatuses and institutions. In this scenario, the social organizations and the social fabric itself, which were already stretched thin, became further weakened by new heavy regulatory and bureaucratic controls. In response to these limitations, we observed that civil society has chosen to resume its path outside the regulated institutional framework and search for new sources of reference in which to ground and resignify the deliberative nature of citizen participation and democracy (CCCV 2020).

CCCV Participatory Action Research Actions: Ten Years of Commitment to Active Citizenship

Throughout CCCV's experiences, sociopraxis has been our core practice. We acknowledge that social change can only be achieved through practices and actions, even if CCCV was born from the need to reflect on the city. We have been committed to concrete actions where changes in practice can be promoted. Although rethinking the city and citizenship are valuable conceptual results of the CCCV, through PAR projects using PM, CCCV has also designed and engaged in multiple diverse actions that have affected human interactions and the built space in the city.

Following PAR principles and in sync with a sociopraxis approach, CCCV began opening spaces of dialogue through "citizen forums" with the populations of different sectors of the city and social movements, about their experiences and expectations. A review of the past ten years shows that the organization has conducted three kinds of activities: (1) building conceptual frameworks based on guiding principles for the exercise of citizenship – which are presented in the section on CCCV Key Concepts; (2) identifying the need to raise awareness about citizen perceptions and opinions as a source for public decision making; and (3) promoting dialogues around knowledges and spaces of reflection to create proposals based on the lessons of the trajectories and struggles of Cuenca's social movements and the experiences of the city's residents. To showcase how our experiences and results have evolved over time, we offer the central experiences from three time periods.

First stage: thinking about the city as a collective (2009–2011)
In 2010, after conceptual debates, CCCV committed itself to promoting active citizenship around the issues discussed and promoted in the national constitutional process. The collective took on a critical stance and hosted multiple discussions trying to relate this new national legal framework to the space of the city. To this end, the CCCV carried out a "Citizen Forums Initiative." CCCV organized open discussions to consider the development of Cuenca given two key principles in the constitution: the Right to the City and *Sumak Kawsay* or Good Living. These discussions led to a deeper understanding of two kinds of publics – a state public and a non-state one. CCCV, which includes geographers, also carried out a collective mapping of Cuenca actors, identifying possible collaborators to build bridges between different perspectives and demands. The objective of the mapping and talks was to systematize, contrast, and face the diversity of concepts, understandings, and aspirations across the city. Part of what emerged was a fuller understanding of Cuenca as a diverse city. Given this finding CCCV realized that we needed to create a space for intercultural bonding to learn to live in diversity.

In the first year of our work, we were able to build relationships in some sectors of Cuenca to activate ourselves around a new way of doing politics and exercising citizenship to influence the design, construction, and transformation of the city as a public good and ethical project. Our dialogical methodology succeeded in involving more people in CCCV who were interested in contributing their ideas, dreams, and knowledge. With this success, we organized an intercultural week and created a communication campaign that showcased the diverse reality of the city.

Based on the results from the citizen forums, CCCV decided to conduct the first Survey of the Quality-of-Life Perceptions in Cuenca. The Sociology Department of the University of Cuenca supported our project. The survey was designed based on ideas shared at the citizen conversation tables in order to gather information on topics relevant to people's lives. It included questions on city aesthetics, environment, social equality, consumption, care of animals, satisfaction with life in Cuenca, transportation and mobility, safety, social support, housing, education, health, sports, culture, employment, public services, municipal management, institutional trust, transparency and accountability, personal and collective values, and lifestyles, etc.

To develop the survey (the first of its kind in Cuenca), in 2011, we followed the model of other surveys conducted in Latin America, incorporating from the Ecuadorian context not only *Sumak Kawsay* and the Right to the City, but also the recognition of the role of municipal governments as those responsible for the management of cities as laid out in the Organic Code of Territorial Organization Autonomy and Decentralization (COOTAD 2010). This first survey

(CCCV 2011) cemented the name of the collective as Colectivo Cuenca Ciudad para Vivir (Cuenca Collective Dedicated to Cuenca as a "City to Live," www.cccv.ec/).

This first survey not only gathered data on how people experience the city in diverse ways depending on their economic, social, gender, and ethnic position, it also allowed us to understand the metabolism (dynamic processes and structures) of the city, the causes and consequences of its growth, and the differences between the social and political forces that drive the city's future direction. CCCV aimed to analyze different aspects related to the city and its citizenship in order to create an informed conceptual structure and set of priorities for its work.

Our survey has contributed to citizen debates about lived realities in Cuenca as well as specific demands on topics of interest. We use the information when we make demands and negotiate with local authorities, who have in turn used the data to draft ordinances, develop baseline data, and elaborate public policy, especially on issues of mobility or transportation, and citizen security.

The results of the surveys reflect the real motivations and interests of the city's citizens. The majority of respondents believe that Cuenca has the resources and characteristics for its residents to experience a good life. These results also provoked a debate on the state and non-state dimensions of "the public." With the information gathered in the surveys, dialogues were developed between different actors that broadened citizens' visions of possibilities for our desired city. The systematization of findings has allowed citizens, academia, and public administration to carry out analyses that problematize reality in a more comprehensive way to improve the quality of decisions.

Second stage: activating the city (2012–2016)

Several of our projects during the second stage of CCCV positioned us as an active social collective at the local and national levels. We created and conducted the second Survey of Perception of the Quality of Life in Cuenca in 2012, the third in 2015, and the fourth in 2016. By repeating our surveys, we were able to identify changes in the perceptions of *cuencanos*, and to carry out analyses over time. The surveys on perceptions did not provide for a full representation of the city, but they did allow us to understand the dynamics of the major forces operating in its context as well as the changes in human behavior in the use and occupation of the city as a shared space. To return the data to community members and make the results of our efforts accessible to the general public, we created handouts with tables of citizen interest. In so doing, we sought to promote a continuous process of information sharing and reflection so as to deepen analysis and awareness of the themes from the survey data. Environmental pollution was identified as one of the top priorities so we developed videos on healthy lifestyles in the city to show the pollution processes ruining the city.

In another important accomplishment CCCV signed an interinstitutional agreement with the four universities in Cuenca to carry out capacity-building processes of citizenship called *Catedra Abierta de Educacion Ciudadana y Cultura de la Convivencia* (courses open to the public on Citizen Education and Culture of Coexistence). These had the objective: "to develop a community of wisdoms and knowledges that promote teaching-learning processes on Civic Education and the Culture of Coexistence, through the creation of programs and interactive projects that develop and disseminate competencies, skills and abilities for exercising an active and responsible citizenship, framed in the values of equity, solidarity, co-responsibility, justice and peace." Between 2013 and 2016, CCCV organized two sets of *Catedra Abierta*, called "Rediscovering Cuenca" and "Inside the City." In 2013, 56 people participated; in 2015, 98 did; and in 2018, in a third version approximately 90 people did. Although CCCV put out an open call for participants, we emphasized recruiting young people studying different fields at the universities. The *Catedras Abiertas* aimed to generate information about recreational activities in the city as well as providing the experience of new forms of participation in the city's development. We appreciated the students' interdisciplinary reflections on their experiences as inhabitants of Cuenca.

CCCV has trained more than 200 citizen leaders. Most of them were university students so that in their professional practice, they will integrate social commitment and service to the city values in their work and lives. Delegates from various social organizations and public institutions participated in the *Catedras Abiertas*, strengthening the focus on solidarity and collective rights. This training process is developed using PM that have enhanced the participation in more organic social processes. As a consequence, many of those trained are currently leaders of the city's social movements on issues such as the environment, feminist groups, and cultural groups.

In 2013, CCCV joined a recycling initiative organized by the city whose goal was to bring together public and private actors and community-based organizations to design public policies to improve the quality of life and working conditions for people dedicated to garbage collection in Cuenca. CCCV supported this project with a number of activities such as an information and awareness campaign on the work of waste pickers and recycling at home. We conducted a qualitative research project on the perception of solid waste management and recycling in Cuenca, and organized citizen roundtables to prepare the new recycling ordinance in Cuenca.

The collaborative work with the waste pickers has been one of the most important political spaces for CCCV's efforts. The waste pickers are one of the most vulnerable groups in the city. Most of them are very low-income families dedicated to their work for the well-being of the environment. In general, their work is not valued by either public administrators or the rest of the population. Organizing with waste pickers incorporates gender-based efforts in our work through the empowerment of the primarily female heads of families. In the last four years, we have actively participated in "Public Round Tables for Recycling," where we could host discussions and negotiate with the municipal authorities in order to influence a reformulation of the current recycling ordinance.

Turning to political education goals, in 2014 CCCV organized an education campaign about the local elections, "Informed Vote," to share the stances of mayoral and county board candidates of the province on relevant topics. Our goal was to create an informed public opinion on issues that had already been raised by CCCV in the forums, workshops, and surveys.

In the fall of 2016, the United Nations organized Habitat III, a conference on Housing and Sustainable Housing Development in Quito. Prior to the Quito gathering, CCCV organized the "International Meeting of Emerging and Sustainable Cities: Approaches to Citizenship Looking towards Habitat III." The Cuenca event brought together 120 people both Ecuadorian and foreign to discuss urban issues including the proposed Urban Agenda that would be part of Habitat III. During the three days of our event, people explored and debated how we as citizens from countries of the global south should position ourselves in the face of international agendas such as the Urban Agenda from the United Nations, and what could be our claims, alternatives, and commitments. It was an important event because it generated a critical vision on global approaches that tend to homogenize representations of cities. Through our international gathering in Cuenca, we engaged in retrospective analyses to identify the lessons from our collective and other alternative visions to the current world models that are developed with a commercial and speculative logic, where cities are envisioned as ideal sites for surplus capital investment. We were also able to exchange ideas and knowledge with citizen groups from other places such as Brazil and Colombia.

The "Declaration of Cuenca" that we created is a letter of introduction that systematizes and validates the issues and approaches that CCCV is promoting.[3] Currently, the Declaration of Cuenca continues to be a benchmark for both our organizational capacity and demonstrates our commitment to convening for social participation. During the three days, not only did we discuss the priority themes of the cities, but we also effectively applied pedagogies based in PAR techniques such as collaborative mapping and group participant observation. This process brought together our collective imagination as we developed the agreements to guide our public praxis towards our shared goal.

Third stage: participating in political and public policy arenas (2017–2019)
From October 2018 to February 2019, in the context of the electoral campaign for a new mayor and city and county officials, CCCV took on a new initiative: to collectively construct a Citizen's Agenda. The resulting document aimed to be a tool for political negotiation with those who sought to become the local government. In partnership with the FARO group of Quito (https://grupofaro.org), another entity similar to CCCV, we organized five citizen forums to collectively develop the new Citizen Agenda. In our efforts we drew from the results from previous PAR efforts, the Citizen Perception Surveys and the *Catedras*. Around 500 people and 15 specialists participated in these forums. Each citizen forum focused on a theme:

1. Mobility, connectivity, and public space.
2. Social inclusion, productivity, and employment.
3. Municipal public management.
4. Water and environmental management.
5. Cultural management, identity, and tourism.

Each theme was divided into three sub-arenas such that ideas were gathered and plans formulated for 15 urban issues. In the forums, topic experts served as facilitators for information sharing, proposal making, and evaluation. At the end of each forum, we asked the experts to share the work group results in order to receive feedback from the rest of the participants, and to validate the information and proposals. In keeping with our approach, the forums were part of a participatory process, supported by an open call for people to join in, followed by a substantial diffusion of the results.

At the end of the five community-based forums, CCCV organized a sixth forum with an interdisciplinary group of academics, social movement leaders, and experts in the relevant fields to analyze the information gathered in the forums. The aim of this last forum was for individuals already involved in the research, design, and management of the themes in Cuenca to provide feedback on the proposed solutions.

The Citizen Agenda contains first-hand information that allowed us to extract the citizens' imaginaries around the axes worked on:

• Mobility, connectivity, and public space in Cuenca: "We dream of a connected, accessible and healthy city, where everyone can move safely and comfortably."

- Water management, protection of water sources, and environment in Cuenca: "We dream of a responsible citizenry caring and preserving our natural environment as part of a fair and ethical coexistence."
- Municipal public management of Cuenca: "We dream of a city as a common good, spatially just, humane and supportive, where residents live happily and in harmony with nature."
- Social inclusion and quality of life of the inhabitants of Cuenca. "We dream of a city where all people matter without discrimination or hate speech and practices."
- Cultural management, identity, and tourism in Cuenca. "We dream of a city that values its historical memory, lives its tangible and intangible heritage, takes care of it, enjoys it, builds it and tells its inhabitants and visitors."

The call for the forums was well received because the selected topics responded to previously identified citizens' concerns. Furthermore, participants have come to recognize and respect the work of CCCV as a facilitator committed to holding the city accountable. Holding the forums during an electoral season encouraged democratic participation and motivated civil society to assume an active role in democratic processes. Finally, the forums succeeded because we were able to create spaces for citizens to propose co-responsible solutions to the city's problems. One of the key outcomes was the development of shared questions for evaluating mayoral candidates' work plans because these were broadcast by the media and could be used by all the citizens to become more informed and active. In February 2019, CCCV and Faro together organized a candidate debate based on the results of the forums and the strategic questions. Through these projects, *cuencanos* became and were seen as interlocutors with the local government, which allowed them to become part of a channel of participation demanding that the government act in response to people's shared demands.

Once the new mayor was elected, CCCV presented the Citizen Agenda to him and distributed it broadly to the public. The mayor signed an agreement to carry out the demands of the population and to incorporate the recommendations in his plans and policies. The Citizen Agenda became the first collectively constructed document that collects and presents the expectations of a city imagined by its residents. This document is now a mandatory read for new city authorities. The Citizen Agenda has created a means for CCCV to follow up on how the city's work plans have incorporated its citizens' proposals.

CONCLUSION: THE PATH CONTINUES – COMBINING PARTICIPATORY ACTION RESEARCH AND COMMUNITY DEVELOPMENT

CCCV is a dynamic civil society organization that aims to promote reflection and deliberation on urban conflicts so as to change Cuenca's political culture. Using sociopraxis and PAR as epistemological and action frameworks, we have raised questions, offered solutions, and changed citizen participation practices. CCCV advocates that we need to rethink our ways of living, revamp the quality of our relationships, and transform the city. We seek to change our styles of learning and acting, that is, the ways in which we face everyday life problems (Villasante 2006). We seek to strengthen our community organization to be a force for the Right to the City to strengthen the participation, diversity, and social justice elements of urban decisions and interventions.

CCCV, alongside other local social movements, has for many years been developing knowledges about our communities and critiques of the dominant system. We have also developed proposals which include new ways of thinking and doing to improve different ways of living. CCCV is convinced that individuals' experiences are a source of knowledge. As a collective, we articulate, validate, and present our work as effective practices to use, transform, and live in the city. CCCV advocates for creative styles of organizing and exercising citizenship.

Through the work of its early years, CCCV became recognized as a key actor in the city that organizes a strictly citizen space defending collective rights. CCCV members frequently participate in important public opinion spaces. After ten years on our path, CCCV's most important lessons have emerged in and through the interactions, attitudes, and perceptions of *cuencanos*, in other words, in the citizen ethic that is at the heart of our community. The members of CCCV are people who come together to debate from different experiences and hold different kinds of employment positions. As such, CCCV can also be considered a network. The members serve as connectors with other groups, people, social movements, institutions, and social struggles. We are aware that our organic organization as a network allows us to easily circulate information, to build social capital and legitimacy, and to enable reflexivity, auto-criticism, and creativity.

CCCV has contributed to participatory territorial management in two ways. On the one hand, since deliberation and political praxis cannot be delegated, CCCV has focused on changing political culture and strengthening citizen organization by articulating social struggles, and opening multi-actor spaces of dialogue and proposal co-creation. On the other hand, CCCV has influenced public decision making by negotiating with local authorities. In general, CCCV conceives of society as a network in which CCCV members serve as social brokers driving critical community involvement in decision making. We help ourselves and others grapple with situations of power and establish bridges between groups, policy-makers, and professionals in different disciplines. Core to our efforts is the doing – or praxis – for by moving from ideas to actions, we gain new knowledge and potential for change. As we share our knowledges, we move from individual rights to collective rights.

The political impact of the CCCV comes from hard work in citizen participation, using PAR and PM. As we have nurtured common interpretations of reality, and developed collective proposals with concrete demands of people for public administrators, we have managed to bring decision makers and the general public closer together, to dialogue about city management and policies. As a result, our efforts are accepted and seen as legitimate by Cuenca's citizens and public authorities who now take into account our collective's demands. Nevertheless, as part of our commitment, we continue to evaluate, critique, and strengthen our efforts as part of the process of real transformation.

We hope that sharing our lessons and experiences motivates people to interrupt their lived realities and to inspire actors in other places to embrace their creative capacity for transformation while always remaining grounded in their local experiences. Social participation and praxis boosts creative collaboration which in turn generates:

- Solidarity: participation makes it possible to experience "otherness" directly; that is, an understanding of the condition of the Other.
- Development of collective solutions and imaginaries: these originate in the democratic exercise of the power to present our ideas in dialogue, to consider with respect the ideas

of others, and to evaluate our knowledge in the light of the knowledge of others. We have found a multiplier effect with creative, multiple, shared, and innovative knowledge.

- Appropriation of power: this includes valuing and recognizing our knowledges, experiences, and history.
- Construction of commitment: the commitment to act with social responsibility is configured in those knowledges that generate solidarity, collective thought, and the appropriation of power. The effect of producing commitment is constituted precisely by going through the experience that we can in fact effectively influence the circumstances that affect our lives.

NOTES

1. We thank Adrienne Falcón for her assistance translating this chapter.
2. See the UNESCO description at: https://whc.unesco.org/en/list/863.
3. The full declaration is available on the CCCV website: www.cccv.ec/download/PlanteamHabIII _00_Declaratoria_Planteamientos_HIII.pdf.

REFERENCES

Adams, Suzi, Paul Blokker, Natalie Doyle, John Krummel, and Jeremy Smith. 2015. Social imaginaries in debate. *Social Imaginaries*, 1(1), 15–52.
Boal, Augusto. 1974. *Teatro del oprimido y otras poéticas políticas*. Buenos Aires: Ediciones de la Flor.
Boff, Leonardo. 2009. Otro mundo es posible. Presentation at the World Social Forum gathering in Belem Brazil. www.elblogalternativo.com/2009/11/05/otro-mundo-es-posible-presentacion-con-la -conferencia-de-leonardo-boff-en-el-forum-social-de-brasil-2009/
Brenner, Neil, Peter Marcuse, and Margit Meyer. 2012. *Cities for People, Not for Profit: Critical Urban Theory and the Right to the City*. London: Routledge.
Cabrera Natasha and Elisa Bernal Reino. 2020. Turismo, patrimonio urbano y justicia social. El caso de Cuenca (Ecuador). *Anales de geografía de la Universidad Complutense*, 40(1), 11–29.
CCCV. 2011. Encuesta de percepción ciudadana sobre la calidad de vida en Cuenca-Ecuador 2011.
CCCV. 2012. Encuesta de percepción ciudadana sobre la calidad de vida en Cuenca-Ecuador 2012.
CCCV. 2015. Encuesta de percepción ciudadana sobre la calidad de vida en Cuenca-Ecuador 2015.
CCCV. 2016. Declaratoria de Cuenca: Planteamientos de la ciudadanía para Hábitat III. Cuenca-Ecuador. www.cccv.ec/download/PlanteamHabIII_00_Declaratoria_Planteamientos_HIII.pdf
CCCV. 2017. Encuesta de percepción ciudadana sobre la calidad de vida en Cuenca-Ecuador 2017.
CCCV. 2019. Agenda ciudadana para Cuenca: Reflexiones, propuestas y demandas para Cuenca desde la ciudadanía. Cuenca-Ecuador.
CCCV. 2020. 10 años de apuesta por la ciudadanía activa. www.cccv.ec/download/20201130_CCCV _SistematizacionExperiencia_10a.pdf
CEPAL. 2016. South American Social and Economic Panorama 2016. www.cepal.org/en/publications/ 40888-south-american-social-and-economic-panorama-2016
Ciudadana, L. O. D. P., Pleno, E. 2011. Ley orgánica de participación ciudadana. Quito.
Constitución del Ecuador. 2008. Registro Oficial, 20.
COOTAD, C. 2010. Código Orgánico de Organización Territorial. *Autonomía y Descentralización*. www.oas.org/juridico/pdfs/mesicic4_ecu_org.pdf
De Sousa Santos, Boaventura. 2014. Más allá del pensamiento abismal: de las líneas globales a una ecología de saberes. http://biblioteca.clacso.edu.ar/ar/libros/coedicion/olive/05santos.pdf
Del Campo Tejedor, Alberto. 2017. Antropología perspectivista o el giro ontológico. Crítica de un paradigma no tan nuevo. *Revista Pucara*, 28: 11–54.

Descola, Philippe. 2014. Modes of being and forms of predication. *HAU: Journal of Ethnographic Theory*, 4(1), 271–280.

Dussel, Enrique. 1994. *Historia de la filosofía y filosofía de la liberación.* Bogota: Editorial Nueva América.

Dussel, Enrique. 2001. *Hacia una filosofía política crítica* (Vol. 12). Bilbao: Desclée de Brouwer.

Dussel, Enrique. 2011. *Filosofía de la liberación. Fondo de cultura económica.* Mexico, DF: FCE.

Fals Borda, Orlando. 1985. *El problema de cómo investigar la realidad para transformarla: por la praxis.* Bogota: Tercer Mundo.

Fals Borda, Orlando. 2001. Participatory (action) research in social theory: Origins and challenges. In P. Reason and H. Bradbury (Eds), *Handbook of Action Research: Participative Inquiry and Practice* (pp. 27–37). London: Sage.

Ferrán, Roque. 2020. Hacia un paradigma de los cuidados. *BORDES*, 17, 23–30. file:///C:/Users/Usuario/Downloads/764-Texto%20del%20art%C3%ADculo-1394-1-10-20200915.pdf

Freire, Paulo. 1993. Pedagogía de la esperanza: un reencuentro con la pedagogía del oprimido. Mexico, DF: Siglo XXI.

Gattino, Silvia. 2013. Cuidados, solidaridad para con la naturaleza y en las relaciones sociales: política, estrategia, arte y apuesta. *Erasmus: Revista para el diálogo intercultural*, 15(2), 133–147.

Hayes, Matthew. 2020. The coloniality of UNESCO's heritage urban landscapes: Heritage process and transnational gentrification in Cuenca, Ecuador. *Urban Studies*, 57(15), 3060–3077.

Harvey, David. 2012. *Rebel Cities: From the Right to the City to the Urban Revolution.* London: Verso.

Hermida, Maria Augusta, Carla Hermida, Natasha Cabrera, and Christian Calle. 2015. La densidad urbana como variable de análisis de la ciudad. El caso de Cuenca, Ecuador. *EURE Revista de Estudios Urbano Regionales*, 41(124), 25–44.

Holloway, John. 2003. *Cambiar el mundo sin tomar el poder.* Buenos Aires: Herramienta.

Instituto nacional de estadísticas y censos. 2017. Ecuador en Cifras. www. ecuadorencifras. gob. ec/documentos/web-inec/Sitios/LIBRO buen vivir/files/assets/downloads/page 0032. pdf

Lake, Daniel and Joel Wendland, Joel. 2018. Practical, epistemological, and ethical challenges of participatory action research: A cross-disciplinary review of the literature. *Journal of Higher Education Outreach and Engagement*, 22(3), 11–42.

Lalander, Richard and Pablo Ospina Peralta. 2012. Movimiento indígena y revolución ciudadana en Ecuador. *Cuestiones políticas*, 28(48), 13–50.

Lander, Edgardo. 2010. Estamos viviendo una profunda crisis civilizatoria. *América Latina en movimiento*, 452, 1–3.

Lefebvre, H. 1996. *Writings on cities*, translated by E. Kofman and E. Lebas. Cambridge, MA: Blackwell.

McAdam, Doug. 1982. *Political Process and the Development of Black Insurgency.* Chicago: University of Chicago Press.

Pérez, Julia Rey and Alicia Tenze. 2018. La participación ciudadana en la Gestión del Patrimonio Urbano de la ciudad de Cuenca (Ecuador). *Estoa. Revista de la Facultad de Arquitectura y Urbanismo de la Universidad de Cuenca*, 7, 229–254.

Robles, Lomeli, Dilean Jafte, and Joanne Rappaport. 2018. Imagining Latin American social science from the global south: Orlando Fals Borda and participatory action research. *Latin American Research Review*, 53(3).

Snow, David, E. Burke Rochford, Steven Worden, and Robert Benford. 1986. Frame Alignment Processes, Micromobilization, and Movement Participation. *American Sociological Review*, 51(4), 464–481.

Stoecker, Randy. 2003. Understanding the development-organizing dialectic. *Journal of Urban Affairs*, 25(4), 493–512.

Svampa, Maristella. 2016. El Antropoceno, un concepto que sintetiza la crisis civilizatoria. *La izquierda diario*. www.laizquierdadiario.com/El-Antropoceno-un-concepto-que-sintetiza-la-crisis-civilizatoria

Theodore, Nic, Jaimie Peck, and Neil Brenner. 2011. *Neoliberal Urbanism: Cities and the Rule of Markets.* Oxford: Blackwell.

United Nations. 2016. Habitat III regional report: Latin America and the Caribbean. https://habitat3.org/wp-content/uploads/HabitatIII-Regional-Report-LAC.pdf

United Nations Educational Scientific and Cultural Organization. n.d. Historic centre of Santa Ana de los Ríos de Cuenca. https://whc.unesco.org/en/list/863

Villasante, Tomas. 1998. Redes y socio-praxis. In *Cuatro Redes para Mejor-Vivir*. Buenos Aires: Lumen-Hvmanitas.

Villasante Tomas. 2006. *Desbordes creativos: estilos y estrategias para la transformación social*. Madrid: Catarata.

Villasante Tomás. 2014. Participación e integración social. *Boletín CF+ S*, 3.

Villasante, Tomás. R. and Pedro M. Gutiérrez. 2006. Redes y conjuntos de acción: para aplicaciones estratégicas en los tiempos de la complejidad social. *Redes. Revista hispana para el análisis de redes sociales*, 11. https://revistes.uab.cat/redes/article/view/v11-n2-vilasante-martin

Zemelman, Hugo and Guadalupe Valencia Garcia. 1990. Los sujetos sociales, una propuesta de análisis. *Acta sociológica*, 3(2), 89–104.

20. Leading with locally produced knowledge: development in Jemna, Tunisia

Ihsan Mejdi and Celeste Koppe

In 2011 the people of Jemna, a rural town in the south of Tunisia, reclaimed agricultural lands through non-violent direct action. The land had previously been occupied by colonizers and authoritarian leaders, and during the 2011 Tunisian revolution locals staged sit-ins and protests to eventually take control of the land. The people of Jemna proceeded to successfully manage agricultural production, using profits to implement several ongoing community development projects. Throughout this process, community leaders managed to defy critics of decentralization by creating and sustaining an association in which they used participatory planning to facilitate discussions and an inclusive decision-making process for – and effective management of – the agricultural lands and development projects.

The experience of community development in Jemna is uniquely grassroots when it comes to the knowledge used to claim and manage the local resources. Collective memory and heritage, paired with the democratic opening created by a popular revolution, motivated locals to reclaim the land, and traditional values propelled the community to organize their economic and development activities to reflect a solidarity economy. The case of Jemna thus highlights the importance of locally produced knowledge within marginalized post-colonial communities, as well as the ability of the community to identify traditional values and translate them into effective community development. This chapter also argues that the potential of this localized knowledge and tradition is not limited to the community itself, but rather it can be better understood through participatory action research to benefit communities in similar conditions.

THE TWO DIMENSIONS OF MARGINALIZED KNOWLEDGE

The First Dimension: Developed versus Developing Countries

Despite recent trends in international development to involve local communities in decision-making processes, leading actors from developed countries still view underdeveloped nations as lacking the knowledge to improve. Moreover, these external actors continually value, for the most part, scientific and technical information over traditional forms of knowledge along with a firm understanding of context and complexities of the target community (Cummings et al. 2019). For example, they place more importance on the possession of and experience with technology, rather than the capacity to identify the roots of problems and implement sustainable solutions by utilizing the awareness of internal actors. This dynamic of marginalization translates into the theory and practice of community development as external researchers and practitioners define their roles in the process in relation to local actors. Through this process, a hierarchy forms in which external actors acquire more privilege than the internal actors as a result of the types of knowledge they prioritize.

The gradual transition from needs-based community development (or problem-centric) to asset-based community development (ABCD) that began in the 1970s represents a step forward in terms of changing the hierarchical recognition of knowledge within community development approaches (Nel 2018). The former, which involves an external evaluator who identifies problems and then provides donations or services, perpetuated a psychology in which community members internalized and then became defined by their deficits – whether it be a lack of material resources or knowledge (Khadka 2012; Kretzmann and McKnight 1996). The latter encourages community members to focus on their internal resources in order to problem solve with the tools, or resources, they excel at (Nel 2018). Mathie and Cunningham (2003) note that through this reorganization of roles and focus, community members are no longer clients but are able to fully engage as active citizens. Alsop (2005) expands on this realization of citizenship, stressing the need for external actors to view members of the community as not only citizens, but citizens with capabilities.

The role of the external actor as someone from outside of the community, or country, continues to be key in approaches to development. An evaluation of the ABCD approach showed that, in many cases, governments implemented the strategy to shift responsibilities onto the community while ignoring discussions surrounding the roots of inequality. Especially in situations in which governments or external actors played a role in discrimination or injustice, they dismiss their potential role in correcting histories of oppression through this approach (MacLeod and Emejulu 2014). Rather than participating as a productive stakeholder, the external actor neglects their responsibility in development and thus neglects the importance of the target community altogether – including the locally produced knowledge. Khadka (2012) presents a mixed-method approach for community development to avoid this dismissal of responsibility. He advocates for a combination of ABCD and the human rights-based approach (HRBA), which engages citizens through ABCD while increasing the accountability of governments and their institutions. In such a situation, community members hold the power to make decisions and lead development, while HRBA ensures that historical injustices and marginalization do not undermine their efforts.

This mixed-methods approach addresses the pitfalls of ABCD because, as Broberg and Sano (2018) explain, it recognizes inequality and discrimination as the main causes of poverty. When this principle is established, community members conceptually transform from passive recipients into active rights holders. They become citizens with entitlements (Alsop 2005). The outcome of this approach, then, is strengthened citizenship through universal rights. The role of external actors when implementing HRBA tends to be defined as empowering community members through education, increasing legal capacity and providing legal services, and also advocating as allies (Gready and Ensor 2005). With these roles in mind, the external actor brings knowledge of rights to sensitize citizens and contributes by providing technical knowledge related to law and policy.

Other studies show that external actors make a larger impact when providing critical resources and ways to pressure governments to respect the rights of communities and citizens (Storeng et al. 2019). In exchange for incentives such as increases in development aid, recipient governments are more inclined to follow internationally recognized treaties and policies regarding human rights. These findings suggest that external actors are most effective when performing the role of ally or advocate, while locally produced knowledge is sufficient in promoting understandings of inequalities and injustices.

Yet, the forms that knowledge and participation take in this context create an intersection between community development and participatory action research. The knowledge prioritized determines the power dynamics of participation, which is the key pitfall of community development theory and practice. In contrast, PAR has the potential to make space for a critical look at how knowledge is created, and moreover which types of knowledge are honored and later applied. This chapter therefore explores this potential, drawing on Fals Borda and Rahman's theory of conscientization (1991), which facilitates a critical recovery of history by allowing internal actors to develop their self-knowledge of history and culture.

The Second Dimension: Urban versus Rural, the Center versus Regions

The second dimension of marginalized knowledge occurs at the national level in developing states between the central governments based in the capital city and communities on the periphery. Development in this sense materializes as either state-led, top-down projects or participatory, grassroots initiatives. The capital city center holds the reputation of modernization and industrialization, and possesses more resources than the traditional, rural communities at the margins (Salman 2017; Vaughan 1995). In most cases, the central government controls and carries out all processes such as voting, tax collection, and resource distribution. This often involves individuals born and raised in the capital having a larger influence on, for example, how and when a school is built than the members of the community the school will serve. Therefore, political decentralization is key to community development because of its potential to localize and legitimize political authority and decision-making processes (Vaughan 1995). At its core, political decentralization means creating and empowering local government bodies to oversee tax collection and resource distribution and implement government services within their local communities. By inverting the previous top-down hierarchy of centralized government, political decentralization has the potential to be a facilitator of ABCD and HRBD as it would ultimately divest power from external actors (those coming from the capital) into the internal actors (local community members).

Research undertaken by political scientists demonstrates that the effects of political decentralization depend on the circumstances of the particular country (Salman 2017; Storeng et al. 2019). A study focused on decentralization in Uganda, Rwanda, and South Africa shows particularly how governments have the power to shape decentralization to fit the needs of their countries, as well as implement political decentralization in an effective manner, if they are committed to the strategic political structure. It argues that the country's policies have the power to carry out decentralization, with an emphasis on electoral decentralization as the cornerstone of deconcentrating power and resources in order to build a more democratic state (Cheema and Rondinelli 2007). A more general study shows that in the late twentieth century 76 percent of developing countries supported some degree of political decentralization whether it is facilitated by subnational or local elections. The United Nations Development Programme and World Bank then commended these countries for improved governance and human development (Work 2002). In essence, researchers and the international development community believe that political decentralization can be achieved through proper leadership on behalf of governing politicians to cement democracy at the grassroots level.

Yet, the language of top-down decentralization used by international development agencies like the World Bank and International Monetary Fund is post-political, meaning their word choice explicitly does not allow the process to address historical injustices (Salman 2017).

For example, the development models favored by these actors view "centered growth" as unavoidable and employ the language of "leading" and "lagging" regions instead of "privileged" and "marginalized" (Salman 2017). The central governments of the target countries also tend to employ these terms used by their implementation partners while grassroots civil society organizations and activists stress the language that brings historical inequalities to the forefront. A close reading of development terms here shows concrete forms of marginalization within both dimensions, the second of which will be elaborated in the following paragraphs.

In the case of Tunisia, the need for the government to decentralize is clear. Scholars attribute regional disparities as one of the leading causes of the 2011 revolution (Aldana and Fassi 2016). Historically, the coastal regions have received more resources and attention to infrastructure than the interior regions within the country, leaving rural areas like Kasserine, Sidi Bouzid, and Gafsa considerably underdeveloped in terms of the economy, government services, and the overall standard of living. Protests in these areas played a large role in inciting protests around the country to overthrow Ben Ali in hopes of creating a democratic state that would ultimately administer justice to these regions.

However, the reluctance of states with strong central governments to engage in this power-sharing system shows they are skeptical of the capabilities of the local communities (Aldana and Fassi 2016). On top of that, the historic regional disparities have been perpetuated by post-revolutionary central governments in the form of "multiple marginalizations" (Sadiki 2019: 1) or systematic socio-economic and political inequalities. As of 2017 the Tunisian government relies on a timeline of 27 years for central authorities to fully hand over decision-making power and financial authority to local authorities (Fida 2016). This ambiguous and prolonged transfer of authority to locally elected government officials then created a situation in which voters went to the polls in 2018 without knowing what explicit duties or powers the candidates under consideration would hold – or if they would be invested with any capabilities at all to practically apply the promises on which they campaigned (Muasher and Yerkes 2018). Ultimately, the hesitation of the central government to increase the role of local representatives in the governance of their jurisdiction undermines locally produced knowledge and participatory forms of development at the national level, which theoretically cements the second dimension of marginalization.

JEMNA IN SOUTHERN TUNISIA: A CASE IN CONTEXT

In 2011, the Middle East and North Africa witnessed mass protests that led to the overthrow of authoritarian regimes. In Tunisia, where these protests started, long-time dictator Zin El-Abidin Ben Ali was ousted after a wave of demonstrations swept across the country from December 17 to January 14. Crackdowns on opposition figures and parties in Tunisia, corruption, and lack of freedoms characterize Ben Ali's years in power. Specifically, interior regions of the country suffered these injustices more so than coastal areas as his regime marginalized the former in order to invest and further develop in the latter; a phenomenon known as regionalism.

The problem of regionalism in Tunisia did not start with Ben Ali. Since its independence from France in 1956, the North African country's developmental strategies have resulted in severe socio-economic disparities. Uneven development is most visible between the thriving north with its coastal regions and the marginalized internal zones. The spatial dichotomy is rooted in an economic duality (Aldana and Fassi 2016) whereby the north benefits from a dynamic export-oriented sector and public investment in infrastructure (Gouider and Nouira 2015), whereas the inland regions remain economically stagnant and marked by high unemployment rates and low-quality infrastructure. This is coupled with a concentration of a small dominant political and economic elite in the urban center Tunis, the capital, and the coastal region of the Sahel (Sadiki 2019). Roughly, the sense of marginalization experienced by local actors at the periphery can be conceptualized as a reaction to a complex history of symbolic and material inequalities. It is a reaction to social, political, and economic exclusion experienced throughout the periods of colonialism, post-independence state formation, and the 23 years of the ousted Ben Ali's rule.

A month of protests started following Mohamed Bouazizi's act of self-immolation on December 17, 2010. The municipal police in Sidi Bouzid, hometown of street vendor Bouazizi, confiscated the cart that he used to sell fruits on the street. To protest this, Mohamad Bouazizi set himself on fire in public. Yet, his act was not a mere protest of municipal police practices. Rather, it was a reaction to a lived socio-economic condition marked by unemployment, poverty, and marginalization. Large segments of the Tunisian society shared Bouazizi's sentiment – especially unemployed youth. Protesters came together with the main slogan of, "employment, freedom, and dignity!" Tunisians' success in toppling the regime snowballed to other Arab countries. On February 11, Hosni Mubarak, the president of Egypt, stepped down under street pressure after 29 years in power. The same fate awaited the presidents of Libya and Yemen in 2011. This event, which changed the face of the Middle East and North Africa in 2011 and still impacts its politics today, is known in the media and academia as the Arab Uprisings/Revolutions. More recently, Algerians and Sudanese took to the streets and demanded change. Demonstrators in both countries succeeded in bringing about change at the regime level. Even though the actions of protesters took place in 2019, for many, what happened in Algeria and Sudan echoed the spirit of the 2011 Arab Revolutions.

In this context, this chapter sheds light on the experience of Jemna, an internal marginalized town in southern Tunisia where the local community participated in the mass demonstrations of 2011. The case of Jemna (and the local community's participation in protest) is not only an episode of contentious politics (Tilly 2008). During the 2011 Tunisian revolution, the community, capitalizing on the event, marched towards a date palm oasis of 400 hectares, claimed it, managed it collectively, and used its revenues to implement developmental projects locally.

Jemna is a town in the southwest of Tunisia. It administratively belongs to the governorate of Kebili (Nefzaoua region). With 7,000 inhabitants, Jemna is geographically located in a region famous for its production of the high-quality "Deglet-Nour" dates. The European Union importation of dates is 90 percent Deglet-Nour and these come mainly from Tunisia and Algeria. In Tunisia, "the date-growing sector accounts for 4% of total agricultural production, 7% of plant production and 12% of agricultural exports" (Ben-Amor et al. 2015: 2).

However, Jemna remains marginalized in terms of investments and infrastructure despite its natural richness and contribution to the flourishing date-growing sector in Tunisia. This is not peculiar to Jemna. Indeed, other internal regions of Tunisia, such as Gafsa, suffer from marginalization whilst at the same time contributing immensely to the economy of the country. Facts such as these explain, to a large extent, why Bouazizi set himself on fire in Sidi Bouzid, and why protests that led to the removal of the president in 2011 started in Tunisia's internal regions.

Historical March towards the Oasis

When the news of Mohamad Bouazizi's self-immolation spread across Tunisia in the winter of 2010–2011, people began protesting in support of the street vendor's cause and to denounce the already existing problems of unemployment, corruption, and lack of freedom. Similarly, in Jemna, the inhabitants took to the streets in what became not only an act of solidarity with Bouazizi, but a nationwide popular revolution against the regime.

Historically, during the periods (1) of French colonialism in Tunisia (1881–1956), (2) of post-independence state formation, and (3) under Ben Ali's rule (1987–2011), Jemna had its share of marginalization. Thus, when the revolution broke out in 2011, the inhabitants capitalized on the political moment to make not only immediate claims, but also historical ones.

On January 12, two days before toppling Ben Ali's regime, akin to thousands of Tunisians throughout the country, hundreds of Jemnis were in the streets of the town, participating in what they refer to as "the revolution of freedom and dignity." They set the local police station on fire, something almost all protesters did in different parts of Tunisia in January 2011. Following this, the demonstrators started shouting; "Stil ... Stil," the name of the oasis they would later claim. Other inhabitants joined the demonstration and a march towards the Stil oasis started. Interlocutors we talked with told us that no one planned to direct the demonstration from the streets of the town to the oasis: "It was spontaneous." Yet, we understood from our interviews and conversations with members of the local community who participated in the march that a shared historical consciousness amongst the inhabitants of the town existed; the participants in the demonstration and march were aware of the *longue durée* land struggle in Jemna.

The oasis that the local community wanted to claim during the revolution was historically under common ownership of the inhabitants of Jemna. Our interlocutors told us that in the town many have their oases which are agricultural lands for the cultivation of dates. Yet, in addition to private oases that people in Jemna have, they all share one oasis which remains under common ownership. During the period of French colonialism in Tunisia, the local community in Jemna had been subject to processes of land dispossession. The colonizers controlled the oasis and forced Jemnis to work in their own land under a corvée law. In 1922 the French decided to start an agricultural company; Société Commericale et Agricole du Sud Tunisien, to benefit from date production in Jemna and in the region of Nefzaoua at large. The company's buildings still stand today in Jemna's oasis, including a fortified house at the heart of the oasis where colonizers who managed the oasis previously lived.

In 1956 Tunisia gained its political independence from France, yet the French kept controlling 300,000 hectares out of 450,000 hectares of agricultural land in Tunisia. On May 12, 1964, Habib Bourguiba, the leader of independence, issued a law, "which nationalised all the farmlands held by foreigners. By this law, 300,000 hectares passed into the domain of the Tunisian state" (Ayeb and Bush 2019: 104). Throughout these processes, the local community in Jemna was waiting to regain its control over the oasis, which they considered as their ancestors' land that was taken by the French. However, even after independence the inhabitants could not manage their oasis. This time, a national, postcolonial modernization project was initiated and required the nationalization of agricultural lands:

> The Tunisian peasantry was subjected to a policy of massive dispossession of their lands. The New Minister of Planning and Finance, Ahmed Ben Sala, wanted to recover the small farmers' land to con-

stitute large Cooperative Production Units, directly managed by state officials. Their main objective was to accelerate the mechanisation and modernization of the agricultural sectors of the economy, especially industry, considered as the strategic engine and the condition of overall economic development. (Ayeb and Bush 2019: 104)

The goal of the Cooperative Units for Agricultural Productions according to the policy makers was to "modernize agriculture and at the same time to achieve the objectives inherent in the education of the people" (Ayeb and Bush 2019: 105). However, the execution of the plan from 1960 to 1970 failed and the state had to shift its policy towards liberalization. "At that time, the state accelerated economic reforms towards a progressively aggressive uncontrolled neoliberalism. That period marked the use of the state to promote the interests of the leading politicians, their clients and power brokers in Tunis and rural Tunisia" (Ayeb and Bush 2019: 108). In this context, the oasis of Jemna was handed to the state-owned Tunisian Company of Dairy Industry (STIL) which managed the oasis from 1972 to 2002. Until today the local community in Jemna calls the oasis Stil, referring to the aforementioned period, or "the Moamer oasis," which stands for "the colonizer's oasis."

During Ben Ali's rule, the oasis was privatized and handed to two businessmen close to the regime. When the 2011 revolution broke out, the local community decided to march towards the oasis to claim it and kick out the investor who was managing it. Everyone in the town knew how the investor benefited from Ben Ali's crony capitalism and they also knew that they rightfully owned the oasis. The march was intended to restore their "ancestors' oasis," something for which they had been waiting for almost a century. Claiming the oasis marked only the start of a unique experience in Jemna from 2011 to the present time.

We will later shed light on how stories about the land and its history circulated in Jemna and became a tool of knowledge production and mobilization in the process of forging a model of community development.

Community Planning and Participatory Work: Setting the Ground for a Community-Led Development Model

When the protesters reached the oasis, they found a few workers who used to work for the two investors who were then managing the oasis. Interlocutors said that they wanted everything to be peaceful and thus asked the workers to take their material and leave the oasis. The protesters then discussed what they should do next and agreed to organize a sit-in which meant that they capitalized on the revolution to claim a "revolutionary" legitimacy. They determined that no one should be in the oasis but the inhabitants of the town. They would be physically there, defending their ancestors' land with their presence in the land, and with their bodies.

The sit-in lasted for approximately three months. In Jemna, everyone participated in one way or another. Jemnis set up tents inside the oasis, and someone always occupied the tents to keep the sit-in going. Others would come and stay until late into the night and then return to their homes. Female interlocutors in Jemna said that even though they did not participate directly by being in the oasis, they were providing the participants with food, blankets, mattresses, and clothes, etc. The members of the local community who were occupying the oasis also created an atmosphere of festivity. They would listen to songs, sing, and recite poems while gathering around the bonfire at night. In addition, during the first days following Ben Ali's fall, they formed Committees for the Protection of the Revolution (or the Revolutionary Safeguard Committees):

The popular insurrection then became radicalized. Demonstrations, strikes, and sit-ins in Tunis and the interior of the country were organized and coordinated by people's committees called "Revolutionary Safeguard Committees." These committees were elected by the revolutionaries on the spot to ensure the safety of citizens, especially during the first sixty days after the ousting of Ben Ali. (Aleya-Sghaier 2012: 24)

The oasis sit-in participants formed their local committee in Jemna as well. The role of the committee was to ensure the safety of citizens and their properties in the neighborhoods as police stations were burned throughout the country during the uprising. Yet, in Jemna the committee's role was also to organize public gatherings where everyone could speak and share their ideas to deliberate over the future of the oasis and how it should be managed. Meetings were held in the oasis and at the center of the town and lasted for hours and days.

Two main opinions emerged from the public meetings. Some thought of dividing the 400 hectares into smaller pieces of land which would later be shared among community members in Jemna. This option did not have as many supporters as the other, which supported keeping common ownership of the oasis and providing community benefit from its revenues to implement projects locally and ultimately employ youth in Jemna.

From 2011 to 2012 the inhabitants of the town managed the land collectively. They first collected donations through which they could buy the materials needed to work the land. Interlocutors said that the oasis needed maintenance as the investors did not care much about the trees' surrounding: "for them it was only about the fruit bunch ... they wanted to get the harvest and sell it. That's all." Many in the town participated in the process, some by working on the land and others by taking care of logistics and financial matters. In the first year, and always under the umbrella of the Committee for the Protection of the Revolution, the local community maintained the oasis's soil and wells, planted new date trees, and increased the number of workers from 7 to 113. From 2011 to 2012, the community's first experience of managing the date trees of the Stil oasis resulted in a revenue of approximately US$350,000. They used this amount to pay the roughly US$120,000 in order to maintain the land and cultivate it until the harvest. Throughout the public meetings, inhabitants would discuss what projects the town needed and how the profit should be used to benefit the community.

In 2012, a year after the events of the 2011 Tunisian revolution, the country moved to a phase of democratic transition. Tunisians elected a Constituent Assembly on October 23, 2011 that drafted a new constitution. These processes of institutionalizing the revolution meant that committees formed during the revolution by ordinary people had to be dissolved as police forces were functioning and able to protect citizens and properties. In Jemna, those who were part of the committee and had organized public gatherings and meetings to talk about the oasis and the projects to be implemented decided to form an official association (unlike the committees which were formed by people in neighborhoods during the revolution). Most inhabitants welcomed the idea, and they formed the Association for the Protection of Jemna's Oases (APJO) in 2012.

APJO consisted of ten members who participated as volunteers and were committed to continue the management of the oasis and the planning for the projects to be implemented locally using the revenues of dates. The local community voted democratically to choose the members of APJO. A list of candidates was circulated and members of the local community chose the names they wanted to be elected. Those who obtained the support of the majority were later appointed as members of APJO. The head of the association, Taher Tahri, for instance, is a retired teacher known for his activism within Tunisia's General Labor Union (UGTT) and the Tunisian League for Human Rights. His role as an internal actor (Fals Borda and Rahman 1991), as will be demonstrated in the next section of this chapter, was pivotal in the success of Jemna's experience.

From 2011 to 2016 APJO managed the oasis and sold the harvest through public tenders. In the period between 2011 and 2016 Taher Tahri met several state officials (from the Ministry of Agriculture and the Ministry of State Affairs) and politicians and discussed the situation of the association and the oasis with them. Tahri told us that all officials he met acknowledged the right of Jemnis to their land, but because of the uncertainties of democratic transition none of them could help the association to have a legal framework for managing the oasis. Ministers were changed and governments reshuffled frequently (from 2011 to 2020, Tunisia had nine prime ministers). The instability of the democratic transition made channels of dialogue between the local community and state officials complicated. Legally, the oasis was still considered a state property. In 2017, the Ministry of Agriculture issued a statement allowing APJO to continue its management of the land temporarily until finding a legal and institutional framework that would organize the activities of APJO. Such a decision, according to members of the community we talked with, shows that even the state acknowledged the success of the association and the right of the Jemnis to their land.

Within only five years of APJO's management of the oasis (2011–2017) the revenues reached more than US$800,000. APJO did not only succeed in creating job opportunities for the youth in the town with the revenues of date production, but also implemented the following projects from 2011 to the time of this writing:

- Construction of a covered marketplace, an indoor sports center, a mini-football pitch, classrooms in primary schools, and a public Hammam.
- Maintenance of an autism center for children, schools' sanitary facilities, a cemetery, and a youth cultural house.
- Donations of equipment to the police station (a printer) and local medical center (air conditioners and an ambulance).
- Regular financial aid to students, poor families, a theatre club, Ithar-Charity Association, an association with the developmental goals, Women's Ulfa Charity Association, a music club, Jemna's Calligraphy Association, and Jemna's Chess Association.

Further, APJO donates to associations in nearby towns and organizes annual events to honor outstanding students from Jemna and these areas. Zied, a member of APJO, told the co-author, Celeste, that now the association is studying the implementation of three major projects: a recreational space for families and children in the town; the creation of greenhouses to diversify agricultural activities and not rely only on date production; and a laboratory to enhance the production and maintenance of the quality of dates. The laboratory project, Zied said, will be supervised by an agricultural engineer from the town and implemented in collaboration with the Tunisian Arid Regions Institute.

LOCAL KNOWLEDGE LEADING TO LOCAL DEVELOPMENT

Critical Recovery of History

In Jemna there is a shared historical awareness about the land struggle. Many interlocutors narrated the history of the town with relation to colonialism, the post-independence state, and Ben Ali's regime whenever we asked them about the act of occupying the oasis in 2011. In this context, "narrative activity provides tellers with an opportunity to impose order on otherwise disconnected events, and to create continuity between past, present, and imagined worlds" (Ochs and Capps 1996: 19). The locally narrated stories had the power to mobilize the community around the demand of restoring their oasis and served as catalysts for action.

The role of stories in the actions of the local community can be understood in line with what Fals Borda and Rahman call "conscientization": "Conscientization is a process of self-awareness-raising through collective self-inquiry and reflection. This permits exchange of information and knowledge but is opposed to any form of teaching or indoctrination" (Fals Borda and Rahman 1991: 17).

The event of claiming the oasis in 2011 was a revolutionary moment for the local community in Jemna. During the sit-ins, gatherings, or public meetings organized by the Committee for the Protection of the Revolution or later APJO, inhabitants would not only deliberate about the projects to implement in the town, but they would also invoke the history of the oasis and the town. History thus informs present action. The 2011 revolution is lived and imagined both as a moment of rupture in the political structures and as a continuation of the historical struggle of the inhabitants in the town to regain control over the oasis. When asked about why the oasis was not divided, our interlocutors would invoke history and talk about a tradition of solidarity in Jemna. For the local community, their actions reflect their past when the town was home to teachers and Sufi men, such as Sidi Ibrahim Jemni (1628–1721) and Sidi Moussa Jemni (1708–1771) who established a tradition of "feeding the needy and helping the poor." When they talk about the demonstration that took place on January 12, 2011, they invoke their past of resistance against colonial France, Habib Bourguiba, and Ben Ali. They act in the present, yet their acts are informed by the past, not necessarily as documented in books but as narrated locally.

The local community knew stories about how their ancestors referred to the date tree as "the tree of seven blessings" to denote the many uses of the tree and its fruit. Historically, without date trees, water springs, and wells, people would not have settled and survived in Jemna. As one of our interlocutors said, "oases were the center of the economy of the town." Another story circulates in Jemna about how in the 1980s the local community started building a school by collecting donations. Thus, when APJO implemented infrastructure projects in schools using the date revenue, the members of the association invoked the past of the local community, a past marked by solidarity and altruism.

When Ihsan visited the Alnajah primary school in Jemna, the director showed him classrooms built by APJO in 2017 and, while there, Ihsan noticed that there were still classrooms under construction. The director of the school told Ihsan that it was only when the association started to add classrooms that the Ministry of Education realized the school needed maintenance:

the Ministry is always late … when they started to construct classrooms I showed them the ones done by the APJO and I told them that they should follow the same style … you know when they build something it is usually done with zero creativity … all state buildings are the same … but this time they had an example to follow and they did.

Jemnis also frequently narrate stories about colonialism. Our interlocutor talked about Merillon and Mauss de Rolley, two colonists who lived in Jemna and exploited the inhabitants, forcing them to work in the oasis. With the colonial-imperial encounter, the local agency of Jemnis regarding the oasis became subject to colonial administration and the dynamics of colonial capital. These dynamics redefined land along the lines of profit and interest and the Jemni oasis became integrated within a capital system of a colonial space (Steinmetz 2017).

The colonial encounter in Jemna, the presence of Merillon and Maus, and the creation of Société Commericale et Agricole du Sud Tunisien reflected the macro logic of the imperial-colonial moment. Merillon thus came to rationalize Jemna's date economy. His strategies were informed by recent knowledge about the land, the climate, and "the natives." There were monographs, reports, studies, and statistics about Jemna and other regions of Tunisia. There were also friends in neighboring Algeria and the metropole who could transfer their colonial know-how to boost production. For Merillon and Maus there was nothing sophisticated about land, date palms, and Jemnis. Everything was simple, "legible," and measurable, yet "every act of measurement was an act marked by the play of power relations" (Scott 1998). Every act of imprisoning Jemnis, silencing them, forcing them to sign pledges and work the land, was an act of domination and subordination.

In contrast, for Jemnis, the oasis and its dates had a social use and a significance beyond the utilitarian and "practical reason" (Sahlins 1976). It is through the social, economic, and moral meaningfulness of oases that Jemnis could make sense of their identity. This vision and imagination of land contrasted with the narrowness of colonial vision. For the French colonialists, or even for Bourguiba, the leader of the post-independence modernization project, "the [oasis] as a habitat disappears and is replaced by the [oasis] as an economic resource to be managed efficiently" (Scott 1998: 13).

Through narrating stories about their past, the local community in Jemna engaged in a process of "self-awareness-raising" (Fals Borda and Rahman 1991: 17). Their awareness of how the colonizers' or the state's top-down modernization projects resulted in their marginalization in the past directed and guided their actions in the present. Additionally, the 2011 revolution presented a moment of democratic opening that allowed for such discussions and talks about the past to take place. Community development and participation were then preceded by a moment of "critical recovery of history" (Fals Borda and Rahman 1991: 8).

Internal and External Actors

In addition to the abstract processes of critical recovery of history and conscientization, the case of Jemna showcases how local and marginalized communities can capitalize on locally produced knowledge to organize, plan, and achieve development.

After the occupation of the oasis in 2011, recall that the local community in Jemna faced a major decision of either keeping common ownership of the land or dividing it among the inhabitants. Similarly, community members later collectively debated which projects should be implemented in these public gatherings in which they discussed the needs of the town and the available resources. The Committee for the Protection of the Revolution organized public gatherings to discuss this. To ensure as many Jemnis as possible attended the gatherings, the Committee for the Protection of the Revolution, and later on APJO, would share the event, date, and time by driving through neighborhoods announcing the details through a loudspeaker, posting on social media, spreading the word through personal networks, and distributing flyers and hanging them by the entrances of cafes and shops.

Clearly the ways in which APJO managed the land and viewed development differed from how the previous investors, the STIL company or the state, did. The local community's know-how was derived from their own experiences of farming. The members of APJO, and almost every family in Jemna, have a private land or oasis where they grow dates. The culture of date cultivation is strongly embedded in the Jemni collective identity. Thus, the local community didn't need any "experts" on farming to show them how things should be done. In contrast, our interlocutors insisted, including Taher Tahri, the head of APJO, that they wanted to show the state they could deal with the problem of uneven development by capitalizing on the land and their knowledge about date cultivation, which they inherited from their ancestors. Furthermore, the sense of belonging to the land and the understanding that the natural resources of the oasis would go towards the development of the town encouraged inhabitants to volunteer and participate.

Both internal and external actors (Fals Borda and Rahman 1991) participated in Jemna's experience. The head of APJO, Taher Tahri, for instance, was one of the main influential internal actors. His symbolic capital as a respected retired French teacher in the town, coupled with his activism within Tunisia's UGTT and the Tunisian League for Human Rights, allowed him to access different networks and mobilize activists and politicians to support Jemna's unique experience of self-development. For instance, Tahri, through his networks, mobilized Jemni and other Tunisian diaspora in France to support the experience of Jemna and visited them in Paris in 2016. When negotiations between APJO and the Ministry of State Affairs or the Ministry of Agriculture took place, Tahri drew on his experience with the UGTT and League for Human Rights to negotiate with state officials and communicate the demands and aspirations of the local community. His mastery of French also allowed him to communicate with French-speaking journalists and academics who were interested in the experience of Jemna. In 2019, a group of Middle Eastern studies master's students from Lund University visited Jemna to learn about the developments. As some of them knew French, Tahri could easily talk to them about the experience of Jemna. Ihsan was there that day, and he observed closely how Tahri was narrating the events whilst students were taking notes and asking questions. The scene was indeed very telling, and one could easily see how popular knowledge originating from a local experience of a marginalized community in the global south can inspire researchers and students from the north.

Moreover, a number of "catalytic external agents" (Fals Borda and Rahman 1991: 6) participated in the process, including a group of civil society activists and students who initiated the national campaign to support the experience of Jemna. These activists organized what they called the Jemna Oases Solidarity Group upon a decision taken by the Ministry of State to declare the oasis and its revenue a state property. On October 8, 2016, the solidarity group organized a caravan from the capital city of Tunis and called on people including journalists, politicians, and human rights activists to visit Jemna to learn about their experience (Alkniss 2019).

In addition to these activities, Jemna's solidarity group started a hashtag on social media that read "Support Jemna. Common good before private profit" to inform people about the dispute between the state and local community. All this was coupled with the organization of events in the capital city to discuss the problems of state-owned lands and the development strategies in the internal regions of Tunisia. The pressure of civil society activists and increased visibility of the local community's success in implementing projects locally pushed the Ministry of State Properties to issue a statement allowing APJO to manage the land while resuming negotiations to find a legal framework that would organize their activities.

Other external agents included academics, both from Tunisia and outside, who were interested in Tunisia's democratic transition and Jemna's experience (see Ben-Slimane et al. 2020). And lastly, collective blogs such as Nawaat.org, legal-agenda.com, and news platforms, meshkal.org, increased the visibility of Jemna's developmental model.

As a result of the growing interest in Jemna's experience since 2011, and the collective efforts of both the internal and external actors in "linking up the local dimension to regional, and at a later stage, to the national and the international levels" (Fals Borda and Rahman 1991: 6), the Tunisian parliament passed a draft law of solidarity economy on June 17, 2020. During the parliamentarian session, the members of parliament cited Jemna's experience and praised it as the inspiration behind the bill. And even though the law is yet to be enacted, it has already offered the local community a legal framework to carry on their developmental projects in the future. For members of the local community, the bill translated both their historical land struggle and the ethos of the 2011 revolution. In Jemna, one of our interlocutors told Ihsan in 2019 that the absence of a law that regulates APJO's activity does not mean that the association must stop those activities. Rather, a new law has to be enacted, he said. One that puts into consideration the 2011 revolution as an event capable of reversing the history of political, social, and economic marginalization in rural Tunisia. Thus, the case of Jemna also opens spaces for thinking about how political transitions, such as Tunisia's ongoing democratic transition, are lived and imagined at the local level where politics does not manifest solely at the institutional level, but also in the lived history that informs marginalized actors' political participation in the present.

CONCLUSION

Jemna's promising experience of self-development in the context of a rural community belonging to a developing country highlights the fact that, when it comes to approaches to community development, locally produced knowledge must be seen as key to the process and not just a factor in facilitating externally created projects or solutions. Furthermore, the case of Jemna shows the power of community knowledge situations in which democratic opportunities allow for ownership and local leadership and participation. All actors of the development process must be cautious of different levels of marginalization, and how these varying cycles of marginalization operate at both the international and national levels. External actors should define their role as assistants to local leaders and participants. Ultimately, community development cannot be successful in an apolitical manner. Successful approaches to development require achievement in the sphere of politics to ensure that improvements continue in a systematic way in the future. The case of Jemna demonstrates also the potential for participatory action research in the context of Tunisia's democratic transition. The democratic opening offered space for the marginalized to restore historical, social, and political agency; this was coupled with the efforts of external agents to increase the visibility of Jemna's experience.

REFERENCES

Aldana, Alfonso Medinilla and Sahra El Fassi. 2016. *Tackling Regional Inequalities in Tunisia*. Brussels: ECDPM.

Aleya-Sghaier, Amira. 2012. "The Tunisian Revolution: The Revolution of Dignity." *Journal of the Middle East and Africa* 3(1): 18–45.

Alkniss, Ali. 2019. "Jemna: Struggle over Land: The State against the Local Community." *Les Cahiers Du FTDES* 2: 203–236.

Alsop, Ruth. 2005. *Power, Rights and Poverty: Concepts and Connections*. Washington, DC: World Bank.

Ayeb, Habib and Ray Bush. 2019. *Food Insecurity and Revolution in the Middle East and North Africa: Agrarian Questions in Egypt and Tunisia*. London: Anthem Press.

Ben-Amor, Rihab, Encarnación Aguayo, and M. Dolores De Miguel-Gómez. 2015. "The Competitive Advantage of the Tunisian Palm Date Sector in the Mediterranean Region." *Spanish Journal of Agricultural Research* 13(2): 1–8.

Ben-Slimane, Karim, Rachida Justo, and Nabil Khelil. 2020. "Institutional Entrepreneurship in a Contested Commons: Insights from Struggles over the Oasis of Jemna in Tunisia." *Journal of Business Ethics* 166(4): 673–690.

Broberg, Morten and Hans-Otto Sano. 2018. "Strengths and Weaknesses in a Human Rights-Based Approach to International Development: An Analysis of a Rights-Based Approach to Development Assistance Based on Practical Experiences." *International Journal of Human Rights* 22(5): 664–680.

Cheema, G. Shabbir and Dennis A. Rondinelli. 2007. *Decentralizing Governance: Emerging Concepts and Practices*. Washington, DC: Brookings Institution Press.

Cummings, Sarah, Anastasia A. Seferiadis, Jeroen Maas, Joske F. G. Bunders, and Marjolein B. M. Zweekhorst. 2019. "Knowledge, Social Capital, and Grassroots Development: Insights from Rural Bangladesh." *Journal of Development Studies* 55(2): 161–176.

Fals Borda, Orlando and Muhammad Anisur Rahman. 1991. *Action and Knowledge: Breaking the Monopoly with Participatory Action Research*. Lexington, KY: Apex Press.

Fida, Nasrallah. 2016. "Carter Center Calls for Improvements in Electoral Legislation, and for Municipal and Regional Elections." Atlanta, GA: The Carter Center. www.cartercenter.org/news/pr/tunisia-092816.html

Gouider, Abdessalem and Ridha Nouira. 2015. "Regional Inequality of Public Investment in Infrastructure in Tunisia." *European Academic Research* 3(7): 8527–8554.

Gready, Paul and Jonathan Ensor. 2005. *Reinventing Development? Translating Rights-Based Approaches from Theory into Practice*. London: Zed Books.

Khadka, Raj. 2012. *Switching Gears: From Needs to Assets Based Approach to Community Development in Nepal*. SSRN Scholarly Paper. ID 2047887. Rochester, NY: Social Science Research Network.

Kretzmann, John and John P. McKnight. 1996. "Assets-Based Community Development." *National Civic Review* 85(4): 23–29.

MacLeod, Mary Anne and Akwugo Emejulu. 2014. "Neoliberalism with a Community Face? A Critical Analysis of Asset-Based Community Development in Scotland." *Journal of Community Practice* 22(4): 430–450.

Mathie, Alison and Gord Cunningham. 2003. "From Clients to Citizens: Asset-Based Community Development as a Strategy for Community-Driven Development." *Development in Practice* 13(5): 474–486.

Muasher, Marwan and Sarah Yerkes. 2018. "Decentralization in Tunisia: Empowering Towns, Engaging People." *Carnegie Endowment for International Peace*. https://carnegieendowment.org/2018/05/17/decentralization-in-tunisia-empowering-towns-engaging-people-pub-76376

Nel, Hanna. 2018. "A Comparison between the Asset-Oriented and Needs-Based Community Development Approaches in Terms of Systems Changes." *Practice* 30(1): 33–52.

Ochs, Elinor and Lisa L. Capps. 1996. "Narrating the Self." *Annual Review of Anthropology* 25: 19–43.

Sadiki, Larbi. 2019. *Regional Development in Tunisia: The Consequences of Multiple Marginalization*. Doha: Brookings Doha Center.

Sahlins, Marshall David. 1976. *Culture and Practical Reason*. Chicago, IL: University of Chicago Press.

Salman, Lana. 2017. "What We Talk about When We Talk about Decentralization? Insights from Post-Revolution Tunisia." *L'Année Du Maghreb* 16: 91–108.

Scott, James C. 1998. *Seeing Like a State: How Certain Schemes to Improve the Human Condition Have Failed*. New Haven, CT: Yale University Press.

Steinmetz, George. 2017. "The Octopus and the Hekatonkheire: On Many-Armed States and Tentacular Empires." In *The Many Hands of the State*, edited by K. J. Morgan and A. S. Orloff. Cambridge: Cambridge University Press, pp. 369–394.

Storeng, Katerini T., Jennifer Palmer, Judith Daire, and Maren O. Kloster. 2019. "Behind the Scenes: International NGOs' Influence on Reproductive Health Policy in Malawi and South Sudan." *Global Public Health* 14(4): 555–569.

Tilly, Charles. 2008. *Contentious Performances*. Cambridge: Cambridge University Press.

Vaughan, Olufemi. 1995. "Assessing Grassroots Politics and Community Development in Nigeria." *African Affairs* 94(377): 501–518.

Work, Robertson. 2002. "Overview of Decentralization Worldwide: A Stepping Stone to Improved Governance and Human Development." *Philippine Journal of Public Administration* 24.

21. Relationship as resistance: partnership and *vivencia* in participatory action research

José Wellington Sousa

Participatory action research (PAR) in its different forms has become an attractive way to produce knowledge and advance academic careers while serving civil society. In this endeavor, discussions around how to build effective partnerships between university and community groups have gained relevance in academic circles. Although researchers involved in PAR recognize the relevance of democratizing knowledge creation and furthering social justice, power imbalances between partners still need to be addressed. Part of the issue is how difficult it is for academics to break free from individualistic and capitalist academic culture. Consequently, researchers are inclined to perceive relationships through a utilitarian and instrumental lens and consequently as a necessary strategy in the academic political economy. Meanwhile, community groups, mostly marginalized, feel used and see little to gain by partnering with higher education institutions for research or any other service (Ross and Stoecker 2017). Given this scenario, how can academics, including myself, reimagine better ways to engage with community groups?

In this chapter, I am revisiting the concept of partnership by looking back at the southern critical tradition of PAR such as Paulo Freire's *Pedagogy of the Oppressed* and Orlando Fals Borda's idea of *vivencia*. I argue that by doing this we will be able to receive valuable insights on how to engage in more authentic subject-to-subject relationships with the community. I am employing the term *southern critical tradition* to emphasize that PAR originated in the global south as a social movement to dismantle oppressive social structures (Leal 2011). Hence, PAR is ultimately an approach for people to organize themselves, learn together, and transform their own reality. In other words, PAR is primarily a community development model that has research as part of the framework (Ledwith 2020; Stoecker 1999). Furthermore, the idea of the global south goes beyond geographic location; it evokes an understanding that PAR serves the interests of those who are marginalized and oppressed in society (Greenwood and Levin 2011) rather than institutions.

This chapter is situated in the tension between PAR as a research approach and as a community development model. By taking this into consideration, I start my reflection by drawing from my experience as a community development practitioner in the Brazilian Amazon on a less utilitarian and more relational basis. Then, I use my own story as an experiential basis to think about how partnership has been portrayed in both the global north and south. Due to confidentiality, I use pseudonyms for the community members as well as the non-profit organization that I worked with. Finally, I draw from Paulo Freire's and Orlando Fals Borda's insights to argue that a more collectivist and people-centered way to engage with community groups is a form of resistance against the institutional status quo. Consequently, it has the potential to lead us towards more community-driven projects in which building relationships is not a strategy, but a way to be in the world.

THIS RIVER IS MY STREET: MY EXPERIENCE AS A STARTING POINT

I was born in Pará, the second largest Brazilian state and part of the Amazon Region. Yet, I was raised in a family with European roots from a different and more economically dynamic part of the country. Though I was surrounded by the Amazonian reality, I only embraced the local culture after becoming an adult. A significant part of this process was my studies on regional development and relationship building with Amazonian traditional peoples. The song titled *Esse rio é minha rua* [This river is my street], composed by local artists Ruy Barata and Paulo Barata, beautifully expresses the reality of the ribeirinhos (river peoples), one of the largest traditional populations of the region. This song includes elements of the popular way of speaking and portrays animals and Amazonian myths that are part of the everyday life of the rural northern population of Brazil (Costa 2008). It expresses the knowledge that comes from the waters – *os saberes das águas* – which brings forth the imaginary and relational way of living (Pojo et al. 2014). Pojo et al. (2014) elucidate that in this relational way of living, humans form community with nature and find in the waters the main representation of their social, economic, political, and cultural identity.

River people communities echo Ferdinand Tönnies' notion of community (*Gemeinschaft*). According to Peet and Hartwick (2015), for Tönnies, community refers to "groups based on family and neighborhood bonds that engender feelings of togetherness" (130). However, Tönnies was describing the features of a pre-capitalist society which was destined to disappear with the advancement of capitalism (Lira and Chaves 2016). Yet, Lira and Chaves (2016) clarified that river people communities as well as other traditional communities of the Amazon such as indigenous, quilombola (descendants of runaway African slaves), and extractive communities are not pre-capitalist. On the contrary, they are non-capitalist.

Costa (1995) explained non-capitalist rationality of economic agents by basing himself on Marx and Chayanov. He argued that traditional Amazonian populations hold a peasant economic rationality whereby the need for investment is oriented by the necessities of family reproduction. Indeed, this rationality, in addition to the accumulation of ancestral knowledge and a particular habitus – a specific disposition of mind and body (Bourdieu 1986) – gives these populations the quality of being a traditional people group (Costa 2005; Prado 2018). In the Amazon, Costa (2005) claimed, this peasant rationality remains and therefore contradicts capitalist projects encouraged in the region since the 1980s. Instead, a peasant rationality suggests an alternative development project based on a diverse and family-based economic production which may lead to decentralization of the means of production and income and consequently to more social equity. According to Costa (2005), this alternative development model has relatively low environmental risks. However, it depends on institutional incentives and relies on associational life and knowledge sharing among the production units to succeed.

Becoming a Community Development Practitioner

I began my journey as a community development practitioner with river peoples and quilombolas in 2011 as a volunteer with Healthcare Outreach, an international faith-based and voluntary-based non-profit organization. Healthcare Outreach mobilized medical doctors, dentists, and other citizens to provide basic medical and dental services and hygiene education to river communities in the northeast of Pará. The medical and dental outreaches were done in partnership with different Municipal Social Assistance Departments and Base Ecclesial Communities (BECs) in that region.

My walk with Amazonian traditional communities challenged my abstract, economist, and management-oriented "head knowledge" on development. Never before had "blah," the expression Freire (2005) used to describe the word deprived of the dimension of action, made so much sense to me. Indeed, the reality of traditional peoples of the Amazon invited me to abandon my verbalism and the fear that comes with it to embrace the relational experience of *praxis*, the Freirean radical interaction of reflection and action. While I was supporting health promotion outreaches, I was also discovering the potential of people-centered development and PAR, including the asset-based community development philosophy, to help marginalized groups assess and transform their own reality (Chambers 1997; Mathie and Cunningham 2008). Initially only by reading, I was amazed about the idea that marginalized populations are not powerless in shaping their own future. While working with Healthcare Outreach, I also volunteered with a community-based organization in Jinja, Uganda. In Jinja, I witnessed rural villagers coming together to discuss the future of their savings group and celebrating the success of its members' entrepreneurial initiatives. Savings groups are groups formed by community members with the goal of saving collectively and allowing participants to take out small loans to start and/or invest in their business (Cassidy and Fafchamps 2018). This was a great example of self-determination right before my eyes!

In this process, I was thrilled by James Yen's 1920 credo that drove China's rural reconstruction movement. The version of Yen's credo[1] cited by Wetmore and Theron (1998: 42) states: "Go to and live among the people; learn from, plan with and work with people; Start with what they know and build on what they have; teach by showing; learn by doing ... Its purpose is not to conform but to transform; not relief but release." This credo motivated me to support Amazonian people in community-led initiatives in order to break the pattern of outsiders only providing services to community groups. Community-led development aims to support and empower local people in assessing and mobilizing their assets to build their communities from the inside out (Mathie and Cunningham 2008). It implies moving from a service-driven initiative toward a mode of participation whereby "local people set their own agenda and mobilize to carry it out in the absence of outside initiators and facilitators" (Negri et al. 1998: 4). In this context, my work involved supporting existing and new community-led entrepreneurial, educational, and cultural initiatives as a collaborator and even a consultant (Stoecker 1999). Therefore, I was not looking to initiate a project, but to engage in long-term relationships and serve the community interests by living with them, dialoguing, and joining forces when new ideas and projects sprung up. A few years later, while deepening my understanding on community development/PAR, I was able to perceive indications of this kind of community engagement in the work of Paulo Freire and Orlando Fals Borda. It was these findings that inspired me to write this chapter.

While working with Healthcare Outreach I was invited to implement a community development school to equip both local and outsider practitioners to do community work in the Amazon and beyond. The school, which still exists, is a non-formal training program on a voluntary and, to some extent, cost-recovery basis. As program director, I incorporated the idea that people should lead their own process of development as a core part of the program. Furthermore, reflecting on the faith-based orientation of Healthcare Outreach, the school is founded on the theological understanding that relationships are an intrinsic aspect of human existence and that poverty and oppression are expressions of broken relationships. In this sense, broken relationships affect the spiritual, psychological, social, and environmental aspect of human life as well as broader social, economic, and political structures (Myers 2012). Hence, development work is about reconciling relationships while people become more of what they were created to be – fully human (Corbett and Fikkert 2012).

Go to and Live among the People: Engaging with the Community of Arapapuzinho

My relationship with the Arapapuzinho river community, which is also a quilombola community, began around 2015 through the intermediation of the Secretaria Municipal de Assistência Social de Abaetetuba [Municipal Secretariat for Social Assistance of Abaetetuba]. We were introduced to Maria, the BEC leader, and Seu João, leader of the Associação das Comunidades Remanescentes de Quilombo das Ilhas de Abaetetuba (ARQUIA) [Association of the Quilombola Communities of Abaetetuba], who was also from Arapapuzinho. This association, as many others in Brazil, is rooted in the rise of social movements in the 1980s and part of a long-term struggle for racial democracy (Gonçalves 2017). Recognizing that a community is of quilombo descent ensures the people's collective right to the land, cultural protection, and access to public policies (Leite 2008). The BECs also are relevant actors as allies in the quilombolas' struggle by supporting people in the process of community organizing for action and change. Rooted in Liberation theology, the work of BECs is part of what Mendieta (2005) called critical Latinamericanism, which is characterized by resistance against different forms of imperialism, including capitalism, and by alignment with the cause of the oppressed.

The relationship I had with the people of Arapapuzinho made the community a potential place to host the community development students' practicum. Yet, engaging with Arapapuzinho was possible not only because of the relationship I built with the community leaders and members through the health promotion initiatives. I have to acknowledge the collectivist orientation of land- and river-based people as well as the community organizing culture built by the work of community activists such as Seu João and Maria. For instance, ARQUIA was founded in 2001 as a local expression of a multilevel struggle for collective land rights. The association is a collective representing the communities of the islands of the municipality of Abaetetuba. Through ARQUIA's work, in 2002 the collective land right was guaranteed to the communities of Alto e Baixo Itacuruçá, Campopema, Jenipaúba, Acaraqui, Igarapé São João, Arapapu, and Itacuruça (Instituto de Terras do Pará 2002). Furthermore, the association is also known as a place for women's emancipation (Santos and Oliveira 2019). According to Santos and Oliveira (2019), women from Arapapuzinho, like Maria, are politically active as ARQUIA board members and have become a reference for others in the community. They also affirmed that the association is a space where the women can construct experiences of freedom and self-determination in order to change their own reality.

The community leaders agreed with our proposal, and we were welcomed into the community. The community members also lent us a canoe and a place to live during the time we were there. Differently from what Healthcare Outreach was used to, my vision was to lead the students and engage with the community as learners in a long-term relationship and see what initiatives we could support. In this endeavor, the focus was on the community and their vision of change rather than service oriented towards students' learning. The emphasis on community and change echoes Stoecker's (2016) notion of liberatory service learning to some degree. Nevertheless, my team and I were not intentional about applying an emancipatory and conflict-based approach per se. In essence, our focus was on bonding with community members and exploring opportunities to support and join local initiatives by relying on the potential of the organizational life already in place. A few years later, despite acknowledging the value of the learning experience and great ties created with community members, I realized the limitation of this approach to challenge power dynamics, and create greater community impact.

The idea of having nothing more than just a relationship as a starting point for a community development initiative was new for both the community leaders and my team. Apparently, they were used to non-profits and public agencies partnering with them closely based on what Chambers (1997) defined as a "things paradigm of development" where local people are beneficiaries of centralized projects with pre-set goals. Maria, who also was a teacher in the community and our guide, mentioned that the community members were used to research visits that could be classified more in terms of extractive research. In this mode of research, knowledge is removed from the communities and commonly presented and validated by outsider academic specialists and/or used by policy makers (Gaudry 2011). This kind of research benefits the academic groups more than the community groups and becomes material for publication which means career advancement (Gaudry 2011). For instance, she mentioned that people used to come from the university and/or government and ask people to attend focus groups and participate in interviews. However, after they left, they were likely to never see each other again. In addition, the community could not see the immediate impact of this kind of research in their everyday life, even though there were lots of promises.

In building relationships with the people of Arapapuzinho, it was evident that the notion of bonding and bridging social capital came into play. Bonding social capital is defined as "dense and strong ties that facilitate exclusive reciprocity and mutual obligations" (Kim 2006: 37). Kim (2006) affirmed that this kind of relationship of solidarity is commonly seen between family members and ethnic community members and is based on "similarity, informality, and intimacy" (37). In Arapapuzinho, bonding is evident. If people are not blood related, they still have strong ties because they share life together. Francisca, a community member of a neighboring river, once told me that no one goes hungry in the community because people can just knock on each other's door and share a meal. Although we should be aware of the power struggles and inequalities that exist within the community, the people are generally inclined to support one another in times of need, personally and through the work of the CEB's pastoral commissions.

My community development students and I were outsiders welcomed into that community. The relationship between our team and the community members can be defined in terms of bridging social capital. Bridging social capital is defined as weak ties between people, which means that relationships are formed with "individuals outside of one's immediate or localized network" (Macinko and Starfield 2001: 392). According to Macinko and Starfield (2001), bridging social capital benefits the community through new information and opportunities which work as leverage for community development. However, despite the fact that, theoretically, bridging social capital would be the appropriate term to define the relationship between our team and the community members, we were still strengthening our ties with the people. This process was facilitated by living with them, joining in informal conversations with our neighbors on our porches, farming together, attending their religious ceremonies, playing soccer with them at the end of the day, and so on. Local culture also helped facilitate this process. Overall, Brazil is a collective oriented society. As such, "people are born into extended families or other in-groups, which continue to protect them in exchange for loyalty"

(Mor Barak 2017: 176). In Brazilian culture, particularly in northern Brazil, the African proverb "it takes a village to raise a child" is the way to live. People make their neighbors their family, which involves a strong sense of mutual obligation. Indeed, people take care of each other (Mor Barak 2017). On one hand, this helps mask racism and social inequalities. On the other hand, community life is still a great source of support to overcome social struggles.

My point is that even though our team members were outsiders and were in the community to work with the people, the work was still informed by collectivist values. I am suggesting that, as people spend time and work together, they are more likely to develop relatively strong ties characterized by trust, flexibility, and reciprocity (Kim 2006). Drawing from the literature on interpersonal relationships in the workplace, professional relationships within a collectivist society are more likely to develop into a relatively family-like relationship (Mor Barak 2017). Our work dynamic was characterized by flexibility; there was no pre-set agenda defined by ourselves alone. This approach made it possible for our team to participate in the everyday life of the people, but not as participant observation researchers where a dichotomy researcher/researched still exists. We were building a relationship beyond work relations which was based on life sharing and a hope for a better future. In this process, we enjoyed playing soccer, talking for hours sitting on the improvised benches in front of our neighbors' houses sharing stories, laughing, and even crying together. There was no rush, just the enjoyment of the moment. We could also feel the affection of the elders when they advised us as one of their own. It was very clear to us, and the cultural aspect helped in this understanding, that relationships are not a strategy but a way of being in the world.

A Participatory Action Research Experience with a Youth Group

Working with river people by looking to foster community-driven initiatives taught me that if one really wants to be focused on relationships and learning, one should relinquish his/her own ideas of what a community development project should look like. At the end of the day, my students and I used to spend time with the youth sitting and talking around the soccer field. In one of our conversations, I was able to share with them about community mapping, appreciative inquiry, and how it could be a tool for new initiatives. Community mapping is a PAR visual method whereby people draw the community geographic space as it relates to the physical, economic, and/social aspects of their group (Loewenson et al. 2014). This method is a tool for reflection based on the community issue the group wants to address. Furthermore, appreciative inquiry proposes an assessment driven by the positive changes that take place in the group. The data collected inspires the vision of what the group might become which drives the planning and implementation process. In this sense, participatory mapping informed by an appreciative process might work as leverage for action with self-esteem and hope (Williamson 2000).

The group of young people got excited about the exercise. The fun part of working without deadline constraints and focusing on the learning process is to see what will come out of the process. Furthermore, my assumption was that regardless of what they decided to do, the learning involved in the initiative such as democratic decision making, critical reflection and inclusion, asset mapping, and mobilizing would build capacity for them to engage in greater community-driven projects later on. Williamson (2000) defined this learning process as inner development. According to Williamson (2000), this inner development implies that the community development process is primarily focused on people's self-concept, leadership and interrelationship skills, and organizational development, which is the basis for structural changes. This idea of inner development expresses what kind of community development we were attempting to experience with the people of Arapapuzinho.

We did not schedule the exercise, but one day a group of youth involved in the BEC's youth commission visited us. We started to talk about the community and what they could do together. As the conversation unfolded, we found ourselves on the floor with papers and pencils drawing by candlelight and reflecting about what makes their community a good place to live and their vision for the community. According to those involved in the exercise, they had never thought about their own community in such a positive way: as an abundant community. In addition, they expressed excitement for what they could do after the reflexive exercise.

As an outcome of the exercise they decided to visit and support the elders in the community, especially those who could not come to community gatherings because of health-related limitations. On one hand, this youth group taught me that relationship- and process-based community development requires outsiders to relinquish their own development ideas, otherwise it would become a colonizing and top-down community development project wrapped in a beautiful participatory discourse. On the other hand, it seemed like relationships are not just the means but also the ends of community development. Indeed, for Arapapuzinho, strong community ties are the support basis for any other infrastructural project.

My intention is not to fall into an essentialist view of Amazonian traditional people and/ or deny the interpersonal tensions existing in collectivist cultures such as the Brazilian, particularly indigenous, culture. However, the relational and collective way of being in the world, which is common in cultures from the global south, particularly among Amazonian traditional peoples, can give us insight on engaging in partnerships through PAR in a more people-centered and relational way. Fundamentally, the river people and quilombolas invited me into a deeper relationship, forming community with them by living, learning, and exploring new possibilities for enhancing community well-being with them. This relational way of living challenges our task-oriented academic lifestyle, which is more likely to be reflected in the way we do research and community development.

PARTICIPATORY ACTION RESEARCH: FROM THE GLOBAL SOUTH TO THE GLOBAL NORTH

My lived experience in the Amazon was an important experiential base (Clandinin and Connelly 2000) that drew my attention to relationships as intrinsic to the PAR framework. This understanding makes the concept of partnership central in academic discussions, particularly when it comes to relationships between community members and outside researchers (Wallerstein and Duran 2008). Partnership expresses the idea of association between people, people working together, and collaboration. Sobrinho and Vasconcellos (2012: 26) explained that partnership involves "cooperation, trust and synergy between individuals and organisations to achieve a common objective." They also asserted that this process is facilitated by trust and the self-organization capacity of partners. Yet, partnership is a result of institutional frameworks that are able to encourage specific behaviors (Sobrinho and Vasconcellos 2012).

This emphasis on relationships becomes more evident when one acknowledges and takes a closer look into the global south critical roots of PAR. In essence, PAR is defined as a social movement starting in the 1960s and 1970s (Glassman and Erdem 2014) in Latin America,

Tanzania, and India, and hereafter recognized as relevant in the global north (Tandon and Hall 2014). As a social movement, PAR implies a process of action-oriented learning within a context of solidarity in order to bring about radical transformation of unjust social, economic, and political structures (Leal 2011). In this sense, PAR is conceived as a counter-hegemonic practice led by ordinary people to dismantle systems of oppression (Hall 1993). Ledwith (2020) described this process as community development. Her notion of community development implies an "ongoing dynamic of research, critical education and community action in symbiotic relation" (135). This statement suggests that PAR is better understood as community development that contains research as part of its framework rather than a research approach in itself. In this process, people come together to engage in the creation of knowledge in action. Yet, the quality of the relationships, particularly partnerships, in this "coming together" is a fundamental aspect for successful knowledge creation, action, and consequently to move towards desired outcomes.

PAR also relies on the principle of "putting research capabilities in the hands of the deprived and disenfranchised people so that they can transform their lives for themselves" (Park 1993: 1). By being a people-led practice, the "real" researchers are the common people rather than academics (Park 1993). This rearticulation of who the researcher really is echoes Gramsci's (1971) idea that "all men are intellectuals" (9), which is the basis of his concept of organic intellectuals. These intellectuals are leaders nurtured by and committed to the struggle of their class (Bowd et al. 2010). As holders of a critical consciousness rooted in lived experience (Gaventa 1993), they are responsible for raising the critical consciousness of their people and organizing them for transformative action (Ledwith 2016).

Gramsci's thoughts had a great influence on the work of theorists of the global south such as Brazilian adult educator Paulo Freire and Colombian sociologist Orlando Fals Borda (Gutberlet et al. 2014). These two theorists are prominent contributors to the foundation of PAR and its many ramifications. Following the Gramscian tradition, Fals Borda (1992) and Freire (2005) believed in the emancipatory power of the lived experience of the common people. Fals Borda (1992) argued that the popular knowledge that comes from peasants and the working class has its own rationality and is able to challenge deformed versions of history portrayed in academic texts. Thus, popular knowledge has a relevant role in providing a critical perspective on hegemonic discourses of history and society. In the same way, Freire (2005: 44) stated that "the great humanistic and historical task of the oppressed [is] to liberate themselves and their oppressors as well ... Only power that springs from the weakness of the oppressed will be sufficiently strong to free both." Fals Borda and Freire are not saying that popular wisdom is flawless, but as Fals Borda (1992) explained, it is a valid source of knowledge and able to orient action on its own terms.

PAR promotes the idea of people-led development and research (Mathie and Alma 2016), but does not imply that academic researchers should not be a part of it. Indeed, PAR is a collaborative approach that brings people together who are interested in seeing change. This may include academics and/or any other outsider. In essence, collaboration is one of PAR's pedagogical principles. As an approach that originates in the global south, PAR is informed by Freire's dialogical pedagogy of praxis (Gutberlet et al. 2014). Praxis is defined as a radical interaction between reflection and action performed in dialogue and solidarity among those who want to change their world (Freire 2005). Praxis is sine qua non for people to experience their ontological and historical vocation: the ongoing process of becoming fully human. In this sense, people become more fully human by becoming critically conscious of "the way they exist in the world with which and in which they find themselves" (83). This process of conscientization (*conscientização*) does not happen in isolation and without the integration of reflection and action. In other words, through critical reflection, people's existence in the world and with the world becomes the object of their cognition and action. This makes transformation possible.

For Freire, the ultimate goal of education is the people's humanization by facilitating the "emergence of critical consciousness and critical intervention in reality" (2005: 81) leading to the production of history and culture (Glass 2001). For this kind of education to happen, teachers must recognize that students are subjects, and therefore, cognitive actors. Thus, in a subject-to-subject relationship students and teachers co-teach and co-learn, and pursue together their ontological vocation as partners (Freire 2005). Indeed, this relational dynamic is also expected in the PAR process. The community, once seen as an object of research, rises up as a subject, as partners in the research process (Wallerstein and Duran 2008). Consequently, both the community and academic researchers share power and exercise power (Hanson and Ogunade 2016) while educating themselves and transforming the world.

Even though the notion of partnership is key to the PAR framework, Muhammad Rahman, another southern PAR theorist and practitioner from Bangladesh, establishes that PAR is an approach that belongs primarily to the people. In his own words, PAR is the "people's own independent inquiry" (Rahman 1991: 17). Rahman (1991) is strongly skeptical towards any initiative started by academic researchers. He agrees with Freire and Fals Borda on the emancipatory power of the wisdom and consciousness of the people. For Rahman (1991), any mobilization initiated by a vanguard body, such as by those who exercise power over the means of knowledge production, "contains seeds of newer forms of domination" (14). Therefore, in order to avoid any tendency of superiority and control by academic researchers, he suggests that academics should be invited by the people on their own initiative if they judge it necessary to do so. This is also a way to counter any tendency of subservience of people who are victims of oppressing structures.

Throughout the years, PAR has been gaining legitimation in academic circles as an action-oriented research approach, particularly in the global north. The birth of the UNESCO Chair on Community-Based Research and Social Responsibility represented a step forward in moving PAR from the margin to the center (Hall 1992; Tandon and Hall 2014). Indeed, UNESCO is a western supranational organization well known for its power to create educational paradigms which shape ways of thinking and doing education (Grace 2013). This legitimation is also perceived through the availability of government funds towards research built around university–community partnerships. On one hand, these are institutional incentives towards university–community partnerships and contribute to the creation of a knowledge democracy by validating different ways of knowing (Hall et al. 2016). On the other hand, PAR is portrayed as a collaborative research approach while its social movement and community development orientation fade away.

In this new momentum, PAR is less defined as a community-led or popular process of knowledge production to transform structures of oppression (Hall et al. 2016) and more as "a collaborative enterprise between academic researchers (professors and students) and community members" (Strand et al. 2003a: 6). In this sense, PAR becomes a tool for "the systematic creation of knowledge that is done with and for community for the purpose of addressing a community-identified need" (Strand et al. 2003b: 8). Hence, university researchers design governance structures and research methods that ensure the participation of the community members affected by the phenomenon under study (Hacker 2013). However, the process of knowledge creation does not necessarily imply a critique of society or an analysis of power, but it is focused on the pragmatic usage of knowledge (Adelman 1993). Furthermore, even though researchers and community members should still engage as equal partners throughout the research process, the power dominance bounces back to academic researchers. This becomes evident when one considers that most of PAR efforts are initiated by university researchers (Viswanathan et al. 2004), and according to Nation et al. (2011), whoever initiates the partnership holds the most power. Then, the other party collaborates by negotiating and accommodating issues related to the research.

Despite disruptions in PAR's southern and critical tradition, PAR researcher-practitioners commonly stand on the ground that traditional social research represents interpretation by an elite of professionals, generally western researchers (Tandon 1988). They recognize that traditional social research reinforces a colonial relationship and dependency between the Western world and former colonies (Wallerstein and Duran 2008). In this sense, whether emphasizing the leadership of community groups or proposing a collective ownership of the research, these researcher-practitioners are aware of the moral commitment to dismantling the binary subject/object by proposing a subject-to-subject relationship between community groups and researchers. In essence, achieving this ideal of engaging community members as equal partners becomes the most important issue among action-oriented research practitioners (Wallerstein and Duran 2008), bringing forth different ways of establishing partnership.

Nevertheless, one should also not ignore that higher education institutions, as the hegemonic pole of the binary university–community, are power/knowledge mediums. As such, they are known for their socio-historic practice of constructing objects and defining who the inhabitants of the margins are (Spivak 2009). This is the case of the creation of the community as an object of study; the community has a long history existing as an object before academics recognize groups that take up this subject position as partners. The same can be said about outsider community development agencies, whose practice, wrapped in good intentions, takes the risk of being rooted in colonialism and marginalization (Mizzi and Hamm 2013). In this center–margin politics, community groups learn how to engage and respond to a university's scripts as they interact in the social space, which manifests a kind of colonized imagination (Goulet et al. 2011).

For instance, in a conversation with Seu João, the ARQUIA leader, he was very eager to know about the services my team and I were bringing into the Arapapuzinho community. He went on by mentioning different experiences with development agencies that had brought projects with pre-set goals into the community. I am not saying that Seu João was wrong. However, I noticed that his question had more to do with "I know how this business works" rather than excitement towards our potential work with the community. Yet, I also heard stories from community members, including Maria, of how these projects came full of hope and promises, but were not sustainable long term. Some community members mentioned how the community was hurt by them, causing resistance to new outside initiatives. Another issue that came up in conversations was how academics and practitioners involved in those projects were more focused on getting the task done and delivering services than on the people impacted by the services.

Complaints about the difficulty of academics and practitioners connecting with the community do not only arise in Arapapuzinho. For instance, Ross and Stoecker (2017) analyzed the perception of residents of the Lower 9th Ward of New Orleans about higher education community engagement experiences after Hurricane Katrina. They explained that this ward was highly exposed to various higher education initiatives whether research or service, including PAR. These initiatives aimed to produce knowledge and support the community in recovering from the traumatic event as well as the consequences of poverty and marginalization exposed by the hurricane. Ross and Stoecker (2017) found that in the very end community members did not differentiate between traditional and participatory forms of research. In addition, residents did not feel emotional support from the researchers when compared to the volunteers. Community members also felt a sense of research fatigue, noted a lack of benefits from the research, and perceived that academic researchers invaded and used them to achieve their own research goals.

The observation of the Lower 9th Ward residents makes me wonder to what extent community-based researchers are engaging with community members by holding a utilitarian and consequently instrumental view of relationships. A utilitarian perspective of relationships sees them as "one among many inputs to an impersonal utility-calculus" (Tiffany 2006: 1). This concept resonates with the idea of instrumental relationships in which people build task-oriented relationships (Halpern 2005) and reciprocity expresses the idea of exchange of service for data (TallBear 2014). This understanding leads to a perception of partnership as strategy. On one hand, this is not a problem when both partners believe that the relationship will bring mutual benefit. On the other hand, it becomes a problem when the community groups do not feel engaged and feel used by the academics. This is more likely to happen due to the individualistic and capitalist academic culture characterized by a competitive market intensified by the ongoing decline of research funds (Mendoza et al. 2012). The dangerous consequence of this culture is people's alienation from themselves and from one another (Marx 1964). Nevertheless, when people see each other as holders of intrinsic worth, they are more likely to put people first, which leads to a more relational reciprocity. In Ross and Stoecker's (2017) example, a relational reciprocity was found in the relationship between residents and volunteers, rather than residents and researchers.

The same problem is also found in organization-driven community development initiatives in which service is the main focus. In my experience with the Arapapuzinho and surrounding communities, organizational priorities were rarely shaped and/or driven by community members. Many times, I resisted organizational pressure to bring unnecessary short-term international teams into communities, which commonly meant disruption in the work already taking place. The long-term local team would move the focus from the community to the visitors by channeling efforts towards language translation and making sure that the visitors were engaged in daily activities. In addition, the local team recurrently had to attend to organizational demands to provide educational activities for kids and women that were neither asked for by the community nor based on local knowledge and resources. I am not saying that these activities did not contribute to the community's well-being. However, I am questioning the process of design and implementation of these activities. These examples show my struggle with an institutionalized form of community engagement in which outsiders create parameters for and prioritize learning and service rather than community and change (Stoecker 2016).

Strand et al. (2003b) affirmed that in order for successful engagement to occur, particularly between university and community, partners should share a common worldview and agree on goals to be achieved and strategies employed in the research. In the partnership, those involved should share power and strive for clear communication. They also argued that when these elements are in place, partners are more likely to have their interests satisfied and their abilities improved. Nevertheless, the partnership should be based on a relationship of trust, mutual respect, empathy, and flexibility. Essentially, while the agreements around power sharing, goals, and strategies provide basic infrastructure for the research collaboration to happen, elements such as trust, respect, and empathy make the enterprise run smoothly. The more the purpose of the research envisions empowerment of the community, the more long term the partnership is and the more the community participates in each stage of the research.

However, it seems like the more researchers have to engage with land-based groups and groups of collectivist orientation and relational worldview such as indigenous peoples, the more academics are invited to leave behind a utilitarian perspective of relationships. They are invited to engage in partnerships based on the notion of relationships as an ontological necessity. In other words, reality is intrinsically relational; it is made up of a "profound interconnectedness of all existence" (Stewart-Harawira 2005: 155). Indeed, this is a condition to balance all things whereby hurting the other also means to hurt oneself (Stewart-Harawira 2005). This understanding of relationship resonates with the notion of covenantal ethics in which researchers and community members engage in a partnership that goes beyond a contractual relationship; it expresses the idea that "people are always dependent on and thus delivered over to one another" (Hilsen 2014: 195). Such a worldview can be also situated as a southern perspective regardless of geographic location; it is southern for its position of marginality (Greenwood and Levin 2011), particularly in academic circles.

PAR with indigenous communities evokes this interconnectedness and this kind of covenantal ethics. For example, Tobias et al. (2013) described their PAR experience with an Anishinaabe group, one of the indigenous peoples located where we now call Canada and the United States. According to the authors, to have an Anishinaabe person as both the leader of the academic team and a community member was essential for the project's success; it created a strong relationship based on a relational history. In addition, having the researchers live for a while by the community's geographic location fostered a relationship of accountability and reciprocity. Lastly, making roles clearly known to those involved and training and hiring local people as research assistants helped equalize power.

Castleden et al. (2012) advised that, in order to build relationships with indigenous communities and perform PAR in a more egalitarian way, indigenous organizations should mediate encounters between indigenous communities and researchers. In addition, they encourage the involvement of researchers in cultural activities and community events. They also suggest that researchers should visit friendship centers and respectfully listen to elders, leaders, and community members about their issues. Such relationships can bring forth research ideas and help researchers familiarize themselves with community-specific cultural protocols and values, which contribute to the success of the research. Castleden et al. (2012) encouraged relational ethics which still find little space in the university among the need for grant writing and the demand for publication throughout the year. They also clarify that even though a community agrees to a partnership, it does not mean that the research starts immediately. As the title of Castleden et al.'s (2012) paper suggested, "I spent the first year drinking tea."

I see the same emphasis on relationship, particularly the idea of covenantal ethics, in the scholarship and practice of Paulo Freire and Orlando Fals Borda. Looking into the work of these southern PAR pioneers is an important step towards thinking critically in order to reimagine partnership between institutions and community groups by going beyond a utilitarian and instrumental perspective of relationship.

PARTNERSHIP REVISITED: *COMPANHEIRISMO* AND *VIVENCIA* IN PARTICIPATORY ACTION RESEARCH

The same invitation I received from Yen's credo and the river people and quilombolas is also made by PAR southern theorists such as Paulo Freire and Fals Borda. It is widely known among PAR scholars and practitioners that Paulo Freire proposes a relational pedagogy that provides a framework for subject-to-subject relationships between researchers and community members. As I mentioned before, Fals Borda does the same through his concept of *vivencia*. It becomes more evident by taking a closer look at their contribution.

Companheirismo: Freire's Concept of Partnership

Freire's (2005) emancipatory pedagogy implies dialogue, critical thinking, and mutual humanization. For these elements to work, Freire (2005) explained that teachers' efforts, as revolutionary humanist educators, "must be imbued with a profound trust in people and their creative power. To achieve this, they must be partners of the students in their relations with them" (75). This partnership implies humility and love and those involved in the process must trust each other, which is a condition to make the partnership stronger. This makes the ideal of subject-to-subject relationship and dialogue possible.

This notion of partnership assumes that students are cognitive subjects as much as teachers are. Yet, the English word partnership does not fully express the depth of the relationship Freire is referring to. Partnership was the translation found for the word *companheirismo*. However, as a Brazilian, I am arguing that the word *companheirismo* has emotional and relational implications that perhaps the word partnership does not allow an English-speaking person to grasp. This insight comes from my back and forth reading of the Portuguese and English versions of *Pedagogy of the Oppressed*. My conclusion after reading the two versions of Freire is that, while the English translation captures my mind, the original book captures my heart. I read Freire with my mind in English, but I feel his ideas in Portuguese.

Freire (2016) gives insights into the meaning of *companheirismo* by implying that the practice of an emancipatory educator is informed by *convivência* [to live with] and *simpatia* [to support; to have appreciation and affection for someone]. In essence, *convivência* and *simpatia* together is expressed by the idea of solidarity in the English translation. Indeed, Gaztambide-Fernández (2012) affirmed that solidarity is a Freirean fundamental concept; it guides the liberatory and dialogic relationship between oppressors and oppressed. However, according to Gaztambide-Fernández (2012), even though the concept of solidarity is relevant, Freire left it undertheorized. Nevertheless, a Freirean notion of solidarity may be clarified by *companheirismo*. This Portuguese word expresses togetherness, which also relates to *convivência*; it entails the notion of camaraderie, familiarity, sharing of life, fellowship, and brotherhood; it echoes the verb *simpatizar*.

To some degree, *companheirismo* may echo the South African idea of comradery (von Kotze and Walters 2017). Comradery involves people working together in opposition to a common enemy; in South Africa's case, apartheid (von Kotze and Walters 2017). Yet, Adler and Steinberg (2000) explained that as comrades, people are not only united by fighting a common enemy and/or sharing an organizational form, but also share a vision for the future. The concept of comradery relates to Freire's notion of *companheirismo* because, as in the South African context, Freire's pedagogy is placed within an emancipatory framework. Furthermore, as in the notion of comradery, *companheirismo* also implies solidarity (Freire 2005), yet a political solidarity (Gaztambide-Fernández 2012). Gaztambide-Fernández (2012) explained that political solidarity characterizes the relationship between people who work together in mutual support and emotional cohesion toward a common goal or against a common enemy. The relationship between political solidarity and the notion of *companheirismo* becomes clearer when one considers that the 35th president of Brazil and founding member of the Workers' Party, Luiz Inácio Lula da Silva, refers to his supporters as *companheiros* (comrades, partners).

By considering that *companheirismo* and political solidarity are related, it is possible and quite easy to perceive solidarity as a strategy. According to Kip (2016), the strategic dimension of solidarity is commonly emphasized by communist thinkers. Kip (2016) supported his statement by mentioning Vladimir Lenin, who defines solidarity as a discipline without which the cause of the working class is hopeless. Kip (2016) also mentioned that radicals very often take solidarity as the support of a cause through "writing letters, signing petitions, and attending rallies" (396), which may generate positive impact. The problem with this perspective is that solidarity becomes instrumental, hence a technical requirement to achieve a goal. This instrumental gaze of solidarity seems to find a good fit into individualistic societies such as the United States and Canada (Hofstede 2001). People from individualistic societies perceive themselves as "separate individuals with primary responsibility for themselves and their very immediate family only" (Mor Barak 2017: 176). In this sense, it is more likely that words such as solidarity and partnership can be interpreted and experienced by people from the north through an individualist and therefore instrumental gaze.

Solidarity in Freire's term is found in *conviver* and *simpatizar* or in living, sharing, supporting, and having affection for one another. This is possible through a relationship between equals in a subject-to-subject relationship. It is through this kind of relationship that people become *companheiros*. I am not rejecting the functionality of political solidarity, but I am arguing that *companheirismo* goes beyond its instrumental aspect. *Companheirismo* is a relational word and one can better grasp its meaning by considering the nationality, culture, and life of Paulo Freire. When I read the account of Freire's life provided by Ledwith (2016), I cannot dissociate it from our warm Brazilian culture, especially in the rural areas of the north and northeast of Brazil. As in the Amazon, a collectivist trait is also found in northeastern Brazil (Oberg 2013). In this sense, when Ledwith (2016) explained that Freire shared his life with young people who lived in poverty, I am able to picture the dialectic reality formed by struggle and a sense of community in our popular neighborhoods. In this context, *companheiros* are formed and nurtured. In this sense, the political solidarity that comes out of this context is less instrumental because people live together. This process of *conviver* creates *simpatia* and a sense of community which implies trust and mutual support. Therefore, solidarity among *companheiros* seems to be relational and less utilitarian, which does not mean less effective.

Conviver and *simpatizar* were the basis of my experience with the people of Arapapuzinho. Living with the people and positioning myself as a learner created a relationship of mutual *simpatia* which led to reciprocity. In this process, working together also means caring for each other which makes friendship and *companheirismo* possible. I am separating friendship from *companheirismo* for a didactic purpose. The people of Arapapuzinho and I are friends because by living and working together we developed ties of affection that exist without the mediation of a community development project. In friendship there is *simpatia*, affection and reciprocity.

Yet, we became *companheiros* because our ties of affection bring with it a purpose of learning through community-driven initiatives.

University researchers/practitioners and community members are able to perceive one another as equals when their community development and/or PAR practice is entrenched in a relationship of *companheirismo*. This kind of relationship requires researchers and practitioners to deepen their relationship with community members to the point that the ties between both partners are stronger, which evokes a quasi-bonding social capital. I am using the term "quasi" to express the understanding that despite their background differences, including class, bonding social capital can be potentially created through *conviver* and *simpatizar*, which is the basis for a subject-to-subject relationship. This echoes the ideas of covenantal relationship and interconnectedness that allow people to see one another as holders of intrinsic worth and put the other first. In practical terms, it has to do with "[acting] in the best interest of others" (Hilsen 2014: 195). It also means academics/practitioners resisting the individualistic and capitalism academic culture by engaging and inhabiting the world that they are learning from, building a relationship of "family, friend, and/or colleague" (TallBear 2014: 3) – *companheiros* – and exploring multiple and continuous ways to give back that goes beyond any one-time project (Bhan 2014). Hence, relationship becomes a resistance against a dehumanizing institutional culture that alienates us from one another.

Vivencia: Fals Borda's Pathway for *Companheirismo*

Indeed, when academic researchers are invited into the community's everyday life, they are invited for *vivencia*, a Spanish word meaning experience. Fals Borda referred to *vivencia* as "authentic commitment" (1991: 4); an "immersion in the field conditions and identification with local communities that combine research and action" (1996: 81). The concept of *vivencia* also gives insight into the nature of the relationship between community members and academic researchers. According to Fals Borda, it goes beyond a participant observation relation whereby researchers immerse in the culture and lives of a people (Calhoun 2002). In participant observation, the researcher still objectifies community groups. In other words, there is no subject-to-subject relationship, but a subject knowing an object. There is no commitment (Fals Borda 1996), only the curiosity of an anthropological mind. *Vivencia* is an invitation to participate through immersion in and commitment to the reality of the people while they transform their world. In this, a subject-to-subject relationship becomes real.

Freire's invitation to *companheirismo* is reinforced by Fals Borda's notion of *vivencia*. According to Fals Borda (1991), through *vivencia*, "we intuitively apprehend its essence; we feel, enjoy and understand it as reality, and we thereby place our own being in a wider, more fulfilling context" (4). *Vivencia* is research through lived experience (Smith 1997). Fals Borda, in an interview posted on YouTube by Villasante (2017), speaks about his own *vivencia* with river peoples of Colombia. Fals Borda states:

> If you want to get to the essence of the river culture subject, you must get away from that privileged group a little and walk, swim and row with the fishermen and hunters of the area. From these human elements ... I know that they have mastered one of the techniques that combine the aquatic with the land. They are the ones who will give you the explanation of what the river culture is really like and among these explanations comes the concept of the already well-known amphibian culture ... And I also had the privilege of living with them, spending time with them in their houses, in their hammocks, and not only in populated places. I preferred going to the smaller people.[2]

Fals Borda's interview challenges academic researchers to leave their comfort zone. If one is doing PAR in an urban and/or in the same city where one's home university is placed, it is relatively easy to visit the people and retreat back to campus. However, Fals Borda's experience required a bit more than just a few minutes or hours of driving to join people in research. It involved a radical immersion into the reality of the common and marginalized people. Fals Borda's interview reminds me of my own *vivencia*. Indeed, it was by living in river communities that I have improved my swimming skills, learned how to row, and learned how to climb an açaí palm tree. I remember the day when one of my students and I joined Seu Tião (a community member) in the management of his açaí palm tree field. We canoed from the front of his house to a stream surrounded by the jungle where his field was located. We helped him manage his field by using a machete to remove unwanted plants. As we worked together, Seu Tião told us stories about how he learned the technique from his father who used to take him to the field and how he hoped to do the same with his child.

I am not saying that Fals Borda's experience is more meaningful because it took place in a reality commonly unknown by academic researchers in the global north. My intention is to emphasize the quality of Fals Borda's engagement with the people's reality. *Vivencia* requires this kind of radical engagement whether in an urban or rural setting, whether in the global north or global south. This is radical because researchers and practitioners have to leave their privileged group to live with and commit to the people (Fals Borda 1996). In other words, by living with the marginalized, academic researchers and people come together to perform "research in and of life" (Smith 1997: 245) in order to achieve social transformation (Fals Borda 1991). Fals Borda is not clear about academic-practitioners leaving their privileged position and consequently comfort zone. Nevertheless, this "leaving" is beyond a geographic displacement, but entails a mindset transformation potentially unleashed through critical reflection and transformative learning.

The concept of *vivencia* implies *convivência* and *simpatia*, which necessarily implies *companheirismo* between academic researchers and the people. While I am tempted to say that *vivencia* is a foundational methodological aspect of PAR, it should not be taken as simply a step to take or a box to check for implementing community development and research projects. Researcher-practitioners should understand *vivencia* in the light of interconnectedness and covenantal ethics. In other words, *vivencia* is not a methodology per se, but a way of being in the world. In the same way, PAR is not a research approach per se, but community in action, a social movement to transform the world.

RELATIONSHIP AS RESISTANCE

The acknowledgment that PAR is historically rooted in critical southern tradition has great implications to knowledge democracy. It opens up room for lived experiences and epistemologies other than western ones as well as creating a space for dialogue and mutual learning between the global north and south. Going back to PAR's roots reminds academic researchers that PAR is critical and, as such, it aims to resist dehumanizing discourses and proposes interventions that reveal people's hope and vision of a better world (Roy 2016). This includes resisting the capitalist and consequently individualistic academic culture which leads to the alienation of ourselves and one another which is particularly evident in a utilitarian view of relationship and partnership that threatens community-engaged scholarship. How then do we resist such a view? What can we learn from southern theorists such as Paulo Freire and Fals Borda in order to help PAR scholars and practitioners in this endeavor?

The original text of Freire's *Pedagogy of the Oppressed* suggests that what was translated as partnership reveals more than just the idea of working together for a common goal, but expresses a more collectivist and relational way of being with one another in order to bring about change. The notion of *companheirismo* implies a partnership whereby affection and political solidarity do not lose each other, but build rapport for transformation. When academic researchers and community groups are willing to build a relationship of *companheirismo*, this relationship is no longer a strategy, but evokes the notion of relationship as an ontological necessity (Ledwith and Springett 2010; Reason and Bradbury 2001). In other words, relationships are intrinsic to human existence as much as praxis is.

Partnership as *companheirismo* also evokes Fals Borda's concept of *vivencia*. This is an invitation for academics and community members to live with and experience life with one another as an ontological given and the basis for consciousness and transformative action. In this sense, *companheirismo* and *vivencia* become both a way of being in the world and methodological aspects of PAR. For academics, the kind of relationship that *companheirismo* and *vivencia* suggest means resisting the academic political economy and being committed to the humanization of both themselves and community members. In resisting through relationships, we can create possibilities for de-alienation of the self and de-alienation from one another, which is the basis for subject-to-subject relationships whether in the global north, global south, or in between.

NOTES

1. Slightly different versions of Yen's credo or poem are found in the community development literature. For example, Dizon (2012), Sihlongonyane (2009), and Wetmore and Theron (1998).
2. Free translation.

REFERENCES

Adelman, C. 1993. "Kurt Lewin and the Origins of Action Research." *Educational Action Research*, 1(1), 7–24.

Adler, G. and Jonny Steinberg, eds. 2000. *From Comrades to Citizens: The South African Civics Movement and the Transition to Democracy*. London: Palgrave Macmillan.

Bhan, Gautam. 2014. "Moving from 'Giving Back' to Engagement." *Journal of Research Practice*, 10(2), Article N14.

Bourdieu, Pierre. 1986. "The Forms of Capital." In *Handbook of Theory and Research for the Sociology of Education*, edited by J. Richardson. Westport, CT: Greenwood, pp. 241–258.

Bowd, R., Alpaslan Ozerdem, and Derese G. Kassa. 2010. "A Theoretical and Practical Exposition of 'Participatory' Research Methods." In *Participatory Research Methodologies: Development and Post-Disaster/Conflict Reconstruction*, edited by A. Ozerden and R. Bowd. Farnham: Ashgate, pp. 3–18.

Calhoun, Craig. 2002. *Dictionary of the Social Sciences*. New York: Oxford University Press.

Cassidy, Rachel and Marcel Fafchamps. 2018. "Banker My Neighbour: Matching and Financial Intermediation in Savings Groups." *CEPR Discussion Paper*, No. DP12715.

Castleden, Heather, Vanessa S. Morgan, and Christopher Lamb. 2012. "'I spent the first year drinking tea': Exploring Canadian University Researchers' Perspectives on Community-Based Participatory Research Involving Indigenous Peoples." *The Canadian Geographer*, 56(2), 160–179.

Chambers, Robert. 1997. *Whose Reality Counts?* London: Intermediate Technology.

Clandinin, D. Jean and F. Michael Connelly. 2000. *Narrative Inquiry: Experience and Story in Qualitative Research*. San Francisco, CA: Jossey-Bass.

Corbett, Steve and B. Fikkert, eds. 2012. *When Helping Hurts: How to Alleviate Poverty without Hurting the Poor and Yourself*. 2nd ed. Chicago, IL: Moody Publishers.

Costa, Francisco. 1995. "O Investimento na Economia Camponesa: Considerações teóricas." *Revista De Economia Política*, 15(1), 83–100.

Costa, Francisco. 2005. "Questão Agrária e Macropolíticas para a Amazônia." *Estudos Avançados*, 19(53), 131–156.

Costa, Tony. 2008. "Música do Norte: Intelectuais, Artistas Populares, Tradição e Modernidade na Formação da 'MPB' no Pará (Anos 1960–1970)." Master's thesis, Instituto de Filosofia e Ciências Humanas, Universidade Federal do Pará, Belém.

Dizon, Josefina. 2012. "Theoretical Concepts and Practice of Community Organizing." *Journal of Public Affairs and Development*, 1(1), 89–123.

Fals Borda, Orlando. 1991. "Some basic ingredients." In *Action and knowledge: Breaking the Monopoly with Participatory Action-Research*, edited by O. Fals Borda and M. A. Rahman. New York: Apex Press, pp. 3–12.

Fals Borda, Orlando. 1992. "La Ciencia y el Pueblo: Nuevas Reflexiones." In *La Investigación-acción Participativa: Inicios y Desarrollos*, edited by M. Salazar. Madrid: Editorial Popular, pp. 59–75.

Fals Borda, Orlando. 1996. "A North-South Convergence on the Quest for Meaning." *Qualitative Inquiry*, 2(1), 76–87.

Freire, Paulo. 2005. *Pedagogy of the Oppressed*. 30th ed. New York: Continuum.

Freire, Paulo. 2016. *Pedagogia do Oprimido*. 60th ed. São Paulo: Paz & Terra.

Gaudry, Adam. 2011. "Insurgent Research." *Wicazo Sa Review*, 26(1), 113–136.

Gaventa, John. 1993. "The Powerful, the Powerless, and the Expert: Knowledge Struggles in an Information Age." In *Voices of Change: Participatory Research in the United States and Canada*, edited by P. Park, M. Brydon-Miller, B. Hall, and T. Jackson. London: Bergin & Garvey, pp. 21–40.

Gaztambide-Fernández, Rubén. 2012. "Decolonization and the Pedagogy of Solidarity." *Decolonization: Indigeneity, Education and Society*, 1(1), 41–67.

Glass, Ronald. 2001. "Paulo Freire's Philosophy of Praxis and the Foundations of Liberation Education." *Educational Researcher*, 30(2), 15–25.

Glassman, Michael and Gizem Erdem. 2014. "Participatory Action Research and Its Meanings: Vivencia, Praxis, Conscientization." *Adult Education Quarterly*, 64(3), 206–221.

Gonçalves, Ana. 2017. "Políticas Públicas para Quilombolas: A Construção da Cidadania na Comunidade Remanescente de Quilombo do Baú." Master's thesis, Instituto de Ciências Humanas, Universidade Federal de Juiz de Fora, Juiz de Fora.

Goulet, Linda, Warren Linds, Jo-Ann Episkenew, and Karen Schmidt. 2011. "Creating a Space for Decolonization: Health through Theatre with Indigenous Youth." *Native Studies Review*, 20(1), 89–116.

Grace, André. 2013. *Lifelong Learning as Critical Action: International Perspectives on People, Politics, Policy, and Practice*. Toronto: Canada Scholar's Press.

Gramsci, Antonio. 1971. *Selections from the Prison Notebooks*. New York: International Publishers.

Greenwood, Davydd and Morten Levin. 2011. *Introduction to Action Research*. Thousand Oaks, CA: SAGE.

Gutberlet, Jutta, Cystal Tremblay, and Carmen Moraes. 2014. "The Community-Based Research Tradition in Latin America." In *Higher Education and Community-Based Research*, edited by R. Munck, L. McIlrath, B. Hall, and R. Tandon. New York: Palgrave Macmillan, pp. 167–180.

Hacker, Karen. 2013. *Community-Based Participatory Research*. Los Angeles: SAGE.

Hall, B. 1992. "From Margins to Center? The Development and Purpose of Participatory Research." *The American Sociologist*, 26(1), 15–28.

Hall, B. 1993. "Introduction." In *Voices of Change: Participatory Research in the United States and Canada*, edited by P. Park, M. Brydon-Miller, B. Hall, and T. Jackson. London: Bergin & Garvey, pp. xiii–xxxii.

Hall, B., Rajesh Tandon, Walter Lepore, Wafa Singh, Angela Easby, and Crystal Tremblay. 2016. "Theoretical Pedagogical Framework for Community-Based Research." In *Knowledge and*

Engagement: Building Capacity for the Next Generation of Community-Based Researchers, edited by R. Tandon, B. Hall, W. Lepore, and W. Singh. New Delhi: PRIA, pp. 7–38.

Halpern, Robert. 2005. "Instrumental Relationships: A Potential Relationship Model for Inner-City Youth Programs." *Journal of Community Psychology*, 33(1), 11–20.

Hanson, Cindy and Adeyemi Ogunade. 2016. "Caught Up in Power: Exploring Discursive Frictions in Community Research." *Gateways: International Journal of Community Research and Engagement*, 9(1), 41–57.

Hilsen, Anne Inga. 2014. "Covenantal Ethics." In *The SAGE Encyclopedia of Action Research*, edited by D. Coghlan and M. Brydon-Miller. London: SAGE, pp. 195–196.

Hofstede, Geert. 2001. *Culture's Consequences: Comparing Values, Behaviors, Institutions, and Organizations across Nations*. 2nd ed. Thousand Oaks, CA: SAGE.

Instituto de Terras do Pará. 2002. "Título de Reconhecimento de Dominio Coletivo (No. 2001/274554). Belém: INTERPA.

Kim, Hyoung. 2006. "Assessing the Role of Social Capital in the Community Development Field: A Multi-Level Analysis." PhD dissertation, University of Georgia, Athens, GA.

Kip, Markus. 2016. "Solidarity." In *Keywords for Radicals: The Contested Vocabulary of Late-Capitalist Struggle*, edited by K. Fritsch, C. O'Connor, and A. Thompson. Chico: AK Press, pp. 391–398.

Leal, P. A. 2011. "Participation: The Ascendancy of a Buzzword in the Neo-Liberal Era." In *The Participation Reader*, edited by A. Cornwall. London: Zed Books, pp. 70–81.

Ledwith, Margaret. 2016. *Community Development in Action: Putting Freire into Practice*. Chicago, IL: Policy Press.

Ledwith, Margaret. 2020. *Community Development: A Critical and Radical Approach*. 3rd ed. Bristol: Policy Press.

Ledwith, Margaret and Jane Springett. 2010. *Participatory Practice: Community-Based Action for Transformative Change*. Bristol: Policy Press.

Leite, Ika. 2008. "O Projeto Político Quilombola: Desafios, Conquistas e Impasses Atuais." *Revista Estudos Feministas*, 16(3), 965–977.

Lira, Talita and Maria Chaves. 2016. "Comunidades Ribeirinhas na Amazônia: Organização Sociocultural e Política." *Interações*, 17(1), 66–76.

Loewenson, Rene, Asa Laurell, Christer Hogstedt, Lucia D'Ambruoso, and Zubin Shroff. 2014. *Participatory Action Research in Health Systems: A Methods Reader*. Harare: TARSC, AHPSR, WHO, IDRC Canada, and Equinet.

Macinko, James and Barbara Starfield. 2001. "The Utility of Social Capital in Research on Health Determinants." *Milbank Quarterly*, 79(3), 387–427.

Marx, Karl. 1964. *Economic and Philosophic Manuscripts of 1844*. New York: International Publishers.

Mathie, Alison and Eileen Alma. 2016. *Participant Manual: Action Research for Citizen-Led Change*. Antigonish: Coady International Institute.

Mathie, Alison and Gord Cunningham. 2008. *From Clients to Citizens: Communities Changing the Course of Their Own Development*. Rugby: Practical Action.

Mendieta, Eduardo. 2005. "Re-Mapping Latin American Studies: Postcolonialism, Subaltern Studies, Post-Occidentalism and Globalization Theory." *Dispositio*, 25(52), 179–202.

Mendoza, Pilar, Aaron M. Kuntz, and Joseph B. Berger. 2012. "Bourdieu and Academic Capitalism: Faculty 'Habitus' in Materials Science and Engineering." *Journal of Higher Education*, 83(4), 558–581.

Mizzi, Robert and Z. Hamm. 2013. "Canadian Community Development Organization, Adult Education, and the Internationalization of a Pedagogical Practice." In *Building on Critical Traditions: Adult Education and Learning in Canada*, edited by T. Nesbit, S. Brigham, N. Taber, and T. Gibb. Toronto: Thompson Educational Publishing, pp. 342–352.

Mor Barak, Michalle. 2017. *Managing Diversity: Towards a Globally Inclusive Workplace*. 4th ed. Los Angeles: SAGE.

Myers, Bryant. 2012. *Walking with the Poor: Principles and Practices of Transformational Development*. New York: Orbis Books.

Nation, Maury, Kimberly Bess, Adam Voight, Douglas Perkins, and Paul Juarez. 2011. "Levels of Community Engagement in Youth Violence Prevention: The Role of Power in Sustaining Successful University-Community Partnerships." *American Journal of Community Psychology*, 48(1), 89–96.

Negri, Bérengère, Elizabeth Thomas, Aloys Ilinigumugabo, Ityai Muvandi, and Gary Lewis. 1998. *Empowering Communities: Participatory Techniques for Community-Based Programme Development* (Vol. 2). Nairobi: Centre for African Family Studies.

Oberg, Lurdes. 2013. "Individualismo e Coletivismo: Reflexões a Partir da Ótica de Mulheres de uma Comunidade." *Polêm!Ca*, 12(2), 192–202.

Park, Peter. 1993. "What Is Participatory Research? A Theoretical and Methodological Perspective." In *Voices of Change: Participatory Research in the United States and Canada*, edited by P. Park, M. Brydon-Miller, B. Hall, and T. Jackson. London: Bergin & Garvey, pp. 1–19.

Peet, Richard and Elaine Hartwick. 2015. *Theories of Development: Contentions, Arguments, Alternatives*. 3rd ed. New York: Guilford Press.

Pojo, Eliana, Lina Elias, and Maria Vilhena. 2014. "As Águas e os Ribeirinhos: Beirando Sua Cultura e Margeando Seus Saberes." *Revista Margens Interdisciplinar*, 8(11), 176–198.

Prado, Mariana. 2018. "Traditional Populations, Land Rights, and Environmental Justice: The Challenges of the Amazon." Brazil Institute. Think Brazil. www.wilsoncenter.org/blog-post/traditional-populations-land-rights-and-environmental-justice-the-challenges-the-amazon

Rahman, Mohammad. 1991. "The Theoretical Standpoint of PAR." In *Action and Knowledge: Breaking the Monopoly with Participatory Action-Research*, edited by O. Fals Borda and M. A. Rahman. New York: Apex Press, pp. 13–23.

Reason, Peter and Hilary Bradbury. 2001. *Handbook of Action Research: Participative Inquiry in Practice*. London: SAGE.

Ross, J. Ashleigh and Randy Stoecker. 2017. "The Emotional Context of Higher Education Community Engagement." *Journal of Community Engagement and Scholarship*, 9(2): 7–18.

Roy, Carole. 2016. *Documentary Film Festivals: Transformative Learning, Community Building and Solidarity*. Rotterdam: Sense Publishers.

Santos, Antonilda and Mara Oliveira. 2019. "A Participação Política das Mulheres da Comunidade Remanescente de Quilombos Arapapuzinho no Município de Abaetetuba Associadas na ARQUIA." *Estudos IAT*, 4(2), 28–41.

Sihlongonyane, Mfaniseni. 2009. "'Community Development' as a Buzz-Word." *Development in Practice*, 19(2), 136–147.

Smith, Susan. 1997. "Deepening Participatory Action-Research." In *Nurtured by Knowledge: Learning to Do Participatory Action-Research*, edited by S. Smith, D. Williams, and N. Johnson. New York: Apex Press, pp. 173–263.

Sobrinho, Mário and Ana Maria Vasconcellos. 2012. "Local Organizations Capacity and Its Influence on Partnership with Local Government for Rural Development in Brazilian Amazonia." *Amazônia, Organizações e Sustentabilidade*, 1(1), 25–44.

Spivak, Gayatri. 2009. *Outside in the Teaching Machine*. New York: Routledge.

Stewart-Harawira, Makere. 2005. "Cultural Studies, Indigenous Knowledge and Pedagogies of Hope." *Policy Futures in Education*, 3(2), 153–163.

Stoecker, Randy. 1999. "Are Academics Irrelevant? Roles for Scholars in Participatory Research." *American Behavioral Scientist*, 42(5), 840–854.

Stoecker, Randy. 2016. *Liberating Service Learning and the Rest of Higher Education Civic Engagement*. Philadelphia, PA: Temple University Press.

Strand, Kerry, Marullo, Sam, Cutforth, Nick, Stoecker, Randy, and Donohue, Patrick. 2003a. "Principles of Best Practice for Community-Based Research." *Michigan Journal of Community Service Learning*, 9(3), 5–15.

Strand, Kerry, Marullo, Sam, Cutforth, Nick, Stoecker, Randy, and Donohue, Patrick. 2003b. *Community-Based Research and Higher Education: Principles and Practices*. San Francisco, CA: Jossey-Bass.

TallBear, Kim. 2014. "Standing with and Speaking as Faith: A Feminist-Indigenous Approach to Inquiry." *Journal of Research Practice*, 10(2), Article N17.

Tandon, Rajesh. 1988. "Social Transformation and Participatory Research." *Convergence* 21(2/3), 18.

Tandon, Rajesh and Budd Hall. 2014. "Majority-World Foundations of Community-Based Research." In *Higher Education and Community-Based Research*, edited by R. Munck, L. McIlrath, B. Hall, and R. Tandon. New York: Palgrave Macmillan, pp. 53–68.

Tiffany, Evan. 2006. "Can Utilitarians Have Friends?" Burnaby: SFU. www.sfu.ca/~etiffany/teaching/phil120/utilitarianism_love.html

Tobias, Joshua, Chantelle Richmond, and Isaac Luginaah. 2013. "Community-Based Participatory Research (CBPR) with Indigenous Communities: Producing Respectful and Reciprocal Research." *Journal of Empirical Research on Human Research Ethics*, 8(2), 123–140.

Villasante, Tomas. 2017. "Orlando Fals Borda Concepto Sentipensante." YouTube. https://youtu.be/mGAy6Pw4qAw

Viswanathan, M., A. Ammerman, E. Eng, G. Garlehner, K.N. Lohr, D. Griffith, S. Rhodes, C. Samuel-Hodge, S. Maty, L. Lux, L. Webb, SF Sutton, T. Swinson, A. Jackman, and L Whitener. 2004. "Community-Based Participatory Research: Assessing the Evidence: Summary." *AHRQ Evidence Report Summaries*. Rockville: Agency for Healthcare Research and Quality.

von Kotze, Astrid and Shirley Walters, eds. 2017. *Forging Solidarity: Popular Education at Work*. Rotterdam: Sense Publishers.

Wallerstein, Nina and Bonnie Duran. 2008. "The Theoretical, Historical, and Practice Roots of CBPR." In *Community-Based Participatory Research for Health: From Process to Outcomes*. 2nd ed., edited by M. Minkler, and N. Wallerstein. San Francisco, CA: Jossey-Bass, pp. 25–46.

Wetmore, Stephen and Francois Theron. 1998. "Community Development and Research: Participatory Learning and Action: A Development Strategy in Itself." *Development Southern Africa*, 15(1), 29–54.

Williamson, John. 2000. "Practical Community Empowerment: Concepts, Organizational Issues and the Process." *MCC Occasional Paper* No. 27. Mennonite Central Committee.

22. Re-storying participatory action research: a narrative approach to challenging epistemic violence in community development

Daniel Bryan and Chelsea Viteri

In a participatory action research (PAR) project on Indigenous epistemologies, the A'í-Cofán[1] community of Bavoroe created this seven-minute play: Two community members well versed in the practice of ancestral medicine are accepted to medical school at a prestigious local university where they struggle against new and contrasting ways of being and knowing. Whether the alarm that wakes them up in the morning, the constant sounds of traffic outside their window, the ways professors teach, or how fellow students look at them, everything feels foreign. Half-way through the play they are exhausted and make the decision to dress and talk like the other students, replacing their traditional necklaces for neckties. Suddenly, using the power of theater, time speeds up and their bodies are thrust through their day-to-day actions as if they no longer control them. Rather, a dominant external force turns their lives into a hurried routine, and before the audience knows it, six years fly by in 60 seconds. They do not know how, and maybe not even why, but at the end of the play, they have become doctors. Time slows back down to normal so news sources, social media, and the academy can celebrate this pioneering accomplishment: the first A'í-Cofán in history to graduate as physicians.

Our narrative approach to PAR and community development (CD) includes enacting stories with local community members to embody the conflicts we hope to transform. The Bavoroe play, which demonstrates an aggressive process of acculturation, is not easy to watch, and since we[2] participate in the entire creative process, it is even harder to act in. What we see and feel is the embodiment of what De Sousa Santos (2007) refers to as "epistemicide" – the suppression, even invisibilization, of non-Western epistemologies – representing an integral part of an ongoing colonial project of domination over territory and resources, not to mention over human stories and bodies.

The challenges this theatricalization presents to our colleagues from Bavoroe, balanced with the conflicts we feel as PAR researchers, represent what we intend to explore in this chapter. We will compare the experiences from the Indigenous epistemologies project with those from another PAR project on gender and Hip Hop that we facilitated one year earlier in the city of Quito. There, instead of creating plays, we theatricalized focus groups by carrying them out in cyphers.[3] In both projects it became apparent that, while the Eurocentric approach to knowledge creation has made innumerable contributions to contemporary life, non-Western epistemologies and ontologies have been excluded, even obliterated, in its name.

For most of us, epistemicide is a subtle violent act that we never perceive. However, it results in collective biases towards what is legitimate knowledge and who is a legitimate knower. It is hard to admit but many of our perceptions, whether conscious or subconscious, are limited to a Western legacy tied to colonial and patriarchal violence. For example, one intent of this book is to find greater synergies between PAR and CD. Yet, in spite of this volume's commitment to

CD as "led by communities ... excluding projects imposed upon place-based communities by outsiders" (Introduction, this volume), our work with communities indicates an epistemic fear of the word "development," which De Sousa Santos (2011) refers to as a colonial construct related to a false promise of infinite growth, continuous progress, and globalization for all. In other words, Eurocentric knowledge promotes certain ways of knowing that function as an epistemic barrier to CD.

A central precept of PAR is accounting for and including different ways of knowing (Hall and Tandon 2017; Heron 1996; Reason and Bradbury 2008), and it can serve as a decolonizing methodology (Ascanio and Villareal 2017; Fals Borda 2006b; Tuck 2016); however, by examining Indigenous research projects (Zavala 2013) or when PAR researchers evaluate their own work with decolonizing/decolonial lenses (Gill et al. 2012) we recognize that PAR is not exempt from epistemic violence. Carrying out PAR with a limited epistemological framework is little more than "offspring of a specifically Western modernity" (Stern 2019: 440), resulting in work that is extractive and exploitative. It is synonymous with carrying out De Sousa Santos's "development" disguised as Stoecker and Falcón's progressive CD (see 'Introduction', this volume).

Zavala (2013) and Hall and Tandon (2017) recommend reconnecting with the emancipatory roots of PAR and Fals Borda reminds us to see PAR as "not only as a research methodology but also as a philosophy of life that would convert its practitioners into 'thinking-feeling persons'" (2006a: 31). In this chapter, we explore PAR as a decolonial and epistemologically plural "philosophy of life" by diving into the "thinking-feeling" world.[4] Via a narrative, arts-based approach to PAR, we seek to engage different ways of knowing as well as the spaces where PAR is carried out, and we wonder if such an approach can achieve what Reason and Bradbury declare the "primary purpose of action research ... to liberate the human body, mind and spirit in search for a better, freer world" (2008: 5). We also wonder how this narrative approach can further ground CD in the stories of the people, liberating it from the epistemic violence associated with "development" while contributing to greater systemic change.

We begin by providing a brief literature review of "epistemicide" and narrative/embodied methodologies. We continue by describing the numerous organizations and communities involved in the two case studies and the strategies we used during those projects, as well as how we reflect on them post facto for the purposes of this study. Then, we explore the case studies in relationship to the frameworks and offer observations for scholar-practitioners in the fields of PAR and CD.

EPISTEMIC VIOLENCE AND PARTICIPATORY ACTION RESEARCH

In the Bavoroe play, we identify the key elements of what De Sousa Santos calls "abyssal thinking," referring to an imaginary yet abyssal and oppressive line that separates ways of knowing in our world. The line, a construct of Western modernity, invisibilizes entire epistemologies by classifying them as "incomprehensible magical or idolatrous practices" (2007: 51). The actors/community members take a metaphorical leap across the abyss, leaving behind magic and idolatry to enter a new epistemological reality "whereby the hegemonic eye, located in civil society, ceases to see and indeed declares as nonexistent the state of nature" (2007: 50).

In this chapter, we pull from a body of work that seeks to understand the complex and multi-faceted characteristics of the "abyssal line" as correlated with PAR and CD, and consequently higher education as a whole. It calls upon the Latin American(ist) collective of scholars from the modernity/coloniality research program (MC), which equates epistemic domination with a "coloniality of knowing" (Escobar 2007). Inherently linked to a coloniality of knowing, Quijano (2007) examines how power has been colonized, first by codifying social discriminations according to categories such as race and ethnicity, and then by colonizing the imaginations of those who are being dominated. When knowing, power, and imaginations are colonized, it becomes the very lived human experience, or the "coloniality of being" (Maldonado-Torres 2007), that is most dramatically felt.

While the primary focus of PAR and MC is the transformation of the lived reality of communities, neither can be separated from higher education. Boidin et al. link the university to modernity's dependency on universal knowledge, or universalism, which "has been complicit with processes of not only class exploitation but also processes of racial, gender, and sexual dehumanization" (2012: 2). They call for transcending disciplinary divisions and the creation of a "pluriversity." Reason and Bradbury echo this sentiment, reminding us that universities are beholden to the Cartesian model, a Western paradigm that has taught us "the world is made up of separate things." However, the "participation" in PAR insists "that we are embodied beings part of a social and ecological order, and radically interconnected with all other beings" (2008: 8).

The "pluriversity" encourages the practice of pluriversal thinking, or epistemological pluralism, which acknowledges epistemology as a spatial and relational construct, not solely a temporal or cause-and-effect one. In other words, decolonizing knowing does not simply refer to the reordering of knowing; rather, it means decolonizing *where* and *how* knowledge is constructed. Decolonial theorists have spent decades defining these pluriversal spaces. De Sousa Santos (2008) argues that our obsession with the "monoculture of linear time" has divided epistemologies into "forward" and "backward" thinking, and recommends a spatial construct of epistemology, an "ecology of knowledges" where different ways of knowing can intersect (De Sousa Santos 2007). Walsh urges "epistemic interculturality," which evolves from "other thinking" in "spaces and places that modernity ... could never have and could not imagine" (2012: 15). Escobar (2007) called for "worlds and knowledges otherwise" before proposing "designs for the pluriverse" (Escobar 2018). Finally, Mignolo and Tlostanova (2006) evoke the space of the border, situating our thinking on the exteriority of modernity/coloniality, from where the subaltern can "delink" from the coloniality of knowing and being without denying their existence. For Mignolo (2012), border thinking is a creative transcendence of Cartesian thought that includes other ways of knowing such as sensing and feeling.

MC's large body of work calls for disrupting preconceived epistemic assumptions and points to development, including CD, as tools for promoting a dominant ideology (Escobar 2011). Their work suggests that CD must actively counteract this ideology or coloniality will permeate any CD project, mirroring macro-level epistemicide on the micro scale. MC regularly turns to Indigenous knowledge(s) for counteracting the violence of development ideologies while working toward a sustainable future (Breidlid 2013).

Several scholars call for collaborative PAR spaces to reflect pluriversal spaces. Stern (2019) summons Homi Bhabha's "Third Space" (Bhabha and Rutherford 2006), or a space where researchers and locals can transcend the scientific and the subaltern, while Pyrch asks us to leave our prison-like boxes and meet in a circle that "reflects the very essence of our spiritual selves" (2007: 210). We acknowledge the challenges of defining a "third space" and hope that our recommendations and conclusions at the end of this chapter represent steps toward naming them in ways that perceive PAR as an essential tool in CD. For contextualization (for this and other chapters in this volume), it is important to recognize "third spaces" as beyond physical spaces. While, in part, they clearly represent the physical places where local community researchers and external scholar practitioners come together to practice PAR, the "third space" is also the imagined working space from where our collective dreams for CD are planted, cultivated, and harvested.

STORYTELLING, EMBODIMENT, AND PARTICIPATORY ACTION RESEARCH

Using a *storytelling* lens, we can observe the Bavoroe play from a different perspective. Instead of focusing on the play's content, we witness the process of embodying narrative. The actors/community members are no longer just telling a story or making social commentary. "Embodiment refers to the double sense of the body as both experiencing living in the world and as a context for knowing about the world" (Ritenburg et al. 2014: 69), leading us to recognize the acting of the play as elemental to being and knowing.

Although the ways we create and share stories have changed over the millennia, storytelling has been central to human survival for tens of thousands of years (Gottschall 2012). It is our species' ability to represent life in fiction that catapulted us up the food chain in an unprecedentedly short amount of time (Harari 2018). We create myths to connect to the mystery of life, to organize ourselves in groups, to teach our young and to grapple with conflict, and even though modern times are radically different from those of our hunter-gatherer ancestors, our brains are basically the same, and the function of stories is relatively unchanged (Campbell 1991). At their core, whether studied by comparative mythologists (see Campbell 1991), cognitive psychologists (see Bruner 1998), or marketing researchers (see Godin 2005), stories construct our truth.

Nevertheless, while it is clear that stories guide our behaviors and actions, only recently have they begun to challenge dominant epistemological paradigms in Western academia (Datta 2017; Fairbanks 1996). Uzendoski (2012) argues that Western scholarship on storytelling, especially oral tradition, implies a lack of civilization and backwardness. This underappreciation, especially as a methodological approach to creating knowledge, reflects the epistemic violence and colonial legacy of the academy, deeming non-Western epistemologies and ontologies inferior, savage, or uncivilized (Grosfoguel 2015; Smith 2012). According to Smith (2012), this legacy has led Indigenous peoples to see *research* as a "dirty word," equal to being objectified and classified as fauna and flora. Indigenous ways of being are perceived as "other" stories, or spectacles to be discovered, unrelated to knowledge creation. This approach to research negates their human essence, resulting in the erasure of entire knowledge systems (Caxaj 2015; Christensen 2012; Stewart 2009).

For Indigenous peoples, storytelling is the "central medium for knowledge transmission" (Little Bear 2000) and the core of their worldviews (Caxaj 2015; Datta 2017). It also serves as a method to recover from colonization (Iseke 2013), to rename reality while remembering and preserving collective memory (McLeod 2000), and to revitalize Indigenous epistemologies, ontologies, and identities (Uzendoski 2012). Storytelling creates bridges between Western and

Indigenous knowledge, providing spaces where both forms of knowing and being can coexist (Bishop 1999; Datta 2017).

In Hip Hop, stories come through the movement's four main elements (rap, DJing, break-dance, and graffiti). Urban youth use these elements to tell stories that shape their identities in ways that challenge dominant power structures (Navarro 2016) while simultaneously connecting them to a broader global community (Motley and Henderson 2008). Osumare (2001) argues what unites the Hip Hop community across borders is a sense of connected marginality, allowing, for example, marginalized youth from Quito to relate with the songs and stories of marginalized Black Americans. Even though there is a globalized Hip Hop culture, each Hip Hop community adds their context, symbols, and languages to tell stories that embrace their own realities.

Storytelling opens the door to a fairer, more representative and emancipatory form of research, blurring the lines between who is the knower, who is the researcher, and who are the participants (Bishop 1999), echoing Freire's (1973) insistence that knowledge is always created by a "we" and not an "I." It embraces Augusto Boal's (2013) interpretation of the Greek "metaxis," or what Linds calls the "in-between," where a physical and social space is situated "between the real and the fictional ... between participants and their role in the play ... between the actor's meaning of the play and how meaning emerges" (2005: 114). Storytelling frees community researchers to reflect, create, question, and choose stories from their own context and worldview (Bishop 1999), empowering scholars "to see knowing as it is enacted in each moment of the present, not as something which already exists" (Linds 2005: 114–115). Storytelling creates opportunities for communities to set their own agendas, ones that begin with their very bodies and open doors to research that is emancipatory.

PARTICIPATING ORGANIZATIONS AND COMMUNITIES WITH PROJECT DESCRIPTIONS

The common thread for both case studies is the Ecuadorian non-profit organization, Fundación Pachaysana, for which we are founding team members. Pachaysana is an educational organization of local and international educators, teaching artists, development specialists, and community organizers that applies a decolonial framework to community-based study abroad, CD, and PAR. The name, Pachaysana, is the fusion of two Kichwa words: *pacha* refers to the world or the time-space continuum, and *aysana* means balance. It is indicative of the organization's mission to create equilibrium between knowledge-creation, education, and development practices.

The first case study is a project called "Gender, Hip Hop and Healing," (HH) which we carried out with two Quito-based collectives/cultural centers, the Nina Shunku Association and Casa Machankara. Nina Shunku is a group of urban youth educators, artists, activists, and community organizers who use graffiti, breakdance, DJing, and rap to instigate social change and recreate communal/collective identity. Casa Machankara is a cultural center that conjoins cultural production with environmental activism and holistic healing. Its founding members are artists and activists with direct ties to the Hip Hop community.

The HH project came out of a broader effort to raise awareness and stimulate change in gender dynamics within Quito's Hip Hop community. The process began as a three-week Theatre of the Oppressed (Boal 1979) workshop, hosted by Casa Machankara, and was open to anyone with interest in the topic. Members of the Hip Hop community participated as attendees and guest speakers/facilitators, which is how Nina Shunku became involved. The workshop revealed the need and interest to challenge dominant gender paradigms in the Hip Hop community, leading Machankara, Nina Shunku, and Pachaysana to create the PAR project.

Pachaysana procured a grant from a United States (US) university[5] and the project was carried out by two principal local researchers from Machankara, two student-researchers from the US university that funded the grant, a local steering committee composed of representatives from Machankara and Nina Shunku, and one Pachaysana staff member whose role was to support all participants. The research implemented creative methods to collect stories and perspectives from members of the Hip Hop community and a bibliographical study of PAR, gender, and Hip Hop methodologies/pedagogies. The project's ultimate goal was a short documentary film to raise awareness about gender dynamics within the Hip Hop community and to contribute to building a culture of diversity and inclusion.

The second case study, a project called "Indigenous Storytelling from the Amazon: Reimagining Diversity and Inclusion via Epistemologies of the South" (IS), was carried out with two Indigenous communities from the Ecuadorian Amazon, the A'i-Cofán community of Bavoroe and the Kichwa community of Tzawata. It was financed by an award for innovation in diversity and inclusion sponsored by a US-based non-profit organization.

Bavoroe and Tzawata are small communities of 10 and 20 families. Bavoroe is part of the greater Cofán-Dureno community in the province of Sucumbios. For over 50 years, the oil industry has severely impacted its way of life, resulting in the contamination of water sources, health problems, and political divisions among community members. Tzawata rests on the banks of the Ansu River in the province of Napo. Its inhabitants are involved in a longstanding legal and political struggle against an international mining company over the rights to their ancestral lands. Previously, Pachaysana had worked with each community for several years, but never together on the same project. With Bavoroe, Pachaysana was concluding the preliminary phase of a project to preserve and promote A'i-Cofán myths. With Tzawata, Pachaysana was wrapping up a series of storytelling and identity workshops with community youth.

The IS project emerged from a multi-faceted dialogue among the communities, Pachaysana, and some of Pachaysana's university partners in Ecuador and the US. As these different actors got to know each other in different contexts, they grew more curious about how academic institutions and Indigenous communities approach diversity and inclusion, and whether epistemological diversity is valued. Together they dreamed up a "ways of knowing" project as a potential bridge between academia and Indigenous communities. It began with community members from Tzawata and Bavoroe living in each other's communities and exploring their ways of knowing and being. With the support of Pachaysana staff and international student interns, they created an interactive "ways of knowing" workshop series (which included the play from the beginning of this chapter) they hoped would impact policies, curricula, and pedagogies in diversity and inclusion. They facilitated the workshop series at a private Ecuadorian university in Quito and hope to take it to universities in the US.[6]

RESEARCH STRATEGY

Although independent of each other, both the HH and IS projects sought to create knowledge that would boost CD. They practiced what Gaudry calls "insurgent research" by "promoting community-based action that targets the demise of colonial interference within our lives and communities" (2011: 114). Both projects planned to share knowledge with a larger public and influence a broader dialogue on what it means to "know something" and how diverse ways of knowing impact CD. Both projects established small working groups that applied narrative-based methods to knowledge creation and included international students who collaborated with the local communities in the narrative-based dialogues and assisted coordinators with bibliographical research.

We, the authors of this chapter, participated as the coordinators on both projects, bringing the groups together, establishing spaces for the narrative-based PAR activities, and leading dialogue-generating activities among all participants. Our goal was to reveal lessons learned and forge new paths for CD. In reflecting on the two case studies, we call on Somekh's *Through the Looking Glass* metaphor, "when Alice passed through the mirror she was radically re-challenged, finding herself this time in a world where reality had radically shifted again" (2005: 4).

We bring complex stories to the work and hope that this exploration (writing and sharing this chapter) will "radically shift us again" as researchers, practitioners, and people who share a "here and now" with the communities. As a mestiza, biracial, bicultural woman from Ecuador and as a white male from the US living in Ecuador for over 20 years, our identities have been impacted by the community projects and the community projects have been impacted by our identities. In and through our work in PAR and CD we seek to redistribute power and foster reciprocal and just relationships, and our identities, colored by different privileges and oppressions, are in constant negotiation. In both these projects we did not hide our stories, and when tensions and conflicts emerged due to our identities, we engaged in a recurrent questioning of ourselves and rethinking of how we can create a more just exchange.

Finally, we never approached PAR and CD as separate processes that require bridging. Rather, we treated PAR as a powerful tool *of* and *for* CD. We recognize PAR as community members participating (the "P") in actively making changes to their lived realities (the "A") by creating knowledge according to their diverse ways of knowing (the "R"). PAR roots CD in the reality, desires, and definitions of the community, and it actively opposes the imposition of top-down development.

CASE STUDIES

The HH and IS projects incorporated a narrative-based methodology that fosters epistemologically plural spaces for exchange and relationship building. We embrace this narrative approach by weaving observations of both projects into parallel narratives. In doing so, we recognize that the projects involved participants from different cultures and were carried out in distinct regions of Ecuador. Thus, we emphasize that this is our weaving, for only we lived both experiences. We hope that our work inspires further weaving, even interweaving, to understand the power and/or usefulness of a narrative-based methodology in PAR and how that might guide CD toward the progressive.

We intertwine dozens of stories that we lived with local participants while influenced by the following questions, which we use to organize our observations and reflections. (1) How is a narrative approach to PAR liberating, decolonial, and epistemologically plural? Or to reflect Reason and Bradbury (2008), how can a narrative approach to PAR liberate the human (and we suggest "collective") body, mind, and spirit in search for a better, freer world? (2) What is the relationship between a narrative approach to PAR and the collaborative third/elusive/decolonial space? What does this space entail and what does it look like? How can we apply the tensions and negotiations in this space to CD?

Before addressing these questions directly, we share our experiences as metaphorical stories with three primary aspirations: (1) to thrust readers and ourselves into the worlds of the projects where we can interrelate with the narratives as both spectator and actor, or what Boal (1979) calls "spect-actors"; (2) to situate the reader and ourselves somewhere between knowing and unknowing, in De Sousa Santos's (2007) "abyssal line"; and (3) to encourage the reader to think beyond the words on the page and make sensory connections, weaving them into their own work or life experiences. (In doing so, we interweave together.)

Narrative 1: The Cypher: Hip Hop's Circle of Healing and Oppression

It is a warm Friday afternoon and our group of community-based and international PAR researchers are traveling to Casa Machankara on Quito's busiest public transportation system, the Trole. No one knows why but Fridays seem to have double the traffic as other days and the trolleybus is especially crowded. Our bodies are mashed together with the other travelers, and for a time, our world is the absence of space in a rolling box. It is such an invasive feeling that all you can do is share uncomfortable smiles with your friends, wait impatiently for your eventual stop, and hope no one is stealing your cell phone.

We get off the trolleybus and walk two blocks to Casa Machankara, taking a moment to observe the Machanagara River that runs right by the front door. Its sewage-stained appearance and smell are a constant reminder of the world we live in, a world that reeks of injustice, yet that flows hopefully toward a brighter future. As we head into Machankara, we notice the group of rappers arriving. They have come to participate in a creative focus group to explore gender dynamics in Quito's Hip Hop community. We share some pleasantries, acknowledge that everyone has arrived with their own personal baggage, and invite all to create a space conducive to sharing.

Without hesitation or discussion, we form a circle with our bodies. This seemingly simple act, similar to huddles in sports or children's games like "duck-duck-goose," brings an energy to the group that is unmistakably powerful. For the Hip Hop community, a circular space where all can express their truth is the *cypher* (Levy et al. 2018). It is a space within a place that only exists because it can simultaneously *disconnect from* and *connect to* all other spaces and places. A rapper strikes up the beat-box and one by one the others enter the center of the cypher to rap a prepared strophe or freestyle riff. With each rap, it becomes clear that this experience is symbolic of our entire project.

The cypher has a rhythm that connects it to a greater community. As we rap, we know that others are rapping in their own cyphers all around the world. The beat that we hear is the heartbeat of Hip Hop and it tells us that we belong, that we are worthy, and that we have something valuable to express, no matter where we come from, what we look like, or what our abilities are. At this moment, in this space, we are the ones sustaining the beat. Tomorrow, it might be others from the Hip Hop community, like breakdancers, DJs, or graffiti artists. Together we are expressing ourselves and making the magic that famed Hip Hop artist Afrika Bambaataa (Gosa 2015) calls "knowledge," the element of Hip Hop that links us all together.

While swaying to the beat, we realize that the cypher is not only a space for each person to share their truth, it is a circle for creating knowledge. Yet, the cypher does not follow the codes of academia, and by creating and engaging the circle, we recognize the silenced voices from society's margins. In the Trole we felt silenced by the mass of humanity all around us, and on the riverbank we felt helpless in the face of violent acts against that which gives us life; however, in the cypher, those who have been silenced by society's hegemonic codes are creating knowledge with their own code. The cypher is the code. And that is when we realize that the cypher is both a space and language at once. In other words, the cypher is not just a space for creating knowledge, the cypher is knowledge itself.

Then, we start to think about the cypher as a circular, knowledge-creating line of human bodies that acknowledges an "out there" and "in here." The dominant narrative, based on a legacy of patriarchal and colonial violence, is "out there," where access to power means you ascribe to a certain way of being. When we step into the center of the cypher and are "in here," we feel immediately powerful, as if the margins have become the center of existence. Suddenly this line intrigues us more. It forms the circle, but it is also a border, and by changing the position of our bodies, or turning our gaze outward and then back inward, we notice that we are situated in the "in-between," providing us observational and reflective power.

By focusing on the situatedness of the line, we can also observe the pitfall of overly romanticizing Hip Hop, acting as if social injustices "out there" could never penetrate our idealized "in here." Our most basic observations reveal that certain "in here" power dynamics mirror "out there" ones. As two women rappers enter the center of the cypher and rap about their struggles against patriarchy, we feel very self-conscious about being in the line. Their words not only question the male-centered power dynamics within Hip Hop, they question the cypher itself. Their protest echoes our own lived experiences in the Hip Hop PAR project, recalling when we felt disparaged, even threatened, if we dare question the purity of the movement. Suddenly, the cypher feels suffocating and the women rappers return to the line, silent … or silenced. We wonder if they feel as liberated and trapped as we feel. Surely, they need the cypher to liberate themselves from injustice, but they also fear its power to replicate the very oppressions we are all fighting.

The cypher comes to a close, yet we continue to straddle the line, inspired and disappointed. Hip Hop seeks to change the world, and the energy of the circle, coupled with verses for social justice, energized and healed us. Yet, Hip Hop is not isolated from the world of the Trole or the Machángara that it is fighting to change, and we must recognize when it is replicating, maybe even accentuating, the violence it purports to transcend and transform. We now understand that to explore changes in Hip Hop and to understand our own roles as PAR research-practitioners we must reimagine the cypher itself.

Narrative 2: Listening to the Aguarico River

Our PAR group is sitting in an apartment in Quito, shellshocked after receiving terrible news. We try to process what happened by telling stories of the experiences we have lived together during this project, and our guiding memory is of course the river.

We remember the sun setting as we crossed the Aguarico River in a motorized canoe. Heading to the road that would take most of us back to our homes, we enjoyed the fresh breeze and radiant sunlight on our faces, but we did not speak. Instead, the river was speaking. What it said to us after living together as a makeshift family for two weeks was probably the same as it was saying when we arrived. We just weren't listening then.

We had met up at the riverbank in the mid-morning and those of us who were not from the area immediately marveled at Aguarico's beauty. When imagining the biodiversity within its waters and in the rainforest that surrounds it, balanced against 60 years of contamination from the oil industry, we could not help but see the river as an act of nature's resilience. We observed the river with compassion, but we were not yet listening to it.

That was the day our unusual family, composed of four Indigenous youth from two Amazon nations, two Quiteñans and one foreigner, boarded the canoe that would take us to Bavoroe. During that initial crossing, we admired how well the A'í-Cofán know their river. With patches of rapids and shallow spots all around, yet hidden from sight by the heavily sedimented waters, it felt as if going to the community was a sort of aquatic obstacle course. For the Quiteñans and foreigner, this "knowing" of the river fit perfectly with our topic of Indigenous epistemologies; however, we were just forcing the metaphor from our outsiders' perspective. We were not listening.

Bavoroe is just a short walk from the river's edge, and our gracious hosts helped us feel right at home. For a few hours each day we participated in workshops to explore our ways of knowing and being. The rest of the day we ate, hiked through the jungle, sang in various languages (Kichwa, A'íngue, Spanish, and English), told scary stories, and of course bathed in the river … together. There was something about living together, being curious about one another and truly listening to our stories that made everything flow. It was enchanting. And now, as we melancholically remember crossing the river back to our homes, we know why. The river was the magic that bonded our family together. Without intending, we had begun to listen. How?

Every afternoon we would play games in the river and laugh until our stomachs hurt before watching the sun go down once more. We knew that the road the oil industry had built was just on the other side, but we felt free and far away from that world of exploitation and hegemonic expectations. We could also sense Bavoroe's town center nearby, but we never worried what the community thought of our frolicking. In some ways, the river felt like her own unapologetically powerful space that just wanted to share a bit of her freedom with us. In other ways, she flowed with such fierce assurance, letting us know no one can stop her, capture her, or even define her. All at once, the river was our space and no one's. We gave into the moment of being together in that river, and in doing so we listened to her.

The PAR workshops did not take place in the river, but in a spiritual way maybe they did. By sharing our lives in and with the river we felt encouraged to share in the workshops. Whether stories of healing, nurturing, and inspiration, or of injustice, violence, and toxicity, we listened to and found validation in each other. We felt purified by each other as if we were in the river.

But today, in Quito, we are nothing less than enraged by the visa rejection letters our friends from Bavoroe received from the US Consulate. Since crossing the river back to the "real world," we had dreamed of contributing to a movement for greater epistemic justice by helping transform how colleges and communities relate to one another. It was our way to share the river with others. The river had made us feel unstoppable and realize that our stories were important, even urgent. But today, reality kicked us out of the river, or maybe it kicked the river out of us.

Was the river nothing more than a dreamland? We went from feeling unstoppable to feeling like we are not enough, or that some of us are not enough. Why did the river not warn us, or at least remind us that the legacy of colonialism could be more powerful than our makeshift family? Did the river trick us? Or were we still not truly listening?

Our friends from Bavoroe tell us that the river speaks to them in dreams, and we should not idealize her, just as we should not idealize the world we dream about creating. As the Aguarico gives us life, she is also polluted. We must listen to her whole story, not just what we want to hear. In doing so, we will begin to hear ourselves in her story and recognize that we are enough. The river is asking us to listen, and if we do, change will come.

The Questions

How is a narrative approach to participatory action research liberating, decolonial, and epistemologically plural?

We hope the narratives we shared for each project inspired you to dream up images of the cypher at Casa Machankara and the Aguarico River flowing by the community of Bavoroe. If so, what you see in your imagination is different from what others see, and unless you have visited, your images are quite different from "real life." However, that is also the point. Each one of your images is influenced by your ways of being and knowing, and by imagining you perform a joyous and liberating act. A narrative approach to PAR embodies a similar process, and when done over and over again it becomes part of CD. It resonates with Reason and Bradbury's claim that PAR is "a verb rather than a noun" (2008: 5).

Both projects used stories to question and interlink our diverse lived realities. Each time we told a story, defined by its characters, conflict, place, theme, etc., it led to a different story with different characteristics, and eventually we would weave the numerous stories into a collective story. This process, for which we now utilize the verbs "to story" and "to re-story" (see Kimmerer 2013), helped us realize the complexity and interconnectivity of our lives, as well as life itself. Interconnecting stories cannot be understood by breaking them down into parts or by comparing them, just as a human being or a community cannot be understood that way. By focusing on how stories are created, interconnected, and recreated, re-storying PAR embraces epistemic and ontological complexity. But what does re-storying PAR mean?

When a PAR research team (locals and outsiders) engages a space with the purpose of interweaving our stories to create knowledge that challenges dominant paradigms, we are re-storying PAR. Interweaving means learning to listen to each other's stories as we learned to listen to the river, and it means being vulnerable to complexity and connections (for us, the essence of "thinking-feeling"). Re-storying PAR enriches the practice's roots in critical pedagogy, evoking Joe Kincheloe's notion of "radical listening" (Tobin 2009), or the act of listening to everyone and everything that is around and inside us. Additionally, as the cypher revealed "in heres" and "out theres" linked to colonial and patriarchal legacies, re-storying PAR reveals space as knowledge. When we simply create a space to hear under-represented voices (for example, the women rappers), it does not mean we have radically listened to the voices or the space, and it certainly does not mean we are all working together to create a new story.

Re-storying PAR sets the groundwork for re-storying CD. The dominant story of development, shaped by Western epistemologies and neoliberalism, has influenced CD's dominant story (Kenny 2016). According to neoliberalism, development is the truth and CD is make-believe, but that is precisely how re-storying PAR can influence CD, by making us believe it is the truth, and convert that truth into a lived reality. Of course, the trick is to listen and create those stories together. The men rappers in the cypher heard the women rappers within a context of their battle against development, yet they did not realize that the women's critique was challenging how development prevented CD within the cypher and the Hip Hop community.

In both projects, when we truly listened to our co-researchers, we could feel a certain magic, as if we were no longer creating stories in space. Instead, it was as if the stories and space were creating us. We learned that re-storying is not done *in* a workshop room or *in* a community or *on* a computer. It is done *in, from, as, across, between,* and *through* multiple spaces, converting the question "where is knowledge created" into a more complicated and wondrous one, which leads us back to De Sousa Santos's abyssal line.

Hall and Tandon refer to the abyssal line as an invisibilizing space where everything on the other side is "beyond truth or falsehood" (2017: 12), resulting in the Global North being "stuck in a rut in the path of history that does not allow for the existence of histories other than the universal history of the west" (2017: 13). The vastness and divisiveness of the line immobilizes the West; however, to challenge epistemicide our experiences suggest we need not cross the abyss. Rather, we need to see the abyss as a knowledge-creating space and create a relationship with the line. Through re-storying, our PAR researchers formed a "thinking-feeling" relationship with the abyssal line. With the cypher, we discovered that it is more than a geometrical figure representing "out there" and "in here," and with the river, the abyssal line transformed from a "vastness between them and us" into a "vastness within us." The stories helped us see inside ourselves and feel the vastness as both oppression and opportunity.

Re-storying PAR also questions the "situatedness" of knowledge, challenging the premise that "all research is undertaken by someone somewhere" (Genat 2009: 108). For example, while the cypher looks like one space, it is not. It is a pluriversal space whose identity is dependent on the existence of cyphers around the world, and the stories told *in* and *from* multiple cyphers form the Hip Hop community. Stories have the power to situate and un-situate us at the same time. When we tell stories in a place composed of multiple spaces, we recognize the line forming the cypher as an embodiment of Mignolo's (2012) "border thinking." It forms a knowledge-creating space, transforming marginalization into a border of bodies between modernity and "worlds otherwise."

This way of discussing research may feel irrational, disjointed, and unrooted; however, it is because we have embodied a tradition in which we afford intellectual property to a person for creating knowledge according to a proper procedure (indeed it feels inappropriate to only put our names as authors of this chapter). The storytelling approach to PAR not only feels like rewriting knowledge; but also rewriting what knowledge means, who owns it, and how we relate to it. In re-storying, those invisibilized by the abyssal line realize their "knowing" is as important, or more so, than the academy's, and alternative development paradigms that perceive community as composed of all forms of existence become more understandable. It is like "braiding sweetgrass," or living in the continuous re-storying of our relationships with the natural world and our ancestors (Kimmerer 2013). Perhaps when we heard the Aguarico, we were also hearing the ancestors who fished and bathed in its waters, or perhaps we were hearing our dreams from the evening before. Indigenous knowledge creation spaces permeate our sleep (Noroña 2020) and the stories we created on the banks of that river belong to all our relations.

We imagine that CD scholar-practitioners will find it difficult to integrate storytelling, especially stories from our dreams, into their work. Nevertheless, as Ledwith (2020) suggests, the diversity and fluidity of what it means to live in and work with communities necessitates new CD approaches. The stories we create in PAR are not just a useful tool for CD, they are part of a new approach and reveal it as a pluriversal undertaking.

Embracing a dreamlike space in PAR and CD rejects De Sousa Santos's "monoculture of linear time" (2008), but it does not escape the Western world of limits characterized by disciplinary boundaries, deadlines, and budgets. We wove stories together as if in dreams, revealing new paths to explore; however, the calendar forced us to choose only a few. This left too much power in Pachaysana's hands, resulting in us portraying the violence we hoped to transform. We surely silenced voices and we could have made a difference by placing greater intentionality on forming the elusive third space.

What is the relationship between a narrative approach to participatory action research and the collaborative third/elusive/decolonial space?

We entered each project wondering how storytelling cultivates third spaces in PAR, and as we reflect, we realize just how elusive these spaces are. We do not constitute a third space by bringing the different parties together in a shared physical space; rather, third spaces are more story than place. We felt the third space thriving when we engaged in the process of re-storying, which became more apparent when that space/story was interrupted by hegemonic dynamics from the outside world (e.g., the rejection of visa applications). The third space we created in the IS project felt more like a story than in the HH project; therefore, we answer our question by identifying how we engaged and embodied the IS third space in a more liberating and effective way.

First, we acknowledge that Pachaysana structured the third spaces differently between the two projects. For each, we supported and guided the diverse participants in creating a non-hierarchical working space; however, as Gill et al. remind us, even the most liberatory PAR projects suffer from "the hegemony of modernism, monolingualism, eurocentrism and colonialism" (2012: 1). In the HH project, despite our "decolonizing" agenda, we often felt we were promoting academic hegemony by focusing on how the collaborative workspace could produce important work for host communities and academia. In the IS project, while we worked hard every day, we also played hard every day. We embraced the unstructured spaces as much as the structured ones, and found that both are needed to form a third space. Through the lens of CD, with the HH project, we formed a space that pushed for desired results, while in the IS project we shaped our space to create a story and trusted it would bring results.

Next, how we storied and re-storied our "thinking-feeling" selves enhanced (or limited) the possibilities of the third space. In the HH project we *articulated* "thinking-feeling," and it often felt real; however, in the IS project we *practiced* "thinking-feeling" by living/being together. In one project, we embraced the Hip Hop movement and its healing potential, while in the other we engaged Indigenous epistemologies to explore, identify, and embrace richer versions of ourselves and each other. This makes evident a circular dynamic where the "thinking-feeling" space is informed by our relationships and vice versa. We put the circle into motion when we stop treating PAR as a philosophy and methodology and begin treating it as a collective way of living, knowing, and being. With HH we tried to identify an existing truth and turn out a CD project, whereas with IS we were "living together fruitfully ... not trying to pin down one truth, but to articulate one of many truths, that are creative, liberating for ourselves and others" (Reason 2003: 116). With less focus on development and more focus on community, IS quickly evolved into a CD project with which everyone felt greater ownership.

We argue that the purpose and potential of the third space is to reimagine how we create knowledge, unlearn systemic and embodied injustices, and transform oppressive relationships into ones that are based on recognition, solidarity, and healing. A third space echoes Augusto Boal's (2013) aesthetic space (also, rehearsal space), referring to how the space becomes a mirror for humans to self-observe, reflect, and take action by rehearsing transformations to their reality. Mirroring our stories to one another is a vulnerable act that requires a supportive community to create and embrace the space. It is also a liberatory experience because we recognize each other while building a story together. In the HH project, our group's inner relationships were weakened by tensions from gender dynamics, leading us to force the mirroring. This made the work feel heavy, even unsafe. In the IS project, living together translated into seeing each other. The space became the mirror, and by seeing ourselves in the other, we felt supported, strong, and safe. We carried the load by playfully and compassionately pushing each other toward their dreams for CD and collective change.

Seeing ourselves in the mirror reveals the "in-between," which is dependent on living and working *in* and *with* uncertainty (referring to the mysterious space between us and our reflections). The cypher and the river were ideal in-between spaces, but we approached the uncertainty differently. We knew the cypher was symbolic of many truths, including those each rapper carried into the circle. We could feel the rhythm and easily conceptualize the cypher as a space for resisting hegemonic, "out there" power structures and encouraging alternative "in here" realities. Yet, we did not feel or embrace the uncertainty of the cypher. The space felt like a quick and easy "world otherwise," meaning as an alternative space it was too certain. Our action was to simply occupy it, diminishing its potential to build and challenge relationships. Once the participants shared their truths and the cypher concluded, the lack of uncertainty resulted in a cathartic experience instead of a "thinking-feeling" one. In contrast, we did not occupy the third space of the river as a place to purge ourselves. We lived the river and she lived in us. The uncertainty of our relationship with the third space forced us to continuously re-story it into our lives and work. The river was exemplary of metaxis, or the in-between *from*, *through*, *by*, and *with* which we liberated each other, together.

RECOMMENDATIONS

Our recommendations are focused on applying a greater level of intentionality to using narrative for shaping and naming PAR/CD third spaces. These recommendations are not instructions, nor do we call for focusing all PAR/CD on a narrative approach. We outline them, intertwined with a story from the IS project, hoping the narrative guides readers toward the potential of re-storying their own PAR and CD work.

> After sharing the last of five workshops on Indigenous Storytelling at one of Ecuador's most prestigious universities, we gather under a large tree on campus to reflect. There is an overwhelming feeling of relief. We had done it! Anita[7] celebrates, "Think about it! For years we are taught to work hard to make it to a university like this one, where we should study even harder and bring back all that we learn to help our communities." She loses herself in thought and we patiently wait, enjoying a bit of silence. "But we had it all wrong. Today, we showed them knowledge does not just come from these buildings. Our communities are universities too, we just do it differently." Nestor punctuates this last phrase, "Because we are different."

Scholars and practitioners in PAR and CD continuously question relationships (knowledge to practice, academy to community, subject to object, etc.), and our first recommendation is to broaden the relational scope by seeing *thinking-feeling* as a doorway to ontological exchange. We entered both projects focused on exploring different ways of knowing; however, we owe our success in the IS project to opening up space and time for the exchange of ways of being. The space of ontological exchange is the *thinking-feeling space*, which creates a sense of peaceful vulnerability that frees us to radically listen to the other. The narrative approach to PAR suggests third spaces are *thinking-feeling spaces* as much as they are workspaces or creative spaces.

> Anita exhales deeply, "Honestly, when I walked onto campus, I thought they might make me feel ashamed for being different or because we only have high school diplomas. At times I felt lost, focused on the 'us' and 'them'!" We talk more and realize our work is not about comparing or figuring out how we are similar and different. Rather, our work is about experiencing "them" in "us" and "us" in "them." In creating this work, we often lacked direction, and while uncomfortable, we embraced the process and its ambiguity. Sitting under this tree, we realize the uncertainty made our relationships grow stronger.

Our second recommendation is to embrace the "abyssal line," including all the discomfort associated with its lack of definition. In both projects, we felt the narrative approach to PAR was most engaged and effective when we perceived our third space as a rehearsal *in* and *with* the abyssal line, referring to exploring *knowing* from a situatedness on (or feeling of) the epistemological in-between. By inhabiting this space as a rehearsal room, we freed ourselves, albeit only partially and temporarily, from certain epistemological limits. For example, we were no longer restricted to the Cartesian "separate things" worldview or to define concepts like *participant action research* and *community development* as nouns or proper nouns. Because the line is where and how we harmonize our relational co-existence, the concepts became verbs. In our space and time, PAR was "participants acting-researching" and CD was "communal developing." The narrative approach to PAR converts the third space into a *rehearsal space* where we can create and believe in a new story.

> Nestor intervenes, "Yeah, it was hard, but once we began telling our stories …" He stops for a moment, thinking about his words carefully. "No … once we began sharing our stories, it all changed." Sharing is the key. Sharing our stories and interconnecting them with others is what makes the whole project work, because the interconnections never stop. But it is also the hardest part, because we have to make ourselves vulnerable over and over again. Feeling somewhere between vulnerability and invincibility, not sure what to say next, Nestor smiles as if to say, "We keep walking."

Third, we recommend transcending the bridge metaphor. We approached both projects thinking that we (PAR/CD scholar-practitioners) build bridges to connect people ("us" and "them") and worlds ("here" and "there"); however, bridges can be more of an escape than spaces for relationship building and knowledge creation. Indeed, a bridge helps us cross from one side to another, but when passing above the river can we truly listen to her? A bridge can help us compare the world of one side with the other but it feels separate from both. This separation makes it easy to be distracted by the voices in our heads, hearing the local community, the academic community and our personal relations all at once. Yet, when we walked into the river, its rushing waters quieted the voices as much as they washed away certain epistemic limitations. The narrative approach to PAR advocates for getting wet and dirty in the *in-between space* more than a bridge that passes over it.

> Javier is deep in thought, staring intently at a dandelion on the ground. He quietly adds, "But in creating the stories for this project we also furthered our own stories and our people's stories. We are always working on our stories, but usually without thinking about it. If we aren't thinking about how we make the stories we don't realize how others impose their ways, making us become who they want us to be. And that is the most important part. Someone or something is trying to steal our stories and give us others to believe in." Anita simply has to jump in, "It is like our play! That 'someone' or 'something' is trying to manipulate us to give them our land, our knowledge, or our resources. They want us to be part of their story. But we resist! Our stories are how we resist and they make us resilient." Nestor lies down on the grass, looks towards the sky and whispers, "our stories are our survival." We all follow Nestor's lead, lying on the grass to admire the clouds and celebrate each other's company.

Being a "thinking-feeling" person is hard because it exposes our vulnerability. As much as entering the river is a joyful act, it is also a painful one. If we intend for her waters to heal or transform us, we must accept that "radically listening" to her will reveal some of our most painful wounds. We must enter the river (or the cypher) with a sense of ceremony and play. Ceremonially, we honor the union of our PAR group (the formation of a new, yet temporary family-community), while playfully setting forth to create stories as children do. In essence, we are creating theater, and to make the play we must play, and in the act of playing we are ceremoniously "seeing in the act of seeing … our most human quality" (Boal 2013: 13). The narrative approach to PAR and CD proposes we build a *ceremonial playground space* where knowledge, even development, comes from the play that makes us most human.

CONCLUSIONS

In re-storying PAR and CD we feel the violent acts of colonization and coloniality as offenses against our thinking-feeling selves, as attacks on our bodies and relationships, and as an attempt to invisibilize the river and cypher. The Cartesian approach to research does not colonize by squashing out ways of knowing and being; rather, it colonizes by invisibilizing the spaces where people of diverse ontologies and epistemologies come together to re-story the world. It invisibilizes the third elusive decolonial space, and in doing so, it takes away our sacred site for interconnecting stories and weaving the fabric of CD. The story under the tree at the university shows us that the magical space for which we have given four names (the *thinking-feeling space*, the *rehearsal space*, the *in-between space*, and the *ceremonial-playground space*) is also where we plant the seeds of CD. Yet, we have learned that these spaces cannot be colonized, only forgotten, lost in the abyssal line. The narrative approach to PAR restores our relationship with these spaces and empowers us to re-story our hopes and dreams for CD.

You may say that providing four names to one space is uncertain or unfinished, but that is the nature of pluriversal spaces, as it is the nature of knowing and being. If we cannot name our identities and stories in a single term, then the same must hold true for our work in PAR and CD. Our job is not to provide certainty and our job is not to finish. Our job is to re-story the world.

NOTES

1. A'í-Cofán is one way of writing the name of those who are typically referred to as the Cofán Nation. Cofán is an imposed name from outsiders, but also the name that is most commonly used by its own people. A'í is the most culturally appropriate way of referring to the nation, whose language is A'íngue. Cofán is sometimes written with a "K," or "Kofán."
2. In this chapter, unless the context implies a specific connotation, the word "we" refers to the authors. When identifying our PAR research team, composed of community members and outside researchers, we will specify this.
3. A cypher is the name of the circle that rappers, dancers, etc. create where each artist can enter the middle to express their creativity while the rest sway, bob, or snap in support.
4. We use "thinking-feeling" throughout the chapter; however, it is more than a reference to Fals Borda's (2006a) citation. "Thinking-feeling" is a decolonizing methodology that questions Cartesian logic in PAR.
5. A top-tier research university in the Midwest.
6. A tour was planned for March 2020, however, the visa applications of the Bavoroe participants were rejected.
7. Names have been changed.

REFERENCES

Ascanio, Adriana C. and Karen M. Villarreal. 2017. "La IAP como alternativa metodológica para el cambio social: un análisis desde distintas perspectivas." *Jangwa Pana*, 16(1): 90.

Bhabha, Homi K. and Jonathan Rutherford. 2006. Third Space. *Multitudes*, 3: 95–107.

Bishop, Russell. 1999. "Collaborative Storytelling: Meeting Indigenous People's Desires for Self-Determination." Paper presented at the World Indigenous People's Conference, Albuquerque, New Mexico, June 15–22.

Boal, Augusto. 1979. *Theatre of the Oppressed*. Theater Communications Group.

Boal, Augusto. 2013. *The Rainbow of Desire: The Boal Method of Theatre and Therapy*. New York: Routledge.

Boidin, Capucine, James Cohen, and Ramón Grosfoguel. 2012. "Introduction: From University to Pluriversity: A Decolonial Approach to the Present Crisis of Western Universities." *Human Architecture: Journal of the Sociology of Self-Knowledge*, 10(1): 1–7.

Breidlid, Anders. 2013. *Education, Indigenous Knowledges, and Development in the Global South: Contesting Knowledges for a Sustainable Future* (Vol. 82). New York: Routledge.

Bruner, Jerome. 1998. "The Narrative Construction of Reality." *Critical Inquiry*, 18(1): 1–21.

Campbell, J. 1991. *The Power of Myth*. New York: Anchor.

Caxaj, Susana C. 2015. "Indigenous Storytelling and Participatory Action Research." *Global Qualitative Nursing Research*, 2: 1–12.

Christensen, Julia. 2012. "Telling Stories: Exploring Research Storytelling as a Meaningful Approach to Knowledge Mobilization with Indigenous Research Collaborators and Diverse Audiences in Community-Based Participatory Research." *The Canadian Geographer/Le Géographe Canadien*, 56(2): 231–242.

Datta, Ranjan. 2017. "Decolonizing Both Researcher and Research and Its Effectiveness in Indigenous Research." *Research Ethics*, 14(2): 1–24.

De Sousa Santos, Boaventura. 2007. "Beyond Abyssal Thinking: From Global Lines to Ecologies of Knowledges." *Binghamton University Review*, 30(1): 45–89.

De Sousa Santos, Boaventura. 2008. "The World Social Forum and the Global Left." *Politics and Society*, 36(2): 247–270.

De Sousa Santos, Boaventura. 2011. "Epistemologías del sur." *Utopia y praxis latinoamericana*, 16(54): 17–39.

Escobar, Arturo. 2007. "Worlds and Knowledges Otherwise." *Cultural Studies*, 21(2–3): 179–210.

Escobar, Arturo. 2011. *Encountering Development: The Making and Unmaking of the Third World* (Vol. 1). Princeton, NJ: Princeton University Press.

Escobar, Arturo. 2018. *Designs for the Pluriverse: Radical Interdependence, Autonomy, and the Making of Worlds*. Durham, NC: Duke University Press.

Fairbanks, Colleen M. 1996. "Telling Stories: Reading and Writing Research Narratives." *Journal of Curriculum and Supervision*, 11(4): 320–340.

Fals Borda, Orlando. 2006a. "Participatory (Action) Research in Social Theory: Origins and Challenges." In P. Reason and H. Bradbury (Eds), *The Handbook of Action Research* (pp. 27–37). New York: Sage.

Fals Borda, Orlando. 2006b. "The North–South Convergence: A 30-Year First-Person Assessment of PAR." *Action Research*, 4(3): 351–358.

Freire, Paulo. 1973. *Education for Critical Consciousness*. New York: Seabury Press.

Gaudry, Adam J. P. 2011. Insurgent Research. *Wicazo Sa Review*, 26(1):113–136. doi: 10.1353/wic.2011.0006

Genat, Bill. 2009. "Building Emergent Situated Knowledges in Participatory Action Research." *Action Research*, 7(1): 101–115.

Gill, Hartej, Kadi Purru, and Gloria Lin. 2012. "In the Midst of Participatory Action Research Practices: Moving towards Decolonizing and Decolonial Praxis." *Reconceptualizing Educational Research Methodology*, 3(1): 1–15.

Godin, Seth. 2005. *All Marketers Are Liars: The Power of Telling Authentic Stories in a Low-Trust World*. London: Penguin.

Gosa, Travis L. 2015. "The Fifth Element: Knowledge." In J. A. Williams (Ed.), *The Cambridge Companion to Hip-Hop* (pp. 56–70). Cambridge: Cambridge University Press.

Gottschall, Jonathan. 2012. *The Storytelling Animal: How Stories Make Us Human*. Boston, MA: Mariner Books.

Grosfoguel, Ramón. 2015. "The Structure of Knowledge in Westernized Universities: Epistemic Racism/Sexism, Westernized Universities and the Four Genocides/Epistemicides of the Long Sixteenth Century." In M. Araújo. and S. R. Maeso (Eds), *Eurocentrism, Racism and Knowledge* (pp. 23–46). New York: Palgrave Macmillan.

Hall, Budd. L. and Rajesh Tandon. 2017. "Decolonization of Knowledge, Epistemicide, Participatory Research and Higher Education." *Research for All*, 1(1): 6–19.

Harari, Yuval. N. 2018. *Sapiens: A Brief History of Humankind*. New York: Harper Perennial.

Heron, John. 1996. *Co-operative Inquiry: Research into the Human Condition*. London: Sage.

Iseke, Judy. 2013. "Indigenous Storytelling as Research." *International Review of Qualitative Research*, 6(4): 559–577.

Kenny, Sue. 2016. "Community Development Today: Engaging Challenges through Cosmopolitanism?" *Community Development Journal*, 51(1): 23–41.

Kimmerer, Robin. W. 2013. *Braiding Sweetgrass: Indigenous Wisdom, Scientific Knowledge and the Teachings of Plants*. Minneapolis, MI: Milkweed Editions.

Ledwith, Margaret. 2020. *Community Development: A Critical Approach*. Bristol: Policy Press.

Levy, Ian., Christopher Emdin, and Edmund Adjapong, E. 2018. "Hip-Hop Cypher in Group Work." *Social Work with Groups*, 41(1–2): 103–110.

Linds, Warren. 2005. "Dancing (in) the In-between." In J. Cohen-Cruz and M. Schutzman (Eds), *A Boal Companion: Dialogues on Theater and Cultural Politics* (pp. 114–124). New York: Routledge.

Little Bear, Leroy. 2000. "Jagged Worldviews Colliding." In M. Battiste (Ed.), *Reclaiming Indigenous Voice and Vision* (pp. 77-85). Vancouver: University of British Columbia Press.

Maldonado-Torres, Nelson. 2007. "On the Coloniality of Being: Contributions to the Development of a Concept." *Cultural Studies*, 21(2–3): 240–270.

McLeod, Neal. 2000. "Cree Narrative Memory." *Indigenous Voices from the Great Plain/Voix Autochtones Des Prairies*, 19(20): 37–61.

Mignolo, Walter. D. 2012. *Local Histories/Global Designs: Coloniality, Subaltern Knowledges, and Border Thinking*. Princeton, NJ: Princeton University Press.

Mignolo, Walter. D. and Madina Tlostanova. 2006. "Theorizing from the Borders: Shifting to Geo-and Body-Politics of Knowledge." *European Journal of Social Theory*, 9(2): 205–221.

Motley, Carol. M. and Geraldine R. Henderson. 2008. "The Global Hip-Hop Diaspora: Understanding the Culture." *Journal of Business Research*, 61(3): 243–253.

Navarro, Jenell. 2016. "WORD: Hip-Hop, Language, and Indigeneity in the Americas." *Critical Sociology*, 42(4–5): 567–581.

Noroña, María. 2020. *Peripheries of Extraction in the Amazon of Ecuador: An Analysis of Indigenous Territory, Livelihoods and Voices.* Doctoral dissertation, University of Oregon. ProQuest. https://scholarsbank.uoregon.edu/xmlui/handle/1794/25211?fbclid=IwAR2lbFq5x_LlZC1X1wAJv_vVnQqT8jsTb8wJ1i-GR21-9IMrg1TFtyjHY60

Osumare, Halify. 2001. "Beat Streets in the Global Hood: Connective Marginalities of the Hip Hop Globe." *Journal of American Culture*, 24(1–2): 171–181.

Pyrch, Timothy. 2007. "Participatory Action Research and the Culture of Fear." *Action Research*, 5(2): 199–216.

Quijano, Anibal. 2007. "Coloniality and Modernity/Rationality." *Cultural Studies*, 21(2–3): 168–178.

Reason, Peter. 2003. "Pragmatist Philosophy and Action Research: Readings and Conversation with Richard Rorty." *Action Research*, 1(1): 103–123.

Reason, Peter and Hilary Bradbury (Eds). 2008. *Handbook of Action Research: Participative Inquiry and Practice* (2nd ed.). New York: Sage.

Ritenburg, Heather, Alannah E. Y. Leon, Warren Linds, Denise M. Nadeau, Linda Goulet, Margaret Kovach, and Mary Marshall. 2014. "Embodying Decolonization: Methodologies and Indigenization." *AlterNative: An International Journal of Indigenous Peoples*, 10(1): 67–80.

Smith, Linda. 2012. *Decolonizing Methodologies* (2nd Ed.). London: Zed Books.

Somekh, Bridget. 2005. *Action Research: A Methodology for Change and Development.* New York: McGraw-Hill Education.

Stern, Thomas. 2019. "Participatory Action Research and the Challenges of Knowledge Democracy." *Educational Action Research*, 27(3): 435–451.

Stewart, Suzanne L. 2009. "One Indigenous Academic's Evolution: A Personal Narrative of Native Health Research and Competing Ways of Knowing." *First Peoples Child and Family Review*, 4(1): 57–65.

Tobin, Kenneth. 2009. "Tuning into Others' Voices: Radical Listening, Learning from Difference, and Escaping Oppression." *Cultural Studies of Science Education*, 4: 505–511.

Tuck, Eve, in conversation with Michelle Fine. 2016. "Inner Angles: A Range of Ethical Responses to/with Indigenous and Decolonizing Theories." In N. Denzin and M. Giardina (Eds), *Ethical Futures in Qualitative Research: Decolonizing the Politics of Knowledge.* New York: Routledge.

Uzendoski, Michael A. 2012. "Beyond Orality." *HAU: Journal of Ethnographic Theory*, 2(1): 55–80.

Walsh, Catherine. 2012. "'Other' Knowledges, 'Other' Critiques: Reflections on the Politics and Practices of Philosophy and Decoloniality in the 'Other' America." *Transmodernity*, 1(3): 11–27.

Zavala, Miguel. 2013. "What Do We Mean by Decolonizing Research Strategies? Lessons from Decolonizing, Indigenous Research Projects in New Zealand and Latin America." *Decolonization: Indigeneity, Education and Society*, 2(1): 55–71.

Index

Printed and bound by CPI Group (UK) Ltd, Croydon, CR0 4YY

27/03/2025

14649533-0001